An Introduction to
the History of Psychology

An Introduction to
the History of Psychology

B. R. Hergenhahn
Hamline University

WADSWORTH PUBLISHING COMPANY
Belmont, California
A Division of Wadsworth, Inc.

This book is dedicated with deep gratitude to Madelon Cassavant —sine qua non of my writing projects.

Psychology Editor: Kenneth King
Production Editor: Vicki Friedberg
Managing Designer: Andrew H. Ogus
Print Buyer: Karen Hunt
Designer: Cecilia Brunazzi
Copy Editor: Gregory Gullickson
Cover Design: Andrew H. Ogus

The cover illustration is a detail of the head of
Psyche from "Cupid and Psyche's Bath," School
of Giulio Romano, Palazzo del Te, Mantua.
© Scala New York/Florence.

Printed in the United States of America

3 4 5 6 7 8 9 10—90 89 88 87

0-534-06072-2

Library of Congress Cataloging-in-Publication Data

Hergenhahn, B. R., 1934–
    An introduction to the history of psychology.

    Bibliography: p.
    Includes indexes.
    1. Psychology—History. I. Title.
BF81.H39 1986   150'.9   85-22478
ISBN 0-534-06072-2

CONTENTS

CHAPTER 12

Behaviorism   232

CHAPTER 13

Neobehaviorism   262

CHAPTER 16

Psychoanalysis 340

CHAPTER 17

Third Force Psychology 374

CHAPTER 18

Psychology Today 400

PREFACE

For reasons that I will elaborate in Chapter 1, writing a history of psychology textbook is an especially difficult task. There are the questions of where to begin such a history, what approach to take in writing it, and what to include. How an author answers these questions reveals the author's biases and determines the nature of the history text that he or she writes. As an overview of this book, I will briefly present my answers to these three questions.

First, I begin my coverage of psychology's history with the early Greek philosophers. Several current texts focus on psychology's history after psychology became a discipline independent of philosophy in the late 1800s. I contend, however, that it is impossible to understand why psychology took the form it did without first knowing the events that occurred during the centuries preceding psychology's emergence as a separate discipline. Also, it would be impossible to understand the many kinds of psychology that appeared in modern times without first knowing their ancient origins.

Second, my approach to reporting psychology's history is to combine several approaches. In explaining why psychology takes different forms at different times, some authors emphasize the Zeitgeist, or the spirit of the times. This approach stresses the cultural and societal variables in psychology's history. Another approach is to concentrate on the works of the great individuals in psychology's history—for example, Plato, Aristotle, Descartes, Freud, and Darwin. Still another approach is to trace ideas or concepts over time. Using the latter approach, one might note how ideas or concepts such as the mind, abnormality, the unconscious, memory,

learning, or perception have changed over the centuries. This text combines all three approaches to the history of psychology.

Third, rather than emphasizing one kind of psychology (for example, experimental), I attempt to give all kinds of psychology sympathetic coverage. Through the years, psychology has borrowed heavily from religion, philosophy, and the natural sciences. To minimize any of these influences would distort psychology's history. Furthermore, although for the last 100 years psychology has made major efforts to be a science, it has not always succeeded. To concentrate a history of psychology text exclusively on scientific psychology is to ignore not only most of psychology's history, but much contemporary psychology as well.

It is popular these days for histories of psychology to suggest that modern psychology has *evolved* from earlier psychology. This contention seems to me to be incorrect. The term *evolution* implies a gradual improvement over time as a function of some kind of selection process—for example, survival of the fittest. To say that contemporary psychology evolved from earlier kinds of psychology suggests that today's psychology is demonstrably better than that of the past. Although this may be true in some cases, it does not appear to be generally true. It is accurate to say that psychology as we know it today is the result of past influences, but to say that it evolved from earlier brands of psychology misrepresents psychology's history. In this text we will trace the history of the many influences that manifest themselves in contemporary psychology.

I agree with the contention of Evans (1984,

p. 18) that psychology, whether modern or ancient, has always addressed the three basic questions:

1. *How do I come to know the things I know?* To address this question, psychologists study such topics as sensation, perception, cognition, genetics, learning, and memory.

2. *How do I come to feel the things I feel?* To answer this question, psychologists study such topics as physiology, biochemistry, motivation, beliefs, values, and attitudes.

3. *How do I come to do the things I do?* To answer this question, psychologists study human behavior, ranging from simple reflexes to complex social interactions.

Thus, throughout history, psychologists have been interested in discovering how we gain knowledge about ourselves and the world, what determines how we feel about that knowledge, and what determines if and how we act upon that knowledge.

During any attempt to answer the three basic questions above, more specific questions arise, and they too, have been part of psychology at least since the time of the early Greek philosophers. This book will review various proposed answers to the following persistent questions in psychology:

• What is the nature of human nature?

• How are the mind and body related?

• To what extent is behavior determined, and to what extent is it free?

• What proportion of what we do or think is genetically determined, and what proportion comes from experience?

• How much do humans have in common with other animals?

• To what extent are human behavior and thought rational?

• Can psychology be a science, and if so, what kind of science?

Although it may be true that psychologists have always addressed the same basic questions, the way they have addressed these questions has varied widely, and many factors are involved. Culture, political and societal climate, the presence of insightful individuals, technology, and developments in fields outside of psychology all influence what form psychology will take at any given time and place in history. Perhaps the most influential variable determining how one attempts to answer psychology's basic questions is one's assumptions about human nature. Each conception of human nature emphasizes certain human attributes and minimizes others. For example, if one assumes that humans are rational animals, then studying the logical thought processes by which humans reach conclusions is very important. But if one assumes that humans are complex machines, or that environmental events alone determine human behavior, then there is no sense in studying rational thought, since one is assuming that it does not exist. Furthermore, for those psychologists assuming that all human behavior is determined, studying free will would be nonsensical; but for those psychologists who believe in free will, studying how humans choose from among various alternatives is vital.

Thus, there is not one psychology, but many. Each kind of psychology embraces a conception of human nature that determines which answers to psychology's basic questions are acceptable and which are not. Likewise, the assumptions one makes about human nature also dictate the methodologies that one will employ while seeking answers to various questions. Each conception of human nature creates what Kuhn (1972) calls a paradigm, a set of beliefs that a group of researchers shares. In this text we will explore psychology's various paradigms. We will trace their origins and attempt to determine their current status.

I hope that by reading this text, the student will be better able to put psychology in perspective. I also hope that the student will *not* see psychology's history as a steady evolution toward a better understanding of people. A fair study of the history of psychology will reveal mistakes, the importance of the Zeitgeist (the spirit of the times), the influence of great individuals, the importance of developments in other disciplines (for example, biology and physics), and a periodic preoccupation with trivia. It will also reveal that psychology has been a human enterprise consisting of advances, errors, breakthroughs, fads and fashions, and occasional temper tantrums. The history of psychology is very human.

Of all the writing projects I have attempted, *An Introduction to the History of Psychology* has been by far the most difficult but perhaps the most satisfying. The manuscript has undergone many revisions. Editors, academic reviewers, and my students evaluated early drafts of the manuscript and made many useful suggestions. I found the comments, criticisms, and questions of Lynne Alexander, Tamara Bush, Sandra Klein, and Ryan Tibbits most helpful. They graciously used various drafts of the manuscript as texts for their independent-study projects in the history of psychology. Their responses on 18 essay examinations corresponding to the 18 chapters of the manuscript allowed me to gauge how well each chapter presented the material.

I also wish to thank the following people for their reviews of the manuscript. They offered many valuable comments: David C. Edwards, Iowa State University; Michael W. Gaynor, Bloomsburg State College; Curtis Gilgash, University of Tampa; Jack Holmes, University of Wisconsin at Stevens Point; John D. Kelton, Davidson College; David E. Leary, University of New Hampshire; and L. W. McCallum, Augustana College.

I would especially like to thank Robert Verbrugge of the University of Connecticut for his honest and insightful comments. He read the manuscript with great care, showing a deep understanding of psychology's history. He pulled no punches in his review, yet he showed sensitivity and kindness in making his recommendations.

I would also like to thank some of my colleagues at Hamline University who helped me considerably, sometimes without knowing it. Over many cheeseburgers and bowls of chili, I had the chance to pick the keen minds of Clifford Creswell (chemistry), John Harrigan (political science), and David Lukowitz (history). Perhaps now these three will know why I steered so many of our conversations in mysterious directions. When specific questions arose, I sought the knowledge of several colleagues at Hamline. These people responded kindly: Duane Cady (philosophy), Nancy Holland (philosophy), and Tim Polk (religion). Also, through the years, whenever our paths crossed, Jerry Weiss, professor of psychology at Macalester College, and I talked about the history of psychology. I benefited greatly from these discussions.

I also wish to express my deep appreciation to my colleagues in Hamline's psychology department. It has become habitual for Jerry Greiner, Kim Guenther, Charles LaBounty, and Matt Olson to cover for me when projects such as this one take up my time and energy. These endeavors would be impossible without their support, understanding, and friendship.

In a project of this magnitude, the importance of an outstanding typist cannot be exaggerated. I've worked with Madelon Cassavant, to whom this book is dedicated, on all of my writing projects the last 10 years. As I said in another of my books, "No Madelon—no book." She is not only an expert typist but also an understanding and supportive friend for which I thank her.

Finally, I must confess that I have selfishly taken advantage of Sherry Green's 11 years of experience in the publishing business. As

Madelon finished typing each chapter, Sherry would proofread it. Sherry's keen eye caught many mistakes, which are inevitable in a large manuscript. Also, Sherry, with Lynne Alexander, was instrumental in tracking down elusive references used in the text—all this for compensation too paltry to mention.

To the people I have mentioned above, I again express my appreciation. Each of them has had a positive influence on this text.

ACKNOWLEDGMENTS

Alexander, F. G., & Selesnick, S. T.: Excerpts from *The History of Psychiatry*. © 1966 by the Estate of Franz Alexander, M.D., and Sheldon Selesnick, M.D. Reprinted by permission of Harper & Row Publishers, Inc. Allen & Unwin (Publishers) Ltd.

Boring, E. G.: Excerpts from *A History of Experimental Psychology* (2nd ed.), pp. ix, 17, and 257. © 1950, renewed 1978. Reprinted by permission of Prentice-Hall, Inc.

Brainerd, C J.: Excerpts from *Piaget's Theory of Intelligence*, 1978, pp. 2 and 3. Reprinted by permission of Prentice-Hall, Inc.

Bruno, F. J.: Excerpts from *The Story of Psychology*. © 1972 by Holt, Rinehart & Winston, Inc. Reprinted by permission of CBS College Publishing.

Cohen, D.: Excerpts from *J. B. Watson: The Founder of Behaviourism*, 1979. Reprinted by permission of Routledge & Kegan Paul PLC and the author.

Darwin, F.: Excerpts from *The Autobiography of Charles Darwin and Selected Letters*, 1959. Reprinted by permission of Cover Publications, Inc.

Esper, E. A.: Excerpts from *A History of Psychology*, 1964. Reprinted by permission of W. B. Saunders & Company.

Evans, R. B.: Excerpts from J. Brozek (Ed.), *Explorations in the History of Psychology in the United States*, 1984. Reprinted by permission of Associated University Presses, Inc.

Fancher, R. E.: Excerpt from *Pioneers of Psychology*. Reprinted by permission of W. W. Norton & Company, Inc. Copyright © 1979 by Raymond E. Fancher.

Fraser, A. C.: Excerpts from John Locke, *An Essay Concerning Human Understanding*, 1959. Reprinted by permission of Dover Publications, Inc.

Freud, S.: Excerpt from *Civilization and Its Discontents*, in J. Strachey (Ed. and Trans.), *Standard Edition of the Complete Psychological Works of Sigmund Freud*. Reprinted by permission of Sigmund Freud Copyrights Ltd., the Institute of Psycho-Analysis and the Hogarth Press, and W. W. Norton & Company, Inc.

Hall, C. S., & Lindsay, G.: Excerpts from *Theories of Personality* (3rd ed.), 1978. Reprinted by permission of John Wiley & Sons, Inc.

Heidbreder, E.: Excerpts from *Seven Psychologies*, pp. 330–331, 389, 391–392, 400–401, 410–411, and 425–426. © 1933; renewed 1961. Reprinted by permission of Prentice-Hall, Inc.

Hergenhahn, B. R.: Excerpts from *An Introduction to Theories of Learning* (2nd ed.), 1982, pp. 41–42, 262, 265, 267, and 285. Reprinted by permission of Prentice-Hall, Inc.

Hergenhahn, B. R.: Excerpts from *An Introduction to Theories of Personality* (2nd ed.), 1984, pp. 47 and 268. Reprinted by permission of Prentice-Hall, Inc.

Jones, W. H. S.: Excerpt from *Hippocrates* (Vols. 1 and 2), 1923. Reprinted by permission of Putnam Publishing Group.

Koffka, K.: Excerpt from *Principle of Gestalt Psychology*. Copyright 1935 by Harcourt Brace Jovanovich, Inc.; renewed 1963 by Elizabeth Koffka. Reprinted by permission of Harcourt Brace Jovanovich, Inc., and Routledge & Kegan Paul PLC.

Kuhn, T. S.: Excerpts from *The Structure of Scientific Revolutions* (2nd ed.), 1973. Reprinted by permission of the University of Chicago Press.

Lachman, R., and Lachman, J. L.: Excerpts from *Cognitive Psychology and Information Processing*, 1979. Reprinted by permission of Lawrence Erlbaum Associates, Inc., Publishers.

Lafleur, L. J.: Excerpts from *Discourse on Method and Meditations.* © 1960 by Liberal Arts Press, reprinted by permission of the publisher, Bobbs-Merrill Educational Publishing, Indianapolis, Indiana.

Leahey, T. H.: Excerpts from *A History of Psychology*, 1980, pp. 216, 218, 306, and 385. Reprinted by permission of Prentice-Hall, Inc.

McDougall, W.: Excerpts from *Introduction to Social Psychology*, 1908. Reprinted by permission of Methuen & Company Ltd., U.K.

McDougall, W.: Excerpt from *Outline of Psychology.* Copyright 1923 by Charles Scribner's Sons; copyright renewed 1951 by Anne A. McDougall. Reprinted by permission of Charles Scribner's Son's and Methuen & Company, Ltd., U.K.

MacLeod, R. B.: Excerpts from the *Persistent Problems of Psychology*, 1975. Reprinted by permission of Humanities Press International, Inc., Atlantic Highlands, N. J.

Maddi, S. R., & Costa, P. T.: Excerpt from *Humanism in Personology: Allport, Maslow, and Murray*, published by Aldine Publishing Company, 1972. Reprinted by permission of Salvatore Maddi.

Maslow, A. H.: Excerpts from *Motivation and Personality* (2nd ed.). © 1970 by Abraham H. Maslow. Reprinted by permission of Harper & Row, Publishers, Inc.

Maslow, A. H.: Excerpts from *The Psychology of Science: A Reconnaissance.* © 1966 by Abraham H. Maslow. Reprinted by permission of Harper & Row, Publishers, Inc.

Mischel, W.: Excerpt from *Introduction to Personality* (3rd ed.), published by Holt, Rinehart & Winston, 1981. Reprinted by permission of CBS College Publishing.

Murphy, G.: Excerpt from *Psychological Thought from Pythagoras to Freud.* © 1949 by Harcourt Brace & World, Inc.; renewed 1977 by Gardner Murphy. Reprinted by permission of the publisher.

Popper, K.: Excerpts from *Conjectures and Refutations*, New York: Basic Books, 1963, and London: Routledge & Kegan Paul, ninth imprint, 1984. Reprinted by permission of Karl Popper.

Robinson, D. N.: Excerpts from *An Intellectual History of Psychology*, 1976, and *An Intellectual History of Psychology* (rev. ed.), 1981, published by Macmillan Publishing Company, Inc.

Rogers, C. R.: Excerpt from *On Becoming a Person: A Therapist's View of Psychotherapy*, 1961. Reprinted by permission of Houghton Mifflin Company and Constable & Company, U.K.

Rogers, C. R.: Excerpts from "A Theory of Therapy, Personality, and Interpersonal Relationships, as Developed in the Client-Centered Framework," in S. Koch (Ed.), *Psychology: A Study of Science* (Vol. 3), 1959. Reprinted by permission of McGraw-Hill, Inc.

Russell, B.: Excerpts from *Wisdom of the West.* © 1959 J. G. Ferguson Publishing Company. Reprinted by permission of J. G. Ferguson Publishing Company.

Severin, F. T.: Excerpts from *Discovering Man in Psychology: A Humanistic Approach*, 1973. Reprinted by permission of McGraw-Hill, Inc.

Sigerist, H. E.: Excerpt from *A History of Medicine, Vol. 1: Primitive and Archaic Medicine*, 1951. Reprinted by permission of Oxford University Press.

Titchener, E. B.: Excerpts from *A Textbook of Psychology*, 1910. Reprinted by permission of Macmillan Publishing Company.

Watson, J. B.: Excerpts from *Behaviorism*, 1925, and *Behaviorism* (rev. ed.), 1930. Reprinted by permission of W. W. Norton & Company, Inc.

Watson, R. I.: Excerpts from *The Great Psychologists* (4th ed.), 1978. Reprinted by permission of Lippincott/Harper & Row.

Wertheimer, M.: Excerpt from *A Brief History of Psychology*, 1970. Reprinted by permission of CBS College Publishing.

Wertheimer, M.: Excerpts from *A Brief History of Psychology* (rev. ed.). Copyright © 1970 and 1979 by Holt, Rinehart & Winston, Inc. Reprinted by permission of CBS College Publishing.

Woodworth, R. S.: Excerpts from *Contemporary Schools of Psychology*, published by the Ronald Press Company, 1931. Reprinted by permission of John Wiley & Sons, Inc.

An Introduction to
the History of Psychology

CHAPTER 1

Introduction

The way in which psychology has been defined has changed as the focus of psychology has changed. At various times in history, psychology has been defined as the study of the psyche or mind, of the spirit, of consciousness, and more recently as the study of, or the science of, behavior. Perhaps, then, we can arrive at an acceptable definition of modern psychology by observing what psychologists are currently focusing on. Here is what we see:

- Some psychologists are seeking the biological correlates of mental events.

- Some attempt to account for individual differences among people in such areas as personality, intelligence, and creativity.

- Some seek to understand humans by studying nonhuman animals.

- Some study unconscious motivation.

- Some are primarily interested in perfecting therapeutic tools that can be used to help mentally disturbed individuals.

- Some focus on the information-processing techniques that people use in adjusting to the environment or in problem solving.

- Still others study how humans change as a function of the maturational process.

Furthermore, we see that though some psychologists are rigorous scientists, others maintain that the scientific method cannot be applied to the study of humans. These are just a few of the activities and points of view that we find among contemporary psychologists.

It should be clear that no single definition of psychology could take into consideration the wide variety of activities engaged in by the more than 50,000 members of the American Psychological Association, not to mention the many other psychologists around the world. It seems best to say simply that psychology is defined by the professional activities of psychologists. These activities are characterized by a rich diversity of methods, topics of interest, and assumptions about human nature. A primary purpose of this book is to examine the origins of modern psychology and to show that most of the concerns of today's psychologists are manifestations of themes that have been part of psychology for hundreds or, in some cases, thousands of years.

PROBLEMS IN WRITING A HISTORY OF PSYCHOLOGY

Where to Start

Literally, *psychology* means the study of the psyche or mind, and this study is as old as the human species. The ancients, for example, attempted to account for dreams, mental illness, emotions, and fantasies. Was this psychology? Or did psychology commence when explanations of human cognitive experience, such as those proposed by the early Greeks, became more systematic? Plato and Aristotle, for example, created elaborate theories that attempted to account for such processes as memory, perception, and learning. Is this the point at which psychology started? Or did psychology come into existence when it became a separate science in the nineteenth century? It is common these

3

days to begin a history of psychology at the point where psychology became a separate science. This latter approach is unsatisfactory for two reasons: (1) it ignores the vast philosophical heritage that molded psychology into the kind of science that it eventually became, and (2) it omits important aspects of psychology that are outside the realm of science. Although it is true that since the mid-nineteenth century psychology has, to a large extent, embraced the scientific method, there have been highly influential psychologists, before and after the mid-nineteenth century, who did not feel compelled to follow the dictates of the scientific method. Their work cannot be ignored.

Our coverage of the history of psychology will not go back to the conceptions of the ancients, although we believe that such conceptions are within the domain of psychology. Space does not permit such a comprehensive history. Rather, we will start with the major Greek philosophers, since their explanations of human behavior and thought processes are the ones that philosophers and psychologists have been reacting to ever since the time of the Greeks.

What to Include

Typically, in determining what to include in a history of anything, one generally traces those people, ideas, and events that led to what is important now. This approach ignores what could have been and concentrates on what is. We, too, will take this approach by looking at the way psychology is today and then attempting to show how it became that way.

Using the present state of psychology as a guide in writing its history involves at least one major danger. R. I. Watson (1971, p. 313) calls such an approach to history **presentism**. Presentism implies that the present state of a discipline represents its highest state of development and that earlier events led to this state. In this view, the latest is the best. Although we

are using present psychology as our guide to what to include in psychology's history, we do not believe that current psychology is necessarily the best psychology. The field is simply too diverse to make such a judgment. At present, psychology is exploring many topics, methods, and assumptions. Which of these explorations will survive for inclusion in future history books is impossible to say. Our use of psychology's present as a frame of reference, therefore, does not rest on the assumptions that psychology's past necessarily evolved into its present or that current psychology represents the best psychology.

Although presentism provides a guide for deciding what individuals, ideas, and events to include in our history of psychology, there remains the question of how much detail to include. If, for example, one attempted to trace all of the causes of an idea, one would be engaged in an almost infinite regression. In fact, after attempting to track down the origins of an idea or concept in psychology, one is left with the impression that nothing is ever entirely new. Seldom, if ever, is a single individual solely responsible for an idea or a concept. Rather, individuals are influenced by other individuals, who in turn were influenced by other individuals, and so on. History, then, can be viewed as an almost unending stream of interrelated events. The "great" individuals are typically those who synthesize ideas that have previously existed in nebulous form into a clear, forceful point of view.

In writing a history, this infinite regression cannot ever be fully documented; attempting to do so would involve so many details that the book would become too long, as well as boring. The usual solution is to omit a large amount of information, so any history must be selective. Typically, only those individuals who did the most to develop or popularize an idea are covered. For example, Charles Darwin is generally associated with evolutionary theory, when in fact evolutionary theory existed in one form or another for thousands of years before Darwin. Darwin documented and reported evidence supporting evolutionary theory in a way that made the theory's validity hard to ignore. Thus, although Darwin was not the first to formulate evolutionary theory, he did much to substantiate and popularize it, and we therefore associate it with his name. The same is true for Freud and the notion of unconscious motivation.

In this book, we will focus on those individuals who either did the *most* to develop an idea, or, for whatever reason, have become closely associated with an idea. This, of course, does not do justice to many important individuals who could be mentioned, and to other individuals who are lost to antiquity or who were not loud or lucid enough to demand historical recognition.

Choice of Approach

Once the material to be included in a history of psychology has been chosen, the choice of approach remains. One could emphasize such nonpsychological factors as developments in other sciences, political climate, technological advancement, and economic conditions. Together, these and other factors create a **Zeitgeist**, or a spirit of the times, which many historians consider vital to the understanding of any historical development. Or one could emphasize the works of great individuals such as Plato, Aristotle, Descartes, Darwin, or Freud. Or one could focus on the historical development of an idea or concept and show how various individuals or events contributed to its change through the years. For example, one could focus on how the idea of mental illness has changed throughout history.

In his approach to the history of psychology, E. G. Boring (1957) stresses the importance of the Zeitgeist in determining whether, or to what extent, an idea or point of view will be accepted. Clearly, ideas do not occur in a vacuum. A new idea, in order to be accepted or even considered, must be compatible with existing ideas. In other words, a new idea will be tolerated only if it arises within an environment that can assimilate it. An idea or point of view that arises before people are prepared for it will be resisted or rejected. The important point here is that validity is not the only criterion by which ideas are judged; psychological and sociological factors are at least as important. New ideas are always judged within the context of existing circumstances. If new ideas are close enough to existing ideas, they will at least be understood; whether they are accepted, rejected, or ignored is another matter. If new ideas are too far removed from existing ones, they will not be understood well enough even to be critically evaluated.

Our approach will involve the Zeitgeist, great individuals, and the evolution of ideas. We will attempt to show that sometimes the spirit of the times seems to produce great individuals and sometimes great individuals influence the spirit of the times. We will also show how great individuals and the general climate of the times can both help to change an idea or a concept. In other words, our approach will be **eclectic** in that it will use whatever approach seems best able to illuminate an aspect of the history of psychology.

WHY STUDY THE HISTORY OF PSYCHOLOGY?

Perspective

As we have seen, ideas are seldom, if ever, born full-blown. Rather, they evolve over a long period of time. Seeing ideas in their historical perspective allows the student to more fully appreciate the subject matter of modern psychology, while seeing the problems and questions being dealt with currently in psychology as manifestations of problems and questions that have persisted for many centuries is humbling and sometimes even frustrating. After all, if psychology's problems have been worked on for centuries, should they not be solved by now? On the other hand, it is exciting to know that one's current studies have been shared, and contributed to, by some of the greatest minds in human history.

Greater Understanding

With greater perspective comes deeper understanding. With a knowledge of history, the student need not take on faith the importance of the subject matter of modern psychology. A student with an historical awareness knows where psychology's subject matter came from and why it is considered important. Just as one gains a greater understanding of a person's current behavior by learning more about that person's past experiences, so does one gain a greater understanding of current psychology by studying its historical origins. Boring (1957) makes this point in relation to experimental psychologists:

> The experimental psychologist . . . needs historical sophistication within his own sphere of expertness. Without such knowledge he sees the present in distorted perspective, he mistakes old facts and old views for new, and he remains unable to evaluate the significance of new movements and methods. In this matter I can hardly state my faith too strongly. A psychological sophistication that contains no component of historical orientation seems to me to be no sophistication at all. (p. ix)

Recognition of Fads and Fashions

While studying the history of psychology, one is often struck by the realization that a point of view does not always fade away because it is wrong; rather, some points of view fade away simply because they become unpopular. What is popular in psychology varies with the Zeitgeist. For example, when psychology first emerged as a science and was closely tied to the biological sciences, the emphasis was on "pure" science—that is, on the gaining of knowledge without any concern for its usefulness. Later, when Darwin's theory became popular, psychology shifted its attention to those things that allowed humans to live more effective lives. Today the emphasis in psychology is on cognitive processes, which have been the focus of concern throughout most of psychology's history. The major exception was during the brief dominance of behaviorism, when the study of cognitive (and physiological) events was unpopular.

In her presidential address to the International Society for Cell Biology, entitled "Fashion in Cell Biology," H. B. Fell (1960) points out that not recognizing that fashions occur in science may lead to wasted time and energy:

> In science, as in the world of dress, fashions recur. . . . There is one form of recurrence that is wholly regrettable, and which is one of the unfortunate consequences of the vast expansion of research and the monstrous and unwieldy literature that it now produces. I will mention a small example of the sort of thing I have in mind. In the 1920's some of my colleagues did a rather extensive series of experiments which they duly published. A few years ago, an account of an almost identical research with the same results appeared in one of the journals, but with no mention of the earlier study. One of my colleagues wrote and pointed this out to the author, who replied that he never quoted any literature prior to 1946. (p. 1625f.)

With such examples of how research topics move in and out of vogue in science, we see again that "factuality" is not the only variable determining whether or not an idea is accepted. Studying the emotional and societal factors related to the accumulation of knowledge allows the student to place currently accepted knowledge into a more realistic perspective. Such a perspective allows the student to realize that what body of knowledge is accepted as important or as "true" is at least partially subjective and arbitrary. As Zeitgeists change, so does what is considered fashionable in science, and psychology has not been immune to this process.

Avoiding Repetition of Mistakes

George Santayana once said, "Those who do not know history are doomed to repeat it." Such repetition would be bad enough if it involved only successes, since so much time and energy would be wasted. It is especially unfortunate, however, if mistakes are repeated. As we shall see in this text, psychology has had its share of mistakes and dead ends. One mistake was believing that the faculties of the mind could be strengthened with exercise, just as one would strengthen his or her biceps. One dead end may have been the entire school of structuralism, whose members attempted to isolate the elements of thought by using the introspective method. It is generally thought that the efforts of the structuralists, although extremely popular at the time, were sterile and unproductive. Yet it was important for psychology that such an effort was made, for we learned that such an approach led to little that was useful. This, and other important lessons, would be lost if the errors of the past were repeated because of a lack of historical information.

A Source of Valuable Ideas

By studying history, one may discover ideas that were developed at an earlier time but, for one reason or another, remained dormant. In the history of science there are several examples of an idea taking hold only after it was rediscovered long after it had originally been proposed. This fact fits nicely into the Zeitgeist interpretation of history, suggesting that some conditions are better suited for the acceptance of an idea than others. The notions of evolution, unconscious motivation, and conditioned

responses had been proposed and reproposed several times in history before they were offered in an atmosphere that allowed their critical evaluation. No doubt there are still many potentially fruitful ideas in psychology's history waiting to be tried again under new circumstances.

Curiosity

Instead of asking the question "Why study the history of psychology?" it might make more sense to ask "Why not?" Many people study American history because they are interested in America, and younger members of a family often delight in hearing stories about the early days of the family's elderly members. In other words, it is natural to want to know as much as possible about a topic or person of interest, including a topic's or a person's history. There is no reason for psychology to be an exception.

Studying the history of psychology allows the student to place modern psychology in historical perspective, understand modern psychology more thoroughly, recognize that what is popular in psychology is often determined by societal and/or emotional factors, see past mistakes so that they need not be repeated, discover potentially useful ideas, and satisfy his or her own curiosity about something deemed important.

WHAT IS SCIENCE?

At various times in history, influential individuals (for example, Galileo and Kant) have claimed that psychology could never be a science because of its concern with subjective experience. Many natural scientists still believe this, and a large number of psychologists would not argue with them. Clearly, how one writes a history of psychology will be influenced by whether or not psychology can be considered a science. In order to answer the question of whether or not psychology is a science, however, we must first attempt to define science. Science came into existence as a way of answering questions about nature by examining nature directly, rather than by church dogma, past authorities, superstition, or by abstract thought processes. From science's inception, its ultimate authority has been empirical observation (that is, the direct observation of nature), but there is more to science than simply observing nature. To be useful, observations must be organized or categorized in some ways, and the ways in which they are similar to or different from other observations must be noted. After noting similarities and differences among observations, many scientists take the additional step of attempting to explain what they have observed. Science, then, is often characterized as having two major components: (1) empirical observation and (2) theory. According to Clark Hull (1943), these two aspects of science can be seen in the earliest efforts of humans to understand their world:

> Men are ever engaged in the dual activity of making observations and then seeking explanations of the resulting revelations. All normal men in all times have observed the rising and setting of the sun and the several phases of the moon. The more thoughtful among them have then proceeded to ask the question, "Why? Why does the moon wax and wane? Why does the sun rise and set, and where does it go when it sets?" Here we have the two essential elements of modern science: The making of observations constitutes the empirical or factual component, and the systematic attempt to explain these facts constitutes the theoretical component. As science has developed, specialization, or division of labor, has occurred; some men have devoted their time mainly to the making of observations, while a smaller number have occupied themselves with the problems of explanation. (p. 1)

The two major components of science can also be seen in the definition of science offered by S. S. Stevens (1951): "Science seeks to generate confirmable propositions by fitting a formal system of symbols (language, mathematics, logic) to empirical observation" (p. 22).

Combination of Rationalism and Empiricism

What makes science such a powerful tool is the fact that it combines two ancient methods of attaining knowledge: **rationalism** and **empiricism**. The rationalist believes that mental operations of some sort must be employed before knowledge can be attained. For example, the rationalist says that the validity or invalidity of certain propositions can be determined by carefully applying the rules of logic. The empiricist maintains that the source of all knowledge is sensory observation. True knowledge, therefore, can only be derived from or validated by sensory experience. After centuries of inquiry it was discovered that by themselves rationalism and empiricism had limited usefulness, so science combined the two positions and knowledge has been accumulating at an exponential rate ever since.

The rational aspect of science keeps it from being a way of collecting an endless array of disconnected empirical facts. Since the scientist must somehow make sense out of what he or she observes, theories are formulated. A **scientific theory** has two main functions: (1) it organizes empirical observations, and (2) it acts as a guide for future observations. The latter function of a scientific theory generates what Stevens refers to as confirmable propositions. In other words, a theory suggests propositions that are tested experimentally. If a proposition generated by a theory is confirmed through experimentation, the theory gains strength; if the proposition is not confirmed by experimentation, the theory loses strength. If the theory generates enough erroneous propositions, it must be either revised or abandoned. Thus, scientific theories must be testable. That is, they must generate hypotheses that can be validated or invalidated empirically.

Another feature of science is that it seeks to discover lawful relationships. A **scientific law** can be defined as a consistently observed relationship between two or more classes of empirical events. For example, when X occurs, Y also occurs. Science then uses theories to find and explain lawful, empirical events. By stressing lawfulness, science is proclaiming an interest in the general case rather than the particular case. Traditionally, science is not interested in private or unique events but in general laws that can be **publicly observed and verified**. That is, a scientific law is general, and because it describes a relationship between empirical events, it is available for anyone to verify.

It should be clear that since a main goal of science is to discover lawful relationships, science must assume that what is being investigated is lawful. For example, the chemist must assume that chemical reactions are lawful, and the physicist must assume that the behavior of atomic and subatomic particles is lawful. The assumption that what is being studied is characterized by lawful relationships is called **determinism**. The determinist assumes that everything that occurs is a function of a finite number of causes, and that if these causes were known, an event could be predicted with complete accuracy. Note that it does not matter that *all* of the causes of an event can never be known; the determinist simply assumes that they exist, and that as more causes are known, predictions become more accurate. For example, almost everyone would agree that the weather is a function of a finite number of variables, such as sunspots, high-altitude jet streams, and barometric pressure; and yet weather forecasts are always probabilistic, because many of these variables change constantly and others are simply unknown. The *assumption* underlying weather prediction, however, is determinism. *All sciences assume determinism.*

REVISIONS IN THE TRADITIONAL VIEW OF SCIENCE

The traditional view of science involves empirical observation, theory formulation, theory testing, theory revision, prediction, the search for lawful relationships, and the assumption of determinism. It should be noted, however, that there are prominent philosophers of science who would take issue with some aspects of the traditional view of science. Among them are Karl Popper and Thomas Kuhn.

Popper's View of Science

Popper disagrees with the traditional description of science in two fundamental ways. First, he disagrees that scientific activity starts with empirical observation. According to Popper, the older view of science implies that scientists wander around making observations and then attempt to explain what they have observed. Popper (1963) shows the problem with such a view:

> Twenty-five years ago I tried to bring home the same point to a group of physics students in Vienna by beginning a lecture with the following instructions: "Take pencil and paper: carefully observe, and write down what you have observed!" They asked, of course, *what* I wanted them to observe. Clearly the instruction, "observe!" is absurd . . . observation is always selective. It needs a chosen object, a definite task, an interest, a point of view, a problem. (p. 46)

So for Popper, scientific activity starts with a problem, and the problem determines what observations scientists will make. The next step is to propose a solution to the problem, and finally attempts are made to find fault with the proposed solution. Popper, then, sees scientific method as involving three stages: problems, theories (proposed solutions), criticism.

What distinguishes a scientific theory from a nonscientific theory, according to Popper, is the **principle of refutability**. A scientific theory must be refutable. Contrary to what many believe, if any conceivable observation agrees with a theory, the theory is weak, not strong. Popper spends a great deal of time criticizing the theories of Freud and Adler for this reason. Without exception, everything a person does can be seen as supportive of either of these theories. Popper contrasts such theories with that of Einstein, which predicted events that, if not observed, would refute the theory. Thus Einstein's theory, unlike the theories of Freud and Adler, was refutable and therefore scientific. According to Popper, the fact that no observation can be specified that would falsify astrology makes astrology unscientific. Here is how Popper (1963) summarizes his views on scientific theory:

(1) It is easy to obtain confirmations, or verifications, for nearly every theory—if we look for confirmations.

(2) Confirmations should count only if they are the result of risky predictions; that is to say, if, unenlightened by the theory in question, we should have expected an event which was incompatible with the theory—an event which would have refuted the theory.

(3) Every "good" scientific theory is a prohibition: it forbids certain things to happen. The more a theory forbids, the better it is.

(4) A theory which is not refutable by any conceivable event is non-scientific. Irrefutability is not a virtue of a theory (as people often think) but a vice.

(5) Every genuine test of a theory is an attempt to falsify it, or to refute it. Testability is falsifiability; but there are degrees of testability: some theories are more testable, more exposed to refutation, than others; they take, as it were, greater risks.

(6) Confirming evidence should not count except when it is the result of a genuine test of the theory; and this means that it can be presented as a serious but unsuccessful attempt to falsify the theory. . . .

(7) Some genuinely testable theories, when found to be false, are still upheld by their admirers—for example, by introducing *ad hoc* some auxiliary assumption, or by re-interpreting the theory *ad hoc* in such a way that it escapes refutation. Such a procedure is always possible, but it rescues the theory from refutation only at the price of destroying, or at least lowering, its scientific status. (pp. 36–37)

Does this mean Popper believes that nonscientific theories are useless? Absolutely not! He says (1963):

Historically speaking all—or very nearly all—scientific theories originate from myths, and . . . a myth may contain important anticipations of scientific theories. . . . I thus [feel] that if a theory is found to be non-scientific, or "metaphysical" . . . it is not thereby found to be unimportant, or insignificant, or "meaningless," or "nonsensical." (p. 38)

Thus, Popper uses falsification as a means of distinguishing between a scientific and a nonscientific theory, but not between a useful and useless theory. Many theories in psychology fail Popper's test of refutability because they are stated in such general terms that they are confirmed by almost any observation. Such theories lack scientific rigor but are often still found to be useful. Freud's theory is an example.

Kuhn's View of Science

We have seen that until recently it was widely believed that the scientific method guaranteed objectivity, and that science produced information in a steady, progressive way. It was assumed that within any science there were knowable "truths," and that following scientific procedures allowed a science to systematically approximate those truths. In his book *The Structure of Scientific Revolutions*, Thomas S. Kuhn (1973) has changed that conception of science by showing science to be a highly subjective enterprise.

According to Kuhn, it is not uncommon in the physical sciences for one point of view to be shared by most members of a science. In physics or chemistry, for example, most researchers share a common set of assumptions and/or beliefs about their subject matter. Kuhn refers to such a widely accepted point of view as a **paradigm**. For those scientists accepting a paradigm, it becomes *the* way of looking at and analyzing the subject matter of their science. Once a paradigm is accepted, the activities of those accepting it become a matter of exploring the implications of that paradigm. Kuhn refers to such activities as **normal science**. Normal science provides what Kuhn calls a "mopping-up" operation for a paradigm. While following a paradigm, then, scientists explore in depth the problems defined by the paradigm and utilize the techniques suggested by the paradigm while exploring those problems. Although a paradigm restricts the range of phenomena scientists deal with, it does guarantee that certain phenomena are studied thoroughly. Kuhn (1973) says:

> By focusing attention upon a small range of relatively esoteric problems, the paradigm forces scientists to investigate some part of nature in a detail and depth that would otherwise be unimaginable. . . . During the period when the paradigm is successful, the profession will have solved problems that its members could scarcely have imagined and would never have undertaken without commitment to the paradigm. And at least part of that achievement always proves to be permanent. (pp. 24–25)

That is the positive side of having research guided by a paradigm, but there is also a negative side. Although normal science allows for the thorough analysis of the phenomena a paradigm focuses on, it blinds scientists to other phenomena and perhaps better explanations for what they are studying. As Kuhn (1973) says:

> Mopping-up operations are what engage most scientists throughout their careers. They constitute what I am here calling normal science. Closely examined, whether historically or in the contemporary laboratory, that enterprise seems an attempt to force nature into the preformed

and relatively inflexible box that the paradigm supplied. No part of the aim of normal science is to call forth new sorts of phenomena; indeed, those that will not fit the box are often not seen at all. Nor do scientists normally aim to invent new theories, and they are often intolerant of those invented by others. Instead, normal-scientific research is directed to the articulation of those phenomena and theories that the paradigm already supplies. (p. 24)

A paradigm, then, determines what constitutes a research problem *and* how the solution to that problem is sought. In other words, a paradigm guides all of the researcher's activities. More important, however, is the fact that researchers become emotionally involved in their paradigm; it becomes part of their lives, and is therefore very difficult to give up.

Then how do scientific paradigms change? According to Kuhn, not very easily. First, there must be persistent observations that a currently accepted paradigm cannot explain; these are called anomalies. Usually a single scientist or a small group of scientists will propose an alternative viewpoint, one that will account for most of the phenomena that the prevailing paradigm accounts for and will also explain the anomalies. Kuhn indicates that there is typically great resistance to the new paradigm, and that converts to it are won over very slowly. Eventually, however, the new paradigm wins out and displaces the old one. According to Kuhn, this describes what happened when Einstein challenged the Newtonian conception of the universe. Now the Einsteinian paradigm is generating its own normal science and will continue to do so until it is overthrown by another paradigm.

Kuhn portrays science as a method of inquiry that combines the objective scientific method and the emotional makeup of the scientist. Science progresses, according to Kuhn, because scientists are forced to change their *belief systems;* and belief systems are very difficult to change, whether for a group of scientists or for anyone else.

What has all of this to do with psychology?

Psychology has been described as a preparadigmatic science (Staats, 1981), since it does not have one widely accepted paradigm but seems to have several that exist simultaneously. For example, in psychology today we see paradigms that can be labeled behavioristic, functionalistic, cognitive, neurophysiological, psychoanalytic, and existential-humanistic. Some see this multiple-paradigm or preparadigmatic situation as negative, and insist that psychology is ready to synthesize all of its paradigms into one unified paradigm. For example, Staats (1981) says:

> Our science [psychology] is presently characterized by separatism, a feature that has a pervasive effect and that constitutes an obstacle to scientific progress. The concept of separatism describes our science as split into unorganized bits and pieces, along many dimensions. Divisions exist on the basis of theory, method, and the types of findings that are accepted, as well as on the basis of student training, organizational bodies such as divisions, journals and individual strivings. Our field is constructed of small islands of knowledge organized in ways that make no connection with the many other existing islands of knowledge. (p. 239)

According to Staats (1981), psychology is ready to become a single-paradigm science, and it should become one:

> A unified theory of large scope might be enormously advantageous to psychology and . . . we must begin generally to allocate a part of our resources to the development of a unified science. . . . My view is that our science requires development of the methodology for the creation of such theory, as well as development of methods and standards of evaluation of theories in terms of their unity and comprehensiveness. (pp. 239–240)

Others do not agree with Staats, saying either that it is more productive to have several paradigms or that, because we are studying humans, several paradigms are inevitable. In any case, like it or not, psychology does have a number of viewpoints, and whether this suggests prematurity as a science is irrelevant; it is simply how things are at this moment.

Popper versus Kuhn

A major source of disagreement between Kuhn and Popper concerns Kuhn's concept of normal science. As we have seen, Kuhn says that once a paradigm has been accepted, most scientists busy themselves with research projects dictated by the paradigm—that is, doing normal science. For Kuhn, a paradigm creates a puzzle, and individual scientists seek pieces of the puzzle until either the puzzle is completed or the paradigm is replaced by a new one. For Popper, what Kuhn calls normal science is not science at all. Scientists attempt to solve problems, he says, not fill in pieces of a puzzle. Furthermore, for Kuhn, paradigms develop and are accepted for psychological and/or sociological reasons. For Popperian science such factors are foreign; problems exist and proposed solutions either pass the rigorous attempts to refute them or they do not. Thus, Kuhn's analysis of science stresses subjective factors, and Popper's analysis stresses logic. Robinson (1981) suggests, and we agree, that the views of both Kuhn and Popper may be correct.

> In a conciliatory spirit, we might suggest that the major disagreement between Kuhn and Popper vanishes when we picture Kuhn as describing what science has been historically, and Popper asserting what it ought to be. (p. 24)

Even with the revisions suggested by Popper and Kuhn, many of the traditional aspects of science remain. Empirical observation is still considered the ultimate authority, lawful relationships are still sought, theories are still formulated and tested, and determinism is still assumed.

IS PSYCHOLOGY A SCIENCE?

Is psychology a science or not? The scientific method has been used with great success in psychology. There have been, and are, experimental psychologists who have demonstrated lawful relationships between classes of environmental events (stimuli) and classes of behavior, and they have devised rigorous, refutable theories to account for those relationships. The theories of Hull and Tolman are examples, and there are many others. Other psychologists work hand in hand with chemists and neurologists who are attempting to determine the biochemical correlates of memory. Other scientifically oriented psychologists have been working on the psychological effects of weightlessness as part of our country's space program and still others have helped design the equipment used by astronauts during spaceflight. In fact, we can safely say that scientifically oriented psychologists have provided a great deal of useful information in every major area of psychology—for example, learning, perception, memory, personality, intelligence, motivation, and psychotherapy.

These scientifically oriented psychologists are willing to assume determinism while studying humans. The kind of determinism assumed, however, varies. Those psychologists attempting to explain human behavior in terms of physical events (for example, brain mechanisms, biochemistry, environmental stimuli, and response mechanisms) assume **physical determinism**. The following comments from Schwartz and Lacey (1982) nicely illustrate the kind of physical determinism that places the cause of human behavior in the environment:

> Behavior theory emphasizes that environmental events play the key role in determining human behavior. The source of action lies not inside the person, but in the environment. By developing a full understanding of how environmental events influence behavior, we will arrive at a complete understanding of behavior. It is this feature of behavior theory—its emphasis on environmental events as the determinants of human action—which most clearly sets it apart from other approaches to human nature. . . . If behavior theory succeeds, our customary inclination to hold people responsible for their actions, and look inside them to their wishes, desires, goals, intentions, and so on, for

explanations of their actions, will be replaced by an entirely different orientation . . . one in which responsibility for action is sought in environmental events. (p. 13)

Other scientifically oriented psychologists emphasize cognitive events (for example, information-processing strategies, perceptions, values, and beliefs) as the determinants of behavior, thereby assuming **psychical determinism**. Among the psychologists assuming psychical determinism are those who stress the importance of mental events of which we are conscious, and those, like Freud, who stress the importance of mental events of which we are not conscious. The scientifically oriented psychologists, in addition to accepting some kind of determinism, also seek general laws, develop theories, and use empirical observation as their ultimate authority in judging the validity of those theories. So, psychology is definitely a science, but the situation is more complicated.

First, there are psychologists who believe that human behavior is determined but that the causes of behavior cannot be accurately measured. With this belief, these psychologists are accepting Heisenberg's **uncertainty principle**. The German physicist Werner Karl Heisenberg (1901–1976) found that the very act of observing an electron influences its activity and casts doubt on the validity of the observation. Heisenberg concluded from this that nothing can ever be known with certainty in science. This principle, when translated into psychology, says that although human behavior is indeed determined, we can never learn the causes of behavior, since in attempting to observe them we change them. Also, the experimental setting itself may act as a confounding variable in the search for the causes of human behavior. Psychologists accepting this point of view believe that there are specific causes of behavior but that they cannot be accurately known. Such a position is called **indeterminism**. Another example of indeterminancy is Immanual Kant's

(1724–1804) conclusion that a science of psychology was impossible because the mind could not be objectively employed to study itself. R. B. MacLeod (1975) summarizes Kant's position:

> Kant challenged the very basis of a science of psychology. If psychology is the study of "the mind," and if every observation and every deduction is an operation of a mind which silently imposes its own categories on that which is being observed, then how can a mind turn in upon itself and observe its own operations when it is forced by its very nature to observe in terms of its own categories? *Is there any sense in turning up the light to see what the darkness looks like?* (p. 146, italics added)

There are also psychologists who completely reject science as a way of studying humans. These psychologists, usually working within either a humanistic or an existential paradigm, believe that the causes of behavior are found in one's self, ego, or psyche and are self-generated. For this group, behavior is freely chosen rather than determined by physical or cognitive causes. This belief in free will is contrary to the assumption of determinism, and therefore the endeavors of these psychologists are nonscientific. Such a position is known as **nondeterminism**. For the nondeterminist, since the individual freely chooses courses of action, he or she alone is responsible for them. The concept of personal responsibility is but one of the many points of disagreement for the determinist and the nondeterminist.

Whether or not we consider psychology a science, then, depends upon which aspect of psychology we focus on. Sigmund Koch (1981), a highly respected psychologist and philosopher of science, answers the question "Is psychology a science?" in a way that stresses psychology's nonscientific nature:

> I have been addressing this question for 40 years and, over the past 20, have been stable in my view that psychology is not a single or coherent discipline but rather a collection of studies of varied cast, some few of which may qualify as science, while most do not. (p. 268)

Psychology should not be judged too harshly because some of its aspects are not scientific or are even antiscientific. Science as we now know it is relatively new, whereas the subject matter of most, if not all, sciences is very old. What is now studied scientifically was once, as Popper has noted, studied philosophically. First came the nebulous categories that were debated for centuries in a nonscientific way. This debate readied various categories of inquiry for the "fine-tuning" that science provides. Frequently scientific method is applied to topics that have evolved for a long time and are therefore ready for the kind of polishing that science provides. Therefore, the importance of prescientific inquiry should not be overlooked, since such inquiry has often provided the concepts that were later studied more objectively using the scientific method.

In psychology today there is inquiry on all levels. Some concepts have a long philosophical heritage and are ready to be treated scientifically; other concepts are still in their early stages of evolution and are not ready for scientific treatment; and still other concepts, by their very nature, may never be amenable to scientific inquiry. It seems that all of these levels and kinds of inquiry are necessary for the growth of psychology, and that all feed off of each other. Also, we have seen that many subjective factors play an important role in the evolution of science, bringing scientific and nonscientific inquiry closer together. Indeed, a new field of interest called the psychology of science has opened up.

PERSISTENT QUESTIONS IN PSYCHOLOGY

Many of the questions psychology is now attempting to answer are the same questions it has been attempting to answer from its inception. Only the methods for dealing with these persistent questions change.

What Is the Nature of Human Nature?

How much of our animal heritage remains in human nature? For example, are we inherently aggressive and hostile? Yes, say the Freudians. Is human nature basically good and nonviolent? Yes, say members of the humanistic camp such as Rogers and Maslow. Or is our nature neither good nor bad but neutral, as the behaviorists such as Watson and Skinner claim? The behaviorists maintain that experience makes a person good or bad or whatever the person is. Do humans possess a free will? Yes, say the existential psychologists; no, say the scientifically oriented psychologists. Associated with each of psychology's paradigms is an assumption about the nature of human nature, and each of these assumptions has a long history. Throughout this text we will sample these conceptions about human nature, as well as the methodologies they generate.

How Are the Mind and the Body Related?

The question of whether there is a mind, and if so, how it is related to the body is as old as psychology itself. It is a question that every psychologist must address either explicitly or implicitly. Through the years almost every conceivable position has been taken on the mind-body relationship. Some psychologists attempt to explain everything in physical terms; for them, even so-called mental events are ultimately explainable in terms of the laws of physics and/or chemistry. These individuals are called **materialists**, and they are also called **monists** because they attempt to explain everything in terms of one kind of reality. Other psychologists take the other extreme and claim that everything is mental, saying that even the so-called physical world is a creation of the human mind. These individuals are called **idealists**, and they too are monists because they attempt to explain everything in terms of human consciousness or perception. Most psychologists, however, accept the existence of both physical and cognitive events and assume that the two are governed by different principles. Such a conception is called **dualism**. The dualist believes that there are physical events and ideas about physical events. Once it is assumed that both a physical and a mental realm exist, the question becomes how the two are related. For the monist, of course, there is no mind-body problem.

One answer that the dualist proposes to the mind-body question is that the two interact. That is, the mind influences the body and the body influences the mind. According to this **interactionistic** conception, the mind is capable of initiating behavior. This was the position taken by Descartes and is the one taken by most members of the humanism-existentialism camp. Another answer to the mind-body question is that bodily experiences cause mental events, but that mental events cannot cause behavior. This position is called **epiphenomenalism** because it claims that mental events are simply by-products (epiphenomena) of physical experience, and as such have no causal relationship to behavior. Another answer the dualists offer is that an environmental experience causes both mental events and bodily responses *at the same time*, and that the two are totally independent of each other. This position is referred to as **psychophysical parallelism**.

According to another dualistic position, called **double aspectism**, a person cannot be divided into a mind and a body but is a unity that experiences things physiologically and mentally at the same time. Mental events and physiological events are two aspects of the same thing—the person. Mind and body do not interact, nor can they ever be separated. They are simply two aspects of each experience we have as humans. Other dualists maintain that there is a **preestablished harmony** between bodily and mental events. That is, the two kinds of events are different but are coordinated by some external agent—for example, God. Finally, in the seventh century Malebranche suggested that when a desire occurs in the mind God causes the body to act. Likewise, when something happens to the body, God causes the corresponding mental experience. Malebranche's position on the mind-body relationship is called **occasionalism**.

All of the above positions on the mind-body question are represented in psychology's history, and we will therefore encounter them throughout this text. Chisholm's whimsical summary of the proposed mind-body relationships is shown in Figure 1.1.

Nativism versus Empiricism

To what extent are human attributes such as intelligence determined by genetics and to what extent are they determined by experience? The nativists emphasize the role of genetics in their explanation of the origins of various human attributes, while the empiricists emphasize the role of experience. Those who consider some aspect of human behavior instinctive, or who take a stand on human nature as being good, bad, gregarious, and so on, are also nativists. The empiricist, on the other hand, claims that humans are the way they are because of the experiences they have had. Obviously this question is still unresolved. The nativism-empiricism controversy is closely related to the question concerning the nature of human nature. For example, those who claim that humans are aggressive by nature are saying that humans are genetically predisposed to be aggressive.

Freedom versus Determinism

Do human beings possess a free will? If so, a science of human behavior is not possible, since, as we have seen, science assumes determinism. That is, if human behavior varies as a function of a person's will, it is not subject to scientific investigation. Though existential psychologists

take this position, most psychologists accept a deterministic model while studying humans. But to say that human behavior is determined is not the same thing as saying that a physical event is determined. Even when a psychologist accepts that human behavior is determined, the question remains, "Determined by what?" In psychology, the physical determinist looks for causes of behavior in stimulation from the environment, sensory apparatus, brain mechanisms, genes, the biochemistry of the body, or a combination of these, as well as in other physical events.

There is another group of psychologists, however, who look for the major causes of behavior in one's subjective experience. For these psychologists, a person's beliefs, perceptions, values, attitudes, and/or expectations are the primary causes of behavior. This psychical determinism creates special problems. Since these cognitive determinants are private and impossible to measure directly, it seems to these psychologists that a person's behavior is not determined by the same kinds of things that the physical determinist assumes it is. Rather, it appears that much behavior is under the control of a person's subjective reality and is therefore **self-regulated**. That is, a person ponders the array of cognitive material available, *selects* from it, and then acts accordingly. Whether or not such behavior is "free"—that is, not determined—depends upon one's definition of freedom. The psychical determinist argues that those emphasizing subjective reality merely shift the causes of behavior from physical reality to subjective reality, and that behavior is therefore still determined. Also, the determinist maintains that these subjective experiences are caused by the various experiences a person has had, and are therefore themselves subject to scientific scrutiny. The psychical determinist assumes that as more is learned about a person's beliefs, values, attitudes, expectations, and so on, his or her behavior will appear more lawful and more predictable. Thus, according to the

FIGURE 1.1 Chisholm's depictions of various mind-body relationships (Redrawn from Taylor, 1963, p. 130). Used by permission of Roderick M. Chisholm.

psychical determinist, behavior can be self-regulated and still not be free.

For most, but not all, contemporary psychologists, the argument is over whether the causes of human behavior are physical or mental, rather than whether human behavior is determined or free. Once it is assumed, however, that the causes of behavior are cognitive rather than physical, the job of the psychologist attempting to explore the causes of human behavior becomes much more complex. It is a job unlike that in any other science.

The Rationality of Human Behavior and Thought

Many psychologists maintain that it is possession of language that allows humans to engage in the complex reasoning that allows for intel-

ligent behavior. According to these psychologists, sensory experience must be pondered in a rational way before accurate knowledge can be attained. Thus they follow in the rationalist tradition, which postulates an active mind. Other psychologists do not agree. They say that the brain, rather than providing a mechanism for rational thought, is more or less a complex switchboard that coordinates sensory events with appropriate behavior. For them, rational thought plays a minor role at best in human conduct, and they see the mind as more passive than active.

Still other psychologists say that much of human behavior is motivated by the emotions or by unconscious determinants and is therefore irrational. Freud, for example, believed that most human behavior is motivated by variables that the individual is unaware of. The question of whether human thought and behavior are rational, mechanistic, or irrational is closely related to the mind-body question, and we shall return to it often in this text.

How Are Humans Related to Other Animals?

The major question here is whether humans are qualitatively or quantitatively different from other animals. If the difference is quantitative (one of degree), then at least something can be learned about humans by studying other animals. The school of behaviorism grew directly out of animal research and maintained that the same principles govern the behavior of both "lower" organisms and humans. For the behaviorist, the results of animal research can be readily generalized to the human level. Representing the other extreme are the humanists and the existentialists, who believe that humans are unique in the animal kingdom and that nothing important about humans can be learned by studying nonhuman animals. The majority of psychologists can be placed somewhere between the two extremes, saying that some things can be learned about humans by studying other animals and some things cannot. Currently, all of these positions are represented in research on language. Some psychologists maintain that language has been demonstrated in chimpanzees; others say only humans possess "true" language. Still others say that rudimentary language has been demonstrated in chimpanzees but that human language is much more complex.

What Is the Origin of Human Knowledge?

The study of knowledge is called **epistemology**. The epistemologist asks such questions as, "What can we know?" and "What are the limits of knowledge?" and "How is knowledge arrived at?" Psychology has always been involved in epistemology, since one of its major concerns has been determining how humans gain information about themselves and their world. The empiricist insists that all knowledge is derived from sensory experience, which is somehow registered and stored in the brain. The rationalist agrees that sensory information is often, if not always, an important first step in attaining knowledge, but argues that the mind must then actively transform this information in some way before knowledge is attained. The nativist would say that some knowledge is innate. Plato and Descartes, for example, believed that many ideas were a natural part of the mind.

In answering epistemological questions, the empiricists postulate a **passive mind** that represents physical experiences as mental images and recollections. In other words, the passive mind is seen as reflecting cognitively what is occurring, or what has occurred, in the physical world. Physical experiences that occur consistently in some particular pattern will be represented cognitively in that pattern and will tend to be recalled in that pattern. The rationalists, however, postulate an **active mind** that *transforms* the data from experience in some important way. Whereas a passive mind is seen as representing physical reality, the active mind is seen as a mechanism by which physical reality is organized, pondered, understood, or valued. For the rationalist, the mind adds something to our mental experience that is not found in our physical experience.

For the empiricist, then, knowledge consists of the accurate description of physical reality as it is revealed by sensory experience and recorded in the mind. For the rationalist, knowledge consists of concepts and principles that can be arrived at only by a pondering, active mind. The empiricist, rationalist, and nativist positions, and various combinations of them, have always been part of psychology, and in one form or another they are still with us today. In this text we will see how these three major philosophical positions have manifested themselves in various ways throughout psychology's history.

SUMMARY

Psychologists have long been interested in the contents and mechanisms of thought, the bodily processes that bring the individual into contact with the physical environment, and the ways in which these mental and physical events are related, if they are related at all. Although such concerns probably go back to the dawn of civilization, our version of the history of psychology begins with the early Greeks. Our approach to writing this text exemplifies presentism, since current psychology is used as a guide in determining what to cover historically. In presenting the history of psychology, this text combines coverage of great individuals, persistent ideas, the spirit of the times, and contributions from other fields. Such a combined approach is referred to as eclectic. By studying the history of psychology a student gains perspective and a deeper understanding of modern psychology. Also, he or she will learn that sometimes social and/or cultural conditions determine what is emphasized in psychology. Finally, by studying the history of psychology, previous mistakes can be avoided, potentially important ideas can be discovered, and the natural curiosity about something thought to be important can be satisfied.

Traditionally, science was viewed as starting with empirical observation and then proceeding to development of theory. Theories were evaluated in terms of their ability to generate predictions that were either supported by experimental outcome or not. Theories that generated predictions that were confirmed became stronger and those making erroneous predictions were revised or abandoned. By linking empirical observation and theory, science combined the philosophical schools of empiricism and rationalism. Science assumes determinism and seeks general laws. Karl Popper disagrees with the traditional view of science, saying that scientific activity does not start with empirical observation but with a problem of some kind that guides the scientist's empirical observations. Furthermore, Popper maintains that if a scientific theory is consistently confirmed, it is more likely a bad theory than a good one. A good theory must make risky predictions that, if not confirmed, refute the theory. In order to be classified as a scientific theory, a theory must specify in advance the observations that, if made, would refute it. What distinguishes a scientific theory from a nonscientific theory is the theory's ability to be falsified or refuted. Thomas Kuhn also disagrees with the traditional view of science. Kuhn's analysis of science stresses sociological and psychological factors. At any given time scientists accept a general framework within which they perform their research, a framework Kuhn calls a paradigm. A paradigm determines what constitutes research problems and determines how those problems are solved. Which paradigm is accepted by a group of scientists is determined as much by subjective factors as by objective factors. For Popper, scientific activity is guided by problems, while for Kuhn, scientific activity is guided by a paradigm that scientists believe to be true.

Some aspects of psychology are scientific and some are not. Psychologists who are willing to assume physical or psychical determinism while studying humans are more likely to have a scientific orientation than those unwilling to make that assumption. Nondeterminists assume that human behavior is freely chosen and therefore not amenable to scientific analysis. The indeterminist believes that human behavior is determined but that the determinants of behavior cannot be known with certainty. Psychology need not apologize for its nonscientific aspects, since these aspects have often made significant contributions to the understanding of humans. Often the concepts developed by nonscientific psychologists are later fine-tuned by psychologists using the scientific method.

Many of the questions that have persisted throughout psychology's history were summarized. They include the following: What is the nature of human nature? How are the mind and body related? To what extent are human attributes determined by heredity (nativism) as opposed to experience (empiricism)? How rational are human behavior and thought? To what extent are humans free, and to what extent is their behavior determined by knowable causes? How are humans related to other animals? What are the origins of human knowledge?

DISCUSSION QUESTIONS

1. Discuss the choices that must be made before writing a history of psychology.

2. What is gained by studying a history of psychology?

3. Discuss why psychology was described as both a science and a nonscience. Include in your answer the characteristics of science that some psychologists are not willing to accept while studying humans.

4. In what ways does Popper's view of science differ from the traditional view?

5. Why does Popper consider Freud's theory to be nonscientific?

6. Summarize Kuhn's views on how sciences change. Include in your answer the definitions of the terms *paradigm* and *normal science.*

7. Should psychology aspire to becoming a single-paradigm discipline or not? Defend your answer.

8. Summarize the various views of human nature that were discussed in the text.

9. Summarize the various proposed answers to the mind-body question. Include in your answer definitions of the terms *monism, dualism, materialism, idealism, interactionism, psychophysical parallelism, epiphenomenalism, preestablished harmony, double aspectism,* and *occasionalism.*

10. Discuss the nativist and empiricist explanations of human attributes.

11. Is human behavior free or determined? Defend your answer. Include in your answer a discussion of self-regulated behavior.

12. Is human thought rational? Defend your answer.

13. What can be learned about humans by studying other animals? Frame your answer around the phenomenon of language.

14. Describe how each of the following would explain how we gain knowledge: the empiricist, the rationalist, and the nativist.

15. Define *physical determinism, psychical determinism, indeterminism,* and *nondeterminism.*

16. Distinguish between a passive and an active mind.

GLOSSARY

Active mind A mind that transforms, interprets, understands, and/or values physical experience. The rationalists assume an active mind.

Determinism The belief that everything that occurs does so because of known or knowable causes, and that if these causes were known in advance, an event could be predicted with complete accuracy.

Double aspectism The belief that bodily and mental events are inseparable. They are two aspects of every experience.

Dualist Anyone who believes that there are two aspects to humans, one physical and one mental.

Eclectic Taking the best from a variety of points of view. The approach to the history of psychology taken in this text is eclectic because it combines coverage of great individuals, the evolution of ideas and concepts, the spirit of the times, and contributions from other disciplines.

Empiricism The belief that the basis of all knowledge is sensory experience.

Epiphenomenalism The contention that bodily experiences cause mental events, but that the mental events do not in turn cause bodily activity.

Epistemology The study of the nature of knowledge.

Freedom The condition in which human actions vary as a function of one's own will and not as a function of measurable causes.

Idealist Anyone who believes that the ultimate reality consists of ideas or perceptions and is therefore not physical.

Indeterminism The contention that even though determinism is true, attempting to measure the causes of something influences those causes, making it impossible to know them with certainty. This contention is also called Heisenberg's uncertainty principle.

Interactionism A proposed answer to the mind-body question that maintains that bodily experiences influence the mind and that the mind influences the body

Materialist Anyone who believes that everything in the world is material (physical), including those things that others refer to as mental.

Mind-body question The question concerning how the cognitive aspects of humans are related to their physical aspects.

Monist Anyone who says there is only one reality. Materialists are monists because they believe that everything is reducible to material substance. Idealists are also monists because they believe that everything, including the material world, is the result of human consciousness and is therefore mental.

Nativism The belief that important human attributes such as intelligence are genetically determined.

Nondeterminism The belief that human thought and/or behavior is freely chosen by the individual and is therefore not caused by antecedent physical or mental events.

Normal science According to Thomas Kuhn, the research activities performed by scientists as they explore the implications of a paradigm.

Occasionalism The belief that the relationship between the mind and body is mediated by God.

Paradigm A point of view shared by many scientists while exploring the subject matter of their science.

Passive mind A mind that reflects cognitively one's experiences with the physical world. The empiricists assume a passive mind.

Physical determinism The kind of determinism that stresses material causes of behavior.

Physical reality Those objects and events that constitute the physical world.

Preestablished harmony The belief that bodily events and mental events are correlated because both were designed to run identical courses.

Presentism Use of the current state of a discipline as a guide in writing the discipline's history.

Principle of refutability Popper's contention that for a theory to be considered scientific it must specify the observations that, if made, would refute the theory. In order to be considered scientific, a theory must make risky predictions.

Psychical determinism The kind of determinism that stresses cognitive causes of behavior.

Psychophysical parallelism The contention that experiencing something in the physical world causes both bodily and mental activity at the same time, with no causal relationship between the bodily and mental events.

Public observation The stipulation that scientific laws must be available for any interested person to verify. Thus, science is interested in general, empirical relationships that are publicly verifiable.

Rationalism The philosophical belief that knowledge can be attained only by engaging in some kind of mental activity.

Science Traditionally, science has been viewed as the systematic attempt to rationally categorize or explain empirical observations. Recently, Popper has described science as a way of rigorously testing proposed solutions to problems, and Kuhn has emphasized the importance of paradigms that guide the research activities of scientists.

Scientific law A consistently observed relationship between classes of empirical events.

Scientific theory Traditionally, a proposed explanation of a number of empirical observations; or, according to Karl Popper, a proposed solution to a problem.

Self-regulated behavior Behavior that varies as a function of one's own subjective experience rather than as a function of the physical environment.

Subjective reality A person's own conscious experience.

Uncertainty principle See **Indeterminism.**

Zeitgeist The spirit of the times.

CHAPTER 2

The Early Greek Philosophers

THE WORLD
OF PRECIVILIZED HUMANS

Imagine yourself living about 15,000 years ago. What would your life be like? It seems safe to say that in your lifetime you would experience most of the following: lightning, thunder, rainbows, the phases of the moon, death, birth, illness, dreams (including nightmares), meteors, an eclipse of the sun or moon, and perhaps one or more earthquakes, tornadoes, or volcanic eruptions. Since these events would touch your life directly, it seems natural that you would want to account for them in some way, but how? Many of these events—for example, lightning—cannot be explained by the average citizens of civilized countries even today; but we have faith that scientists can explain such events, and we are comforted and less fearful. However, as an early human, you would have no such scientific knowledge to draw upon, and therefore you would be on your own. We mentioned in the last chapter that thoughtful humans have always made empirical observations and then attempted to explain those observations. Although observation and explanation became key components of science, the explanations early humans offered were anything but scientific.

The earliest attempts to explain natural events involved a projection of human attributes onto nature, which was seen as alive with human emotions. For example, the sky or earth could become angry or could be tranquil, just as a human could. Looking at all of nature as though it were alive is called **animism**, and the projection of human attributes onto nature is called **anthropomorphism**; both were involved in early attempts to make sense out of life (Cornford, 1957; Murray, 1955). The early human made no distinctions between animate (living) and inanimate objects, or between material and immaterial things.

Another approach to explanation assumed that a ghost or spirit dwelt in everything, including humans, and that these spirits were as real as anything else. The events in nature and human conduct were both explained as the whims of the spirits that resided in everything. The word *spirit* is derived from the Latin word for "breath" (Hulin, 1934, p. 7). Breath (later spirit or ghost) is what gives things life, and when it leaves a thing death results. This spirit can sometimes leave the body and return, as was assumed to be the case in dreaming. Also, since one can dream of, or think of, a person after his or her biological death, it was assumed that the person must still exist; for it was believed that if something could be thought of, it must exist. With this logic, anything the mind could conjure up was assumed to be real; therefore, imagination and dreams provided an array of demons, spirits, monsters, and later, gods, who lurked behind all natural events.

Since an array of spirits with human qualities was believed to exist, it seemed a natural impulse to attempt to communicate with the spirits and otherwise influence them. If, for example, a spirit was providing too much or too little rain, an attempt was made to persuade the spirit to modify its influence. Likewise, a sick person was thought to be possessed by an evil spirit that had to be coaxed to leave the body or be driven out.

Elaborate methods evolved that were designed to influence the spirits, and such methods were called **magic**. It was believed that the spirits could be influenced by appropriate words, ceremonies, or human actions.

As rudimentary as these beliefs were, they at least gave early humans the feeling that they had some control over their fate. Sigerist (1951) describes how pervasive these magical practices were in ancient Egypt and Babylonia:

> Like the Egyptian, and even more so, the Babylonian lived in a world that was haunted by evil spirits. They were everywhere, in the dark corners of the house, in the attic, in ruins, and on waste lands; they roamed the streets of the city at night, hid behind rocks and trees on the open land ready to attack you when you passed by; they rode howling with the storm wind. There was not a place where you could feel safe. Yet, it would be a great mistake to assume that the life of the Babylonian was one of perpetual terror, far from it. If you led a righteous life, worshipping the gods, keeping the ghosts of your ancestors in the Underworld by feeding them with regular offerings, if you respected taboos and possessed the necessary amulets and charms, there was no reason why you should be afraid of spirits. They were kept in check and had no power over you, although it happened here and there that they attacked a man without apparent reason. (p. 442)

Humans have always needed to understand, predict, and control nature. Animism, anthropomorphism, magic, religion, philosophy, and science can all be seen as efforts to satisfy those needs.

THE FIRST PHILOSOPHERS

Magic, superstition, and mysticism, in one form or another, dominated attempts to understand nature for most of early history. It was therefore a monumental step in human thought when *natural* explanations were offered instead of supernatural ones. Such explanations, although understandably simple, were offered by the early Greeks. Philosophy began when natu-ral explanations replaced supernatural ones, but these early philosophies were not devoid of animism and anthropomorphism. What makes them significant is their shift in emphasis away from the supernatural.

Thales

As noted in Chapter 1, no idea is born full-blown within a single individual. **Thales** (624–546 B.C.), although often referred to as the first philosopher, had a rich intellectual heritage. He traveled to Egypt and Babylonia, both of which enjoyed advanced civilizations that no doubt influenced him. For example, the knowledge of geometry that Thales demonstrated had been known for centuries by the Egyptians. In Egypt and Babylonia, however, knowledge was either practical (geometry was used to lay out the fields for agricultural purposes) or was used primarily in a religious context (knowledge of anatomy and physiology was used to prepare the dead for their journey into the next world). Thales was important because he *emphasized* natural explanations and minimized supernatural ones, but he did view the universe as alive. His position was a **vitalistic** one as opposed to a **materialistic** one, which views all nature as consisting of inanimate matter. Thales believed that a vital force permeated matter, giving it the power to move. For him, moving matter was the same as living matter. Although Thales viewed nature as alive, he did not see it as possessed by spirits with human characteristics.

Thales searched for that *one* substance or element from which everything else is derived. The Greeks called such a primary element or substance a **physis**, and those who sought it were **physicists**. Physicists to this day are searching for the "stuff" from which everything is made. Thales concluded that the physis was water, since many things seem to be a form of water, life depends on water, water exists in many forms (such as ice, steam, hail, snow, clouds, fog, and dew), and some water is found in everything. This conclusion that water is the primary substance has considerable merit. As Bertrand Russell (1959) observes:

> The most important of Thales' views is his statement that the world is made of water. This is neither so far fetched as at first glance it might appear, nor yet a pure figment of imagination cut off from observation. Hydrogen, the stuff that generates water, has been held in our time to be the chemical element from which all other elements can be synthesized. The view that all matter is one is quite a reputable scientific hypothesis. As for observation, the proximity of the sea makes it more than plausible that one should notice that the sun evaporates water, that mists rise from the surface to form clouds, which dissolve again in the form of rain. The earth in this view is a form of concentrated water. The details might thus be fanciful enough, but it is still a handsome feat to have discovered that a substance remains the same in different states of aggregation. (pp. 16–17)

In addition to this achievement, Thales also was able to predict eclipses, developed methods of navigation based on the stars and planets, and applied geometric principles to the measurement of such things as the heights of buildings. He is even said to have cornered the market on olive oil by predicting weather patterns. Such practical accomplishments brought great fame to Thales and respectability to philosophy. Thales showed that knowledge of nature, which minimized supernaturalism, could provide power over the environment, something humans had been seeking from the dawn of history.

Anaximander

Anaximander (611–545 B.C.), who studied with Thales, argued that even water was a compound of more basic material. According to Anaximander, the physis was something that had the capability of becoming anything. This something he called the "boundless" or the "indefinite." Anaximander also proposed a rudimentary theory of evolution stating that humans had evolved from fish, and he used fossils to support his argument. We can see how the physical environment can influence one's philosophizing. Both Thales and Anaximander lived near the shores of the Mediterranean Sea, and its influence on their philosophies is obvious.

Heraclitus

Impressed by the fact that everything in nature seemed to be in a constant state of flux or change, **Heraclitus** (540–475 B.C.), therefore, assumed fire to be the physis, since in the presence of fire everything is transformed into something else. To Heraclitus, the overwhelming fact about the world was that nothing ever "is"; rather, everything is "becoming." Nothing is either hot or cold, but is becoming hotter or colder; nothing is young but is becoming older; nothing is fast or slow, but is becoming faster or slower. Heraclitus's position is summarized in his famous statement "No man steps into the same river twice." Heraclitus meant that the river becomes something other than what it was when it was first stepped into.

Heraclitus believed that all things existed somewhere between polar opposites—for example, night-day, life-death, winter-summer, up-down, heat-cold, sleeping-waking. For Heraclitus, one end of the pole defined the other, and the two poles were inseparable. For example, only through injustice can justice be known, and only through health can illness be known. In other words, as Hegel would say many centuries later, "Everything carries within itself its own negation."

Heraclitus raised an epistemological question that has persisted to this day: How can something be known if it is constantly changing? If something is different at two points in time, and therefore not really the same object, how can it be known with any certainty? Does not knowledge require permanence? It was at this point in history that the senses became a questionable means of acquiring knowledge, since they could only provide information about a constantly changing world. In answer to the question "What can be known with certainty?" empirical events could not be included, since they were in a constant state of flux. Those seeking something unchangeable, and thus knowable, had two choices. They could choose something that was physical but undetectable by the senses, as the atomist and the Pythagorean mathematicians did; or they could choose something mental (for example, ideas or the soul), as Plato and the Christians did. Both groups believed that anything experienced through the senses was too unreliable to be known. Even today, the goal of science is to discover laws that are abstractions *derived* from sensory experience. Scientific laws are derived rationally and are considered mental abstractions; when manifested in the empirical world, they are only probabilistic.

The search for something that can be known with certainty is one of the longest in history, and it continues. In the realm of modern personality theory this search manifests itself in an effort to discover what gives a person his or her identity or individual personality. A person stands, sits, walks, is healthy, is sick, and is older than he or she was a year or even a moment ago. Yet, through all of these and many other changes, we still refer to the person as the same person. What are we responding to? What is it that makes the person appear to be the same person in spite of the fact that the empirical events constituting that person are in a constant state of flux? Another way of asking this question is, What would need to change before we would refer to him or her as a different person?

Parmenides

Taking a view exactly the opposite of Heraclitus's, **Parmenides** (540–470 B.C.) believed that all change was an illusion. There is only one reality; it is finite, uniform, motionless, and fixed, and can be understood only through reason. Thus, for Parmenides, knowledge is attained through thought, since sensory experience provides only illusion. Parmenides supported his position with logic. Like the earliest humans, he believed that being able to speak or think of something implied its existence, since we cannot think of something that does not exist. Bertrand Russell (1945) summarizes Parmenides' argument as follows:

> When you think, you think of something; when you use a name, it must be of something. Therefore both thought and language require objects outside themselves, and since you can think of a thing or speak of it at one time as well as another, whatever can be thought or spoken of must exist at all times. Consequently there can be no change, since change consists in things coming into being and ceasing to be. (p. 49)

Fifteen hundred years later, St. Anselm (A.D. 1033–1109) used the same argument to "prove" the existence of God. If one can think of a perfect being, he said, there must be a being as real as the one thought of. Zeno of Elea, a disciple of Parmenides, used logical arguments to show that motion was an illusion. He said that for an object to go from point A to point B, it must first go half the distance between A and B. Then it must go half the remaining distance, then half of that distance, and so on. Since there is an infinite number of points between any two points, the process can never stop. Also, the object must pass through an infinite number of points in a finite amount of time, and this is impossible. Therefore, it is logically impossible for the object ever to reach point B. The fact that it seems to do so is a weakness of the senses. This reasoning, usually known as **Zeno's paradox**, is often expressed in the following form: if one runner in a race is allowed to leave slightly before a second runner, the second runner can never overtake the first runner no matter how slow the first runner is or how swift the second runner is.

We have in Parmenides and in Zeno examples of how far unabated reason can take a person. They concluded that either logic, mathematics, and reason were correct, or the information provided by the senses was, and they opted for logic, mathematics, and reason. The same mistake has been made many times in history. Other misconceptions can result from relying exclusively on sensory data. It was not until science emerged in the sixteenth century that **rationalism** and **empiricism** were wed, and sensory information provided that which was reasoned about. Science, therefore, minimized the extremes of both rationalism and empiricism.

Heraclitus and Parmenides provide a kind of Kuhnian clash of paradigms, one paradigm viewing the world as permanent and knowable through reason, and the other viewing the world as constantly changing and known through the senses. Various combinations of these two points of view are found throughout psychology's history.

Pythagoras

Largely through his influence on Plato, **Pythagoras** (582–500 B.C.) has had a significant influence on Western thought. Pythagoras postulated that the basic explanation for everything in the universe was found in numbers and in numerical relationships. He noted that the square of the hypotenuse of a right-angle triangle is exactly equal to the sum of the squares of its other two sides. Although this came to be called the Pythagorean theorem, it had probably been known to the Egyptians (Murphy, 1968, p. 6). Pythagoras also observed that a harmonious blending of tone results when one string on a lyre is exactly twice as long as another. Pythagoras took these and several other observations and created a school of thought that glorified mathematics. He and his followers applied mathematical principles to almost every aspect of human existence, creating what Esper

(1964) describes as "a great muddle of religious mysticism, music, mathematics, medicine, and cosmology" (p. 52).

According to the Pythagoreans, numbers and numerical relationships, although abstract, were nonetheless real and exerted an influence on the empirical world. The world of numbers existed independently of the empirical world and could be known in its pure form only through reason. When conceptualized, the Pythagorean theorem is exactly correct and applies to all right-angle triangles that ever were or ever will be. As long as the theorem is applied rationally to imagined triangles, it is flawless, but when applied to actual triangles, the results are not absolutely correct. This is because there are no perfect triangles in the empirical world. In fact, according to the Pythagoreans, *nothing* is perfect in the empirical world. Perfection is found only in the abstract mathematical world that lies beyond the senses, and therefore can be embraced only by reason.

The Pythagoreans assumed a dualistic universe, one part abstract, permanent, and intellectually knowable (like that proposed by Parmenides) and the other empirical, changing, and known through the senses (like that proposed by Heraclitus). Sensory experience, then, cannot provide knowledge. In fact, such experience interferes with the attainment of knowledge and should be avoided. This point of view grew into outright contempt for sensory experiences and for bodily pleasures, and the Pythagoreans launched a crusade against vice, lawlessness, and bodily excess of any kind. Members of this school imposed long periods of silence on themselves so as to enhance clear, rational thought. Moreover, they attempted to cleanse their minds by imposing certain taboos (for example, against eating flesh or beans) and by hard physical and mental exercise.

The Pythagoreans believed that the universe was characterized by a mathematical harmony and that everything in nature was interrelated. Following this paradigm, they encouraged women to join their organization (it was *very* unusual for Greeks to look upon women as equal to men in any area), argued for the humane treatment of slaves, and developed medical practices based on the assumption that health resulted from the harmonious workings of the body and illness resulted from some kind of imbalance or discord.

The belief that experiences of the flesh are inferior to those of the mind—a belief that plays such an important role in Plato's theory and is even more important in early Christian theology—can be traced directly to the Pythagoreans. Eventually Plato became a member of their organization. He based his Academy on Pythagorean concepts, and above the entrance was a sign that read, "Let no one without an understanding of mathematics enter here." Pythagoras would have been very pleased.

Pythagoras postulated two worlds, one physical and one abstract, the two interacting with each other. Of the two, the abstract was considered the better. Pythagoras also postulated a dualism in humans, claiming that, in addition to the flesh of the body, we have reasoning powers that allow us to attain an understanding of the abstract world. Furthermore, reasoning is a function of the soul, which the Pythagoreans believed to be immortal. Pythagoras's philosophy provides one of the first clear-cut mind-body dualisms in the history of Western thought.

Empedocles

Empedocles (554–495 B.C.) was a disciple of Pythagoras. Instead of one physis, Empedocles suggested four elements from which everything in the world is made: earth, fire, air, and water. Humans, too, consist of these four elements, with earth forming the solid part of the body, water accounting for the liquids in the body, air providing the breath of life, and fire providing our reasoning ability. Empedocles was the first philosopher to offer a theory of perception. He

assumed that each of the four elements mentioned above was found in the blood. Objects in the outside environment throw off tiny copies of themselves called "emanations" or **eidola**, which enter the blood through the pores of the body. Like attracts like, so the eidola will combine with the element that is like them in the blood, the fusion of external elements with internal elements resulting in perception. Empedocles believed that the matching of eidola with their corresponding internal elements occurred in the heart.

Democritus

Democritus (460–370 B.C.) said that all things are made of tiny, indivisible parts called atoms. The differences among things are explained by the shape, size, number, location, and arrangement of atoms. Atoms themselves were believed to be unalterable, but they could have different arrangements; so although the actual atoms do not change, the objects they are made of can change. Humans, too, are bundles of atoms, and the soul or mind is made up of smooth, highly mobile fire atoms that give us our mental characteristics. For Democritus, therefore, animate, inanimate, and cognitive events were reduced to atomic activity. Since the behavior of atoms was thought to be lawful, Democritus's view was deterministic. It was also a materialistic monism, since everything was explained in terms of the arrangement of atoms, and there was no separate life force. Democritus's view was also **elementistic** because no matter how complex something was, Democritus believed it could be explained in terms of atoms and their activity.

Democritus agreed with Empedocles that perceptions and sensations arise when atoms emanate from the surfaces of objects, but he said that eidola enter the body through one of five sensory systems and are transmitted to the brain. Upon entering the brain, the emanations sent by an object cause the highly mobile fire

TABLE 2.1 Galen's extension of Hippocrates' theory.

Humor	Temperament	Characteristic
Phlegm	Phlegmatic	Sluggish, unemotional
Blood	Sanguine	Cheerful
Yellow bile	Choleric	Quick-tempered, fiery
Black bile	Melancholic	Sad

atoms to form a copy of them. This match between eidola and atoms in the brain causes perception. Democritus stressed that eidola are not the object itself, and that the match between the eidola and the atoms in the brain may not be exact. Therefore, there may be differences between the physical object and what the physical object is perceived to be. The problem of determining what is gained or lost as objects in the environment are experienced through the senses has been one of the most persistent in psychology.

Democritus placed thinking in the brain, emotion in the heart, and appetite in the liver. He discussed five senses: vision, hearing, smell, touch, and taste. And he suggested four primary colors: black, red, white, and green, from which all colors were derived. Since he believed that all bodily atoms scattered at death, he also believed that there was no life after death. His was the first completely naturalistic view of the universe, devoid of any supernatural considerations. Although his view contained no gods or spirits to guide human action, Democritus did not condone a life of hedonism (pleasure seeking). He preached moderation, as did his disciple Epicurus one hundred years later.

Hippocrates and Galen

Hippocrates (460–375 B.C.) is often referred to as the Father of Medicine. Up to his time, illness was largely explained as a result of possession by evil spirits or demons. For example, epilepsy was called the "sacred disease," suggesting possession by an evil spirit. Hippocrates disagreed, saying that all illness had natural and not supernatural causes. Hippocrates agreed with Empedocles that everything was made from four elements: earth, air, fire, and water, and that humans, too, were made up of these elements. In addition, however, Hippocrates associated the four elements with four humors in the body. He associated earth with phlegm, air with blood, fire with yellow bile, and water with black bile. Individuals in whom the humors are properly balanced are healthy; an imbalance among the humors results in illness. We will have more to say about Hippocrates when we review the treatment of the mentally ill in Chapter 15.

About 500 years after Hippocrates, **Galen** (A.D.130–200) associated the four humors of the body with four temperaments. If one of the humors dominated, the person would display the characteristics associated with that humor. Galen's extension of Hippocrates' theory can be summarized as shown in Table 2.1.

Galen's extension of Hippocrates' views created the first rudimentary theory of personality, as well as a way of diagnosing illness that was to dominate medicine for about the next 14 centuries.

THE RELATIVITY OF TRUTH

The step from supernatural explanations of things to natural ones was enormous, but perhaps too many philosophers took it. Various philosophers found the basic element (physis) to be water, fire, numbers, the atom, and the boundless, and some philosophers found more than one basic element. Some said that things are constantly changing, others that nothing changes, and still others that some things change and others do not. Furthermore, most of these philosophers and their disciples were outstanding orators who presented and defended their views forcefully and with convincing logic. Where does this leave the individual seeking the truth? Such an individual is much like the modern college student who goes to one class and is convinced of something (for example, psychology is a science) only to go to his or her next class to be convinced of the opposite (psychology is not a science). Which is true? One group of philosophers concluded that there was not just one truth, but many. These philosophers were called **Sophists**. The Sophists were professional teachers of rhetoric and logic who believed that effective communication determined whether or not an idea was accepted, rather than the idea's validity. Truth was considered relative, and therefore no single truth was thought to exist. This belief marked a major shift in philosophy. The question was no longer "What is the universe made of?" but "What can humans know and how can they know it?" In other words, there was a shift toward epistemological questions.

Protagoras

Protagoras (480–411 B.C.), the best-known Sophist, summarized the Sophists' position with his famous saying "Man is the measure of all things, of things that are, that they are; and of things that are not, that they are not." This statement is pregnant with meaning. First, it means that truth depends on the perceiver rather than on physical reality. Second, since perceptions vary with the previous experiences of the perceiver, they will vary from person to person. Third, what is considered to be true will be, in part, culturally determined, since one's

culture influences one's experiences. Fourth, to understand why a person believes as he or she does, one must understand the person. According to Protagoras, therefore, each of the preceding philosophers was presenting his own subjective point of view rather than the objective "truth" about physical reality. Paraphrasing Heraclitus's famous statement, Protagoras said, "Man never steps into the same river once," since the river is different for each individual *to begin with*. Protagoras's position is probably more compatible with modern psychology than that of any other Greek philosopher. It is also compatible with Kuhn's view of science. Kuhn would say that each of the great philosophers created a paradigm that defined a set of problems and suggested the manner in which those problems should be solved. As was noted in the preceding chapter, paradigms are ways of viewing things and do not provide a final truth about the world.

The relativist nature of truth that the Sophists suggested was distasteful to many who wanted "truth" to be more than the projection of one's own subjective reality onto the environment. As we have seen, the views of Heraclitus had previously caused the same concern. Among those most concerned was Socrates, who both agreed and disagreed with the Sophists.

Socrates

Socrates (470–399 B.C.) agreed with the Sophists that individual experience is important (witness his famous expressions "know thyself" and "an unexamined life is not worth living), but he disagreed with the Sophists' contention that no truth exists beyond personal opinion. In his search for truth, Socrates used a method sometimes called **inductive definition**, which started with an examination of instances of such concepts as beauty, love, justice, or truth and then moved on to such questions as "What is it that *all* instances of beauty have in common?"

In other words, Socrates asked what it is that makes something beautiful, just, or true. In this way he sought to discover general principles from examining isolated examples. It was thought that these general principles, or concepts, transcend their individual manifestations and are therefore stable and knowable. For Socrates, these principles constituted knowledge, and the goal of life was to gain knowledge. When one's conduct is guided by knowledge, it is necessarily moral. For example, if one knows what justice is, one acts justly. For Socrates, knowledge and morality were intimately related; knowledge is virtue, and improper conduct results from ignorance. Unlike most of the earlier philosophers, Socrates was concerned mainly with what it means to be human and the problems related to human existence.

In 399 B.C., when Socrates was 70 years old, he was accused of not respecting the city gods and of corrupting the youth of Athens. He was tried, convicted, and sentenced to death. The wisdom of Socrates, however, was perpetuated and greatly elaborated by his famous student, Plato. Plato requires more attention than other philosophers because his theory created a theme that runs all through the history of psychology and continues to exert an influence on modern psychology.

Socrates

PLATO

The writings of **Plato** (437–347 B.C.) need to be divided into two periods. During the first period, Plato was essentially reporting the thoughts and methods of his teacher, Socrates. When Socrates was executed, however, Plato went into self-imposed exile in southern Italy, where he came under the influence of the Pythagoreans. After he returned to Athens, he founded his own school, the Academy, and his subsequent writings combined the Socratic method with the mystical Pythagorean philosophy. Like Socrates, Plato wished to find some-

thing permanent that could be the object of knowledge, but his search for permanence carried him far beyond the concepts or principles that Socrates had settled for.

The Theory of Forms or Ideas

According to the Pythagoreans, although numbers and numerical relationships were abstractions (that is, they could not be experienced through the senses), they were nonetheless real and could exert an influence on the empirical world. The result of the influence, however, was believed to be inferior to the abstraction

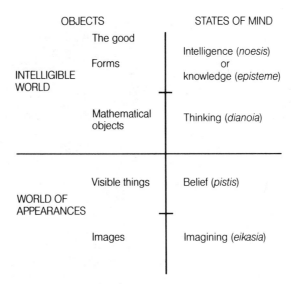

OBJECTS   STATES OF MIND

The good

Forms   Intelligence (*noesis*)
or
knowledge (*episteme*)

INTELLIGIBLE
WORLD

Mathematical
objects   Thinking (*dianoia*)

Visible things   Belief (*pistis*)

WORLD OF
APPEARANCES

Images   Imagining (*eikasia*)

FIGURE 2.1 Plato's analogy of the divided line. (From Cornford's translation of Plato's *Republic,* 1968, p. 222.)

that caused the influence. As we have already mentioned, the Pythagorean theorem is absolutely true when applied to abstract (imagined) triangles, but is never completely true when applied to a triangle that exists in the empirical world (for example, one that is drawn on paper). This is because the lines making up the right angle will never be exactly even. The Pythagoreans took this view and from it developed a philosophy that condemned bodily experience and glorified rational thought.

Plato took the next step. For him, everything in the empirical world was a manifestation of a pure form (idea) that existed in the abstract. Thus, chairs, chariots, rocks, cats, dogs, and even people were inferior manifestations of pure **forms**. For example, the thousands of cats that one encounters are but inferior copies of an abstract idea or form of "catness" that exists in pure form in the abstract. This is true for every object for which we have a name. What we experience through the senses results from the interaction of the pure form with matter, and since matter is constantly changing and is experienced through the senses, the result of the

interaction must be less perfect than the pure idea before that idea interacts with matter. Plato replaced the principle that Socrates sought with the concept of form as the aspect of reality that was permanent enough to be known, but he agreed with Socrates that knowledge could be attained only through reason.

The Analogy of the Divided Line

What, then, becomes of those who attempt to gain knowledge by examining the empirical world via sensory experience? According to Plato, they are doomed to ignorance or, at best, opinion. The only true knowledge involves grasping the forms themselves, and this can be done only by rational thought. Plato summarizes this point of view with his famous **analogy of the divided line**, which is illustrated in Figure 2.1.

Imagining is seen as the lowest form of understanding, since it is based on images—for example, a portrait of a person, which is once removed from the person. Reflections in the water are also images, since they too are a step removed from the objects reflected. We are slightly better off confronting the objects themselves rather than their images, but the best we can do even when confronting objects directly is to form beliefs about them. Beliefs, however, do not constitute knowledge. Still better is the contemplation of mathematical relationships, but mathematical knowledge is still not the highest kind, since it often depends on events in the empirical world, and many of its relationships exist only by definition. That is, mathematical relationships are assumed to be true, but these assumptions could conceivably be false. To think about mathematics in the abstract, however, is better than dealing with images or empirical objects. The highest form of thinking involves embracing the forms themselves, and true intelligence or knowledge results *only* from an understanding of the abstract forms. The "good" or the "form of the good" constitutes the highest form of wisdom, since it encompasses all of the other forms and shows their interrelatedness. The form of the good is like the sun, in that it illuminates all of the other forms and makes them knowable. It is the highest truth. Later, in Christian theology, the form of the good was equated with God.

The Allegory of the Cave

In the **allegory of the cave** (see Cornford, 1968, pp. 227–231) Plato describes fictitious prisoners who have lived their entire lives in the depths of a cave. The prisoners are chained so they can see only forward. Behind them is a road over which individuals pass, carrying a variety of objects. A fire is situated in such a way that it projects shadows of the travelers and the objects onto the wall in front of the prisoners. For the prisoners, the projected shadows constitute reality. Plato then describes what might happen if one of the prisoners were to escape his bondage and leave the cave. Turning toward the fire would cause his eyes to ache, and he might

decide to return to his world of shadows. If not, he would eventually adjust to the flames and see the individuals and objects that he had previously seen only shadows of. Plato now asks us to suppose that the prisoner continues his journey and leaves the cave. Once in the "upper world," the prisoner would be blinded by sunlight. Only after a period of adjustment could he see things in this "upper world" and recognize that they were more real than the things he had experienced in the cave. Finally, Plato asks us to imagine what might happen to the escaped prisoner if he went back into the cave to enlighten his fellow prisoners. Still partially blinded by such an illuminating experience, the prisoner would find it difficult to readjust to the previous life of shadows. He would make mistakes in describing the shadows and in predicting which objects would follow which. This would be evidence enough for his fellow prisoners that no good could come from leaving the world of shadows. In fact, anyone who attempted to lead the prisoners out of the shadowy world of the cave would be killed.

The bound prisoners, of course, represent humans who confuse the shadowy world of sense experience with reality. The prisoner who escapes represents the rare individual whose actions are governed by reason instead of sensory impressions. The escaped prisoner sees the real objects (forms) responsible for the shadows in the cave (sensory information) and thus embraces true knowledge. After such an enlightening experience, an effort is often made to steer others away from ignorance and toward wisdom. The plight of Socrates is evidence of what can happen to the individual attempting to free others from the chains of ignorance.

The Reminiscence Theory of Knowledge

How does one come to know the forms if they cannot be known through sensory experience? The answer to this question involves the most mystical aspect of Plato's theory. Plato's answer was influenced by the Pythagorean notion of the immortality of the soul. According to the Pythagoreans, the highest form of thought was reason, which was a function of the immortal soul. Plato expanded this idea and said that before the soul is implanted in the body, it dwells in pure and complete knowledge; that is, it dwells among the forms. After the soul enters the body, this knowledge begins to be contaminated by sensory information. The only way to arrive at true knowledge is to ignore sensory experience and focus one's thoughts on the contents of the mind. To Plato, all knowledge is *innate* and can be attained only through **introspection**, which is the searching of one's *inner* experiences. At most, sensory experience can only remind one of what was already known. Therefore, for Plato, all knowledge comes from **reminiscence**, from remembering the experiences the soul had before entering the body. We see, then, that Plato was a **nativist** as well as a **rationalist**, since he stressed mental operations as a means of arriving at the truth (rationalism) and he stressed that the truth ultimately arrived at was inborn (nativism). He was also an **idealist**, since he believed that the highest reality was the idea or form.

The Nature of the Soul

We saw above that Plato believed the soul to have a rational component that was immortal, but Plato also believed that there were two other components of the soul: the courageous and the appetitive. The courageous and appetitive aspects of the soul were part of the body, and thus mortal. With his concept of the three-part soul, Plato postulated a situation in which humans were almost always in a state of conflict, a situation not unlike the one Freud depicted many centuries later. According to Plato, the body has appetites (needs such as hunger, thirst, and sex) that must be met and that play a major motivational role in everyday life. Humans also have varied emotions—such as fear, love, and rage—

that seek expression. However, if true knowledge is to be attained, the person must suppress the needs of the body and concentrate on rational pursuits, such as introspection. Since bodily needs do not go away, the person must spend considerable energy keeping them under control—but they must be controlled. The supreme goal in life, according to Plato, should be to free the soul as much as possible from the adulterations of the flesh. In this he agreed with the Pythagoreans.

Plato realized that not everyone was capable of intense rational thought, and he believed that in some individuals the appetitive aspect of the soul would dominate, in others the courageous aspect of the soul would dominate, and in still others the rational aspect would dominate. In his *Republic* he created a utopian society in which the three kinds of individuals would have special functions. Those in whom the appetitive aspect dominated would be workers and slaves, those in whom courage dominated would be soldiers, and those in whom reason dominated would be philosopher-kings. In Plato's scheme there is an inverse relationship between concern with bodily experiences and one's status in society. In Book V of the *Republic*, Plato forcibly states his belief that societies have little chance of survival unless they are led by individuals with the wisdom of philosophers:

> Until philosophers are kings, or the kings and princes of this world have the spirit and power of philosophy, and political greatness and wisdom meet in one, and those of commoner natures who pursue either to the exclusion of the other are compelled to stand aside, cities will never have rest from their evils . . . then only will this our state have a possibility of life and behold the light of day. (Jowett's translation, p. 473)

Plato's Legacy

Since science depends on empirical observation, it is clear why Plato's theory did little to promote science and much to inhibit it. Plato created a dualism that divided the human into a body, which was material and imperfect, and a mind (soul), which contained pure knowledge. Furthermore, the rational soul was immortal. Had philosophy remained unencumbered by theological concerns, perhaps Plato's theory would have been challenged by subsequent philosophers and gradually displaced by more tempered philosophic views. Aristotle, in fact, went a long way in modifying Plato's position, but the challenge was aborted. The mysticism of early Christianity was combined with Platonic philosophy, creating unchallengeable religious dogma. When Aristotle's writings were rediscovered centuries later, they were also carefully modified and assimilated into church dogma. It was not until the Renaissance that Platonism (and Aristotelianism) was finally questioned openly and largely discarded.

ARISTOTLE

Plato's most famous student was **Aristotle** (384–322 B.C.), who joined Plato's Academy when he was only 17 and Plato was 60. Aristotle developed a system that was in some ways similar to Plato's, but in important ways it was very dissimilar. Aristotle was the first philosopher to treat extensively many topics that were later to become part of psychology. In his vast writings he covered memory, sensation, sleep, dreams, geriatrics, and learning. He also began his book *De Anima* ("On the Soul") with what is considered to be the first history of psychology.

The Basic Difference between Plato and Aristotle

Both Plato and Aristotle were primarily interested in first principles, or truths that went beyond the mere appearance of things, but their methods for arriving at those principles were distinctly different. For Plato, true reality was found in the forms that existed *independent* of nature and that could only be arrived at by

Aristotle

THE BETTMANN ARCHIVE, INC.

ignoring sensory experience and turning one's thoughts inward (that is, by introspection). For Aristotle, certain abstract principles were knowable, but they could only become known by studying nature. He believed that if enough individual manifestations of a principle were investigated, eventually one could infer the general principle that they exemplified. Aristotle, then, was a rationalist, but it was the information furnished by the senses that was the object of rational thought.

The general principles that were thought to be real and knowable have been referred to in different ways through the years—for example, as first principles or universals. In each case it was assumed that something basic existed that could not be determined only by studying individual instances or manifestations of the abstract principle involved. Some kind of rational activity was needed in order to find the principle underlying individual cases. The search for first principles or universals characterized most early philosophy and, in a sense, continues in modern science as the search for laws governing empirical events.

For Plato, first principles were arrived at by pure thought; for Aristotle, they were arrived at by examining nature directly. For Plato, all knowledge existed independent of nature; for Aristotle, nature and knowledge were inseparable. In Aristotle's view, therefore, the body was not a hindrance in the search for knowledge, as it was for Plato and the Pythagoreans. Also, Aristotle disagreed with Plato on the importance of mathematics. For Aristotle, mathematics was essentially useless, his emphasis being on the careful examination of nature by observation and classification. Aristotle was director of a research center in Athens called the Lyceum, where an incredibly large number of observations of physical and biological phenomena were made. The observations were then classified, and categories into which they were placed defined. Through this method of observation, definition, and classification, Aristotle compiled what has been called an encyclopedia of nature. He was interested in studying the things in the empirical world and learning what their functions were.

Since Aristotle sought to explain several psychological phenomena in biological terms, he can be considered the first physiological psychologist. Robinson (1981) says:

> When we study the philosophers before Aristotle, we can uncover, here and there, a psychological orientation that is materialist in tone . . . however, no predecessor could possibly or plausibly lay claim to the title of an early physiological psychologist, and this is precisely the title we may assign to Aristotle. He was the first authority to delineate a domain specifically embracing the subject matter of psychology and, within that domain, to restrict his explanations to principles of a biological sort. That the entire body of Aristotelian philosophy does not fit into a materialist mold is clear. . . . But on the narrower issues of learning, memory, sleep and dreams, routine perceptions, animal behavior,

emotion, and motivation, Aristotle's approach is naturalistic, physiological, and empirical. (pp. 81–82)

The views of Plato and Aristotle concerning the sources of knowledge set the stage for epistemological inquiry that has lasted until the present. Almost every philosopher, and most psychologists, can be evaluated in terms of their agreement or disagreement with the views of Plato or Aristotle.

Causation and Teleology

To truly understand anything, according to Aristotle, we must know four things about it. That is, everything has four causes:

1. *Material cause.* What an object is made of. For example, a statue is made of marble.

2. *Formal cause.* The particular form or pattern of an object. For example, a piece of marble takes on the form of Venus.

3. *Efficient cause.* The force that transforms the matter into a certain form. An example is the energy of the sculptor.

4. *Final cause.* The purpose for which an object exists. In the case of a statue, this purpose may be to bring pleasure to those who view it.

Since for Aristotle everything in nature exists for a purpose, his theory is **teleological**. But by purpose, Aristotle did not mean conscious intention. Rather, he meant that everything in nature has a function that is built into it. This built-in purpose or function is called **entelechy**. The entelechy keeps an object moving or developing in its prescribed direction until its full potential is reached. For example, the eye exists to provide vision, and it continues developing until it does so. The final cause of living things is part of their nature; it exists as a potentiality from the organism's very inception. An acorn has the potential to become an oak tree, but it cannot become an olive tree. In other words, the purpose or entelechy of an acorn is to become an oak tree.

The Hierarchy of Souls

For Aristotle, a soul was what gives life; therefore, all living things possess a soul. The soul provides a living thing's entelechy or inner purpose, as well as its formal, efficient, and final causes. According to Aristotle, there were three kinds of souls, and a living thing's potential was determined by what kind of a soul it possessed.

1. *Vegetative or nutritive soul.* Possessed by plants. It allows only growth, the assimilation of food, and reproduction.

2. *Sensitive soul.* Possessed by animals but not plants. In addition to the above functions, organisms that possess a sensitive soul sense and respond to the environment, experience pleasure and pain, and have a memory. Aristotle said that information about the environment is provided by the five senses: sight, hearing, taste, touch, and smell. Unlike earlier philosophers (for example, Empedocles and Democritus), Aristotle did not believe objects sent off tiny copies of themselves (eidola). Rather, he felt that perception was explained by the motion of objects that stimulate one of the senses. The movement of environmental objects created movements through different media, and each of the five senses was maximally sensitive to movements in a certain medium. For example, seeing resulted from the movement of light caused by an object, hearing and smelling resulted from the movement of air, and taste and touching from movement of the flesh. In this way, Aristotle explained how we could actually sense environmental objects without those objects sending off physical copies of themselves. Unlike Plato, Aristotle believed we could trust our senses to yield an accurate reflection of the environment.

3. *Rational soul.* Possessed only by humans. It provides all of the functions of the other two souls, but in addition allows thinking or rational thought.

As important as sensory information was to Aristotle, it was only the first step in acquiring knowledge. In other words, *sensory experience was a necessary but not a sufficient element in the attainment of knowledge.* In the first place, each sensory system provides isolated information about the environment that, by itself, is not very useful. For example, seeing a baby tossing and turning provides a clue as to its condition, hearing it cry provides another clue, smelling it may give a clue as to why it is so uncomfortable, and touching may reveal that it has a fever. It is the information from all of the senses together that allows for the most effective interactions with the environment.

Aristotle postulated a **common sense** as the mechanism that coordinated the information from all the senses. The common sense, like all other mental functions, was assumed to be located in the heart. The job of common sense was to synthesize sensory experience, thereby making it more meaningful. Secondly, sensory information, even after it was synthesized by common sense, could provide information only about particular instances of things. **Passive reason** involved the utilization of synthesized experience for getting along effectively in everyday life, but it did not result in an understanding of first principles. The abstraction of first principles from one's many experiences could be accomplished only by **active reason**, which was considered the highest form of thinking. Aristotle, therefore, delineated levels of knowing or understanding much like Plato's divided line. These levels were as follows:

- *Active reason*—the abstraction of principles from synthesized experience

- *Passive reason*—utilization of synthesized experience

- *Common sense*—synthesized experience

- *Sensory information*—isolated experiences

An example of how these levels of understanding are related might be to experience electricity through the senses of sight (seeing an electrical discharge), pain (being shocked), and hearing (hearing the electrical discharge). These experiences would correspond to the level of sense reception. The common sense would indicate that all of these experiences had a common source—electricity. Passive reason would indicate how electricity could be used in a variety of practical ways, while active reason would seek the laws governing electricity and an understanding of its nature. What started as a set of empirical experiences ends as a search for the principles that can explain those experiences.

The active-reason part of the soul provides humans with their highest purpose. Just as the ultimate goal of an acorn is to become an oak tree, the ultimate goal of humans is to engage in active reason. Aristotle also believed that acting in accordance with one's nature caused pleasure, and that acting otherwise brought pain. In the case of humans, engaging in active reason was the source of greatest pleasure. On this matter, Aristotle was essentially in agreement with Socrates and Plato. Also, because Aristotle postulated an inner potential in humans that may or may not be reached, his theory represents psychology's first self-actualization theory. The theories of Jung, Maslow, and Rogers may all be seen as modern examples of Aristotle's belief in the human entelechy.

With his concept of active reason, Aristotle inserted a mystical or supernatural component into an otherwise naturalistic theory. The active-reason part of the soul was considered immortal, but when it left the body upon death, it carried no recollections with it. It was considered a mechanism for pure thought and was believed to be identical for all humans. It was not judged in accordance with the moral character of its prior possessor, and there was no union or reunion with God. The active-reason part of the soul went neither to heaven nor hell. Later, however, the Christianized version of the Aristotelian soul was to be characterized by all these things.

Another mystical component in Aristotle's theory was his notion of the **unmoved mover**. For Aristotle, everything in nature had a purpose that was programmed into it. This purpose, or entelechy, explained why a thing was like it was, and why it did what it did. But if everything in nature has a purpose, what causes that purpose? To avoid an infinite regression of causes, Aristotle postulated an unmoved mover, or that which caused everything else but was not caused by anything itself. For Aristotle, the unmoved mover set nature in motion and did little else; it was a logical necessity, not a deity. Along with Aristotle's notion of the immortal aspect of the soul, the Christians also found his unmoved mover very much to their liking.

Memory and Recall

In keeping with his empirical thrust, Aristotle explained memory and recall as the results of sense perception. This contrasts with Plato's explanation, which was essentially nativistic. **Remembering**, for Aristotle, was a spontaneous recollection of something that had been previously experienced. For example, you see a person and remember that you saw that person before, and perhaps engaged in a certain conversation. **Recall**, however, involves an actual mental search for a past experience. It was in conjunction with recall that Aristotle postulated his now famous laws of association. The **Law of Similarity** states that if we think of something, we will tend to think of things similar to it. The **Law of Contrast** states that if we think of something, we will also tend to think of things that are its opposite. The **Law of Contiguity** states that if we think of something, we will also tend to think of things that were experienced along with it. Aristotle also implied the **Law of Frequency**, which states that the more times something is experienced, the easier it will be to recall. Aristotle's laws of association were to become the basis of learning theory for more than two thousand years. In fact, the concept of mental association is still at the heart of most theories of learning. The belief that one or more laws of association can be used to explain the origins of ideas or to explain how complex ideas are formed from simple ones came to be called **associationism**. Recently, Weimer (1973) described Aristotle's influence on modern psychology as follows:

> A moment's recollection . . . shows that Aristotle's doctrines are at the heart of contemporary thought in epistemology and the psychology of learning. The centrality of associationism as the mechanism of the mind is so well known as to require only the observation that *not one single learning theory* propounded in this century *has failed to base its account on associative principles.* (p. 18)

We said in Chapter 1 that no idea is invented by a single person. Even Aristotle, one of the great thinkers of all time, extended or modified the thoughts of previous philosophers. We have already mentioned that many philosophers shared his search for universals. Even the laws of association, usually attributed to Aristotle, can be clearly seen in the following passage from Plato's *Phaedo:*

> And yet what is the feeling of lovers when they recognize a lyre, or a garment, or anything else which the beloved has been in the habit of using? Do not they, from knowing the lyre, form in the mind's eye an image of the youth to whom the lyre belongs? And this is recollection. In like manner anyone who sees Simmias may remember Cebes; and there are endless examples of the same thing . . . and recollection is most commonly a process of recovering that which has already been forgotten through time and inattention . . . so much is clear—that when we perceive something, either by the help of sight, or hearing, or some other sense, from that perception we are able to obtain a notion of some other thing like or unlike which is associated with it but has been forgotten. (from Jowett, 1942, pp. 105–108)

Aristotle made several mistakes. For example, he assigned thinking and common sense to the heart and claimed that the main function of the brain was to cool the blood. He also believed that the number of species of living things in the world was fixed, and thereby denied evolution. But compared to his many positive contributions, these mistakes were minor. Although many of his observations were incorrect, he did observe almost everything, and in doing so, he brought Greek philosophy to new heights.

Aristotle died in 322 B.C., at the age of 62. His death marked the end of the Golden Age of Greece, which had started about 300 years earlier with the philosophy of Thales. Most, if not all, of the philosophical concepts that have been pursued ever since the Golden Age of Greece were produced during this period. After Aristotle's death, philosophers began either to rely on the teaching of past authorities, or they turned their attention to questions concerning models for human conduct. It is to the latter concerns that we turn in the next chapter.

SUMMARY

Primitive humans looked upon everything in nature as if it were alive; there was no distinction between the animate and the inanimate—this was called animism. Moreover, there was a tendency to project human feelings and emotions onto nature, and this was called anthropomorphism. A spirit or ghost was thought to reside in everything, giving it life. The course of natural events was explained in terms of the whims and wishes of these resident spirits. The dwelling of a spirit in humans explained such things as dreams and illness, and the spirit's permanent departure resulted in death, although when the body died the spirit was thought to continue living. An array of magical practices evolved that were designed to influence various spirits. These practices gave humans the feeling that they had some control over nature.

The first philosophers emphasized natural explanations instead of supernatural ones. They sought a primary element, called the physis, from which everything was made. For Thales the physis was water, for Anaximander it was the boundless, for Heraclitus it was fire, for Parmenides it was the "one" or "change-lessness," for Pythagoras it was number, for Democritus it was the atom, and for Hippocrates and Empedocles there were four primary elements: water, earth, fire, and air.

The debate between Heraclitus, who believed everything was constantly changing, and Parmenides, who believed nothing ever changed, raised a number of epistemological questions such as, "What, if anything, is permanent enough to be known with certainty?" and, "If sensory experience provides information only about a continually changing world, how can it be a source of knowledge?" These and related questions have persisted to the present.

Most of the first philosophers were monists, since they made no distinction between the mind and the body; whatever element or elements they arrived at were supposed to account for everything. In Pythagoras, however, we have a full-fledged dualism between the mind and the body and between the physical and the abstract. Numbers were abstractions but were real, and they could be known only by rational thought, not by sensory experience. Sensory experience could only inhibit attainment of abstract knowledge and was to be avoided. The mind, or soul, was thought to be immortal. The mind-body dualism that the Pythagoreans emphasized has remained part of philosophy, psychology, and even natural science.

The Sophists concluded that there were many equally valid philosophical positions. "Truth" was believed to be a function of a person's education, personal experiences, culture, and beliefs, and whether or not this "truth" was accepted by others depended upon one's communicative skills. Socrates agreed with the Sophists that truth was subjective, but he also believed that a careful examination of one's subjective experiences would reveal certain concepts or principles that were stable and knowable and could be used to generate proper conduct.

Plato, influenced by the Pythagoreans, took Socrates' belief an additional step by saying that principles, ideas, or concepts had an independent existence, just as the Pythagorean number did. For Plato, ideas or forms were the ultimate reality, and they could be known only by reason. Sensory experience leads only to ignorance—or at best, opinion—and should be avoided. The soul, before becoming implanted in the body, dwells in pure and complete knowledge, which can be remembered if one turns one's thoughts inward and away from the empirical world. For Plato, knowledge results from remembering what the soul experienced prior to its implantation in the body. This is called the reminiscence theory of knowledge. Plato believed that the rational powers of the mind (rationalism) should be turned inward (introspection) in order to rediscover ideas that had been present at birth (nativism).

Aristotle was also interested in principles instead of isolated facts, but unlike Plato, he felt that the way to find principles was to examine nature. Instead of urging the avoidance of sensory experience, he claimed that it was the source of all knowledge. Aristotle's brand of rationalism relied heavily on empiricism since he believed that principles are derived from the careful scrutiny of sensory observations. He distinguished between living things and nonliving things, believing that all living things contain an entelechy that determines their potential. An acorn, for example, has the potential to become an oak tree. There are three categories of living things: those possessing a vegetative soul, those possessing a sensitive soul, and those possessing a rational soul. Humans alone possess a rational soul, which has two functions: passive reason and active reason. Passive reason ponders information from the five senses and from the common sense, while the common sense synthesizes sensory information. Active reason is used to isolate enduring principles that manifest themselves in sensory experience. Aristotle considered active reason immortal. He also postulated an unmoved mover that was the entelechy for all of nature; it caused everything else but was not itself caused by anything. Aristotle distinguished between memory, which was spontaneous, and recall, which was the active search for a recollection of a past experience. It was with regard to recall that Aristotle postulated his laws of association—the laws of similarity, contrast, contiguity, and frequency.

DISCUSSION QUESTIONS

1. Describe some of the events that may have concerned primitive humans, and discuss how humans accounted for and attempted to control these events.

2. What distinguished the attempts of the first philosophers to understand nature from the attempts of those who preceded them?

3. Why were the first philosophers called physicists? List the physes arrived at by Thales, Anaximander, Heraclitus, Parmenides, Pythagoras, Empedocles, and Democritus.

4. What epistemological question did Heraclitus's philosophy raise?

5. Give examples of how logic was used to defend Parmenides' belief that change and motion were illusions.

6. How did the Sophists differ from the philosophers who preceded them? What was their attitude toward knowledge? In what way did Socrates agree with the Sophists and in what way did he disagree?

7. What, for Socrates, was the goal of philosophical inquiry? What method did he use in pursuing that goal?

8. Describe Plato's theory of forms or ideas.

9. In Plato's philosophy, what was the analogy of the divided line?

10. Summarize Plato's cave allegory. What points was Plato making with this allegory?

11. Discuss Plato's reminiscence theory of knowledge.

12. Compare Aristotle's attitude toward sensory experience with that of Plato.

13. According to Aristotle, what were the four causes of things?

14. Discuss Aristotle's concept of entelechy.

15. Discuss the relationship among sensory experience, common sense, passive reason, and active reason.

16. In Aristotle's philosophy, what was the function of the unmoved mover?

17. Describe the laws of association that Aristotle proposed.

GLOSSARY

Active reason According to Aristotle, the faculty of the soul, that searches for the abstract principles that manifest themselves in the empirical world. Aristotle thought that the active-reason part of the soul was immortal.

Allegory of the cave Plato's description of individuals who live their lives in accordance with the shadows of reality provided by sensory experience instead of in accordance with the true reality beyond sensory experience.

Analogy of the divided line Plato's illustration of his contention that there is a hierarchy of understanding. The lowest kind of understanding is based on images of empirical objects. Next highest is an understanding of empirical objects themselves, which results only in opinion; next is an understanding of abstract mathematical principles; next is an understanding of the forms; the highest understanding (true knowledge) is an understanding of the form of the good, and includes a knowledge of all the forms and their organization.

Anaximander (611–545 B.C.) Suggested the "infinite" or "boundless" as the physis and also formulated a rudimentary theory of evolution.

Animism The belief that an entity dwells in everything in nature, giving things life.

Anthropomorphism The projection of human attributes onto nonhuman things.

Aristotle (384–322 B.C.) Believed sensory experience to be the basis of all knowledge, although the five senses and the common sense provided only the information from which knowledge could be derived. Aristotle also believed that everything in nature had an entelechy (purpose) within it that determined its potential. Active reason, which was considered the immortal part of the human soul, provides humans with their greatest potential, and therefore fully actualized humans engage in active reason. Since everything was thought to have a cause, Aristotle postulated an unmoved mover that caused everything in the world but was not itself caused.

Associationism The philosophical belief that mental phenomena, such as learning, remembering, and imagining, can be explained in terms of the laws of association.

Common sense According to Aristotle, the faculty located in the heart that synthesizes the information provided by the five senses.

Democritus (460–370 B.C.) Offered atoms as the physis. Everything in nature, including humans, was explained in terms of atoms and their activities. His was the first completely naturalistic view of the world and of humans. There was no mind-body distinction and no immortal soul. Democritus also refined Empedocles' theory of perception. According to Democritus, eidola from environmental objects enter the body through one or more of the five sensory systems and are transmitted to the brain, where the highly mobile fire atoms form copies of them. This match between eidola and the fire atoms results in perception. Democritus's philosophy was materialistic, deterministic, and elementistic.

Efficient cause According to Aristotle, the force that transforms a thing.

Eidolon (plural, **eidola**) A tiny replication that a number of early Greek philosophers thought emanated from the surfaces of things in the environment, allowing the things to be perceived.

Elementism The belief that complex processes can be understood in terms of the elements they consist of.

Empedocles (495–435 B.C.) Postulated earth, fire, air, and water as the four basic elements from which everything is made. He was also the first philosopher to suggest a theory of perception.

Empiricism The belief that knowledge is based upon sensory experience.

Entelechy According to Aristotle, the purpose for which a thing exists; it remains a potential until actualized. Active reason, for example, is the human entelechy, but it remains only a potential in many humans.

Final cause According to Aristotle, the purpose for which a thing exists.

Formal cause According to Aristotle, the form of a thing.

Galen (A.D. 130–200) Associated each of Hippocrates' four humors with a temperament, thus creating a rudimentary theory of personality.

Heraclitus (540–475 B.C.) Suggested fire as the physis, since in its presence nothing remained the same. He viewed the world as in a constant state of flux.

Hippocrates (460–370 B.C.) Considered the Father of Medicine, assumed that disease had natural causes not supernatural ones. Health prevails when the four humors of the body are in balance, disease when there is an imbalance.

Idealist One who believes that the ultimate reality consists of abstract ideas. Plato was an idealist.

Inductive definition The technique used by

Socrates that examined many individual examples of a concept to see what they all had in common.

Introspection The examination of one's own subjective experiences.

Law of Contiguity A thought of something will tend to cause thoughts of things that are usually experienced along with it.

Law of Contrast A thought of something will tend to cause thoughts of opposite things.

Law of Frequency The more often something is experienced, the easier it will be to recall it.

Law of Similarity A thought of something will tend to cause thoughts of similar things.

Magic Various ceremonies and rituals that are designed to influence spirits.

Material cause According to Aristotle, what a thing is made of.

Materialistic view of the world The view that everything in nature is ultimately reducible to some inanimate substance, such as atoms.

Nativist One who believes that an important human attribute is innate and therefore not derived from experience.

Parmenides (540–470 B.C.) Believed that all change was an illusion, and therefore that the world was solid, fixed, and motionless.

Passive reason According to Aristotle, thinking about things in the world as they appear after they are filtered through the common sense.

Physicist A person who searches for or postulates a physis.

Physis A primary substance or element from which everything is derived.

Plato (437–347 B.C.) Strongly influenced by the Pythagoreans, postulated the existence of an abstract world of forms or ideas that, when manifested in matter, make up the objects in the empirical world. The only true knowledge is that of the forms, a knowledge that can be gained only by reflecting on the innate contents of the soul. Sensory experience interferes with the attainment of knowledge and should be avoided.

Protagoras (480–411 B.C.) A Sophist who taught that "man is the measure of all things." In

other words, what is considered true varies with a person's personal experiences; therefore, there is no objective truth, only individual opinion.

Pythagoras (582–500 B.C) Believed that an abstract world consisting of numbers and numerical relationships exerted an influence on the physical world. He created a dualistic view of humans by saying that in addition to our body we had a mind (soul), which, through reasoning, could understand the abstract world of numbers. Furthermore, our soul was immortal. Pythagoras's philosophy had a major influence on Plato and, through Christianity, on the entire Western world.

Rationalism The belief that knowledge is attained through some sort of mental operation.

Rational soul According to Aristotle, possessed only by humans. It incorporates the functions of the vegetative and sensitive souls and, in addition, allows thinking about events in the empirical world (passive reason) and the abstraction of the principles that characterize events in the empirical world (active reason).

Recall For Aristotle, the active mental search for past experiences.

Remembering For Aristotle, the passive recollection of past experiences.

Reminiscence theory of knowledge Plato's belief that knowledge is attained by remembering the experiences the soul had when it dwelt among the forms before entering the body.

Sensitive soul According to Aristotle, possessed by animals. It allows the functions provided by the vegetative soul and in addition provides the ability to interact with the environment and to retain the information gained from that interaction.

Socrates (470–399 B.C.) Disagreed with the Sophists' contention that there is no objective truth but only subjective opinion. Socrates believed that by examining a number of individual manifestations of a principle or concept, the general principle or concept itself could be discovered. These general abstractions were stable and knowable, and when known, they generated moral behavior.

Sophist A paid teacher of such subjects as rhetoric and logic who believed that truth was relative.

Teleology The belief that nature is purposive.

Thales (624–546 B.C.) Often called the first philosopher because he emphasized natural instead of supernatural explanations of things. He believed water to be the primary element from which everything else was derived.

Theory of forms Plato's contention that the ultimate reality consists of the abstract ideas or forms that correspond to all objects in the empirical world. Knowledge of these abstractions is innate and can be attained only through introspection.

Unmoved mover According to Aristotle, that which gave nature its purpose or final cause, but was itself uncaused. In Aristotle's philosophy, the unmoved mover was a logical necessity.

Vegetative soul The soul possessed by plants. It allows only growth, the intake of nutrition, and reproduction.

Vitalistic view of the world The view that everything in nature is alive but not necessarily inhabited by anthropomorphic spirits.

Zeno's paradox The assertion that in order for an object to pass from point A to point B, it must first traverse half the distance between those two points and then half of the remaining distance and so forth. Since this process must occur an infinite number of times, Zeno concluded that an object could logically never reach point B.

CHAPTER 3

After Aristotle: A Search for the Good Life

After Sparta defeated Athens in the Peloponnesian War (431–404 B.C.), the Greek city-states began to collapse, and the Greek people became increasingly demoralized. In this postwar atmosphere Socrates, Plato, and Aristotle flourished, but a gulf was beginning to develop between philosophy and the psychological needs of the people. Shortly after Aristotle's death (322 B.C.), the Roman invasions into Greek territory began, making an already unstable situation even more uncertain. In this time of great personal strife, complex and abstract philosophies were of little comfort. A more wordly philosophy was needed, a philosophy that addressed the problems of everyday living. The major questions were no longer "What is the nature of physical reality?" or "What and how can humans know?" but rather, "How is it best to live?" or "What is the nature of the good life?" or "What is worth believing in?" In response to the latter questions emerged the philosophies of the Skeptics, Cynics, Epicureans, Stoics, and finally the Christians.

SKEPTICISM AND CYNICISM

Both **Skepticism** and **Cynicism** were critical of other philosophies, contending that these other philosophies were either completely false or irrelevant to human needs. As a solution, Skepticism promoted a suspension of belief in anything, and Cynicism promoted a retreat from society.

Pyrrho

Pyrrho (360–270 B.C.) founded the school of Skepticism based on a mistrust of any so-called first principles or universal truths. No matter what one believed, it could turn out to be false, and therefore one could avoid the frustration of being wrong by simply not believing in anything. There was a kinship between the Sophists, who believed that many views were probably true, and the Skeptics, who believed that most if not all views were equally false.

Antisthenes and Diogenes

Antisthenes (445–365 B.C.) completely lost faith in philosophy and renounced his comfortable upper-class life. He believed that society, with its emphasis on material goods, status, and employment, was a distortion of nature and should be avoided. Questioning the value of art, mathematics and learning, Antisthenes preached a back-to-nature philosophy that involved a life free from wants and passions and from the many conventions of society. He thought that true happiness depended upon self-sufficiency. **Diogenes** (412–323 B.C.), a disciple of Antisthenes, was said to live an extremely primitive life and was given the nickname "cynic," which means doglike. Originally, the Cynic was one who retreated from society and lived close to nature. It is said that Diogenes broke his only bowl when he saw a child drinking with cupped hands (Robinson, 1976, p. 100).

Epicurus

EPICUREANISM AND STOICISM

Both **Epicureanism** and **Stoicism** were responses to the claim of the Skeptics and Cynics that philosophy had nothing useful to say about everyday life. Both were philosophies that spoke directly to the moral conduct of humans, and both were based on the empirical world.

Epicurus

Epicurus (341–270 B.C.) based his philosophy on Democritus's atomism but rejected his determinism. According to Epicurus, the atoms making up humans never lose their ability to move freely, hence he postulated free will. Epicurus agreed with Democritus that there was no after-life, since the soul was made up of freely moving atoms that scattered upon death. Atoms were never created or destroyed; they were only rearranged. It followed that the atoms comprising an individual would become part of another configuration following the individual's death. However, it was assumed that nothing was retained or transferred from one configuration to another. In this way, Epicurus freed humans from one of their major concerns: What is life like after death, and how should one prepare for it? The good life must be attained in this world, for there is no other.

Epicurean philosophy maintained that all knowledge was based upon sensory experience. Through association with physical objects, both memory and conscious ideas come to reflect physical reality. Our senses provide us with our only way of gaining knowledge, and according to Epicurus they can be trusted. Humans also have the capacity to experience pleasure and pain, experiences that are at the heart of Epicurean philosophy.

According to Epicurus, the goal of life was individual happiness, but his notion of happiness was not a simple **hedonism** (that is, seeking pleasure and avoiding pain). He was more interested in a person's long-term happiness, which could be attained only by avoiding extremes. Extreme pleasures are short-lived and ultimately result in pain or frustration, so humans should strive for the tranquility that comes from a balance between the lack of something and an excess of it. Therefore, humans cannot simply follow their impulses to attain the good life; reason and choice must be exercised in order to provide a balanced life, which in turn provides the greatest amount of pleasure over the longest period of time. For Epicurus, the good life was free, simple, rational, and moderate.

Zeno of Citum

Because **Zeno of Citum** (333–262 B.C.) taught in a school that had a *stoa poikile,* a covered hallway of many colors, his philosophy came to be known as Stoicism (Russell, 1959, p. 110). Zeno believed that the world was ruled by a divine plan, and that everything in nature, including humans, was there for a reason. The Stoics believed that to live in accordance with nature was the ultimate virtue. The most important derivative of this "divine plan" theory was the belief that whatever happens, happens for a reason, that there are no accidents. Translated onto the human level, this meant that whatever happened to a person happened for a reason, and that it must simply be accepted as part of the plan. The good life involved accepting one's fate with indifference, even if suffering was involved. Indeed, courage in the face of danger was considered most admirable. Material possessions were not highly valued, because they could be lost or taken away. Virtue alone was important. All people were expected to accept their stations in life and perform their duties without question. The joy in life came in knowing that one was participating in a master plan, even if that plan was incomprehensible to the individual. The only personal freedom was in choosing whether or not to act in accordance with nature's plan. When the individual's will was compatible with natural law, the individual was virtuous. When it was not, the individual was immoral. This philosophy, of course, was abhorrent to the Epicurean, who believed that certain governments should be rejected because they do not maximize pleasure and minimize pain.

In the Roman Empire, Stoicism won out over Epicureanism because Stoicism was compatible with the Roman emphasis on law and order. As long as the Roman government provided minimal happiness and safety, Stoicism remained the accepted philosophy, but then the Roman Empire began to fail. There was government corruption, crop failures, and economic problems, and the barbarian invasions could not be stopped. The people sought a new definition of the good life, one that would provide comfort and hope in perilous times. It was time to look toward the heavens for help. Before turning to the Christian alternative, however, we must look briefly at another philosophy that became part of Christian thought.

NEOPLATONISM

In addition to Stoicism and Epicureanism, there appeared in Rome renewed interest in Plato's philosophy. **Neoplatonism**, however, stressed the most mystical aspects of Plato's philosophy and minimized its rational aspects. The following two examples of Neoplatonist philosophers should make it easy to see why, when the Christian theologians sought a philosophical basis for their religion, Neoplatonism was very appealing.

Philo

Nicknamed the "Jewish Plato," **Philo** (25 B.C.–A.D. 50) viewed humans as having a higher self and a lower self. The higher self is the spiritual component, and it is immortal. The lower self is the body, which includes the senses. Evil results from bodily experiences, which should be minimized or avoided. We can see that Philo emphasized the spiritual aspect of Plato's philosophy.

Plotinus

Plotinus (A.D. 205–270) urged a mystical reunion with the "world soul." The world soul was like the world postulated by the Pythagoreans and by Plato as existing beyond sensory experience, and one should attempt to live in this world soul as fully as the bonds of flesh permit. Plotinus believed that by entering trances he was able to enter this world beyond appearances. He viewed worldly matters as largely irrelevant. Like Plato and all the Neoplatonists, Plotinus saw the body as the soul's prison. Through intense meditation, the soul could be released from the body and dwell among the eternal and the changeless. Plotinus believed that all humans were capable of such transcendental experiences, and encouraged them to have them, since no other experience was more important or satisfying. To the Stoic's definition of the good life as quiet acceptance of one's fate and the Epicurean's seeking of pleasure, we can now add a third suggestion—the turning away from the empirical world in order to enter a union with those eternal things that dwell beyond the world of flesh. Plotinus's theory was not itself Christian, but it strongly influenced subsequent Christian thought.

MacLeod (1975) notes that there are five classical doctrines of human nature: the relativistic doctrine of the Sophists, which claimed that human nature was a function of one's experiences; the materialistic doctrine of the atomists, which claimed that everything in nature, including humans, was made of atoms, and that everything both mental and physical could be explained by the movement and arrangement of atoms; the idealistic doctrine of the Pythagoreans and Plato, which claimed that the ultimate reality consisted of abstractions such as numbers, forms, or ideas; the teleological doctrine of Aristotle, which claimed that everything in nature, including humans, had a purpose built into it; and the religious doctrine, which emphasized the immortal soul and the word of God above all else. It is to the religious doctrine of human nature that we turn next.

EMPHASIS ON SPIRIT

The Roman period lasted from about 30 B.C. to about A.D. 300. At the height of its influence, the Roman Empire included the entire Western world, from the Near East to the British Isles. The imperial expansion of the Roman Empire, and then its collapse, brought a number of influences to bear on Roman culture. One such influence came from the religions of India and Persia. Indian *Vedantism,* for example, taught

that perfection could be approximated by entering into semiecstatic trances. Another example is **Zoroastrianism**, which taught that individuals are caught in an eternal struggle between wisdom and correctness on the one hand, and ignorance and evil on the other. All good things were thought to derive from the brilliant, divine sun, and all bad things from darkness. Another influence came from Greek culture. Generally, the Romans recognized the importance of Greek scholarship and sought to preserve and disseminate it. Although both Stoicism and Epicureanism became Roman philosophies, they originated in Greek philosophy, and this was also true of Neoplatonism. Another major influence on Roman thought was the Hebrew religion. The Hebrews believed in one Supreme God who, unlike the rather indifferent Olympian and Roman gods, was concerned with the conduct of individual humans. The Hebrews also had a strict moral code, and if an individual's conduct was in accordance with this code, God rewarded the person; if it was not, God punished the person. Thus, individuals were responsible for their transgressions. It was from this mixture of many influences that Christianity emerged. The city of Alexandria, in Egypt, provided the setting where the Eastern religions, the Hebrew tradition, and Greek philosophy all combined to form early Christian thought.

Jesus

Of course, the Christian religion centered around **Jesus** (4 B.C.–A.D. 30), who taught, among other things, that knowledge of good and evil is revealed by God, and that once revealed, such knowledge should guide human conduct. But Jesus himself was not a philosopher. As Brett (1965) describes him, he was a simple man with limited goals:

> Jesus himself had no speculative interests, his concern being primarily with the religious development of the individual. In his attitude to

the learned he typified the practical man of simple faith and intuitive insight who trusts experience rather than a book and his heart rather than his head. He knew intuitively what to expect from people and the influences which shape their development of character. A brilliant diagnostician and curer of souls, he had little interest in formalizing or systematizing his assumptions. (pp. 143–144)

None of the philosophers who formalized the teachings of Jesus ever met him. How much of Jesus' original intent survived the various attempts at formalization is still a matter of speculation. In any case, those who claimed that Jesus was the Son of God were called Christians. But before it was to become a dominant force in the Western world, Christianity needed a philosophical basis, and this was provided to a large extent by Plato's philosophy. The early Christian church is best thought of as a blending of the Judeo-Christian tradition with Platonism—or, more accurately, with Neoplatonism. This blending did not occur suddenly, but gradually, and reached its peak in Augustine. As the blending of the Judeo-Christian tradition and the Platonic philosophy proceeded, there was a major shift in emphasis from the rational (emphasized by Greek philosophy) to the spiritual (emphasized in the Judeo-Christian tradition).

St. Paul

The many influences converging on early Christianity are nicely illustrated in the work of **St. Paul** (A.D. 5–67), the first to claim and preach that Jesus of Nazareth was the Messiah. Paul was a Roman citizen whose education involved both Hebrew religion and Greek philosophy. From the Hebrew tradition he learned that there was one God who created the universe and who shapes the destiny of mankind. God is omniscient (knows everything) omnipresent, (is everywhere), and omnipotent (has unlimited power). Humans fell from a state of grace in the Garden of Eden, and ever since, they have been seeking atonement for this origi-

nal sin. To these Hebrew beliefs, Paul added the belief that God had sacrificed his Son to atone for one shared transgression—that is, original sin. This sacrifice made a personal reunion with God possible. In a sense, each individual was now able to start life with a clean slate.

In his training in Greek philosophy, St. Paul was especially influenced by Plato. Paul took Plato's notion that true knowledge can be attained only by escaping from the influence of sensory information and transformed it into a battle between the soul, which contains the spark of God, and the desires of the flesh. But then he did something that most Greek philosophers would have found abhorrent: he placed faith above reason. Faith alone can provide personal salvation. The good life is no longer defined in terms of rationality but in terms of one's willingness to surrender one's existence to God's will. God is the cause of everything, knows everything, and has a plan for everything. By believing—by having faith—one affiliates himself or herself with God and receives his grace. By living a life in accordance with God's will, one is granted the privilege of spending eternity in God's grace when one's mortal coil is shed. For many, given their earthly conditions, this seemed like a small price to pay for eternal bliss.

Paul's efforts left major questions for future theologians to answer. Given the fact that God is all-knowing and all-powerful, is there any room for human free will? And given the importance of faith for salvation, what is the function or value of human reason? Or the questions can be stated in slightly different terms. Given the fact that everything is determined by God's will, why did God apparently give humans the ability to choose? And if we are incapable of understanding God's plan—and, indeed, if it is not necessary for us to do so—why do we possess reasoning powers? There was also a third question: Given the fact that God is perfect and loving, what accounts for the evil in the world? Following St. Paul, theologians were to agonize

THE BETTMANN ARCHIVE, INC.

St. Augustine

over these and related questions for many centuries.

The human was now clearly divided into three parts: the body, the mind, and the spirit. As with the Pythagoreans, Plato, and the Neoplatonists, the body was the major source of difficulty. The spirit was the spark of God within us and was the most highly valued aspect of human nature. Through our spirit we are capable of becoming close to God, and of course the spirit was viewed as immortal. The mind, the rational part of humans, was seen as caught between the body and the spirit—sometimes serving the body, which is bad, and at other times serving the spirit, which is good. St. Paul describes the situation nicely:

> We know that the law is spiritual; but I am not. . . . I do not even acknowledge my own actions as mine, for what I do is not what I want to do, but what I detest. But if what I do is against my will, it means that I agree with the

law and hold it to be admirable. But as things are, it is no longer I who perform the action, but sin that lodges in me. For I know that nothing good lodges in me—in my unspiritual nature . . . the good which I want to do, I fail to do; but what I do is the wrong which is against my will; and if what I do is against my will, clearly it is no longer I who am the agent. (Romans 7:14–20)

This state of conflict involving the good, the bad, and the rational is not unlike the one described by Freud many centuries later. The early Christians left unanswered the question of how one comes to know God. Is God to be known through the Scriptures, through revelation, or through reason, or is God's existence to be taken entirely on faith? It is this question that St. Augustine addressed, as well as the question concerning the function of the human will.

St. Augustine

St. Augustine (A.D. 354–430) concentrated almost exclusively on human spirituality. About the physical world one needs to know only that God created it. Augustine shared with the Pythagoreans, Plato, the Neoplatonists, and the earlier Christians a contempt for the flesh. When thoughts are focused on God, there is little need for worldly things. Arrival at true knowledge requires the passage from an awareness of the body to sense perception, to an internal knowledge of the forms (universal ideas), and finally to an awareness of God, the author of the forms. For Augustine, as for the earlier Christians, ultimate knowledge consisted of knowing God. The human was seen as a dualistic being consisting of a body not unlike that possessed by animals, and a spirit that was close to, or part of, God. The war between the two aspects of human nature, already present in Platonic philosophy, became the Christian struggle between heaven and hell—that is, between God and the Devil.

The will. God speaks to each individual through his or her soul, *but the individual need not* *listen.* According to Augustine, individuals were free to choose between the way of the flesh (Devil), which was sinful, and the way of God, which led to everlasting life in heaven. The human ability to choose explains why evil is present in the world: evil exists because people choose it.

The insertion of free will into Christian theology made several things possible. With freedom comes responsibility. If an individual chooses correctly (that is, to live in accordance with God's will), he or she will be rewarded by God's grace. If one chooses incorrectly, one is denied an afterlife in heaven; but more immediately, if the person chooses incorrectly, he or she feels guilty. According to Augustine, people have an **internal sense** that helps them evaluate their experiences by providing an awareness of truth, error, personal obligation, and moral right. Deviation from this internal sense causes the feeling of guilt. In fact, one need not actually act contrary to this internal sense to feel guilty, but only *intend* to do so. Just thinking about doing something sinful will cause as much guilt as actually *doing* something sinful. All of this results in behavior being controlled internally rather than externally. That is, instead of behavior being controlled by externally administered rewards and punishments, it is controlled by personal feelings of virtue or guilt.

Augustine was very instrumental in shifting the locus of control of human behavior from the outside to the inside. For him, the acceptance of free will made personal responsibility meaningful. Because individuals were personally responsible for their actions, it was possible to praise or blame them, and people could feel good or bad about *themselves* depending upon what choices they made. If one periodically chose evil over good, however, one need not feel guilty forever. By disclosing the actual or intended sin (for example, by confession) one was forgiven and again could pursue the pure Christian life.

The Christian alternative had wide appeal. To people suffering hunger, plague, and war, a religion that focused on a more perfect, non-physical world was comforting. To slaves and others with low status, a feeling of justice came from knowing that all humans were created in God's image and were finally judged by the same criteria. The poor were consoled by learning that material wealth was irrelevant to living the good life. Criminals did not need to remain criminals; they could be forgiven and given the opportunity for salvation, just like anyone else. All humans were part of a brotherhood; our origins were the same as were our goals. Eternal life with God in heaven was available to everyone, and to attain it all one needed to do was live a Christian life.

Knowing God. For Augustine, one did not need to wait for the death of the body to know God; knowledge of God was attainable within an individual's lifetime. Before arriving at this conclusion, Augustine needed something about human experience of which he could be certain. He searched for something that could not be doubted, and finally concluded that the fact that he doubted could not be doubted. In Book 20, Chapter 10 of *On The Trinity*, Augustine says:

> Who ever doubts that he himself lives, and remembers, and understands, and wills and thinks, and knows, and judges? Seeing that even if he doubts, he lives; if he doubts, he remembers why he doubts; if he doubts, he understands that he doubts; if he doubts, he wishes to be certain; if he doubts, he thinks; if he doubts, he knows that he does not know; if he doubts, he judges that he ought not to assert rashly. Whosoever therefore doubts about anything else, ought not to doubt of all these things; which if they were not, he would not be able to doubt of anything. (Hadden, 1912, pp. 133–134)

Thus, Augustine established the validity of inner, subjective experience. (As we shall see in the next chapter, Descartes used the same technique to arrive at his famous conclusion, "I think, therefore I am.") The internal sense could be trusted, but not outer (sensory) experience. For Augustine, then, a second way of knowing God (the first being the Scriptures) was **introspection**, or the examination of one's inner experiences. We see here the influence of Plato, who also believed that truth must be attained through introspection. Augustinian introspection, however, became a means of achieving a personal communion with God. According to St. Augustine, the feeling of love that one experiences when one is contemplating God creates an ecstasy unsurpassed among human emotions. Such a feeling is the primary goal of human existence, and anything that is compatible with achieving such a state of ecstasy is good while anything that distracts from its achievement is bad. Faith, and a personal emotional union with God, became the most important ingredients of human existence. Reason, which had been supreme for the Greeks, became inferior not only to faith but to human emotion as well. Reason remained in an inferior position for almost 1000 years, during which time the writings of Augustine prevailed and eventually provided the cornerstone of church dogma. Augustine had demonstrated that the human mind could know itself without confronting the empirical world. Since the Holy Spirit dwelled in this realm of pure thought, intense, highly emotional introspection was encouraged. Such introspection carried the individual farther within himself or herself and farther away from the empirical world.

By A.D. 395, Christianity was the official religion of the Roman Empire. Church dogma was no longer challengeable, and it wielded tremendous power. The questions with which the church grappled concerned inconsistencies within church doctrine. The question of what was true had already been answered, and there was no need to look elsewhere. People were either believers or heretics, and heretics were dealt with harshly. Once established as the official religion, Christianity became more and more powerful. The church owned vast properties, the Pope could make or break kings, and

priests controlled the behavior, feelings, and thoughts of the citizens. The eight crusades against the Moslems between 1095 and 1291 showed the power of Christianity to organize its followers to stop the Islam influence that had been spreading so rapidly throughout Europe.

In this climate the writings of Aristotle were rediscovered. Many centuries earlier, mainly because of the conquests of Alexander the Great, the Greek influence had been spread over a large area in which Greek philosophy, science, and art came to flourish. In fact, many believe that the Greeks overextended themselves and were unable to control their empire. When the Romans began to invade this empire, many Greek scholars fled into territories later conquered by the Arabs. These scholars carried with them many Greek works of art and philosophy, among them the works of Aristotle. Aristotle's works were preserved in the great Islamic mosques and were used to develop Arabic philosophy, religion, mathematics, and medicine. Under the influence of Islam, the Arabs moved west, and under the influence of Christianity the European armies moved east. The clash between the two resulted in the bloody holy wars, but it also brought the West back into contact with Aristotle's philosophy. At first, church authorities welcomed Aristotle's writings; then, after more careful analysis, the works were banned. It was clear that in order for Aristotle's thoughts to be "accepted," they needed to be Christianized.

Long before Aristotle's writings were rediscovered by the West, however, the Arabs were using them. In fact, more than 200 years before the West attempted to Christianize Aristotle's philosophy, several Arab philosophers busied themselves attempting to make it compatible with Islam.

THE ARABIC INFLUENCE

The years between about 500 and 800 are often referred to as the Dark Ages, but they are only dark with reference to the Western world. During this time, Islam was a powerful force in the world. The followers of Mahomet conquered Persia, Syria, Egypt, North Africa, and Spain. Also during this time, Arab philosophers translated, studied, and expanded on the ancient wisdom of Greece and Rome. By utilizing this wisdom, the Arabs were able to make great strides in medicine, science, and mathematics, subjects that were of greatest interest during the expansion of the Islamic empire because of their practical value. When conditions stabilized, however, there was greater interest in making the ancient wisdom compatible with Mohammadanism. Although these efforts focused mainly on Aristotle's philosophy, Neoplatonism was also very influential. The Arabic translations of the Greek and Roman philosophers, and the questions that were raised in attempting to make this ancient wisdom compatible with Islam, were utilized many years later when the Christians attempted the same thing; and in a surprising number of ways, the two efforts were similar.

Avicenna

THE BETTMANN ARCHIVE, INC.

Avicenna

Despite the fact that there were many outstanding Arabic philosophers, we will briefly mention only two. **Avicenna** (980–1037) wrote books on many topics, including medicine, mathematics, logic, metaphysics, Moslem theology, astronomy, politics, and linguistics. Although in most of his work he borrowed heavily from Aristotle, he made modifications in Aristotle's philosophy that persisted for hundreds of years.

In his analysis of human thinking, Avicenna started with the five external senses—vision, hearing, touch, taste, and smell. Then he turned to the "interior senses" (a term borrowed from Augustine), postulating seven interior senses arranged in a hierarchy. First is the common sense, which synthesizes the information provided by the external senses. The next interior sense is retentive imagination, the ability to remember the synthesized information

from the common sense. Next are compositive animal imagination and compositive human imagination. Compositive imagination allows both humans and animals to learn what to approach or avoid in the environment. For animals this is a strictly associative process. Those objects or events associated with pain are subsequently avoided, and those associated with pleasure are subsequently approached. Human compositive imagination, however, allows the creative combination of information from the common sense and from the retentive imagination. For example, humans can imagine a unicorn without ever having experienced one. Nonhuman animals do not possess this ability. Next in the hierarchy is the estimative power, the innate ability to make judgments about environmental objects. Lambs may have an innate fear of wolves, and humans may have an innate fear of spiders and snakes, or there may be a natural tendency to approach the things conducive to survival. Although Aristotle hinted at the idea, this was one of the first clear suggestions that some behavior may be instinctive. Next in the hierarchy is the ability to remember the outcomes of all of the information processing that occurs lower in the hierarchy, and finally there is the ability to use that information.

Although Aristotle postulated only three internal senses (common sense, imagination, and memory) and Avicenna seven, Avicenna was essentially an Aristotelian. His major departure from Aristotle's philosophy concerns the active intellect. For Aristotle, the active intellect was used in understanding the universal principles that could not be gained simply by observing empirical events. For Avicenna, the active intellect took on supernatural qualities; it was the aspect of humans that allowed them to understand the cosmic plan and to enter into a relationship with God. For Avicenna, an understanding of God represented the highest level of intellectual functioning. About the significance of Avicenna's work to subsequent philosophical development in the West, Robinson (1981) says:

> Had it not been for Avicenna and his colleagues in the Islamic world of the eleventh century, the philosophical achievements of twelfth- and thirteenth-century Europe—achievements based so sturdily upon Aristotelianism—are nearly unimaginable. (p. 145)

Averroës

Averroës (1126–1198) disagreed with Avicenna that human intelligence is arranged in a hierarchy with only the highest level able to bring humans into contact with God. According to Averroës, all human experiences reflect God's influence. In almost everything else, Averroës agreed with Avicenna, and he too was basically an Aristotelian. Averroës' writings are mainly commentaries on Aristotle's philosophy, with special emphasis on Aristotle's work on the senses, memory, sleep and waking, and dreams. Also, following Aristotle, Averroës said that the soul dies with the body. Only the active intellect survives death, and since the active intellect is the same for everyone, nothing personal survives death. This was of course contrary to Christian thought, and Averroës' interpretation of Aristotle was labelled "Averroism" and was severely attacked by later Christian philosophers.

It was almost time for the Western world to assimilate Aristotelianism into its religious beliefs, but an intermediate step needed to be taken. Human reasoning powers, which had been minimized in St. Augustine's philosophy but were so important in Aristotle's philosophy, had to be made respectable again. Reason and faith had to be made compatible. We shall mention only two of the philosophers who took on this important task.

RECONCILIATION OF FAITH AND REASON

St. Anselm

In *Faith Seeking Understanding*, St. Anselm (1033–1109) argued that perception and reason can and should supplement Christian faith. Although St. Anselm was basically an Augustinian, this acceptance of reason as a means of understanding God and his will represented a major departure from tradition, which had emphasized faith. St. Anselm exemplified how reason can be used within the Christian faith with his famous **ontological argument** for the existence of God. This is a complex argument, but essentially it says that if we can think of something, something must be causing the thought. That is, when we think of things, there must be real things corresponding to those thoughts. St. Anselm beckons us to continue thinking of a being until we can think of none better or greater, a being "than which nothing greater can be conceived." This perfect being that we have conjured up is God, and since we can think of him, he exists. St. Anselm was one of the first Christian theologians to attempt to use logic to support religious belief.

Peter Lombard

Also an Augustinian, **Peter Lombard** (1100–1164) argued even more forcefully for the place of reason within Christianity than did St. Anselm. Perhaps even more important, Lombard insisted that God could be known by studying his works. There is no need to escape from the empirical world to understand God; one can learn about God by studying the empirical world. Thus, for Lombard, there were three ways to learn about God: faith, reason, and the study of God's works (the empirical world). Philosophers such as St. Anselm and Lombard helped to create a receptive atmosphere for the works of Aristotle, which were about to have a major and long-lasting impact on Western philosophy.

SCHOLASTICISM

The holy wars had brought the Western world into contact with the works of Aristotle. The question now was what to do with these works. At first the works were condemned as pagan, but eventually an attempt was made to modify Aristotle's philosophy and incorporate it into Christian dogma. Some of the keenest minds in the history of Western thought took on the monumental task of synthesizing Aristotle's philosophy and Christian theology and showing what implications that synthesis had for living one's life. This synthesis came to be called **Scholasticism**.

Peter Abelard

Peter Abelard (1079–1142) marks the shift toward Aristotle as *the* philosopher in Western philosophy. Besides translating Aristotle's writings, Abelard introduced a method of study that was to characterize the Scholastic period. In question-and-answer form he outlined the logical consequences of philosophical assumptions. This was an excellent way of preparing for any debate that might occur over an issue. It was also an effective way of testing the validity of various assumptions. Abelard taught that if God exists, all methods of inquiry should prove that fact. The believer, then, has nothing to fear from logic, reason, or the direct study of nature. In the philosophies of Lombard and Abelard we see the seeds of science being planted. But lest one receive the impression that the established church initially met Aristotle's philosophy with open arms, it should be pointed out that the Pope ordered Abelard to stop teaching, and soon thereafter Abelard died, a lonely and frustrated man.

Albertus Magnus

Albertus Magnus (1193–1280) was one of the first Western philosophers to make a comprehensive review of Aristotle's works, as well as of the interpretations of Aristotle's works by the Moslem scholars. This was no mean feat, considering that the church still regarded Aristotle as a heretic. Magnus presented Aristotle's views on sensation, intelligence, and memory to the church scholars and attempted to show how human rational powers could be used to achieve salvation. Following Aristotle, Magnus performed detailed observations of nature, and he himself made significant contributions to botany. He was among the first since the Greeks to attempt to learn about nature by making careful empirical observations. But as instrumental as Abelard and Magnus were in bringing Aristotle's philosophy into the Christian tradition,

St. Thomas Aquinas

works and the Christian tradition. This was a major feat, but it had an important negative aspect. Once Aristotle's ideas were assimilated into church dogma, they were no longer challengeable. In fact, Aristotle's writings became almost as sacred as the Bible. This was unfortunate, because much of what Aristotle had said, later turned out to be false. With Aristotle, as earlier with Plato, the church emphasized those ideas that were most compatible with its theology. Ideas that were not compatible were either changed or ignored. Although this "Christianization" was easier to perform with Plato's philosophy than with Aristotle's, Aristotle did say several things that, with minor shifts and embellishments, could be construed as supporting church doctrine—for example, his thoughts on active reason and on the unmoved mover.

The Aristotelian emphasis on reason was so great that it could not be ignored. After all, the huge body of information Aristotle had generated was a product of empirical observation guided by reason. This emphasis on reason placed the church in a difficult position, since from its inception it had emphasized revelation, faith, and spiritual experience and minimized empirical observation and rationality. It turned out that Aquinas's greatest task (and achievement) was the reconciliation of faith and reason, which he accomplished by arguing effectively that *reason and faith are not incompatible.* For Aquinas, as for the other Scholastics, all paths led to the same truth—God and his glory. Thus, God could now be known through revelation, through Scripture, through examination of inner experience, or through logic, reason, and the examination of nature.

Although sensory information was again accepted as an accurate source of knowledge, Aquinas, following Aristotle, said that the senses could provide information only about particulars, not about universals, which reason must abstract from sensory information. Rea-

the greatest Scholastic of all was St. Thomas Aquinas.

St. Thomas Aquinas

St. Thomas Aquinas (1225–1274) did as much as anyone to synthesize Aristotle's philosophical son and faith cannot conflict because they both lead to the same ultimate reality, God. The philosopher uses logical proof and demonstration to verify God's existence, while the Christian theologian takes the existence of God on faith. Both arrive at the same truth but by different means. Humans alone are capable of reasoning and thereby pondering many possible solutions to problems, since the behavior of animals is governed solely by associative memory or by instinct. Aquinas spent considerable time discussing the differences between humans and "lower" animals. The biggest difference he recognized was that nonhuman animals do not possess souls, and therefore salvation is not available to them.

Aquinas's synthesis of Aristotelian and Christian thought was bitterly argued within the church but was finally accepted as official church doctrine. (Aquinas's work, with some modifications, remains the cornerstone of Catholicism to this day.) Aquinas's work eventually had several effects: it divided reason and faith, making it possible to study them separately; it made the study of nature respectable; and it showed the world that argument over church dogma was possible. Although Aquinas's goal was to strengthen the position of the church by admitting reason as a means of understanding God, his work had the opposite effect. Several philosophers following Aquinas argued that faith and reason could be studied separately. That is, they argued that reason could be studied without considering its theological implications. Philosophy without religious overtones was becoming a possibility—a possibility that had not existed for well over 1,000 years.

Aquinas, at least partially, shifted attention away from the heavens and back to earth, although his emphasis was still on the heavens. This shift had to occur before the Renaissance could take place. The Renaissance was still a long way off, however, and the church still controlled most human activities.

Limitations of Scholastic Philosophy

It is one thing to examine nature and try to arrive at the principles that seem to govern it, as most Greek philosophers did; it is another thing to assume that something is true and then attempt to make nature conform to that truth. The Christian theologians attempted to do the latter. During the time from Augustine to Aquinas, scholarship consisted of demonstrating the validity of church dogma. New information was accepted only if it could be shown to be compatible with church dogma; if this was not possible, the information was rejected. The "truth" had been found, and there was no need to search elsewhere. What was needed was an elaboration of the principles upon which the Christian faith depended and logical arguments that defended the faith.

Although the Scholastics were outstanding scholars and hair-splitting logicians, they offered little of value to either philosophy or psychology. They were much more interested in maintaining the status quo than in revealing any new information. Certainly, there was little concern with physical nature, except for those aspects that could be used to prove God's existence or to show something about God's nature. As with the major Greek philosophers who preceded them, the Scholastics searched for the universal truths or principles that were beyond the world of appearance. For the Pythagoreans it was numerical relationships; for Plato it was the pure forms or ideas; for Aristotle it was the entelechy, which gave a class of things its essence; and for the Scholastics it was the idea of God. All assumed that there was a higher truth beyond the one that could be experienced through the senses. For all, a knowledge of universals, principles, or abstractions was the only true knowledge.

As was mentioned earlier, once Aquinas separated faith and reason, it was only a matter of time before there would be those wishing to exercise reason while remaining unencumbered by faith. William of Occam was one who took this step. In so doing, he challenged the whole idea of universals or first principles, thus dealing a severe blow to Scholasticism.

WILLIAM OF OCCAM: A TURNING POINT

William of Occam (sometimes spelled *Ockham*, 1300–1349), a British-born Franciscan monk, accepted Aquinas's division of faith and reason, and pursued the latter. Occam believed that in explaining things, no unnecessary assumptions should be made—in other words, that explanations should always be kept as simple as possible. This belief that extraneous assumptions should be "shaved" from explanations or arguments came to be known as **Occam's razor**.

Occam applied his "razor" to the debate concerning the existence of universals. As we have seen, some scholars believed that universal ideas or principles existed, and that individual empirical experiences were only manifestations of those universals. Those believing in the independent existence of universals were called **realists**. On the other hand, some scholars believed that so-called universals were nothing more than verbal labels used to describe groups of experiences that had something in common. Those believing that universals were nothing more than convenient verbal labels were called **nominalists**. Since Occam saw the assumption that universals had an independent existence as unnecessary, he sided with the nominalists, arguing forcefully that so-called universals were nothing more than mental habits. For example, since all cats have certain features in common, it is convenient to label all objects with those features as cats. The same thing is true for dogs, trees, books, or any other class of objects or experiences. According to Occam, the fact that experiences have features in common allows us to use general labels to describe those experiences; but the use of such labels does not mean

that there is a pure idea, essence, or form that exists beyond our experiences. Occam believed we could trust our senses to tell us what the world was really like, that we could know the world *directly* without needing to worry about what lurked beyond our experience.

Occam changed the question concerning the nature of knowledge from a metaphysical problem to a psychological problem. He was not concerned with a transcendent reality that could be understood only by abstract reasoning or intense introspection. For him, the question was how the mind classifies experience, and his answer was that we habitually respond to similar objects in a similar way. We apply the term *female* to a person because that person has enough in common with others we have called female.

In his empiricism, Occam went beyond Aristotle. Aristotle believed that sensory experience was the basis of knowledge, but that reason needed to be applied in order to extract from individual experiences knowledge of universals and essences. For Occam, sensory experience was the basis of knowledge—*period*. Occam's philosophy marks the end of Scholasticism. Despite the church's efforts to silence them, Occam's views were widely taught and can be viewed as the beginning of modern empirical philosophy. Indeed, we see in Occam a strong hint of the coming Renaissance. In spite of his radical empiricism, Occam was still a Franciscan monk and he believed in God. He did say, however, that God's existence could never be confirmed by studying nature, since there was nothing in nature that directly proved his existence. God's existence, then, must be accepted on faith.

THE SPIRIT OF THE TIMES BEFORE THE RENAISSANCE

During the fourteenth and fifteenth centuries, philosophy still served religion, as did everyone and everything else. There were two classes of people, believers and nonbelievers. The latter, if they could not be converted, were physically punished, imprisoned, or killed, and they were considered either stupid or possessed by the devil. There was no in-between. Superstition and magic were rampant. If the God contemplated through introspection was real, so must other objects of thought be real, such as demons and monsters. Astrology was extremely popular and magic was practiced almost everywhere. Superstition was not confined to the peasant, but was also shared by kings, scholars, and clergy.

All bodily experiences were seen as inferior to spiritual ones, but sex became the worst sin of all. Attitudes toward sex and toward women went hand in hand. The early Christians perpetuated the negative attitude toward women that the Greeks and Romans had demonstrated. Plato, for example, believed that women and the lower animals were degenerated forms of men (Esper, 1964, p. 80). Likewise, Aristotle felt that a man was superior to a woman and therefore should rule his house, his children, and his wife as a king rules his kingdom and his subjects (Esper, 1964, p. 192). There were three kinds of women: those who were promiscuous and therefore sinful; mothers, who did their duty by having children; and virgins, who were glorified. When men gave in to sexual desire it was thought to be the woman's fault, and even mothers were not entirely free from ridicule.

There is no doubt that the negative attitude toward women found in much Greek and Roman philosophy was assimilated into the Christian religion; this, in turn, has contributed to many of the problems that women experience today. Unfortunately, many things rooted in the distant past are extremely difficult to change, something that is especially true when beliefs become part of religious or any other kind of dogma that claims to be the final truth.

Clearly, this was not a time of open inquiry. To use Kuhn's terminology, inquiry was characterized by a single paradigm: the Christian conception of humans and the world. Although Kuhn was mainly concerned with science, his notion of paradigms can be applied to other fields of inquiry as well. As with other paradigms, the Christian paradigm determined what was acceptable as a problem and what counted as a solution. Philosophers were engaged in "normal philosophy," which, like normal science, is concerned only with exploring the implications of the accepted paradigm. Little creativity is involved in either normal science or normal philosophy. Kuhn tells us that in order for there to be a paradigm shift, anomalies must arise within the accepted paradigm; that is, consistent observations that cannot be explained must occur. As the anomalies persist, a new paradigm gradually gains recruits and eventually overthrows the old paradigm. The process is long and difficult and often traumatic for the early dissenters from the old paradigm. In the period before the Renaissance, anomalies were appearing everywhere in Christian doctrine, and it was clear that church authority was on the decline. Because open inquiry had been stifled for too long, for centuries there was little philosophical, scientific, or even theological growth. For progress to occur, the authority of the church had to be broken, and the cracks were beginning to appear almost everywhere.

SUMMARY

After Aristotle's death, philosophers began to concern themselves with principles of human conduct and asked the question "What constitutes the good life?" Pyrrho preached Skepticism. To him, nothing could be known with certainty, so why believe anything? The Skeptic did not commit himself or herself to any particular belief. Antisthenes advocated a back-to-nature approach to life, since he saw society as a distortion of nature that should be rejected. A simple life, close to nature and free of wants and passions, was best. Antisthenes' position was later called Cynicism. Epicurus said the good life involved seeking the greatest amount of pleasure over the greatest amount of time.

Such pleasure did not come from having too little or too much, but from a life of moderation. Zeno of Citum, the founder of Stoicism, claimed that the good life involved living in harmony with nature, which was designed in accordance with a divine plan. Since everything happens for a reason, one should accept whatever happens with courage and indifference. The Stoics believed material possessions to be unimportant, and they emphasized virtue (the acceptance of one's fate).

Clearly, the preceding moral philosophers were often contradictory, and they lacked a firm philosophical base. This problem was "solved" when philosophers switched their attention from ethics to religion. In Alexandria, there was a mixture of Greek philosophy, Hebrew traditions, and Eastern religions. Philo, a Neoplatonist, combined the Hebrew tradition with Plato's philosophy and created a system that glorified the spirit and condemned the flesh. Plotinus, another Neoplatonist, urged the embracing of the "world soul" through trances. These transcendental experiences were valued much more than any physical experience that one could have. St. Paul claimed Jesus to be the Son of God and thereby established the Christian religion.

St. Augustine said that humans can know God through intense introspection. The ecstasy that comes from cognitively embracing God was considered the highest human emotion and could only be achieved by avoiding or minimizing experiences of the flesh. By postulating human free will, Augustine accomplished several things: he explained evil as the result of humans choosing evil over good, humans became responsible for their own destiny, and personal guilt became an important means of controlling behavior. Augustine claimed that an internal sense reveals to each person how he or she should act as a Christian. Acting contrary to this internal sense, or even intending to act contrary to it, causes guilt. In making this claim, Augustine changed the locus of control of human behavior from outside the person to inside the person.

During the so-called Dark Ages, Arabic culture flourished and expanded throughout Europe. Arab scholars translated the works of the Greek and Roman philosophers and used this wisdom to make great advances in medicine, science, and mathematics. Avicenna and Averroës concentrated mainly on the works of Aristotle, translating and expanding them and attempting to make them compatible with Islam.

Before the Western World could embrace Aristotle's philosophy, human reasoning powers had to be made respectable. St. Anselm and Lombard were instrumental in showing that reason and faith were compatible, while Abelard and Magnus were among the first Western philosopher/theologians to embrace the work of Aristotle. Those who attempted to synthesize Aristotle's philosophy with the Christian religion were called Scholastics. The greatest Scholastic was St. Thomas Aquinas, and the major outcome of his work was the acceptance of both reason and faith as ways of knowing God. Before Aquinas, faith alone had been emphasized. The acceptance of reason as a means of knowing God made the examination of nature, the use of logical argument, and even debate within the church itself respectable. Many believe that Aquinas inadvertently created an atmosphere that led ultimately to the decline of church authority and therefore to the Renaissance.

Within the church, there was a debate between the realists and the nominalists. The realists believed in the existence of universals, of which individual empirical events were only manifestations. The nominalists believed that so-called universals were nothing more than verbal labels applied to classes of experience. William of Occam sided with the nominalists by explaining universals as mental habits. Occam took this position because it required the fewest assumptions. The belief that of two or more adequate explanations of the same thing, the explanation requiring the fewest assumptions should be chosen, came to be called Occam's razor.

In the heyday of early Christianity, a largely negative social climate prevailed. There was widespread superstition and fear, persecution of disbelievers, and discrimination against women. Any action or thought not in accor-

dance with church dogma was a sin. The minimum amount of sexual activity was tolerated so that humans could reproduce, anything beyond that being considered a hideous sin. The church had absolute power, and any dissension was dealt with harshly. Clearly, the spirit of the times was not conducive to open, objective inquiry.

DISCUSSION QUESTIONS

1. Briefly state what constituted the good life according to Pyrrho, Antisthenes, Epicurus, and Zeno of Citum. Also, indicate the names that were given to their points of view.

2. What five doctrines of human nature did MacLeod suggest? Briefly summarize each.

3. Describe the factors that contributed to the development of early Christian theology.

4. What characterized St. Paul's version of Christianity?

5. Summarize the philosophy of Neoplatonism.

6. Discuss the importance of free will in Augustine's philosophy.

7. How did Augustine change the locus of control of human behavior from forces outside the person to forces inside the person?

8. What did Augustine feel humans could be certain of, and how did he arrive at his conclusion? How, according to Augustine, could humans experience God, and what kind of emotion resulted from this experience?

9. In what way were the Dark Ages dark? Explain.

10. What was the importance of Avicenna and Averroës to Western thought?

11. How did the work of St. Anselm and Lombard prepare the Western world for the acceptance of Aristotle's philosophy?

12. What was St. Anselm's ontological argument for the existence of God?

13. What was the significance of the work of Abelard and Magnus?

14. How, according to Aquinas, can humans know God? What are some of the implications of Aquinas's position?

15. What was Scholasticism? Give an example of what the Scholastic did.

16. Summarize the debate between the realists and the nominalists.

17. Was William of Occam a realist or a nominalist? Explain.

18. What was Occam's razor?

GLOSSARY

Abelard, Peter (1079–1142) The first Western philosopher/theologian to emphasize the works of Aristotle.

Antisthenes (445–365 B.C.) Founder of Cynicism.

Averroës (1126–1198) An Arabic scholar who

attempted to make Aristotelian philosophy compatible with the Moslem religion.

Avicenna (980–1037) An Arabic scholar who translated and modified Aristotelian philosophy and attempted to make it compatible with Islam.

Cynicism The belief that the best life is one lived close to nature and away from the rules and regulations of society.

Diogenes (412–323 B.C.) Like his mentor, Antisthenes, advocated retreating from society and living a simple life close to nature.

Epicureanism The belief that the best life is one of long-term pleasure resulting from moderation.

Epicurus (341–270 B.C.) Founder of Epicureanism.

Hedonism The belief that the good life consists of seeking pleasure and avoiding pain.

Internal sense The internal knowledge of moral right that individuals use in evaluating their behavior and thoughts. Postulated by St. Augustine.

Introspection The examination of one's own subjective experiences.

Lombard, Peter (1100–1164) Insisted that God could be known through faith, reason, or the study of his work in nature.

Magnus, Albertus (1193–1280) Made a comprehensive review of Aristotle's work. Following Aristotle's suggestion, he also made careful, direct observations of nature.

Neoplatonism Philosophy that emphasized the most mystical aspects of Plato's philosophy. Transcendental experiences were considered the most significant kind of human experience.

Nominalism The belief that so-called universals are nothing more than verbal labels or mental habits that are used to denote classes of experience.

Occam's razor The belief that of several alternative explanations, the one that makes the fewest assumptions should be accepted.

Ontological argument for the existence of God St. Anselm's contention that if we can think of something, it must be real. Since we can think of a perfect being (God), that perfect being must exist.

Philo (25 B.C.–A.D. 50) A Neoplatonist who combined Hebrew theology with Plato's philosophy. Philo differentiated between the lower self (the body) and a spiritual self, which is made in God's image. The body is the source of all evil; therefore, in order for the spiritual self to develop fully, one should avoid or minimize sensory experience.

Plotinus (A.D. 205–270) A Neoplatonist who emphasized the importance of embracing the "world soul" through intense cognitive effort. These cognitive, subjective experiences were much more important than physical experiences.

Pyrrho (360–270 B.C.) Founder of Skepticism.

Realism The belief that abstract universals exist and that empirical events are only manifestations of those universals.

St. Anselm (1033–1109) Argued that sense perception and rational powers should supplement faith (see also **ontological argument for the existence of God**).

St. Augustine (A.D. 354–430) After having demonstrated the validity of inner, subjective experience, said that one can know God through introspection as well as through the revealed truth of the Scriptures. Augustine also wrote extensively on human free will.

St. Paul (A.D. 5–67) Founded the Christian church by claiming that Jesus was the Son of God. St. Paul placed the soul or spirit in the highest position among the human faculties, the body in the lowest, and the mind in a position somewhere between these two.

St. Thomas Aquinas (1225–1274) Epitomized Scholastism. He sought to "Christianize" the works of Aristotle and to show that both faith and reason lead to the truth of God's existence.

Scholasticism The synthesis of Aristotelian philosophy with Christian teachings.

Skepticism The belief that all beliefs can be proved false, so that to avoid the frustration of being wrong, it is best to believe nothing.

Stoicism The belief that one should live according to nature's plan and accept one's fate with indifference, or in the case of extreme hardship, with courage.

Vedantism The Indian religion that emphasized the importance of semiecstatic trances.

William of Occam (1300–1349) Denied the contention of the realists that what we experience is but a manifestation of an abstract principle. Instead, he sided with the nominalists who said that so-called abstract principles, or universals, were nothing more than verbal labels that we use to describe classes of experiences. For Occam, reality is what we experience directly; there is no "higher" reality beyond our senses.

Zeno of Citum (333–262 B.C.) Founder of Stoicism.

Zoroastrianism The Persian religion that equated truth and wisdom with the brilliance of the sun, and ignorance and evil with darkness.

CHAPTER 4

The Beginnings of Modern Psychology

The Renaissance is generally dated from approximately 1450 to 1600, although many historians would date its beginning much earlier. **Renaissance** means "rebirth," and during this period the tendency was to go back to the more open-minded method of inquiry that had characterized early Greek philosophy. It was a time when Europe gradually switched from being God-centered to being human-centered. If God existed, he existed in nature; therefore, to study nature was to study God. Also, since God had given humans the faculties to create works of art, why not exercise those faculties to the fullest? The new view was that there was more to humans than their souls; they had reliable sensory systems, too, so why not use them? They had reasoning powers, so why not exercise them? And they had the capacity for enjoyment, so why not enjoy? After all, God, in his infinite wisdom, must have given humans these attributes for a reason. Attention was diverted from the heavens, where the Pythagoreans, Platonists, and early Christians had focused it, to the world. Nowhere is this spirit of the times better illustrated than in the work of the Renaissance humanists.

RENAISSANCE HUMANISM

Major Themes

The term **humanism**, as it applies to the Renaissance, does not mean "humanitarianism." That is, it does not refer to a deep concern about the welfare of humans. Nor does it refer to humaneness—that is, treating one's fellow humans with respect, sensitivity, and dignity. As it applies to the Renaissance, the term *humanism* denotes an intense interest in human beings, as if we were discovering ourselves for the first time. Interest was focused on a wide range of human activities. How do we think, behave, and feel? What are we capable of? These and related questions are reflected in the four major themes that characterize Renaissance humanism.

1. *Individualism*. There was great concern with human potential and achievement. The belief in the power of the individual to make a positive difference in the world created a spirit of optimism.

2. *Personal religion*. Although all of the Renaissance humanists were devout Christians, they wanted religion to be more personal and less formal and ritualistic. They argued for a religion that could be personally experienced rather than one that the church hierarchy imposed upon people.

3. *Intense interest in the past*. The Renaissance humanists fell in love with the past. The works of the early Greek and Roman poets, philosophers, and politicians were of special interest. Renaissance scholars wanted to read what the ancients had really said, instead of someone's interpretation of what they had said. They sought to assign correct authorship to old manuscripts, since several manuscripts had been incorrectly attributed to certain authors, and they attempted to expose forgeries. These activities exposed Renaissance scholars to a wide range of viewpoints from the past, and many of these

views found considerable support among the humanists. For example, much previously unknown philosophy of Plato was discovered, resulting in a wave of interest in Plato. In 1462, **Marsilio Ficino** (1433–1499) founded a Platonic Academy in Florence. He sought to do for Plato's philosophy what the Scholastics had done for Aristotle's. Among the humanists, almost every early Greek and Roman philosophy had its adherents, but Plato was especially influential. Even some extremely old Eastern religions were rediscovered, stimulating great interest in the occult.

4. *Anti-Aristotelianism.* Many of the humanists believed that the church had gone too far in its embracing of Aristotle's philosophy, to the point where Aristotle's philosophy was as authoritative as the Bible. It was not uncommon for a passage from Aristotle to be used to settle a theological dispute. To the humanists this was ridiculous, since Aristotle had been only human, and like any human he was capable of error. To the regret of the humanists, Aristotle's philosophy had been used to create a set of rules, regulations, and beliefs that one had to accept in order to be a Christian. Accepting church dogma became more important than one's personal relationship with God, and therefore the humanists attacked church dogma harshly. Although there were many interesting Renaissance humanists, space permits only a brief review of a few of them.

Francesco Petrarch

So influential was **Francesco Petrarch** (1304–1374) that many historians argue that his writings mark the beginning of the Renaissance. Clearly, all of the themes discussed above are found in Petrarch's work. Above all else, Petrarch was concerned with freeing the human spirit from the confines of medieval traditions, and the main target of his attack was Scholas-

ticism. He felt that the classics should be studied as the works of humans and not be interpreted or embellished by others. He had a low opinion of those who used the classics to support their own beliefs, saying of these interpreters, "Like those who have no notion of architecture, they make it their profession to whitewash walls." An obvious example of this kind of interpreter is the Scholastic.

Like most Renaissance humanists, Petrarch urged a return to a personal religion like that described by St. Augustine—a religion based upon the Bible, personal faith, and personal feelings. He felt that Scholasticism, in its attempt to make religion compatible with Aristotelian rationalism, had made it too intellectual. Petrarch also argued that a person's life in this world is at least as important as life after death. God wanted humans to use their vast capabilities, not inhibit them, Petrarch argued. By actualizing the potential God has given to us, we can change the world for the better. By focusing on human potential, Petrarch stimulated the explosion of artistic and literary endeavors that characterized the Renaissance.

Giovanni Pico

Giovanni Pico (1463–1494) argued that God had granted humans a unique position in the universe. Angels are perfect and thus have no need to change, while animals are bound by their instincts and cannot change. Humans alone, being between angels and animals, are capable of change. By *choice*, they are capable of leading almost any kind of life and embracing almost any point of view. Pico insisted that all philosophies had common elements; for example, they reflected human rationality and individuality. He argued further that, if properly understood, the major philosophical viewpoints were essentially in agreement. All points of view, therefore, should be studied objectively with the aim of discovering what they have in common. Pico sought peace among philosophical and religious rivals. All human works, he said, should be respected.

Martin Luther

Martin Luther (1483–1546) was extremely upset with what Christianity had become in his day. His view of Christianity, like those of the other humanists, was much more in accordance with Augustine's view than with Aquinas's. Luther was especially opposed to the Catholic church's sale of indulgences, which allowed sinners to reduce the retribution for their sins by paying a fee to church officials. God alone, he preached, determined what was sinful and how sinfulness was to be dealt with. But the sale of indulgences was not the only thing wrong with the church: in Luther's eyes, the church had drifted far from the teachings of Jesus and the Bible. Jesus had preached the glory of the simple life devoid of luxury and privilege, but the church had come to value these things and to engage in too many formal rituals. For Luther, the major reason for the downfall of Catholicism was its assimilation of Aristotle's philosophy, and Luther had harsh words for Aristotle:

> What are the universities . . . but . . . schools of Greek fashion and heathenish manners full of dissolute living, where very little is taught of the Holy Scriptures and of the Christian faith, and the blind heathen teacher, Aristotle, rules even further than Christ. Now, my advice would be that the books of Aristotle, the "Physics," the "Metaphysics," "Of the Soul," "Ethics," which have hitherto been considered the best, be altogether abolished. . . . My heart is grieved to see how many of the best Christians this accursed, proud, knavish heathen has fooled and led astray with his false words. God sent him as a plague for our sins. (Blucher, 1946, p. 630)

The Catholic church's response to the criticisms of Luther and others was to make Aquinas's Christianized version of Aristotle's philosophy official church dogma that all Christians were expected to follow. Having failed in their efforts to reform the Catholic church, Luther and others began promoting their own version of Christianity. The result was the **Reformation**, which divided Western Christianity into the Protestant and the Roman Catholic churches, and the dispute over which version of Christianity was correct soon divided Europe into two warring factions.

Desiderius Erasmus

Like Pico, **Desiderius Erasmus** (1466–1536) was opposed to a fanatical belief in anything. Erasmus was fond of pointing out mistakes in the classics, claiming that anything created by humans could not be perfect. He exposed exorcism and alchemy as nonsense, attacking these and other forms of superstition and begging people to take their lessons from the simple life of Jesus instead of from the pomp and circumstance of the organized church. He believed that war was caused by fanaticism and was nothing more than homicide, and he was especially disturbed by bishops who became rich and famous because of war. Eclectic and practical, Erasmus was a keen observer of the world and its problems. During the Reformation he could not side with either the Catholics or the Protestants and was condemned by both.

There were many other Renaissance humanists. Some manifested the power of the individual in art (Leonardo da Vinci, 1452–1519), some in politics (Niccoló Machiavelli, 1469–1527), some in education (Juan Luis Vives, 1492–1540), and some in literature (William Shakespeare, 1564–1616). The emphasis was always the same—the individual. Now to be judged by their work instead of their words, people were seen as having the power to change things for the better rather than simply accepting the world as it was or hoping that it would become better. Although the Renaissance humanists added nothing new in philosophy or psychology, the belief that individuals could act upon the world to improve it was conducive to the development of science. During the Renaissance, art, literature, and architecture benefited from human endeavor. The age of science was still in the future.

To say the least, the Renaissance was a paradoxical time. On the one hand, there was an explosion of interest in human potential, coupled with great human achievements. In this respect, the Renaissance resembled classical Greece and Rome. On the other hand, it was a time of persecution, superstition, witch hunting and burning, fear, torture, and exorcism. While astrologers and alchemists were generally highly regarded and popular, abnormal individuals were treated with extreme harshness. Wars destroyed much of France and Germany, the Black Death cut Europe's population nearly in half, there were major famines, and syphilis was epidemic. Yet in spite of all this, there was almost unparalleled creativity. The Renaissance displayed the best and worst of humanity—the stuff from which modern philosophy and psychology emerged.

FURTHER CHALLENGES TO CHURCH AUTHORITY

The Renaissance and the breakdown of church authority went hand in hand. Church dogma consisted of fixed truths such as there being exactly seven heavenly bodies in the solar system, the earth being the center of the solar system, humans being created in God's image, and the earth being flat. Gradually, these "truths" were challenged, and each successful challenge focused suspicion on other "truths." Once begun, the questioning increased rapidly, and the church tried desperately to discourage these challenges to its authority. Church scholars attempted to show that contradictions were only apparent. Failing in this, they attempted to impose censorship, but it was too late: the challenging spirit was too widespread. The decline

in the church's authority was directly related to the rise of a new spirit of inquiry that took as its ultimate authority empirical observation instead of the Scriptures, faith, or revelation. Gradually church dogma was replaced by the very thing it had opposed the most—the direct observation of nature without the intervention of theological considerations. But the transition, although steady, was slow and painful. Many Renaissance scholars were caught between theology and science, either because of personal beliefs or because of fear of retaliation by the church. They reported their observations with extreme caution, and in some cases they requested that their observations be reported only after their deaths.

There is no single reason for this reawakening of the spirit of objective inquiry; several factors are believed responsible. One was Aquinas's acceptance of reason and examination of nature as ways of knowing God. Once sanctioned by the church, the human capacity to reason was focused everywhere, including on church dogma. Another factor was the work of the humanists, which recaptured the spirit of open inquiry reflected in the classics. The humanists also stressed the human potential to act upon the world and change it for the better. In addition, the following events are considered factors in the acceptance of the objective study of nature because they weakened the authority of the church:

- Marco Polo's explorations (1254–1324)
- Invention of the printing press by Johann Gutenberg (1450)
- Discovery of America (1492)
- Luther's challenge to Catholicism (1517)
- Magellan's circumnavigation of the globe (1522)

These and other events expanded the known world. The discovery that the earth was round and filled with strange peoples with strange customs created many problems for the church; for example, a long debate occurred concerning whether "savages" found in America had souls or not (it was decided that they did). The printing press made the widespread, accurate, and rapid exchange of ideas possible. And as we have seen, Luther's challenge to Catholicism resulted in the development of the Protestant movement, which argued against centralized church authority and for increased individualism within the Christian religion. People, said Luther, should have the right to interpret the Bible for themselves.

As influential as the above events were, however, it was the work of a few astronomer-physicists that was most detrimental to church dogma and most influential in creating a new way of examining nature's secrets. That new way was called science.

COPERNICUS, KEPLER, AND GALILEO

Nicolaus Copernicus

Nicolaus Copernicus (1473–1543) argued successfully that rather than the sun revolving around the earth (the geocentric theory), the earth revolved around the sun (the heliocentric theory). Copernicus was well aware that his observation directly opposed church dogma, and therefore arranged for his work to be published only after his death. Probably more important than the observation itself was the fact that it questioned the place of humankind in the universe. Were we favored by God and therefore placed in the center of the universe, or not? If not, why not? If the church was wrong about this vital fact, what else was it wrong about? Were there other solar systems that contained life? If so, how were they related to ours, and which did God favor? **Giordano Bruno** (1548–1600) speculated that there were other

Nicolaus Copernicus

life-containing solar systems, and he was burned at the stake for his speculations. Bruno's fate helps explain the caution exhibited by scientists and philosophers during these times.

Johannes Kepler

Johannes Kepler (1571–1630) supported Copernicus's heliocentric theory, and through observation and mathematical deduction he worked out the laws of planetary motion. For example, he found that the paths of the planets around the sun were elliptical rather than circular. Kepler also studied vision directly and found that environmental objects project an inverted image onto the retina. This observation contrasted with earlier theories that explained vision as the result of the projection of exact copies of objects directly into the sense receptors. Kepler also questioned our ability to perceive things correctly when the image projected onto the retina is upside down, but he left that problem for others to solve.

Galileo Galilei

Galileo Galilei (1564–1642) challenged Aristotle's contention that heavy objects fall faster than lighter ones by *demonstrating* that both fall at the same rate. In 1609 he made a telescope and discovered four moons of Jupiter. This made 11 bodies in the solar system, not 7 as the church had insisted. Most people refused to look through Galileo's telescope because they felt that to do so was an act of heresy. Galileo differentiated between the physical characteristics of things (later called primary qualities) and things as they are perceived (later called secondary qualities). In the area of sound, for example, vibrations could be studied directly, but the hearing resulting from those vibrations could not. According to Galileo, science could investigate only primary qualities; secondary qualities were too subjective, and therefore could not be studied scientifically. Thus, Galileo excluded from science much of what is now included in psychology, and many modern natural scientists refuse to accept psychology as a science for the same reason that Galileo did not accept it.

Galileo viewed the universe as a perfect machine whose workings could be understood in mathematical terms. Burtt (1932) quotes Galileo:

> Philosophy is written in that great book which ever lies before our eyes—I mean the universe—but we cannot understand it if we do not first learn the language and grasp the symbols in which it is written. This book is written in the mathematical language, and the symbols are triangles, circles, and other geometric figures, without whose help it is impossible to comprehend a single word of it; without which one wanders in vain through a dark labyrinth. (p. 75)

We see in Galileo a great deal of the Pythagorean philosophy, as well as a belief in universals. For Galileo, an experiment was performed in order to discover a universal law, which, when discovered, could be used to deduce many other instances of that law. Galileo relied much more on mathematical reasoning than he did on empirical experimentation, and on the question of realism versus nominalism, he was on the side of realism. For Galileo, the experiment was a vehicle for discovering universal truth about the universe.

Aristotle was a prime target of Galileo's. Using mathematical reasoning and empirical observation, Galileo discredited one Aristotelian "truth" after another—thus, of course, attacking the very core of church dogma. At the age of 70, Galileo was brought before the Inquisition and made to recant his beliefs. For the several years that he lived afterward, he is said to have felt severe guilt for having denied something that he truly believed. Only recently did the church admit wrongdoing in the condemnation of Galileo and his views. It was the work of Copernicus, Kepler, and especially Galileo that Newton expanded into a conception of the universe that was to have a profound influence on psychology.

FRANCIS BACON

Francis Bacon (1561–1629) and Galileo were contemporaries, but their approaches to science were very different. Galileo sought principles that could be expressed mathematically and from which deductions could be made, an approach that actually required very little experimentation. The important thing for Galileo was to discover the laws that governed the physical world. Once such laws had been isolated and expressed mathematically, a large number of manifestations of those laws could be deduced. (**Deduction** involves predicting a particular event from a general principle.) Bacon, on the other hand, demanded science based on **induction**. According to Bacon, science should include no theories, no hypotheses, no mathematics, and no deduction, but should stay close to the facts of observation. He felt that anyone doing research with preconceived notions would tend to see nature in light of those preconceptions. In other words, Bacon felt that holding a theory was likely to bias one's observations, and he offered Aristotle as an example of a biased researcher. Bacon said that since Aristotle had assumed that the objects in nature were governed by final causes, Aristotle's research confirmed the existence of final causes. Esper (1964) says:

> [Bacon] declared that when we assume "final causes and apply them to science, we are carrying into nature what exists only in our imagination. Instead of understanding *things*, we dispute about *words*, which each man interprets to suit himself." (p. 290)

Bacon distrusted rationalism because of its emphasis on words, and he distrusted mathematics because of its emphasis on symbols. In his book *Of the Proficience and Advancement of Learning Divine and Human* (1605), Bacon says, "Words are but the images of matter . . . to fall in love with them is [like falling] in love with a picture." Bacon trusted only the direct observation and recording of nature. With his radical empiricism, Bacon made it clear that the ultimate authority in science was to be empirical observation. No authority, no theory, no words, no mathematical formulation, no belief, and no fantasy could displace empirical observation as the basis of factual knowledge.

But Bacon did not avoid classifying empirical observations. He believed that after many observations generalizations could be made, and similarities and differences among observations noted. Bacon's generalizations were used to describe classes of events or experiences. They were not principles from which predictions could be made. Again, Bacon's approach to science was inductive, whereas Galileo's was deductive.

Bacon summarized the four sources of error that he felt could creep into scientific investigation in his famous "idols."

Francis Bacon

- *The idol of the cave*: personal biases that result from one's own experiences, education, or feelings.

- *The idol of the tribe*: agreed-upon ways of thinking that are part of a culture and that result in cultural prejudice.

- *The idol of the marketplace*: biases that result from being overly influenced by the traditional meanings of words. Verbal labels often distort what is really there.

- *The idol of the theater*: blind allegiance to dogma, authority, or tradition.

Bacon also insisted that science seek practical information—that is, information that is useful in solving human problems. For Bacon, *useless* and *worthless* meant the same thing. (Bacon died of pneumonia that he caught while stuffing a chicken with ice to test the benefits of refrigeration.)

Bacon is a pivotal figure because of his extreme skepticism concerning all sources of knowledge except the direct examination of nature. He urged that nature itself be the only authority in settling epistemological questions. We see in Bacon an insistence that observations

René Descartes

at La Flèche, he, like other students at the time, studied the writings of Plato, Aristotle, and the early Christian philosophers. At that time education consisted of logically demonstrating the validity of revealed truths (scholasticism). After his graduation from La Flèche, Descartes roamed freely and sampled many of life's pleasures, finally taking up residence in St. Germain, a suburb of Paris. It was here that Descartes observed a group of mechanical statues that the queen's fountaineers had constructed for her amusement. The statues contained a system of water pipes that, when activated by a person stepping on a hidden floor-plate, caused a series of complex movements and sounds. As we shall see shortly, this idea of complex movement being caused by a substance flowing through pipes was to have a profound influence on Descartes's later philosophy.

be made without any philosophical, theological, or personal considerations. Skepticism concerning information from the past also characterized the first great philosopher of the new age, René Descartes, to whom we turn next.

RENÉ DESCARTES

Born of wealthy parents on March 31, 1596, in La Haye, France, **René Descartes** (1596–1650) was truly a Renaissance man; at one time or another, he was a soldier, a mathematician, a philosopher, a scientist, and a psychologist. In addition, he was a man of the world who enjoyed gambling, dancing, and adventure. But he was also an intensely private person who preferred solitude and avoided emotional attachments with people. At a time when his fame had begun to grow, he moved to Holland; and while he was there he moved 24 times without leaving a forwarding address, so that he would not be bothered.

As one might expect, Descartes was a very bright child. His parents enrolled him in a progressive school at La Flèche when he was 10 years old; he graduated when he was 16. While

Descartes's Search for Philosophical Truth

About the time Descartes moved to St. Germain he experienced an intellectual crisis. It occurred to him that everything he had ever learned was useless, especially philosophy. He noted that philosophers had been seeking truth for centuries but had been unable to agree among themselves about anything, and he concluded that nothing in philosophy was beyond doubt. This realization thrust Descartes into deep depression. In 1618 he enlisted in the army, but found that the military was as ignorant of the truth as was philosophy.

In 1618 an event occurred that was a turning point in Descartes's life. Descartes was attempting to make sense out of a mathematical problem posted on a public wall, and since it was written in Flemish, he sought the help of a bystander. The person whose assistance he sought turned out to be Isaac Beeckman, an internationally known physician and mathematician. Beeckman and Descartes became close friends and spent considerable time engaged in intellectual conversations. During this time Descartes wrote his first original essay (on music), which he dedicated to Beeckman. Usually Descartes explored his many new ideas during intense meditation while lying in bed, and during one of these meditations one of his greatest insights occurred. Descartes invented analytic geometry after watching a fly in his room. He noted that he could precisely describe the fly's position at any given instance with just three numbers: the fly's perpendicular distances from two walls and from the ceiling. Generalizing from this observation, Descartes showed how geometry and algebra could be integrated, making it possible to represent astronomical phenomena such as planetary orbits with numbers. The invention of analytic geometry made mathematics much more practical than it had been.

Descartes then sought other areas of human knowledge that could be understood with the same certainty as analytic geometry. Stimulated by his success in mathematics, he summarized his four rules for attaining certainty in any area:

> The first rule was never to accept anything as true unless I recognized it to be certainly and evidently as such: that is, carefully to avoid all precipitation and prejudgment, and to include nothing in my conclusions unless it presented itself so clearly and distinctly to my mind that there was no reason or occasion to doubt.
>
> The second was to divide each of the difficulties which I encountered into as many parts as possible, and as might be required for an easier solution.
>
> The third was to think in an orderly fashion when concerned with the search for truth, beginning with the things which were simplest and easiest to understand, and gradually and by degrees reaching toward a more complex knowledge, even treating, as though ordered, materials which were not necessarily so.
>
> The last was, both in the process of searching and in reviewing when in difficulty, always to make enumerations so complete, and reviews so general, that I would be certain that nothing was omitted. (LaFleur, 1960, p. 15)

Thus began Descartes's search for philosophical truth. He resigned himself to doubt everything that could be doubted and to use whatever was certain just as one would use axioms in mathematics. That is, that which was certain could be used to deduce other certainties. After a painful search, Descartes concluded that the only thing of which he could be certain was the fact that he was doubting, but doubting was thinking and thinking necessitated a thinker. Thus, he arrived at his celebrated conclusion *Cogito, ergo sum* (I think, therefore I am). In this way, Descartes established the certainty of his own thought processes, a certainty that, for him, made the introspective search for knowledge valid.

Assuming this validity, Descartes further analyzed the content of his thought and found that some ideas were experienced with such clarity and forcefulness that they needed to be accepted as true, and yet they had no counterparts in the empirical world. Descartes thought that such ideas were innate—that is, they were natural components of the mind. Among the innate ideals, Descartes included those of unity, infinity, perfection, the axioms of geometry, and God. Since God exists and is perfect and will not deceive humans, we can trust the information provided by our senses. However, even sensory information must be clear and distinct before it can be accepted as valid. *Clear* means that the information is represented clearly in consciousness, and *distinct* means that the conscious experience cannot be doubted or divided for further analysis. Descartes gives the example of seeing a stick partially submerged in water and concluding that it is bent. Seeing the apparently bent stick provides a clear cognitive experience, but further analysis, like removing the stick from the water, would show that the experience was an illusion. Thus, Descartes concluded that rational processes were valid and that knowledge of the physical world gained through the senses could be accepted, since God would not deceive us; but even sensory information had to be analyzed rationally in order to determine its validity. Clearly, like Plato and the early Christian philosophers, Descartes was a

rationalist; and like many of those who preceded him in this tradition, he was also a
nativist. Descartes's belief in innate ideas was to
be the most severely attacked aspect of his philosophy.

Although Descartes's philosophy was anchored in rational processes, he created an entirely mechanistic conception of all animal
behavior and much of human behavior. In his
view, animals responded to the world in a way
that could be explained in terms of physical
principles. In order to understand these principles, we must recall Descartes's observation of
the statues in St. Germain.

The Reflex

Descartes took the statues at St. Germain as a
model to explain all animal behavior and much
human behavior (that is, Descartes explained
both the behavior of the statues and the behavior of animals in terms of mechanical principles). The sense receptors of the body were like
the pressure plates that started the water flowing through the tubes so that it could activate
the statues. Descartes thought of the nerves as
hollow tubes containing "delicate threads" that
connected the sense receptors to the brain.
These threads were connected to the cavities or
ventricles of the brain, which were filled with
animal spirits. (The concept of animal spirits
goes back to Galen [130–200], who said that the
presence of animal spirits distinguished the
organic from the inorganic world. Descartes described animal spirits as a gentle wind or a subtle flame.) The delicate threads were ordinarily
taut, so that when an external event stimulated
a sense organ, the threads were tightened further and opened a "pore" or "conduit" in the
corresponding brain area; the pore then released animal spirits into the nerves. When the
animal spirits flowed to the appropriate muscles, they caused the muscles to expand and
thus bring about behavior. Descartes gives as an
example a person's foot coming near a flame.

The heat causes a pull on the threads connected
to cavities of the brain containing animal spirits.
The pull opens one or more of these cavities,
allowing animal spirits to travel down small,
hollow tubes (nerves) to the foot muscles, which
in turn expand and withdraw the foot from the
flame.

By saying that both animal and human interactions with the environment were reflexive,
Descartes made it legitimate to study nonhuman animals to learn more about the functioning of the human body. He did a great deal
of dissecting and concluded from his research
that not only could interactions with the environment be explained through mechanical
principles, but so could digestion, respiration,
nourishment and growth of the body, circulation of the blood, and even sleeping and dreaming.

Descartes's explanation of sleep begins by
noting that while organisms are awake, the cavities of the brain are so filled with animal spirits
that the brain tissue engulfing a cavity expands
slightly, increasing the tautness of the delicate
threads and thus making them maximally responsive to sensory stimulation. Through the
day, the amount of animal spirits in the brain
cavities diminishes and the tissue surrounding
them becomes lax, whereupon the delicate
threads become slack. Under these conditions,
the organism is not very responsive to the environment, and we say it is asleep. There are
random flows of animal spirits in the cavities,
and every now and then isolated cavities will be
filled, their connecting threads becoming tight.
This causes the random, disconnected experiences we refer to as dreams.

The Mind-Body Interaction

As mentioned above, Descartes believed that all
animal behavior and internal processes could be
explained mechanically, as well as much of
human behavior and many internal processes.
There was, however, an important difference

between humans and other animals. Only humans possessed a mind that provided consciousness, free choice, and rationality. Furthermore, the mind was nonphysical and the body physical—that is, the body occupied space, but the mind did not. By saying that the nonphysical mind could influence the physical body, Descartes confronted the ancient mind-body problem head-on. What had been implicit in many philosophies from the time of Pythagoras was explicit in Descartes's philosophy. He clearly stated that humans possessed a body that operated according to physical principles and a mind that did not, and that the two interacted (influenced each other). The question, of course, is how this interaction occurs.

Since the mind was thought of as nonphysical, it could not be located anywhere. Descartes felt that the mind permeated the entire body. Still, Descartes sought a place where the mind exerted its influence on the body. He sought a structure in the brain because the brain stored the animal spirits. Also, the structure had to be unitary because our conscious experience, although often resulting from stimulation coming from the two eyes or two ears, is unitary. Finally, the structure had to be uniquely human, since humans alone possess a mind. Descartes chose the pineal gland because it was surrounded by animal spirits (what we now call cerebrospinal fluid), it was not duplicated like other brain structures, and (he erroneously believed) it was found only in the human brain. It was through the pineal gland that the mind willed the body to act or to inhibit action. When the mind willed something to happen, it stimulated the pineal gland, which in turn stimulated appropriate brain areas, causing animal spirits to flow to various muscles and thus bringing about the willed behavior.

Since the mind is free, it can inhibit or modify the reflexive behavior that the environment would elicit mechanically. Emotions are related to the amount of animal spirits involved in a response; the more animal spirits, the stronger the emotion. Emotions are experienced consciously as *passions* such as love, wonder, hate, desire, joy, anger, or sadness. According to Descartes, the will can and should control the passions so that virtuous conduct results. If, for example, anger is experienced and angry behavior is appropriate, the mind will allow, or even facilitate, such behavior. If, however, such behavior is seen as inappropriate, the mind will attempt to inhibit it. In the case of an intense passion, the will may be unable to prevent the reflexive behavior, and the person will act irrationally. We see in this portion of Descartes's philosophy the kind of conflict between animal needs and rationality that became so prominent in Freud's theory.

Descartes's Contributions to Psychology

Impressed by the work of the physicists, Descartes attempted a completely mechanistic explanation of many bodily functions, including behavior. He focused attention on the brain as an important mediator of behavior, and he specified the mind-body relationship with such clarity that it could be supported or refuted by others. His notion of innate ideas became a notion that other philosophers could react to. By actually investigating the bodies of animals to learn more about their functioning, he gave birth to both physiological and comparative psychology. His work on conflict did not focus on sinful versus moral behavior, but on animal versus rational behavior; he was interested in the kind of conflict Freud later studied. His mechanistic analysis of reflexive behavior can be looked upon as the beginning of both stimulus-response and behavioristic psychology. Finally, because of his use of introspection to find clear and distinct ideas, Descartes can be looked upon as an early phenomenologist. The phenomenologist studies intact, meaningful, conscious experience without dissecting it in any way.

Descartes's view of the mind-body relationship has come to be known as **psychophysical interactionism**, and it has stimulated debate right up to the present. After Descartes, some philosophers elaborated the mechanical side of his theory by saying that humans were *nothing but* machines and that the concept of mind was unnecessary. Others stressed the cognitive side of his philosophy, saying that rationality was the most important aspect of humans. In any case, what followed Descartes was, in one way or another, a reaction to him; and for that reason, he is often considered the father of modern philosophy in general and of modern psychology in particular.

The church banned Descartes's books because it felt they led to atheism. As a result, Descartes slowed down his writing and instead communicated personally with small groups or individuals who sought his knowledge. One such individual was Queen Christina of Sweden, who invited Descartes to be her philosopher-in-residence, and he accepted. Unfortunately, the queen insisted on being tutored at five o'clock each morning, and one day Descartes had to travel to the palace before sunrise during a severe Swedish winter. After only six months in Sweden, Descartes caught pneumonia and died on February 11, 1650, at the early age of 53.

ISAAC NEWTON

Isaac Newton (1642–1727) was born the year that Galileo died. Like Galileo, Newton conceived of the universe as a complex, lawful machine created by God. Guided by these conceptions, he developed differential and integral calculus (Leibniz made the same discovery independently), developed the universal theory of gravity, and did pioneer work in optics. Newton created a conception of the universe that was to prevail in physics and astronomy for more than two centuries, until Einstein revised it. His methods of verification included observa-

tion, mathematical deduction, and experimentation. In Newton, who was deeply religious, we have a complete reversal of the earlier faith-oriented way of knowing God: since God made the universe, studying it objectively was a way of understanding God.

Although Newton believed in God as the creator of the universe, Newton's work pushed God farther into the background. God created the universe and set it in motion, but that exhausted his functions; and after Newton, it was but a short step to removing God altogether. Likewise, it was only a matter of time before humans, too, would be viewed and analyzed as just another machine that operated in accordance with Newtonian principles.

Perhaps Newton's most significant contribution was his universal Law of Gravitation. According to this law, *all* objects in the universe attract each other. The amount of attraction is directly proportional to the product of the masses of the bodies and inversely proportional to the square of the distance between the bodies. This single law was able to explain the motion of all physical bodies everywhere in the universe. To Newton, the universe was a machine that God had created; it operated according to principles that humans could discover, and Newton found that these principles could be expressed precisely in mathematical terms—thus his conclusion that "God was a mathematician." Newton did a great deal to revive the kind of materialism Democritus had originally suggested.

MacLeod (1975, pp. 105–108) lists the principles of Newtonian science:

1. Although God is the creator of the world, he does not actively intervene in the events of the world. It is therefore inappropriate to invoke his will as an explanation of any particular thing or event in the material world.

2. The material world is governed by natural laws, and there are no exceptions to these laws.

3. There is no place for purpose in natural law, and therefore Aristotle's final causes must be rejected.

4. Whatever happens does so because of natural laws.

5. Occam's razor is to be accepted. Explanations must always be as simple as possible. In Book III of his *Principia*, Newton gives this advice: "We are to admit no more causes of natural things than such as are both true and sufficient to explain their appearances."

6. Natural laws are absolute, but at any given time our understanding is imperfect. Therefore, scientists often need to settle for probabilities rather than certainty. This is because of human ignorance, not because of any flexibility in natural laws.

7. Natural events can never be explained by postulating properties inherent in them. Bodies fall, for example, not because of an inherent tendency to fall, as Aristotle had assumed, but because of various forces acting upon them.

8. Classification is not explanation. To note that chasing cats seems to be a characteristic of dogs does not explain *why* dogs tend to chase cats.

The astronomers' successes with mathematical deduction and empirical observation stimulated scholars in all fields and launched a spirit of curiosity and experimentation that has lasted until this day. Likewise, the success that resulted from viewing the universe as a machine was to have profound implications for psychology. Science had become a proven way of unlocking nature's secrets, and it was embraced with intense enthusiasm. In many ways, science was becoming the new religion. MacLeod (1975) says:

For centuries the Church had been impressing on man the limitations of his own wisdom. The mind of God is unfathomable. God works in a mysterious way his wonders to perform. Man

Isaac Newton

must be content with partial understanding; the rest he must simply believe. For a Galileo or a Newton such a restriction of human curiosity was unacceptable. The scientist was willing to concede that some things may be ultimately unintelligible except on the basis of faith; but as he stubbornly continued to observe, measure and experiment, he discovered that more and more of the puzzles of nature were becoming clear. He was actually explaining in natural terms phenomena that had hitherto been unintelligible. Small wonder, then, that the new science began to generate a faith that ultimately science would displace theology. There is little evidence that in the sixteenth and seventeenth centuries such a faith was more than a dim hope. Nevertheless the seeds had been sown; scientists were uncovering more and more of the secrets of nature; and more and more explanations were now being given "without benefit of clergy." (p. 105)

The philosophers and scientists of the sixteenth and seventeenth centuries that we have reviewed in this chapter were transitional figures. In their lives we see a mixture of religious subjectivity and the need to be completely objective. These thinkers were not anti-religion; they were anti-dogma. Most of them felt that their work was revealing God's secrets. What made them different from those who had preceded them was their refusal to allow past beliefs or methods to influence their inquiries; and in fact, their investigations were motivated by apparent errors in previously accepted dogma. The eighteenth century is generally referred to as the Age of Enlightenment because explanations became completely free of theological considerations. During this time the older philosophies of empiricism and rationalism reached new heights; however, the romantic movement developed as a reaction against those philosophies that viewed the human intellect as a product of experience (empiricism) or as completely rational (rationalism). The romantics focused mainly on the emotional makeup of humans. In the next three chapters, we will review the developments in empiricism, rationalism, and romanticism.

SUMMARY

Renaissance humanism had four major themes: a belief in the potential of the individual, an insistence that religion be more personal and less institutionalized, an intense interest in the classics, and a negative attitude toward Aristotle's philosophy. The humanists did much to break the authority of the organized church and of Aristotle's philosophy; this had to happen before a scientific attitude could be developed. Although the Renaissance was a troubled time, it was a time of great curiosity and creativity. As the power of the church deteriorated, inquiry became increasingly objective, since findings no longer needed to fit church dogma. Copernicus demonstrated that the earth was not the center of the solar system, while Kepler found that the paths of the planets were not circular but elliptical. Galileo found, among other things, that all material bodies fell at the same rate; and using a telescope, he discovered four of Jupiter's moons. Galileo concluded that the universe was lawful and that the results of experiments could be summarized mathematically. He also concluded that a science of psychology was impossible because of the subjective nature of human thought processes.

Francis Bacon wanted science to be completely untainted by past mistakes, and therefore urged that scientific investigations be inductive and devoid of theories, hypotheses, and mathematical formulations. Bacon also wanted science to be aimed at the solution of human problems. He described four sources of error that can creep into scientific investigation: the idol of the cave, or biases resulting from personal experience; the idol of the tribe, or cultural prejudice; the idol of the marketplace, or biases due to the traditional meanings of words; and the idol of the theater, or blind acceptance of authority or tradition.

Like Bacon, Descartes wanted a method of inquiry that would yield knowledge about which one could be certain. Descartes doubted everything except for the fact that he doubted, and thus concluded that introspection was a valid method for seeking truth. Descartes also decided that sensory information could be trusted because God had created our sensory apparatus and would not deceive us. Taking his inspiration from mechanical statues that he had observed, Descartes concluded that all animal behavior and much human behavior was mechanical. He likened sense receptors to pressure plates that, when stimulated, pulled on tiny strings in the nerves. When pulled, the strings opened pores in the brain that allowed animal spirits to move back down the nerves into the muscles, causing them to expand. The expanding muscles, in turn, caused behavior. Descartes saw the mind and body as interacting; that is, the body can influence the mind, and the mind can influence the body. Such a view is called psychophysical interactionism. Descartes also believed that the mind contained several innate ideas, and that emotional behavior, experienced consciously as a passion, was determined by the amount of animal spirits involved in the behavior. Descartes brought much attention to the mind-body relationship, caused great controversy over innate ideas, stimulated animal research (and thus physiological and comparative psychology), and was the first to describe the reflex, a concept that was to become extremely important in psychology.

Newton viewed the universe as a complex, lawful, knowable machine that had been created and set in motion by God. Like Bacon, he wanted a science that was completely objective,

but that is where the similarity between the two men's views of science ends. Unlike Bacon's, Newton's science was highly theoretical and mathematical. Furthermore, Newton was much less concerned with relevance than Bacon was. Newton's success in explaining much of the physical universe in terms of a few basic laws had a profound influence on science, philosophy, and eventually psychology. In fact, Newtonian science was so successful that people began to believe science had the potential to answer all questions. In a sense, science was becoming the new religion.

DISCUSSION QUESTIONS

1. Describe the four themes that characterized Renaissance humanism, and give an example of each.

2. Why is the Renaissance referred to as a paradoxical period?

3. Describe the individuals and events that challenged and weakened church authority.

4. Summarize Francis Bacon's view of science

5. Describe the idols of the cave, marketplace, theater, and tribe.

6. Summarize Descartes's view of the mind-body relationship.

7. What was it that Descartes thought he could be certain of? Once this certainty was arrived at, how did Descartes use it in further developing his philosophy?

8. What were Descartes's contributions to psychology?

9. In general, what attitude toward religion did the individuals covered in this chapter have?

10. What was Newton's conception of science? Briefly compare and contrast Newton's conception of science with Bacon's.

11. Discuss Newton's influence on science, philosophy, and psychology.

GLOSSARY

Animal spirits The substance Descartes thought was located in the cavities of the brain. When this substance moved, via the nerves, from the brain to the muscles, the muscles swelled and behavior was instigated.

Bacon, Francis (1561–1629) Urged an inductive, practical science that was free from the misconceptions of the past and from any theoretical considerations.

Bruno, Giordano (1548–1600) Suggested that many solar systems may contain life. For his belief he was burnt at the stake.

Copernicus, Nicolaus (1473–1543) Demonstrated that the earth rotated around the sun, and therefore that the earth was not the center of the solar system, as the church had maintained.

Deduction The method of reasoning by which conclusions must follow from certain assumptions, principles, or facts. If there are five people in a room, for example, one can deduce that there are also four; or, if it is assumed that everything in nature is there for a purpose, then one can conclude that humans, too, are on earth for a purpose. Deductive reasoning proceeds from the general to the particular.

Descartes, René (1596–1650) Believed that much human behavior can be explained in mechanical terms, that the mind and the body interact, and that the mind contains innate ideas. With Descartes began comparative-physiological psychology, stimulus-response psychology, phenomenology, and a debate over whether or not innate ideas exist. Descartes also focused attention on the nature of the relationship between the mind and the body.

Erasmus, Desiderius (1466–1536) A Renaissance humanist who opposed fanaticism, religious ritual, and superstition.

Ficino, Marsilio (1433–1499) Founded a Platonic Academy in 1462 and sought to do for Plato's philosophy what the Scholastics had done for Aristotle's.

Galilei, Galileo (1564–1642) Showed several of Aristotle's "truths" to be false and, by using a telescope, extended the known number of bodies in the solar system to 11. Galileo argued that science could deal only with objective reality, and that since human perceptions were subjective, they were outside the realm of science.

Humanism A point of view that existed during the Renaissance. It emphasized four themes: individualism, a personal relationship with God, interest in classical wisdom, and a negative attitude toward Aristotle's philosophy.

Idol of the cave Bacon's term for personal biases that result from one's experiences.

Idol of the marketplace Bacon's term for error that results when one accepts the traditional meanings of the words used to describe things.

Idol of the theater According to Bacon, the inhibition of objective inquiry that results

when one accepts dogma, tradition, or authority.

Idol of the tribe Bacon's term for biases that result from cultural beliefs.

Induction The method of reasoning that moves from the particular to the general. After a large number of individual instances are observed, a theme or principle common to all of them might be inferred. Deductive reasoning starts with some assumption, whereas inductive reasoning does not.

Kepler, Johannes (1571–1630) By observation and mathematical deduction determined the elliptical paths of the planets around the sun. Kepler also did pioneer work in optics.

Luther, Martin (1483–1546) Was especially disturbed by corruption within the church and by the church's emphasis on ritual. He believed that a major reason for the church's downfall was its embracing of Aristotle's philosophy, and he urged a return to the personal religion that St. Augustine had described. His attack of the established church contributed to the Reformation, which divided Europe into two warring camps.

Newton, Isaac (1642–1727) Co-invented differential and integral calculus and discovered the lawfulness of the universe. Newton saw the universe as a complex machine that God had created and set in motion.

Petrarch, Francesco (1304–1374) A Renaissance humanist referred to by many historians as the Father of the Renaissance. He attacked Scholasticism as stifling the human spirit and urged that the classics be studied not for their religious implications but because they were the works of unique human beings. He insisted that God had given humans their vast potential so that it could be utilized. Petrarch's views about human potential helped stimulate the many artistic and literary achievements that characterized the Renaissance.

Pico, Giovanni (1463–1494) Maintained that humans, unlike angels and animals, were capable of changing themselves and the world. He felt that all philosophical positions should be respected, and the common elements among them sought.

Psychophysical interactionism The contention that the mind and the body influence each other.

Reformation The attempt of Luther and others to reform the Christian church by making it more Augustinian in character. The failure of this effort resulted in the division of western European Christianity into Protestantism and Roman Catholicism.

Renaissance The period from about 1450 to about 1600 when there was a rebirth of the open, objective inquiry that had characterized the early Greek philosophers.

CHAPTER 5

Empiricism, Materialism, and Positivism

Descartes was so influential that most of the philosophies that developed after him were reactions to some aspect of his philosophy. The major reactions to Descartes's philosophy were concentrated in several regions of Europe. The British philosophers denied Descartes's contention that some ideas are innate, saying instead that all ideas are derived from experience. These British empiricists attempted to explain the functioning of the mind as Newton had explained the functioning of the universe. That is, they sought a few principles or laws that could account for all human cognitive experience.

The French philosophers accepted Descartes's contention that all animal behavior and much human behavior could be explained in terms of mechanistic principles, and they went further, saying that *all* human activity could be explained by such principles. According to Descartes, what distinguishes humans from other animals is the fact that, among other things, humans possess a mind equipped with innate ideas and a free will. The French materialists denied the existence of such a mind and said that humans and other animals differed only in degree of complexity.

The German philosophers, instead of denying the existence of a mind, made an active mind central to their conception of human nature. In general, they postulated a mind that acted upon sensory information and that thereby gave this information meaning it otherwise would not have. For the German rationalists, knowing the operations of this active mind was vital in determining how humans confronted and understood their world.

Scattered throughout Europe, the romantic philosophers rebelled against the views of the empiricists, materialists, and rationalists. All these philosophies concentrated on one aspect of humans and neglected others. The romantics urged a focus on the total human, a focus that included two things the other viewpoints either minimized or neglected: human feelings and the uniqueness of each individual.

After Descartes, and to a large extent because of him, the ancient philosophies of empiricism, materialism, rationalism, and romanticism were presented more clearly and in greater detail than they had ever been before. It was from the modern manifestations of these philosophies that psychology as we know it today emerged. In this chapter we will review British empiricism and French materialism. In Chapter 6 we will review German rationalism and in Chapter 7 romanticism.

BRITISH EMPIRICISM

Unfortunately, the term **empiricist** has meant many things through the years. Some say that any philosopher who claims sensory information is important in attaining knowledge can be called an empiricist. Using such a definition, even Descartes could be called an empiricist, since for him many ideas came from experience. In psychology, empiricism is often contrasted with mentalism; but this is a mistake since, as we shall see, the early empiricists were very mentalistic. In fact, their main research tool was introspection, and their main goal was to explain subjective experience. In this text we will use the definition of empiricism that Robinson (1976) offers:

> Empiricism . . . is the epistemology that asserts that the evidence of sense constitutes the primary data of all knowledge; that knowledge cannot exist unless this evidence has first been gathered; and that all subsequent intellectual processes must use this evidence and only this evidence in forming valid propositions about the real world. (p. 198)

Thus, although other epistemological approaches may utilize sensory experience as part of their explanation of the origins of knowledge, for the empiricist, sensory experience is of supreme importance.

Thomas Hobbes

Although he follows in the tradition of William of Occam and Francis Bacon, **Thomas Hobbes** (1588–1679) is often referred to as the founder of British empiricism. Hobbes was educated at Oxford and was friends with both Galileo and Descartes. He also served as Francis Bacon's secretary for a short time. Hobbes felt strongly that the church should be subordinate to the government, a radical idea at the time.

Hobbes believed not only that the behavior of individual humans could be explained in terms of laws like those discovered by Kepler and Galileo, but that there could also be a science of society. Once human nature was understood, that knowledge could be used to design a society in which war was minimized or eliminated and personal happiness maximized. The first step in developing a science of society was to stop using vague and subjective terminology and to stop looking for abstract universal principles. Rather, we should look upon a human as a body in motion and upon society as humans in motion. According to Hobbes, there are two kinds of motion (behavior): involuntary and in-

tentional. Intentional behavior is aimed at satisfying the needs of the body. Some needs are innate, such as those that must be met for survival. Most needs, however, are learned from experience. What facilitates the satisfaction of our needs is considered good, and what prevents the satisfaction of our needs is bad. Thus, what is considered good or bad will vary from person to person if their needs are different. Hobbes denied free will, saying that what appears to be choice is nothing more than a verbal label we use to describe the attractions and aversions we experience while interacting with the environment.

According to Hobbes, government is important because without it humans would be in a constant state of war with each other in their attempts to satisfy their needs. In other words, unless interfered with, humans would selfishly seek power over others so as to guarantee the satisfaction of their own personal needs. The function of society, according to Hobbes, is to satisfy as many needs as possible and also to prevent people from fighting with each other. Human behavior is determined by reward and punishment, and acts that appear benevolent or altruistic are in fact selfish. The nineteenth-century **utilitarians** (for example, Jeremy Bentham) greatly respected Hobbes's philosophy, saying that the best society was the one that provided the greatest good for the greatest number of individuals.

Hobbes believed that anything that existed must be physical and therefore could be explained in terms of the laws of physics. Unlike the mind Descartes postulated, the mind Hobbes postulated was physical and therefore subject to the laws of nature. Hobbes rejected a mind-body interaction and instead assumed a **materialistic monism**. Thus, the movement of the atoms in the brain caused cognitive experience. The content of the mind came from sensory experience alone; that is, there were no innate ideas. Like other empiricists, Hobbes assumed that complex cognitive experience was derived from simple cognitive experience, and that simple cognitive experience resulted from sensory experience.

Most of the empiricists use the concept of association as the glue that holds mental experience together. Why, they ask, should ideas be experienced or remembered in a meaningful order? Hobbes acknowledged contiguity and frequency as two laws of association. The laws of association, of course, go back at least as far as Aristotle; and most, if not all, of the empiricists use one or more of them to explain how the memories of various experiences are held together in some lawful way. The effort to explain mental phenomena such as learning, memory, and perception in terms of associative principles is called **associationism**, which is closely related to empiricism. By assuming that both the mind and the body were physical, Hobbes was taking the materialistic position that later dominated French philosophy. We can see the major elements of both British empiricism and French materialism in Hobbes's work, as well as the materialistic **hedonism** seen in behaviorism centuries later.

John Locke

THE BETTMANN ARCHIVE, INC.

John Locke

Like Hobbes, **John Locke** (1631–1704) was educated at Oxford, where he studied medicine, the classics, and Descartes. In time, Locke was to become the most influential political philosopher in Europe. He contended that since abilities came from experience and were not inherited, each individual should be given equal opportunity in a society. Furthermore, the only power that a government should have was that given to it by the people. These were radical views in a Europe governed by inherited monarchies. Locke vigorously opposed Descartes's notion of innate ideas, saying that if the mind contained innate ideas, then all humans should have those ideas, and clearly they do not. Where, then, do all the ideas that humans have come from? Locke answered the question as follows in his famous book *An Essay Concerning Human Understanding* (1690):

Let us then suppose the mind to be, as we say, white paper void of all characters, without any ideas. How comes it to be furnished? Whence comes it by that vast store which the busy and boundless fancy of man has painted on it with an almost endless variety? Whence has it all the materials of reason and knowledge? To this I answer, in one word, from *experience*; in that all our knowledge is founded, and from that it ultimately derives itself. Our observation, employed either about external sensible objects, or about the internal operations of our minds perceived and reflected on by ourselves, is that which supplies our understandings with all the materials of thinking. These two are the fountains of knowledge, from whence all the ideas we have, or can naturally have, do spring. (Fraser, 1959, p. 104)

Sensation and reflection. For Locke, there were two kinds of cognitive experience: ideas that were caused by sensory stimulation and ideas caused by reflection of the remnants of prior sensory experience. Furthermore, ideas could be simple or complex. A simple idea, like an atom, could not be divided or analyzed further. Complex ideas were composites of simple ideas, and therefore could be analyzed to search for their component parts (simple ideas). It is often overlooked that Locke's philosophy, although basically empirical, was very nativistic. Ideas were derived from experience, but the ability to think about ideas and to perceive and remember them were powers of the mind *not* derived from experience—that is, they were innate. This is exemplified in Locke's concept of reflection. Reflection, the second fountain of knowledge referred to in the above quotation, is the mind's ability to reflect upon itself. About reflection, Locke (1690) says:

> This source of *ideas*, every man has wholly in himself: and though it be not sense, as having nothing to do with external objects; yet it is very like it, and might properly enough be called internal sense. But as I call the other *sensation*, so I call this *reflection*, the ideas it affords being such only, as the mind gets by reflecting on its own operations within itself . . . the term operations here I use in a large sense, as comprehending not barely the actions of the mind about its ideas, but some sort of passions arising sometimes from them, such as is the satisfaction or uneasiness arising from any thought. (Fraser, 1959, p. 105)

For Locke, then, the information that the senses provided was the stuff the mind thought about and had emotional responses toward. This is the empirical component in Locke's philosophy. The ability of the mind to analyze, reflect upon, and feel emotion toward such information, however, was not derived from sensory experience. Such faculties of the mind were innate. Thus Locke's philosophy, although labelled empirical, is strongly nativistic. Locke opposed the notion of specific innate *ideas* but not innate faculties of the mind.

The association of ideas. With his concept of association, Locke again demonstrates that his philosophy is both empirical and nativistic. He

says that some ideas are associated because they naturally belong together, such as when the odor of baking bread causes one to have the idea of bread. These are the safest and surest kinds of associations because they are determined by a natural relationship. Other associations are learned by chance, custom, or mistake. The prejudices that parents teach their children exemplify learned associations (for example, all red dogs are violent). These learned associations lead to errors in understanding, whereas natural associations cannot. Here is how Locke (1690) distinguishes between natural and learned associations:

> Some of our *ideas* have a natural correspondence and connexion one with another: it is the office and excellency of our reason to trace these, and hold them together in that union and correspondence which is founded in their peculiar beings. Besides this there is another connexion of *ideas* wholly owing to chance or custom; *ideas* that in themselves are not at all kin, come to be so united in some men's minds, that 'tis very hard to separate them, they always keep in company, and the one no sooner at any time comes into the understanding but its associate appears with it; and if they are more than two which are thus united, the whole gang, always inseparable, show themselves together. (p. 395)

Primary and secondary qualities. The distinction between primary and secondary qualities is the distinction that several early Greeks, and later Galileo, made between what is physically present and what is experienced psychologically. The **primary qualities** of an object are its physical characteristics, such as solidity, mobility, shape, and weight. The **secondary qualities**, such as taste, smell, color, and sound, are produced in the perceiver of the object. Although Locke did not elaborate on it much, the distinction between primary and secondary qualities was very important to subsequent philosophers and remains an important issue in modern psychology.

With his "paradox of the basins," Locke dramatically demonstrated the existence of secondary qualities. One might ask, Is temperature a characteristic of the physical world? In other words, is it not safe to assume that objects in the physical world are hot or cold or somewhere in between? Looked at in this way, temperature would be a primary property. Locke beckons his readers to take three water basins: one containing water with a temperature of 40° C (Basin A), one containing water of 80° C (Basin B), and the other containing water of 60° C (Basin C). If a person places one hand in Basin A and the other in Basin B, one hand will feel hot and the other cold, supporting the contention that hot and cold are properties of the water (that is, that temperature is a primary property). Next, Locke instructs the reader to place both hands in Basin C, which contains the water at 60° C. To the hand that was previously in Basin A, the water in Basin C will feel warm, and to the hand that was previously in Basin B, the water will feel cold, even though the temperature of the water in Basin C is physically the same for both hands. Thus, Locke forcefully demonstrates that the experiencing of heat and cold is subjective, and that temperature is therefore a secondary property. Again, determining the relationship between what is physically present and what is perceived is one of psychology's oldest and most persistent problems.

Government by the people and for the people. Locke attacked not only the notion of innate ideas, but also the notion of innate moral principles. He believed that much dogma was built on the assumption of one innate moral truth or another, and that people should seek the truth for themselves, rather than having it imposed on them. For this and other reasons, empiricism was considered to be a radical movement that sought to replace religion based on revelation with natural law. Very influential politically, Locke challenged the divine right of kings and proposed a government by and for the people. His political philosophy, like that of

George Berkeley

Hobbes, was accepted enthusiastically by the nineteenth-century utilitarians; and it was very influential in the drafting of America's Declaration of Independence.

George Berkeley

Born in Ireland and educated at Trinity College in Dublin, **George Berkeley** (1685–1753) became an ordained minister at the age of 24 and had made significant contributions to both philosophy and psychology by the time he was 28. He traveled extensively throughout Europe and America, and although he never made it west of New England in his quest to convert the "savages" to Christianity, the city of Berkeley, California, and the University of California campus there bear his name.

Secondary qualities. Whereas Locke assumed a relationship between primary qualities (the physical world) and secondary qualities (perception), Berkeley could make no such assumption. For him, the only reality of which we could be aware was our perceptions. If there was a physical world, we could never experience it directly.

Berkeley's motto was *Esse est percipi,* or "To be is to be perceived." Berkeley did believe in the existence of a physical world even though we could never experience it. He took the physical world on faith because he believed in a benevolent God who would not deceive us (much as Descartes had believed). According to Berkeley, God perceives the world and thereby gives its existence, and the fact that our ideas correspond to the physical world is the result of God's benevolence. It is God's perception of the world that saves Berkeley's position from **solipsism**, the belief that the only reality is one's own subjective awareness. Berkeley's philosophy is not far from the modern phenomenological position, according to which a person's subjective interpretation of reality is more important in determining behavior than is physical reality.

Berkeley posed some problems that remain unsolved. For example, if it is true that we do not confront the physical world directly but only through our sense receptors, neural pathways, and brain mechanisms, it is still unclear exactly how these mechanisms influence our conception of physical reality. Many philosophers and psychologists have argued, for example, that the brain transforms sensory data, and in so doing creates mental events not found in the sensory data itself. Kant, the Gestalt psychologists, and Piaget all say that the mind, in a sense, projects a structure on the world that is not really characteristic of physical reality. If this is true, what we experience subjectively does not conform to physical reality. We will have more to say about this when we talk about Immanual Kant in the next chapter, and again in Chapter 14 when we discuss Gestalt psychology.

Theory of visual perception. In his book *An Essay towards a New Theory of Vision* (1709), Berkeley proposed one of the first theories of visual perception based on empiricism. He criticized Descartes's "natural geometry" explanation of distance, according to which the experience of distance was determined by the visual angle that an object subtended on the retina. Berkeley's explanation was based on the association of physical cues with visual experience. For example, the sensations caused by the convergence and divergence of the eyes as objects move closer or farther from a person are associated with the size of an object. A distant object will become associated with certain kinesthetic sensations and will eventually be seen as far away. Thus, it is not the geometric angle an object projects on the retina that determines the object's perceived distance; rather, the association of various bodily sensations with visual experiences articulates one's visual experiences in terms of size, distance, and depth.

Berkeley also distinguished between perception and imagination. Perceptions are vivid ideas, and imagination involves less vivid ideas. This, of course, is not the distinction between primary and secondary qualities, since for Berkeley the mind could know only what Locke had called secondary qualities.

Idealistic monism. As we have already noted, any philosophical position claiming that all of reality is composed of one thing is called a *monism.* With Hobbes, we had a materialistic monism, since he believed everything, even the mind, to consist of matter. With Berkeley, we have an *idealistic monism,* since he felt that the only reality was perception or ideas. Philosophies like Locke's and Descartes's are dualistic because they speak of two realities, one mental and one physical.

David Hume

Born in Edinburgh, Scotland, **David Hume** (1711–1776) was educated at the University of Edinburgh. Although reared in the Calvinistic tradition of Scottish Presbyterianism, he became an outspoken atheistic political theorist. Hume created a philosophy much like Berkeley's, only without God. In other words, Hume agreed with Berkeley that we could know only our subjective experience; but unlike Berkeley, he did not believe that we could be sure our thoughts corresponded to a physical world. Hume could not accept Berkeley's claim that God ensured an accurate relationship between our ideas and the physical world. Therefore, for Hume, there was no reason to believe that our subjective experiences were necessarily valid reflections of the physical world. Unlike Berkeley, Hume was a solipsist, since he believed that the only reality we could ever know was our own subjective experience.

According to Hume, our experience is divided into *impressions*, which are strong and vivid, and *ideas*, which are faint copies of impressions. Both impressions and ideas may be simple or complex. Impressions are usually complex because we seldom experience anything through just one sense modality, while complex ideas occur because of the clustering that results from *association*. Hume said that similar ideas clustered together in memory; this is the **Law of Resemblance** (sometimes called the Law of Similarity). He also said that things experienced together in space or time were mentally clustered together; this is the **Law of Contiguity**. All conclusions we make about the physical world are based on our subjective experience, since there is no way for us to experience the physical world directly. Thus, these conclusions may or may not be true. Hume said that even the notion of cause and effect was nothing more than a habit of thought. For example, if we repeatedly see event B follow event A, we are tempted to say that A causes B, but the apparent cause-and-effect relationship is in our mind and not necessarily in the physical world. We do, however, have an innate tendency to generalize from our experience. Knowledge comes from impressions, ideas, associations, and generalizations, not from reasoning.

Hume trusted impressions more than ideas, since he felt that through imagination, ideas could be combined in ways that had no corre-

David Hume

spondence with the real world. For example, it is possible to imagine a unicorn by combining a number of simple ideas, but just because we can imagine a unicorn does not mean that unicorns exist. The safest way to truth, according to Hume, is to analyze either the impressions or the ideas that are closely linked to impressions. Other ideas can lead to conclusions that are too far removed from reality. The belief that truth is to be found by sticking close to the empirical facts was later to be called positivism, and we shall review this approach to philosophy later in this chapter.

David Hartley

Educated at the University of Cambridge, **David Hartley** (1705-1757) was originally trained for the clergy, but his interest in biology caused him to seek a career as a physician. In his book *Observations of Man, His Frame, His Duty and His Expectations* (1749), Hartley attempted to establish a physiological basis for associations. He borrowed from Newton the idea that stimuli in the physical world are vibratory in nature. According to Hartley, stimuli from the environment set up vibrations in the nerves (which he believed were solid and not hollow, as Descartes had believed), and the nerves set up vibrations in the brain. The vibrations in the brain are experienced as the idea (mental representation) of the physical object that caused the vibrations to begin with. Unlike Hobbes, Hartley was not a monist; he was dualist because he distinguished between the mental (ideas) and the physical (vibrations). His brand of dualism is called **epiphenomenalism** because he believed that physical events (vibrations in the nerves and brain) cause mental events (ideas), but that mental events do not influence the body. Epiphenomenalism is depicted in Figure 1.1 (see p. 17).

Hartley believed further that vibrations continued in the brain after the external stimulations that caused them had ceased. He called these lingering vibrations **vibratiuncles** and he proposed two laws of association—contiguity and frequency. According to these laws, physical events experienced together become associated in memory, and the more often they are experienced together, the stronger the association. Furthermore, if a group of physical events is typically experienced at the same time, or in close succession, the entire group is clustered together in memory; and if any member of the group is again experienced, there is a tendency to remember the entire group. Hartley (1749) puts this idea as follows:

> Any sensation A, B, C, etc. by being associated with one another a sufficient number of times, gets such a power over the corresponding ideas a, b, c, etc. that one of the sensations A, when impressed alone, shall be able to excite in the mind b, c, etc. the ideas of the rest. (I, prop. 10)

Hartley's notion that experiences consistently occurring together are recorded in the brain as an interrelated package, and that one element in the package will make one conscious of the entire package, is amazingly modern. For example, contrast the above quotation from Hartley with the following statement Donald Hebb made in 1972:

> Cell-assemblies that are active at the same time become interconnected. Common events in the child's environment establish assemblies, and then when these events occur together the assemblies become connected (because they are active together). When the baby hears footsteps, let us say, an assembly is excited; while this is still active he sees a face and feels hands picking him up, which excites other assemblies—so that "footsteps assembly" becomes connected with the "face assembly" and the "being-picked-up assembly." After this has happened, when the baby hears footsteps only, all three assemblies are excited; the baby then has something like a perception of a mother's face and the contact of her hands before she has come in sight—but since the sensory stimulations have not yet taken place, this is ideation or imagery, not perception. (p. 67)

James Mill

James Mill (1773–1836) was a Scotsman educated at the University of Edinburgh. His book *Analysis of the Phenomena of the Human Mind* (1829) is regarded as the most complete summary of associationism ever offered. In this book, Mill attempted to show that the mind consisted of only sensations and ideas held together by contiguity. He maintained that any mental experience could be reduced to the simple ideas that made it up. Thus, James Mill gave us a conception of the mind based on Newtonian physics. For Newton, the universe could be understood as consisting of material elements held together by physical forces and behaving in a predictable manner. For Mill, the mind consisted of mental elements held together by the laws of association, and therefore mental experience was as predictable as were physical events.

For Mill, the elements of thought were sensations and their copies, ideas. Just as physical elements could combine to form complex objects and substances, mental elements could combine to form complex mental experiences. However, no matter how complex a mental experience was, it was always possible to reduce the experience to the simple elements that made it up. Mill (1829) makes this point as follows:

> Brick is one complex idea, mortar is another complex idea; these ideas, with the ideas of position and quantity, compose my idea of a wall. My idea of a plank is a complex idea, my idea of a rafter is a complex idea, my idea of a nail is a complex idea.
>
> These, united with the same ideas of position and quantity, compose my duplex idea of a floor. In the same manner my complex ideas of glass, wood, and others, compose my duplex idea of a window; and these duplex ideas, united together, compose my idea of a house, which is made up of various duplex ideas. How many complex, or duplex ideas, are all united in the idea of furniture? How many more in the idea of merchandise? How many more in the idea called Every Thing? (Rand, 1912, p. 482)

In this quotation, things like bricks, planks, and nails are referred to as complex ideas because they are made up of simple ideas such as color, shape, and texture.

John Stuart Mill

James Mill supervised the early education of his son, **John Stuart Mill** (1806–1873). James Mill's attempt at using associative principles in raising his son must have been at least partially successful, since John Stuart had learned Greek by the time he was three, Latin and algebra by eight, and logic by twelve.

John Stuart Mill felt that his father's analysis of the associative process was extreme, and instead of accepting the notion that complex ideas were aggregates of simple ideas, he proposed a kind of **mental chemistry**. He was impressed by the fact that often chemicals would combine and produce something entirely different from

John Stuart Mill

THE BETTMANN ARCHIVE, INC.

the elements that made them up, such as when hydrogen and oxygen combine to produce water. Also, Newton had shown that when all the colors of the spectrum were combined, white light was produced. John Stuart Mill believed that the same kind of thing happened in the mind. That is, it was possible for elementary ideas to fuse and to produce an idea that was different from the elements that made it up. J. S. Mill (1843) describes mental chemistry as follows:

> The laws of the phenomena of the mind are sometimes analogous to mechanical, but sometimes also to chemical laws. When many impressions or ideas are operating in the mind together, there sometimes takes place a process of a similar kind to chemical combination. When impressions have been so often experienced in conjunction, that each of them calls up readily and instantaneously the ideas of the

whole group, those ideas sometimes melt and coalesce into one another, and appear not as several ideas but one, in the same manner as when the seven prismatic colors are presented to the eye in rapid succession, the sensation produced is that of white. But in this last case it is correct to say that the seven colors when they rapidly follow one another *generate* white; so it appears to me that the Complex Idea, formed by the blending together of several simpler ones, should, when it really appears simple, (that is, when the separate elements are not consciously distinguishable in it) be said to *result from*, or be *generated by*, the simple ideas, not to *consist* of them . . . these are cases of mental chemistry: in which it is possible to say that the simple ideas generate, rather than that they compose, the complex ones. (p. 558)

J. S. Mill's belief that some cognitive experiences we have are different from the elements that make them up reappears in Gestalt psychology, which we will cover in Chapter 14.

Alexander Bain

Born in Aberdeen, Scotland, **Alexander Bain** (1818–1903) lived most of his life there. Although he was the son of a weaver, Bain became a prominent professor of psychology at the University of Aberdeen and is credited with writing the first systematic textbooks of psychology in English (*The Senses and the Intellect*, 1855, and *The Emotions and The Will*, 1859). Bain's books were to remain standard texts in psychology for nearly 50 years. In addition to writing the first textbooks in psychology in English, Bain was the first to write a book on the relationship between the mind and the body (*Mind and Body*, 1872); and in 1876 he founded *Mind*, which is generally considered the first journal devoted exclusively to psychological issues. Bain also wrote a biography of James Mill and had a lifelong friendship with John Stuart Mill.

In preparation for writing *The Senses and The Intellect* (1855), Bain made it a point to digest the most current information on neurology, anatomy, and physiology. He then attempted to show how these biological processes were related to psychological processes. His text was modern in the sense that it started with a chapter on neurology, a practice most introductory psychology textbooks have followed ever since. After Bain, the major effort in psychology was to explore the relationships among physiological and psychological processes, an effort that continues to this day. Bain was the first to attempt to relate real physiological processes to psychological phenomena. Hartley had earlier attempted to do this, but his physiological principles were imaginary.

On the mind-body issue, Bain accepted the position of *psychophysical parallelism*, the contention that every experience causes both a physical (biological) and a mental reaction but that the two do not interact. Since each human experience causes both physical and psychological reactions, the psychologist must be aware of the principles of biology as well as the principles of consciousness. This, too, has a very modern ring. There is currently a debate as to whether Bain was the last of the older empirical-associationistic psychologists or the first of the new physiologically oriented psychologists. In either case, his place in the history of psychology is secure.

For Bain, the mind had three components: feeling, volition, and intellect. The intellect was explained by the laws of association. Bain accepted the older associative laws of contiguity (things experienced together are remembered together) and frequency (the more often things are experienced together, the stronger the tendency to remember them together). Bain added the **law of compound association**, which states that although individual experiences may be too weak to revive memory, several weak associations may combine and thereby be strong enough to revive memory. He also added the **law of constructive association**, which states that the mind has the power to rearrange associations into combinations that differ from actual experience. In other words, the mind can rearrange memories of various experiences into an almost infinite number of combinations. The law of constructive association was thought to account for the imagination and creativity that characterized poets, artists, inventors, and the like.

Another of Bain's contributions to modern psychology was his treatment of **voluntary behavior** (volition). Unlike reflexive behavior, which is triggered by some known external stimulus, voluntary behavior is spontaneous and is a function of the mind rather than of external stimulation. In his analysis of voluntary behavior, Bain drew heavily upon the notion of *hedonism*. **Jeremy Bentham** (1748–1832) had taken the ancient concept of hedonism (from the Greek word *hedone*, meaning "pleasure") and made it the cornerstone of his political/ethical theory:

> Nature has placed mankind under the governance of two sovereign masters, pain and pleasure. It is for them alone to point out what we ought to do, as well as to determine what we shall do. On the one hand the standard of right and wrong, on the other the chain of causes and effects, are fastened to their throne. They govern us in all we do, in all we say, in all we think: every effort we can make to throw off their subjection will serve but to demonstrate and confirm it. (Bentham, 1879/1961, Ch. 1, Sec. 1)

Bain explains the development of voluntary behavior as follows. First, when some need such as hunger or the need to be released from confinement occurs, there is random or spontaneous activity. Second, some of these random movements will produce conditions necessary for satisfying the need; these are called "Happy Hits." Third, the activities that bring need satisfaction are remembered. And fourth, next time the organism is in this situation, it will perform the activities that previously brought about need satisfaction. Actions that are performed

because of their previous effectiveness in a given situation are voluntary rather than reflexive. Bain (1859) offers the example of an animal learning to escape from confinement:

> The repeated connection between the feeling [of displeasure through confinement] and this one movement (at first accidentally stumbled upon) would end in a firm association between the two; there would be no more fumbling and uncertainty; the random tentatives, arising through spontaneity and the spasmodic writhings of pain, would give place to the one selected and appropriate movement and should have a full-grown volition adapted to the case. (p. 322)

Bain essentially described trial-and-error learning, which was to become so important to E. L. Thorndike several years later. We also see in Bain's writings the rudiments of reinforcement theory, which came to dominate psychology in the 1940s and remains an important part of contemporary psychology. Bain introduced physiology into both empiricism and associationism. His work demonstrated a compatibility between philosophy and the natural sciences that would shortly lead to the development of experimental psychology.

FRENCH MATERIALISM

The empiricists and (as we shall see in the next chapter) the rationalists had one important thing in common; they were both attempting to explain subjective reality. They differed as to its origins, as to what they thought we could be certain of, and as to whether or not anything in the mind was innate, but they both directed their attention toward an understanding of human consciousness. Another philosophical movement that emerged in the seventeenth and eighteenth centuries focused on something other than consciousness. Instead, it modeled itself after physics and looked upon humans as machines. This movement was called **materialism**, and it had a profound influence on psychology. The materialists believed that everything, including human morality, reason, and feeling, could be explained in terms of matter in motion. For them, psychology was to be looked upon as a branch of physics.

As we have already noted, the philosophical rebellions that characterized the Renaissance were not directed at religion but at religious dogma. With few exceptions, the great philosophers and scientists of the period were deeply religious men. For Robinson (1976) this raises a very interesting question:

> It is instructive to pause and to note a remarkable feature of contemporary psychology: no major spokesman for the discipline, no figure identified as one responsible for its methods and concerns, none who has provided a theory of consequence to contemporary endeavors, has argued that the religious message is necessary for an understanding of human psychology. Stated another way, we recognize that in the fifteen centuries beginning in A.D. 200, there is no record of a serious psychological work devoid of religious allusion and that, since 1930, there has not been a major psychological work expressing a need for spiritual terms in an attempt to comprehend the psychological dimensions of man. (p. 279)

According to Robinson, the reasons for the dramatic shift cannot be found in the increased popularity of science or in the historic tensions between rationalism and empiricism. For Robinson, the reason for the shift can be traced back to the point where humans were likened to machines. The metaphor of human beings as machines was stimulated by the work of Copernicus, Kepler, Galileo, and Newton. The question became, If everything else in the universe can be explained in terms of mechanical laws, why should not humans, too, obey those laws? For some, the answer was that humans could indeed be explained completely as natural phenomena; that is, like the universe, humans were also machines.

Pierre Gassendi

Descartes had separated the mind and the body and had said that the human body, like the bodies of other animals, followed mechanical laws, but that the mind was free and possessed innate ideas. Almost immediately, it was recognized that all human activity could be explained without recourse to a mind. For example, **Pierre Gassendi** (1592–1655), who is considered the founder of modern materialism (an honor that could as easily be given to Hobbes), asked why "lower" animals could move themselves quite well without the aid of a mind, and yet humans needed one. Why not ascribe the operations attributed to the mind to the functions of the brain (which is physical)? In other words, Gassendi saw no reason for postulating an unextended mind to explain any human activity. We were nothing but matter, and therefore we could be studied and understood like anything else in the universe. Gassendi suggested a natural monism not unlike the one that the early Greek atomists such as Democritus and later the Epicureans had suggested. He had many followers, and we shall review the works of three of them below.

Julien de La Mettrie

Julien de La Mettrie (1709–1751) rejected the idea that rationality was unique to humans. In his book *L'Homme Machine* (Man a Machine), published in 1748, he describes a continuity of thought processes from the lowest animals to the highest (humans). According to La Mettrie, we are not completely rational, and other animals are not completely irrational. Nor are humans to be seen as fallen angels who are only inferior images of God. We are simply part of nature and differ only in degree from other organisms. La Mettrie believed that monkeys and apes had the potential to use symbols (for example, language), an idea borne out in recent years; and he believed further that seeing ourselves as continuous with nature would create a more positive attitude toward nature and would generate a moral life in pursuit of simple pleasures instead of a life governed by religious superstition. Like the British empiricists, La Mettrie accepted hedonism as the major motive for human activity.

Although Descartes is often given credit for creating comparative and physiological psychology, some believe La Mettrie should be given more recognition. Actually, La Mettrie saw no need for a separate discipline of psychology, since all human activity could be explained by the mechanistic laws of physiology.

Etienne Bonnot de Condillac

Etienne Bonnot de Condillac (1715–1780) attempted to reduce human understanding to a single principle, *sensation*. He deeply respected Locke, but believed Locke had given the mind too many unnecessary powers, such as reflection, attention, and memory. Condillac denied all these powers and said that all mental experience was derivable from simple sensations. To make his point, Condillac asks us to imagine a statue that has the sense of smell and the ability to experience pleasure and pain. Although the statue would be devoid of the mental faculties Locke had postulated, Condillac attempts to demonstrate that his statue could still understand the world as humans do. The statue does not have the ability to reflect, and attention is explained by the fact that stronger sensations dominate weaker ones. But Condillac seems to cheat a bit when it comes to memory, since his statue is capable of recognizing sensations the second time they occur. Although Condillac denies a faculty of memory, somehow his statue has the ability to store its experiences. In any case, Condillac attempted to show that many cognitive activities previously thought to be due to various powers of the mind could be understood in terms of simple sensations, a few basic emotions, and perhaps memory.

Claude Helvetius

Claude Helvetius (1715–1771) agreed with Condillac that the mind at birth was devoid of both ideas and rational powers, but disagreed with La Mettrie's contention that humans come into the world with complex behavioral tendencies and with the ability to utilize symbols. In Helvetius's view, *all* human attributes came from environmental experience. Like the modern behaviorist, he saw this as something positive. An environment could be manipulated, whereas a person's genetically determined faculties could not be. For this reason, like the modern behaviorist, Helvetius had great faith that education could improve individuals. People were what they experienced and retained; therefore, through control of experiences (education), social skills and even genius could be taught. Helvetius's position has much in common with that of the modern behaviorists.

POSITIVISM

As the success of the physical sciences spread throughout Europe, and as religious doctrine became increasingly suspect, a new belief emerged: the belief that perhaps science could solve all human problems. For many, scientific knowledge was the only objective knowledge; therefore, it was the only information one could believe in. For these individuals, science took on some of the characteristics of a religion.

Auguste Comte

One such individual was **Auguste Comte** (1798–1857). For him, the only thing we can be sure of is what is publicly observable—that is, sense experiences that can be shared with other individuals. The data of science are publicly observable and therefore can be trusted. For example, scientific laws are statements about

THE BETTMANN ARCHIVE, INC.

Auguste Comte

how empirical events vary together, and once determined they can be experienced by any interested party. Comte's insistence on equating knowledge with empirical observations was called **positivism**. Positivism can be seen as an extension of empiricism and materialism, although one can be either an empiricist or a materialist without necessarily being a positivist. One influence of positivism on psychology was the rejection of mentalism. Since mental events such as ideas could not be experienced publicly, they were outside the realm of science and were suspect. Likewise, the introspective method that was used to explore the mind was to be rejected as dubious. Comte felt that psychology, because of its concentration on mental events and its use of introspection, was "an idle fancy, and a dream, when it is not an absurdity." The *outcome* of mental activity could be examined, however, and individual and group *behavior* could be studied scientifically. Comte coined the term *sociology* to describe such a study.

Comte also believed that cultures passed through three stages of evolution in the way that they explained things. The first stage is *theological*, and explanations are based on superstition and mysticism. In the second stage, which is *metaphysical*, hidden forces or principles replace religious explanations. During the third and highest stage of development, the *scientific*, all explanations are objective and directed at publicly observed phenomena. Comte also used the term *sociology* to describe how different cultures compared in terms of the development described above.

Logical Positivism

Positivism gradually evolved into what was called **logical positivism**. Comte wanted science to be mainly descriptive and to avoid theory. Logical positivism, however, divided science into two parts: the empirical and the theoretical. In other words, it wedded empiricism and rationalism. S. S. Stevens's definition of science in Chapter 1 indicates how these two philosophical systems are combined in science. By accepting theory as part of science, the logical positivists in no way reduced the importance of empirical observation. In fact, the ultimate authority for the logical positivist was, and is, empirical observation, and theories are considered useful only if they help to clarify what is observed.

One way in which the logical positivists influenced psychology was by insisting that all psychological concepts be operationally defined. An **operational definition** ties a concept to some empirical referent. Such a definition attempts to establish what we can look at in the empirical world to determine whether, or how much, an organism has learned, how intelligent an organism is, how much anxiety a person is experiencing, and so on. In other words, the operational definition is an attempt to convert an otherwise subjective term into a set of empirical operations. For a while, **operationism** was the rage in psychology, but soon it was all but given up. Today the position in psychology that best reflects the spirit of logical positivism, including the insistence on operational definitions, is that of Clark Hull, the great learning theorist. Most others, including the logical positivists themselves, abandoned a strict operationism because it was too restrictive; it excluded from science concepts that were too nebulous to be defined operationally but were still useful in suggesting new avenues of research and methods of inquiry. Perhaps the most important reason that logical positivism failed, however, was the discovery that it did not accurately describe how science was practiced even by its most effective practitioners. Individuals such as Thomas Kuhn (see Chapter 1) have shown that the behavior of scientists is determined as much by beliefs, biases, and emotions as by axioms, theories, or logic.

Another outcome of positivism and logical positivism was the belief that all sciences were essentially the same. Since they all followed the same principles and made the same assumptions, and since they all attempted to explain empirical events, why should they not use the same terminology? The push for unification of the sciences and for a common vocabulary among the sciences (including psychology, since the logical positivists did not have the same low opinion of psychology that Comte did) was called **physicalism**. The science proposed as a model for the other sciences was physics.

In later chapters we will see many examples of the deep and lasting effect of positivism and logical positivism on psychology.

SUMMARY

A group of British philosophers opposed Descartes's notion of innate ideas, saying that all ideas were derived from experience. Those who claimed that experience was the basis of all knowledge were called empiricists. Hobbes insisted that all human activity was ultimately reducible to physical principles; thus, he was a materialist as well as an empiricist. He believed that the function of a society was to satisfy the needs of individuals and to prevent individuals from fighting among themselves. Locke was an empiricist who distinguished between primary qualities, or the attributes of physical things, and secondary qualities, or the perception of physical things. Berkeley said that we could know only secondary qualities (perceptions), but that we could trust our perceptions of the physical world to be accurate, since God would not deceive us. He also proposed an empirical theory of distance perception.

Hume agreed with Berkeley that the only thing we experienced directly was our own subjective experience, but disagreed with Berkeley's faith that our perceptions accurately reflected the physical world. For Hume, we could never know anything about the physical world, since all we ever experienced was thought and habits of thought. Hartley attempted to couple empiricism and associationism with a rudimentary conception of physiology, and his work turned out to be surprisingly similar to the more modern work of Donald Hebb. James Mill pushed empiricism and associationism to their logical conclusion by saying that all ideas could be explained in terms of experience and associative principles. He also said that even the most complex ideas could be reduced to simpler ones. John Stuart Mill disagreed with his father's contention that simple ideas remained intact as they combined into more complex ones. He maintained that simple ideas underwent a fusion, and that the complex idea they produced could be quite different from the simpler ideas that made it up. J. S. Mill's idea of fusion was called mental chemistry. Alexander Bain was the first to write a psychology text in English, to write an entire book on the relationship between the mind and the body, to utilize known neurophysiological facts in explaining psychological phenomena, and to found a psychology journal. He explained voluntary behavior in terms of hedonism and trial-and-error behavior, and he added the laws of compound association and constructive association to the list of traditional laws of association.

The materialists, including Hobbes, Gassendi, La Mettrie, Condillac, and Helvetius, sought to explain all human activity—including mental activity—in terms of physical principles. They viewed humans as complex machines. Comte created a position called positivism, according to which only scientific information could be considered valid. Anything not publicly observable was suspect, and therefore all subjective experience was rejected as a proper object of study. Comte suggested that cultures progressed through three stages in their attempt to explain things: the theological, the metaphysical, and the scientific. Positivism was later expanded into logical positivism, which accepted scientific theory that was rational. For the logical positivist, however, the ultimate authority was still empirical observation. The logical positivists insisted that all scientific concepts be operationally defined—that is, defined in terms of the procedures followed when measuring the concept. The insistence that all scientific concepts be operationally defined is called operationism.

DISCUSSION QUESTIONS

1. Define *empiricism*.

2. Why was Hobbes referred to as a materialist? What functions did Hobbes see government as having?

3. According to Locke, what was the difference between primary and secondary qualities? How did the "paradox of basins" demonstrate this difference?

4. Explain Berkeley's statement "To be is to be perceived." What saved Berkeley's position from solipsism?

5. Summarize Berkeley's explanation of distance perception.

6. Differentiate between a materialistic and an idealistic monism.

7. For Hume, what was the only reality? Summarize Hume's analysis of causation.

8. In what way was Hartley's empirical philosophy different from the others? What was Hartley's position on the mind-body problem?

9. Compare the position of James Mill with that of his son John Stuart Mill. Be sure to include in your answer the concept of mental chemistry.

10. Summarize Alexander Bain's contributions to psychology. Include in your answer the new laws of association that he added and his treatment of voluntary behavior.

11. List the materialists covered in this chapter and describe each of their contributions. What model did the materialists use in their explanation of human activities?

12. What did Comte mean by *positivism*? Describe the stages that Comte felt cultures went through in the way they attempted to explain things.

13. Explain the difference between positivism and logical positivism.

14. What is an operational definition? Give an example. What is operationism?

15. Explain the relationship between empiricism and associationism.

GLOSSARY

Associationism The belief that memories are held together in some meaningful way by one or more of the laws of association. Such laws include contiguity, frequency, similarity, and contrast.

Bain, Alexander (1818–1903) The first to attempt to relate the known physiological facts to psychological phenomena. He also wrote the first psychology text in English, and he founded psychology's first journal (1876). Bain explained voluntary behavior in much the same way that modern learning theorists later explained trial-and-error behavior. Finally, Bain added the law of compound association and the law of constructive association to the older, traditional laws of association.

Bentham, Jeremy (1748–1832) Said that the seeking of pleasure and the avoidance of pain governed most human behavior. Bentham also said that the best society was one that did the greatest good for the greatest number of people.

Berkeley, George (1685–1753) Said that the only thing we experienced directly was our own perceptions, or what Locke called secondary qualities. Berkeley offered an empirical explanation of the perception of distance, saying that we learn to associate the sensations caused by the convergence and divergence of the eyes with different distances. Berkeley also distinguished between perception, which involved vivid ideas, and imagination, which involved faint ideas.

Comte, Auguste (1798–1857) The founder of positivism and coiner of the term *sociology*. He felt that cultures passed through three stages in the way they explained things: the theological, the metaphysical, and the scientific.

Condillac, Etienne Bonnot de (1715–1780) Maintained that all human mental attributes could be explained using only the concept of sensation, and that it was therefore unnecessary to postulate any "powers" of the mind.

Empiricist One who believes that all knowledge is derived from sensory experience.

Epiphenomenalism The belief that bodily events cause mental events but that mental events do not cause bodily events.

Gassendi, Pierre (1592–1655) Generally considered the father of modern materialism, Gassendi saw humans as nothing but complex physical machines, and he saw no need to assume a nonphysical mind.

Hartley, David (1705–1757) Combined empiricism and associationism with rudimentary physiological notions. Hartley arrived at the surprisingly modern notion that sensations are grouped according to the law of contiguity, and that after they have been grouped, experiencing any member of the group alone stimulates the memory of the entire group.

Hedonism The contention that the major motive for human behavior is the seeking of pleasure and the avoidance of pain.

Helvetius, Claude (1715–1771) Agreed with Condillac that all human attributes were derived from experience. Since Helvetius denied the importance of genetically determined skills, he placed great emphasis on education as a means of improving individuals.

Hobbes, Thomas (1588–1679) Believed that the primary motive in human behavior was the seeking of pleasure and the avoidance of pain. For Hobbes, the function of government is to satisfy as many human needs as possible and to prevent humans from fighting with one another. Hobbes believed that all human activity, including mental activity, could be reduced to atoms in motion, and therefore he can be classified as a materialist.

Hume, David (1711–1776) Agreed with Berkeley that we could experience only our own subjective reality, but disagreed with his contention that we could assume certain things about the physical world because God would not deceive us. For Hume, we can be sure of nothing. Even the notion of cause and effect, which is so important to Newtonian physics, is nothing more than a habit of thought. Hume distinguished between impressions, which are vivid, and ideas, which are faint copies of impressions.

La Mettrie, Julien de (1709-1751) Believed humans were machines that differed from other animals only in complexity. La Mettrie's belief in the continuity among all animals did much to stimulate physiological and comparative psychology.

Law of compound association Although a single experience may be too weak to revive a memory, several weak experiences may combine and thus become strong enough to trigger a memory.

Law of constructive association The mind can rearrange the memories of various experiences so that the creative associations formed are different from the experiences that gave rise to the associations.

Law of Contiguity The tendency for physical events that are experienced together to be remembered together.

Law of Resemblance The tendency for similar ideas to cluster together in memory (also called the **Law of Similarity**).

Locke, John (1632-1704) An empiricist who denied the existence of any innate ideas but who assumed many nativistically determined powers of the mind. Locke distinguished between physical attributes (primary qualities) and the perception of those physical attributes (secondary qualities). The different kinds of ideas included those caused by sensory stimulation, those caused by reflection, simple ideas, and complex ideas, which were composites of simple ideas.

Logical positivism An expanded form of the original positivist position. It included scientific theory. As with positivism, however, the ultimate authority in science was empirical observation.

Materialism The belief that everything human, including conscious experience, can be explained by physical principles. Following Newton's conception of the universe, the materialists viewed humans as nothing more than complex machines.

Materialistic monism The belief that all human activity, including subjective experience, can

be reduced to and explained by something physical, such as atoms in motion.

Mental chemistry The process by which individual sensations can combine to form a new sensation that is different from any of the individual sensations that make it up.

Mill, James (1773-1836) Maintained that all mental events consisted of sensations and ideas (copies of sensations) held together by association. No matter how complex an idea was, Mill felt that it could be reduced to simple ideas.

Mill, John Stuart (1806-1873) Disagreed with his father, James, that complex ideas could be reduced to simple ideas. J. S. Mill proposed a process of mental chemistry according to which complex ideas could be distinctly different from the simple ideas (elements) that made them up.

Operational definition The specification of the procedures that are to be followed when measuring whatever is being defined.

Operationism The belief that all scientific concepts should be operationally defined.

Physicalism The belief that all sciences should share common concepts and a common vocabulary and that physics should act as a model for all the sciences.

Positivism The contention that only scientific facts—facts that can be observed directly—can be trusted. The positivist rejects all mentalism, and therefore the introspective method.

Primary qualities Attributes of physical objects.

Psychophysical parallelism The contention that every experience has both a physical (biological) and a mental component, with no interaction between the two.

Secondary qualities The perceptions caused by physical objects.

Solipsism The belief that the only knowable reality is one's subjective experience.

Utilitarian A person who believes that the best society or government is one that provides the greatest good for the greatest number of individuals. Jeremy Bentham was a utilitarian.

Vibratiuncles According to Hartley, the vibrations that linger in the brain after the initial vibrations caused by external stimulation have ceased.

Voluntary behavior According to Bain, behavior that first emitted randomly and accidentally and that happens to satisfy a need. Thereafter, when the same need is present in a similar situation, that behavior will arise voluntarily.

CHAPTER 6

Rationalism

The preceding chapter began by defining *empiricism* as the belief that sensory experience is the basis of all knowledge. All of the philosophers covered in the preceding chapter assumed the importance of sensory information, though most used introspection to analyze what happened to that information after it had arrived in the mind. Clearly, the term *empiricism* is not to be contrasted with *mentalism*. All of the early empiricists postulated a mind in which such things as association, reflection, imagination, and generalization took place. What distinguishes the empiricist from the rationalist, then, is not whether or not they postulated a mind; rather, it is the *kind* of mind they postulated. The empiricists tended to accept a **passive mind**—that is, a mind that acts upon sensory information and the memories of such information in an automatic, mechanical way. And they used the laws of association to explain most mental phenomena. As we have mentioned, the British empiricists, under the influence of Newton, were attempting to explain all mental events using a few laws or principles. The French tended to be even more extreme, suggesting that there was no need for the concept of mind. All mental phenomena, they claimed, could be explained by physiological processes and association.

What, then, is a rationalist? The **rationalist** tends to postulate an **active mind**, a mind that acts upon the information from the senses and gives it meaning it otherwise would not have. For the rationalist, the mind adds something to

sensory data, rather than simply passively organizing and storing it in memory. Typically, the rationalist assumes innate mental structures, principles, operations, or abilities that are used in analyzing the world. There are truths about the world, but they cannot be ascertained simply by experiencing the world; such truths must be arrived at by such processes as logical deduction, analysis, and argument. For the empiricist, hedonism, experience, and memory determine how a person acts. They even determine one's morality. For the rationalist, however, there are reasons for acting one way or another. For example, there are moral principles, and if they are understood and acted upon they result in moral behavior. The empiricist tends to emphasize *causes* of behavior, whereas the rationalist tends to emphasize *reasons* for behavior. And while the empiricist emphasizes induction (that is, the accumulation of experience and the generalizations from it) the rationalist emphasizes deduction. Given certain sensory data and certain rules of thought, certain things must follow. It should be no surprise that mathematics has always been more important to the rationalist than to the empiricist.

Just as Bacon is looked upon as the founder of modern empiricism, Descartes is looked upon as the founder of modern rationalism. Both Bacon and Descartes had the same motive: to overcome the mistakes and mysticism of the past. In the remainder of this chapter we will review the work of several of the rationalists who helped mold modern psychology.

BARUCH SPINOZA

Baruch Spinoza (1632–1677) was a Jew reared in the Christian city of Amsterdam at a time when Descartes's philosophy was very popular. Eventually Spinoza's philosophy led to his excommunication from the Jewish religion, but the fact that he was Jewish prevented him from entering the circle of Christian intellectuals. Spinoza was a maverick who really did not fit comfortably anywhere. Alexander and Selesnick (1966) describe Spinoza's situation:

> Judged a heretic because of his pantheism and refutations of the anthropomorphic God-image of the Jewish and Christian religions, Spinoza was publicly excommunicated by the elders of the synagogue when he was twenty-seven years old. The Jews in his community were forbidden to communicate with him in any way; they were forbidden to enter a room in which he was present or to read one line of his writings. He supported himself by teaching and by polishing lenses. He earned barely enough to live on, yet he consistently refused to accept gifts and annuities offered to him by his admirers, among them Henry Oldenbury, the secretary of the Royal Society of England, Leibniz, the great philosopher, and Huygens, the physicist. He also refused a pension offered to him by Louis XIV, because the King expected Spinoza to dedicate his next book to him; and he turned down the chair of philosophy at the University of Heidelberg because he would not have been allowed to challenge the concepts of Christianity. (p. 97)

Descartes had separated God, the mind, and matter. He was severely criticized for conceptualizing God as a power that set the world in motion and then was no longer involved in it. Following Descartes, one could study the world without theological considerations, and this is essentially what Newton did.

For Spinoza, God did not start the world in motion and then leave it; Spinoza believed God to be present everywhere in nature. In fact, Spinoza equated God and nature. To understand the laws of nature was to understand God.

Spinoza thus rejected the anthropomorphic image of God that both the Christians and Jews accepted. Although Spinoza's God did not judge humans, Spinoza still considered it essential that we understand God. That is, Spinoza insisted that the best life was one lived with a knowledge of the causes of things. Since natural law (God) governed everything in the universe, everything was determined by natural causes, including human thoughts and behavior. The closest we could get to freedom was understanding what caused our behavior or thoughts. According to Spinoza, humans did not possess free will. The murderer was no more responsible for his behavior than was a river that flooded a village. If the causes of both were understood, however, the aversive events could be controlled or prevented.

Continuing in his efforts to create a unified view of the world, Spinoza proposed a unique solution to the mind-body problem. Rather than viewing the mind and body as two different but interacting systems, as Descartes had viewed them, Spinoza viewed the mind and body as two aspects of the same thing—the living human being. The mind and body were inseparable; anything happening to the body was experienced as emotions and thoughts. Thus, Spinoza combined physiology and psychology into one unified system. Spinoza's position on the mind-body relationship has been called **psychophysical double-aspectism** or **double-aspect monism**, and is depicted in Figure 1.1 (p. 17).

Spinoza believed the master motive for human behavior and thought to be self-preservation. Whatever enhances self-preservation is "good," and whatever interferes with it is "bad." Since for Spinoza emotions and ideas are inseparable, when we ponder ideas of events that enhance our chances for survival, we experience positive emotions such as love; and when we ponder ideas of events that threaten our existence, we experience negative emotions such as hate. Pondering ideas of events that have caused both pleasure and pain arouses opposing emotions of love and hate, causing what Spinoza called "vacillation of the soul" or what later writers would call conflict. Clear thinking (that is, knowing the causes of things) is conducive to survival, and therefore humans are born with an urge to understand the laws of nature (God).

An aspect of humans that could reduce the probability of survival is the experience of passion. Unlike an emotion, which is linked to a specific thought, passion is not associated with any particular thought. A child's love for its mother is an emotion, whereas a general emotional upheaval exemplifies passion, since it is not directed at anything specific. Since passion can cause nonadaptive behavior, it must be harnessed by reason. Behavior and thoughts guided by reason are conducive to survival; but behavior and thoughts guided by passion are not. By understanding the causes of passion, reason gives one the power to control passion, just as knowing why rivers flood villages allows the control of floods. If we replace the term *passion* with *unconscious determinants of behavior*, we see how similar Spinoza's position is to Freud's. Alexander and Selesnick (1966, p. 96) actually refer to Spinoza as the greatest of the pre-Freudian psychologists.

Spinoza attempted to synthesize what had been separated for centuries. For him, the mind and the body were inseparable, as were ideas and emotions. And since God and nature were the same thing, there was no need for conflict between religion and science. Almost all versions of psychology that later developed reflected some aspect of Spinoza's philosophy.

Before turning to other rational philosophers and psychologists, we will first briefly review another position on the mind-body relationship that was taken in Spinoza's time. We mention Malebranche's position mainly to show that almost every conceivable relationship between the mind and body has been proposed at one time or another.

NICOLAS DE MALEBRANCHE

A mystically oriented priest, **Nicolas de Malebranche** (1638–1715) accepted Descartes's separation of the mind and body but disagreed with his explanation of how the two interacted. For Malebranche, God mediated mind and body interactions. For example, when a person has a desire to move an arm, God is aware of this desire and moves the person's arm. Likewise, if the body is injured, God is aware of this and causes the person to experience pain. In reality there is no contact between mind and body, but there appears to be because of God's intervention. A wish to do something becomes the occasion for God to cause the body to act, and for that reason this point of view became known as **occasionalism**. This view of the mind-body relationship can be referred to as a parallelism with divine intervention. Without the divine intervention, the activities of the mind and the body would be causally unrelated, and we would have psychophysical parallelism. Malebranche's position on the mind-body relationship is depicted in Figure 1.1 (p. 17). Malebranche reverted to a much earlier explanation of the origins of knowledge, suggesting that ideas were not innate and that they did not come from experience. Instead, they came only from God, and we could know only what God revealed to our souls.

GOTTFRIED WILHELM VON LEIBNIZ

Like several of the rationalists, **Gottfried Wilhelm von Leibniz** (1646–1716), a contemporary of both Newton and Locke, was a great mathematician. In fact he co-invented differential calculus independently of Newton. His father was a professor of moral philosophy at the University of Leipzig, which Leibniz entered at the age of 15. His early education included the

Gottfried Wilhelm von Leibniz

act appropriately, but experience does not cause ideas. There is no way that the confrontation between sense organs and the physical world can cause something purely mental (for example, an idea). For this reason, Leibniz rejected the mind-body dualism of Descartes—that is, because it is impossible for something physical to cause something mental.

Mind, according to Leibniz, is simply substance that cannot be reduced to anything else or be derived from anything else. The mind exemplifies a **monad**. Everything in the world consists of monads that are unique and independent of each other (*monad* is the Greek word for "individual" or "unity"). The mind and the body, each being a monad, exist independently of each other but are in harmony. Whatever harmony exists among monads was created by God. According to Leibniz, since God created the world, it cannot be improved upon. In Voltaire's *Candide*, Leibniz appears as a foolish professor who continues to insist, even after observing tragedy after tragedy, that "this is the best of all possible worlds."

Sometimes monads are so minute that the influence of just one, or a few of them, cannot make us aware of them. Bruno (1972) gives the following example:

> Let us say that you are sitting in your home and a drop of rain falls on the roof. Do you hear it? Probably not. If only one drop falls, we are conscious of no sound; but if many drops fall we have the complex experience of hearing rain fall on the roof. We say we hear rain; we do not say we hear individual drops. Yet it would appear that the complex experience of hearing the rain must be made up of the simpler experiences of hearing the drops of rain fall. Still, if we cannot hear an individual drop, why is it we can hear the rain at all? (p. 51)

Leibniz would answer the question by saying that each raindrop creates a **petites perception**, or a perception below the level of awareness. Each monad experienced individually causes a petites perception. As more monads are added to the experience, their combined force is even-

Greek and Roman classics and the works of Bacon, Descartes, and Galileo.

Leibniz's argument was mainly with Locke, who claimed that all knowledge was derived from experience and that the mind registered, stored, and organized ideas in accordance with the laws of association. For the empiricists, ideas derived from experience and acted upon by the laws of association *were the mind*; but according to Leibniz, the mind existed prior to these experiences, and therefore it was the mind that received and acted upon them. Leibniz responded to Locke's description of the mind as a *tabula rasa* by saying that there was nothing in the mind that had not first been in the senses, *except the mind itself*. Leibniz proposed a mind that acted upon sensory information in order to determine its significance.

For Leibniz, experience is necessary because it focuses attention on the thoughts already in us and allows us to organize our thoughts and

THE BETTMANN ARCHIVE, INC.

tually enough to cause awareness, or what Leibniz called **apperception**. This is why, according to Leibniz, we cannot hear one raindrop but we can hear several of them together. There is a continuum between the unconscious and the conscious. Leibniz was among the first philosophers to postulate the unconscious mind. Leibniz referred to the point at which an experience becomes strong enough to cause awareness as the **limen**, or threshold. We are aware of experiences above the threshold, but experiences below the threshold remain unconscious. Leibniz's concept of threshold was to become extremely important when psychology became a science in the late 1800s.

On the mind-body question, Leibniz assumed a psychophysical parallelism. Because of the harmony created by God, the monads of the mind and those of the body are always in agreement, but they do not interact. In addition to disagreeing with the interactionism of Descartes, Leibniz disagreed with the occasionalists, who maintained that the mind and body were coordinated through God's continuous intervention. According to Leibniz, God created all the monads so that there is a lasting harmony among them. Leibniz asks that we imagine two identical, perfect clocks that have been set to the same time at the same moment. Afterward, the clocks will always be in agreement but will not interact. For Leibniz, this describes how the mind and body are related: they are always in agreement, because God planned it that way, but they are not causally related. This **pre-established harmony** form of psychophysical parallelism is depicted in Figure 1.1 (p.17).

THOMAS REID AND FRANZ JOSEPH GALL

Like Hume, **Thomas Reid** (1710–1796) was a Scotsman. Unlike Hume, however, Reid represented rationalism instead of empiricism. Reid opposed the skepticism about our ability to know the physical environment that Berkeley and especially Hume showed. Reid said that since all humans were convinced of the existence of physical reality, it must exist. "All mankind," he said, "could not be wrong and go against the wisdom of the ages." If Hume's logic caused him (Hume) to conclude that we could never know the physical world, then, said Reid, something was wrong with Hume's logic. We can trust our impressions of the physical world because it makes *common sense* to do so. We are naturally endowed with the abilities to deal with and make sense out of the world. If reasoning denies either these human abilities or the physical world, it must be faulty. According to Reid (1764):

> When a man suffers himself to be reasoned out of the principles of common sense, by metaphysical arguments, we may call this *metaphysical lunacy*. (Lehrer and Beanblossom, 1975, p. 119)

Reid felt that it was just plain silly to deny the existence of the physical world. In his book *Inquiry into the Human Mind on the Principles of Common Sense* (1764), Reid describes what life would be like if we did not assume that our senses accurately reflected reality:

> I resolve not to believe my senses. I break my nose against a post. . . . I step into a dirty kennel; and after twenty such wise and rational actions, I am taken up and clapped into a madhouse. (Lehrer and Beanblossom, 1975, p. 86)

Reid defends the existence of reasoning powers by saying that even those who claim that reasoning does not occur are using reasoning to doubt its existence. The mind reasons, and the stomach digests food. Both the mind and stomach do their jobs because they are innately disposed to do so, and to ask why the mind reasons is like asking why the stomach digests food. Reason is necessary so that we can control our emotions, appetites, and passions, and so that we can understand and perform our duty to God and other humans.

Reid and his followers believed that the skeptics reduced human dignity by either denying reasoning powers or by likening humans to machines. Members of this **Common Sense School of Thought** also felt that physiological explanations of associations, like those Hartley proposed, reduced human dignity. Reid said that consciousness occurred too rapidly to depend on physiological processes, and that it therefore must come from God.

Reid did not believe that consciousness was formed by one sensation being added to another. Rather, we experience objects immediately as units because of our power of perception. We perceive the world *directly* in terms of meaningful units, not as isolated sensations that are then combined via associative principles. We will see this belief again in Kant's philosophy and later in Gestalt psychology. In addition to perception, Reid proposed more than 20 other powers or faculties of the mind— for example, self-preservation, pity, desire, gratitude, duty, imagination, judgment, moral taste, will, and memory. Reid believed that these faculties were located in specific places in the brain and that they were not derived from experience—that is, they were innate. Those who postulated such faculties of the mind or brain were later called **faculty psychologists**, and Reid is often referred to as the father of modern faculty psychology.

Franz Joseph Gall (1758–1828), a German physician, took an additional step by saying that the faculties did not exist to the same extent in all humans. He believed that if a faculty were well developed in a person, that person would have a bump or protrusion on the part of the skull corresponding to that faculty. If a faculty were underdeveloped, there would be a hollow or depression on the corresponding area of the skull. Thus, Gall believed that the magnitude of one's faculties could be determined by examining the bumps and depressions on one's skull. Such an analysis was called **phrenology**.

Phrenology had two lasting effects on psychology:

> First, it led to research designed to discover the function of various parts of the brain. It was this very research, however, that disproved the assumptions upon which phrenology was based. Second, many faculty psychologists believed that the faculties became stronger with practice just like the biceps become stronger with practice. For this reason, the faculty psychologists were said to have taken a "mental muscle" approach to learning. Learning, to them, meant strengthening faculties by practicing those traits associated with them. One could improve one's reasoning abilities, for example, by formally studying such topics as mathematics or Latin. The belief that a particular course or training would strengthen certain faculties was called *formal discipline*, a concept that provides one answer to the question of how learning transfers from one situation to another. (Hergenhahn, 1982, pp. 41–42)

We will have more to say about phrenology in Chapter 8 when we discuss early developments in physiological psychology, and again in Chapter 11 when we discuss functionalism.

IMMANUEL KANT

Immanuel Kant (1724–1804) was born in Königsberg, Prussia, and never traveled more than 40 miles from his birthplace in the 80 years of his life (Boring, 1957, p. 246). Kant was educated at the University of Königsberg and taught there until he was 73, when he resigned because he was asked to stop including his views on religion in his lectures. He became so famous in his lifetime that philosophy students came from all over Europe to attend his lectures, and he had to keep changing restaurants to avoid admirers who wanted to watch him eat his lunch. Kant's famous books *Critique of Pure Reason* (1781) and *Critique of Practical Reason* (1788) set the tone of German rationalist philosophy and psychology for generations.

Kant started out as a disciple of Leibniz, but

reading Hume's philosophy caused him to wake from his "dogmatic slumbers" and attempt to rescue philosophy from the skepticism that Hume had created toward it. Hume had argued that all conclusions we reached about anything were based on subjective experience, since that was the only thing we ever encountered directly. According to Hume, all statements about the nature of the physical world or about morality were derived from ideas and the feelings that ideas aroused, as well as from the way ideas were organized by the laws of association. Even causation, which was so important to many rationalists, was reduced to a habit of the mind in Hume's philosophy. For example, even if B always follows A, and the interval between the two is always the same, we cannot ever conclude that A causes B, since there is no way for us to verify an actual causal relationship between the two events. For Hume, rational philosophy, physical science, and moral philosophy were all reducible to subjective psychology. Therefore, nothing could be known with certainty, since all knowledge was based on the interpretation of subjective experience.

Kant set out to prove Hume wrong by demonstrating that some truths were certain and were not based on subjective experience. He focused on Hume's analysis of the concept of cause. Kant agreed with Hume that this concept corresponded to nothing in experience. In other words, nothing in our experience suggests that one thing causes another. But, asks Kant, if the notion of cause does not come from experience, *where does it come from*? Kant argued that the very ingredients necessary even for thinking in terms of a causal relationship could not be derived from experience, and therefore must exist *a priori*, or independent of experience. Kant did not deny the importance of sensory data, but felt strongly that the mind must add something to that data before knowledge could be attained; that something was the *a priori* (innate) categories of thought. These categories perform logical functions on the evi-

Immanuel Kant

dence of the senses, and thereby give it its meaning. According to Kant, what we experience subjectively has been filtered through the pure concepts of the mind and is therefore more meaningful than it would otherwise have been. Kant included the following in his list of *a priori* pure concepts, or what have been called categories of thought: unity, totality, cause and effect, reality, negation, possibility-impossibility, existence-nonexistence.

Without the influence of these and other categories, our sensory experience would have far less meaning. For example, we could never make statements beginning with the word *all*, since we never experience all of anything. According to Kant, the fact that we are willing at some point to generalize from several particular experiences to an entire class of events merely specifies the conditions under which we employ the innate category of totality, since the word *all* can never be based on experience. In this way, Kant showed that although the empiricists had been correct in stressing the importance of experience, a further analysis of the very experience that the empiricists referred to revealed the importance of rational principles.

Kant also attempted to rescue moral philosophy from what empiricists had reduced it to—utilitarianism. According to Kant, just as there are categories of thought upon which our knowledge of the physical world is based, there are also *a priori* rational principles upon which moral principles are based. For Kant, it was not enough to say that certain experiences felt good and others did not; he asked what rule or principle was being applied to those feelings and making them desirable or undesirable. He called the rational principle that governed, or should govern, moral behavior the **categorical imperative**, according to which a person should always act in such a way that the basis of his or her actions could serve as a universal law for everyone to follow. This innate moral principle exists in all people, but each individual is free to act in accordance with it or not; those who choose to act contrary to it experience guilt. Whereas the empiricists' analysis of moral behavior emphasized hedonism, Kant's was based upon a rational principle.

We have in Kant a rationalism that relies heavily on both sensory experience and innate knowledge. Kant has had a considerable influence on psychology, and from Kant's time until the present there has been a lively debate in psychology concerning the importance of innate factors in such areas as perception, language, cognitive development, and problem solving. The modern rationalistically oriented psychologists side with Kant by stressing the importance of genetically determined brain structures or operations. The empirically oriented psychologists insist that such psychological processes are best explained as resulting from sensory experience and the passive laws of association, thus following in the tradition of British empiricism and French materialism. Although Kant's influence was clearly evi-

dent when psychology emerged as an independent science in the late 1800s, Kant never believed that psychology could become an experimental science. The mind, he said, does not stand still and wait to be analyzed; it is constantly changing and therefore cannot be objectively studied. Furthermore, the categories of thought do not result from experience and are not reducible to biological or mechanical laws. The way to understand the *a priori* categories of thought is by rational deduction, not by empirical induction. Throughout psychology's history, many prominent psychologists have shared Kant's conclusion that a science of mental life was impossible.

JOHANN FRIEDRICH HERBART

At the age of 18, **Johann Friedrich Herbart** (1776–1841) entered the University of Jena in East Germany, where he pursued his interest in Kant's philosophy. After his undergraduate training, he moved to the University of Göttingen, where he obtained his doctorate and wrote his first books. As a testimony to his success, Herbart was invited to the University of Königsberg to occupy the position Kant had held. Herbart was only 33 at the time, and he remained at Königsberg for 24 years, after which he returned to the University of Göttingen because the Prussian government had shown antagonism toward his educational research. He remained at Göttingen until his death.

Herbart agreed with Kant's contention that psychology could never be an experimental science, but he believed that the activities of the mind could be expressed mathematically—and in that sense, that psychology *could* be a science. The reason Herbart denied that psychology could become an experimental science was that he felt experimentation necessitated the dividing up of its subject matter; and since the mind acted as an integrated whole, it could not be fractionated. For this reason, Herbart was very much opposed to faculty psychology, which was so popular in his day.

Herbart borrowed his concept of the idea from the empiricist. Following Leibniz, however, he assumed that ideas contained a force or energy of their own, and therefore he denied the validity of the laws of association. Herbart's system has been referred to as "psychic mechanics" because Herbart believed that ideas had the power to attract or repel other ideas and that they struggled to gain expression in consciousness. The same idea may at one time be given conscious expression and, at another time, be unconscious. In Herbart's view, therefore, an idea is never forgotten; it is either experienced consciously or it is not. Herbart's position represented a major departure from that of the empiricists, since they believed that ideas, like Newton's particles of matter, were buffeted around by forces external to them. Herbart agreed that ideas were derived from experience, but he maintained that once they existed, they had a life of their own. For Herbart, an idea was like an atom with energy and consciousness of its own—a conception that was very much like Leibniz's conception of the monad.

The Apperceptive Mass

Not only was Herbart's view of the idea very close to Leibniz's view of the monad, but Herbart also borrowed the concept of apperception from Leibniz. According to Herbart, at any given moment compatible ideas gather in consciousness and form a group. This group of compatible ideas constitutes the **apperceptive mass**. Another way of looking at the apperceptive mass is to equate it with attention; that is, the apperceptive mass contains all of the ideas to which we are attending.

It is with regard to the apperceptive mass that ideas compete with each other. An idea outside of the apperceptive mass (that is, an idea of which we are not conscious) will only be allowed to enter the apperceptive mass if it is compatible with the other ideas contained in the apperceptive mass at the moment. If the idea is not compatible, the ideas in the apperceptive mass will mobilize their energy to prevent the idea from entering. Thus, only those ideas that are compatible with the ideas in the apperceptive mass will be permitted to leave the unconscious mind and enter awareness. In Herbart's system, the same idea may at one time be conscious and at other times unconscious, depending on the nature of the apperceptive mass. MacLeod (1975) gives an example:

> If we combine the ideas of "about three feet long," "straight," "made of wood," "useful for measurement," we have the idea of yardstick; to add the idea "yellow" merely makes it a yellow yardstick. Let us add another idea, "having only one end," and what happens? A yellow yardstick with only one end is nonsense; either the original idea collapses or the new idea is rejected. Thus, with all mental processes, the existing apperceptive mass determines the extent to which the new ideas can be assimilated. (p. 187)

Sometimes, if enough similar ideas are rejected, they can combine their energy and force their way into consciousness, thereby displacing the existing apperceptive mass. Again, MacLeod (1975) gives an example:

> Think for example, of the time when the earth was believed to be flat. The movements of the sun, the moon, and the stars required some explanatory ingenuity, but the common sense belief was not seriously challenged. Gradually, however, evidence supporting a different hypothesis grew more and more convincing. In Herbartian terms, the rejected ideas mobilized their forces and eventually shattered the existing apperceptive mass. Today, the notion that the earth is spherical is part of the common apperceptive mass. An incompatible idea would be promptly rejected. (p. 187)

Again borrowing from Leibniz, Herbart used the term *limen* or *threshold* to describe the border between the conscious and the unconscious. Although the details need not concern us here, Herbart mathematically quantified the apperceptive mass, the limen, and the conflict among ideas, making him the first to apply a mathematical model to psychology.

Educational Psychology

In addition to being the first mathematical psychologist, many consider Herbart to be the first educational psychologist. He applied his theory to education by offering the following advice to teachers:

1. Review the material that has already been learned.

2. Prepare the student for new material by giving an overview of what is coming next. This creates a receptive apperceptive mass.

3. Present the new material.

4. Relate the new material to what has already been learned.

5. Show applications of the new material and give an overview of what is to be learned next.

For Herbart, then, a student's existing apperceptive mass, or mental set, must be taken into consideration when presenting new material. Material not compatible with a student's apperceptive mass will simply be rejected. Herbart's theory of education comes very close to the more modern theory of Piaget. Piaget says that in order for teaching to be effective, it must start with what a student is able to assimilate into his or her cognitive structure. If information is too incompatible with a student's cognitive structure, it simply will not be learned. If we substitute the term *apperceptive mass* for *cognitive structure*, we see a great deal of similarity between the theories of Herbart and Piaget.

GEORG WILHELM FRIEDRICH HEGEL

Georg Wilhelm Friedrich Hegel (1770–1831) was born in Stuttgart and learned Latin from his mother. Later, at Tübingen University, he concentrated on the Greek and Roman classics. After receiving his doctorate in 1793, he studied the historical Jesus and what the best minds through history had thought the meaning of life to be. Hegel was forced to change teaching jobs several times because of political unrest in Europe, but in 1818 he accepted one of the most prestigious academic positions in Europe, the chair in philosophy at the University of Berlin. Hegel remained at Berlin until he succumbed to a cholera epidemic on November 14, 1831.

Like Spinoza, Hegel saw the universe as an interrelated unity, which he called "the absolute idea." The only true understanding, according to Hegel, is an understanding of this absolute idea. True knowledge can never be attained by examining isolated instances of anything unless those instances are related to the "whole." Russell (1945) describes this aspect of Hegel's philosophy:

> The view of Hegel, and of many other philosophers, is that the character of any portion of the universe is so profoundly affected by its relation to the other parts and to the whole, that no true statement can be made about any part except to assign its place in the whole. Thus, there can be only one true statement; there is no truth except the whole truth. (p. 743)

The process that Hegel proposed for seeking knowledge was not unlike the one Plato proposed. First, one must recognize that sense impressions are of little use unless one can determine the general principle or idea that they exemplify. Once general ideas or principles are understood, the next step is to determine how those principles or ideas are related to each other. When one sees the interrelatedness of all principles and ideas, one experiences the absolute idea, which is similar to Plato's form of the good.

Hegel believed that both human history in general and the human intellect in particular evolved toward the absolute idea via the **dialectic process**. In studying Greek history, Hegel observed that one philosopher would take a position that another philosopher would then negate; then a third philosopher would develop a view that was intermediate between the two opposing views. For example, Heraclitus said that everything was constantly changing. Parmenides said that nothing ever changed, and Plato said that some things changed and some did not. The dialectic process involves a *thesis* (one point of view), an *antithesis* (a contrary point of view), and a *synthesis*, which is a compromise between the thesis and the antithesis. When a cycle is completed, the previous synthesis becomes the thesis for the next cycle, and the process repeats itself continually. In this manner, both human history and the human intellect evolve toward the absolute idea.

Hegel's belief that the whole is more important than particular instances led him to conclude that the state (government) was more important than the individuals that made it up. In other words, for Hegel, people existed for the state. This is exactly opposite of the position taken by Locke, who said that the state existed for the people.

We find Hegel's influences in a number of places in psychology. As we shall see in Chapter 8, Hegel strongly influenced Fechner, and thereby the development of psychophysics and ultimately the school of structuralism. Some see Freud's concepts of the id, ego, and superego as manifestations of the dialectic process (for example, Robinson, 1976, p. 338). Others see the roots of self-actualization theory (for example, the theories of Jung, Rogers, and Maslow) in

Georg Wilhelm Friedrich Hegel

THE BETTMANN ARCHIVE, INC.

Hegel's philosophy. Others see in it the beginnings of phenomenology, which ultimately manifested itself in Gestalt, humanistic, and existential psychology.

The rationalists of the seventeenth and eighteenth centuries perpetuated the tradition of Plato, St. Augustine, St. Thomas, and Descartes, a tradition that is still very much alive in psychology in many areas. In fact, insofar as modern psychology is scientific, it is at least partially a rational enterprise. As was mentioned in Chapter 1, scientific theory is a combination of empiricism and rationalism. In other words, it is now believed that a mere collection of empirical facts is meaningless unless analyzed in terms of some rational principle.

SUMMARY

Empiricism emphasizes sensory experience and the laws of association in explaining the intellect and the contents of the mind. The rationalist, in addition to accepting the importance of sensory information, postulates an active mind that acts upon and thereby transforms the information furnished by the senses. For the rationalist, the mind is *more than* a collection of ideas derived from sensory experience and held together by the laws of association. Although there is considerable overlap between empiricism and rationalism, the former postulates a passive mind and the latter an active mind.

Spinoza equated God with nature, and in so doing was excommunicated from both the Jewish and Christian religions. According to Spinoza, if humans acted in accordance with the laws of nature, their behavior was determined; only unnatural behavior was free. The former was considered desirable and the latter undesirable. For Spinoza, there was one basic reality and it was reflected in both the mind and the body. Therefore, bodily processes and thoughts were merely two aspects of the same thing. This proposed solution to the mind-body problem is called psychophysical double-aspectism. Malebranch believed that there was a mind and a body, but that they did not interact. Rather, God coordinated them. That is, if there was an idea in the mind, God was aware of it and caused the body to act appropriately. Such a belief became known as occasionalism.

Leibniz suggested that the universe was made up of indivisible entities called monads. All monads are self-contained and do not interact with other monads. Furthermore, all monads contain energy and possess consciousness. The harmony among monads was created by God and therefore cannot be improved upon. Experiencing one minute monad, or a small number of minute monads, creates a *petites perception*, which takes place below the level of awareness. If, however, enough minute monads are experienced together, their combined influence crosses the limen or threshold, and they are apperceived or experienced consciously.

Thus, for Leibniz, the difference between a conscious and an unconscious experience depends upon the number of monads involved.

Reid felt that the empiricists had degraded humans by equating the intellect with ideas derived from experience. He also opposed Hume's skepticism. Reid felt that we could accept the physical world as it appeared to us because it made common sense to do so. Human consciousness could not be explained by assuming that one sensation was added to another via the laws of association. Rather, Reid postulated powers of the mind or mental faculties to account for conscious phenomena. Later, Gall expanded faculty psychology into phrenology, according to which individuals differed with regard to the faculties, and the various faculties could be strengthened by practicing the activities associated with them.

Kant agreed with Hume that any conclusions we reached about physical reality were based on subjective experience. However, Kant asked where concepts such as cause and effect came from if we never directly experienced causes of things. His answer was that several categories of thought were innate and that sensory information was filtered through those categories, which thus modified what we experienced consciously. For Kant, then, the mind changed sensory information and made it more meaningful than it otherwise would be. Kant's influence on modern psychology is seen mainly in Gestalt psychology.

Herbart disagreed with the empiricists, who likened an idea to a Newtonian particle whose fate was determined by forces external to it. Rather, Herbart likened an idea to a Leibnizian monad; that is, he saw ideas as having an energy and a consciousness of their own. Also, he saw ideas as striving for conscious expression. The group of compatible ideas of which we are conscious at any given moment forms the apperceptive mass; all other ideas are in the unconscious. It is possible for an idea to cross the threshold between the unconscious and the conscious mind if that idea is compatible with the ideas making up the apperceptive mass; otherwise, it is rejected. Herbart attempted to express mathematically the nature of the apperceptive mass, the threshold, and the conflict between ideas, making him the first to apply mathematics to psychological phenomena. He is also considered to be the first educational psychologist, since he applied his theory to educational practices. He said, for example, that if a student was going to learn new information, it must be compatible with the student's apperceptive mass.

Like Spinoza, Hegel believed the universe to be an interrelated unity. For Hegel, the only true knowledge was that of unity, which he called "the absolute idea." Hegel believed that the human intellect advanced by a process he called "the dialectic," which involves a thesis (an idea), an antithesis (the negation of that idea), and a synthesis (a compromise between the original idea and its negation). The synthesis then becomes the thesis of the next stage of development. As this process continues, humans approximate an understanding of "the absolute idea."

The popularity of such topics as information processing, decision making, Gestalt psychology, and science in general is evidence of the rationalists' influence upon modern psychology.

DISCUSSION QUESTIONS

1. In general, what are the basic differences between the empiricist and the rationalist philosophies?

2. Distinguish between the mind as active and the mind as passive.

3. What was Spinoza's conception of nature? What was his position on the mind-body relationship?

4. Summarize Spinoza's position on the issue of free will versus determinism.

5. What was Malebranche's position on the mind-body relationship?

6. Discuss Leibniz's concepts of monads, petites perception, and apperception.

7. What was Reid's argument with the empiricists? According to Reid, what was the nature of the mind?

8. Define *phrenology*. Who was responsible for starting phrenology, and what effects has it had on psychology?

9. What did Kant mean by an *a priori* category of thought? According to Kant, how do such categories influence what we experience consciously?

10. What did Kant mean by *categorical imperative*?

11. How did Herbart's concept of the idea differ from those of the empiricists?

12. Discuss Herbart's notion of the apperceptive mass. For example, how does the apperceptive mass determine which ideas are experienced consciously and which are not? Include in your answer Herbart's concept of the limen or threshold.

13. How did Herbart apply his theory to educational practices?

14. Discuss Hegel's notion of "the absolute idea." Describe the dialectic process by which Hegel felt the absolute idea was approximated.

15. Give examples of how rationalistic philosophy has influenced modern psychology.

16. Do you find yourself leaning toward either the empiricist or rationalist camp? Summarize your position and why you hold it.

GLOSSARY

Active mind A mind equipped with genetically determined categories or operations that are used to analyze, organize, or modify sensory information. The rationalists postulated such a mind.

Apperception A conscious experience.

Apperceptive mass According to Herbart, the cluster of interrelated ideas that we are conscious of at any given moment.

Categorical imperative According to Kant, the moral directive that we should always act in such a way that our actions could be used as a basis for everyone else's actions.

Common Sense School of Thought The position, first proposed by Reid, that we can assume the existence of the physical world and of human reasoning powers because it makes common sense to do so.

Dialectic process The process involving an original idea, the negation of the original idea, and a synthesis of the new idea and its negation. The synthesis then becomes the starting point (the idea) of the next cycle of the developmental process.

Faculty psychology The belief that the mind consists of several powers or faculties.

Gall, Franz Joseph (1758–1828) Believed that the strengths of mental faculties varied from person to person and that they could be determined by examining the bumps and depressions on a person's skull. Such an examination came to be called phrenology.

Hegel, Georg Wilhelm Friedrich (1770–1831) Like Spinoza, believed the universe to be an interrelated unity. Hegel called this unity "the absolute idea," and he thought that human history and the human intellect progressed via the dialectic process.

Herbart, Johann Friedrich (1776–1841) Likened ideas to Leibniz's monads by saying that they had energy and a consciousness of their own. Also, according to Herbart, ideas strive for consciousness. Those ideas compatible with a person's apperceptive mass are given conscious expression, while those that are not remain below the limen in the unconscious mind. Herbart is considered to be the first mathematical and educational psychologist.

Kant, Immanuel (1724–1804) Believed that there were several innate categories of thought through which sensory information was filtered before it was experienced consciously.

Leibniz, Gottfried Wilhelm von (1646–1716) Felt that the universe consisted of indivisible units of experience called monads. God had created the arrangement of the monads, and therefore this was the best of all possible worlds. If only a few minute monads were experienced, a petites perception resulted, which was unconscious. If enough minute monads were experienced at the same time, apperception occurred, which was a conscious experience.

Limen (threshold) For Leibniz and Herbart, the border between the conscious and the unconscious mind.

Malebranche, Nicolas de (1638–1715) Contended that the mind and body were separate but that God coordinated their activities.

Monad According to Leibniz, an indivisible unit of experience.

Occasionalism The belief that bodily events and mental events are coordinated by God's intervention.

Passive mind A mind whose contents are determined by experience. It contains a few mechanistic principles that organize, store, and generalize sensory experiences. The British empiricists postulated such a mind.

Petites perception According to Leibniz, a perception that occurs below the level of awareness because only one or a few minute monads are involved.

Phrenology The examination of the bumps and depressions on the skull in order to determine the strengths of various mental faculties.

Preestablished harmony Leibniz's contention that God had created the monads comprising the universe in such a way that there was a continuous harmony among them. This explained why mental and bodily events were coordinated.

Psychophysical double-aspectism (also called **double-aspect monism**) The contention that bodily events and mental events reflect two aspects of the same basic reality.

Rationalist Anyone who accepts a philosophy that postulates an active mind, a mind that must act upon sensory information in some way before valid knowledge can be attained.

Reid, Thomas (1710–1796) Thought that the empiricists had degraded humans by ques-

tioning their ability to know the physical world and by attempting to explain mental processes physiologically. Reid said that we could trust our impressions of the physical world because it made common sense to do so. He also postulated an active mind containing several faculties.

Spinoza, Baruch (1632–1677) Equated God with nature and said that nature was an interrelated unity. Spinoza believed that bodily processes and mental processes reflected two aspects of the same basic reality. This position is called psychophysical double-aspectism.

CHAPTER 7

Romanticism and Existentialism

ROMANTICISM

Not everyone believed that the truth was to be found by exercising the intellect, as the rationalists maintained, or by examining the ideas derived from experience, as the empiricists maintained. There were those who insisted that both rationalism and empiricism were overlooking the truest source of valid information— human nature itself. Humans, they said, have not only an intellect and ideas derived from experience, but feelings or emotions as well. Those emphasizing the importance of human feelings were called **romantics**. They believed that rational thought had often led humans astray in their search for valid information, and that empiricism reduced people to unfeeling machines. According to the romanticists, the best way to find out what humans were really like was to study the *total* person, not just his or her rational powers or empirically determined ideas.

The rational, empirical, and material philosophers of the Enlightenment had attempted to create political systems based on their philosophies, and they had failed. According to the romantics, these philosophers had failed because they viewed humans as victims of experience or vehicles by which some grandiose rational principle was manifested. During the romantic movement, between the late 1700s and the middle of the 1800s, there was great emphasis on human emotions, instincts, and uniqueness. The good life was defined as one lived honestly in accordance with one's inner nature. The great philosophical systems were no longer to be trusted, and in general science was seen as antithetical—or at best irrelevant— to understanding humans. The inner world of humans replaced the outer world as the focus of philosophical concern. Coan (1977) summarizes the romantic movement:

> The romantics exalted the emotions and the senses over reason and the intellect, and they had a higher regard for the creative artist than for the scientific thinker. With this movement there was a stress on imagination and fantasy, on religious mysticism, on symbolism, and on beauty in nature and art. (p. 38)

In addition to a disenchantment with rationalism, empiricism, materialism, and positivism, there were other reasons for the romantic movement. According to Alexander and Selesnick (1966):

> In European politics, after the fall of Napoleon, internal affairs took precedence over great international conquests and rivalries. Led by the Austrian statesman Prince Metternich (1773–1859), the guiding spirit of the reactionary movement, Germany, Russia, and France, with the consent and tacit cooperation of England, agreed at the Congress of Vienna (1814–1815) to restore absolutism, order, and religion. The rulers of these countries saw enemies not in each other but in their own peoples, who had been aroused by the slogans of the revolution and who resisted becoming "subjects" again. The ruling class fought this internal foe by suppression. The police state, Metternich's masterwork of political suppression, appeared. Informers and secret agents lurked everywhere. Politicial action was replaced by words and loud but ineffective songs about freedom and the death of tyrants. Most men, however, withdrew to their own homes and sought hap-

Jean Jacques Rousseau

THE BETTMANN ARCHIVE, INC.

piness in the small events of daily life. . . . Interest in personal destiny replaced grandiose participation in public events and revolutionary action to reform the world. Consequently the experiences of everyday life were invested with an exaggerated emotional content so that love affairs, passionate involvements, friendships, and personal intrigues became all-important. The world citizen of the eighteenth century, actively bent on creating a new society according to the abstract universal principles of reason, was succeeded by the petty bourgeois content to creep into the secluded corner of his own small world.

In this kind of social atmosphere interest in psychology, history, and idealistic philosophy flourish, for the mind turned selfward has to become aware of the depths of the inner life. (p. 134)

Thus, people were disenchanted not only with philosophy but with the political systems that had been based upon philosophical systems. Once again in history the time was right for turning away from the external world and toward one's subjective experiences. Rousseau is usually thought of as the father of romanticism, and to his philosophy we turn next.

Jean Jacques Rousseau

Jean Jacques Rousseau (1712–1778) was born in Geneva, and his mother died giving him birth—something for which his father never forgave him. Rousseau suffered from poor health all his life, and in his early years he moved from place to place and from job to job. Arriving in Paris at the age of 30, he joined a group of influential Parisian intellectuals, though he himself had had no formal education. Rousseau was an intensely private person and did not like the social life of the city. In 1756 he left Paris for the quiet of the country. But in 1762, publication of his two most famous works, *The Social Contract* and *Emile*, ended Rousseau's tranquil country life. Within a month of the publication of these two books, the city of Paris condemned him and his hometown of Geneva issued a warrant for his arrest. He was forced to spend the next four years as a refugee. Finally, in 1766, David Hume offered Rousseau refuge in England. Eventually, the opposition to Rousseau's ideas faded and Rousseau returned to Paris, where he remained until his death.

Feelings versus reason. Rousseau began *The Social Contract* (1762) with the statement "Man is born free and yet we see him everywhere in chains." His point was that all governments in Europe at the time were based upon a faulty assumption about human nature—the assumption that humans needed to be governed. The only justifiable government, according to Rousseau, was one that allowed humans to reach their full potential and to fully express their free will. The best guide for human conduct was a person's honest feelings and inclinations. "The first impulses of the heart," he said, "are always right." Rousseau distrusted reason, organized religion, science, and societal laws as guides for human conduct. His philosophy became a defense for Protestantism because it supported the notion that God's existence could be defended on the basis of individual feeling and did not depend on the dictates of the church:

> Rousseau's defence of the feelings as against reason has been one of the powerful influences in the shaping of the romantic movement. Amongst other things it has set Protestant theology on a new path that sharply differentiates it from the [Catholic] doctrine, which is in the philosophic tradition of the ancients. The new Protestant approach dispenses with proofs for the existence of God, and allows that such information wells up from the heart unaided by reason. Likewise, in ethics Rousseau contends that our natural feelings point in the right direction, whereas reason leads us astray. (Russell, 1959, p. 237)

The noble savage. Looking at natural impulses to understand humans was not new with Rousseau; we saw in Chapter 5 that Hobbes did the same thing. The major difference between Hobbes and Rousseau is the conclusion they reached about the nature of human nature. For Hobbes, human nature was animalistic, selfish, and needed to be controlled by government—a view of human nature that was also accepted by the many theologians and philosophers who said that reason had to constantly control the brutish human impulses. Rousseau completely disagreed, saying that humans were born basically good.

He claimed that if a **noble savage** could be found (that is, a human not contaminated by society), we would have a human whose behavior was governed by feelings but who would not be selfish. Rousseau believed that humans were, by nature, social animals who wished to live with other humans in harmony. If humans were permitted to develop freely, they would become happy, fulfilled, free, and socially minded. They would do what was best for themselves

and for others if simply given the freedom to do so. Rousseau's writing strongly influenced leaders of both the French and American revolutions.

Education. Education, according to Rousseau, should not consist of pouring information into children in a highly structured school. Rather, education should create a situation in which a child's natural abilities and interests could be nurtured. For Rousseau, the child naturally had a rich array of positive instincts, and the best education was one that allowed these impulses to become actualized.

In his famous book *Emile* (1762), Rousseau describes what he considers the optimal setting for education. A child and his tutor leave civilization and return to nature, and in this setting the child is free to follow his own talents and curiosities. The tutor responds to the child's questions rather than trying to impose his views on the child. As the child matures, abilities and interests change, and thus what constitutes a meaningful educational experience changes. It is always the child's natural abilities and interests, however, that guide the educational process. The current interest in "free" or "open" schools can be traced back directly to Rousseau's philosophy, as can the movement to "deschool" society. Rousseau's philosophy also appears in the modern self-actualization theories of Maslow and Rogers.

Johann Wolfgang von Goethe

A poet, a dramatist, a scientist, and a philosopher, **Johann Wolfgang von Goethe** (1749–1832) was one of the most revered individuals in the intellectual life of Germany in the late eighteenth and early nineteenth centuries. Goethe is usually thought of as the initiator of the "storm and stress" period in literature. In his literary works and in his philosophy, he viewed humans as being torn by the stresses and conflicts of life. Life, he felt, consisted of opposing forces such as love and hate, life and death, and good and evil. The goal of life should be to embrace these forces rather than to deny or overcome them. One should live life with a passion and aspire continuously for personal growth. Even the "darker" aspects of human nature could provide stimulation for personal expansion. The idea of being transformed from one kind of being (unfulfilled) into another kind (fulfilled) was common within the romantic movement.

In 1774 Goethe wrote *The Sorrows of Young Werther*, a novella about a young man who has love problems. So vividly are these problems portrayed that the book resulted in an epidemic of suicides. In 1808 Goethe published *Faust*, considered one of the greatest literary works of all time. As *Faust* begins, old Dr. Faust is filled with despair and is contemplating suicide. The Devil appears and makes a deal with him: in exchange for Faust's soul, the Devil will transform the old man into a radiant and handsome youth. The young Faust then begins his search for a source of happiness so great that he would choose to experience it forever. Faust finally bids time to stand still when he encounters people allowed to express their individual freedom. He sees that human liberty is the ultimate source of happiness.

Although most of the romantics were antiscience, Goethe was not. He wrote a book attempting to refute Newton's theory of color vision and proposing his own theory in its place. It turned out that Goethe's theory was incorrect, but his methodology had a major impact on later psychology. Goethe demonstrated that sensory experiences could be studied by introspection. Furthermore, he insisted that intact, meaningful psychological experience should be the object of study, rather than meaningless, isolated sensations. This insistence that whole, meaningful experiences be studied came to be called *phenomenology*. Many years before Darwin, Goethe also proposed a theory of evolution according to which one species of living thing could gradually be transformed into another. Rather than denying the importance of science, Goethe saw science as limited; he believed that many important human attributes were beyond the grasp of the scientific method.

Because of his significant influence on the entire German culture, Goethe has had many influences on the development of psychology. One famous psychologist whom Goethe's writings influenced directly was Carl Jung, later a colleague of Freud:

> In my youth (around 1890) I was unconsciously caught up by this spirit of the age, and had no methods at hand of extricating myself from it. *Faust* struck a cord in me and pierced me through in a way that I could not but regard as personal. Most of all, it awakened in me the problems of opposites, of good and evil, of mind and matter, of light and darkness. (Jung, 1963, p. 235)

Goethe's writings also influenced Freud. Both Jung's and Freud's theories emphasize the conflicting forces operating in one's life, and both theories focus on conflict, frustration, and perpetual struggle between animal impulses and civilized behavior. Also, both Freud and Jung maintained that animalistic urges were not to be eliminated but harnessed and used to enhance personal growth. All of these ideas appear in Goethe's writings.

Arthur Schopenhauer

An important German philosopher, **Arthur Schopenhauer** (1788–1860) was influenced by Kant and by ancient philosophies from India and Persia. For Schopenhauer, the fundamental impulse in human existence was the will to survive. This will causes humans to experience an unending cycle of needs and need satisfaction. It is this overwhelming drive toward self-preservation that accounts for most human behavior, not the intellect and not morality. Most human behavior, then, is irrational. Because Schopenhauer believed that human behavior reflected relentless, irrational striving instead of enlightened rationality, his philosophy has been characterized as pessimistic. "In the heart of every man," Schopenhauer said, "there lives a wild beast." The primitive, unconscious will to survival is the ultimate cause of everything we say, do, or think. Like the other romantics, Schopenhauer saw the intellect as secondary to human feelings, impulses, and strivings. Insofar as we seek knowledge and rationality, we enter into conflict with our true irrational nature.

Because its purpose is to perpetuate the human species but not necessarily the individual, the will to live can sometimes cause problems for individuals. This is why, according to Schopenhauer, even a person suffering from a painful terminal disease finds it very difficult to take his or her life, even when this might be the rational thing to do. Likewise, the animalistic impulses related to survival can, and often do, conflict with the societal circumstances in which a person finds himself or herself. Individuality is lost in the needs whose satisfaction allows survival of the species.

Even though these powerful, irrational forces are a natural part of human existence, humans can and should rise above them. With great effort, humans are capable of approaching nirvana, a state characterized by freedom from irrational strivings. Schopenhauer anticipated Freud's concept of sublimation when he said that some relief or escape from the irrational forces within us could be attained by immersing ourselves in music, poetry, or art. Also, one could attempt to counteract these irrational forces, especially the sex drive, by living a life of asceticism.

Schopenhauer also spoke of repressing undesirable thoughts into the unconscious and of the resistance encountered when attempting to recognize repressed ideas. Freud (1938, p. 939) credited Schopenhauer as being the first to discover these processes, but Freud claimed that he himself had discovered the same processes independently of Schopenhauer.

In Freud's theory we see much of Schopenhauer's philosophy. In addition to the ideas of

Friedrich Nietzsche

repression and sublimation, Freud shared Schopenhauer's belief that irrational forces were the prime motivators of human behavior and that the best we could do was minimize their influence. Both men were therefore pessimistic.

Friedrich Nietzsche

Like Schopenhauer, **Friedrich Nietzsche** (1844–1900) believed that humans were basically irrational. Unlike Schopenhauer, however, Nietzsche felt that the instincts should not be repressed or sublimated but should be given full expression. Even aggressive tendencies should not be inhibited. For Nietzsche, the main motive for human behavior was the **will to power**. This motive can be fully satisfied if a person acts as he or she feels—that is, acts in such a way as to fully satisfy all of the instincts. In *The Antichrist* (1895), Nietzsche says:

Life itself appears to me as an instinct for growth, for survival, for the accumulation of forces, for power: whenever the will to power fails there is disaster. (No. 6)

The will to power is the tendency to gain mastery over one's self and one's destiny. If given expression, the will to power causes a person to seek new experiences and to ultimately reach his or her full potential. Such individual growth cannot be inhibited by conventional morality, and thus must go "beyond good and evil." People reaching their full potential are "supermen" because standard morality does not govern their lives. Instead, they rise above such morality and live independent, creative lives.

Although Nietzsche's views changed over time, the position most often attributed to him is the one portrayed in *Thus Spake Zarathustra* (1893) and *Beyond Good and Evil* (1886). In general, Nietzsche felt that religious notions were delusions, and that accepting them was a regression to childhood. And science was not much better. Nietzsche saw both science and Christianity as ways of restricting full human experience, and he thought that the only way to live a full life was to affirm one's nature fully and deny nothing.

Thus, both Schopenhauer and Nietzsche believed that irrational instincts strongly influenced human behavior. But while Schopenhauer believed that such instincts should be repressed, Nietzsche felt that they should be expressed. Freud was influenced most by Schopenhauer, whereas one of Freud's early followers, Alfred Adler, was influenced more by Nietzsche.

Like the other romantics, both Nietzsche and Schopenhauer stressed the irrational (emotional) side of human nature, both believing that science had neglected this aspect of human nature. This was also the belief of Sören Kierkegaard, the founder of existential philosophy:

Both Schopenhauer and Nietzsche recognized that one limitation of natural science is that it

offers no access to a most essential principle of life, the irrational nature of human existence. Nietzsche considered that modern science alienated man from his self, a view that was shared by the Danish theologian Sören Kierkegaard (1813–1855), the philosophic Godfather of existentialism. Man's one-sided preoccupation with the exploration of the universe, Kierkegaard said, had made him lose contact with what is nearest to him—his own self; only a return to the original ideals of preinstitutionalized Christianity could give back to human existence the meaning that had been stripped from it by science. (Alexander and Selesnick, 1966, p. 169)

We turn next to Kierkegaard's existential philosophy.

EXISTENTIALISM

The romantics were not the only ones who rebelled against rationalism, empiricism, materialism, and positivism. There was another group of philosophers that emphasized the importance of meaning in one's life and one's ability to choose freely from among many possible approaches to life. These philosophers were called **existentialists**, and they stressed freedom of choice and the uniqueness of each individual. For the existentialists, the fact that humans possessed a free will was not necessarily positive. Freedom carried responsibility, since one could not blame the conditions of one's life on God, the environment, or inheritance. Thus freedom led to anxiety. To reduce this anxiety, many individuals attempted to give up their freedom through blind conformity, domination of others, or detachment from the world. For the existentialists, the most important aspects of humans were their personal, subjective interpretations of life and the choices they made in light of those interpretations. Like the romanticists, the existentialists saw inner experience and feeling as the only valid guide for one's behavior. One of the earliest existential philosophers was Sören Kierkegaard.

Sören Kierkegaard

A Danish theologian and philosopher, **Sören Kierkegaard** (1813–1855) is generally considered the first existentialist, although Nietzsche developed similar ideas at about the same time and independently of Kierkegaard. Kierkegaard's ideas received little attention in his lifetime. He was ridiculed by other philosophers, the public press, and by his fellow townspeople, who considered him eccentric. As a student, Kierkegaard rejected Christianity and was a devout follower of Hegel. Later, the situation was reversed when he rejected Hegel and embraced Christianity. The Christianity that Kierkegaard accepted, however, was not that of the institutionalized church. He was an outspoken critic of the established church for its worldliness and its insistence on the acceptance of prescribed dogma. He said that the most meaningful relationship with God was a purely personal one that was arrived at through an individual's free choice, not one whose nature and content were dictated by the church.

Authentic and inauthentic lives. Kierkegaard was concerned that too many Christians were praying reflexively and accepting religious dogma without really understanding it. More generally, he saw little correspondence between what people actually thought or felt and what they did or said. According to Kierkegaard, such individuals were experiencing *self-alienation*. Self-alienated individuals have lost touch with their true feelings and therefore live *inauthentic lives*. The self-alienated individual's life is guided by culture, dogma, or the desires of other individuals instead of by what is subjectively true for him or her. An **inauthentic life** is characterized by guilt, dread, and despair—feelings that only a life of commitment growing out of one's true feelings and perceptions can minimize. To live an **authentic life** means accepting full responsibility for one's life. Thus humans are in a very difficult situation; either a

Sören Kierkegaard

person is authentic (that is, he or she is totally responsible for his or her life whether it is pleasant or unpleasant), or a person fails to exercise his or her freedom and becomes self-alienated, and therefore experiences guilt, dread, and despair. Such a choice characterizes human existence.

Kierkegaard rejected Hegel's philosophy because he felt that it placed too much emphasis on the logical and the rational and not enough on the irrational and feeling side of human nature. For the same reason, Kierkegaard rejected science as too mechanistic: he thought it prevented us from viewing humans as emotional and choosing beings. The ultimate state of being for Kierkegaard was arrived at when the individual decided to embrace God and take God's existence on faith, without needing a logical, rational, or scientific explanation of why or how the decision was arrived at.

For Kierkegaard, self-awareness, freedom of choice, self-realization, and the concept of God were all closely linked. To be self-aware involves the realization that one is free to choose among many alternatives in life. The more self-aware people are, the more aware they are of their possibilities in living. Only after one accepts his or her freedom, and the many possibilities for life that such freedom provides, can one enter into a personal relationship with God.

Anxiety and guilt. The realization of personal freedom, however, necessitates the experience of anxiety. Choice carries with it the possibility of being wrong, or at least the necessity of change; and being wrong or changing both carry with them uncertainty and therefore anxiety. Freedom, then, is not pleasant, and accepting it and acting upon it take personal courage. Since the road to self-awareness and growth necessarily involves anxiety, many people deny their true natures. But such an escape—not exercising one's freedom—causes *guilt*. The dilemma that humans are in, therefore, is to accept and act upon their freedom and thus experience anxiety, or to deny their freedom and thus experience guilt. According to Kierkegaard, there is a constant conflict between anxiety and guilt.

People use a variety of strategies to avoid the anxiety that comes from acceptance of human freedom. One is to believe that one's destiny is governed by fate and that one has no control over it. A second strategy is what Kierkegaard called "shutupness," which is living a withdrawn, isolated life and thereby reducing drastically the number of choices available. Third, one can accept rigid, narrow, dogmatic beliefs and use them as a guide for making one's choices. Each of these strategies denies true human nature, therefore causing guilt and preventing the actualization of human potential. For Kierkegaard, the only honest way to deal with anxiety and guilt is to recognize them as the inevitable consequences of personal growth and to confront them as such. When this is done, one will have as his or her *goal* the attainment of full freedom and will accept the associated anxiety; but since one can never reach this goal, one will necessarily experience a certain amount of guilt.

Approximation of personal freedom. Kierkegaard said that the approximation of full personal freedom occurred in stages. The first is the **aesthetic stage**. At this stage, people are open to experience, and they seek out many forms of pleasure and excitement. But they do not recognize their ability to choose. People operating at this level are either hedonistic or intellectual, and such an existence ultimately leads to boredom and despair. The second stage is the **ethical stage**. People operating at this level accept the responsibility of making choices but use as their guide ethical principles established by others—for example, church dogma. Although Kierkegaard considered the ethical level higher than the aesthetic level, people operating on the ethical level were still not recognizing and acting upon their full personal freedom. Kierkegaard referred to the highest level of existence as the **religious stage**. At this stage, people recognize and accept their freedom and enter into a personal relationship with God. The nature of this relationship is not determined by convention or by generally accepted moral laws, but by the nature of God and by one's self-awareness. A person existing on this level sees possibilities in life that often run contrary to what is generally accepted, and therefore tends to be a nonconformist.

Kierkegaard and Nietzsche

Nietzsche was apparently unaware of Kierkegaard's work, yet he developed ideas that were in many ways similar to Kierkegaard's. Like Kierkegaard, Nietzsche rejected what was conventionally accepted, such as the organized church and science. For both men, Hegelian philosophy was a favorite target, and both men preached reliance on direct personal experience. The major difference between the two was that Kierkegaard accepted the existence of God, whereas for Nietzsche God did not exist. Like Kierkegaard, Nietzsche tended to alienate others; and he experienced severe emotional turmoil, which in his later years led finally to psychosis.

Today romanticism and existentialism have combined to form the third force movement in psychology, which the theories of Adler, Allport, May, Maslow, and Rogers exemplify. In Chapter 17 we will explore third force psychology in greater detail.

SUMMARY

The philosophies of empiricism, materialism, positivism, and rationalism pictured humans as complex machines, products of experience, or highly rational beings operating in accordance with lofty, abstract principles. In the opinion of some, however, these philosophies all left something important out of their analyses—the irrational or emotional aspect of humans. Those stressing the importance of human irrationality were called romantics. In general, the romantics emphasized inner, personal experience and distrusted science and the philosophers who pictured humans as products of experience, as machines, or as totally rational beings.

Rousseau is usually considered the father of romanticism. He believed that the best society was one that allowed humans to act in accordance with their own natures. People, he said, are basically good and will do what is best for themselves and for other people if given the freedom to do so. Education should take into consideration a child's natural curiosity rather than attempting to mold a child as if he or she were a lump of clay or a blank tablet. Goethe, who was a scientist, poet, and philosopher, viewed life as consisting of choices between conflicting forces (for example, good and evil, and love and hate). He felt that the best life was one lived with passion, one that resulted in self-expansion. And he felt that the physical sciences, although they were effective in providing useful information about the physical world, were of limited value when it came to understanding people.

According to Schopenhauer, humans experience a constant conflict between their irrational and rational sides. The most powerful motive for human activity is the will for survival, but since this will is for the survival of the entire species, it sometimes causes problems when manifested in the life of an individual. Irrational desires can be sublimated into such rational pursuits as music, art, and poetry. Also, the rational mind can repress irrational thoughts and hold them in the unconscious mind. For Schopenhauer, irrationality is something rationality must inhibit. Nietzsche agreed with Schopenhauer that many human desires are irrational but disagreed with him that they should be repressed or sublimated. For Nietzsche, the basic human motive is the will to power, which is satisfied when a person acts as he or she feels. Acting upon irrational instincts causes a person to have new experiences, and thus to develop greater potential as a person. According to Nietzsche, science, religion, rationalism, and empiricism stifle irrationality and thereby inhibit human development.

Another reaction against empiricism and rationalism was existentialism. The existentialist stressed freedom of choice, subjective experience, personal responsibility, and the uniqueness of the individual. Kierkegaard is generally considered the first existential philosopher. According to Kierkegaard, the only authentic life is one lived in accordance with one's true feelings. One cannot live an authentic life while conforming to someone else's values. Freedom to choose creates uncertainty, which in turn creates anxiety. To grow as an individual, one must make choices, and therefore one must experience anxiety. On the other hand, the person who does not exercise his or her freedom will experience guilt. Life, then, is a constant struggle between anxiety and guilt.

The influence of the romantic movement in modern psychology appears mainly in psychoanalysis, and most currently in such existential/humanistic theories as those of Rogers, Maslow, and May.

DISCUSSION QUESTIONS

1. What was romanticism a reaction against? Discuss the major features of the romantic movement.

2. What assumptions did Rousseau make about human nature? For Rousseau, what was the best kind of society? Educational system?

3. What did Rousseau mean by his statement "Man is born free yet we see him everywhere in chains"?

4. What did Rousseau and Hobbes have in common? Over what did they disagree?

5. How did Goethe view life? What was his attitude toward science?

6. How did Schopenhauer feel that the irrational side of humans should be dealt with? Give examples.

7. How did Nietzsche feel that the irrational side of humans should be dealt with? On what did Schopenhauer and Nietzsche agree?

8. What did Nietzsche mean by *the will to power*?

9. Define *existentialism*. What is meant by the statement "Freedom causes anxiety"?

10. What do existentialism and romanticism have in common?

11. What was Kierkegaard's attitude toward religion?

12. For Kierkegaard, what was the difference between an authentic and an inauthentic life?

13. What did Kierkegaard mean when he said life involved choosing between anxiety and guilt?

14. Describe what Kierkegaard referred to as the three stages toward full personal freedom.

15. Give a few examples of those who represent romanticism and existentialism in modern psychology.

GLOSSARY

Aesthetic stage According to Kierkegaard, the first stage in the growth toward full personal freedom. At this stage, the person delights in many experiences but does not exercise his or her freedom.

Authentic life According to Kierkegaard, a life that is freely chosen and lived in accordance with one's true feelings.

Ethical stage According to Kierkegaard, the second stage in the growth toward full personal freedom. At this stage, the person makes ethical decisions but uses principles developed by others as a guide in making them.

Existentialist One who believes that humans are free to choose their own destinies. Like the romantics, the existentialists stress the importance of inner experience and are anti-science.

Goethe, Johann Wolfgang von (1749–1832) Believed that life was characterized by choices

between opposing forces, and that much about humans was forever beyond the grasp of science.

Inauthentic life According to Kierkegaard, a life that is lived in accordance with values formulated by others and is therefore not freely chosen.

Kierkegaard, Sören (1813–1855) Considered the father of existentialism. He believed that humans were what they chose to be and that exercising one's free will caused anxiety, but that not exercising it caused guilt.

Nietzsche, Friedrich (1844–1900) Believed that humans had powerful irrational instincts and that, in order for humans to reach their full potential, these instincts must be given full expression.

Noble savage Rousseau's term for a human not contaminated by society. Such a person would live in accordance with his or her true feelings, would not be selfish, and would live harmoniously with other humans.

Religious stage According to Kierkegaard, the third stage in the growth toward full personal freedom. At this stage, the person recognizes his or her freedom and enters into a personal relationship with God.

Romantic An individual who stresses the uniqueness of each person and who values emotional experience much more than rationality. According to the romantic, people can, and should, trust their own natural impulses.

Rousseau, Jean Jacques (1712–1778) Considered the father of the romantic movement. Rousseau believed that human nature was basically good, and that the best society and educational system allowed humans to be free to express themselves.

Schopenhauer, Arthur (1788–1860) Believed that humans had powerful irrational instincts that must be repressed or sublimated by the rational mind.

Will to power Nietzsche's term for the desire to reach one's full potential by giving full expression to both rational and irrational impulses.

CHAPTER 8

Early Developments in Physiology and the Rise of Experimental Psychology

Scientific achievements of the eighteenth century allowed ancient philosophical questions to be examined in new, more precise ways. Much had been learned about the physical world and it was now time to direct scientific method toward the study of the mechanisms by which we come to know the physical world. Basically, the question was, "By what mechanisms do empirical events come to be represented in consciousness?" Everything from sense reception to motor reactions was studied intensely, and this study eventually gave birth to experimental psychology. If one is interested in discovering the origins of psychology, one needs to go back to the early Greeks. If, however, one is interested in the origins of *experimental* psychology, one must look to early developments in physiology, anatomy, neurology, and even astronomy.

INDIVIDUAL DIFFERENCES

It was astronomers who first realized that the kind of knowledge human physiology provided might be useful to all sciences. In 1795, the astronomer Nevil Maskelyne and his assistant David Kinnebrook were setting ships' clocks according to when a particular star crossed a hairline in a telescope. Maskelyne noticed that Kinnebrook's observations were .8 second slower than his, and he relieved Kinnebrook of his duty. Twenty years later, the incident came to the attention of the German astronomer Friedrich Bessel (1784–1846), who speculated that the error had not been due to incompetence but

to *individual differences* among observers. Bessel set out to compare his observations with those of his colleagues, and indeed found systematic differences among them. This was the first **reaction time** study, and it was used to correct differences among observers. This was done by calculating **personal equations**. For example, if .8 second was added to Kinnebrook's reaction time, his observations could be equated with Maskelyne's. Bessel found systematic differences among individuals and a way to compensate for those differences, but his findings did not have much of an impact on the early development of experimental psychology. As we shall see, the early experimental psychologists were interested in learning what was true about human consciousness in *general*; therefore, when individual differences were found among experimental subjects, those differences were generally attributed to sloppy methodology. Later in psychology's history (after Darwin), a study of individual differences was to be of supreme importance.

Bessel did, however, show that the observer influenced observations; and since all of science was based upon human observation, it was now necessary to learn more about the processes that converted physical stimulation into conscious experience.

THE BELL-MAGENDIE LAW

Charles Bell (1774–1842) found that when nerves on the back (dorsal) side of the spinal cord were destroyed, an animal became insen-

THE BETTMANN ARCHIVE, INC.

Johannes Müller

sitive to environmental stimulation. Working independently of Bell, **Francois Magendie** (1783–1855) destroyed the nerves on the front (ventral) side of the spinal cord and found that animals lost their ability to *respond* to stimulation, though they could still detect it. For an animal with its ventral nerves destroyed, a painful stimulus elicits cries of pain, but the animal is incapable of withdrawing its limb from the source of pain. Bell and Magendie had shown that the dorsal nerves of the spinal cord carry sensory information to the brain and that the ventral nerves carry impulses from the brain to the muscles. Thus, the distinction between sensory nerves and motor nerves, which both Galen (131–200) and Descartes (1596–1650) had earlier suggested, had been confirmed experi-

mentally. The distinction between sensory and motor nerves came to be known as the **Bell-Magendie Law**.

Often in history an important discovery is made at the wrong time and is ignored, thus showing the importance of the Zeitgeist. Wertheimer (1979) offers the Bell-Magendie Law as an example:

> This discovery [the Bell-Magendie Law] was hailed as very significant, since it showed that specific mental functions are mediated by different anatomical structures. It incidentally also serves to reemphasize the vagaries of history: the same fact had already been pointed out by Eristratus of Alexandria, about 300 B.C., and was reiterated by the great physician Galen during the second century A.D. (who, incidentally, disagreed with Aristotle about the locus of the mind: Aristotle placed it in the heart, Galen in the brain). It is curious that the same "important fact" has to be rediscovered periodically. (p. 25)

THE DOCTRINE OF SPECIFIC NERVE ENERGIES

The Bell-Magendie Law indicated that nerves were neither hollow tubes transmitting animal spirits to and from the brain nor general mechanisms performing both sensory and motor functions. Bell and Magendie had verified two different kinds of nerves with two different functions. **Johannes Müller** (1801–1858) expanded the Bell-Magendie Law by devising the **doctrine of specific nerve energies**. Müller said that there were five kinds of sensory nerves, each containing a characteristic energy, and that when they were stimulated, a characteristic sensation resulted. In other words, each nerve responded in its own characteristic way *no matter how it was* stimulated. For example, stimulating the eye with light waves, electricity, pressure, or by a blow to the head will all cause visual sensations. DuBois-Reymond, one of Müller's students, went so far as to say that if we could cut and cross the visual and auditory nerves, we would hear with our eyes and see with our ears.

Müller's detailed experimental research put to final rest the old emanation theory of perception, according to which tiny copies of physical objects went through the sensory receptors, along the nerves, and to the brain, causing an image of the object. According to this old view, any sensory nerve could convey any sensory information to the brain.

Although Müller claimed that various nerves contained their own specific energy, he did not think that all the sense organs were equally sensitive to the same stimulus. Rather, each of the five kinds of sense organs was maximally sensitive to a certain kind of stimulation. Müller called this "specific irritability," and it was later referred to as **adequate stimulation**. The eye is most easily stimulated by light waves, the ear by sound waves, the skin by pressure, and so on. The eye can be stimulated by pressure, but pressure is a less adequate stimulus for vision than is a light wave. As we experience the environment, this differential sensitivity of the various senses provides an array of sensations. Müller agonized over the question of whether the characteristics of the nerve itself or the place in the brain where the nerve terminated accounted for specificity. He concluded that the nerve was responsible, but subsequent research proved brain location to be responsible.

The most significant implication of Müller's doctrine for psychology was that the nature of the central nervous system, and not the nature of the physical stimulus, determines our sensations. According to Müller, we are aware not of objects in the physical world but of various sensory impulses. An ardent Kantian, Müller felt that he had found the physiological equivalent of Kant's mental faculties. According to Kant, sensory information is filtered through the mental faculties before it is experienced consciously. For Müller, the nervous system is the intermediary between physical objects and con-

sciousness. Kant's nativism stresses mental categories, whereas Müller's stresses physiological mechanisms. In both cases, sensory information is modified, and therefore what we experience consciously is different from what is physically present.

Müller was one of the greatest experimental physiologists of his time. His *Handbuch der Physiologie der Menschen* (Handbook of Human Physiology, 1833–1840) summarized what was known about human physiology at the time. Müller also established the world's first institute for experimental physiology in Berlin. Most of those destined to become the most prominent physiologists of the nineteenth century studied with Müller, including Helmholtz, to whom we turn next.

HERMANN VON HELMHOLTZ

Many consider **Hermann von Helmholtz** (1821–1894) to be the greatest scientist of the nineteenth century. As we shall see, he made significant contributions in physics, physiology, and psychology. Helmholtz was born on August 31, 1821, in Potsdam, Germany. His father was a teacher who did not have enough money to pay for the scientific training that his son desired. Fortunately, the government had a program by which talented students could go to medical school free if they agreed to serve for eight years as army surgeons following graduation. Helmholtz took advantage of this program and enrolled in the Berlin Royal Friedrich-Wilhelm Institute for Medicine and Surgery when he was 17 years old. While in his second year of medical school, he began his studies with Johannes Müller.

Although Helmholtz accepted many of Müller's conclusions, the two men still had basic disagreements, one of them over Müller's belief in **vitalism**. In biology and physiology, the vitalism-antivitalism problem is much like the

THE BETTMANN ARCHIVE, INC.

Hermann von Helmholtz

or of anything else from the realm of science. Helmholtz sided with the materialists, who believed that the same laws applied to living and nonliving things, as well as to mental and nonmental events. So strongly did Helmholtz and several of his fellow students believe in antivitalism that they signed the following oath (some say in their own blood):

> No other forces than the common physical-chemical ones are active within the organism. In those cases which cannot at the time be explained by these forces one has either to find the specific way or form of their action by means of the physical mathematical method, or to assume new forces equal in dignity to the physical-chemical forces inherent in matter, reducible to the force of attraction and repulsion. (Bernfeld, 1949, p. 171)

Helmholtz obtained his medical degree at the age of 21 and was inducted into the army. While in the army, he was able to build a small laboratory and to continue his early research, which concerned metabolic processes in the frog. Helmholtz demonstrated that food and oxygen consumption were able to account for the total energy that an organism expended. He was thus able to apply the already popular **principle of conservation of energy** to living organisms. According to this principle, which had been previously applied to physical phenomena, energy is never created or lost in a system but is only transformed from one form to another. This principle was later to play an important role in Freud's theory of the mind. When applied to living organisms, the principle was clearly in accordance with the materialist philosophy, since it brought physics, chemistry, and physiology closer together. In 1847 Helmholtz published a paper entitled "The Conservation of Force," and it was so influential that he was released from the remainder of his tour of duty in the army.

In 1848 Helmholtz was appointed lecturer of anatomy at the Academy of Arts in Berlin.

mind-body problem in philosophy and psychology. The vitalists maintained that life could not be explained by the interactions of physical and chemical processes alone. For the vitalists, life was "more than" a physical process and could not be reduced to such a process. Furthermore, because it was not physical, the "life force" was forever beyond the scope of scientific analysis. Müller was a vitalist. The antivitalists, on the other hand, saw nothing mysterious about life and assumed that it could be explained in terms of physical and chemical processes. Therefore, there was no reason to exclude the study of life

The following year, he was appointed professor of physiology at Königsberg, where Kant had spent his entire academic life. It was at Königsberg that Helmholtz conducted his now famous research on the speed of nerve conduction.

The Rate of Nerve Conduction

Helmholtz disagreed with Müller not only over the issue of vitalism but over the supposed speed of nerve conduction. Müller had maintained that nerve conduction was almost instantaneous, making it too fast to measure. His view reflected the ancient belief, still very popular during Müller's time, that there was a vital, nonmaterial agent that moved instantaneously and determined the behavior of living organisms. Many earlier philosophers had believed that the mind or the soul controlled bodily actions, and that since the mind and soul were inspired by God, their effect throughout the entire body was instantaneous. Those believing in either animal, vital spirits or in a nonmaterial mind or soul felt that measuring the speed of nerve conduction was impossible.

Helmholtz, however, excluded nothing from the realm of science, not even the rate of nerve conduction. To measure the rate of nerve conduction, Helmholtz isolated the nerve fiber leading to a frog's leg muscle. He then stimulated the nerve fiber at various distances from the muscle and noted how long it took the muscle to respond. He found that the muscular response followed more quickly when the motor nerve was stimulated closer to the muscle than when it was stimulated farther away from the muscle. By subtracting one reaction time from the other, he was able to conclude that the nerve impulse traveled at a rate of 90 feet per second. Helmholtz then turned to humans, asking his subjects to respond by pushing a button when they felt their leg being stimulated. He found that reaction time was slower when the toe was stimulated than when the thigh was

stimulated; and he concluded, again by subtraction, that the rate of nerve conduction in humans was between 165 and 330 feet per second. This aspect of Helmholtz's research was significant because it showed that nerve impulses were indeed measurable—that in fact they were fairly slow. This was taken as further evidence that physical-chemical processes were involved in our interactions with the environment, instead of some mysterious process that was immune to scientific scrutiny. Helmholtz's finding was to bring psychology even closer to the physical sciences.

Although the measure of reaction time was extremely useful to Helmholtz in measuring the speed of nerve conduction, he found that reaction time varied considerably among subjects and even for the same subject at different times. He concluded that reaction time was too unreliable to be used as a valid measure and abandoned it. Support for his doubts came years later when more precise measurements indicated that the nerve conduction speeds he had reported were too low. But this does not detract from the importance of Helmholtz's pioneering research on the rate of nerve conduction.

Helmholtz's Theory of Perception

Although Helmholtz felt that the physiological apparatus of the body provided the mechanisms for **sensation**, he felt that the past experience of the observer was what converted sensations into **perceptions**. In explaining the transformation of sensations into perceptions, Helmholtz relied heavily on the notion of **unconscious inference**. According to Helmholtz, to label a visual experience a "chair" involves the application of a great deal of previous experience, as does looking at railroad tracks converging in the distance and insisting that they are parallel. Likewise, we see moving pictures as moving because of our prior experience with events that create a series of images across the retina. And we learn from experience that perceived distance is inversely related to the size of the retinal image. For Helmholtz, the perception of depth arises because the retinal image an object causes is slightly different on the two retinas. Previous experience with such retinal disparity causes the unconscious inference of depth. Helmholtz was very reluctant to use the term *unconscious inference*, since it suggested the kind of mysterious process that would violate his oath, but he could not find a better term.

Helmholtz supported his empirical theory of perception with the observation that individuals who were blind at birth and then acquired sight needed to learn to perceive, even though all the sensations furnished by the visual apparatus were available. His classic experiments with lenses that distorted vision provided further evidence. Helmholtz had subjects wear lenses that displaced the visual field several inches to the right or left. At first, the subjects would make mistakes in reaching for objects; but after several minutes *perceptual adaptation* occurred, and even while wearing the glasses, the subjects could again interact accurately with the environment. When the glasses were removed, the subjects again made mistakes for a short time but soon recovered.

One by one, Helmholtz took the supposed innate categories of thought Kant had proposed and showed how they were derived from experience. Concerning the axioms of geometry, which Kant had assumed were innate, Helmholtz said that if our world were arranged differently, our axioms would be very different. Helmholtz and Kant agreed, however, on one important point: the perceiver transforms what the senses provide. For Kant, this transformation was accomplished when sensory information was filtered through the innate faculties of the mind. For Helmholtz, the transformation occurred when sensory information was embellished by an individual's past experience. Kant's account of perception was therefore nativistic, and Helmholtz's was empiricistic. With his notion of unconscious inference, Helmholtz came very close to what would later be considered part of psychology, but he never considered himself a psychologist. He felt that psychology was too closely allied with metaphysics, and he wanted nothing to do with metaphysics.

Helmholtz's Theory of Color Vision

Helmholtz performed his work on vision between 1853 and 1868 at the Universities of Königsburg, Bonn, and Heidelberg, and he published his results in the three-volume *Handbook of Physiological Optics*. Many years before Helmholtz's birth, Thomas Young (1773–1829) had proposed a theory of color vision very similar to Helmholtz's, but Young's theory had not been widely accepted. Helmholtz changed Young's theory slightly and buttressed it with experimental evidence. The theory we present here has come to be called the **Young-Helmholtz theory of color vision** (also called the **trichromatic theory**).

In 1672 Newton had shown that if white sunlight was passed through a prism, it emerged as a band of colored lights with red on one end of the band, then orange, yellow, green, blue, and finally violet. The prism separated the various wavelengths that together were experienced as white. Early speculation was that a different wavelength corresponded to each color, and that different color experiences resulted from experiencing different wavelengths. However, Newton himself saw difficulties with this explanation. By mixing various wavelengths, it became clear to him that the property of color was not in the wavelengths themselves but in the observer. For example, white is experienced either if all the wavelengths of the spectrum are present or if the wavelengths corresponding to the colors red and blue-green are combined. Likewise, a person cannot distinguish the sensation of orange caused by the single wavelength corresponding to orange from the sensation of orange caused by mixing red and yellow. The question was how to account for the lack of correspondence between the physical spectrum and subjective experience.

Helmholtz's answer was to expand Müller's doctrine of specific nerve energies by postulating three different kinds of color receptors on the retina. It was already known that various combinations of three primary colors—red, green, and blue-violet—could produce all other colors. Helmholtz speculated that there were three kinds of color receptors corresponding to the three primary colors. If a red light was shown, the so-called red receptors were stimulated, and one had the sensation of red; if a green light was shown, the green receptors were stimulated, and one had the experience of green, and so on. If all the primaries were shown at once, one experienced white. If the color shown was not a primary color, it would stimulate various combinations of the three receptors, resulting in a subjective color experience corresponding to the combination of wavelengths present. For example, presenting a red and a green light simultaneously would produce the subjective color experience of yellow. Also, the same color experience could be caused by several different patterns of the three receptor systems firing. In this way Helmholtz explained why many physical wavelengths give rise to the same color experience.

The Young-Helmholtz theory of color vision was extremely helpful in explaining many forms of color blindness. For example, if a person lacks one or more of the receptor systems corresponding to one of the primary colors, he or she will not be able to experience certain colors subjectively, even though the physical world has not changed. The senses, therefore, actualize elements of the physical world that otherwise exist only as potential experiences.

Helmholtz was continually amazed at the way physiological mechanisms distorted the information a person received from the physical world, but he was even more amazed at the mismatch between physical events and psychological sensations (for example, the experience of color). He expressed his feelings as follows:

> The inaccuracies and imperfections of the eye as an optical instrument, and the deficiencies of the image on the retina, now appear insignificant in comparison with the incongruities we have met with in the field of sensation. One might almost believe that Nature had here contradicted herself on purpose in order to destroy any dream of a preexisting harmony between the outer and the inner world. (Kahl, 1971, p. 192)

For Helmholtz there was no active mind to compensate for, or add to, sensory information. We are left to do commerce with the world utilizing a sensory system that only partially reflects what is physically out there.

Helmholtz's Theory of Auditory Perception

For audition, as he had done for color vision, Helmholtz further refined Müller's doctrine of specific nerve energies. He found that the ear was not a single sense receptor but a highly complex system of receptors; and he found that when the main membrane of the inner ear, the basilar membrane, was removed and uncoiled, it was shaped much like a harp. Assuming that this membrane was to hearing what the retina was to seeing, Helmholtz speculated that the different fibers along the basilar membrane were sensitive to differences in the frequency of sound waves. The short fibers responded to the higher frequencies, the longer fibers to the lower frequencies. A wave of a certain frequency caused the appropriate fiber of the basilar membrane to vibrate, thus causing the sensation of sound corresponding to that frequency. This process was called *sympathetic vibration*, and it can be demonstrated by stimulating a tuning fork of a certain frequency and noting that the string on a piano corresponding to that frequency also begins to vibrate. Helmholtz assumed that a similar process occurred in the middle ear, and that through various combinations of fiber stimulation one could explain the wide variety of auditory experiences we have. This is often referred to as the **resonance place theory of auditory perception**. Variations of Helmholtz's place theory persist today, but there are still auditory phenomena that no theory can explain.

Helmholtz's Contributions

Helmholtz went a long way in experimentally substantiating the empirical-materialistic conception of the human mind. He showed that nerve transmission was not instantaneous, as had previously been believed, but that it was rather slow and reflected the operation of physical processes. More than anyone before him, Helmholtz showed with experimental rigor the mechanisms by which we do commerce with the physical world, mechanisms that could also be explained in terms of objective physical laws. Although he found that the match between what was there physically and what was experienced psychologically was not very good, he could explain the discrepancy in terms of the properties of the receptor systems and the unconscious inferences of the observer. No mystical, unscientific forces were involved. Helmholtz's work brought physics, chemistry, physiology, and psychology closer together. In so doing, it paved the way for the emergence of experimental psychology, which was in many ways an inevitable step after Helmholtz's work.

Helmholtz realized a lifelong ambition when he was appointed professor of physics at the University of Berlin in 1871. In 1882 the German emperor granted him noble status, and thereafter his name was Hermann *von* Helmholtz. In 1893 Helmholtz came to America to see the Chicago World's Fair and to visit with William James. On his way back to Germany, he fell down aboard ship and broke his hip. Never fully recovering, he died the following year.

EARLY RESEARCH ON BRAIN FUNCTIONING

To review early brain research, we must start by going back to Gall, on whom we commented in Chapter 6. Gall's assumptions about brain functioning have set the course of brain research right up to the present.

Franz Joseph Gall

For reasons that we shall consider shortly, **Franz Joseph Gall** (1758–1828) is usually reviewed negatively in the history of psychology, but Gall made several contributions to the study of brain functioning. For example, he studied the brains of several animal species, including humans, and was the first to suggest a relationship between cortical development and mental functioning. He found that larger, better-developed cortexes were associated with more intelligent behavior. This discovery of the correlation between mind and brain alone qualifies Gall for recognition in the history of psychology.

Like many others at the time, Gall accepted the widely held Kantian belief that faculties of the mind acted upon and transformed sensory information and initiated certain behavior patterns, but he went several steps beyond traditional faculty psychology. First, he assumed that the faculties resided in *specific locations* in the brain. Second, he assumed that humans possessed faculties in different degrees and that these individual differences were innate. Third, he assumed that the bumps and indentations on the surface of the skull could be used to index the magnitude of the underlying faculties. The examination of the shape of the skull in order to determine a person's strong or weak faculties came to be called **phrenology**, a term that Gall rejected but that one of his associates, *Johann Casper Spurzheim* (1776–1832), made popular.

Gall's idea was not a bad one. In fact, Gall was among the first to attempt to relate certain overt behavior patterns to specific brain functions. The problem was with the kind of evidence he would accept as demonstrating this relationship. He would observe that someone had a pronounced personality characteristic and also that he or she had a well-developed brain structure, and then he would attribute the one to the other. After observing such a relationship in one individual, he would generalize it to all individuals.

In their research on the mental faculties, some of Gall's followers even exceeded his shoddiness. As Fancher (1979) says:

> If Gall himself was cavalier in his treatment of evidence, he attracted followers who raised such tendencies almost to an art form. When a cast of the right side of Napoleon's skull indicated a phrenological analysis markedly at variance with the Emperor's known characteristics, the phrenologists unhesitatingly replied that his true personality was reflected on the left side— a cast of which was conveniently missing. When Descartes's skull was examined, it was found to be exceptionally small in the parts associated by phrenology with the rational faculties. The phrenologists retorted that Descartes's rationality had always been overrated. (p. 53)

The scientific community failed to take Gall seriously, so he took his ideas directly to the public through lectures and demonstrations. He was widely accepted among nonscientists and made a considerable amount of money. This is not to say, however, that phrenology had no support among scientists. A journal dedicated to the topic of phrenology was begun in 1823 and continued in publication until 1911, or for 88 years. And phrenology's impact on education has lasted to this day (see Hergenhahn, 1982, pp. 41–42).

Pierre Flourens

It was not enough to claim that the phrenologists were wrong in their assumptions; the claim had to be substantiated scientifically. This was the goal of **Pierre Flourens** (1794–1867), who pioneered the use of extirpation, or ablation, in brain research. His approach was to destroy part of the brain and then note the

behavioral consequences of the loss. Like Gall, Flourens assumed that the brains of lower animals were similar in many ways to human brains, so he used organisms such as dogs and pigeons as his research subjects. He found that removal of the cerebellum disturbed an organism's coordination and equilibrium, that ablation of the cerebrum resulted in passivity, and that destruction of the semicircular canals resulted in loss of balance.

When he had examined the entire brain, Flourens concluded that there was some localization; but contrary to what the phrenologists believed, the cortical hemispheres did not have localized functions. Instead, they functioned as a unit. Seeking futher evidence of the brain's interrelatedness, Flourens observed that animals sometimes regained functions that they had lost following ablation. Thus, at least one part of the brain had the capacity to take over the function of another part. Years later, Karl Lashley would make this same observation. Flourens's fame as a scientist, and his conclusion that the cortex functioned as a unit, effectively silenced the phrenologists. Subsequent research, however, would show that they had been silenced too quickly.

Paul Broca

Using the **clinical method**, **Paul Broca** (1824–1880) cast doubt on Flourens's conclusion that the cortex acted as a whole. Boring (1957) describes Broca's observation:

> Broca's famous observation was in itself very simple. There had in 1831 been admitted at the Bicetre, an insane hospital near Paris, a man whose sole defect seemed to be that he could not talk. He communicated intelligently by signs and was otherwise mentally normal. He remained at the Bicetre for thirty years with this defect and on April 12, 1861, was put under the care of Broca, the surgeon, because of a gangrenous infection. Broca for five days subjected him to a careful examination, in which he satisfied himself that the musculature of the larynx and articulatory organs was not hindered in normal movements, that there was no

other paralysis that could interfere with speech, and that the man was intelligent enough to speak. On April 17 the patient—fortunately, it must have seemed, for science—died; and within a day Broca had performed an autopsy, discovering a lesion in the third frontal convolution of the left cerebral hemisphere, and had presented the brain in alcohol to the Societe d'Anthropologie. (p. 71)

Thus Broca was the first to observe a behavior disorder and then locate the part of the brain causing it. Other speech researchers have implicated the area on the left side of the cortex that Broca found to be damaged, and the area has been named **Broca's area**. The localizing of a function on the cortex supported the phrenologists and damaged Flourens's contention that the cortex acted as a unit. Unfortunately for the phrenologists, however, Broca did not find the speech area to be where the phrenologists had said it would be.

Gustav Fritsch, Edward Hitzig, and David Ferrier

Electrically stimulating the exposed cortex of a dog **Gustav Fritsch** (1838–1927) and **Edward Hitzig** (1838–1907) made two important discoveries. First, the cortex was not insensitive, as had been previously assumed. Second, they found that when a certain area of the cortex was stimulated, muscular movements were elicited from the opposite side of the body. Stimulating different points in this *motor area* of the brain stimulated movements from different parts of the body. Thus, another function was localized on the cortex. **David Ferrier** (1843–1928) found a cortical area corresponding to the skin senses, and later researchers found visual and auditory areas.

Wilder Penfield and Karl Spencer Lashley

Unexpected confirmation of all the preceding studies on localization of cortical function came accidentally from **Wilder Penfield** (1891–

1976). Working at the Montreal Neurological Institute at McGill University, Penfield and his colleagues were seeking surgical treatment for epilepsy. Dealing only with severely epileptic patients who had given their consent, Penfield stimulated all areas of the cortex and noted the results. Stimulation of the motor areas produced involuntary movements on the opposite side of the body; stimulation of the sensory area caused patients to report various sensations, such as tingling or pressure, in various parts of their body; stimulation of the visual area produced lights, colors, flashes, and other visual sensations; and stimulation of the auditory areas produced a variety of sound sensations. In some cases dreamlike states or complex memories were elicited. Penfield (1958) describes the report of a 26-year-old woman who was being stimulated near the temporal region of the cortex:

> Yes, I hear voices. It is late at night, around a carnival somewhere—some sort of traveling circus—I just saw lots of big wagons that they use to haul animals in. (p. 29)

The evidence seemed clear; there was a great deal of localization of function on the cortex, just as the phrenologists had maintained. These findings, however, did not support phrenology. Seldom was a function (faculty) found where the phrenologists had said it was. Furthermore, the phrenologists had spoken of faculties such as vitality, firmness, love, and kindness, but the researchers instead found sensory and motor areas. These findings extended the Bell-Magendie Law to the brain. It looked very much like the brain was a complex switchboard where sensory information was projected and where it in turn stimulated appropriate motor responses. The localization studies seemed to favor the empirical-materialistic view rather than the rationalist view. This switchboard conception of the brain was later to be challenged by the work of such researchers as **Karl Spencer Lashley** (1890–1959), who found *both* localization and *unity* in the cortex. That is, Lashley found that there were specialized areas on the cortex, but that they were related to other areas; and if one area was destroyed, other areas could take over its function. To a large extent, Lashley's view goes back to the viewpoint of Flourens, but Lashley did not deny that there was some localization of function.

By now it was clear that physical stimulation gave rise to some kind of subjective sensation that was somehow housed in the brain. The next step in psychology's evolution toward becoming an experimental science was to examine *scientifically* how sensory stimulation was systematically related to conscious experience.

THE RISE OF EXPERIMENTAL PSYCHOLOGY

The very important difference between what was physically present and what was experienced psychologically had been recognized and agonized over for centuries. This was the distinction that had caused Galileo to conclude that a science of psychology was impossible, and Hume to conclude that we could know nothing with certainty. Kant amplified this distinction when he claimed that the mind embellished sensory experience, and of course Helmholtz reached the same conclusion with his concept of unconscious inference. This is the distinction between primary and secondary qualities, and it is directly related to the ancient mind-body problem.

With advances in science, much had been learned about the physical world—that is, about physical stimulation. Also, as we have seen, much had been learned about the sense receptors that convert physical stimulation into nerve impulses and about the brain structures where those impulses terminate. There was never much doubt about the existence of consciousness; the problem was in determining what we were conscious of and what caused consciousness. By now it was widely believed that conscious sensations were triggered by

Ernst Weber

ARCHIVES OF THE HISTORY OF AMERICAN PSYCHOLOGY

brain processes, which themselves were initiated by sense reception, but the question remained: How are the two domains (mental sensations and the neural processes) related?

Without measurement, science is impossible. Therefore, it was assumed that a science of psychology was impossible unless consciousness could be measured as objectively as the physical world. Furthermore, once measured, mental events would have to be shown to vary in some systematic way with physical events. Ernst Weber and Gustav Theodor Fechner first took this important step.

Ernst Weber

Obtaining his doctorate from the University of Leipzig in 1815, **Ernst Weber** (1795–1878) taught there until his retirement in 1871. Weber was a physiologist who was interested in the senses of touch and kinesthesis (muscle sense).

Weber's work on touch. For the sensation of touch, Weber attempted to determine the least spatial separation at which two points of touch on the body could be discriminated. He did this by simultaneously applying two points of pressure to a subject's skin. The smallest distance between the two points at which the subject reported sensing two points instead of one was called the **two-point threshold**. Weber found the smallest two-point threshold on the tongue (about one millimeter), and the largest in the middle of the back (about 60 millimeters). He assumed that the differences in thresholds at different places on the body resulted from the anatomical arrangement of the sense receptors for touch—the more receptors, the finer the discrimination. Note that Weber was stimulating his subjects *physically* and asking them to report on the *conscious experience* resulting from that stimulation. Furthermore, Weber was seeking, and finding, a *systematic* relationship between the stimulation and the subject's introspective report.

Work on kinesthesis. Even more important than Weber's work on touch was his work on kinesthesis. Weber sought to determine the smallest difference between two weights that could be discriminated. To do this he had his subjects lift one weight (the standard), which remained the same during a series of comparisons, and then lift other weights. The subject was to *report* whether the varying weights were heavier, lighter, or the same as the standard weight. He found that when the variable weights were only slightly different from the standard, they were judged to be the same as the standard. Through a series of such comparisons, Weber was able to determine the **just noticeable difference** (j.n.d.) that the subject could detect between the standard and the variable weight.

Weber was truly amazed to find that the just noticeable difference was a constant fraction of the standard weight, and that fraction was $\frac{1}{40}$. For example, if the standard weight were 40

grams, the variable weight would have to be 41 grams to be judged heavier or 39 grams to be judged lighter than the standard. If the standard weight were 160 grams, the variable weight would have to be 164 grams or 156 grams to be judged heavier or lighter than the standard. This finding—that j.n.d.'s were a constant fraction of the standard weight—was later called **Weber's Law** and can be considered the first quantitative law in psychology's history. *This was the first statement of a systematic relationship between physical stimulation and a psychological experience.* Chaplin and Krawiec (1979) summarize the importance of Weber's work:

> These experiments marked a fundamental shift in the status of psychology. The new science had at last severed its ties with mental philosophy, and the court of last resort for the resolution of psychological issues was no longer philosophical debate but an appeal to empirical investigation. Weber thus allied psychology with the natural sciences and blazed the way for the *experimental* investigation of human behavior. (p. 39)

But since Weber was a physiologist, psychology was not his primary concern. It was Fechner who realized the implications of Weber's work for psychology, and who saw in it the possible resolution of the mind-body problem.

Gustav Theodor Fechner

Gustav Theodor Fechner (1801–1887) was a brilliant, complex, and unusual individual. Following in the Hegelian tradition, Fechner was a spiritualist. He believed that physical objects were only manifestations of a homogeneous spirit, a view not unlike that of the Pythagoreans and Plato. All his life he fought materialism, which he called the "night view"; it contrasted with the "day view," which emphasized mind, spirit, and consciousness. His mysticism can be seen in the titles of several books he wrote under the pen name Dr. Mises—for example, *Concerning the Mental Life of Plants* (1836) and *Zend Avesta, Or Concerning Matters of Heaven and the Hereafter* (1851).

Fechner was the son of a village pastor. At the age of 16 he began his studies in medicine at the University of Leipzig (where Weber was) and obtained his degree in 1822 at the age of 21. For the next ten years Fechner was interested mainly in physics, and at the age of 31 he was appointed professor of physics at Leipzig. About this time he had a "nervous breakdown" and also injured his eyes while looking at the sun through colored glasses. Fechner entered a state of depression that was to last several years and result in his interests turning from physics to philosophy. From his philosophical interest in the relationship between the mind and the body sprang his interest in psychophysics. He wanted desperately to solve the mind-body problem in a way that would satisfy the materialistic scientists of his day. Fechner's mystical philosophy taught him that the physical and the mental were simply two aspects of the same underlying reality. Thus, he accepted the double-aspect monism Spinoza had postulated. But to say that there was a demonstrable relationship between the mind and the body was one thing; proving it was another matter. According to Fechner (see Boring, 1957, pp. 270–280), the solution to the problem occurred to him the morning of October 22, 1850, as he was lying in bed. His insight was that a systematic relationship between bodily and mental experience could be demonstrated if a person were asked to report changes in sensations as a physical stimulus was systematically varied. Fechner speculated that in order for mental sensations to change arithmetically, the physical stimulus would have to change geometrically. In testing these ideas, Fechner created the area of psychology that was later called psychophysics.

Psychophysics. As the name suggests, **psychophysics** is the study of the relationship between physical and psychological events. Fechner's

Gustav Theodor Fechner

first step in studying this relationship was to state mathematically what Weber had found and to label the expression Weber's Law:

$$\frac{\Delta R}{R} = K$$

where:

R = *Reiz* (the German word for "stimulus"). In Weber's research this was the standard stimulus.

ΔR = the minimum change in R that could be detected. That is, ΔR = j.n.d.

K = a constant. As we have seen, Weber found this constant to be $\frac{1}{40}$ of R for kinesthesis.

Weber's Law concerns the amount that a physical stimulus must change before it results in the awareness of a difference or in a change of sensation (S). Through a series of mathematical calculations, Fechner arrived at his famous formula, which he felt showed the relationship between the mental and the physical (the mind and the body):

$$S = K \times \text{Log } R$$

This formula mathematically states Fechner's earlier insight. That is, for the magnitude of a sensation to rise arithmetically, the magnitude of the physical stimulus must rise geometrically. This simply means that as a stimulus gets larger, the magnitude of the change must become greater and greater if the change is to be detected. For example, if the stimulus (R) is 40 grams, a difference of only one gram can be detected, whereas if the stimulus is 200 grams, it takes a difference of 5 grams to cause a j.n.d. Fechner's formula also allows for "negative sensations," sensations that do not exceed the threshold necessary for them to be experienced consciously. Thus it is compatible with the earlier notions of petites perception, threshold of consciousness, and the distinction between the conscious and unconscious mind.

Psychophysical methods. After establishing that mental and physical events varied systematically, and thus showing that a science of the mind was indeed possible (contrary to the beliefs of such individuals as Galileo, Hume, and Kant), Fechner employed several methods in further exploring the mind-body relationship.

1. **The method of limits.** With this method, one stimulus is varied and is compared to a standard. To begin with, the variable stimulus can be equal to the standard and then varied, or it can be much stronger or weaker than the standard. The goal here is to determine the range of stimuli that the subject considers to be equal to the standard.

2. **The method of constant stimuli.** Here pairs of stimuli are presented to the subject.

One member of the pair is the standard and remains the same, and the other varies in magnitude from one presentation to another. The subject reports whether the variable stimulus appears greater than, less than, or the same as the standard.

3. **The method of adjustment.** Here the subject has control over the variable stimulus and is instructed to adjust its magnitude so that the stimulus appears equal to the standard stimulus. After the adjustment, the difference between the variable stimulus and the standard stimulus is measured.

These methods are Fechner's major legacy to psychology, and they are still widely used.

Fechner did not solve the mind-body problem; it is still alive and well in modern psychology. Like Weber, however, he did show that it was possible to measure mental events and relate them to physical ones. Many mark the beginning of experimental psychology with the 1860 publication of Fechner's *Elements of Psychophysics*. This seems reasonable. But another important step had to be taken before psychology could emerge as a full-fledged branch of science: psychology needed to be *founded* as a separate discipline. As we shall see in the next chapter, Wilhelm Wundt took that step.

SUMMARY

The discovery of individual differences among astronomers in the recording of astronomical events demonstrated the need, even within the physical sciences, for understanding how the physical world was sensed and mentally represented. An intense investigation of the human sensory apparatus and nervous system followed. Bell and Magendie discovered that some nerves were specialized to carry sensory information to the brain, while others were specialized to carry sensory information from the brain to the muscles of the body. This distinction between sensory and motor nerves is called the Bell-Magendie Law. Müller found that each sensory nerve was specialized to produce a certain kind of energy, which in turn produced a certain kind of sensation. For example, no matter how the optic nerve is stimulated, it will produce the sensation of light. The same is true for all the other sensory nerves of the body. Müller's finding is called the doctrine of specific nerve energies.

Helmholtz is a monumental figure in the history of science. He opposed the belief in vitalism that his teacher, Müller, and others held. The vitalists maintained that life could not be reduced to physical processes, and therefore could not be investigated scientifically. For Helmholtz, nothing was beyond scientific investigation. He showed that the amount of energy an organism expended was directly proportional to the amount of food and oxygen it consumed, thereby showing that the principle of conservation of energy applied to living organisms as well as to physical phenomena. Ignoring the contention that nerve impulses were too fast to be measured, he measured their speed and found them to be remarkably slow.

Helmholtz also differentiated between sensations and perceptions, the former being the raw images provided by the sense receptors and the latter being the meaning that past experience gave to those raw sensations. Through the process of unconscious inference, the wealth of prior experience we have had with objects and events is brought to bear on current sensations, converting them into perceptions. With his notion of unconscious inference, Helmholtz offered an empirical explanation of perception instead of the nativistic explanation that Kant and others had offered. And he extended the doctrine of specific nerve energies to color vision by saying that specific receptors on the retina corresponded to each of the three primary colors: red, green, and blue-violet. If one of the three receptors was missing or inoperative, the person would be blind to the

color the receptor was sensitive to. For Helmholtz, all experiences of color could be explained as the stimulation of one or a pattern of the three kinds of color receptors. Since Young had earlier proposed a similar theory of color vision, the theory became known as the Young-Helmholtz (or trichromatic) theory of color vision.

Helmholtz also explained auditory perception by applying the doctrine of specific nerve energies. He believed that tiny fibers on the basilar membrane each responded to a different frequency, and that our auditory perception resulted from the combination of the various fibers that were being stimulated at any given time. This is called the resonance place theory of auditory perception. Helmholtz's work clearly indicated that there was a difference between what was present physically and what was experienced psychologically. The reason for this difference is that the sensory equipment of the body is not capable of responding to everything that is physically present. Helmholtz's work moved physiology closer to psychology, and thus paved the way for experimental psychology.

Gall was among the first to study systematically the role of the brain in sensation and perception. He believed that the brain contained various faculties and that these faculties were housed in specific locations on the cortex. Furthermore, the strengths of these faculties varied from person to person. Spurzheim, one of Gall's associates, called the study of the skull in order to determine the strength of a faculty phrenology. Flourens experimentally tested many of Gall's assumptions, and although he found some evidence for localization of function in the lower parts of the brain, he concluded that the cortex itself acted as a whole. Because of Flourens's prestige as a scientist, the scientific community rejected phrenology. Using the clinical method, however, Broca did find evidence for a speech center on the cortex. Furthermore, Fritsch and Hitzig found a motor area on the cortex, and Ferrier found a sensory area. Penfield confirmed the existence of motor and sensory areas by stimulating the brains of conscious human subjects. Thus, there did seem to be localization of function on the cortex, but the functions were not the same as those the phrenologists had proposed, nor were they in the locations the phrenologists had proposed.

Weber was the first to attempt to quantify the relationship between a physical stimulus and the sensation it caused. He determined the two-point threshold for various parts of the body by observing the smallest distance between two points of stimulation that would be reported as two points. Working with weights, Weber determined how much heavier or lighter than a standard a weight must be before it was reported as being lighter or heavier than the standard. This was called a just noticeable difference. Weber found that if a weight was ¹⁄₄₀ lighter than the standard, the subject would report that it was lighter; if it was ¹⁄₄₀ heavier than the standard, it would be reported as heavier. A difference in weight of less than ¹⁄₄₀ of the standard went undetected. Weber's work provided the first statement of a systematic relationship between physical and mental events.

Fechner expanded Weber's work by showing that just noticeable differences were related to stimulation in a geometric way. That is, the greater the magnitude of the standard stimulus, the more that needed to be added to or subtracted from it before a difference was noted. In his work on psychophysics, Fechner utilized three methods: the method of limits, by which one stimulus is held constant and another varied in order to determine which values of the variable stimulus are seen as the same as the standard; the method of constant stimuli, by which pairs of stimuli are presented and the subject reports whether one stimulus appears to be greater than, less than, or the same as the other stimulus; and the method of adjustment, by which the subject adjusts the magnitude of one stimulus until it appears to be the same as the standard stimulus. Now that it had been demonstrated that mental events could be studied experimentally, the ground was laid for the founding of psychology as an experimental science.

DISCUSSION QUESTIONS

1. What is the Bell-Magendie Law?

2. Describe the doctrine of specific nerve energies.

3. Define *vitalism*.

4. How did Helmholtz apply the principle of conservation of energy to living organisms?

5. Describe the procedure Helmholtz used to measure the rate of nerve conduction.

6. How did Helmholtz explain perception? Include in your answer a discussion of unconscious inference.

7. Summarize the Young-Helmholtz theory of color vision.

8. Summarize the resonance place theory of auditory perception.

9. Discuss the importance of Helmholtz's work for the development of psychology as a science.

10. Discuss Gall's positive and negative contributions to brain research.

11. Describe Flourens's approach to brain research. What conclusions did he reach concerning the functioning of the brain?

12. Describe Broca's approach to brain research. What conclusions did he reach concerning the functioning of the brain?

13. What approach to brain research did Fritsch and Hitzig take? Did their results support Gall or Flourens? Explain.

14. What significance did Weber's work have for the evolution of experimental psychology?

In your answer, describe Weber's research techniques and his findings.

15. What philosophical problem did Fechner attempt to solve? What solution did he propose?

16. Summarize Fechner's psychophysical methods.

GLOSSARY

Adequate stimulation Stimulation that a sense modality is maximally sensitive to.

Bell, Charles (1774–1842) Discovered, in modern times, the distinction between sensory and motor nerves.

Bell-Magendie Law There are two kinds of nerves: sensory nerves carrying impulses from the sense receptors to the brain, and motor nerves carrying impulses from the brain to the muscles and glands of the body.

Broca, Paul (1824–1880) Found evidence that part of the left side of the cortex was specialized for speech.

Broca's area The speech area on the left side of the cortex.

Clinical method The technique that Broca used. It involved first determining behavior disorders in a living patient and then, after the patient had died, locating the part of the brain responsible for the behavior disorder.

Doctrine of specific nerve energies Each sensory nerve, no matter how it is stimulated, releases an energy specific to that nerve.

Fechner, Gustav Theodor (1801–1887) Expanded Weber's Law by showing that in order for just noticeable differences to vary arithmetically, the magnitude of a stimulus must increase geometrically.

Ferrier, David (1843–1928) Discovered the sensory area of the cortex.

Flourens, Pierre (1794–1867) Concluded that the cortical region of the brain acted as a unity and was not divided into a number of faculties, as the faculty psychologists and the phrenologists had maintained.

Fritsch, Gustav (1838–1927) Along with Hitzig, discovered motor areas on the cortex by directly stimulating the exposed cortex of a dog.

Gall, Franz Joseph (1758–1828) Concluded that mental faculties were housed in specific locations on the cortex.

Helmholtz, Hermann von (1821–1894) A monumental figure in the history of psychology who did pioneer work in the areas of nerve conduction, sensation, perception, color vision, and audition.

Hitzig, Edward (1838–1907) Along with Fritsch, discovered motor areas on the cortex by directly stimulating the exposed cortex of a dog.

Just noticeable difference The smallest amount that must be added to or subtracted from a stimulus before it is judged to be greater or less than a standard stimulus.

Lashley, Karl Spencer (1890–1959) Concluded that although brain functions were localized, they worked together as an interrelated whole.

Magendie, Francois (1783–1855) Discovered, in modern times, the distinction between sensory and motor nerves.

Method of adjustment An observer adjusts a variable stimulus until it appears to be equal to a standard stimulus.

Method of constant stimuli A stimulus is presented at different intensities along with a standard stimulus, and the observer reports whether it appears to be greater than, less than, or equal to the standard.

Method of limits A stimulus is presented at varying intensities along with a standard (constant) stimulus, in order to determine the range of intensities judged to be the same as the standard.

Müller, Johannes (1801–1858) Expanded the Bell-Magendie Law by indicating that each sense receptor, when stimulated, released an energy specific to that particular receptor. This finding is called the doctrine of specific nerve energies.

Penfield, Wilder (1891–1976) Confirmed the existence of motor, sensory, visual, and auditory areas on the cortex by electrically stimulating the exposed cortex of a conscious human.

Perception The mental experience arising when sensations are embellished by the recollection of past experiences.

Personal equation A mathematical formula used to correct for differences in reaction time among observers.

Phrenology The study of the bumps and indentations of the skull in order to determine the strengths and weaknesses of a person's mental faculties.

Principle of conservation of energy The energy within a system is constant. Therefore it cannot be added to or subtracted from, but only transformed from one form to another.

Psychophysics The systematic study of the relationship between physical and psychological events.

Reaction time The period of time between presentation of and response to a stimulus.

Resonance place theory of auditory perception The tiny fibers on the basilar membrane of the inner ear are stimulated by different frequencies of sound. The shorter the fiber, the higher the frequency it responds to.

Sensation The rudimentary mental experience caused by an environmental stimulus.

Two-point threshold The smallest distance between two points of stimulation at which the two points are experienced as two points.

Unconscious inference According to Helmholtz, the process by which the remnants of past experience are added to sensations, thereby converting them into perceptions.

Vitalism The belief that life cannot be explained solely on the basis of physical and biological forces.

Weber, Ernst (1795–1878) Using the two-point threshold and the just noticeable difference, was the first to demonstrate systematic relationships between stimulation and sensation.

Weber's Law Just noticeable differences correspond to a constant proportion of a standard stimulus.

Young-Helmholtz theory of color vision (also called the **trichromatic theory**) Separate receptor systems on the retina are responsive to each of the three primary colors: red, green, and blue-violet.

CHAPTER 9

Structuralism: Psychology's First School

Many, if not all, of the individuals we covered in the preceding chapter planted the seeds that grew into experimental psychology. The honor of formally founding experimental psychology, however, is given to Wilhelm Wundt. In his epoch-making book *Principles of Physiological Psychology* (1874), Wundt stated that his goal was to create a new domain of science. By 1890, he had reached his goal, and psychology's first **school** had been formed. A school can be defined as a group of individuals who share common assumptions, work on common problems, and use common methods. This definition of *school* is very similar to Kuhn's definition of *paradigm*. In both a school of thought and a paradigm, individuals work to explore the problems articulated by a particular point of view. That is, they engage in what Kuhn calls normal science.

By 1890, students from all over the world were traveling to Leipzig to be trained in experimental psychology at Wundt's laboratory. Wundt founded and edited the first journal devoted exclusively to disseminating the results of experimental psychological research. There now appeared to be little doubt that a productive, scientific psychology was possible. A staggering amount of research poured out of Wundt's laboratory, and laboratories similar to his were being established throughout the world, including in the United States.

It was Wundt, then, who took the diverse achievements of many others and synthesized them into a unified program of research that was organized around certain beliefs, procedures and methods. Since one of Wundt's stated goals was to determine scientifically the structure of the mind, his school became known as **structuralism**. As we shall see, however, the term *structuralism*, when used to describe Wundt's work, is misleading.

WILHELM MAXIMILIAN WUNDT

Wilhelm Maximilian Wundt (1832–1920) was born in a village near Heidelberg, Germany, on August 16, 1832. He was the fourth, and last, child of a Lutheran minister. His father's side of the family included historians, theologians, economists, and two presidents of the University of Heidelberg. On his mother's side there were physicians, scientists, and government officials. In spite of the intellectually stimulating atmosphere in which Wundt grew up (or perhaps because of it), he remained a shy, reserved person who was fearful of new situations. Wundt's only sibling to survive infancy was a brother who was eight years his elder and who went away to school. Wundt's only friend his own age was a retarded boy who could barely speak. When Wundt was about eight years old, his education was turned over to a young vicar who worked in his father's church. The vicar was Wundt's closest friend until Wundt entered high school. Wundt's first year in high school was a disaster: he made no friends, daydreamed incessantly, was physically punished by his teachers, and finally failed. The following year, he started high school over, this time in the city of Heidelberg, where his brother and a cousin

Wilhelm Maximilian Wundt

were students. Although he was not an outstanding student, he did much better there.

After graduation from high school, Wundt enrolled in the premedical program at the University of Tübingen. He stayed for a year and then transferred to the University of Heidelberg, where he became one of the top medical students in his class, graduated *summa cum laude*, and placed first in the state medical board examination. After receiving his medical degree in 1855 at the age of 24, he went to Berlin and studied with Johannes Müller, who so influenced Wundt that he decided to pursue a career in experimental physiology instead of medicine. After a year of working and studying at Müller's

institute, Wundt returned to the University of Heidelberg, where he became Helmholtz's laboratory assistant. While Wundt was working for Helmholtz he gave his first course in psychology as a natural science, and he wrote his first book, *Contributions toward a Theory of Sense Perception* (1862). In this book Wundt formed the plan for psychology that he was to follow for the rest of his life. Wundt remained a teacher at Heidelberg until 1874, when he accepted a professorship in inductive philosophy at the University of Zurich in Switzerland. The following year, he was offered an appointment at the University of Leipzig, where he was to teach scientific philosophy. Wundt accepted the appointment and remained at Leipzig for 45 years.

After arriving at the University of Leipzig in 1875, Wundt asked for and received a small demonstration laboratory. In 1879 he founded what many consider to be the first laboratory dedicated to psychological research (as we shall see in Chapter 11, perhaps William James should be given this credit). The university administration was not supportive of Wundt's laboratory, and it was not listed in the catalog until 1885. One reason for this reluctance was the administration's belief that prolonged introspection could drive students insane. In 1881 Wundt began the journal *Philosophical Studies*, the first journal devoted to experimental psychology.

The university administration's opinion of experimental psychology changed when Wundt's lectures became the most popular at the university. In 1889 he was honored by being elected rector of the university. In 1882 he moved from his small one-room laboratory to one with 11 rooms, and in 1897 he was given an entire building, which he helped design. By now Wundt dominated experimental psychology, something he continued to do for three decades.

Wundt was one of the most productive individuals in the history of psychology. Boring (1950) estimates that between 1853 and 1920,

Wundt wrote a total of 53,735 pages. Wundt's primary interest was his work:

> He never was much excited about anything other than his work. Even his wife and family receive no more than one paragraph in his entire autobiography. . . . His dedication went so far that he analyzed his psychological experiences when he was very seriously ill and near death; at one point in his life he was rather intrigued with the idea of experiencing the process of dying. (Wertheimer, 1970, p. 59)

Appropriately, the last thing Wundt worked on was his autobiography, which he finished a few days before he died on August 31, 1920, at the age of 88.

Wundt has been described as humorless and, as we have seen, completely dedicated to his work. Many stories about him substantiate these aspects of his personality. Both aspects appear in the description of Wundt's lecture technique by one of his most famous students, Edward Titchener (1921):

> The [teaching assistant] swung the door open, and Wundt came in. All in black, of course, from boots to necktie; a spare narrow-shouldered figure, stooping a little from the hips; he gave the impression of height, though I doubt in fact if he stands more than 5 ft. 9.
>
> He clattered—there is no other word for it—up the side-aisle and up the steps of the platform: slam bang, slam bang, as if his soles were made of wood. There was something positively undignified to me about the stamping clatter, but nobody seemed to notice it. . . .
>
> Wundt made a couple of mannered movements—snatched his forefinger across his forehead, arranged his chalk,—and then faced his audience with both elbows on [an adjustable book-rest]. A curious attitude, which favours the impression of height. He began his lecture in a high-pitched, weak, almost apologetic voice; but after a sentence or two, during which the room settled down to silence, his full lecturing voice came out, and was maintained to the end of the hour. It is an easy and abundant bass, somewhat toneless, and at times a little barking; but it carries well, and there is a certain persuasiveness, a sort of fervour, in the

delivery that holds your interest and prevents any feeling of monotony.

> . . . The lecture was given without reference to notes; Wundt, so far as I could tell, never looked down once at the book-rest, though he had some little shuffle of papers there between his elbows. . . .
>
> He stopped punctually at the stroke of the clock, and clattered out, stooping a little, as he had clattered in. If it wasn't for this absurd clatter I should have nothing but admiration for the whole proceeding. (pp. 162-163)

Psychology's Goals

Wundt felt that, first of all, psychology must be scientific. He felt that all sciences were based on experience, and that psychology should be no different. But the *kind* of experience psychology would utilize would be different. Whereas other sciences were based upon **mediate experience**, psychology was to be based upon **immediate experience**. The data the physicist utilizes, for example, are provided by various measuring devices such as spectrometers (to measure wavelengths of light) or sound spectrographs (to measure the frequencies and intensities of sound waves). The physicist records the data these devices provide, then uses the data to analyze the characteristics of the physical world. Thus, the experience of the natural scientist is mediated by recording devices and is not direct. For Wundt, the subject matter of psychology was to be human consciousness *as it occurred.* Wundt was not interested in the nature of the physical world, but wanted to understand the psychological processes by which we experience the physical world.

The tool that Wundt proposed for studying immediate experience was **introspection** or self-analysis. The introspection that Wundt demanded was much different from the kind used by St. Augustine to explore the mind to find the essence of God, or by the empiricists to study ideas. Wundt's introspectionists had to be carefully trained to avoid reporting the *meaning* of a stimulus. Wundt sought a description of the

elements of thought, a description of the basic, raw sensations from which more complex cognitive experiences were built. He sought a kind of periodic table for mental elements, like the one physical scientists had developed for the physical elements. The worst thing introspectionists could do would be to name the object of their introspective analysis. If the subjects were shown an apple, for example, the task would be to describe hues and spatial characteristics. Calling the object an apple would be committing what Titchener would later call the **stimulus error**. Wundt wanted his introspectionists to report sensations, not perceptions.

Once the mental elements were isolated, the laws governing their combination into more complex experiences could be determined. Thus Wundt set two major goals for his experimental psychology:

1. To discover the basic elements of thought.
2. To discover the laws by which mental elements combine into more complex mental experiences.

The Elements of Thought

According to Wundt, there were two basic kinds of mental experience: sensations and feelings. A **sensation** occurs whenever a sense organ is stimulated and the resulting impulse reaches the brain. Sensations can be described in terms of *modality* (visual, auditory, taste, and so on) and *intensity* (for example, how loud an auditory stimulus is). Within a modality, a sensation can be further analyzed. For example, a visual sensation can be described in terms of hue (color), brightness, and saturation ("richness" of color). An auditory sensation can be described in terms of pitch, loudness, and timbre ("fullness" of tone). A taste sensation can be described in terms of its degree of saltiness, sourness, bitterness, or sweetness.

Sensations are accompanied by **feelings**. Wundt reached this conclusion while listening to the beat of a metronome. He noted that some

rates of beating were more pleasant than others. From his own introspections, he formulated his **tridimensional theory of feeling**, according to which any feelings can be described in terms of the degree to which they possess three attributes: pleasantness-unpleasantness, excitement-calm, strain-relaxation.

Wundt believed that what we call emotions were various combinations of these elemental feelings. As we shall see later in this chapter, Wundt's student Edward Titchener was to disagree with Wundt's theory of feelings. Wundt found the mental elements to include a large number of sensations and a few feelings, all of which varied along three dimensions. He also mentioned **images**, which are remnants (memories) of sensations.

Perception, Apperception, and Creative Synthesis

Often a discussion of Wundt's system stops with his concern with mental elements and his use of introspection as the means of isolating them. Such a discussion leaves out some of Wundt's most important ideas. To a certain extent, Wundt accepted an associationism, but the brand of association he accepted was that of John Stuart Mill, who said that mental events were *more than* the elements that made them up.

Indeed, sensations are the elements of consciousness, but in everyday life they are rarely, if ever, experienced in isolation. Most often, many elements are experienced simultaneously, and then **perception** occurs. According to Wundt, perception is a passive process governed by the physical stimulation present, the anatomical makeup of the individual, and the individual's past experiences. These three influences interact and determine an individual's perceptual field at any given time. The part of the perceptual field that the individual attends to is *apperceived*. (Wundt borrowed the term **apperception** from Herbart.) Attention and apperception go hand in hand; what is attended to is apperceived. Unlike perception, which is passive and automatic, apperception is active and voluntary. In other words, apperception is under the control of the individual. So strongly did Wundt believe that individuals could direct their attention that he referred to his theory as **voluntarism**. When elements are attended to, they can be arranged and rearranged according to the will of the individual, and thus arrangements never actually experienced before can result. Wundt called this phenomenon **creative synthesis** and felt that it was involved in all acts of apperception.

Contrary to the popular view that Wundt busied himself searching for the cognitive and emotional elements of a static mind, he viewed the mind as active, creative, dynamic, and volitional. Wundt's view of the mind was much more compatible with that of the German rationalists than with the view of the British empiricists. Wundt believed that the apperceptive process was vital for normal mental functioning, and he speculated that schizophrenia could be the result of a breakdown of the attentional processes. If a person lost the ability to apperceive, his or her thoughts would be disorganized and would appear meaningless, as in the case of schizophrenia.

As we have seen, Wundt was interested in sensations; and in explaining how sensations combined into perceptions, he remained close to traditional associationism. With apperception, however, he emphasized attention, thinking, and creative synthesis. These are all processes much more closely aligned with the rationalist tradition than with the empiricist tradition.

Mental Chronometry

In his book *Principles of Physiological Psychology* (1874), Wundt expressed his belief that reaction time could supplement introspection as a technique for studying the elemental contents and activities of the mind. We saw in Chapter 8 that Friedrich Bessel performed the first reaction-time experiment in order to collect data that

could be used to correct for individual differences in reaction times among those observing and reporting astronomical events. Helmholtz used reaction time to determine the rate of nerve conduction, but then abandoned it because he found it to be an unreliable measure.

Franciscus Cornelius Donders. About 15 years after Helmholtz gave up the technique, **Franciscus Cornelius Donders** (1818–1889), a famous Dutch physiologist, began an ingenious series of experiments involving reaction time. First, Donders measured simple reaction time by noting how long it took a subject to respond to a predetermined stimulus (for example, a light) with a predetermined response (for example, pressing a button). Next, Donders reasoned that by making the situation more complicated he could measure the time required to perform various mental acts.

In one experiment, for example, Donders presented several different stimuli to his subjects but instructed them to respond to only one of them, which he designated ahead of time. This required the subjects to discriminate among the stimuli before responding. The arrangement can be diagrammed as follows:

Stimuli:	A	B	C	D	E
			↓		
Response:			c		

The time it took to perform the mental act of discrimination was determined by subtracting simple reaction time from the reaction time that involved discrimination. Donders then made the situation more complicated by presenting several different stimuli and instructing his subjects to respond to each of them differently. This experimental arrangement can be diagrammed as follows:

Stimuli:	A	B	C	D	E
	↓	↓	↓	↓	↓
Responses:	a	b	c	d	e

Donders called reactions under these circumstances *choice reaction time*, and the time required to make a choice was determined by subtracting both simple and discrimination reaction times from choice reaction time.

Wundt's use of Donders's methods. Wundt enthusiastically seized upon Donders's methods, believing that they could provide a **mental chronometry**, that is, an accurate cataloging of the time it took to perform various mental acts. Almost 20 percent of the work done in Wundt's laboratory involved repeating or expanding on Donders's research on reaction time. Wundt felt strongly that such research provided another way (along with introspection) of doing what so many had thought to be impossible—experimentally investigating the mind.

One of the first observations Wundt and his students made was that reaction time varied depending on whether a subject concentrated on the stimulus or on the response. The researchers found that reaction time was about $1/10$ of a second slower if attention was focused on the stimulus. According to Wundt, this was because a subject focusing on an expected stimulus first had to perceive the stimulus and then apperceive it. That is, the subject first had to detect a stimulus and then determine whether it was the one that he or she had been instructed to respond to in a certain way. When attention was focused on the response rather than on the stimulus, subjects typically responded faster but they also made more mistakes. Since these subjects were not concentrating on any particular stimulus, they sometimes responded to stimuli other than the appropriate one. Wundt concluded that apperception took $1/10$ of a second, since that is about how much slower subjects concentrating on the stimulus responded.

Wundt repeated the Donders experiment in which subjects were presented with several stimuli but were instructed to respond to only one of them. Whereas Donders had called the mental operation required for this task *discrimination*, Wundt called it *cognition*. Wundt calculated the time that the mental act of cognition took by subtracting reaction time involving perception (focusing on the response) and reaction time involving apperception (focusing on the stimulus) from the reaction time requiring cognition.

Wundt then replicated what Donders had called a choice experiment by presenting subjects with several stimuli, each requiring a different response. Instead of saying that this arrangement required a choice, as Donders had done, Wundt said that it required an association. The act of association required more time than cognition. The time required to perform the mental act of association was calculated by subtracting the reaction times involving perception, apperception, and cognition from the reaction times found in the association experiment.

Although Wundt was originally optimistic about being able to measure precisely the time required to perform various mental operations, he eventually abandoned his reaction-time studies. One reason was that he, like Helmholtz, found that reaction times varied too much from study to study, from subject to subject, and often for the same subject at different times. More devastating, however, was the fact that introspective reports indicated that the more complicated mental acts Wundt studied were not merely compounds of simpler acts. Wundt had assumed that complex mental acts (for example, association) could be broken down into elemental mental acts (for example, perception, apperception, and cognition). Instead, introspective reports indicated that subjects viewed all of the tasks quite differently. As tasks were changed, the entire consciousness patterns of the subjects changed, and these changed patterns could not be analyzed into elemental mental acts. Wundt's student Oswald Külpe, who discovered that complex mental operations could not be understood in terms of elements, was later instrumental in the development of Gestalt psychology. We will have more to say about Külpe later in this chapter.

The Mind-Body Relationship

Wundt's position on the mind-body problem was like Spinoza's. That is, the mental and the physical were simply two different aspects of one reality. Though these two aspects occurred together, they were not causally related. Wundt (1897) said:

> As a result of this relation, it follows that there must be a relation between all facts that belong at the same time to both experiences of the natural sciences and to the immediate experiences of psychology, for they are nothing but components of a single experience which is merely regarded in the two cases from different points of view. Since these facts belong to both spheres, there must be an elementary process on the physical side, corresponding to every such process on the psychical side. (pp. 317–318)

Thus, Wundt opposed the idea that the mind could be studied apart from the body. Each experience had a bodily aspect and a mental aspect, and the two were inseparable. Like Spinoza's, Wundt's position on the mind-body question was double-aspectism. Wundt felt that when psychology and the other sciences had gathered enough empirical data, a scientific metaphysics would be possible. This metaphysics would involve synthesizing the facts from the various sciences into a comprehensive, interrelated theory of the universe. Like his position on the mind-body relationship, Wundt's hope for a scientific metaphysics shows Spinoza's influence.

Völkerpsychologie

Although Wundt went to great lengths to found experimental psychology as a separate branch of science and spent years performing and analyzing experiments, *he believed strongly that the higher human faculties could never be investigated experimentally.* He believed that the higher mental processes, which had culminated in human culture, could only be studied through histor-ical analysis and naturalistic observation. Such processes could not be systematically manipulated in a laboratory, and therefore were not amenable to experimental investigation. Among the aspects of human culture beyond the scope of laboratory investigation, Wundt included religion, social customs, myths, history, language, morals, art, and the law. Thus, Wundt's approach to the study of the higher mental processes was empirical but not experimental. Wundt studied these processes for the last twenty years of his life, his research culminating in his ten-volume *völkerpsychologie* ("Group" or "Ethnic" psychology). In this work, Wundt emphasizes the study of language, and his long-overlooked conclusions have a strikingly modern ring to them.

According to Wundt, verbal communication begins with a **general impression**, or unified idea, which one wishes to convey. The speaker apperceives this general impression and then chooses words and sentences to express it. The linguistic structures and words the speaker chooses for expressing the general impression may or may not do so accurately; and upon hearing his or her own words, the speaker may say, "No, that's not what I had in mind," and make another attempt at expression. Once the speaker has chosen sentences appropriate for expressing the general idea, the next step is that the listener must *apperceive* the speaker's words. That is, the listener must understand the general impression that the speaker is attempting to convey. If this occurs, the listener will be able to replicate the speaker's general impression by using any number of different words or sentence structures. Verbal communication, then, is a three-stage process: first, the speaker must apperceive his or her own general impression; next, the speaker chooses words and sentence structures to express the general impression; and finally, the listener, after hearing the words and sentences, must apperceive the speaker's general impression. As evidence for this process, Wundt points out that we often retain the *meaning* of a person's words long after we have forgotten the specific words the person used to convey that meaning.

Wundt's system was far more flexible and comprehensive than is commonly believed. One reason Wundt is misunderstood is that people often equate his view of psychology with that of his student Edward Titchener, who was much narrower than Wundt in his approach to psychology.

EDWARD BRADFORD TITCHENER

Born in Chichester, England, **Edward Bradford Titchener** (1867–1927) attended Malvern College, a prestigious secondary school. He then went to Oxford between 1885 and 1890, and his academic record was outstanding. While at Oxford, he developed an interest in experimental psychology and translated the third edition of Wundt's *Principles of Physiological Psychology* into English. Following graduation from Oxford, Titchener went to Leipzig and studied for two years with Wundt. He returned to England but found little interest there in experimental psychology, so he accepted an appointment at Cornell University at Ithaca, New York, where he remained for the rest of his life. When Titchener arrived at Cornell, he was 25 years old.

Titchener ruled his domain with an iron fist. He determined what the research projects would be and which students would work on them. For him, structuralism was the only worthwhile kind of psychology. He was a member of the American Psychological Association but never attended a meeting—even when the national meeting was held in Ithaca. His wife carefully screened all his callers, and although he became a legend at Cornell, a number of his colleagues never met him. As long as Titchener was healthy, structuralism flourished, but when he died of a brain tumor at the age of 60, structuralism essentially died with him.

Psychology's Goals

Titchener agreed with Wundt that psychology should study immediate experience—that is, consciousness. He defined *consciousness* as the sum total of mental experience at any given moment, and *mind* as the accumulated experiences of a lifetime. Titchener set as goals for psychology the determination of the what, how, and why of mental life. The *what* was to be learned through careful introspection. The goal here was a cataloging of the basic mental elements that accounted for all conscious experience. The *how* was to be an answer to the question of how the elements combine, and the *why* was to involve a search for the neurological correlates of mental events.

The Mental Elements

Essentially, Titchener accepted Wundt's conclusions about the elements of thought; but he described them more specifically than Wundt had, and in some cases he disagreed with Wundt's analysis. According to Titchener, there are seven senses (visual, auditory, olfactory, gustatory, cutaneous, kinesthetic, and organic), which can be further subdivided. For example, the cutaneous sense is divisible into the sensations of pressure, cold, warmth, and pain. In his *Outline of Psychology* (1896, p. 67), Titchener concludes that there are over 40,000 identifiable elements of consciousness, most of them related to the sense of vision, with audition next. He also says that there are over 30,000 visual elements alone.

Like Wundt, Titchener included *images* as a separate category of consciousness. An image was simply a remnant of a sensation. Like a sensation, it could vary in terms of *modality* and *intensity*, as Wundt had proposed. Titchener, however, added the attributes of *duration, clearness*, and *extensity*. As we shall see shortly, Titchener equated attention with clearness. Extensity was the impression that a sensation was more or less spread out in space.

It was over Wundt's tridimensional theory of feeling that Titchener and Wundt had one of their most serious disagreements. Titchener argued that feelings occurred along only one dimension, not three, as Wundt had maintained. According to Titchener, feelings can be described only in terms of the pleasantness-unpleasantness dimension. He argued that the other two dimensions Wundt had suggested (tension-relaxation and excitement-calm) were really combinations of sensations and true feelings (pleasantness-unpleasantness). The *what* of psychology, then, included the sensations and feelings that were described in terms of quality, intensity, duration, vividness, and extensity, as well as the feelings that varied in terms of pleasantness.

The Law of Combination

After Titchener had isolated the elements of thought, the next step was to determine *how* they combined to form more complex mental processes. In explaining how elements of thought combined, Titchener rejected Wundt's notions of apperception and creative synthesis in favor of traditional associationism. Thus Titchener's theory was much more mechanistic than Wundt's. Titchener (1910) made the law of contiguity his basic law of association:

> Let us try . . . to get a descriptive formula for the facts which the doctrine of association aims to explain. We then find this: that, whenever a sensory or imaginal process occurs in consciousness, there are likely to appear with it (of course, in imaginal terms) all those sensory and imaginal processes which occurred together with it in any earlier conscious present. . . . Now the law of contiguity can, with a little forcing, be translated into our own general law of association. (pp. 378–379)

What about attention, the process that was so important to Wundt? For Titchener, attention was simply an attribute of a sensation (clearness). Sensations that were attended to were more vivid or clear than those not attended

Edward Bradford Titchener

to. For the *how* of mental processes, then, Titchener accepted traditional associationism, thus aligning himself with the British empiricists.

Neurological Correlates of Mental Events

Rather than accepting the dual-aspect position on the mind-body question as Wundt had done, Titchener accepted epiphenomenalism. That is, he believed that neural processes always precede mental processes. According to Titchener, the closest we can come to understanding the why of mental processes is to understand the neural processes that precede them. Titchener (1910) stated his position as follows:

Physical science, then, explains by assigning a cause; mental science explains by reference to those nervous processes which correspond with the mental processes that are under observation. We may bring these two modes of explanation together, if we define explanation itself as the statement of the proximate circumstances or conditions under which the described phenomenon occurs. Dew is formed under the conditions of a difference of temperature between the air and the ground; ideas are formed under the condition of certain processes in the nervous system. Fundamentally, the object and the manner of explanation, in the two cases, are one and the same. (p. 41)

Ultimately, then, neural processes are the *why* of mental life, if *why* is understood to mean a description of the circumstances under which mental processes occur and not a specification of the causes of mental events.

The Context Theory of Meaning

What do we mean by the word *meaning*? Titchener's answer again involved associationism. Sensations are never isolated. In accordance with the law of contiguity, every sensation tends to elicit images of sensations that were previously experienced along with the sensation. A vivid sensation or group of sensations forms a *core*, and the elicited images form a *context* that gives the core meaning. A rattle may elicit images of the baby who used it, thus giving the rattle meaning to the observer. A picture of a loved one tends to elicit a wide variety of images related to the loved one's words and activities, thus giving the picture meaning. Even with such a rationalist concept as meaning, Titchener's **context theory of meaning** maintains his empiricist and associationist philosophy.

Though Wundt and Titchener had much in common, there were fundamental differences between the two, and clearly their thoughts should not be equated. Wundt's brand of psychology was closer to the thought of the rationalists, such as Leibniz, Spinoza, Hegel, and Kant, than to the thought of the empiricists, such as Hobbes, Locke, Berkeley, and Hume.

For Titchener the reverse was true. Blumenthal (1970, 1975, 1979) has been largely responsible for clarifying Wundt's true position. He speculates that Wundt's early use of the word *element* was responsible for his being misinterpreted by so many:

Today I cannot help but wonder whether Wundt had any notion of what might happen the day he chose the word "Elemente" as part of a chapter title. Later generations seized upon the word with such passion that they were eventually led to transform Wundt into something nearly opposite to the original. (Blumenthal, 1979, p. 549)

It turns out that Wundt was not a structuralist at all. In 1899 it was Titchener who defined the goal of structuralism as describing the *is* of mental life. He was willing to leave the *is for* for others to ponder.

EARLY OPPONENTS OF STRUCTURALISM

Although Wundt and Titchener's structuralism dominated experimental psychology for many years, it was not without its critics. Many of the structuralists' assumptions were adequately challenged, and some of these challenges strongly influenced the development of other schools of psychology.

Franz Brentano

Franz Brentano (1838–1917) became Wundt's most influential rival. He was the grandson of an Italian merchant who had immigrated to Marienburg, the town in Germany where Brentano was born. Like Wundt, Brentano had many prominent relatives: some of his aunts and uncles wrote in the German romantic tradition, and his brother won a Nobel prize for his work on intellectual history. When Brentano was 17 he began studying for the priesthood, but before being ordained he obtained his Ph.D. in philosophy from the University of

Tübingen in 1862. His dissertation was entitled "On the Manifold Meaning of Being According to Aristotle." Two years later he was ordained a priest and in 1866 became a teacher at Würzburg. Brentano eventually left the church because of his disagreement with the doctrine of the Pope's infallibility, his favorable attitude toward Comte's positivism, his criticisms of scholasticism, and his desire to marry. In 1874 he was appointed professor of philosophy at the University of Vienna, where he enjoyed his most productive years. In the same year (1874), Brentano published his most famous work, *Psychology from an Empirical Standpoint.* (Incidentally, this was the same year that Wundt published his *Principles of Physiological Psychology.*) In 1894, pressure from the church forced Brentano to leave Vienna and move to Florence. Italy's entrance into World War I ran contrary to Brentano's pacifism, and he protested by moving to Zurich, where he died in 1917.

Brentano agreed with Wundt that psychology should be empirical, but he disagreed with Wundt over the importance of experimentation. Brentano believed that overemphasizing experimentation (systematic manipulation of one variable and noting its effects on another) diverted the researcher's attention from the important issues. Brentano also disagreed with the structuralists over the importance of knowing the physiological mechanisms behind mental events. Finally, he felt that the search for mental elements implied a static view of the mind that was not supported by the facts. According to Brentano, the important thing about the mind was not what was in it but what it did. In other words, Brentano felt that the proper study of the mind should emphasize the mind's *processes* rather than its contents. If we replace the word *process* with *function*, we can see that Brentano influenced functionalism, psychology's next school.

Brentano's views came to be called **act psychology** because of his belief that mental processes were aimed at performing some func-

Carl Stumpf

tion. Among the mental acts, he included feeling, recall, ideation, perception, judgment, loving and hating, and intention. Brentano saw the mind as dynamic—not static, as the structuralists (especially Titchener) maintained. One of Brentano's most famous students was Sigmund Freud, who took his only nonmedical courses from Brentano. Brentano wrote very little, believing that oral communication was most effective, and his major influence on psychology has come through those whom he influenced personally. Much of what became Gestalt psychology and existential psychology can be traced to Brentano.

Carl Stumpf

Carl Stumpf (1848–1936) studied with Brentano. Stumpf's primary interest was music, and his research eventually earned him a reputation in audition that rivaled that of Helmholtz. His most influential work was his two-volume *Psychology of Tone* (1883 and 1890). Engaging in a major dispute with Wundt over the perception of musical tones, Stumpf maintained that trained musicians were able to make more valid judgments of musical tones then trained introspectionists who were not musicians.

Stumpf argued that mental events should be studied as meaningful units, just as they occur to the individual, and should not be broken down for further analysis. In other words, for Stumpf, the proper object of study for psychology was mental *phenomena*, not conscious elements. This stance led to the phenomenology that was to become the cornerstone of the later school of Gestalt psychology. In fact, the chair that Stumpf occupied at the University of Berlin for 26 years was passed on to the great Gestalt psychologist Wolfgang Köhler. The other two founders of Gestalt psychology, Max Wertheimer and Kurt Koffka, also studied with Stumpf.

Edmund Husserl

Edmund Husserl (1859–1938) studied with Brentano between 1884 and 1886 and then worked with Stumpf, to whom he dedicated his book *Logical Investigations* (1900 and 1901). Husserl accepted Brentano's concept of **intentionality**, according to which mental acts are functional in the sense that they are directed at something outside of themselves. For example, the act of seeing involves seeing something, the act of judging involves judging something, and so on. For Brentano, then, mental acts were the means by which we made contact with the physical world. For Husserl, however, studying intentionality resulted in only one kind of knowledge, that of the person turned outward to the environment. Equally important was the knowledge gained through studying the person turned inward. The former study utilizes introspection to examine the mental acts with which we embrace the physical world. The latter utilizes introspection to examine all subjective experience as it occurs, without the need to relate it to anything else. For Husserl, then, there were at least two kinds of phenomenology: one that focused on intentionality and one that focused on whatever a person experienced subjectively. For example, the former kind would ask what external object the act of seeing intended, while the latter would concentrate on a description of the pure experience of seeing.

In his book *Ideas: General Introduction to Pure Phenomenology* (1913), Husserl suggested a science that concentrated exclusively on examining mental events—that is, on a study of the person turned inward. According to Husserl's **phenomenological psychology**, introspection was to be used to explore the essence of subjective experience; there was no need to establish a physical referent for the subjective experience. Husserl proposed that we study phenomenological experience without any scientific, philosophical, religious, or personal biases. He hoped that by taking such an approach, we could determine the workings of the mind. Since a knowledge of the workings of the mind provided the background for any intellectual pursuit, it would aid science and philosophy.

Husserl's position differed radically from that of the structuralists in that Husserl sought to examine *meanings* and essences, not mental elements, via introspection. He and his subjects would thus commit the dreaded stimulus error. Husserl also differed from his teacher Brentano and his colleague Stumpf by insisting on a pure **phenomenology** with little or no concern for determining the relationship between subjective experience and the physical world.

Brentano, Stumpf, and Husserl all insisted that the proper subject matter for psychology was intact, meaningful psychological experiences. This phenomenological approach was to appear soon in Gestalt psychology and existential psychology. Martin Heidegger, one of the most famous existential thinkers, dedicated his book *Being and Time* (1927) to Husserl. We will have more to say about Husserl when we discuss third force psychology in Chapter 17.

Oswald Külpe

Oswald Külpe (1862–1915) was interested in many things, including music, history, philosophy, and psychology. During the time when he was primarily interested in philosophy, he wrote five books on philosophy for the lay reader, including one on Kant's philosophy. He was majoring in history at the University of Leipzig when he attended Wundt's lectures and became interested in psychology. Under Wundt's supervision, Külpe received his Ph.D. in 1887, and he remained Wundt's assistant for the next eight years. (Külpe dedicated his book *Outlines of Psychology* (1893) to Wundt.) Külpe was primarily responsible for the introspective research that caused Wundt to realize that complex mental operations could not be viewed as compounds of simpler operations. This realization caused Wundt to abandon his reaction-time studies. During his time as Wundt's assistant, Külpe met and roomed with Titchener; and although the two often disagreed, they maintained the highest regard for one another. In fact, Titchener later translated several of Külpe's works into English. In 1894 Külpe moved to the University of Würzburg, where for the following 15 years he did his most influential work in psychology. In 1909 he left Würzburg and went to the University of Bonn, and then to the University of Munich. After Külpe left Würzburg, his interest returned more and more to philosophy. He was working on epistemological questions when he died in 1915, at the early age of 53.

Imageless thought. Although starting out very much in the Wundtian camp, Külpe became one of Wundt's most worthy opponents. Külpe disagreed with Wundt that all thought had to have a specific referent—that is, a sensation, image, or feeling. Külpe felt that some thoughts were *imageless*. Furthermore, he disagreed with Wundt's contention that the higher mental processes (for example, thinking) could not be studied experimentally, and he set out to do so,

using what he called *systematic experimental introspection*. This technique involved giving subjects *problems* to solve and then asking them to report on the mental operations they engaged in to solve them. In addition, subjects were asked to describe the kinds of thinking involved at different stages of problem solving. They were asked to report their mental experiences while waiting for the problem to be presented, during actual problem solving, and after the problem had been solved. Külpe's more elaborate introspective technique indicated that there were indeed imageless thoughts, such as searching, doubting, confidence, and hesitation. In 1901 Karl Marbe, one of Külpe's colleagues, published a study describing what happened when subjects were asked to judge weights as heavier or lighter than a standard weight. Marbe was not interested in the accuracy of the judgments but in *how* the judgments were made. Subjects reported prejudgment periods of doubt, searching, and hesitation, after which they simply made the judgments. Marbe concluded that Wundt's elements of sensations, images, and feelings were not enough to account for the act of judging. There appeared to be a mental act of judging that was independent of what was being judged. Marbe concluded that such an act was imageless.

Mental set. The most influential work coming out of the Würzburg school was that on *Einstellung* or **mental set**. It was found that focusing subjects on a particular problem created a **determining tendency** that persisted until the problem was solved. Furthermore, although this tendency or set was operative, subjects were unaware of it; that is, it operated on the unconscious level. For example, a bookkeeper can balance the books without being aware of the fact that he or she is adding or subtracting. It was found that mental sets could be induced experimentally by instructing subjects to perform different tasks or solve different problems. Mental sets could also result from a person's past experiences. William Ryan, one of the American students working in Külpe's laboratory, provided an example of an experimentally induced set. Ryan showed cards containing various nonsense syllables written in different colors and in different arrangements. Subjects who were instructed to attend to the colors were afterwards able to report the colors present but could not report the other stimuli. On the other hand, subjects instructed to attend to the syllables could report them with relative accuracy but could not accurately report the colors. It appeared that instructions had directed the subjects' attention to certain stimuli and away from others. This demonstrated that environmental stimuli did not automatically create sensations that became images. Rather, the process of attention determined which sensations would and would not be experienced.

Narziss Ach, who was also working in Külpe's laboratory, demonstrated the kind of mental set derived from experience. Ach found that when the numbers 7 and 3 were flashed rapidly and subjects had not been instructed to respond in any particular way, the most common response was to say "ten." Ach's explanation was that the mental set to add was more common than the mental sets to subtract, multiply, or divide, which would have resulted respectively in the responses 4, 21, and 2.3.

Other findings of the Würzburg school. Besides showing the importance of mental set in problem solving, members of the Würzburg school showed that problems had motivational properties. Somehow problems caused subjects to continue to apply relevant mental operations until a solution was attained. The motivational aspect of problem solving was to be emphasized later by the Gestalt psychologists. Wertheimer, one of the founders of the school of Gestalt psychology, wrote his doctoral dissertation under Külpe's supervision.

The Würzburg school showed that the higher mental processes could be studied ex-perimentally and that certain mental processes occurred independently of content (that is, they were imageless). It also indicated that associationism was inadequate for explaining the operations of the mind, and challenged the structuralists' narrow use of the introspective method. Members of the Würzburg school made the important distinction between thoughts and thinking, between mental contents and mental acts. In elaborating these distinctions, members of the school moved closer to Brentano, and away from Wundt and especially Titchener. Members of the Würzburg school and Brentano were both interested in how the mind worked instead of what static elements it contained.

The controversies the Würzburg school caused did much to promote the collapse of structuralism. Was there imageless thought or not? Was it possible, as some maintained, that some individuals had imageless thought and others did not? If so, how would this affect the search for universal truths about the mind? How could introspection be properly used? Could it be directed only at static contents of the mind, or could it be used to study the dynamics of the mind? Most devastating was the fact that different individuals were using the same research technique (introspection) and reaching much different conclusions. More and more, introspection became looked upon as unreliable. This questioning of the validity of introspection as a research tool did much to launch the school of behaviorism.

Hermann Ebbinghaus

Born the son of a merchant near Bonn, Germany, **Hermann Ebbinghaus** (1850–1909) received his Ph.D. from the University of Bonn in 1873. He wrote his dissertation on the philosophy of the unconscious. While roaming Europe after he had received his Ph.D., he found and read a copy of Fechner's *Elements of Psycho-*

physics, which deeply impressed him. Ebbinghaus later dedicated his book *Outline of Psychology* to Fechner, of whom he said, "I owe everything to you." Unaware of Wundt's belief that the higher mental processes could not be studied experimentally, Ebbinghaus proceeded to systematically study learning and memory. Unlike Wundt's critics at Würzburg, who thought that they had argued successfully against associationism and who were inclined toward rationalism, Ebbinghaus was very much in the empiricism-associationism tradition. In fact, his research can be seen as determining the role of the associative principle of frequency in learning and memory.

Ebbinghaus's research finally culminated in a monograph entitled *On Memory* (1885), which marked another turning point for psychology. It was the first time that the processes of learning and memory had been studied as *they occurred*, rather than after they had occurred, as all previous investigators had done. Once Ebbinghaus had opened the door, research on learning rapidly became the most popular topic in experimental psychology, and it remains so today. As testimony to Ebbinghaus's thoroughness, many of his findings are still cited in modern psychology textbooks. With Arthur König, Ebbinghaus founded psychology's second experimental journal, *Journal of Psychology and Physiology of the Sense Organs*, which broke Wundt's monopoly on the publishing of results from psychology experiments. Ebbinghaus was also the first to publish an article on the testing of school children's intelligence. Shortly after he had turned 59, and while he was at the peak of his career, Ebbinghaus died of pneumonia.

In order to study learning as it occurred, Ebbinghaus needed material that no one had previously experienced. That is, he needed material that was free of prior associations. For this, he invented the **nonsense syllable**, which consisted of a vowel between two consonants—for example, XUW, QAT, or CEP. From the 2300 possible nonsense syllables, Ebbinghaus

Hermann Ebbinghaus

THE BETTMANN ARCHIVE, INC.

chose a group to be learned. The group usually consisted of 12 syllables, though he varied the size of the group in order to study rate of learning as a function of the amount of material to be learned. Keeping the syllables in the same order, and using himself as a subject, he would look at each syllable for a fraction of a second. After going through the list in this fashion, he would pause for 15 seconds and go through the list again. He continued in this manner until he could recite each syllable without making a mistake, at which point *mastery* was said to have occurred.

At various time intervals following mastery, Ebbinghaus would relearn the group of syllables. He recorded the number of exposures it took to relearn the material and subtracted that from the number of exposures it took to learn the material to begin with. He called the difference between the two **savings**. By plotting savings as a function of time, Ebbinghaus created psychology's first retention curve. He found that forgetting was most rapid during the first few hours following a learning experience and relatively slow thereafter. And he found that if he *overlearned* the original material (that is, if he continued to expose himself to material after he had attained mastery), the rate of forgetting was considerably reduced. Ebbinghaus also studied the effect of *meaningfulness* on learning and memory. For example, he found that it took about nine times as many exposures to learn 80 nonsense syllables as it did to learn 80 successive syllables from Byron's *Don Juan*, showing that meaningful material was not only learned faster but retained longer.

THE DECLINE OF STRUCTURALISM

In many ways, the decline of the school of structuralism was inevitable. We have seen that interest in the mind is as old as history itself, and the question of how the mind is related to bodily processes goes back at least as far as the early Greeks. Focusing mainly on the physical world, early science was extremely successful, and its success stimulated interest in directing scientific methodology to a study of the mind. Since both empiricists and rationalists alike had long believed that the senses were the gateways to the mind, it is no surprise that sensory processes were among the first things science focused on when it was applied to humans. From there it was but a short, logical step to looking at neural transmission and then at brain mechanisms, and finally at conscious sensations.

Structuralism was essentially an attempt to study scientifically what had been the philosophical concerns of the past. How does sensory information give rise to simple sensations, and how are these sensations then combined into more complex mental events? The major tool of all the structuralists, and even their opponents, was introspection. This, too, had been inherited from the past. Although it was now used scientifically (that is, in a controlled situation), introspection was yielding different results depending on who was using it and what they were looking for. Other arguments against the use of introspection began to appear. It was pointed out that what was called introspection was really *retrospection*, because the event that was reported had already occurred, and therefore what was being reported was a memory of a sensation rather than the sensation itself. Also, it was suggested that one could not introspect on something without changing it—that is, that observation changed what was being observed. It was beginning to appear that those who claimed that a science of the mind was impossible were correct.

Besides the apparent unreliability of introspection, structuralism came under attack for several other reasons. Structuralism either ignored or minimized several developments that researchers outside of the school of structuralism were showing to be important. The study of animal behavior had little meaning for those hoping to find the basic elements of human consciousness, yet others were finding that much could be learned about humans by studying nonhuman animals. The structuralists were not interested in the study of abnormal behavior, even though Freud and others were making significant advances in understanding and treating the mentally ill. Likewise, the structuralists essentially ignored the study of personality, learning, psychological development, and individual differences while others were making major breakthroughs in these areas. Also damaging was the structuralists' refusal to seek *practical* knowlege. Wundt and the other leading structuralists had insisted that they were seeking pure knowledge and were not concerned with applying the principles of psychology to the solution of practical problems. Most important to structuralism's demise, however, was its inability to assimilate one of the most important developments in human history—the doctrine of evolution. For all these reasons, the school of structuralism was short-lived and died within Titchener's own lifetime.

It was now time for a psychological school of thought that would deal with the important areas structuralism neglected, do so within the context of evolutionary theory, and use research techniques that were more reliable and valid than introspection. Titchener himself named this new school functionalism, a school that was concerned with the *what for* of the mind instead of the *what is*. The development and characteristics of the school of functionalism will be the topics of the next two chapters.

SUMMARY

Wundt was the founder of both experimental psychology as a separate discipline and of the school of structuralism. One of Wundt's goals was to discover the elements of thought by having well-trained subjects introspect on their immediate experience. A second goal was to discover how these elements combined to form complex mental experiences. Wundt found that there were two kinds of basic mental experiences: sensations, which could be described in terms of modality and intensity; and feelings, which could be described in terms of the attributes of pleasantness-unpleasantness, excitement-calm, and strain-relaxation. Wundt distinguished among sensations, which were basic mental elements; perceptions, which were mental experiences given meaning by past experience; and apperceptions, which were mental experiences that were the focus of attention.

Since humans can focus their attention on whatever they wish, Wundt's theory is sometimes referred to as voluntarism. By focusing one's attention on various aspects of conscious experience, that experience can be arranged and rearranged in any number of ways, and thus a creative synthesis results from apperception. Wundt believed that if the ability to apperceive broke down, mental illness such as schizophrenia might result. With his concept of apperception, Wundt was closer to the rationalist than to the empiricist tradition.

Wundt initially believed that reaction time could supplement introspection as a means of studying the mind. Following techniques developed by Donders, Wundt presented tasks of increasing complexity to his subjects and noted that more complex tasks resulted in longer reaction times. Wundt believed that the time required to perform a complex mental operation could be determined by subtracting the times it took to perform the simpler operations of which the complex act consisted. Wundt eventually gave up his reaction-time studies because he found reaction time to be an unreliable measure and because he discovered that complex mental operations were not compounds of simpler operations.

On the mind-body question, Wundt held the position of dual-aspectism, and he believed that the higher mental functions could not be studied through experiments but only through historical analysis and naturalistic observation. Wundt considered language to be a higher mental function, and therefore one that could not be studied experimentally. For Wundt, verbal communication began when one person formed a general impression. Next, the person chose to express the general impression. Finally, if the words adequately conveyed the general impression, and if the listener apperceived it, communication was successful.

Titchener created a stronghold for structuralism at Cornell University. For Titchener, sensations and images could vary in terms of modality, intensity, duration, clearness, and extensity, and he found evidence for over 40,000 separate mental elements. Titchener thought that all feelings varied only along the pleasantness-unpleasantness dimension, thus disagreeing with Wundt's tridimensional theory. Following in the empirical-associationistic tradition, Titchener said that attention was only a clear sensation. According to Titchener's context theory of meaning, sensations always stimulate the memories of events that were previously experienced along with those sensations, and these memories give the sensations meaning. There were a number of fundamental differences between Wundt's brand of structuralism and Titchener's.

Those disagreeing with the tenets of structuralism included Brentano, Stumpf, Husserl, Külpe, and Ebbinghaus. According to Brentano, psychology should be an empirical science but not an experimental one. He also felt that it was not necessary to know the neurophysiological correlates of mental events. Brentano proposed that mental processes or acts be studied instead of mental content, and therefore his position is referred to as act psychology. Stumpf, whose primary interest was music, argued that intact, meaningful mental phenomena should be studied instead of meaningless mental elements. Husserl proposed a pure phenomenological approach whereby subjective experiences would be investigated without any preconceptions and without any concern for how such experiences related to the physical world. He also significantly influenced Gestalt psychology and modern existential philosophy.

Through his technique of systematic experimental introspection, Külpe found that the mind possessed processes—not just sensations, images, and feelings—and that these processes were imageless. Examples of imageless thoughts included searching, doubt, and hesitation. Külpe and his colleagues found that a mental set, which could be created either through instructions or through personal experience, provided a determining tendency in problem solving. They also found that once a mental set had been established, humans could solve problems unconsciously. Ebbinghaus demonstrated that Wundt had been wrong in saying that the higher mental processes could not be studied experimentally. Using nonsense syllables, Ebbinghaus systematically studied both learning and memory so thoroughly that his conclusions are still cited in psychology texts today.

Many factors led to the downfall of structuralism. Examples are the unreliability of introspection, the observation that introspection was really retrospection, and the ignoring of psychological development, abnormal behavior, personality, learning, individual differences, evolutionary theory, and practicality.

DISCUSSION QUESTIONS

1. What is meant by a "school" of psychology?

2. For Wundt, what were the goals of psychology?

3. For Wundt, what were the elements of thought and what were their attributes? Include in your answer Wundt's tridimensional theory of feeling.

4. Define the terms *sensation*, *perception*, *apperception*, and *creative synthesis* as they were used in Wundt's theory.

5. Summarize how Wundt utilized reaction time in an effort to determine how long it took to perform various mental operations.

6. Why did Wundt abandon his reaction-time research?

7. Why did Wundt feel it necessary to write his

Völkerpsychologie? What approach to the study of humans did it exemplify?

8. Summarize Wundt's explanation of language.

9. For Titchener, what were the goals of psychology?

10. What did Titchener feel would be the ultimate *why* of psychology?

11. How did Titchener's explanation of how elements combine differ from Wundt's?

12. What was Titchener's context theory of meaning?

13. Compare and contrast Wundt's view of psychology with Titchener's.

14. Summarize Brentano's act psychology.

15. What did Brentano mean by *intentionality?*

16. Describe the observations members of the Würzburg school made that were detrimental to structuralism.

17. Discuss the significance of Ebbinghaus's work to the history of psychology.

18. Summarize Husserl's phenomenological psychology.

19. List the reasons for the decline of structuralism. Include in your answer the various criticisms of introspection.

GLOSSARY

Act psychology The name given to Brentano's brand of psychology because it focused on mental operations or functions. Act psychology dealt with the interaction between mental processes and physical events.

Apperception The process by which attention is focused on certain mental events.

Brentano, Franz (1838–1917) Felt that introspection should be used to understand the functions of the mind rather than its elements. Brentano's position came to be called act psychology.

Context theory of meaning Titchener's contention that a sensation is given meaning by the images it elicits. That is, for Titchener, meaning is determined by the law of contiguity.

Creative synthesis The arrangement and rearrangement of mental elements that can result from apperception.

Determining tendency See **Mental set**.

Donders, Franciscus Cornelius (1818–1889) Used reaction time to measure the time it took to perform various mental acts. Donders subtracted reaction times generated in simple situations (for example, response a to stimulus A) from the reaction times generated by more complicated situations (for example, where several stimuli were presented, but the subject

was instructed to respond to only one of them). Donders felt that by utilizing this subtractive method he could determine the time required to perform increasingly complicated mental acts.

Ebbinghaus, Hermann (1850–1909) The first to study learning and memory experimentally.

Elements of thought According to Wundt and Titchener, the basic sensations from which more complex thoughts are derived.

Feeling The basic element of thought that accompanies each sensation. Wundt felt that emotions consist of various combinations of elemental feelings (see also **Tridimensional theory of feeling**).

General impresson The thought a person has in mind before he or she chooses the words to express it.

Husserl, Edmund (1859–1938) The founder of phenomenological psychology.

Image The memory of a sensation.

Immediate experience Mental experience as it occurs, without interpretation of any kind.

Intentionality Concept proposed by Brentano, according to which mental acts always intend something. That is, mental acts embrace either some object in the physical world or some mental image (idea).

Introspection Reflection upon one's subjective experience.

Külpe, Oswald (1862–1915) Applied systematic experimental introspection to the study of problem solving and found that some mental operations were imageless.

Mediate experience Experience that is given meaning by past experience and is therefore interpreted in some way.

Mental chronometry The measurement of the time required to perform various mental acts.

Mental set A problem-solving strategy that can be induced by instructions or by experience and is utilized without a person's awareness. Another term for mental set is *determining tendency.*

Nonsense syllable Consonant-vowel-consonant combination with little or no meaning. Ebbinghaus used nonsense syllables to study learning and memory.

Perception Mental experience that occurs when sensations are given meaning by the memory of past experiences.

Phenomenological psychology The brand of psychology Husserl proposed, in which subjective experience was to be introspectively explored without any preconceptions.

Phenomenology The study of meaningful mental events as they are experienced, without any dissection or analysis that would destroy that meaning.

Savings The difference between the time it originally takes to learn something and the time it takes to relearn it.

School A group of scientists who share common goals, problems, and methods.

Sensation A basic mental experience that is usually triggered by an environmental stimulus.

Stimulus error Letting past experience influence an introspective report.

Structuralism Psychology's first school of thought. The structuralist's major goal was to describe the structure of the mind.

Stumpf, Carl (1848–1936) Psychologist who was primarily interested in musical perception and who insisted that psychology study intact, meaningful mental experiences instead of searching for meaningless mental elements.

Titchener, Edward Bradford (1867–1927) Led a structuralistically oriented program at Cornell. Titchener's brand of structuralism was much more in the empiricism-associationism camp than was Wundt's.

Tridimensional theory of feeling Wundt's contention that feelings vary along three dimensions: pleasantness-unpleasantness, excitement-calm, and strain-relaxation.

Völkerpsychologie Wundt's ten-volume work, in which he investigated higher mental processes through historical analysis and naturalistic observation.

Voluntarism The name sometimes given to Wundt's theory because of Wundt's belief that through the process of apperception individuals could direct their attention toward whatever they wished.

Wundt, Wilhelm Maximilian (1832–1930) The founder of experimental psychology as a separate discipline and of the school that Titchener later called structuralism.

CHAPTER 10

The Darwinian Influence

Structuralism was a product of Germany. Because it did not fit the American temperament, Titchener's attempt to transplant it to America was not successful. When Titchener arrived at Cornell in 1892, there was a spirit of independence, practicality, and adventure that was incompatible with the authoritarian, dry, and static views of the structuralists as Titchener presented them. That structuralism survived as long as it did in America was testimony to the forceful personality of Titchener himself. The pioneering American spirit was prepared to accept only a point of view that was new and practical and unconcerned with the abstract analysis of the mind. Evolutionary theory provided such a view, and America embraced it like no other country. Not even in England, the birthplace of evolutionary theory, did it meet with the enthusiasm that it received in America. In America, evolutionary theory became *the* dominant theme running through most, if not all, aspects of psychology. The translation of evolutionary theory into psychology created a psychology that was uniquely American, and it caused the center of psychological research to shift from Europe to America, where it has been ever since.

EVOLUTIONARY THEORY BEFORE DARWIN

The idea that both the earth and living organisms change in some systematic way over time goes back at least as far as the early Greeks. Since Greece was a maritime country, it was possible to observe a wide variety of life forms there. Such observations, in addition to the growing tendency toward objectivity, caused some early Greeks to develop a surprisingly modern theory of evolution. Hulin (1934) gives the following examples:

> It was conjectured, for example, that the earth was originally in a fluid state, that evaporation caused the emergence first of land and then of animals, that man originally appeared as an aquatic animal encased in a horny bark which fell away when he emerged on dry land. Another guess was that the earth was originally covered with slime from which living things developed through the influence of the sun's heat. (pp. 10–11)

With such a good start, why did evolutionary theory not develop more fully? To a large extent, the reason is that Plato and Aristotle did not believe in evolution. For Plato, the number of pure forms was fixed forever; the forms themselves did not change. For Aristotle, the number of species was fixed, and transmutation from one species to another was impossible. To the beliefs of Plato and Aristotle, the early Christians added the notion of divine creation as described in the Book of Genesis. God in his wisdom had created a certain fixed number of species, including humans, and this number could be modified only by another act of God, not by natural forces. This religious account of the origin of species put the matter to rest until modern times. MacLeod (1975) summarizes the restrictions placed on early biologists:

> Since the infancy of their science biologists had been constricted by the doctrine of the fixity of

species. According to the account in Genesis each species of plant, fish, bird, and beast had been specially created with special forms and functions, and Aristotle and the Church had sanctified the doctrine. All the biologist could do was observe and classify the forms of plant and animal life and try to make each species meaningful in terms of the presumed purpose of God. (p. 174)

By the eighteenth century, several prominent individuals were postulating a theory of evolution, including Charles Darwin's grandfather, Erasmus Darwin (1731–1802), who believed that one species could be gradually transformed into another. What was missing from these early theories was the mechanism by which the transformation took place. The first to postulate such a mechanism was Jean Lamarck.

In his *Philosophie Zoologique* (1809), **Lamarck** (1744–1829) noted that fossils of various species showed that earlier forms were different from current forms, and therefore that species changed over time. Lamarck concluded that environmental changes were responsible for structural changes in plants and animals. If, for example, due to a scarcity of prey, members of a species had to run faster to catch what few prey were available, the muscles involved in running would become more fully developed because of the frequent exercise they received. If the muscles involved in running were fully developed in an adult of a species, the offspring of this adult would be born with highly developed muscles, which also enhanced their chances for survival. According to Lamarck, any habits adult members of a species developed that were conducive to survival were passed on to their offspring. This process came to be referred to as the **inheritance of acquired characteristics**. In other words, it was assumed that those adults of a species who developed behavioral patterns that allowed them to survive would pass those behavioral patterns on to their offspring. Obviously, those adult members of species who did not adjust adequately to their environment

would not survive, and therefore would produce no offspring. In this way, according to Lamarck, the characteristics of a species would change as conditions changed. Thus, the transmutation of the species.

HERBERT SPENCER

An early follower of Lamarck (and later of Darwin) was **Herbert Spencer** (1820–1903). Spencer took the notion of evolution and applied it not only to animals but to the human mind and to human societies as well. In fact, he applied the notion of evolution to everything in the universe. Everything, according to Spencer, starts as an undifferentiated whole. Through evolution differentiation occurs, so that systems become increasingly complex. This notion also applies to the human nervous sytem, which eons ago was simple and homogenous but through evolution has become highly differentiated and complex. The fact that we now have complex nervous systems allows us to make a greater number of associations, and the greater the number of associations an organism can make, the more intelligent it is. Our highly complex nervous system allows us to make an accurate neurophysiological (and thus mental) recording of events in our environment, and this ability is conducive to survival.

In his explanation of how associations are formed, Spencer relied heavily on the principle of contiguity. Environmental events that occur either simultaneously or in succession are recorded in the brain and give rise to ideas of those events. Through the process of contiguity, our ideas come to map environmental events. Through experience, a person learns which environmental events are conducive to survival (those that cause pleasant feelings) and which are not (those that cause painful feelings). The next step that Spencer took tied his theory directly to Lamarck's. Spencer claimed that an offspring inherited the cumulative associations that its ancestors had learned. Those associations that preceding generations had found to be conducive to survival were passed on to the next generation. That is, there was an inheritance of acquired associations. Spencer's theory was a blending of empiricism, associationism, and nativism, since Spencer believed that the associations gained from experience were passed on to offspring.

Spencer was therefore an associationist, but to associationism he added Lamarck's evolutionary theory. He maintained that frequently utilized associations were passed on to offspring as instincts or reflexes. For Spencer, then, instincts were nothing more than habits that had been conducive to survival for preceding generations. Instincts had been formed in past generations just as habits were formed in an organism's lifetime—through association.

When Darwin's work appeared, Spencer merely shifted his emphasis from acquired characteristics to natural selection. The concept of the **survival of the fittest** (the term was Spencer's, but Darwin later adopted it) applied in either case. Spencer's application of his notion of the survival of the fittest to society was called **social Darwinism**. As Spencer saw it, humans in society, like animals in their natural environment, struggled for survival, and only the most fit survived. According to Spencer, if the principles of evolution were allowed to operate freely, all living organisms would approximate perfection, including humans. The best policy for a government to follow, then, was a laissez-faire policy that provided for free competition among its citizens. Government programs designed to help the weak and poor would only interfere with evolutionary principles and inhibit a society on its course toward increased perfection.

Obviously, Spencer's ideas were compatible with American capitalism. In the United States, Spencer's ideas were taught in most universities, and his books sold hundreds of thousands of copies. Indeed, when Spencer visited the

Charles Darwin

United States in 1882, he was treated like a hero. Even William James, whom many consider the greatest psychologist who ever lived, used Spencer's *Principles of Psychology* (1855) as a textbook. When James published his own textbook in 1890, it too was called *The Principles of Psychology.*

CHARLES DARWIN

Charles Darwin (1809–1882) was born in Shrewsbury, England, in the same year that Lamarck published his book describing the inheritance of acquired characteristics. Darwin's father, Robert, was a prominent physician who had four daughters and two sons, of which Charles was the youngest. At 30 years of age Charles Darwin married his cousin Emma, with whom he eventually had ten children. Darwin never liked or did well in school, but he showed an early interest in collecting things like coins, minerals, and shells. His father sent him to the University of Edinburgh to study medicine, but Darwin found medicine boring. Next, he studied for the clergy at Cambridge, and later he reflected that the three years he had spent there had been wasted academically, but that socially it had been the best time of his life. Darwin received his degree from Cambridge in 1831. Immediately upon graduation, he went on a geological expedition to Wales with some of his friends. Darwin saw the expedition as a temporary way of escaping taking his religious vows. A more permanent escape on the high seas was soon to be available to him.

The Journey of the *Beagle*

At the instigation of one of his instructors, Darwin signed on as an unpaid naturalist aboard the *Beagle*, which the British government was sending on a five-year scientific expedition (1831–1836). There are several unusual facts about this trip. First, the captain of the *Beagle*, Robert Fitz-Roy, who was a firm believer in the Genesis account of creation, wanted a naturalist aboard so that evidence could be gathered that would *refute* the notion of evolution. Furthermore, Darwin himself began the trip as a believer in the biblical explanation of creation (Monte, 1975, p. 59). It was only after reading Sir Charles Lyell's *Principles of Geology* aboard ship that he began to doubt the biblical account. A third fact almost changed the course of history: because Captain Fitz-Roy accepted phrenology, he almost rejected Darwin as the *Beagle's* naturalist because of the shape of Darwin's nose.

On becoming very intimate with Fitz-Roy, I heard that I had run a very narrow risk of being rejected on account of the shape of my nose! He was . . . convinced that he could judge a man's character by the outline of his features; and doubted whether anyone with my nose could possess sufficient energy and determination for the voyage. But I think he was afterwards well satisfied that my nose had spoken falsely. (F. Darwin, 1954, pp. 26–27)

The journey of the *Beagle* began on December 27, 1831, from Plymouth, England. Darwin was 23 years old at the time. The *Beagle* went first to South America, where Darwin studied marine organisms, fossils, and tribes of Indians. Then, in the fall of 1835, the *Beagle* stopped at the Galápagos Islands, where Darwin studied huge tortoises, lizards, sea lions, and 13 species of finch. Of special interest was his observation that tortoises, plants, insects, and other organisms differed somewhat from island to island even when the islands were separated by a relatively short distance. The *Beagle* went on to Tahiti, New Zealand, and Australia; and in October 1836, Darwin arrived back in England, where he went to work classifying his enormous specimen collection.

Back in England

Even after Darwin returned to England, his observations remained disjointed; he needed a principle to tie them together. Reading **Thomas Malthus's** *Essay on the Principle of Population* (1798) furnished Darwin with that principle. Malthus observed that the world's food supply increased arithmetically, while there was a tendency for the human population to increase geometrically. He concluded that food supply and population size were kept in balance by such things as war, starvation, and disease. Darwin embellished Malthus's concept and applied it to animals and plants as well as to humans:

In October 1838, that is, fifteen months after I had begun my systematic enquiry, I happened to read for amusement Malthus on *Population*, and being well prepared to appreciate the struggle for existence which everywhere goes on from long-continued observation of the habits of animals and plants, it at once struck me that under these circumstances favourable variations would tend to be preserved and unfavourable ones to be destroyed. The result of this would be the formation of new species. Here, then, I had at last got a theory by which to work; but I was so anxious to avoid prejudice, that I determined not for some time to write even the briefest sketch of it. (F. Darwin, 1959, pp. 42–43)

About the time Darwin read Malthus's essay, he began to have serious health problems. Along with the realization that what he was working on was revolutionary, these problems caused Darwin to delay the formal publication of his theory for more than 20 years. In fact, there is reason to believe that Darwin's theory would have been published only after his death if it had not been for a forceful demonstration that the time was right for such a theory. In June of 1858, Darwin received a letter from **Alfred Russell Wallace** (1823–1913) describing a theory of evolution almost identical to his own. Wallace, too, had been influenced by Malthus's essay, as well as by his own observations in the Amazon and in the Malay Archipelago. Lyell, the evolutionary geologist, reviewed both Wallace's and Darwin's ideas and suggested that both men read papers at the Linnaean Society on the same day, and they did. Darwin's epoch-making book, *On the Origin of Species by Means of Natural Selection*, was published two months later. By then there was so much interest in evolutionary theory that all 1,500 copies of the book sold on the first day it was available.

Six years after the publication of Darwin's theory, Captain Fitz-Roy committed suicide, perhaps because he felt that he was at least partially responsible for Darwin's theory of evolution (Gould, 1976, p. 34). Because of the abundance of data that Darwin amassed and the thoroughness of his work, we attribute the theory to him and not to Wallace, but what follows may someday be referred to as the Darwin-Wallace theory of evolution.

Darwin's Theory of Evolution

The reproductive capacity of all living organisms allows for many more offspring than can survive in a given environment; therefore, there is a **struggle for survival**. Among the offspring of any species there are vast *individual differences*, some of which are more conducive to survival than others. This results in the *survival of the fittest* (a term that Darwin borrowed from Spencer). For example, if there is a shortage of food in the environment of giraffes, only those giraffes with necks long enough to reach the few remaining leaves on tall trees will survive and reproduce. In this way, as long as food remains scarce, giraffes with shorter necks will tend to become extinct. Thus, a **natural selection** occurs among the offspring of a species. This natural selection of adaptive characteristics from the individual differences occurring among offspring accounts for the slow transmutation of a species over the eons. Evolution, then, results from the natural selection of those accidental variations that prove to have survival value.

In *Origin of Species* Darwin said very little about humans, but later he wrote *The Descent of Man* (1871), in which he made his case that humans were also the product of evolution. Both humans and the great apes, he says, descended from a common, distant primate ancestor. The book ends with the following statement:

Man may be excused for feeling some pride at having risen, though not through his own exertions, to the very summit of the organic scale; and the fact of his having thus risen, instead of having been aboriginally placed there, may give him hope for a still higher destiny in the distant future. But we are not here concerned with hopes or fears, only with the truth as far as our reason permits us to discover it; and I have given the evidence to the best of my ability. We must, however, acknowledge, as it seems to me, that man with all his noble qualities, with sympathy which feels for the most debased, with benevolence which extends not only to other men but to the humblest living creature, with his God-like intellect which has penetrated into the movements and constitution of the solar system—with all these exalted powers—man still bears in his bodily frame the indelible stamp of his lowly origin. (p. 707–708)

Of Darwin's books, the one most directly related to psychology was *The Expression of Emotions in Man and Animals* (1872), in which he argued that human emotions were remnants of animal emotions that had once been necessary for survival. In the distant past, only those organisms capable of such things as biting and clawing survived and reproduced. Somewhat later, perhaps, simply the baring of the teeth or snarling were enough to discourage an aggressor, and therefore facilitated survival. Although no longer as functional in modern society, these emotions that were originally associated with attack or defense are still part of our biological makeup, as can be seen in human reactions under extreme conditions.

Darwin's direct comparison of humans with other animals in *The Expresson of Emotions in Man and Animals*, along with his forceful assertion that humans differed from other animals only in degree, launched modern comparative and animal psychology. It was now clear that much could be learned about humans by studying "lower" animals.

There is no better summary of Darwin's theory than Darwin's own conclusion to *Origin of Species* (1859):

It is interesting to contemplate a tangled bank clothed with many plants of many kinds, with birds singing on the bushes, with various insects flitting about, and with worms crawling through damp earth, and to reflect that these elaborately constructed forms, so different

from each other, and dependent upon each other in so complex a manner, have all been produced by laws acting around us. These laws taken in the largest sense, being Growth with Reproduction; Inheritance which is almost implied by Reproduction; Variability from the indirect and direct action of the conditions of life, and from use and disuse; a Ratio of Increase so high as to lead to a Struggle for Life, and as a consequence of Natural Selection, entailing Divergence of Character and the Extinction of less-improved forms. Thus, from the War of Nature, from famine and death, the most exalted object which we are capable of conceiving, namely, the production of the higher animals, directly follows. There is grandeur in this view of life, with its several powers, having been originally breathed by the Creator into a few forms or into one; and that whilst this planet has gone cycling on according to the fixed law of gravity, from so simple a beginning endless forms most beautiful and most wonderful have been, and are being evolved. (pp. 373–374)

Darwin's Influence

To say the least, Darwin's theory was revolutionary. Robinson (1981) summarizes the reasons that evolutionary theory has always met such great resistance:

If the Bible suggests that all living forms were created at the same time, the Bible is wrong. If Christian teaching insists that God made so many forms of life and no more, Christian teaching is wrong. If philosophers believe that man, through will and accomplishments, has removed himself from natural contexts in which survival never exceeds probability, the philosophers are wrong. (p. 335)

And MacLeod (1975) says:

Darwin's conception of the evolutionary process was so radically new as to represent a revolution in science that was coordinate in importance with the revolutions of Newton and Copernicus. Darwin threw the intellectual world into turmoil, and out of the turmoil there emerged a new doctrine of man that was to give shape to the whole subsequent history of psychology. (p. 176)

As we shall see in the remainder of this chapter, Darwin's ideas ultimately gave birth to a uniquely American kind of psychology—a psychology that emphasized individual differences and their measurement, the adaptive value of thoughts and behavior, and the study of animal behavior. Before discussing American psychology, however, we must first review the works of a man who was an important link between Darwinian theory and American psychology.

SIR FRANCIS GALTON

Erasmus Darwin, the physician, philosopher, poet, and early evolutionary theorist, was the grandfather of both Charles Darwin and **Francis Galton** (1822–1911). Galton was Darwin's cousin, and he was born near Birmingham, England, on February 16, 1822, the youngest of seven children. His father was a wealthy banker and his mother was a half sister of Charles Darwin's father. Receiving his early education at home, Galton could read and write by the age of two and a half. At five he could read any book written in English, and by seven he was reading such authors as Shakespeare for pleasure. But things changed when Galton was sent to a boarding school, where his experiences included flogging, hell-raising, sermons from the teachers, and fights with his fellow students. At 16 he was taken out of boarding school and sent to Birmingham General Hospital to study medicine, and after this practical experience he transferred to King's College in London. He then moved to Cambridge University, where he obtained his degree in 1843. Galton planned on returning to King's College to obtain his medical degree, but when his father died he decided not to, so his formal education ended.

Since Galton was independently wealthy, he could work on what he wanted, when he wanted. After graduation he traveled in Egypt, the Sudan, and the Middle East. Then he came home and socialized with his rich friends for a

Francis Galton

few years—riding, shooting, ballooning, and experimenting with electricity. After consulting with a phrenologist who recommended an active life, Galton decided to join the Royal Geographical Society on a trip to Southwest Africa. The trip lasted two years, and for Galton's creation of a map of previously unexplored territories in Africa, the Royal Geographical Society honored him with their highest medal. Galton was 32 at the time.

We can see in Galton's map-making ability a passion that Galton had all his adult life: the passion to measure things. Concerning Galton's expedition with the Royal Society, Fancher (1979) says:

> One of the things Galton liked best about the expedition—and one of the major reasons for its success—was that it enabled him to indulge

his penchant for measurement. He mastered the sextant, the heliostat, and other navigational and surveying instruments, and returned home with several notebooks full of detailed readings and calculations of the African terrain. He found a rather more unorthodox use for his measuring skill when he encountered some native women who, he wrote home, had figures "that would drive the females of our native land desperate." Wishing to ascertain their measurement without risking a direct approach, Galton "sat at a distance with my sextant, and . . . surveyed them in every way and subsequently measured the distance of the spot where they stood . . . worked out and tabulated the results at my leisure. (p. 260)

In 1853 Galton published his first book, *Narrative of an Explorer in South Africa.* He became a recognized expert on travel in the wild, and the British government commissioned him to teach camping procedures to soldiers. In 1855 he published his second book, *The Art of Travel,* which included information on how to deal with wild animals and savages. For his inventiveness, Galton was elected president of the Royal Geographical Society in 1856.

To further illustrate Galton's passion for measurement, here are a few of his other endeavors:

- In his effort to measure and predict the weather, he invented the weather map and was the first to use the terms *highs, lows* and *fronts.*

- He was the first to suggest that fingerprints could be used for personal identification—a procedure later adopted by Scotland Yard.

- He attempted to determine the effectiveness of prayer (he found it ineffective).

- He tried to determine which country had the most beautiful women.

- He measured the degree of boredom at scientific lectures.

One can imagine Galton's delight when he became aware of his cousin's evolutionary theory, with its emphasis on individual differences.

Galton believed that if there were important individual differences among people, clearly they should be measured and catalogued. This became Galton's mission in life.

The Measurement of Intelligence

Galton assumed that intelligence was a matter of sensory acuity, since humans could know the world only through the senses. Thus, the more acute the senses, the more intelligent a person was. Furthermore, since sensory acuity was mainly a function of natural endowment, intelligence was inherited. And if intelligence was inherited, as Galton assumed, one would expect to see extremes in intelligence run in families. Assuming that high reputation or eminence was an accurate indicator of high intellectual ability, Galton set out to measure the frequency of eminence among the offspring of illustrious parents as compared to the frequency of eminence among the offspring of the general population. For comparison with the general population, Galton studied the offspring of judges, statesmen, commanders, literary men, scientists, poets, musicians, painters, divines, oarsmen, and wrestlers. The results of Galton's research, published in *Hereditary Genius: An Inquiry into Its Laws and Consequences* (1869), were clear; the offspring of illustrious individuals were far more likely to be illustrious than the offspring of nonillustrious individuals. Galton also observed, however, that zeal and vigor must be coupled with inherited capacity before eminence could be attained.

Selective breeding. Galton's conclusion raised a fascinating possibility: *selective breeding.* If intelligence was inherited, could not the general intelligence of a people be improved by encouraging the mating of bright people and discouraging the mating of people who were less bright? Galton's answer was yes. He called the improvement of living organisms through selective breeding **eugenics**, and he advocated its practice, as the following quotation from *Hereditary Genius* (1869) shows:

> I propose to show in this book that a man's natural abilities are derived by inheritance, under exactly the same limitations as are the form and physical features of the whole organic world. Consequently, as it is easy, notwithstanding those limitations, to obtain by careful selection a permanent breed of dogs or horses gifted with peculiar powers of running, or of doing anything else, so it would be quite practicable to produce a highly-gifted race of men by judicious marriages during several consecutive generations. I shall show that social agencies of an ordinary character, whose influences are little suspected, are at this moment working towards the degradation of human nature, and that others are working towards its improvement. I conclude that each generation has enormous power over the natural gifts of those that follow, and maintain that it is a duty we owe to humanity to investigate the range of that power, and to exercise it in a way that, without being unwise towards ourselves, shall be most advantageous to future inhabitants of the earth. (p. 45)

In 1865, Galton proposed that couples be scientifically paired, and that the government pay those possessing desirable characteristics to marry. The government was also to take care of the educational expenses of any offspring.

The nature-nurture controversy. Galton's extreme nativism did not go unchallenged. *Alphonse de Candolle* (1806–1893), for example, wrote a book stressing the importance of environment in producing scientists. Candolle suggested that climate, religious tolerance, democratic government, and a thriving economy were at least as important as inherited capacity in producing scientists.

Such criticism prompted Galton's next book, *English Men of Science: Their Nature and Nurture* (1874). To gather information for this book, Galton sent a questionnaire to 200 of his fellow scientists at the Royal Society. This was the first use of the questionnaire in psychology. The participants were asked many factual questions, ranging from their political and religious backgrounds to their hat sizes. In addition, they were asked to explain why they had become interested in science in general as well as in their particular branches of science. Finally, the scientists were asked whether they felt that their interest in science was innate.

Although the questionnaire was very long, most of the scientists finished it. Most attributed their interest in science to genetic factors. Galton noticed, however, that a disproportionate number of the scientists were Scottish, and that these scientists praised the broad and liberal Scottish educational system. On the other hand, the English scientists had very unkind things to say about the English educational system. Based on these findings, Galton urged that English schools be reformed to make them more like Scottish schools. Here Galton was acknowledging the importance of the environment. His revised position was that the potential for high intelligence was inherited, but that it must be nurtured by a proper environment. Galton (1874) clearly stated the **nature-nurture controversy** which is still the focus of much attention in modern psychology:

> The phrase "nature and nurture" is a convenient jingle of words, for it separates under two distinct heads the innumerable elements of which personality is composed. Nature is all that a man brings with himself into the world; nurture is every influence that affects him after his birth. The distinction is clear: the one produces the infant such as it actually is, including its latent faculties of growth and mind; the other affords the environment amid which the growth takes place, by which natural tendencies may be strengthened or thwarted, or wholly new ones implanted. (p. 12)

In his next book, *Inquiries into Human Faculty and Its Development* (1883), Galton further supported his basic nativistic position by studying twins. He found monozygotic (one-egged) twins to be very similar to each other even when they were reared apart, and dizygotic (two-egged) twins to be dissimilar even when they were reared together.

The Word-Association Test

In *Inquiries* (1883), Galton described psychology's first word-association test. He wrote 75 words, each on a separate piece of paper. Then he glanced at each word, and noted his response to it on another piece of paper. He went through the 75 words on four different occasions, randomizing the words each time. Three things struck Galton about this study. First, responses to stimulus words tended to be constant; he very often gave the same response to a word all four times he experienced it. Second, his responses were often drawn from his childhood experience. And third, he felt that such a procedure revealed aspects of the mind never revealed before. Galton (1883) says:

> Perhaps the strongest of the impressions left by these experiments regards the multifariousness of the work done by the mind in a state of half-consciousness, and the valid reason they afford for believing in the existence of still deeper strata of mental operations, sunk wholly below the level of consciousness, which may account for such mental phenomena as cannot otherwise be explained. (p. 145)

Whether Galton influenced Freud is not known, but Galton's work with word association anticipated two aspects of psychoanalysis: the use of free association and the emphasis upon the unconscious mind.

Mental Imagery

Galton was also among the first, if not the first, to study imagery. In *Inquiries* (1883), he reported the results of asking people to imagine the scene as they had sat down to breakfast. He found that the ability to imagine was essentially normally distributed, with some individuals almost totally incapable of imagery and others having the ability to imagine the breakfast scene

flawlessly. Galton was amazed to find that many of his scientist friends had virtually no ability to form images. If sensations and their remnants (images) were the stuff of all thinking, as the empiricists had assumed, why was it that many scientists seemed unable to form and utilize images? Galton also found, not so surprisingly, that whatever a person's imagery ability was, he or she assumed that everyone else had the same ability.

Anthropometry

Also in *Inquiries* (1883), Galton again expressed his belief that intelligence was closely related to sensory acuity, a belief that stimulated him to produce the first intelligence tests, most of which were designed to test sensory acuity. In his test battery, Galton included measures of motor ability because he felt that muscular strength was related to will or determination. He also devised methods for testing the keenness of sight and hearing, color sense, strength of grip (using a dynamometer), and ability to discern small differences in weights. The adjustable whistle that he used to test keenness of hearing is still used today, and is appropriately called a Galton whistle. In 1884 Galton set up what he called an "Anthropometric Laboratory" at London's International Health Exhibition and collected normative data by running 9,337 individuals through many tests, including those just mentioned.

Although intelligence is no longer believed to be related to sensory acuity, Galton's early efforts can be seen as the beginning of the mental testing movement in psychology. Following our review of Galton, we will have more to say about how intelligence testing changed after Galton's efforts.

The Concept of Correlation

The last of Galton's many contributions to psychology that we will consider is his notion of correlation, which has become one of psychology's most widely used statistical methods. In 1888 Galton published an article entitled "Co-Relations and Their Measurement, Chiefly from Anthropometric Data," and in 1889 he published a book entitled *Natural Inheritance*. Both works describe the concepts of correlation and regression. Galton (1888) defined **correlation** (or *Co-Relation*) as follows:

> Two variable organs are said to be co-related when the variation on one is accompanied on the average by more or less variation of the other, and in the same direction. Thus the length of the arm is said to be co-related with that of the leg, because a person with a long arm has usually a long leg, and conversely. . . . (p. 135)

In a definition of *correlation*, the word *tend* is very important. Even in the above quotation, Galton says that those with long arms *usually* have long legs. After planting peas of varying sizes and measuring the size of their offspring, Galton observed that very large peas tended not to have offspring quite as large as they were, and that very small peas tended not to have offspring quite as small as themselves. He called this phenomenon **regression toward the mean**, something he also found when he correlated heights of children with heights of their parents. In fact, Galton found regression whenever he correlated inherited characteristics. Earlier, Galton had observed that eminent individuals only tended to have eminent offspring.

By visually displaying his correlational data in the form of scatterplots, Galton found that he could visually determine the strength of a relationship. Galton's friend **Karl Pearson** (1867–1936) devised a formula that produced a mathematical expression of the strength of a relationship. Pearson's formula produces the now familiar **Coefficient of Correlation** (r).

Galton's Contributions to Psychology

Few individuals in psychology have more firsts attributed to them than Galton. Galton's firsts include study of the nature-nurture question, the use of questionnaires, the use of a word-association test, twin studies, the study of imagery, intelligence testing, and the development of the correlational technique. Everywhere in his work we see a concern with individual differences and their measurement, a concern that was a direct reflection of the influence of Darwin's theory of evolution.

INTELLIGENCE TESTING AFTER GALTON

James McKeen Cattell

The transfer of Galton's testing procedures to the United States was accomplished mainly through the efforts of **James McKeen Cattell** (1860–1944), who had studied with both Wundt and Galton in Europe but had been much more influenced by Galton. At the University of Pennsylvania, Cattell administered Galtonian measures to his students, and in 1890 he published an article summarizing his results in *Mind*. It was in this article that the term *mental test* was used for the first time. In 1891 Cattell moved to Columbia University, where he began administering his tests to entering freshmen. Cattell assumed that if all of his tests were measuring the same thing (intelligence), performance on the tests should be highly correlated. He assumed further that if the tests were indeed measuring intelligence, they should correlate highly with academic success in college. Wissler (1901) tested Cattell's assumptions, finding that the correlations among the tests were very low, and that the correlation between the test results and success in college was nearly zero (Guilford, 1967, p. 6). With such findings, the testing movement in America began to lose its impetus. The emphasis in American psychology was turning toward practicality, and it appeared that the Galton measures were not very useful, at least as far as intelligence was concerned.

Alfred Binet

Alfred Binet

In France, however, a different approach to measuring intelligence was being tried, one that appeared to be more successful than Galton's. It involved *directly* measuring the complex mental operations thought to be involved in intelligence. **Alfred Binet** (1857–1911) championed this method of testing, which was much more in the rationalist than the empiricist tradition.

Binet was born on July 11, 1857, in Nice, France. His father was a physician, as were both of his grandfathers. Although initially following the family tradition by studying medicine, Binet terminated his medical studies and turned to psychology instead. Being independently wealthy allowed Binet to take the time to educate himself, and he read the works of Darwin, Galton, and the British empiricists, among others. He received no formal education in psychology.

Binet began his career in psychology by working wtih Jean Charcot, the world-famous psychiatrist, at La Salpetriere. Like Charcot, Binet conducted research on hypnotism, and he claimed that in one study he had been able to manipulate the symptoms and sensations of a hypnotized subject by moving a magnet to various places around the subject's body. He also claimed that application of the magnet could convert fear of an object, such as a snake, into affection. Binet thought that such findings would have important implications for the practice of medicine in general and for psychiatry in particular, but other researchers were unable to reproduce Binet's findings, and concluded that Binet's results were due to poor experimental control. For example, it was found that Binet's subjects always knew what was expected of them and acted accordingly. When subjects were unaware of the researcher's expectations, they did not exhibit the phenomena that Binet had observed. Thus, suggestion had caused Binet's result, not the magnet. After a long attempt to defend his beliefs, Binet finally admitted that his results had been due to suggestion and not to the magnet's power, and he resigned his position at La Salpetriere in 1890. The humiliation resulting from his public admission of shoddy research procedures haunted Binet all his life. His statement "Tell me what you are looking for, and I will tell you what you will find" (Wolf, 1973, p. 347) was directed at metaphysicians, but Binet knew from personal experience that it could apply to researchers as well.

Fortunately, Binet's second career in psychology was more successful. Without a professional position, Binet directed his attention to the study of the intellectual growth of his two daughters, who were two and a half and four and a half at the time. The tests he created to investigate his children's mental operations were very similar to those Piaget later devised.

He asked, for example, which of two piles contained more objects, and found that the answer was not determined by the number of objects in the piles but by the amount of space the piles took up on the table. Binet also investigated how well his daughters could remember objects that he first showed them and then removed from sight. In 1890 he published three papers describing his research on his daughters.

In 1891 Binet joined the laboratory for physiological psychology at the Sorbonne, where he performed research in such areas as memory, the nature of childhood fears, the reliability of eyewitness testimony, creativity, imageless thought, and graphology. During his years at the Sorbonne, Binet also investigated individual differences in the perception of inkblots—before the famous work of Rorschach. In her outstanding biography of Binet, Theta Wolf (1972) says that Binet was the father of experimental psychology in France, and that he had more of an impact on American psychology than Wundt did. The reader is directed to Wolf's book for more details concerning Binet's many pioneering research endeavors and for the interesting details of his life.

In 1899 **Theodore Simon** (1878–1961), who worked as an intern at a colony for retarded children, asked Binet to collaborate with him on a research program. (It was with Simon that Binet was to develop his famous—or infamous—intelligence tests.) Also in 1899, Binet joined the Free Society for the Psychological Study of the Child, an organization that sought scientifically valid information about children. In 1903 Binet and Simon were appointed to the group that the French government commissioned to study the problems of retarded children in the French schools. It was immediately clear that if retarded children were to receive special education, it was necessary to have an adequate method of distinguishing them from normal children. At the time, variations of Galton's tests were being used to detect mental

retardation, and Binet noted that because of these tests, children who were blind or deaf were erroneously being classified as retarded. Earlier, in 1896, Binet (with Victor Henri) had criticized Galton's measures of intelligence as too sensory and too simple. To replace them, Binet proposed complex tests that were designed to measure cognitive abilities *directly*. Although Binet later reported a person's intelligence in one score, he believed that intelligence consisted of several different kinds of cognitive abilities. In 1896 he suggested that the following processes be studied through tests: memory, imagery, imagination, attention, comprehension, suggestibility, aesthetic appreciation, moral sentiment, force of will, judgment of visual space. Binet's list is evidence of his comprehensive view of intelligence.

Craniometry. As late as 1898, Binet believed that measuring the size of the head was a valid means of measuring intelligence.

> The relationship between the intelligence of subjects and the volume of their head . . . is very real and has been confirmed by all methodical investigators, without exception. . . . As these works include observations on several hundred subjects, we conclude that the preceding propositon is incontestable. (Binet, 1898, pp. 294-295)

With his work on **craniometry**, Binet made the same mistake he had made while studying hypnosis: finding what he was looking for *because* he was looking for it. In 1900 Binet confessed, "I feared that in making measurements on heads with the intention of finding a difference in volume between an intelligent and a less intelligent head, I would be led to increase, unconsciously and in good faith, the cephalic volume of intelligent heads and to decrease that of unintelligent heads" (p. 323).

This tendency for researchers to fulfill their own prophecies was later called **experimenter bias,** or the experimenter effect. It has been found to be an important variable in research. Rechecking his work on craniometry, Binet concluded that his own expectations had influenced many of his observations, and craniometry was soon dropped as a measure of intelligence.

The 1905 Binet-Simon scale and revisions. Binet and Simon offered the **Binet-Simon scale of intelligence** as a valid way of distinguishing between normal and mentally deficient children—a way that was to replace the less reliable physical, social, and educational signs that were being used at the time to identify the retarded. The 1905 scale consisted of 30 tests ranging in difficulty from simple eye movements to abstract definitions. Three of the tests measured motor development, and the other 27 were designed to measure cognitive abilities. Arranged in order of difficulty, so that the more tests a child passed the higher was his or her score, the scale was given to normal children and to children thought to be retarded, all of them between the ages of 3 and 12. As it turned out, the scores of normal children were much higher than those of retarded children.

In 1908 Binet and Simon revised their scale. Their goal now was to go beyond simply distinguishing normal from retarded children, to distinguishing among levels of intelligence for normal children. The tests were administered to children from age 3 to 13. If 75 percent or more of the children of a certain age passed a particular test, the test was assigned to that age level. For example, most four-year-old children could copy a square but not a diamond. In this way, it could be determined whether a given child was performing at, above, or below average. A five-year-old passing the tests that most other five-year-olds also passed was considered to have normal intelligence. But if that child passed only the tests typically passed by four-year-olds, he or she was thought to have below average intelligence. And if the five-year-old passed tests normally passed by six-year-olds, he

or she was thought to have above average intelligence. In other words, a child's intelligence level was determined by how much higher or lower than the norm the child performed. In the 1908 scale, different numbers of tests corresponded to the different age levels; therefore, in 1911 Binet and Simon revised the scale once again so that there were five tests corresponding to each age level. This allowed 1/5 of a year to be added to a child's score for each test the child passed beyond those that were the norm for his or her age.

Intelligence quotient (I.Q.). In 1911 **William Stern** (1871–1938), a German psychologist, introduced the term **mental age**. For Stern, a child's mental age was determined by his or her performance on the Binet-Simon tests. Stern also suggested that mental age be divided by chronological age and the result multiplied by 100 (to remove the decimal), yielding an **intelligence quotient** (I.Q.). Thus the familiar formula for I.Q.

$$I.Q. = \frac{MA}{CA} \times 100$$

Binet was opposed to both the concept of mental age and the use of the intelligence quotient. He felt that intelligence was too complex to be represented by a simple term or number. History shows, however, that Stern's simplifications won out over Binet's opposition. But in any case, Binet and Simon had developed a relatively brief, easy-to-administer measure of intelligence, and it became extremely popular. By the beginning of World War I, the Binet-Simon test was being used throughout most of the world.

Binet's view of the scale. Before reviewing what happened to the Binet-Simon scale in the United States, it is important to review how Binet viewed his scale. First and foremost, Binet saw the scale as a device for identifying children who needed some sort of special education.

Binet strongly believed that children with low test scores could benefit considerably if given special attention. Binet *did not* believe that intelligence level was fixed at birth, and he worried very much about students in classrooms where teachers did believe that intelligence was innately determined. He was appalled by teachers who

> are not interested in students who lack intelligence. They have neither sympathy nor respect for them, and their intemperate language leads them to say such things in their presence as "This is a child who will never amount to anything . . . he is poorly endowed. . . . He is not intelligent at all." How often I have heard these imprudent words. (1909, p. 100)

In Binet's reaction to those who maintained that some children would *never* be able to accomplish some things, he indicates clearly that he did not accept a nativist view of intelligence.

> Never! What a momentous word. Some recent thinkers seem to have given their moral support to these deplorable verdicts by affirming that an individual's intelligence is a fixed quantity, a quantity that cannot be increased. *We must protest and react against this brutal pessimism; we must try to demonstrate that it is founded upon nothing.* (1909, p. 101; italics added)

Binet believed that **mental orthopedics** could prepare disadvantaged children for school. Mental orthopedics consisted of exercises that would improve a child's will, attention, and discipline—all abilities that Binet felt were necessary for effective classroom education. Binet believed that by engaging in mental orthopedics, children learned how to learn.

THE BINET-SIMON SCALE IN THE UNITED STATES

Henry H. Goddard

Henry H. Goddard (1866–1957), who translated the Binet-Simon scale into English, received his Ph.D. from Clark University in 1899

Henry H. Goddard

and became director of the Research Laboratory for the Study of the Feebleminded at the Vineland Training School in New Jersey. Besides administering the translated Binet-Simon scale to the children at the Vineland School, Goddard also administered it to 2,000 public school children in New Jersey. He was shocked to find that many of the public school children performed below the norms for their ages. This especially disturbed Goddard because he believed, like Galton, that intelligence was largely inherited—a belief he thought to be supported by the observation that the children at Vineland often had brothers and sisters who were feebleminded.

Study of feeblemindedness. Goddard decided to investigate the relationship between family background and intelligence more carefully. In 1911 he administered the Binet-Simon scale to Deborah Kallikak, who had been living at the Vineland School since 1897. Although her chronological age was 22, her test performance yielded a mental age of 9, producing an I.Q. of about 40. Goddard coined the term *moron* to denote Deborah's intellectual level. He then traced Deborah's ancestry back to the American Revolution, when Martin Kallikak, Sr., had had a relationship with a "feebleminded" barmaid that resulted in the birth of Martin Kallikak, Jr. After leaving the army, Martin, Sr., married a "worthy girl," and they had seven children. Martin, Jr., eventually married and had ten children. In Goddard's analysis, the descendents of Martin, Sr., and the "worthy girl" represented the "good" side of Deborah's ancestors, and the descendents of Martin, Jr., represented the "bad" side. Goddard found that of Martin, Sr.'s children none were feebleminded, whereas five of Martin, Jr.'s children were feebleminded. In subsequent generations on Martin, Jr.'s side, Goddard found an abundance of mentally defective individuals. In Goddard's time people believed that feeblemindedness was the cause of most criminal, immoral, and antisocial behavior; and Goddard supported this belief by showing that many descendents of Martin, Jr., had been horse thieves, prostitutes, convicts, alcoholics, parents of illegitimate children, or sexual deviates. Of the hundreds of descendents from Martin, Sr.'s marriage, only three had been mentally defective, and one had been considered "sexually loose." Among Martin, Sr.'s descendents had been judges, lawyers, educators, and other prestigious individuals.

Goddard reported his findings in *The Kallikaks: A Study in the Heredity of Feeble-Mindedness* (1912). His research was taken as support for the Galtonian belief that intelligence was genetically determined. Along with Goddard, several of the leading scientists of the day urged that the mentally defective be sterilized or segregated from the rest of society. They contended that since the feebleminded could not be expected to control their own reproduction, the intelligent members of society must control it for them.

If both parents are feeble-minded all the children will be feeble-minded. It is obvious that such matings should not be allowed. It is perfectly clear that no feeble-minded person should ever be allowed to marry or to become a parent. It is obvious that if this rule is to be carried out, the intelligent part of society must enforce it. (Goddard, 1914, p. 561)

No fewer than 20 states passed sterilization laws, and thousands of "undesirables" were sterilized. In some states, the sterilization law was enforced into the 1970s. Galton would have been pleased.

Mental testing and immigration. In the years between 1905 and 1913 millions of individuals migrated from Europe to the United States, and there was growing concern that many of these immigrants might be mentally inferior. The question was how to know for certain. In 1912 the comissioner of immigration invited Goddard to Ellis Island to observe the immigrants. Goddard claimed he could tell that many of the immigrants were mentally defective simply by observing their physical characteristics, but to be sure he administered the Binet-Simon scale. Based upon the test results, many immigrants were labeled mentally defective and thousands were deported. Goddard even went so far as to specify the European countries for which the percentage of mentally defective immigrants was the highest. In general, Goddard concluded that between 40 and 50 percent of the immigrants were morons.

As with his earlier work, Goddard assumed that test performance was due mainly to inherited intelligence and not to educational, cultural, or personal experience—all factors that were later found to profoundly influence performance on the test. But the immigrants were also taking the test under special circumstances, which Gould describes in his book *The Mismeasure of Man* (1981):

For the evident reason, consider a group of frightened men and women who speak no English and who have just endured an oceanic voyage in steerage. Most are poor and have never gone to school; many have never held a pencil or pen in their hand. They march off the boat: one of Goddard's [assistants] takes them aside shortly thereafter, sits them down, hands them a pencil, and asks them to reproduce on paper a figure shown to them a moment ago, but now withdrawn from their sight. Could their failure be a result of testing conditions, of weakness, fear, or confusion, rather than of innate stupidity? Goddard considered the possibility, but rejected it. (p. 166)

Furthermore, the tests were administered by a translator whose accuracy in translating the test into the immigrant's native tongue was taken on faith.

Because of Goddard's efforts, the rate of deportation increased 350 percent in 1913 and 570 percent in 1914. Except for all the common, inexpensive laborers America was losing, Goddard was pleased. In his later years, Goddard radically changed his beliefs by embracing many of Binet's views. For example, he finally agreed that the proper treatment for individuals scoring low on intelligence tests was special education, not segregation or sterilization. But he had already done much damage.

Lewis M. Terman

Terman and the Stanford-Binet. Lewis M. Terman (1877–1956) attained his Ph.D. in 1905 from Clark University, and after holding various positions he joined the faculty at Stanford University in 1910. Terman found that when the Binet-Simon scale was administered to American children, the results were uneven. That is, the average scores of children of various ages were either higher or lower than the chronological age of the age group being tested. For example, Terman observed that items from the Binet-Simon scale were too easy for five-year-olds and too difficult for twelve-year-olds. This caused the mental age of average five-year-olds to be artificially high and that of average twelve-year-olds to be artificially low. Terman added and deleted items from the test until the average score of a sample of children was

Lewis M. Terman

100, no matter what their age. This meant that for each age group tested, the average mental age would equal the group's chronological age. Published in 1916, Terman's revision of the Binet-Simon scale was referred to as the Stanford-Binet. It was revised in 1937 and again in 1960. Throughout most of his career, Terman believed that intelligence was largely inherited and that there were genetically determined differences in intelligence. Furthermore, Terman assumed that low intelligence was the cause of most criminal and other forms of antisocial behavior. For him, a stupid person could not be a moral person.

> Not all criminals are feeble-minded, but all feeble-minded persons are at least potential criminals. That every feeble-minded woman is a potential prostitute would hardly be disputed by anyone. Moral judgment, like business judgment, social judgment, or any other kind of higher thought process, is a function of intelligence. Morality cannot flower and fruit if intelligence remains infantile. (Terman, 1916, p. 11)

Terman attempted to validate his test by correlating test performance with teacher ratings of academic performance, teacher estimations of intelligence, and school grades. He found fairly high correlations in each case, but this was not surprising, since the traits and abilities that schools and teachers valued highly in students were the same traits and abilities that yielded high scores on the Stanford-Binet. Nonetheless, the correlations meant that academic performance could be predicted with some success from test performance. Whether or not the tests were truly measuring native intelligence, however, Terman never determined.

Terman's study of genius. In Terman's day it was widely believed that very bright children were abnormal in more than a statistical sense. One common expression describing such children was "early ripe, early rot," suggesting that if mental ability developed too fast at an early age, not enough would remain for the later years. In order to objectively study the experience of bright children through the years, Terman ran one of the most famous studies in psychology's history. First, he defined genius as a score of 135 or higher on his test. Next, he administered the test to thousands of California school children, and he isolated 1,521 gifted children (850 boys and 671 girls). The average chronological age of the group was 11, and the average I.Q. of the group was 151. Learning everything he could about his subjects—including their interests, family history, educational background, health, physical characteristics, and personality—Terman wanted to study the experiences of group members as they matured through the years. He began his study in 1921 and reported the first results in *Genetic Studies of Genius* (1926). It is important to realize that the term *genetic* can have two meanings. First, it can mean "developmental." When the term is being used in this sense, a "genetic" study is one that traces how something varies as a function of maturation or time. Second, the term *genetic* can refer to the genes or chromosomes responsible for various traits. Terman used the term in the developmental sense.

Terman found that the children had parents with above average educational backgrounds, that the children had learned to read at an early age, that they participated in a wide range of activities, and that their schoolwork was usually excellent. All of this might have been expected; the major question was how these children would fare as they became older. Terman did follow-up studies in 1927–1928, when the average age of the group was about 16, and again in 1939–1940, when the average age was about 29. These studies indicated that test scores were still in the upper 1 percent of the general population, that members of the group still participated in a wide variety of activities and excelled in most of them, and that they were still outstanding academically. Seventy percent of the men and 67 percent of the women had finished college, and 56 percent of the men and 33 percent of the women had gone on for at least one advanced degree. All of these percentages were far higher than for the general population at the time.

The final follow-up that Terman participated in took place in 1950–1952, and it showed that members of the group continued to excel in most of the categories studied. By now, many members of the group had attained prominence as doctors, lawyers, teachers, judges, engineers, authors, actors, scientists, and business people. Others continued to study the group after Terman's death in 1956; in all, the group was studied for about 50 years. For the researchers involved, the results were clear: the gifted child becomes a gifted adult. Terman's study put to rest many mistaken beliefs about gifted children, but it left unanswered the question of whether "giftedness" was inherited or whether it was the result of experience. Terman felt strongly that it was inherited, but subsequent researchers have shown that many of Terman's results can be explained by taking into account the group members' experience. How much of intelligence is genetically determined and how much is environmentally determined is still a hotly contested question in psychology. Most modern researchers, however, concede that both factors are important.

INTELLIGENCE TESTING IN THE ARMED FORCES

When the United States entered World War I in 1917, **Robert M. Yerkes** (1876–1956) was president of the American Psychological Association. Yerkes had obtained his Ph.D. from Harvard in 1902 and had remained there as an instructor in comparative psychology. He called a special meeting of the association to determine how psychologists could help in the war effort. It was decided that psychologists could contribute by devising ways of selecting and evaluating recruits into the armed forces. Upon Goddard's invitation, a small group of psychologists, including Yerkes and Terman, went to the Vineland School to develop psychological tests that were then tried at various army and navy bases. Because the results were encouraging, Yerkes was made an army major and given the job of organizing a testing program for the entire army. The goals of the program were to select out the mentally defective, to classify men in terms of their intelligence level, and to select individuals for special training—for example, to become officers. Yerkes felt that in order to be effective, the test used had to be a group test rather than an individual test, had to measure "native" intelligence, and had to be easy to administer and score. Yerkes' group created a test that met these criteria, but found that 40 percent of the recruits could not read well enough to take the test. The group solved the problem by creating two forms of the test: the *Army Alpha* for the literate individuals and the *Army Beta* for illiterate individuals or for those who spoke and read a langue other than English. For an excellent review of the army tests and the outcomes of the army testing program, see Gould (1981).

The war ended in 1918, and the testing pro-

Robert M. Yerkes

gram was terminated in 1919, by which time over 1,750,000 individuals had been tested. Many people claimed that the army testing program had demonstrated psychology's practicality, but the evidence does not support such a contention. Samuelson (1977) reports that only .005 percent of those tested were recommended for discharge as mentally unfit, and in many cases the army ignored the recommendations. Also, if the army had perceived the testing program as effective, it would not have terminated the program so soon after the war ended.

THE DETERIORATION OF NATIONAL INTELLIGENCE

The use of the Army Alpha and Beta tests rekindled concern about the deterioration of the nation's intelligence level. About half of the white males tested in the army had a mental age of 13 or lower, and the situation was even worse for black soldiers. Goddard's response was that people with low mental ability should not be allowed to vote. Along with Goddard, Terman and Yerkes were very concerned about the deterioration of the nation's intelligence, which they believed immigration and the fact that intellectually inferior individuals were reproducing faster than normal or above normal individuals were causing. In addition to sterilization, these researchers proposed many other restrictions for curing these "evils."

As was common at the time, Yerkes (1923) believed that many of the nation's ills were being caused by people of low intelligence, and that immigration policies were only aggravating the problem:

> Whoever desires high taxes, full almshouses, a constantly increasing number of schools for defectives, of correctional institutions, penitentiaries, hospitals, and special classes in our public schools should by all means work for unrestricted and non-selective immigration. (p. 365)

Fortunately, the extremely nativistic position that Goddard, Terman, and Yerkes represented did not go unchallenged. More and more, people realized that performance on so-called intelligence tests could be explained by such factors as early experience and education. Rather than measuring native intelligence, the tests were apparently measuring personal achievement. It followed that the more privileged a person was in terms of enriching experiences and education, the higher his or her scores would be on so-called intelligence tests. The tests were accused of being socially and racially biased, and generally invalid as measures of intelligence. Even in recent times, however, we find an occasional nativist of the Galtonian kind who believes that intelligence tests measure native intelligence. In 1969, for example, *Arthur Jensen* claimed that performance on I.Q. tests indicated that blacks were genetically less intelligent than whites, and that special or compensatory education could there-

fore never equalize the two groups intellectually. Jensen is in the tiny minority, however, and most psychologists today would attribute differences in test scores to varying educational opportunities or to cultural biases in the tests.

Questions concerning the nature of intelligence, how best to measure intelligence, and how much of intelligence is genetically determined as opposed to environmentally determined are still being addressed in contemporary psychology. In the realm of intelligence testing, the nature-nurture controversy has always manifested itself.

SUMMARY

Evolutionary theory has existed in one form or another since the time of the early Greeks. The biblical account of the origin of species silenced evolutionary theory for many centuries, but by the eighteenth century there was again speculation about the evolutionary process. Lamarck claimed that traits acquired during an individual's lifetime that were conducive to survival were passed on to the individual's offspring. Spencer originally followed Lamarck by saying that frequently used associations were passed on to offspring in the form of reflexes and instincts. Later, Spencer accepted Darwin's version of evolutionary theory and applied it to society by saying that society should allow enough freedom so that those most fit for survival could differentiate themselves from those least fit for survival. This was called social Darwinism.

After his five-year journey aboard the *Beagle*, Darwin realized that in different locations members of a species possessed different characteristics, and that the characteristics of a species changed over time, but he could not explain why. Darwin found the explanation he needed in Malthus's *Essay on the Principle of Population* (1798), in which Malthus observed that a species always produced many more offspring than the food supply could support, but that population was kept in check by such things as starvation and disease. Darwin expanded Malthus's notion into the notion of a general struggle for survival in which only the fittest survived. According to Darwin, many more offspring of a species were born than could survive. There were individual differences among those offspring, and in the struggle for survival, some offspring possessed traits that were conducive to survival, while others did not. Only the fittest offspring would survive. Thus, there was a natural selection of those offspring whose traits were most conducive to survival under the existing circumstances. In his books *The Descent of Man* (1871) and *The Expression of Emotions in Man and Animals* (1872), Darwin demonstrated that the evolutionary process applied to humans as well as to other living organisms.

Darwin's cousin Francis Galton had a passion for measurement. He equated intelligence with sensory acuity, and therefore measured intelligence mainly by measuring the acuity of the senses. Since he believed that intelligence was inherited, he urged the practice of eugenics, or selective breeding, to improve human intelligence. Using psychology's first word-association test, Galton found that responses to stimulus words tended to remain constant, tended to be drawn from childhood experience, and suggested the existence of an unconscious mind. In his research on mental imagery, Galton found that the ability to experience mental images was normally distributed. Galton also observed that although there was a tendency for children to inherit the traits of their parents, there was also a regression toward the mean. That is, extremely tall parents tended to have tall children, but the children tended not to be as tall as the parents. By demonstrating how two things tended to vary together, Galton invented the method of correlation. It was Pearson who created the formula that quantified the magnitude of a correlation by generating a coefficient of correlation.

Cattell brought Galton's notion of intelligence testing to the United States. Wissler's research indicated that Galton's sensory and motor tests were not all measuring the same thing (intelligence), since the correlations among the tests were low. When Wissler found practically no relationship between performance on the tests and performance in college, it was concluded that the tests had little practical value.

In France, Binet took another approach to measuring intelligence. The earlier research of Binet and others had indicated that intelligence consisted of several different mental abilities, such as memory, imagery, attention, comprehension, and judgment. Binet's goal was to devise tests that would directly measure these mental abilities. In response to the French government's request for an instrument that could be used to distinguish reliably between normal and mentally retarded children, Binet and Simon offered their 1905 scale of intelligence. The scale consisted of 30 tests arranged from the simplest to the most difficult. The more tests a child passed, the higher was his or her score. It was assumed that scores varied with intelligence. In 1908 Binet and Simon revised their scale so that it would not only distinguish between normal and retarded children but would distinguish levels of intelligence among normal children as well. They gave the scale to children between the ages of 3 and 13, and all tests that 75 percent or more of the children of a certain age passed were assigned to that age. In this way it became possible to determine whether any particular child was performing at, above, or below the average performance of other children of his or her age. In 1911 Binet and Simon again revised the scale so that five tests corresponded to each age level. This allowed ⅕ of a year to be added to a child's score for each test he or she passed beyond the average for his or her age group. Stern suggested the term *mental age* and also the notion of intelligence quotient (I.Q.). I.Q. was calculated by dividing a child's mental age (score on the Binet-Simon scale) by the child's chronological age and multiplying the quotient by 100.

Goddard translated the Binet-Simon scale into English and administered it to both the retarded children at the Vineland School, where he worked, and to children in the New Jersey public schools. Appalled to find that many public school children performed at a level below their age norm, Goddard believed this poor performance reflected a deterioration in the nation's native intelligence. To investigate the relationship between inheritance and intelligence, Goddard studied the family history of a retarded girl at the Vineland School. He found that one of the girl's distant relatives had had a child by a feebleminded barmaid, and that the line of descendents from that child forward was characterized by mental defectiveness and criminal and antisocial behavior. The man who had fathered the barmaid's child subsequently married a "normal" woman, and their descendents showed a very low incidence of mental defectiveness, many individuals from that side of the family attaining positions of prominence. Goddard and many others took these findings as support for the contention that intelligence was inherited. Many states instituted laws allowing for the sterilization of mentally defective individuals as well as others who were socially undesirable, while the influence of personal experience on intelligence level was essentially ignored.

Fear of the "menace of the feebleminded" directed attention to the immigrants entering the United States. Administration of the Binet-Simon test led to the conclusion that many immigrants were mentally defective, and they were deported back to Europe. The fact that the scale was written in English and many of the immigrants knew little or no English was ignored.

Terman revised the Binet-Simon scale, making it more compatible with American culture and statistically easier to analyze. Terman's revision, called the Stanford-Binet, was used to isolate about 1,500 intellectually gifted children who were then intensely studied throughout their lives. Through the years it was found that members of this group of gifted individuals continued to score in the top 1 percent of the population in intelligence, participated in and excelled at a wide range of activities, and were outstanding academically. Since the study showed that the gifted children became well adjusted, successful, healthy adults, it laid to rest the belief that gifted individuals were psychologically abnormal.

When the United States entered World War I, Yerkes and others concluded that psychology could help in the war effort by devising tests that could be used to classify recruits into the armed forces in terms of their intellectual level. The psychologists developed an Army Alpha test for literate recruits and an Army Beta test for illiterate or non–English-speaking recruits. Although more than 1,500,000 recruits were tested, only a very few were recommended for rejection because of low test performance. The army ignored most of those recommendations anyway, and terminated the testing program shortly after the war ended.

According to the results of the army's testing program, about half of the white males tested had a mental age of 13 or lower, and the situation was even worse for black males. Once again there were proposals for restricting marriage and for widespread sterilization of mentally defective individuals. At this time, however, a growing number of prominent individuals were wondering whether so-called intelligence tests were actually measuring genetically determined intelligence. They argued that test performance was determined more by education and personal experience than by genes, and there was a growing feeling that as more and more people received equal experiential opportunities test performance would also equalize. In other words, it was argued that so-called intelligence tests were more achievement tests than aptitude tests.

Efforts to define intelligence and to determine how best to measure it continue in contemporary psychology. Today, most psychologists believe that inheritance and experience are both factors in intelligence. The argument now mainly concerns the relative contributions of the two factors.

DISCUSSION QUESTIONS

1. Summarize Lamarck's theory of evolution.

2. Describe Spencer's social Darwinism.

3. What were the ironies concerning Darwin's voyage aboard the *Beagle*?

4. Why did Darwin delay publication of his theory for so long? What finally prompted him to publish it?

5. Summarize Darwin's theory of evolution.

6. What did Galton mean when he said that eugenics should be practiced? Where did he stand on the nature-nurtue question?

7. Explain why Galton's measures of "intelligence" were mainly sensory in nature.

8. Summarize Galton's contributions to psychology.

9. In what ways did Binet's approach to intelligence testing differ from Galton's?

10. Describe the 1905 Binet-Simon scale of intelligence. How was the scale changed in 1908 and in 1911?

11. What procedures did Stern suggest for reporting a person's intelligence? Why did Binet oppose these procedures?

12. What conclusions did Goddard reach when he administered the Binet-Simon scale to schoolchildren in the United States?

13. What procedures did Goddard suggest for stopping the deterioration of intelligence in the United States? In suggesting these procedures, what assumption did he make?

14. Summarize the conclusions that Goddard reached when he traced the ancestry of Deborah Kallikak.

15. Try to make a case that Goddard caused many immigrants to be unjustifiably deported.

16. In what important way did Terman modify the Binet-Simon scale?

17. What prompted Terman's longitudinal study of gifted individuals?

18. Summarize the results of Terman's study of gifted individuals.

19. How did Yerkes suggest that psychologists help in the war effort? Was the effort that resulted from this suggestion a success or a failure?

20. What arguments were offered in opposition to the contention that intelligence tests were measuring genetically determined intelligence?

21. Where do most psychologists stand today on the nature-nurture question as it applies to intelligence?

GLOSSARY

Anthropometry Galton's approach to measuring intelligence. Anthropometry consisted of measuring the sensory capacities of individuals.

Binet, Alfred (1857–1910) Found that following Galton's methods of measuring intelligence often resulted in falsely concluding that deaf and blind children had low intelligence. Binet attempted to measure directly the cognitive abilities he thought comprised intelligence.

Binet-Simon scale of intelligence The scale by Binet and Simon devised for measuring directly the various cognitive abilities they felt comprised intelligence. The scale first appeared in 1905 and was revised in 1908 and in 1911.

Cattell, James McKeen (1860–1944) Worked with Galton and developed a strong interest in measuring individual differences. Cattell brought Galton's methods of intelligence testing to the United States.

Coefficient of Correlation (r) A mathematical expression indicating the magnitude of correlation between two variables.

Correlation Systematic variation in two variables.

Craniometry The measurement of head volume to determine intelligence. Binet initially employed this technique, but he eventually dropped it.

Darwin, Charles (1809–1882) Originator of modern evolutionary theory. By showing the continuity between humans and other animals, Darwin strongly influenced psychology.

Eugenics The use of selective breeding to increase the general intelligence of the population.

Experimenter bias The tendency that Binet observed for researchers to find what they were looking for. Binet felt that this self-fulfilling prophecy occurred on the unconscious level. It was later called experimenter bias or the experimenter effect.

Galton, Francis (1822–1911) Under the influence of his cousin Charles Darwin, was keenly interested in the measurement of individual differences. Galton was convinced that intellectual ability was inherited, and therefore recommended eugenics or the selective breeding of humans. He was the first to attempt to systematically measure intelligence.

Goddard, Henry H. (1866–1957) Translated Binet's intelligence test into English and used it to test and classify retarded students. Goddard was an extreme nativist who recommended that the mentally defective be sterilized or institutionalized.

Inheritance of acquired characteristics Lamarck's contention that abilities developed during an organism's lifetime were passed on to the organism's offspring.

Intelligence quotient (I.Q.) A way Stern suggested for quantifying intelligence. Mental age is divided by chronological age, and the quotient is multiplied by 100.

Lamarck, Jean (1744–1829) Proposed that functional characteristics acquired during an organism's lifetime were genetically passed on to the organism's offspring. This was the mechanism by which species were transformed.

Malthus, Thomas (1766–1834) Wrote *Essay on the Principle of Population* (1798), which provided Darwin with the principle he needed for explaining the observations he had made while aboard the *Beagle*. The principle was that many more individuals are born than the environment can support; therefore, there is a struggle for survival.

Mental age According to Stern, a composite score reflecting all of the tests that a child could successfully pass.

Mental orthopedics The procedures that Binet suggested for enhancing determination, attention, and discipline. These procedures would prepare a child for formal education.

Natural selection A key concept in Darwin's theory of evolution. Since more members of a species are born than the environment can support, nature selects those with characteristics most conducive to survival under the circumstances to continue living and to reproduce.

Nature-nurture controversy The debate over whether important attributes are inherited or learned.

Pearson, Karl (1867–1936) Devised the formula that produces the Coefficient of Correlation.

Regression toward the mean The tendency for extremes to become less extreme in one's offspring. For example, the offspring of extremely tall parents tend not to be as tall as the parents.

Simon, Theodore (1878–1961) Collaborated with Binet to develop the first test designed to directly measure intelligence.

Social Darwinism Spencer's contention that, if given freedom to compete in society, the ablest individuals will succeed and the weaker ones will fail.

Spencer, Herbert (1820–1903) First a follower of Lamarck, then of Darwin. Spencer applied Darwinian principles to society by saying that society should maintain a laissez-faire policy so that the ablest individuals could prevail. Spencer's position is called social Darwinism.

Stern, William (1871–1938) Suggested the intelligence quotient (I.Q.) as a means of quantifying intelligence. I.Q. is obtained by dividing mental age by chronological age and multiplying the quotient by 100. Stern also proposed the concept of mental age.

Struggle for survival Situation that arises when there are more offspring of a species than the environment can support.

Survival of the fittest The notion that in a struggle for survival, those organisms with traits most conducive to survival under the circumstances will survive and reproduce.

Terman, Lewis (1877–1952) Revised Binet's test of intelligence, making it more compatible with the American culture. Terman was instrumental in creating the Army Alpha and Army Beta tests. He also conducted a longitudinal study of gifted children and found that, contrary to the belief at the time, gifted children tended to become gifted adults.

Wallace, Alfred Russell (1823–1913) Developed a theory of evolution almost identical to Darwin's, at almost the same time that Darwin developed his theory.

Yerkes, Robert M. (1876–1956) Was responsible for the creation of the Army Alpha and Army Beta tests. Yerkes concluded that the tests could have been more useful if the army had acted upon the results, instead of practically ignoring them. On the nature-nurture question as it applied to intelligence, Yerkes was a nativist.

CHAPTER 11

Functionalism

In Chapter 9 we reviewed Titchener's brand of psychology, which he called structuralism. Because Titchener's psychology was strongly influenced by Wundt, it was largely German in approach and content. We will now look at what psychology was like before Titchener, and before the doctrine of evolution was to combine with the American *Zeitgeist* to create what became America's own brand of psychology.

EARLY AMERICAN PSYCHOLOGY

It is generally assumed that American psychology did not exist before Titchener and William James. In his presidential address to the Ninth International Congress of Psychology at Yale University in 1929, James McKeen Cattell said that a history of American psychology before the 1880s "would be as short as a book on snakes in Ireland since the time of St. Patrick. Insofar as psychologists are concerned, America was then like heaven, for there was not a damned soul there" (1929, p. 12).

To make such a statement, Cattell assumed that only experimental psychology was *real* psychology and that everything else was mental or moral philosophy. Titchener agreed, and he argued forcibly that experimental psychology should be completely separated from philosophy and especially from theology. The problem with Cattell and Titchener's argument is that it ignores the fact that experimental psychology grew out of nonexperimental psychology, and

to understand the former one must understand the latter. Evans (1984) says:

> To deny that there was psychological thought before the 1880's in America is to deny that it existed in Europe before Wilhelm Wundt opened the Leipzig laboratory or in England before Francis Galton opened his laboratory in London. There were in all these places long histories of psychological thought that acted as the substrata for the establishment of various experimental psychologies of the twentieth century. . . .
>
> Nothing emerges from nothing. Before there emerged courses, professorships, and departments in American colleges labeled "psychological," there were people with other titles talking about much the same things, although often under different rubrics and with different intents than those of the twentieth-century psychologists. (p. 18)

In an attempt to set the record straight, Fay wrote *American Psychology before William James* (1939), and Roback wrote *History of American Psychology* (1952), which traces American psychology back to the colonial days. Also, Brŏzek has recently edited a book entitled *Explorations in the History of Psychology in the United States* (1984). For our purposes, however, we will follow Sahakian's (1975) description of the four stages of early American psychology.

Stage One: Moral and Mental Philosophy (1640–1776)

Early in the 136-year period of moral and mental philosophy, psychology included such topics as ethics, divinity, and philosophy. During this time, psychology concerned matters of the soul, and what was taught was not questioned. Thus, to learn psychology was to learn the accepted theology of the day. Like all the other subjects taught at the time, psychology was combined with religious indoctrination. The earliest American universities, such as Harvard (founded in 1636), were modeled after the British universities, whose main purpose was to perpetuate religious beliefs.

A period of "American enlightenment" began in 1714, when John Locke's *Essay Concerning Human Understanding* (1690) arrived in America and had a widespread influence. *Samuel Johnson* (1696–1772), the first president of Columbia University (founded in 1754) embraced Locke enthusiastically and wrote a book containing many of Locke's ideas. This book also contained a number of topics clearly psychological in nature—for example, child psychology, the nature of consciousness, the nature of knowledge, introspection, and perception. Lockean philosophy provided the basis for a logic and a psychology that could be used to support one's religious beliefs. Roback (1952, p. 23) says of this period, "Psychology existed for the sake of logic, and logic for the sake of God."

Stage Two: Intellectual Philosophy (1776–1886)

During the stage of intellectual philosophy, psychology became a separate discipline in America, largely because of the Scottish "common sense" philosophy. As we saw in Chapter 6, the Scottish philosophy of common sense was a reaction against philosophers such as Hume, who maintained that nothing could be known with certainty and that moral and scientific laws were nothing more than mental habits. Scottish philosophers such as *Thomas Reid* (1710–1796) disagreed, saying that sensory information could be accepted at face value. The Scottish philosophers also maintained that self-examina-

tion or introspection yielded valid information, and that morality was based on self-evident intuitions. The "common sense" philosophy had clear implications for theology: the existence and nature of God need not be proved logically, since one's personal feelings could be trusted on these matters.

With the respectability of the senses and feelings established, textbooks written by the Scottish philosophers began to include such topics as perception, memory, imagination, association, attention, language, and thinking. Such a textbook, written by *Dugald Stewart* in 1792 and entitled *Elements of the Philosophy of the Human Mind*, was used at Yale University in 1824.

Soon American textbooks bearing a close resemblance to those of the Scottish philosophers began to appear, such as Noah Porter's *The Human Intellect: With an Introduction upon Psychology and the Soul* (1868). Porter's text represents a transitional period when psychology was leaving the realm of philosophy and theology and becoming a separate discipline. Porter's book defined psychology as the science of the human soul and covered such topics as psychology as a branch of physics, psychology as a science, consciousness, sense perception, development of the intellect, association of ideas, memory, and reason. We can see in Porter's text, and in many other texts of the time, the strong influence of the Scottish "common sense" philosophy, as well as the emphasis on the individual that was later to characterize modern American psychology.

Stage Three: The American Renaissance (1886–1896)

During the American Renaissance, psychology was completely emancipated from religion and philosophy and became an empirical science. In 1886 John Dewey wrote *Psychology*, which described the new empirical science. In 1887 the first issue of the *American Journal of Psychology*,

America's first psychology journal, appeared; and in 1890 William James's *Principles of Psychology* was published. All these events marked the beginning of a psychology that was to emphasize individual differences, adaptation to the environment, and practicality—in other words, a psychology that was perfectly compatible with evolutionary theory. Since the days of the pioneers, Americans had emphasized individuality and practicality, and adaptation to the environment had to be a major concern. This explains why America was such fertile ground for phrenology, mesmerism, and spiritualism—practices that purported to help individuals.

Stage Four: American Functionalism (1896 to present)

During the stage of American functionalism, science, concern for practicality, emphasis of the individual, and evolutionary theory combined into functionalism, America's first school of psychology. Sahakian (1975) marks the beginning of functionalism with the 1896 publication of John Dewey's article "The Reflex Arc in Psychology." This date is somewhat arbitrary. Others mark the formal beginning of American Psychology with the 1890 publication of James's book *The Principles of Psychology*. Whether one accepts Dewey or James as the founder of American psychology, it is clear that the tone set by these men, and by others whom we shall consider below, still permeates American psychology.

WILLIAM JAMES

William James (1842–1910) represents the transition between European psychology and American psychology. His ideas were not fully enough developed to suggest a school of thought, but they contained the seeds that were later to grow into the school of functionalism.

William James

ARCHIVES OF THE HISTORY OF AMERICAN PSYCHOLOGY

Biographical Sketch

William James was born on January 11, 1842, at the Astor House in New York City. His brother Henry, the famous novelist, was born 15 months later. William and Henry's father, who was independently wealthy, believed that his children should receive the best possible education. After enrolling William in several private schools in America, the father decided that European schools would be better; so James attended schools in Switzerland, France, Germany, and England. James's early life was highly stimulating, involving a great deal of travel and exposure to intense intellectual discussions at home.

At 18 years of age, James studied painting; a

year later, in 1861, he enrolled as a chemistry student at Harvard University. He soon switched to physiology to prepare himself for a career in medicine, and in 1864 he enrolled in Harvard's medical school. James's medical studies were interrupted when he accepted an invitation from Louis Agassiz, a famous Harvard biologist and an opponent of Darwinian theory, to go on an expedition to Brazil. Seasick most of the time, James also came down with smallpox, and he decided to return home and continue his medical studies. After he returned home, his health deteriorated further, his eyesight became weak, and he experienced severe back pains. In 1867, James decided to go to Germany and bathe in mineral springs, in hopes of improving his back problems. While in Germany, he continued to read German psychology and philosophy. In his diary, James shares a letter written to a friend in 1867, which shows that this was the time when James discovered Wundt and agreed with Wundt that psychology should attempt to become a science:

> I have blocked out some reading in physiology and psychology which I hope to execute this winter—though reading in German is still disgustingly slow . . . it seems to me that perhaps the time has come for psychology to begin to be a science—some measurements have already been made. . . . Helmholtz and a man named Wundt at Heidelberg are working at it. . . . The fact is, this sickness takes all the spring, physical and mental, out of a man. (1920, Vol. 1, pp. 118–119)

James returned to America and finally obtained his medical degree from Harvard in 1869. After graduation, however, James's health deteriorated further, and he became deeply depressed. Apparently, one reason for his depression was the implications of the German mechanistic physiology and psychology that had so impressed him. It was clear to James that if the mechanistic philosophy was correct, it applied to him as well. This meant that anything that happened to him was predetermined and thus beyond his control. His depression, for example, was a matter of fate, and it made no sense to attempt to do anything about it.

A major turning point in James's life came when he read an essay on free will by Charles Renouvier. After reading this essay, James wrote in his diary:

> I think that yesterday was a crisis in my life. I finished the first part of Renouvier's second "Essais" and see no reason why his definition of free will—"The sustaining of a thought because I choose to when I might have other thoughts"—need be the definition of an illusion. At any rate, I will assume for the present—until next year—that it is no illusion. My first act of free will shall be to believe in free will. . . . Hitherto, when I have felt like taking a free initiative, like daring to act originally, without carefully waiting for contemplation of the external world to determine all for me, suicide seemed the most manly form to put my daring into; now I will go a step further with my will, not only act with it, but believe as well; believe in my individual reality and creative power. (1920, Vol. 1, pp. 147–148)

This change in beliefs cured James's depression, and he became highly productive. Here we have the beginnings of James's **pragmatism**, the belief that if an idea works, it is valid. That is, the ultimate criterion for judging an idea should be the idea's usefulness. At this point we also see the conflict James perceived between the objective, scientific point of view based on determinism and personal, subjective feelings such as the feeling that one's will is free. James used pragmatism to solve the problem. While using scientific method in psychology, he said, it was necessary to assume that human behavior was the result of heredity, habits, and/or instincts. As useful as this method was, however, it had limits. Certain metaphysical questions lay beyond the reach of science, and in dealing with them, a subjective approach was more useful. Therefore, according to James, both a scientific *and* a philosophical approach must be used in the study of human behavior and thought. To assume that all aspects of humans could be known through scientific research, he said, was like a doctor giving all his patients tics because it was the only thing he could cure. If something about humans—for example, free will—could not be studied effectively using a certain method, James said, one did not throw out that aspect of human existence. Rather, one sought alternative methods of investigation. Following his own advice, as he often did, he explored the phenomenon of religious experience and summarized his findings in *The Varieties of Religious Experience* (1902). James's willingness to use methods ranging from anecdotes to rigorous experimentation was further testimony to his belief in pragmatism.

In 1872 James was given the opportunity to teach physiology at Harvard, and he taught for one year. He then toured Europe for a year and again returned to Harvard to teach, but this time his course concerned the relations between physiology and psychology. In 1875 James created a small demonstration laboratory, which he used in teaching his course. This has raised a controversy concerning who should be given credit for establishing psychology's first laboratory, Wundt in 1879 or James in 1875. Usually the credit is given to Wundt, since his laboratory was more elaborate and was designed for research and not merely for teaching demonstrations, but the debate continues.

In 1878 the publisher Henry Holt offered James a contract to write a textbook on psychology. The textbook was finally published 12 years later, in 1890. Although James's *Principles of Psychology* was to revolutionize psychology, James did not think much of it, as he indicates in a letter he sent to the publisher along with the manuscript:

No one could be more disgusted than I at the sight of the book. No subject is worth being treated of in 1000 pages. Had I ten years more, I could rewrite it in 500; but as it stands it is this or nothing—a loathsome, distended, tumefied, bloated, dropsical mass, testifying to nothing

but two facts: 1st, that there is no such thing as a science of psychology, and 2nd, that W. J. is an incapable. (1920, Vol. 1, p. 294)

Contrary to James's opinion of his book, MacLeod (1975) says:

James' *Principles* is without question the most literate, the most provocative, and at the same time the most intelligible book on psychology that has ever appeared in English or in any other language. (p. 15)

Two years later (1892), James published a condensed version of his *Principles*, which came to be called "Jimmey."

In neither James's writings nor in James the man do we find an organized theory. Rather, we find treatment of a wide variety of topics, many of which later researchers pursued. As we shall see, however, the themes of practicality (pragmatism) and individuality permeate most of his writings. James was always willing to entertain a wide variety of ideas ranging from religion, mysticism, faith healing, and psychic phenomena to the most rigorous scientific facts and methods available in psychology at the time. Murphy (1968) summarizes James's *Principles*:

He [James] argued at times for essentially an associationist's viewpoint, at times for a highly integrated oneness of each psychological act. He gave instinct and habit formation a large place, and at the same time looked for cognitive acts of profundity and range, and for the ultimate pinnacle of the life of the mind in the process of the will. He is at the same time evolutionist and mystic, lover of the raw, crude, vague, confused, intellectually unrespectable. At the other end of the spectrum, he is an aspirant to the sharpest clarity and the highest order that mind can achieve. Consistency in ultimate outlook one should not expect to find in the *Principles* even were one to regard it as the creation of a single year. The chapters represent different angles, different phases, different recurring themes evident in twelve years of a great man's life. They must be read as profound literature, often factually correct, modern in spirit, but far more important than either, always challenging, guiding, preparing us for new discoveries. (p. 147)

We will now sample a few of James's more famous notions.

Opposition to Structuralism

Almost everything in *Principles* can be seen as a criticism of structuralism, but James is especially harsh in the following passage (1890):

> Within a few years what one may call a microscopic psychology has arisen in Germany, carried on by experimental methods, asking of course every moment for introspective data, but eliminating their uncertainty by operating on a large scale and taking statistical means. This method taxes patience to the utmost, and hardly could have arisen in a country whose natives could be *bored*. Such Germans as Weber, Fechner . . . and Wundt obviously cannot; and their success has brought into the field an array of younger experimental psychologists, bent on studying the *elements* of the mental life, dissecting them from the gross results in which they are embedded, and as far as possible reducing them to quantitative scales. The simple and open method of attack having done what it can, the method of patience, starving out, and harassing to death is tried; the Mind must submit to a regular *siege*, in which minute advantages gained night and day by the forces that hem her in must sum themselves up at last into her overthrow. There is little left of the grand style about these new prism, pendulum, and chronography-philosophers. They mean business, not chivalry. What generous divination, and that superiority in virtue which was thought by Cicero to give a man the best insight into nature, have failed to do, their spying and scraping, their deadly tenacity and almost diabolic cunning, will doubtless some day bring about. (Vol. 1, pp. 192–193)

Stream of Consciousness

With **stream of consciousness**, James again takes on the structuralists who were busy searching for the *elements* of thought. In the first place, says James, *consciousness is personal*. It re-

flects the experiences of an individual, and therefore it is foolhardy to search for elements common to all minds. Second, *consciousness is continuous and cannot be divided up for analysis*. James (1890) says:

> Let anyone try to cut a thought across in the middle and get a look at its section. . . . The rush of the thought is so headlong that it almost always brings us at the conclusion before we can arrest it. Or if our purpose is nimble enough and we do arrest it, it ceases forthwith to be itself. As a snowflake crystal caught in the warm hand is no longer a crystal but a drop, so, instead of catching the feeling of relation moving to its term, we find we have caught some substantive thing, usually the last word we were pronouncing, statically taken, and with its function, tendency, and particular meaning in the sentence quite evaporated. The attempt at introspective analysis in these cases is in fact like seizing a spinning top to catch its motion, or trying to turn up the gas quickly enough to see how the darkness looks. (Vol. 1, p. 244)

Third, *consciousness is constantly changing*. Even though consciousness is continuous and can be characterized as a steady stream from birth to death, it is also constantly changing. James quotes Heraclitus's aphorism about the impossibility of stepping into the same river twice. For James, the same is true for conscious experience. One can never have exactly the same idea twice, since the stream of consciousness that provides the context for the idea is ever-changing.

Fourth, *consciousness is selective*. Some of the many events entering consciousness are selected for further consideration and others are inhibited. Here James (1890) flirts again with free will:

> We see that the mind is at every stage a theatre of simultaneous possibilities. Consciousness consists in the comparison of these with each other, the selection of some, and the suppression of the rest by the reinforcing and inhibiting agency of attention. (Vol. 1, p. 288)

Finally, and perhaps most importantly, *con-

sciousness is functional. This point permeates all of James's writing, and it is the point from which the school of functionalism evolved. According to James, the most important thing about consciousness—and the thing the structuralists overlooked—was that its purpose was to aid the individual in adapting to the environment. Here we see the powerful influence of Darwin on early American scientific psychology.

Consciousness, then, is personal, continuous, constantly changing, selective, and purposive. There is little in this view that is compatible with the view held by the structuralists.

Habits and Instincts

James believed that both instinct and habit governed human behavior. For example, he believed that humans were both gregarious and aggressive by nature. Whatever instincts we had, however, could be modified by experience. As an activity was repeated, habits formed. Repetition caused the same neural pathways to, from, and within the brain to become more entrenched, making it easier for energy to pass through those pathways. Thus James had a neurophysiological explanation of habit formation, and his neurophysiological account of learning was very close of Pavlov's. According to James (1890), habit makes society possible:

> Habit is thus the enormous fly-wheel of society, its most precious conservative agent. It alone is what keeps us all within the bounds of ordinance, and saves the children of fortune from the envious uprisings of the poor. It alone prevents the hardest and most repulsive walks of life from being deserted by those brought up to tread therein. . . . It dooms us all to fight out the battle of life upon the lines of our nurture or our early choice, and to make the best of a pursuit that disagrees, because there is no other for which we are fitted, and it is too late to begin again. It keeps different social strata from mixing. Already at the age of twenty-five you see the professional mannerism settling down on the young commercial traveller, on the young

doctor, on the young minister, on the young counsellor-at-law. You see the little lines of cleavage running through the character, the tricks of thought, the prejudices, the ways of the "shop," in a word, from which the man can by-and-by no more escape than his coat-sleeve can suddenly fall into a new set of folds. On the whole, it is best he should not escape. It is well for the world that in most of us, by the age of thirty, the character has set like plaster, and will never soften again. (Vol. 1, p. 121)

The Self

James discussed what he called the *empirical self* or the "me" of personality, which consisted of those things that could be empirically determined about a person. James divided the empirical self into three components: (1) the material self, which was everything material that a person could call his or her own, including his or her own body; (2) the social self, which consisted of the various roles a person played in his or her life (this was the person as known by others); and (3) the spiritual self, which consisted of a person's will and moral responsibility. The empirical self was the person as *known*. Above the empirical self James postulated a self as *knower*, or the "I" of personality. This was the aspect of self that did the knowing. James also defined *self-esteem* as a ratio of goals and successes. In other words, the feeling of self-esteem that one experienced was a function of both what one tried (individual goals) and what one accomplished.

Emotions

James reversed the traditional belief that emotion resulted from the perception of an event. For example, it was traditionally believed that we saw a bear, we were frightened, and we ran. According to James, we saw a bear, we ran, and *then* we were frightened. Perception, according to James, caused bodily reactions that were then experienced as emotions. In other words, the emotions we felt depended on what we *did*. James (1890) puts his theory as follows:

> Our natural way of thinking about . . . emotions is that the mental perception of some fact excites the mental affection called the emotion, and that this latter state of mind gives rise to the bodily expression. My theory, on the contrary, is that *the bodily changes follow directly the perception of the exciting fact, and that our feeling of the same changes as they occur IS the emotion*. Common-sense says, we lose our fortune, are sorry and weep; we meet a bear, are frightened and run; we are insulted by a rival, are angry and strike. The hypothesis here to be defended says that this order of sequence is incorrect, that the one mental state is not immediately induced by the other, that the bodily manifestations must first be interposed between, and that the more rational statement is that we feel sorry because we cry, angry because we strike, afraid because we tremble, and not that we cry, strike, or tremble, because we are sorry, angry, or fearful, as the case may be. Without the bodily states following on the perception, the latter would be purely cognitive in form, pale, colorless, destitute of emotional warmth. We might then see a bear, and judge it best to run, receive the insult and deem it right to strike, but we should not actually *feel* afraid or angry. (Vol. 2, pp. 449–450)

Coupled with James's belief in free will, his theory of emotion yields practical advice: *act the way you want to feel*. If we believe James, there is a great deal of truth in Oscar Hammerstein's line, "Whenever I feel afraid, I whistle a happy tune. And soon I'm not afraid." James (1890) says:

> Whistling to keep up courage is no mere figure of speech. On the other hand, sit all day in a moping posture, sigh, and reply to everything with a dismal voice, and your melancholy lingers. There is no more valuable precept in moral education than this, as all who have experience know: if we wish to conquer undesirable emotional tendencies in ourselves we must assiduously, and in the first instance cold-bloodedly, go through the *outward movements* of those contrary dispositions which we prefer to cultivate. The reward of persistency will infallibly come, in the fading out of the sullenness or depression, and the advent of real cheerfulness and kindliness in their stead. (Vol. 2, p. 463)

James had discovered the power of this advice when he decided to believe in free will and thus cured the depression that believing in a strict determinism had caused.

James's theory of emotion provides still another example of the importance of the *Zeitgeist*, since the Danish physician **Carl George Lange** (1834–1900) published virtually the same theory at about the same time. In recognition of the contributions of both men, the theory is now known as the **James-Lange theory of emotion**.

Free Will

Although James did not solve the free will-determinism controversy, he did arrive at a position that he was confortable with. He noted that without the assumption of determinism, science would be impossible; and insofar as psychology was to be a science, it, too, must assume determinism. Science, however, was not everything, and for certain approaches to the study of humans, the assumption of free will might be very fruitful. As James (1890) says:

> Science . . . must constantly be reminded that her purposes are not the only purposes, and that the order of uniform causation which she has use for, and is therefore right in postulating, may be enveloped in a wider order, on which she has no claims at all. (Vol. 2, p. 576)

Pragmatism

Everywhere in James's writings is his belief in pragmatism. According to pragmatism, which is the cornerstone of functionalism, any belief, thought, or behavior must be judged by its consequences. Any belief that helps create a more effective and satisfying life is worth holding, whether such a belief is scientific or religious. Believing in free will was emotionally satisfying to James, so he believed in it. According to the pragmatic point of view, truth is not something "out there" in a static form, waiting to be discovered, as the rationalists maintained. Instead, truth is something that must be gauged by effectiveness under changing circumstances. What works is true, and since circumstances change, truth must be forever dynamic.

James's pragmatic philosophy appears in his description of the methods that psychology should employ. He urged the use of both introspection and experimentation, as well as the study of animals, children, preliterate humans, and abnormal humans. In short, he encouraged the use of any method that would shed light on the complexities of human existence; he believed that nothing useful should be omitted.

In 1907 James wrote *Pragmatism*, in which he delineated two kinds of personality: the *tender-minded* and the *tough-minded*. Tender-minded people are rationalistic (principle-oriented), intellectual, idealistic, optimistic, religious, and dogmatic, and they believe in free will. Tough-minded people, on the other hand, are empiricistic (fact-oriented), sensationalistic, materialistic, pessimistic, irreligious, skeptical, and fatalistic. James saw pragmatism as a way of compromising between the two outlooks. The pragmatist simply takes from each list whatever works in the circumstances at hand, or combines the lists in some way. James (1907) gives the following example:

> There are unhappy men who think the salvation of the world impossible. Theirs is the doctrine known as pessimism.
>
> Optimism in turn would be the doctrine that thinks the world's salvation inevitable.
>
> Midway between the two there stands what may be called the doctrine of meliorism. . . . Meliorism treats salvation as neither necessary nor impossible. It treats it as a possibility, which becomes more and more of a probability the more numerous the actual conditions of salvation become.
>
> It is clear that pragmatism must incline towards meliorism. (pp. 285–286)

James's Contributions to Psychology

James helped to incorporate evolutionary theory into psychology. By stressing what was useful, he represented a major departure from structuralism. He expanded research techniques in psychology not only by accepting introspection, but by encouraging any other technique that promised to yield useful information about people. By studying all aspects of human existence—including behavior, cognition, emotions, volition, and even religious experience—James also expanded the subject matter of psychology. His ideas led directly to the school of functionalism, which we will discuss later in this chapter. Many believe that current psychology in America represents a return to psychology as James described it.

In 1892, when James was 50, he decided that he had said everything he could say about psychology, especially about experimental psychology. He decided to devote his full attention to philosophical matters, something that necessitated his giving up the directorship of the Harvard Psychology Laboratory. To maintain the laboratory's reputation as the best in the country, James sought an outstanding, creative, experimentally oriented psychologist, and certainly one who did not embrace Wundtian psychology. He found such a person in Hugo Münsterberg.

HUGO MÜNSTERBERG

Born in the East Prussian port city of Danzig (now Gdansk, Poland), **Hugo Münsterberg** (1863–1916) was one of four sons of prominent parents. His father was a successful businessman, his mother a recognized artist. Throughout his life, Münsterberg had wide-ranging interests. In his early years, he displayed interest and talent in poetry, foreign languages, music, and acting. Then, while studying medicine at the University of Leipzig, he heard a lecture by Wundt, and his interest switched to psychology. Münsterberg became Wundt's research assistant and received his Ph.D. under Wundt's supervision in 1885. The next year, Münsterberg obtained his medical degree from the University of Heidelberg. In 1887 he was appointed

Hugo Münsterberg

lecturer at the University of Freiburg, where he started a psychology laboratory and began publishing papers on time perception, attentional processes, learning, and memory. In 1888 he published *Activity of the Will*, which James called a masterpiece and Wundt criticized harshly.

During the time when Münsterberg was Wundt's assistant, one of Münsterberg's jobs was to study voluntary activities through introspection. But the two men disagreed over whether the will could be experienced as a conscious element of the mind during introspection. Wundt believed that it could, while Münsterberg felt that it could not. In *Activity of the Will*, Münsterberg reasserted his earlier position on the matter. James was impressed by many of Münsterberg's publications and cited them often in his *Principles of Psychology*. He arranged to meet Münsterberg at the first International Congress of Psychology in 1889, and their relationship strengthened further.

In 1892 James asked Münsterberg to replace him as director of the Harvard Psychology Laboratory, and Münsterberg accepted. For about three years, Münsterberg lived up to James's expectations by supervising a highly productive experimental laboratory. More and more, however, Münsterberg's interests turned to the practical applications of psychological principles. Unlike his mentor Wundt, Münsterberg felt *very* strongly that psychologists should attempt to uncover information that could be used in the "real world." With his efforts, Münsterberg did much to create what is now referred to as **applied psychology**.

Münsterberg's Version of Psychology

Münsterberg refused to define psychology, feeling that any definition would be unnecessarily restrictive. He did, however, distinguish between **causal psychology** and **purposive psychology**. Causal psychology involved the empirical investigation of the relationship between physiological and mental processes, whereas purposive psychology concentrated on willful or goal-directed activities. By delineating these two kinds of psychology, Münsterberg was extending psychology's domain to include both Wundt's brand of psychology and Brentano's. Münsterberg, however, was mainly interested in purposive psychology; and in the next chapter we will see that Münsterberg had a strong influence on William McDougall and Edward C. Tolman, both of whom stressed the importance of purposive behavior.

Clinical Psychology

In an attempt to understand the causes of abnormal behavior, Münsterberg saw many mentally ill people. Since he was seeing them for scientific reasons, he never charged a fee. He applied his "treatment," which consisted mainly of causing his patients to expect to improve, to cases of alcoholism, drug addiction, phobia, and sexual dysfunction, but not to psychosis. He felt that psychosis was caused by deterioration of the nervous system and could not be treated. Along with the suggestion that individuals would improve as the result of his efforts, Münsterberg also employed **reciprocal antagonism**, which involved strengthening the opposite thoughts to those causing problems. Although Münsterberg was aware of Freud's work, he chose to treat symptoms directly and did not search for the underlying causes of those symptoms. In his book *Psychotherapy* (1909), Münsterberg states his view of Freud's theory of unconscious motivation: "The story of the subconscious mind can be told in three words: there is none" (p. 125).

Forensic Psychology

Münsterberg was the first to apply psychological principles to legal matters, thus creating **forensic psychology**. Among other things, he pointed out that eyewitness testimony could be unreliable because sensory impressions could be illusory, suggestion and stress could affect perception, and memory was not always accurate. Münsterberg would often stage various traumatic events in his classroom to show that even when witnesses were attempting to be accurate, there were wide differences in the individual accounts of what had actually happened. Münsterberg urged that psychological methods replace the brutal interrogation of criminals. He felt that harsh interrogation could result in false confessions because some people would want to please the interrogators, some had a need to give in to authority figures, and some very depressed people had a need to be punished. Münsterberg published his thoughts on forensic psychology in his best-selling book *On the Witness Stand* (1908). In this book, Münsterberg described an apparatus that could

detect lying by observing changes such as those in pulse rate and respiration. Others would follow Münsterberg's lead and later create the controversial lie detector.

Industrial Psychology

Münsterberg's *Vocation and Learning* (1912) and *Psychology and Industrial Efficiency* (1913) are usually considered the beginning of what later came to be called **industrial psychology**. In these books, Münsterberg dealt with such topics as methods of personnel selection, methods of increasing work efficiency, and marketing and advertising techniques. To aid in personnel selection, for example, he recommended defining the skills necessary for performing a task and then determining the person's ability to perform that task. In this way, one could learn whether a person had the skills necessary for doing a certain job adequately. Münsterberg also found that whether a task was boring or not could not be determined by observing the work of others. Often, work that some people thought boring interested those doing it. It was necessary, then, to take individual differences into account when selecting personnel and when making job assignments.

Münsterberg's Fate

Because of his work in applied psychology, Münsterberg was well known to the public, the academic world, and the scientific community. William James had made psychology popular within the academic world, but Münsterberg helped make it popular with the general population by showing its practical uses. In addition, Münsterberg had among his personal friends some of the most influential people in the world, including President Theodore Roosevelt and the philosopher Bertrand Russell. By the time Münsterberg died in 1916, however, the general attitude toward him had turned negative, and his death went essentially unnoticed. The main reason for his unpopularity was his desire to create a favorable relationship between America and his native Germany. Never obtaining American citizenship, Münsterberg maintained a nationalistic loyalty toward Germany. He felt that both Germans and Americans had inaccurate stereotypes of each other, and he wrote books attempting to correct them—for example, *The Americans* (1904). As World War I approached, Münsterberg found himself caught up in the American outrage over German military aggression. Even many of his colleagues at Harvard disassociated themselves from him. During this time of extreme anti-German feeling, Münsterberg suffered a fatal stroke as he was lecturing to one of his classes. A year after his death, the United States entered the war against Germany.

Though little of Titchener's work is relevant in contemporary psychology, most of Münsterberg's is still of vital interest. Münsterberg's emphasis on practicality was perfectly compatible with the school of functional psychology that was soon to emerge, a school of thought that still characterizes American psychology.

GRANVILLE STANLEY HALL

In his influence on American psychology, **Granville Stanley Hall** (1844–1924) was second only to William James. As we shall see, Hall was a theorist in the Darwinian tradition, but above all he was an organizer. The number of firsts associated with Hall is unequaled by any other American psychologist.

Hall was born in the small farming town of Ashfield, Massachusetts. In 1863 he enrolled in Williams College, where he learned associationism, Scottish "common sense" philosophy, and evolutionary theory as he prepared for the ministry. Upon graduation in 1867, he enrolled in the Union Theological Seminary in New York City. Here Hall gave indications that perhaps he was not cut out for the clergy. R. I. Watson (1978) says:

During his year in New York, he explored the city with zest, roaming the streets, visiting police courts, and attending churches of all denominations. He joined a discussion club interested in the study of positivism, visited the theater for plays and musicals, tutored young ladies from the elite of New York, visited a phrenologist, and generally had an exciting year. He was not noted for his religious orthodoxy. After preaching his trial sermon before the faculty and students, he went to the office of the president for criticism. Instead of discussing his sermon, the president knelt and prayed that Hall would be shown the errors of his ways! (p. 398)

In 1868 a small grant made it possible for Hall to travel to Germany, where he studied theology and philosophy. He also spent a lot of time in beer gardens and theaters, and engaged in considerable romance.

In 1871 Hall accepted a position at Antioch College in Ohio, where he not only taught English literature, French, German, and philosophy, but served as the librarian, led the choir, and did a little preaching. Also while at Antioch, Hall read Wundt's *Physiological Psychology*. In 1876 he was offered an instructorship of English at Harvard. During his stay at Harvard, Hall became friends with William James, who was only two years his elder. Hall did research in Harvard's medical school, writing up his results as "The Muscular Perception of Space," which he offered as his doctoral thesis in 1878. Harvard was the first institution to offer a Ph.D. in psychology, and in 1878 Hall was the first to attain that degree.

After receiving his Ph.D., Hall returned to Germany, where he studied first with Wundt and then with Helmholtz. Hall was Wundt's first American student. In a letter to James, Hall confessed that he had learned more from Helmholtz than from Wundt.

In 1880, at the age of 36, Hall returned to the United States where, after giving a series of lectures, he was offered a position at Johns Hopkins University. In 1883 Hall set up a working psychology laboratory. It is generally agreed that Wundt founded the world's first psychology laboratory in Leipzig in 1879, and that Hall's laboratory at Johns Hopkins was the first psychology laboratory in America (Boring, 1965, p. 5). (As was previously mentioned, the laboratory James established in 1875 is generally discounted because it was designed for teaching demonstrations rather than research.) While at Johns Hopkins, in addition to founding a psychology laboratory, Hall founded the first American journal dedicated to psychological issues, the *American Journal of Psychology*, which first appeared in 1887. Also while at Johns Hopkins, Hall taught James McKeen Cattell and John Dewey, who were later to become key figures in functionalism.

President of Clark University

In 1888 Hall left Johns Hopkins to become the first president of Clark University in Worcester, Massachusetts, but he also remained a professor of psychology. At Clark, Hall maintained a strong hand in directing and shaping American psychology. According to R. I. Watson (1978):

> Hall was the Great Graduate Teacher of American psychology. By 1893 eleven of the fourteen Ph.D. degrees from American universities had been given by him; by 1898 this had increased to thirty awarded out of fifty-four. (p. 403)

One reason Hall was able to produce so many Ph.D.'s in psychology was that when he left Johns Hopkins, he took most of the best students with him, as well as most of the laboratory equipment (Sahakian, 1975, p. 313).

While at Clark University, Hall invited 26 of the most prominent psychologists in America to meet in Worcester, Massachusetts, to form an association of psychologists. The meeting took place on July 8, 1892, and represents the founding of the American Psychological Association (APA). Some of those who were invited did not attend (for example, William James and John Dewey), but they are considered charter members because they were invited to join and they

supported the association. Hall was elected the first president of the association, and in subsequent years William James and John Dewey would also serve as presidents. From an original membership of 26, the APA now has more than 50,000 members. Wertheimer (1970) jokingly points out that "if the APA continues to grow at the rate it did during the first three-quarters of a century of its existence, by sometime in the twenty-second century, there should be more psychologists than people in the world" (p. 86).

Recapitulation Theory

Hall contributed a great deal to educational psychology, and he started the child psychology movement in America. In 1904 he wrote *Adolescence: Its Psychology and Its Relations to Physiology, Anthropology, Sociology, Sex, Crime, Religion, and Education*. He urged the study of adolescence because he felt that at this stage of development habits learned during childhood were discarded and new adult habits had not yet been learned. During this transitional period, the individual was forced to rely on instincts, and therefore adolescence was a very good time to study human instinctual makeup.

More generally, Hall believed that each individual in his or her lifetime reenacted all of the evolutionary stages of the human race. This is called the **recapitulation theory** of development. For example, our dreams of floating are memories of our protozoan ancestors, who floated on the surface of water, the gill-like structures that appear during prenatal development represent the fish stage of evolution, and the tendency of a very young infant to cling to a horizontal bar reflects the behavior of our ape-like ancestors.

Psychology at Clark University

Hall's 31 years as president of Clark University were colorful to say the least. Under his leadership, psychology dominated Clark, and Clark

ARCHIVES OF THE HISTORY OF AMERICAN PSYCHOLOGY

John Dewey

was a strong competitor with Harvard for top students and faculty. In 1908 Hall decided to invite prominent European psychologists to lecture at Clark. When Hall's faculty decided in 1909 that Ebbinghaus should be invited, Hall invited Sigmund Freud and Carl Jung instead, for Hall had long been interested in Freud's ideas and was among the first to urge sex education in America. Freud and Jung arrived on September 5, 1909, and according to Freud, this visit to Clark did much to further acceptance of his theory throughout the world.

By embracing evolutionary theory, with its emphasis on practicality and adaptation, James, Münsterberg, and Hall paved the way for a kind of psychology that was distinctly different from that of Wundt and Titchener; they had planted the seeds for a psychology that stressed the function of behavior and thought.

FUNCTIONALISM AT THE UNIVERSITY OF CHICAGO

John Dewey

In spite of the fact that **functionalism** was never a well-defined school of thought like structuralism, it is common to attribute its founding to **John Dewey** (1859–1952), even though James, Münsterberg, and Hall certainly laid important groundwork. Dewey was born in Burlington, Vermont, on October 25, 1859. While attending the University of Vermont as an undergraduate, he became interested in philosophy. Following graduation, he taught secondary school for three years before entering Johns Hopkins University to pursue his interests in philosophy. At Johns Hopkins, Dewey had Hall as a teacher, and he wrote his doctoral dissertation on the psychology of Immanuel Kant. Dewey's first academic appointment was at the University of Michigan, where he taught both philosophy and psychology. While at Michigan, Dewey wrote *Psychology* (1886), the first functionalist textbook ever written. It preceded James's *Principles* by four years.

In 1894 Dewey accepted an appointment at the University of Chicago, where he wrote an article that many think marks the formal beginning of the school of functionalism. Sahakian (1975) says:

> 1896 marks the formal date of the birth of functionalism in psychology in the United States, owing to the publication of Dewey's classical critique of the reflex arc theory in psychology. In his "The Reflex Arc Concept in Psychology" (1896), Dewey initiated a new trend in psychology by his protestation against elementism that dominated psychology. (p. 357–358)

Titchener's criticisms of the ideas presented in this paper did much to launch the school of functionalism. Dewey's argument was that to divide the elements of a reflex into sensory processes, brain processes, and motor responses for analysis was artificial and misleading. The three elements of a reflex, said Dewey, must be viewed as a coordinated system that was directed toward a goal, and this goal was usually related to the survival of the organism. Dewey urged that all behavior be looked at in terms of its function—to adapt the organism to its environment. To study elements of the adaptive act in isolation caused one to miss the most important aspect of the act: its purposiveness. We see here a great deal of similarity between Dewey and James. Also, Dewey was espousing the kind of psychology that Münsterberg called purposive.

As an evolutionist, Dewey felt that social change was inevitable, but he also believed that it could be influenced positively by proper plans of action. Dewey was very influential in creating what came to be called "progressive" education in America. He believed that education should be student-oriented rather than subject-oriented, and that the best way to learn something was to do it—thus his famous statement that students *learn by doing*. Dewey was very much opposed to rote memorization, drills, and the view that the purpose of education was to transmit traditional knowledge. Rather, he believed that education should facilitate creative intelligence and prepare children to live effectively in a complex society. In 1904 friction with the education department caused Dewey to resign from the University of Chicago and to accept an appointment at Teachers College at Columbia University where he pursued his interests in education and pragmatic philosophy. He died on June 1, 1952, at the age of 93.

James Rowland Angell

James Rowland Angell (1869–1949) studied in Europe and with James at Harvard, but never obtained a Ph.D. Angell arrived at the University of Chicago in 1894, the same year Dewey arrived, and both men eventually served as presidents of the APA (Dewey in 1899, Angell in 1906). Angell's presidential address, entitled "The Province of Functional Psychology," distinguished between structuralism and functionalism. But it was Titchener who had originally delineated the two kinds of psychology. In his article "The Postulates of a Structural Psychology" (1898), Titchener labeled the kind of psychology concerned with the function (or usefulness) of behavior and thought as "functional." He was opposed to such psychology and insisted that structuralism was the only true psychology. Functionalism, he said, might be a technology, but it was not a science. In spite of Titchener's beliefs, however, functionalism began to take shape as a new school of psychology, and Angell's address helped to define its domain. In his address, Angell made three major points: (1) Functional psychology was interested in mental operations rather than in conscious elements. (2) Mental processes mediated between the needs of the organism and the environment. That is, mental functions helped the organism to survive. Behavioral habits allowed an organism to adjust to familiar situations; but when an organism was confronted with the unfamiliar, mental processes aided in the adaptive process. (3) Mind and body could not be separated; they acted as a unit in an organism's struggle for survival.

Angell was chairman of the psychology department for 25 years. Under his leadership, the University of Chicago became a center of functionalism. Among Angell's famous students were Harvey Carr, whom we consider next, and John B. Watson, who will be featured in the next chapter. In 1921 Angell left Chicago to become president of Yale University, a post he held until 1937.

Harvey Carr

Harvey Carr (1873–1954) obtained his B.A. and M.A. degrees from the University of Colorado and then went to the University of Chicago, where he obtained his Ph.D. in 1905 under the supervision of Angell. Carr stayed at Chicago all of his professional life, and in 1927 he was elected president of the American Psychological Association.

In 1925 Carr wrote *Psychology: A Study of Mental Activity*, in which he defined psychology as the study of mental activity. Mental activity, in turn, was "concerned with the acquisition, fixation, retention, organization, and evaluation of experiences, and their subsequent utilization in the guidance of conduct" (Carr, 1925, p. 1). We see in Carr's definition the functionalist's concern with the learning process. Since learning was a major tool used in adjusting to the environment, it was a major concern of the functionalists. Central to Carr's psychology was what he called the **adaptive act**, which had three characteristics: (1) a motive that acted as a stimulus for behavior (for example, hunger or thirst); (2) an environmental setting, or the situation the organism was in; and (3) a response that satisfied the motive (for example, eating or drinking). Here again, we see the influence of evolutionary theory on functionalism. Needs must be met in order for organisms to survive. Needs motivate behavior until an act satisfies the need, at which point learning occurs; and the next time the organism is in the same situation and experiences the same need, the organism will tend to repeat the behavior that was previously effective. For Carr, both perception and behavior were necessary in adapting to the environment, since how the environment was perceived determined how an organism responded to it. Seeing a wild animal in a zoo and seeing one while walking through the forest would elicit two different reactions.

Although Carr, like the other functionalists, accepted both introspection and objective experimentation as legitimate methods, the latter became the favored research technique. One reason for this was the growing success of animal research, in which introspection was of course impossible. This success suggested a bold step for psychology, a step that John B. Watson eventually took.

FUNCTIONALISM AT COLUMBIA UNIVERSITY

James McKeen Cattell

Functionalism took on a slightly different appearance under the leadership of **James McKeen Cattell** (1860–1944) who, as we noted in Chapter 10, was strongly influenced by Galton. Cattell was born in Easton, Pennsylvania, and obtained his B.A. in 1880 from Lafayette College, where his father was president. He then went to Leipzig to study with Wundt. Cattell wrote a paper on philosophy that won him a fellowship at Johns Hopkins University; and while at Johns Hopkins (1882–1883), he did research in Hall's new psychology laboratory and decided to become a psychologist. In 1883 Cattell returned to Leipzig, where he became Wundt's first experimental assistant. Much to Wundt's dismay, however, Cattell insisted on studying individual differences, something that was contrary to the main thrust of the Leipzig laboratory. Cattell also expressed doubts about the usefulness of introspection. R. I. Watson (1978) describes the situation:

> Contrary to the usual custom of being assigned a problem by Wundt, Cattell worked on his own problems in reaction time. He also became convinced that the introspective efforts directed toward fractionation of the reaction time into perception, choice, and the like, then gospel in Wundt's laboratory, was something he could not carry out and which he doubted others could. The situation reached the point where he did some of his experiments at his lodging rather than in the laboratory, since Wundt would not permit subjects in his laboratory who could not profit from introspection. Though somewhat strained, relations between them never reached a breaking point. Wundt and Cattell did agree on the value of the study of reaction time. In Cattell's eyes it was a valuable tool for the study of the time necessary for mental operation and especially for the investigation of individual differences. (p. 408)

Cattell received his Ph.D. from Leipzig in 1886. Returning to the United States, he taught at Bryn Mawr College and the University of Pennsylvania, before going to London to work with Galton. In Galton, Cattell finally found someone who shared his intense interest in individual differences. Galton confirmed Cattell's conviction that individual differences were important and that they could be objectively measured. Cattell shared Galton's belief in eugenics, and he argued that delinquents and defectives should be sterilized and that bright and healthy individuals should be encouraged to marry.

In 1888 Cattell was given a professorship in psychology at the University of Pennsylvania, and in 1891 he accepted a professorship at Columbia University, where he stayed for 26 years. Cattell did basic research in such areas as reaction time, psychophysics, association, and perception, but he will probably be remembered most for his work on mental tests (a term that he coined). He believed that the measurement of mental processes could make psychology as objective as the physical sciences. In 1890 Cattell said:

> Psychology cannot attain the certainty and exactness of the physical sciences, unless it rests on a foundation of experiment and measurement. A step in this direction could be made by applying a series of mental tests and measurements to a large number of individuals. The results would be of considerable scientific value in discovering the constancy of mental processes, their interdependence, and their variation under different circumstances. (p. 373)

Following Galton, Cattell assumed that mental processes could be measured by studying sensory and motor abilities. In fact, he used many of the same tests that Galton had used—for example, dynamometer pressure, least noticeable difference in weight, and reaction time.

A man of tremendous energy and ambition, Cattell was only 28 years old when he became professor of psychology at the University of Pennsylvania. His professorship was the first in the world to be in psychology and not in philosophy. Also at Pennsylvania, Cattell founded the

Robert Sessions Woodworth

first psychology laboratory designed for undergraduate students. This he did in 1887. In 1895, when only 35 years old, Cattell was elected as the fourth president of the APA, following William James. The year before, along with James Mark Baldwin, he had founded America's second psychology journal, *Psychological Review.*

Soon after Cattell arrived at Columbia in 1891, Robert S. Woodworth and Edward L. Thorndike joined him. They, too, were destined to become leading representatives of functionalism.

Robert Sessions Woodworth

Robert Sessions Woodworth (1869–1962) graduated from Amherst College in Massachusetts. For his M.A. he went to Harvard, where he studied with William James. Woodworth then moved to Columbia and obtained his Ph.D. in 1899 under the supervision of Cattell. Following graduation, he taught physiology in New

York Hospital and then spent a year in England studying with the famous physiologist Sir Charles Sherrington. In 1903 he returned to Columbia, where he stayed for the remainder of his career.

Like all functionalistic psychologists, Woodworth was interested in what people do and *why they do it*—especially the second question. He was primarily interested in motivation, so he called his brand of psychology **dynamic psychology**. Like Dewey, Woodworth disagreed with those who talked about adjustments to the environment as a matter of stimuli, brain processes, and responses. Some psychologists even left out the brain mechanisms and spoke only of S-R (stimulus-response) relationships. Woodworth chose the symbol S-O-R (stimulus-organism-response) for designating behavior, to emphasize the importance of the organism. He used the term *mechanism* much as Carr had used the term *adaptive act*—to refer to the way an organism interacted with the environment in order to satisfy a need. These mechanisms, or adaptive behavior patterns, remained dormant unless activated by a need of some kind. Thus, in the *same* physical environment, an organism would act differently depending on what need or *drive* was present. According to Woodworth, the internal condition of the organism activated the organism's behavior.

Although we have included Woodworth among the functionalists, he was always willing to entertain a wide variety of ideas and believed none of them religiously. Woodworth believed that psychologists should accept valid information about humans no matter where it came from; and he believed that, like himself, most psychologists maintained a middle-of-the-road or eclectic attitude. In 1931 he said:

> Suppose we should organize a world's tournament or olympic contest of psychologists, and should assemble the two or three thousand of them on some large field, with banners raised here and there as rallying points for the adherents of the several schools—a banner here

for Freud, a banner there for Adler, one for Jung, one for McDougall, one for the Gestalt school, one for the behaviorists, and one for the existentialists, with perhaps two or three other banners waving for schools which I have not mentioned. After all the loyal adherents of each school had flocked to their respective banners, there would remain a large body in the middle of the field, or in the grandstand ready to watch the jousting. How many would thus remain unattached? A majority? I am convinced it would be a large majority. (p. 205)

Though often criticized for his eclecticism, Woodworth did not care much. In response to being chided for sitting on the fence instead of getting down and becoming involved in the prevailing controversy, he said (1931), "Well, in support of this position it may be said that it is cooler up here and one has a better view of all that is going on" (p. 216).

Edward Lee Thorndike

Born in Williamsburg, Massachusetts, **Edward Lee Thorndike** (1874–1949) attained a B.A. from Wesleyan University. He then went to Harvard, where he became good friends with William James. In fact, when Thorndike was refused laboratory space at Harvard for doing his animal research, James allowed him to conduct his studies in the basement of the James home. After receiving his M.A. from Harvard, Thorndike accepted a fellowship at Columbia where, like Woodworth, he worked under Cattell's supervision. His doctoral dissertation, entitled "Animal Intelligence: An Experimental Study of the Associative Processes in Animals," was published in 1899 and was republished in 1911 as *Animal Intelligence*. Thorndike's work was to have a monumental influence on psychology, and it can be seen as representing the transition from the school of functionalism to the school of behaviorism. We will review the reasons for all of this shortly, but first we will look at the nature of animal research prior to Thorndike's work.

Animal research before Thorndike. Modern comparative psychology clearly started with the works of Darwin, specifically with the book *The Expression of Emotions in Man and Animals* (1872). Darwin's work was taken a step further by his friend **George John Romanes** (1848–1894), who wrote *Animal Intelligence* in 1882 and *Mental Evolution in Animals* in 1884. In a third book, *Mental Evolution in Man* (1885), Romanes attempted to trace the evolution of the human mind. All of Romanes's evidence was anecdotal, however, and he was often guilty of *anthropomorphizing*, or attributing human thought processes to lower animals. For example, Romanes attributed such emotions as anger, fear, and jealousy to fish; affection, sympathy, and pride to birds; and slyness and keen reasoning power to dogs. Sargent and Stafford (1965) cite an example of the kind of anecdotal evidence Romanes used to demonstrate the similarity between humans and other animals:

> One day the cat and the parrot had a quarrel. I think the cat had upset Polly's food, or something of that kind; however, they seemed all right again. An hour or so after, Polly was standing on the edge of the table; she called out in a tone of extreme affection, "Puss, puss, come then—come then, pussy." Pussy went and looked up innocently enough. Polly with her beak seized a basin of milk standing by, and tipped the basin and all its contents over the cat; then chuckled diabolically, of course broke the basin, and half drowned the cat. (p. 149)

Conway Lloyd Morgan (1842–1936) sought to correct Romanes's errors by applying the principle that has come to be known as **Morgan's Canon**. Morgan states this principle in his *Introduction to Comparative Psychology* (1891):

> In no case may we interpret an action as the outcome of the exercise of a higher psychical faculty, if it can be interpreted as the outcome of the exercise of one which stands lower in the psychological scale. (p. 53)

Sometimes called the law of parsimony, Morgan's Canon can be viewed as a modern exam-

Edward Lee Thorndike

ple of Occam's razor. Morgan sought to shave extraneous assumptions from the explanation of animal behavior. Instead of attributing higher mental abilities to animals, Morgan stressed instinct, habit, and association. He felt that nonhuman animals could not possibly possess many of the human attributes that Romanes and others had attributed to them:

> A sense of beauty, a sense of the ludicrous, a sense of justice, and a sense of right and wrong—these abstract emotions or sentiments, as such, are certainly impossible to the brute. (Morgan, 1891, p. 403)

In his book *Animal Behavior* (1900), Morgan offers what he considers an objective account of how his dog developed the ability to open a garden gate:

> The way in which my dog learnt to lift the latch of the garden gate and thus let himself out

affords a good example of intelligent behavior. The iron gate is held to by a latch, but swings open by its own weight if the latch be lifted. Whenever he wanted to go out the fox terrier raised the latch with the back of his head, and thus released the gate, which swung open. Now the question in any such case is: How did he learn the trick? In this particular case the question can be answered, because he was carefully watched. When he was put outside the door, he naturally wanted to get out into the road, where there was much to tempt him—the chance of a run, other dogs to sniff at, possibly cats to be worried. He gazed eagerly out through the railings on the low parapet wall . . . and in due time chanced to gaze out under the latch, lifting it with his head. He withdrew his head and looked out elsewhere but the gate had swung open. Here was a fortunate occurrence arising out of the natural tendencies of a dog. But the association between looking out just there and the open gate with a free passage into the road is somewhat indirect. The coalescence of the presentative and representative elements into a conscious situation effective for the guidance of behavior was not effected at once. After some ten or twelve experiences, in each of which the exit was more rapidly effected, with less gazing out at wrong places, the fox terrier learnt to go straight and without hesitation to the right spot. *In this case the lifting of the latch was unquestionably hit upon by accident, and the trick was only rendered habitual by repeated association in the same situation of the chance act and happy escape.* Once firmly established, however, the behaviour remained constant throughout the remainder of the dog's life, some five or six years. (p. 144, italics added)

Though there is obviously still great subjectivity in Morgan's report of his dog's behavior, Morgan did describe the trial and error learning that was to become so important in Thorndike's research. It remained for someone to apply Morgan's own canon more rigorously and to bring the investigation of animal learning out of the uncontrolled environment and into the laboratory, where it could be studied more systematically. Thorndike did both.

Thorndike sought a completely objective method of studying animal behavior. Morgan had been on the right track, but had relied too heavily on observations made under uncontrolled circumstances. With naturalistic observation, so many variables are occurring that it is impossible to observe them all at the same time, let alone to know which of them is responsible for the behavior being observed. Thorndike decided to solve these problems by observing animal behavior under controlled laboratory conditions.

Thorndike's puzzle box. To investigate systematically the kind of learning Morgan described above, Thorndike used a **puzzle box** like the one shown in Figure 11.1. Although during his career Thorndike used chicks, rats, dogs, fish, monkeys, and humans as research subjects, his work with the puzzle box involved cats. The box was arranged so that if the animal performed a certain response, the door opened and the animal was allowed to escape; in addition, the animal received a reward, such as a piece of fish. In 1911 Thorndike described the behavior of animals under these circumstances. Note the similarity to Morgan's earlier observation of his dog learning to open the garden gate:

The behavior of all but 11 and 13 [the cats were identified by number] was practically the same. When put into the box the cat would show evident signs of discomfort and of an impulse to escape from confinement. It tries to squeeze through any opening; it claws and bites at the bars or wire; it thrusts its paws out through any opening and claws at everything it reaches; it continues its efforts when it strikes anything loose and shaky; it may claw at things within the box. It does not pay very much attention to the food outside, but seems simply to strive instinctively to escape from confinement. The vigor with which it struggles is extraordinary. For eight or ten minutes it will claw and bite and squeeze incessantly. With 13, an old cat, and 11, an uncommonly sluggish cat, the behavior was different. They did not struggle vigorously or continually. On some occasions they did not even struggle at all. It was therefore necessary

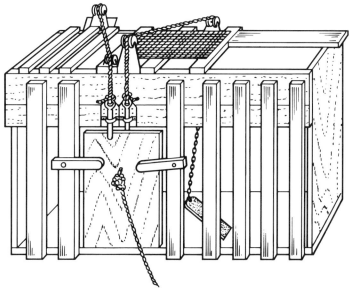

FIGURE 11.1 The puzzle box Thorndike used in his experiments with cats. (Thorndike, 1898)

to let them out of the box a few times, feeding them each time. After they thus associate climbing out of the box with getting food, they will try to get out whenever put in. They do not, even then, struggle so vigorously or get so excited as the rest. In either case, whether the impulse to struggle be due to instinctive reaction to confinement or to an association, it is likely to succeed in letting the cat out of the box. The cat that is clawing all over the box in her impulsive struggle will probably claw the string or loop or button so as to open the door. And gradually all the other nonsuccessful impulses will be stamped out and the particular impulse leading to the successful act will be stamped in by the resulting pleasure, until after many trials, the cat will, when put in the box, immediately claw the button or loop in a definite way. (pp. 35–40)

From these and other observations, Thorndike reached the following conclusions:

1. Learning is incremental. That is, it occurs a little bit at a time rather than all at once. With each successful escape, subsequent escapes were made more quickly.

2. Learning occurs automatically. That is, it is not mediated by thinking.
3. The same principles of learning apply to all mammals. That is, humans learn in the same manner as all other mammals.

With these observations, Thorndike was very close to being a behaviorist. If thinking was not involved in learning, what good was introspection in studying the learning process? And if animals and humans learned in the same way, why not simplify the situation by studying only nonhuman animals?

The Laws of Exercise and Effect. To account for his research findings, Thorndike developed psychology's first major theory of learning. The theory was comprised basically of the associationism and hedonism that had been prevalent for centuries, but Thorndike stated his principles with precision and supported them with ingenious experimentation. His own research findings actually forced him to make major revisions in his own theory. The early version of his theory consisted mainly of the Laws of Exercise and Effect. The **Law of Exercise** had two parts: the **Law of Use** and the **Law of Disuse**. According to the Law of Use, the more often an association was practiced, the stronger it became. This was essentially a restatement of Aristotle's law of frequency. According to the Law of Disuse, the longer an association remained unused, the weaker it became. Taken together, the Laws of Use and Disuse said that we learned by doing and forgot by not doing.

Thorndike's early **Law of Effect** was that if an association were followed by a "satisfying state of affairs" it would be strengthened, and if it were followed by an "annoying state of affairs" it would be weakened. In modern terminology, Thorndike's earlier Law of Effect was that reinforcement strengthened behavior, whereas punishment weakened it.

In September 1929, Thorndike began his address to the International Congress of Psychology with the dramatic statement "I was wrong." He was referring to his early theory of learning. Research had forced him to abandon his Law of Exercise completely, for he had found that practice *alone* did not strengthen an association and that the passage of time *alone* (disuse) did nothing to weaken an association. In addition to discarding the Law of Exercise, Thorndike discarded half of the Law of Effect, concluding that a satisfying state of affairs strengthened an association but that an annoying state of affairs did not weaken one. In modern terminology, Thorndike found that reinforcement was effective in modifying behavior, but punishment was not. With these revisions, Thorndike's theory became very similar to B. F. Skinner's current theory of learning. In fact, all of the major aspects of Skinner's theory first appeared in Thorndike's theory.

Under the influence of evolutionary theory, Thorndike added a behavioral component to associationism. Rather than focusing on the association of one *idea* to another, he studied the association between the environment and behavioral responses. Although Thorndike's brand of psychology is generally seen as being within the framework of functionalism (since Thorndike believed that only useful associations were selected and maintained), his insistence that learning occurred without ideation brought him very close to being a behaviorist.

The transfer of training. In 1901 Thorndike and Woodworth combined their skills to examine the contention of the early faculty psychologists that the faculties of the mind could be strengthened by practicing the attributes associated with them. For example, it was believed that studying a difficult topic, such as Latin, could enhance general intelligence. Such a belief was sometimes called the "mental muscle" approach to education, and sometimes "formal discipline." Thorndike and Woodworth's study, which involved 8,564 high school students, found no support for this contention. Then why did it seem that more difficult courses produced brighter students? Thorndike (1924) answers as follows:

By any reasonable interpretation of the results, the intellectual values of studies should be determined largely by the special information, habits, interests, attitudes, and ideals which they demonstrably produce. The expectation of any large differences in general improvement of the mind from one study rather than another seems doomed to disappointment. The chief reason why good thinkers seem superficially to have been made such by having taken certain school studies, is that good thinkers have taken such studies, becoming better by the inherent tendency of the good to gain more than the poor from any study. When the good thinkers studied Greek and Latin, these studies *seemed* to make good thinking. Now that the good thinkers study physics and trigonometry, these seem to make good thinkers. If abler pupils should all study physical education and dramatic art, these subjects would seem to make good thinkers. . . . After positive correlation of gain with ability is allowed for, the balance in favor of any study is certainly not large. (p. 98)

Thorndike answered the "mental muscle" approach to education with his **identical elements theory of transfer**, which states that the extent to which information learned in one situation will transfer to another situation is determined by the similarity between the two situations. If two situations are exactly the same, information learned in one will transfer completely to the other. If there is no similarity between two situations, information learned in one will be of no value in the other. The implication for education is obvious: schools should teach skills that are similar to those that will be useful when students leave school. Rather than attempting to strengthen the faculties of the mind by requiring difficult subjects, schools should emphasize the teaching of practical knowledge.

Many consider Thorndike the greatest learning theorist of all time. As was mentioned, many of his ideas can be seen in current psychology in the work of B. F. Skinner, whom we will consider in the next chapter. Thorndike is usually considered a functionalist, Skinner a behaviorist. The two men are classified differently because Thorndike's theory employs such terms as *satisfying state of affairs*. If Thorndike was a functionalist, he was one with strong leanings toward behaviorism.

A SUMMARY OF FUNCTIONALISTIC PSYCHOLOGY

Functionalism was never a well-defined school of thought with one recognized leader or an agreed-upon methodology. It is not even clear when functionalism came into existence as a school, if it ever did. Some mark functionalism's beginning with the work of William James, others with the work of John Dewey, and still others suggest Darwin himself. Amidst all of functionalism's diversity, however, there were still common themes running through the work of all those calling themselves functionalists. We

follow Keller (1973, pp. 74–75) in delineating those themes.

1. The functionalists were opposed to elementism as represented by the structuralists.

2. They wanted to understand the function of the mind rather than to provide a static description of its contents. They believed that mental processes had a function—to aid the organism in adapting to the environment.

3. They wanted psychology to be a practical science, not a pure science; and they sought to apply their findings to the improvement of personal life, education, industry, and so on. The structuralists had actively avoided practicality.

4. The functionalists represented the biological tradition rather than the physiological tradition. While the structuralists had been influenced by the careful physiological work of such individuals as Helmholtz, who had traced the path from sensory stimulation to simple mental sensation, the functionalists were more strongly influenced by Darwinian biology, with its emphasis on the struggle for existence. In a sense, the functionalists converted psychology from the Newtonian model of science to a Darwinian model.

5. They urged the broadening of psychology to include research on animals, children, and the abnormal. They also urged a broadening of methodology to include anything that was useful, such as puzzle boxes and mental tests.

6. Their interest in the *why* of mental processes and behavior led directly to a concern with motivation. Since an organism will act differently in the same environment as its needs change, these needs must be understood before the organism's behavior can be understood.

7. They accepted *both* mental processes and behavior as legitimate subject matter for psychology, and most of them saw introspection as a valid research tool. Some functionalists, however, (such as Thorndike) came very close to being behaviorists.

8. All functionalists were directly or indirectly influenced by William James, who in turn had been strongly influenced by Darwin's theory of evolution.

9. They were more interested in what made organisms different from one another than what made them similar.

What happened to functionalism? It did not die as a school, as structuralism had, but was absorbed. According to Chaplin and Krawiec (1979):

As a systematic point of view, functionalism was an overwhelming success, but largely because of this success it is no longer a distinct school of psychology. It was absorbed into mainstream psychology. No happier fate could await any psychological point of view. (p. 53)

And Bruno (1972) says:

Like the mind of William James, American psychology is still a somewhat paradoxical mixture of subjective and objective points of view. Many modern psychologists want to use the tools of science and draw from objective data. Nevertheless, they find themselves unwilling to give up the rich world of inner experience as a source of psychological information. From the point of view of the philosophy of science, the problems in a mixed approach are varied and complex. Nevertheless, practical men often compromise and override glaring contradictions in order to get on with the business at hand. The middle-of-the-road position of the functionalists continues today. (p. 111)

SUMMARY

Before functionalism, psychology in America passed through three stages. During the first stage (1640–1776), psychology was the same as religion and moral philosophy, although some of John Locke's philosophy was taught. During the second stage (1776–1886), the Scottish "common sense" philosophy was taught, but its relationship to religion was still emphasized. During this second period, textbooks began to appear that contained chapters on topics constituting much of today's psychology—for example, perception, memory, language, and thinking. In the third stage (1886–1896), psychology became completely separated from religion, and the groundwork for an objective, practical psychology was laid.

James was instrumental in creating a psychological school of thought that has dominated American psychology right up to the present. James's main target was the elementism of the structuralists. Following Darwin, James felt that mental events and overt behavior always had a function. Rather than studying consciousness as a group of elements that combined in some lawful way, as physical elements do, James viewed consciousness as a stream of ever-changing mental events whose purpose was to allow the person to adjust to the environment. For James, the major criterion for judging an idea was the idea's usefulness, and he applied this pragmatism to the idea of free will. James believed that while working as a scientist, a person had to accept determinism; while not playing the role of scientist, however, the person could accept free will and feel responsible for his or her activities, instead of feeling like a victim of circumstance. James believed that much of behavior was instinctive and much of it learned. According to James and Lange's theory of emotion, first an individual reacts behaviorally and then has an emotional reaction. In many ways, psychology today is the kind of psychology James outlined—a psychology willing to embrace all aspects of human existence and to employ those techniques found to be effective.

James chose Münsterberg to replace him as director of the Harvard Psychology Laboratory. At first, Münsterberg concentrated on performing controlled laboratory experiments, but his interests turned more and more to the application of psychological principles to problems outside of the laboratory. In developing his applied psychology, Münsterberg did pioneer work in clinical, forensic, and industrial psychology. Although he was at one time one of the most famous psychologists in the world, he died in obscurity because of his efforts to improve relations between the United States and Germany at a time when Americans were disgusted with German military and political aggression.

Like James and Münsterberg, Hall was very influential in the development of functionalism. The first person to obtain a Ph.D. specifically in psychology, Hall was Wundt's first American student; he created America's first working psychology laboratory in 1883, and he created the first American journal dedicated exclusively to psychological issues. As president of Clark University, he invited Freud to deliver a series of lectures—lectures that helped psychoanalysis gain international recognition and respect. Hall also founded the American Psychological Association and was its first president. According to his recapitulation theory, human development reflects all of the evolutionary stages that humans passed through before becoming human. Hall did much to stimulate the study of child psychology, and he was among the first to urge that children be given sex education. Along with James and Münsterberg, Hall incorporated Darwinian theory into psychology, and in so doing helped pave the way for the school of functionalism.

Once launched, functionalism was centered at the University of Chicago and Columbia University. At Chicago, Dewey wrote "The Reflex Arc Concept in Psychology," an article thought by many to mark the formal beginning of the school of functionalism. Dewey's text, *Psychology* (1886), was the first functionalist textbook ever written. Also at Chicago was Angell, who had studied with James. During his 25 years as departmental chairman at Chicago, Angell encouraged the growth of functional psychology. Carr was another who furthered the development of functional psychology at Chicago. A key figure in Columbia University's brand of functionalism was Cattell. Though Cattell was Wundt's first experimental assistant, he was more strongly influenced by Galton, with whom he also studied. Like Galton, Cattell was intensely interested in measuring individual differences, and he obtained the first professorship ever awarded in psychology. Another leading figure at Columbia was Woodworth, whose dynamic psychology focused on motivation. In explaining behavior, Woodworth took an eclectic approach.

But perhaps the most influential Columbia functionalist was Thorndike. Thorndike's goal was to study animal behavior objectively, since Darwin's theory had shown that there were only quantitative differences between humans and other animals. Darwin's friend Romanes did rudimentary animal research, but his observations were riddled with anthropomorphism. Morgan's animal work was better because he applied the principle that came to be called Morgan's Canon: no animal action should be explained on a higher level (thinking, reasoning) if it can be explained on a lower level (instinct, neuromechanisms). Morgan's Canon was used to discount the anecdotal evidence that Romanes and others had offered. Although Morgan's work was an improvement over Romanes's, it consisted mainly of uncontrolled naturalistic observations. Thorndike was the first to study animal behavior under controlled laboratory conditions. From his use of the puzzle box with several species of animals, Thorndike concluded that learning occurred one small step at a time rather than all at once, that learning occurred without the involvement of mental processes, and that the same principles of learning applied to all mammals, including humans.

Thorndike summarized many of his observations with his famous Laws of Exercise and Effect. According to his Law of Exercise, the strength of an association varied with the frequency of its occurrence. His Law of Effect stated that if an association was followed by a positive experience, it would be strengthened, whereas if an association was followed by a negative experience, it would be weakened. In 1929 Thorndike revised his theory by discarding the Law of Exercise and salvaging only the half of the Law of Effect that said positive consequences strengthened an association. Negative consequences, he had found, had no effect on an association. Thorndike opposed the old "mental muscle" explanation of the transfer of training, which was an outgrowth of faculty psychology. Thorndike contended that learning would transfer from one situation to another to the degree that the two situations were similar or had common elements. Many of Thorndike's

ideas are found in the contemporary work of Skinner.

In general, functionalistic psychology has the following characteristics: it opposes elementism; it is concerned with the function of mental and behavioral processes; it is interested in the practical application of its principles; it adheres to a Darwinian rather than a Newtonian model; it embraces a wide range of subjects and methodologies; it is extremely interested in motivation; and it is more interested in the differences among individuals than in their similarities. Many believe that current American psychology is best characterized as functionalistic.

DISCUSSION QUESTIONS

1. Briefly describe the four stages of American psychology.

2. Define *pragmatism*.

3. Summarize James's view of consciousness.

4. Try to make the case that James's criticism of structuralism is more valid when directed at Titchener than when directed at Wundt.

5. What did James mean when he said that habit was the "fly-wheel" of society?

6. How did James resolve the controversy over free will and determinism?

7. How did Münsterberg view psychology? Include in your answer his distinction between causal and purposive psychology.

8. Summarize Münsterberg's work in clinical, forensic, and industrial psychology.

9. What was Münsterberg's fate?

10. List G. Stanley Hall's "firsts" in psychology.

11. Describe Hall's recapitulation theory.

12. What was Dewey's argument against the

traditional way of studying the reflex in psychology? What did he propose instead? What part did Dewey's work play in the development of functionalism?

13. Discuss the contributions of Angell and Carr to functionalism.

14. In what way was Cattell's approach to psychology different from that of the other American functionalists?

15. Why was Woodworth's approach to psychology called dynamic psychology?

16. What did Thorndike add to earlier approaches to animal research?

17. Compare Thorndike's theory of learning before and after 1929.

18. How did Thorndike's theory of the transfer of training differ from the earlier theory, which was based on faculty psychology?

19. List the common themes that run through the work of functionalistic psychologists.

20. What was functionalism's fate?

GLOSSARY

Adaptive act Carr's term for a unit of behavior with three characteristics: a need, an environmental setting, and a response that satisfies the need.

Angell, James Rowland (1869–1949) As president of the American Psychological Association and as chairman of the psychology department at the University of Chicago for 25 years, did much to promote functionalistic psychology.

Applied psychology Psychology that is useful in solving practical problems. The structuralists opposed such practicality, but Münsterberg and later the functionalists emphasized it.

Carr, Harvey (1873–1954) An early functionalistic psychologist at the University of Chicago.

Cattell, James McKeen (1860–1944) Represented functionalistic psychology at Columbia University. By working with Galton, Cattell developed a strong interest in measuring individual differences.

Causal psychology Münsterberg's term for the kind of psychology that sought the relationship between physiological and mental processes.

Dewey, John (1859–1952) A key person in the development of functionalistic psychology. Some mark the formal beginning of the school of functionalism with the 1896 publication of Dewey's article "The Reflex Arc Concept in Psychology."

Dynamic psychology The brand of psychology suggested by Woodworth that stressed the internal variables that motivate organisms to act.

Forensic psychology The application of psychological principles to legal matters. Münsterberg is considered the first forensic psychologist.

Functionalism America's first school of psychology. Under the influence of Darwin, the functionalists stressed the role of consciousness and behavior in adapting to the environment.

Hall, Granville Stanley (1844–1924) Created America's first experimental psychology laboratory, founded and became the first president of the American Psychological Association, and invited Freud to Clark University to give a series of lectures. Hall thus helped psychoanalysis receive international recognition, and his recapitulation theory did much to stimulate interest in developmental psychology. Hall was also among the first to advocate giving children sex education.

Identical elements theory of transfer Thorndike's contention that the extent to which learning would transfer from one situation to another was determined by the similarity between the two situations.

Industrial psychology The application of psychological principles to such matters as personnel selection, increasing employee productivity, equipment design and marketing, and advertising and packaging of products.

James, William (1842–1910) Was instrumental in the founding of functionalistic psychology. James emphasized the function of both consciousness and behavior. For him, the only valid criterion for evaluating a theory, thought, or act was whether or not it worked. In keeping with his pragmatism, he claimed that psychology needed to employ both scientific and nonscientific procedures. Likewise, on the individual level, sometimes one must believe in free will and at other times in determinism.

James-Lange theory of emotion The theory that people first respond behaviorally and then have an emotional experience. For example, we run first and then we are frightened. An implication of the theory is that one should act according to the way one wants to feel.

Lange, Carl George (1834–1900) Along with James, proposed the theory that a person's emotional experience followed his or her behavior.

Law of Disuse Thorndike's contention that infrequently used associations became weak. Thorndike discarded this law in 1929.

Law of Effect Thorndike's contention that reward strengthened associations, whereas punishment weakened them. Later, Thorndike revised the law to state that reward strengthened associations but punishment had no effect on them.

Law of Exercise Thorndike's contention that the strength of an association varied with the frequency of the association's use. Thorndike discarded this law in 1929.

Law of Use Thorndike's contention that the more often an association was made, the stronger it became. Thorndike discarded this law in 1929.

Morgan, Conway Lloyd (1852–1936) One of the first to do objective research on animal behavior. Morgan's research consisted of naturalistic observations.

Morgan's Canon The insistence that explanations of animal behavior be kept as simple as possible. Morgan's Canon was suggested as a means of guarding against anthropomorphizing.

Münsterberg, Hugo (1868–1916) Stressed the application of psychological principles in such areas as clinical, forensic, and industrial psychology. In so doing, Münsterberg created applied psychology.

Pragmatism The belief that usefulness is the best criterion for judging something.

Purposive psychology Münsterberg's term for the kind of psychology that studied willful or goal-directed activities.

Puzzle box The experimental chamber Thorndike used for systematically studying animal behavior.

Recapitulation theory Hall's contention that all of the stages of human evolution were reflected in the life of an individual.

Reciprocal antagonism Münsterberg's method of treating mentally disturbed individuals, whereby he would strengthen thoughts that were antagonistic to those causing a problem.

Romanes, George John (1848–1894) One of the first to follow Darwin's lead and study animal behavior. Romanes's research was very subjective, however, and relied heavily on anecdotal evidence.

Stream of consciousness Term for the way James thought the mind worked. James described the mind as consisting of an ever-changing stream of interrelated, purposive thoughts, rather than static elements that could be isolated from each other, as the structuralists had suggested.

Thorndike, Edward Lee (1874–1949) Marks the transition between the schools of functionalism and behaviorism. Thorndike concluded from his objective animal research that learning occurred a little bit at a time, was independent of consciousness, and was the same for all mammals. His final theory of learning was that practice alone had no effect on an association, and that positive consequences strengthened an association but negative consequences did not weaken an association.

Woodworth, Robert Sessions (1869–1962) An influential functionalist at Columbia University who emphasized the role of motivation in behavior.

CHAPTER 12

Behaviorism

THE BACKGROUND OF BEHAVIORISM

Seldom, if ever, has a major development in psychology resulted from the work of one person. This is not to say that single individuals have not been important, but their importance lies in their ability to culminate or synthesize previous work rather than to create a unique idea. The founding of the school of **behaviorism** is a clear example of this. Although John B. Watson is usually given credit for founding behaviorism, we shall see that so much of his thinking was "in the air" that the term *founding* should not be taken to indicate innovation as much as an inevitable outgrowth of the spirit of the times. As we shall see, objective psychology (psychology that insists on studying only those things that are directly measurable) was already well developed in Russia before the onset of behaviorism, and several functionalists were making statements very close to those Watson later made.

As we have seen in the preceding chapters, the school of structuralism relied heavily on introspection as a means for studying the content and processes of the mind; functionalism accepted both introspection and the direct study of behavior. While the structuralist sought a pure science unconcerned with practical applications, the functionalist was more concerned with practical applications than with pure science. Some of the functionalists were impressed by how much could be learned about humans without the use of introspection, and they began to drift toward what was later the behavioristic position. One such functionalist was James McKeen Cattell, whom we encountered in the last chapter. In 1904, a full nine years before Watson's official founding of behaviorism, Cattell said this about psychology:

> I am not convinced that psychology should be limited to the study of consciousness as such, insofar as this can be set off from the physical world. . . . I admire the products of the Herbartian School and the ever-increasing acuteness of introspective analysis from Locke to Ward. All this forms an important chapter in modern psychology; but the scientific results are small in quantity when compared with the objective experimental work accomplished in the past fifty years. There is no conflict between introspective analysis and objective experiment—on the contrary, they should and do continually cooperate. But the rather widespread notion that there is no psychology apart from introspection is refuted by the brute argument of accomplished fact.
>
> It seems to me that most of the research work that has been done by me or in my laboratory is nearly as independent of introspection as work in physics or in zoology. The time of mental processes, the accuracy of perception and movement, the range of consciousness, fatigue and practise, the motor accompaniments of thought, memory, the association of ideas, the perception of space, color-vision, preferences, judgments, individual differences, the behavior of animals and children, these and other topics I have investigated without requiring the slightest introspection on the part of the subject or undertaking such on my own part during the course of the experiments. . . . It is certainly difficult to penetrate by analogy into the consciousness of the lower animals, of savages and of children, but the study of their behavior has already yielded much and promises much more. . . . If I did not believe that

psychology affected conduct and could be applied in useful ways, I should regard my occupation as nearer to that of the professional chess-player or sword swallower than to that of the engineer or scientific physician. . . . I see no reason why the application of systematized knowledge to the control of human nature may not in the course of the present century accomplish results commensurate with the nineteenth century applications of physical science to the material world. (pp. 179–186)

Cattell's statement is clearly within the functionalistic framework, since it stresses the study of both consciousness and behavior and emphasizes the practicality of knowledge; but it also stresses that *much* important information can be attained without the use of introspection. At the time, for example, the study of young children and lower animals was yielding valuable information, and in such research introspection was impossible.

W. B. Pillsbury (1911) provides another example of the Zeitgeist:

> Psychology has been defined as the "science of consciousness" or as the "science of experience subjectively regarded." Each of these definitions has advantages, but none is free from objection. . . . Mind is known from man's activities. *Psychology may be most satisfactorily defined as the science of human behavior.*
>
> Man may be treated as objectively as any physical phenomenon. He may be regarded only with reference to what he does. Viewed in this way the end of our science is to understand human action. (pp. 1–2, italics added)

In addition to the tendency toward the objective study of behavior in psychology, the success of research on animals had much to do with the development of behaviorism. Thorndike, for example, who was technically a functionalist because he did not completely omit consciousness or mentalistic terms from his work, was discovering how the laws of learning that were derived from work on lower animals applied to humans. His work came very close to behaviorism, since he demonstrated that neither thought nor reasoning was involved in the learning process of any organism, including humans. Except for a few subjective terms in his writings, Thorndike could easily be classified as a behaviorist.

The success of animal researchers such as Thorndike created a strain between them and the prominent psychologists who insisted that psychology concentrate on introspective data. (Such data, of course, were impossible to obtain in animal research.) This strain between the animal researchers and the introspectionists created the atmosphere in which behaviorism took on revolutionary characteristics. Woodworth (1931) puts the matter as follows:

> The rapid and interesting development of animal psychology . . . was one of the important predisposing causes for the outbreak of behaviorism.
>
> But the "exciting cause" was the repressive attitude toward animal psychology assumed by those important psychologists of that day who were perfectly clear that psychology was, and must logically be, the study of conscious experience and nothing else. From this major premise they reasoned logically that behavior data were not psychology at all unless translated over into terms of the animal's consciousness. Now since the days of Descartes it had been recognized that you cannot prove consciousness in animals. Shall we assume that all animals, down to the very lowest, are conscious in their behavior, or shall we limit consciousness to animals that learn, or to animals that have a nervous system, or by what criterion shall we draw the line? At best, inference from behavior to consciousness in animals was reasoning by analogy and a leap in the dark. Titchener and others granted that some such inferences might legitimately be drawn, provided caution were used, and that thus animal experiments could throw some light on psychology. But as this leap in the dark was necessary in order to make any psychological use of the behavior data, animal psychology was at best an indirect and relatively unimportant part of our science.
>
> Meanwhile the animal psychologists were obtaining objective results on such problems as instinct and learning, and disliked to be told they must resort to dubious analogies in order to make psychology out of their findings. (pp. 56–57)

As we shall see, J. B. Watson was one of these animal researchers. Before we consider Watson's proposed solution to the problem, however, we must review the work of the Russians, work that was to become the cornerstone of Watson's behaviorism.

RUSSIAN OBJECTIVE PSYCHOLOGY

Ivan M. Sechenov

The founder of Russian objective psychology, **Ivan M. Sechenov** (1829–1905), started out studying engineering but switched to physiology. As part of his training in physiology, he studied with Johannes Müller and Hermann von Helmholtz in Europe. Sechenov sought to explain all psychic phenomena on the basis of associationism, materialism, and positivism—thus showing Helmholtz's influence on him. Sechenov strongly denied that thoughts caused behavior. Rather, he insisted that external stimulation caused *all* behavior. In his classic book *Reflexes of the Brain* (1863/1965), Sechenov puts the matter as follows:

> Since the succession of two acts is usually regarded as an indication of their causal relationship . . . *thought is generally regarded as the cause of action.* When the external influence, i.e., the sensory stimulus, remains unnoticed—which occurs very often—*thought is even accepted as the initial cause of action.* Add to this the strongly pronounced subjective nature of thought, and you will realize how firmly man must believe in the voice of self-consciousness when it tells him such things. But actually this is the greatest of falsehoods: *the initial cause of any action always lies in external sensory stimulation,* because without this thought is inconceivable. (pp. 88–89, italics in the original)

Sechenov did not deny consciousness or its importance, but he insisted that there was nothing mysterious about consciousness and sought to explain it in terms of physiological processes triggered by external events. For Sechenov, both overt behavior and covert behavior (mental processes) were reflexive in the sense that they were both triggered by external stimulation. Furthermore, both resulted from physiological processes in the brain. For Sechenov, the only valid approach to the study of psychology involved the objective methods of physiology. His positivism is apparent in the following passage (1935/1973):

> Physiology will begin by separating psychological reality from the mass of psychological fiction which even now fills the human mind. Strictly adhering to the principle of induction, physiology will begin with a detailed study of the more simple aspects of psychical life and will not rush at once into the sphere of the highest psychological phenomena. Its progress will therefore lose in rapidity, but it will gain in reliability. As an experimental science, physiology will not raise to the rank of incontrovertible truth anything that cannot be confirmed by exact experiments; this will draw a sharp boundary-line between hypothesis and positive knowledge. Psychology will thereby lose its brilliant universal theories; there will appear tremendous gaps in its supply of scientific data; many explanations will give place to a laconic "we do not know"; the essence of the psychical phenomena manifested in consciousness (and, for the matter of that, the essence of all other phenomena of nature) will remain an inexplicable enigma in all cases without exception. And yet, psychology will gain enormously, for it will be based in scientifically verifiable facts instead of the deceptive suggestions of the voice of our consciousness. Its generalizations and conclusions will be limited to actually existing analogies, they will not be subject to the influence of the personal preferences of the investigator which have so often led psychology to absurd transcendentalism, and they shall thereby become really objective scientific hypotheses. The subjective, the arbitrary and the fantastic will give way to a nearer or more remote approach to truth. In a word, *psychology will become a positive science. Only physiology can do this, for only physiology holds the key to the scientific analysis of psychical phenomena.* (pp. 350–351, italics in the original)

Sechenov's objectivity appears clearly in the work of Pavlov and Bechterev, which Watson

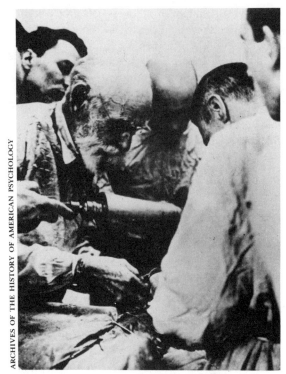

ARCHIVES OF THE HISTORY OF AMERICAN PSYCHOLOGY

Pavlov operating on an experimental animal.

used to support his behaviorism. Though Watson's behaviorism developed out of functionalism and animal psychology, Russian objective psychology was seen as compatible with it.

Ivan Petrovitch Pavlov

Ivan Petrovitch Pavlov (1849–1936) was born in the farming village of Ryazan. Pavlov's father was a village priest, and Pavlov originally studied for the priesthood himself. In 1870, however, he enrolled in the University of St. Petersburg, where he studied the natural sciences. During this time, Pavlov became interested in digestion. Following his undergraduate training, he pursued a degree in medicine at the Military Medical Academy; and after attaining his medical degree, he studied physiology in Germany for two years. Upon returning to Russia, he held a variety of ill-paying jobs until 1890, when he was finally appointed professor of physiology at St. Petersburg's Military Medical Academy. Pavlov was 41 at the time, and he would spend most of the remainder of his career at the academy.

Interest in digestion. During his first ten years at St. Petersberg, Pavlov pursued his interests in the digestive system. At this time, most of what was known about digestion came from studies in which animals had been operated on to expose organs of interest. Often the experimental animals were already dead as their organs were investigated; and if not dead, they were at least highly traumatized by the operation. Noting that little could be learned about normal digestive functioning by studying dead or traumatized animals, Pavlov sought a more effective experimental procedure. He knew of someone who had suffered a severe gunshot wound to the stomach and recovered. The victim's treatment, however, had left an open hole in his body through which his internal organs could be observed. The grateful patient allowed his physician to observe his internal processes, including those of the digestive system.

Although this particular case lacked scientific control, it gave Pavlov the information he needed to perfect his technique for studying digestion. Using the latest aseptic surgical techniques and his outstanding surgical skills, Pavlov prepared a *gastric fistula*—a channel—leading from a dog's digestive organs to outside of the dog's body. Such a procedure allowed the animal to recover fully from surgical trauma before its digestive processes were investigated. Pavlov performed hundreds of experiments to determine how the amount of secretion through the fistula varied as a function of different kinds of stimulation to the digestive system, and his pioneering research won him the 1904 Nobel prize.

Discovery of the conditioned reflex. During his work on digestion, Pavlov discovered the conditioned reflex. As was mentioned Pavlov's method of studying digestion involved a surgical arrangement that allowed the dog's gastric juices to flow out of the body and be collected. While studying the secretion of gastric juices in response to such substances as meat powder, Pavlov noticed that things associated with meat powder also caused stomach secretions—for example, the mere sight of the experimenter or the sound of his or her footsteps. Pavlov referred to these latter responses as "conditioned" because they resulted from an organism's experience. He realized that such reflexes could be explained by the associative principles of contiguity and frequency. Pavlov also realized that by studying conditioned reflexes, which he had originally called "psychic reflexes," he would be entering the realm of psychology. Like Sechenov before him, Pavlov had a low opinion of psychology, with its prevailing mentalism. He resisted the study of conditioned reflexes for a long time because of their apparently subjective nature. After pondering Sechenov's work, however, he concluded that conditioned reflexes, like natural reflexes, could be explained in terms of the neural circuitry and the physiology of the brain. At the age of 50, Pavlov began studying the conditioned reflex. His work would continue for 30 years.

Pavlov's personality. Like Sechenov, Pavlov was positivistic, mechanistic, and totally objective. If researchers in his laboratory used mentalistic terminology to describe their findings, he fined them. Fancher (1979) describes how Pavlov ran his laboratory:

> He was punctual in his arrival at the laboratory, perfectionistic in his experimentation, tyrannical in his control, and unhesitating in docking or firing workers who failed to meet his standards.
> One of the most famous Pavlov stories concerns a worker who was late to the laboratory one day during the Russian Revolution, because he had to dodge skirmishes in the streets. Believing that devotion to science should supersede all other values, Pavlov did not regard that as a proper excuse. According to some versions of the story he fired the worker, though it is more probable he simply issued a reprimand. Less extreme manifestations of this same attitude occurred almost every month, as Pavlov would become irritated when his workers had to take time off to collect their pay. (p. 301)

In private life, however, Pavlov was a completely different person. Fancher (1979) gives the following account of Pavlov outside the laboratory:

> In private life Pavlov was notoriously careless about money, even though he often lived just above the poverty line. Many months he simply forgot to pick up his salary. Once, after he had just won an academic promotion which brought with it a badly needed cash bonus, Pavlov lent an unscrupulous acquaintance most of the sum before he even got home. The money was never seen again. After this, all family financial affairs were conducted by Pavlov's wife, and he was seldom allowed to carry more than loose change. One of the few times he did carry much money was on a visit to the United States, made without his wife. All of his money—more than $800 in small bills—was jammed into a bulky wallet that protruded visibly from his jacket pocket. When Pavlov ventured onto the crowded New York subway, the predictable felony occurred. Fortunately, for him, he was already world famous and the guest of the Rockefeller Institute, which replaced his funds.
> Sometimes Pavlov's impracticality took a sentimental turn. When he was engaged, he spent almost all of his available money on luxuries for his fiancée—candy, flowers, theater tickets, and such. The only practical gift he bought her was a new pair of shoes, which she badly needed for a trip she was planning. She arrived at her destination and opened her trunk, to find only one shoe! Upon writing to Pavlov about the mystery, she received this answer: "Don't look for your shoe. I took it as a remembrance of you and have put it on my desk." (pp. 300–301)

Conditioned and unconditioned reflexes. According to Pavlov, organisms respond to the environment in terms of unconditioned and conditioned reflexes. An **unconditioned reflex** is innate and is triggered by an **unconditioned stimulus**. For example, placing acid in a dog's mouth will increase the dog's saliva flow. The acid is the unconditioned stimulus (UCS), and the increased salivation is the **unconditioned response** (UCR). The connection between the two is genetically determined. A **conditioned reflex** is derived from experience, in accordance with the laws of contiguity and frequency. Before Pavlov's experiment, stimuli such as the *sight* of food powder, the sight of the attendant, and the sound of the attendant's footsteps were considered biologically neutral in the sense that they did not automatically elicit a specific response from the dogs. Pavlov called a biologically neutral stimulus a **conditioned stimulus** (CS). Because of its contiguity with an unconditioned stimulus (in this case food), this previously neutral stimulus developed the capacity to elicit some fraction of the unconditioned response (in this case salivation). When a previously neutral stimulus (that is, a conditioned stimulus) elicits some fraction of an unconditioned response, the reaction is called a **conditioned response** (CR). Thus a dog salivating to the sound of an attendant's footsteps exemplifies a conditioned response. Though Pavlov explained all of this in terms of brain physiology, his explanation need not concern us here.

Conditioning. Through this process of conditioning, the stimuli governing an organism's behavior are gradually increased from a few innate, unconditioned stimuli to countless other stimuli that become associated to unconditioned stimuli by contiguity. Pavlov (1955) explains:

> The basic physiological function of the cerebral hemispheres throughout the . . . individual's life consists in a constant addition of numberless signally conditioned stimuli to the limited number of the initial inborn unconditioned stimuli, in other words, in constantly supple-menting the unconditioned reflexes by conditioned ones. Thus, the objects of the instincts [our desires for food, and the like] exert an influence on the organism in ever-widening regions of nature and by means of more and more diverse signs or signals, both simple and complex; consequently, the instincts are more and more fully and perfectly satisfied, i.e., the organism is more reliably preserved in the surrounding nature. (p. 273)

Since conditioning depends on the unconditioned stimulus, Pavlov called such a stimulus a **primary reinforcer**. Through continuous association with a primary reinforcer, conditioned stimuli take on reinforcing properties and can be used to bring about further conditioning. Since the reinforcement value of conditioned stimuli is derived from primary reinforcers, it is called secondary. If, for example, a bell is sounded just prior to an animal's feeding, the bell will eventually be able to elicit salivation. At the same time, the bell will have developed secondary reinforcing properties and can itself be used to develop further conditioning. If a blinking light now precedes the sounding of the bell, the blinking light will also eventually cause the animal to salivate. This process is called **higher-order conditioning** and is developed through the use of a secondary reinforcer.

If a conditioned stimulus (CS) is continually presented to an organism and is no longer followed by an unconditioned stimulus, the conditioned response (CR) will gradually diminish and finally disappear, at which point **extinction** is said to have occurred. If a period of time is allowed to elapse after extinction and the conditioned stimulus is again presented, the stimulus will elicit a conditioned response. This is called **spontaneous recovery**. For example, if a tone (CS) is consistently followed by the presentation of food powder (UCS), an organism will eventually salivate when the tone alone is presented (CR). If the tone is then presented but not followed by the food powder, the magnitude of the CR will gradually diminish, and finally the tone will no longer elicit a CR (extinction). After a delay, however—even without any further pairing of the tone and food powder—the tone will again elicit a CR (spontaneous recovery).

Generalization and discrimination. Pavlov also found that once conditioning had been established, stimuli similar to the conditioned stimulus would also elicit a conditioned response. He called this **generalization**. For example, if a tone of a certain frequency was used as a conditioned stimulus, tones with a higher or lower frequency would also elicit conditioned responses. Pavlov found that the magnitude of the conditioned response elicited depended on the stimulus's similarity to the actual conditioned stimulus: the more similar a stimulus was to the actual conditioned stimulus, the greater the magnitude of the conditioned response. Pavlov found that generalization could be severely reduced by either prolonged training or differential reinforcement. If, for example, the number of pairings between the conditioned and unconditioned stimulus was far greater than the number needed to establish conditioning, generalization was reduced to only a few stimuli that were very similar to the conditioned stimulus. Likewise, if several related conditioned stimuli were presented during training, but only one was followed by the unconditioned stimulus (primary reinforcement), generalization was drastically reduced. When an organism responds to only the conditioned stimulus used during training, or to stimuli very similar to it, **discrimination** is demonstrated.

The Key to associationism. Pavlov sought to explain all human behavior, both overt and covert, on the basis of innate reflexes, conditioned reflexes, extinction, spontaneous recovery, generalization, and discrimination. He even explained language as a special kind of conditioned reflex system. The physical stimuli we respond to with both conditioned and unconditioned reflexes Pavlov called the **first-signal system**. However, as humans we also learn to respond to *symbols* of physical events. For example, we learn responses to the word *mother* just as we learn responses to our physical mothers. Reactions are conditioned to symbols (for example, words) just as they are conditioned to physical stimuli. Pavlov called our conditioned reaction to symbols the **second-signal system**.

Although Pavlov had a very low opinion of most psychologists (he felt that they were too preoccupied with a study of consciousness and were therefore unscientific), he did have a high opinion of Thorndike. In the following passage, Pavlov even acknowledges Thorndike as the first to do systematic research on the learning process in animals:

> Some years after the beginning of the work with our new method I learned that somewhat similar experiments on animals had been performed in America, and indeed not by physiologists but by psychologists. Thereupon I studied in more detail the American publications, and now I must acknowledge that the honour of having made the first steps along this path belongs to E. L. Thorndike. By two or three years his experiments preceded ours, and his book must be considered as a classic, both for its bold outlook on an immense task and for the accuracy of its results. (1928, pp. 38–40)

Pavlov felt he had discovered the physiological mechanism for explaining the associationism that philosophers and psychologists had been talking about for centuries. He believed that by showing the physiological underpinnings of association, he had put associationism on an objective footing, and that speculation about how *ideas* become associated with each other could finally end. For him, the temporary connections formed by conditioning were what had previously been referred to as associations. Pavlov (1955) says:

> Are there any grounds . . . for distinguishing between that which the physiologist calls the temporary connection and that which the psychologist terms association? They are fully identical; they merge and absorb each other. Psychologists themselves seem to recognize this,

since they (at least, some of them) have stated that the experiments with conditioned reflexes provide a solid foundation for associative psychology, i.e., psychology which regards association as the base of psychical activity. (p. 251)

We shall see later that although Watson used Pavlov's work to support this brand of behaviorism, he either revised or ignored many aspects of Pavlov's work.

Vladimir M. Bechterev

In attempting to develop a completely objective psychology based on physiology, **Vladimir M. Bechterev** (1857–1927) also followed in the footsteps of Sechenov. Like Sechenov and Pavlov, Bechterev studied at St. Petersburg, receiving his doctorate there in 1881, at the age of 24. He then studied with Wundt at Leipzig. In 1885 he returned to Russia to a position at the University of Kazan, where he created the first Russian experimental psychology laboratory. In 1893 he was transferred to St. Petersburg's Military Medical Academy, where he held a chair of psychic and nervous diseases. During this time Bechterev wrote *Objective Psychology* (1907), in which he insisted that psychology concern itself with phenomena that could be studied directly and not with the study of consciousness through introspection or any other means.

Bechterev's ideas. In 1907 Bechterev and his collaborators left the Military Medical Academy to found the Psychoneurological Institute, which was later named the V. M. Bechterev Institute for brain research in his honor. Bechterev summarized his ideas in *General Principles of Human Reflexology: An Introduction to the Objective Study of Personality*, which first appeared in 1917 and reached its fourth edition in 1928. Many of the points in this book are also found in American behaviorism at about the same time. It should be remembered, however, that Bechterev was writing about objective psychology as early as 1885 (see Bechterev, 1973,

p. 19). A few passages from Bechterev's *General Principles of Human Reflexology* (1928/1973) will exemplify his thinking:

In order to assume . . . a strictly objective standpoint in regard to man, imagine yourself in a position of being from a different world and of a different nature, and having come to us, say, from another planet. . . . Observing human life in all its complex expressions, would this visitor from another planet, of a different nature, ignorant of human language, turn to subjective analysis in order to study the various forms of human activity and those impulses which evoke and direct it? Would he try to force on man the unfamiliar experiences of another planetary world, or would this being study human life and all its various manifestations from the strictly objective point of view and try to explain to himself the different correlations between man and his environment, as we study, for example, the life of microbes and lowly animals in general? I think there can be no doubt of the answer. . . .

In following this method, obviously we must proceed in the manner in which natural science studies an object: in its particular environment, and explicate the correlation of the actions, conduct, and all other expressions of a human individual with the external stimuli, present and past, that evoke them; so that we may discover the laws to which these phenomena conform, and determine the correlations between man and his environment, both physical, biological, and, above all, social.

It is regrettable that human thought usually pursues a different course—the subjective direction—in all questions concerning the study of man and his higher activities, and so extends the subjective standpoint to every department of human activity. But this standpoint is absolutely untenable, since each person develops along different lines on the basis of unequal conditions of heredity, education, and life experience, for these conditions establish a number of correlations between man and his environment, especially the social, and so each person is really a separate phenomenon, completely unique and irreproducible, while the subjective view presupposes an analogy with oneself—an analogy not existing in actual fact, at least not in the highest, and consequently more valuable, expressions of a human being.

You will say that we use analogy everywhere, that in everyday life we cannot approach another man without it. All that is, perhaps, true to a certain extent, but science cannot content itself with this, because taking the line of subjective interpretation, we inevitably commit some fallacy. It is true that, in estimating another person, we turn to subjective terminology, and constantly say that such and such a man thinks this or that, reasons in this or that manner, etc. But we must not forget that everyday language and the scientific approach to natural phenomena cannot be identical. For instance, we always say of the sun that it rises and sets, that it reaches its zenith, travels across the sky, etc., while science tells us that the sun does not move, but that the earth revolves round it. And so, from the point of view of present-day science, there must be only one way of studying another human being expressing himself in an integration of various outward phenomena in the form of speech, facial and other expressions, activities, and conduct. This way is the method usually employed in natural science, and consists in the strictly objective study of the object, without any subjective interpretation and without introducing consciousness. (pp. 33–36)

By 1928 Bechterev was aware of the growing tendency toward objective psychology in America and claimed that he was the originator of that tendency:

The literature on the objective study of animal behavior has grown considerably and in America an approach is being made to the study of human behavior, a study which has first been set on a scientific basis on Russian soil in my laboratories at the Military Medical Academy and at the Psychoneurological Institute. (p. 214)

Bechterev versus Pavlov. Who discovered the conditioned reflex? It was neither Bechterev nor Pavlov. Bechterev spends considerable time showing that such reflexes were known for a very long time, saying, for example (1928/1973):

These "psychic" secretions, by the way, attracted attention as early as the 18th century.

Even then it was known that when oats is given to a horse, he secretes saliva before the oats enters his mouth. (p. 403)

Both Bechterev and Pavlov studied conditioned reflexes at about the same time. What Pavlov called a conditioned reflex, Bechterev called an **association reflex**. Bechterev was well aware of Pavlov's research and felt that it had a number of major flaws. In fact, almost every time Bechterev mentions Pavlov in his 1928 book, he has something negative to say about him. Bechterev's major criticisms of Pavlov's "saliva method" include the following:

1. An operation is necessary for collecting gastric juices from the stomach.

2. Pavlov's procedure cannot be easily used on humans.

3. The use of acid to elicit an unconditioned response causes reactions in the animal that may contaminate the experiment.

4. If food is used as an unconditioned stimulus, the animal will eventually become satiated and therefore no longer respond in the desired fashion.

5. The secretory reflex is a relatively unimportant part of an organism's behavior.

6. The secretory reflex is unreliable and therefore difficult to measure accurately. Instead of studying secretion, Bechterev studied motor reflexes. He states his reasons for this as follows (1928/1973):

Luckily, in all animals, and especially in man, who particularly interests us in regard to the study of correlative activity, the secretory activities play a much smaller part than do motor activities, and, as a result of this, and for other reasons also (the absence of an operation, the possibility of exact recording, the possibility of frequent repetition of the stimuli . . . and the absence of any complications as a result of frequent stimulation in experiment) we give unconditional preference, in view of the above-mentioned defects of the saliva method, to the method of investigation of association—motor reflexes of the extremities and of respiration—a method developed in my laboratory. This method, which is equally applicable to animals and to man, and consists in the electrical stimulation on the front paw of the animal, and in man, of the palm or fingers of the hand, or the ball of the foot, with simultaneous visual, auditory, cutaneo-muscular and other stimulations, has as far as I know, not met with any opposition in scientific literature from the time of its publications. (p. 203)

It turns out that Bechterev's concentration on the overt behavior of organisms was more relevant to American behaviorism than was Pavlov's research on secretion. But Pavlov was the one whom Watson discovered, and therefore the name Pavlov became widely known in American psychology. It is another one of those quirks of history that but for the sake of fortuitous circumstances, the name Bechterev could have been a household name instead of Pavlov. And as we shall see, in his application of conditioning procedures, Watson actually followed Bechterev more closely than he did Pavlov.

JOHN B. WATSON AND BEHAVIORISM

Biographical Sketch

John Broadus Watson was born on January 9, 1878, in Greenville, South Carolina. His mother was extremely religious, but his father was not. His father drank, swore, and chased women. This incompatibility finally resulted in Watson's father leaving home in 1891, when Watson was 13 years old. Watson and his father had been close, and his father's departure disturbed him deeply. He immediately became a troublemaker and was arrested twice, once for fighting and once for firing a gun in the middle of Greenville. Later, when Watson was famous, his father sought out his son, but Watson refused to see him.

One can only speculate on the effects of the mother's intense religious convictions in Watson's life, but the origin of Watson's lifelong fear of the dark seems clear (Cohen 1979):

The nurse Emma [Watson's mother] employed told him [Watson] that the devil lurked in the dark and that if ever Watson went a-walking during the night, the Evil One might well snatch him out of the gloom and off to Hell. Emma seems to have done nothing to stop the nurse instilling such terrors in her young son. Most likely, she approved. To be terrified of the Devil was only right and prudent. As a fundamentalist Baptist, she believed that Satan was always prowling. All this left Watson with a lifelong fear of the dark. He freely admitted that he studied whether children were born with an instinctual fear of the dark because he had never managed to rid himself of the phobia. He tried a number of times to use his behaviourist principles to cure himself but he never really managed to do it. As an adult Watson was often depressed, and when he got depressed he sometimes had to sleep with his light on. (p. 7)

Undergraduate years. In spite of his history of laziness and violence in school, Watson somehow managed to get himself accepted to Furman University at the age of 15. Although it is not known why Watson was accepted, Cohen (1979) suggests Watson's persuasive ability as the reason. All his life Watson demonstrated an ability to get what he wanted. While at college, Watson continued to live at home and worked at a chemical laboratory in order to pay his fees. His most influential teacher at Furman was Gordon Moore, who taught philosophy and psychology. The psychology Watson learned involved mainly the works of Wundt and James. All during college, Watson had problems with his brother, Edward, who considered Watson a sinner like his father and therefore a disgrace to the family.

At Furman Watson did well, but not exceptionally well. He should have graduated in 1898, but an unusual event set him back a year. His favorite teacher, Gordon Moore, warned that he would flunk any student who handed his or her examination in backwards. Absent-mindedly, Watson handed in his examination backwards and was flunked. His extra year at Furman, however, earned him an M.A. degree at the age of 21.

Following graduation, Watson taught in a one-room school in Greenville, for which he earned $25 a month. When his mother died, he decided to continue his education outside of the Greenville area, and he applied to both Princeton and the University of Chicago. When he learned that Princeton required a reading knowledge of Greek and Latin, he decided to go to the University of Chicago. Another reason for his decision was that his favorite teacher—Moore, the one who had flunked him—had since joined the faculty at the University of Chicago. So in September 1900, Watson left Greenville for Chicago.

To survive financially, Watson had a room in a boardinghouse and worked as a waiter there to pay for his room and board. He also earned $1.00 per week as a janitor in the psychology laboratory and another $2.00 per week for taking care of the white rats.

The Chicago years. At Chicago, Watson studied the British empiricists with his old teacher, Gordon Moore. Watson especially liked Hume because Hume taught that nothing was necessarily fixed or sacred. Watson took philosophy from John Dewey but confessed that he was unable to understand what Dewey was talking about. Though the faculty member who had the greatest influence on Watson was James Angell, the radical physiologist Jacques Loeb also influenced him. Loeb (1859–1924) was famous for his work on **tropism**, having shown that the behavior of simple organisms could be explained as being automatically elicited by stimuli. Just as plants oriented toward the sun because of the way they were constructed, so animals responded in certain ways to certain stimuli because of their biological makeup. According to Loeb, no mental events were involved in such tropistic behavior; it was simply a

John B. Watson

matter of the stimulation and the structure of the organism. This point of view, which Loeb applied to plants, insects, and lower animals, Watson would later apply to humans as well.

Under the influence of Angell and Henry Donaldson, a neurologist, Watson began to investigate the learning process in the white rat. In 1901 very little was known about animal learning, even though Thorndike had done some objective research by that time. Also in 1901, Small had published an article on the maze-learning ability of the white rat, but the article was as anthropomorphic as the work of Romanes. Thus Watson had little information to draw upon. By the end of 1902, however, he knew more about the white rat than anyone else in America. Also about this time, Watson first began to develop a feeling for behaviorism. "If you could understand rats without the convolutions of introspection, could you not understand people the same way?" (Cohen, 1979, p. 33).

Even though Watson had begun thinking about behaviorism as early as 1902, he resisted mentioning it to his mentor and friend **Angell**, because he knew that Angell believed psychology should include the study of consciousness.

When he finally did tell Angell of his ideas in 1904, Angell responded negatively and told him that he should stick to animals, thus silencing Watson on the subject for four years.

Although Watson suffered a nervous breakdown in 1902, he managed to submit his doctoral thesis in 1903. The title of his thesis, "Animal Education: The Psychical Development of the White Rat," shows that there was still a hint of mentalistic thinking in Watson at this time. The thesis was accepted, and Watson attained his doctorate at 25 years of age, making him the youngest person ever to attain a Ph.D. at the University of Chicago. Donaldson loaned Watson the $350 that was needed to publish the thesis, and it took Watson 20 years to repay the loan.

The University of Chicago hired Watson as an assistant professor for a salary of $600 per year, and he taught courses in both animal and human psychology. For the latter, he even used Titchener's laboratory manuals. During this time Watson married one of his students, Mary Ickes, and 11 months later they had a child. Also about this time, he began his correspondence with Robert Yerkes. Yerkes (1876–1956) was another young animal researcher who, while a student at Harvard, had been encouraged to pursue his interest in comparative psychology. After receiving his Ph.D. from Harvard in 1902, he had been offered an appointment at Harvard as instructor of comparative psychology. In his career, Yerkes studied the instincts and learning abilities of many different species, including mice, crabs, turtles, rats, worms, birds, frogs, monkeys, pigs, and apes; but he is probably best remembered for the work on anthropoid apes that he supervised at the Yerkes Laboratories of Primate Biology in Orange Park, Florida. His involvement in the development of the Army Alpha and Beta tests of intelligence was clearly an extension of his interests in comparative psychology (see Chapter 10). In spite of Yerkes' involvement with animal research and his friendship with Watson, he never accepted Watson's behaviorist position. During the formative stages of behaviorism, Yerkes remained loyal to Titchener.

In 1906 Watson began his research designed to determine what sensory information rats used as they learned to solve a complex maze. He did his research with Harvey Carr, the prominent functionalist. Using six-month-old rats that had previously learned the maze, Watson began systematically to remove one sensory system after another, in hopes of learning which sensory system the rats used to traverse the maze correctly. One by one he eliminated the senses of vision, hearing, and smell. Nothing appeared to make a difference: after full recovery from each operation, the rats were able to traverse the maze accurately. Watson and Carr then took a naive group of rats and performed the same operations, finding that the naive rats learned the maze as well as the rats that had full sensory apparatus. Watson then speculated that perhaps the rats were using their whiskers, but shaving off the whiskers made no difference. Even destroying the sense of taste made no difference. Watson and Carr finally found that the rats were relying on kinesthetic sensations—sensations from the muscles. If the maze was made shorter or longer, after destruction of the kinesthetic sense the rats were confused and made many errors. This discovery of the importance of kinesthetic sensation was to play an important role in Watson's later theory. Watson published the research results in 1907, in an article entitled "Kinesthetic and Organic Sensations: Their Role in the Reactions of the White Rat to the Maze."

In 1907 the Carnegie Institution offered Watson an opportunity to study the migratory instinct of terns, and Watson made several visits to an island off Key West, Florida. Much of Watson's research on instinctive behavior was done in collaboration with Karl Lashley, who was later to make significant contributions to neurophysiological psychology (see Chapter

14). One summer Watson brought Lashley with him to see whether terns in fact had the ability to home. To find out, Lashley took a number of terns to Mobile and some to Galveston and turned them loose. The results were exciting. Without any training, the terns found their way back to the small island, which was about 1,000 miles from where Lashley had released them. Watson and Lashley tried in vain to explain how the terns had accomplished this feat, and in the end, both men turned to other matters. Since Watson has become known for other accomplishments, it is often overlooked that he was one of this country's early ethologists. Watson's early publication (with Lashley) "Homing and Related Activities of Birds" provides an interesting contrast to Watson's later work.

The move to Johns Hopkins. By 1907 Watson had a national reputation in animal psychology, and he was offered a position at Johns Hopkins University. He really did not want to leave the University of Chicago, but he found the offer of $3,000 per year from Johns Hopkins irresistible. Thus Watson arrived in Baltimore in August 1908. At Johns Hopkins, psychology was part of the Department of Philosophy, Psychology and Education, and James Mark Baldwin was chairman of the department. Baldwin was also editor of *Psychological Review*, one of psychology's leading journals. Among Watson's duties was the teaching of human psychology, for which he still used Titchener's manuals. Watson wrote to Titchener about the problems he was having setting up a laboratory at Johns Hopkins, and Watson and Titchener exchanged many letters from that point on. Both men always showed great respect for each other. In Watson's time of great trouble (which we shall discuss shortly), Titchener was the only person who stuck with him.

In December 1909, a significant event occurred in Watson's life: Baldwin was caught in a brothel and was forced to resign from Johns Hopkins immediately. Watson became editor of

the *Psychology Review*, and ultimately he used the journal to publish his views on behaviorism. For many years Watson had been pondering a purely behavioristic position, but when he tried his ideas on those closest to him—for example, Angell and Yerkes—they discouraged him because they both felt that the study of consciousness had an important place in psychology. Watson first publicly announced his behavioristic views in 1908, at a colloquium at Yale University. Again Watson was severely criticized, and again he fell silent. At the time, Watson did not have enough confidence to go to war against established psychology on his own. He also remained silent to avoid offending his friend Titchener. Cohen (1979) reports the following exchange between Watson and Yerkes:

> On 6 February 1910 Watson told Yerkes that, in fact, "I would remodel psychology as we now have it." He would like to expound behaviorism and to put consciousness in its place as an irrelevance but, "I fear to do it because my place here is not ready for it. My thesis developed as I long to develop it would certainly separate me from the psychologist [Titchener]. Titchener would cast me off and I fear Angell would do likewise." The main obstacles were Watson's own inner loyalties. Yerkes urged caution. (p. 62)

Watson gained courage, however, and in 1913 he decided to take another plunge. When asked to give a series of lectures at Columbia University in New York, he used the opportunity to state publicly his views on psychology again. He began his now famous lecture, "Psychology as the Behaviorist Views It" (1913), with the following statement:

> Psychology as the Behaviorist views it is a purely objective experimental branch of natural science. Its theoretical goal is the prediction and control of behavior. Introspection forms no essential part of its methods, nor is the scientific value of its data dependent upon the readiness with which they lend themselves to interpretation in terms of consciousness. The Behaviorist, in his efforts to get a unitary scheme of animal

response, recognizes no dividing line between man and brute. The behavior of man, with all of its refinement and complexity, forms only a part of the Behaviorist's total scheme of investigation. (p. 158)

Published in the *Psychological Review*, which Watson edited, this lecture is usually taken as the formal founding of behaviorism.

The responses immediately began rolling in. Titchener was not upset, because he felt Watson had outlined a technology of behavior that did not conflict with psychology proper; but Angell, Cattell, and Woodworth all criticized Watson for being extreme. After his Columbia lectures, Watson was publicly committed to behaviorism and had no tolerance for any other brand of psychology. As we shall see, Watson's position gradually expanded to the point where it attempted to explain all human behavior.

The ideas that Watson expressed must have been what many psychologists were waiting to hear, because Watson's popularity grew dramatically. In 1914 he was elected president of the Southern Society for Philosophy and Psychology. In the same year, he was elected the 24th president of the American Psychological Association—all this at the age of 36, and only 11 years after receiving his doctorate from the University of Chicago.

Scandal. As rapidly as Watson's influence rose, however, it fell even more rapidly. In 1920 Watson's wife discovered that he was having an affair with Rosalie Rayner, with whom he was doing research on infant behavior, and sued him for divorce. The scandal was too much for Johns Hopkins: Watson was asked to resign, and he did. For all practical purposes this marked the end of Watson's professional career in psychology. He did go on writing about and lecturing on psychology for many years, and he did revise many of his earlier works, but more and more he directed his ideas toward the general public and not toward psychologists. For many years he tried to gain another academic

position in psychology, but the "scandal" had taken its toll, and no college or university would have him. Now his thoughts appeared in popular magazines such as *Harpers, New Republic, McCall's,* and *Cosmopolitan* rather than in professional journals. Watson also appeared on many radio talk shows. The following is a sample of titles of his articles and radio talks:

- "How We Think" (1926)
- "The Myth of the Unconscious" (1927)
- "On Reconditioning People" (1928)
- "Feed Me on Facts" (1928)
- "Why 50 Years from Now Men Wouldn't Marry" (1929)
- "After the Family—What?" (1929)
- "Women and Business" (1930)
- "On Children" (1935)

The last article that Watson wrote was entitled "Why I Don't Commit Suicide." Watson submitted it to *Cosmopolitan*, but it was rejected because it was too depressing.

Advertising work. In 1921 Watson was out of work and broke. He had to find a job. An opportunity arose for him to work for the J. Walter Thompson Advertising Company. The job offered to Watson contrasted sharply with what Watson had grown accustomed to. Cohen (1979) describes the job interview and the job itself:

If Watson had been able to laugh at that point, he must have done so. Resor [the person who interviewed Watson] was a man who had graduated from Yale with no great distinction in 1901. He had sold stoves for his father and had gone on to run a twelve-man office in Cincinnati. In 1916 he had clubbed together with some friends from Yale to buy out the original J. Walter Thompson who had made the agency a small success. Now John B. Watson, who was recognized as being one of the greatest psychologists in the world, who was in the same intellectual league as Freud and Russell and

Bergson, was asking Resor for a job. And Resor gave Watson only a temporary job. And what a job! Resor had to address the annual convention of the Boot Sellers League of America. In order to have the most impressive paper at the convention, he wanted some quick research to be done on the boot market. John B. Watson was given the job of studying the rubber boot market on each side of the Mississippi River from Cairo to New Orleans. It is a measure of Watson that he took to this job without feeling humiliated. He set out to learn it. He did not feel bitter that he had come to this. He always believed in being adaptable, in coping with what he called "life's little difficulties." Most psychologists would have felt this little difficulty as a crushing blow. And, in many ways, it was crushing. Watson wanted to pursue his work on children; he enjoyed his status as a leading professor. But one had to deal with life and, for him, the best way of doing so was to plunge whole-heartedly into it adversity and all. He threw himself into the study of the rubber boot market on the Mississippi. To be immersed even in that was some relief. (p. 161)

Resor asked for letters of recommendation for Watson, and a very supportive one came from none other than Titchener. Cohen (1979) says:

> Watson was always deeply grateful to Titchener for consenting to write a reference and wrote to him in 1922 that "I know, in my heart, that I owe you more than almost all my other colleagues put together." Watson's instinct was just. (p. 172)

Resor hired Watson in 1921, at a salary of $10,000 per year. By 1924 Watson was considered one of the leading people in advertising and was made a vice president of the J. Walter Thompson Company. Titchener wrote and congratulated him, but worried that the promotion would give Watson less time to work on psychology. By 1928 Watson was making over $50,000 per year, and by 1930 over $70,000. Remember that this was in 1930—imagine what the equivalent salary would be today! Even though Watson's accomplishments in advertising were vast, however, his first love was always

psychology, and he regretted for the rest of his life that he was unable to pursue his professional goals, especially his research on children. How psychology would be different today if Watson had not been dismissed from Johns Hopkins in 1920 cannot be known, but surely it would be different.

Watson's Objective Psychology

When Watson discovered Russian objective psychology, he found support in it, but he had arrived at his position independently of the Russians. The main thing Watson and the Russian psychologists had in common was a complete rejection of introspection and of any explanation of behavior based on mentalism. That is, both felt that consciousness could not *cause* behavior; it was merely a phenomenon that accompanied certain physiological reactions caused by stimuli. The Russians were clearly more interested than Watson in explaining the physiology underlying behavior, especially the brain physiology. As time went by, Watson became even less interested in physiology and more interested in correlating stimuli and responses. He called the brain a "mystery box" that was used to account for behavior when the real cause was unknown.

In his 1913 statement on behaviorism, Watson did not mention the work of the Russians, and he said very little about human behavior. And though Watson's first book, *Behavior: An Introduction to Comparative Psychology* (1914), dealt mainly with animal behavior, there was still no mention of the Russian psychologists. Finally, in his presidential address to the American Psychological Association in 1915 (published as "Conditioned Reflex in Psychology" in 1916), Watson suggested that Pavlov's work on the conditioned reflex could be used to explain human as well as animal behavior. But Watson never fully accepted or utilized Pavlovian concepts in his work. As we shall see, he had his own notions concerning the terms *stimulus* and *response*, and concerning the value of reinforcement.

The goal of psychology. In his major work, *Psychology from the Standpoint of a Behaviorist* (1919), Watson fully elaborated a stimulus-response psychology. In a 1913 article, he had stated the goal of psychology as the prediction and control of behavior, and in 1919 he explained further what he meant:

> If its facts were all at hand the behaviorist would be able to tell after watching an individual perform an act what the situation is that caused his action (prediction), whereas if organized society decreed that the individual or group should act in a definite, specific way the behaviorist could arrange the situation or stimulus which would bring about such action (control). In other words, Psychology from the Standpoint of the Behaviorist is concerned with the prediction and control of human action and not with an analysis of "consciousness." (pp. vii–ix)

He goes on to say (1919):

> The goal of psychological study is the ascertaining of such data and laws that, given the stimulus, psychology can predict what the response will be; or, on the other hand, given the response, it can specify the nature of the effective stimulus. (p. 10)

Watson, however, did not use the terms *stimulus* and *response* in as narrow a sense as the Russian reflexologists. For him, a stimulus could be a general environmental situation or some internal condition of the organism. A response was anything the organism did—and that included a great deal. In his book *Behaviorism* (1925), Watson says:

> The rule, or measuring rod, which the behaviorist puts in front of him always is: Can I describe this bit of behavior I see in terms of "stimulus and response"? By stimulus we mean any object in the general environment or any change in the tissues themselves due to the physiological condition of the animal, such as the change we get when we keep an animal from sex activity, when we keep it from feed-

ing, when we keep it from building a nest. By response we mean anything the animal does—such as turning toward or away from a light, jumping at a sound, and more highly organized activities such as building a skyscraper, drawing plans, having babies, writing books, and the like. (pp. 6–7)

Thus Watson's position has been unjustly called "the psychology of twitchism," implying that it is concerned with a specific reflex elicited by a specific stimulus. This criticism is more accurately directed at the Russian reflexologists.

For Watson, there were four kinds of responses. There was *explicit* (overt) *learned behavior,* such as talking, writing, and playing baseball. There was *implicit* (covert) *learned behavior,* such as the increased heart rate caused by the sight of a dentist's drill. There was *explicit unlearned behavior,* such as grasping, blinking, and sneezing. And finally, there was *implicit unlearned behavior,* such as glandular secretions and circulatory changes. According to Watson, everything that a person did, including thinking, fell into one of these four categories.

For studying behavior, Watson proposed four methods: *observation,* either naturalistic or experimentally controlled; the *conditioned-reflex method* that Pavlov and Bechterev had proposed; *testing,* by which Watson meant the taking of behavior samples, and *not* the measurement of "capacity" or "personality"; and *verbal reports,* which Watson treated as any other kind of overt behavior. By now it should be clear that Watson did *not* use verbal behavior as a means of studying consciousness.

Language and thinking. The most controversial aspect of Watson's theory concerned language and thinking. To be consistent in his behavioristic view, Watson had to reduce language and thinking to some form of behavior *and nothing more.* In 1925 he said:

> *Saying* is doing—that is, *behaving.* Speaking overtly or to ourselves (thinking) is just as objective a type of behavior as baseball. (p. 6)

For Watson, then, speech presented no special problem; it was simply a kind of overt behavior. Watson solved the problem of thinking by claiming that thinking was implicit or subvocal speech. Since overt speech was produced by substantial movement of the tongue and larynx, Watson assumed that minute movements of the tongue and larynx accompanied thought. No one ever really found such movements, but Watson assumed that as more sophisticated measuring equipment was developed they would be found. Here is how Watson (1930) describes the evolution from overt speech to implicit speech (thinking):

> The child talks incessantly when alone. At three he even plans the day *aloud*, as my own ear placed outside the keyhole of the nursery door has very often confirmed. Soon society in the form of nurse and parents steps in. "Don't talk aloud—Daddy and Mother are not always talking to themselves." Soon the overt speech dies down to whispered speech and a good lip reader can still read what the child thinks of the world and of himself. Some individuals never make this concession to society. When alone they talk aloud to themselves. A still larger number never go beyond even the whispering stage when alone. Watch people reading on the street car; peep through the keyhole sometime when individuals not too highly socialized are just sitting and thinking. But the great majority of people pass on to the third stage under the influence of social pressure constantly exerted. "Quit whispering to yourself," and "Can't you even read without moving your lips?" and the like are constant mandates. Soon the process is forced to take place behind the lips. Behind these walls you can call the biggest bully the worst name you can think of without even smiling. You can tell the female bore how terrible she really is and the next moment smile and overtly pay her a verbal compliment. (pp. 240–241)

Watson's attempt to reduce thought to subvocal speech aroused great opposition. Woodworth's reaction was typical (1931):

> I may as well tell you in a few words some reasons why I personally do not accept the equation, thought = speech. One is that I often have difficulty in finding a word required to express a meaning which I certainly have "in mind." I get stuck not infrequently, for even a familiar word. Another reason is that you certainly cannot turn the equation around and say that speech = thought. You can recite a familiar passage with no sense of its meaning, and while thinking something entirely different. Finally, thinking certainly seems as much akin to seeing as to manipulating. It seems to consist in seeing the point, in observing relations. Watson's speech habits substituted for actual manipulation fail to show how thinking carries you beyond your previous habits. Why should the combination of words, "Suppose I moved the piano over there," lead to the continuation, "But it would jut out over the window," just as a matter of language habit? Something more than the words must certainly be in the game, and that something consists somehow in seeing the point. (p. 72)

The problem of determining the nature of thought and determining thought's relationship to behavior is as old as psychology and is just as much an issue today as it ever was. Watson did not solve the problem, but neither has anyone else.

The role of instincts in behavior. Watson's attitude toward instincts changed radically over the years. In 1914 instincts played a prominent role in his theory. By 1919 Watson had taken the position that instincts were present in infants but that learned habits quickly displaced them. In 1925 he completely rejected the idea of instincts in humans, contending that there were a few simple reflexes such as sneezing, crying, eliminating, crawling, sucking, and breathing, but no complex, innate behavior patterns called instincts. In 1926 Watson said:

> In this relatively simple list of human responses there is none corresponding to what is called an "instinct" by present-day psychologists and biologists. There are then for us no instincts—we no longer need the term in psychology. Everything we have been in the habit of calling an "instinct" today is a result largely of training—belonging to man's *learned behavior*. (p. 1)

For Watson, *experience* and not genetics made people what they were. Change experience and you change personality. Thus Watson's position ended up as a **radical environmentalism**. Watson goes on (1926):

I would feel perfectly confident in the ultimate favorable outcome of careful upbringing of a *healthy, well-formed baby* born of a long line of crooks, murderers, thieves and prostitutes. Who has any evidence to the contrary? Many, many thousands of children yearly, born from moral households and steadfast parents, become wayward, steal or become prostitutes, through one mishap or another of nurture. Many more thousands of sons and daughters of the wicked grow up to be wicked because they couldn't grow up any other way in such surroundings. But let one adopted child who had a bad ancestry go wrong and it is used as incontestible evidence for the inheritance of moral turpitude and criminal tendencies. (p. 9)

Finally, Watson makes one of the most famous (or infamous) statements in the history of psychology (1926):

I should like to go one step further tonight and say, "Give me a dozen healthy infants, well-formed, and my own specified world to bring them up in and I'll guarantee to take any one at ramdom and train him to become any type of specialist I might select—a doctor, lawyer, artist, merchant-chief and, yes, even into beggarman and thief, regardless of his talents, penchants, tendencies, abilities, vocations and race of his ancestors." I am going beyond my facts and I admit it, but so have the advocates of the contrary and they have been doing it for thousands of years. Please note that when this experiment is made I am to be allowed to specify the way they are to be brought up and the type of world they have to live in. (p. 10)

Watson did, however, allow for genetically determined differences in *structure* that could influence personality characteristics. He says (1926):

So let us hasten to admit—yes, there are heritable differences in form, in structure. Some people are born with long, slender fingers, with delicate throat structure; some are born tall, large, of prize-fighter build; others with delicate skin and eye coloring. These differences are in the germ plasm and are handed down from parent to child. . . . But do not let these undoubted facts of inheritance lead you astray as they have some of the biologists. The mere presence of these structures tell us not one thing about function. . . . Our hereditary structure lies ready to be shaped in a thousand different ways—the same structure mind you—depending on the way in which the child is brought up. (p. 4)

Watson gives the following example of how structure interacts with experience to produce specific behavior patterns (1926):

The behaviorist would *not* say: "He inherits his father's capacity or talent for being a fine swordsman." He would say: "This child certainly has his father's slender build of body, the same type of eyes. His build is wonderfully like his father's. He, too, has the build of a swordsman." And he would go on to say: " . . . and his father is very fond of him. He put a tiny sword into his hand when he was a year of age, and in all their walks he talks sword play, attack and defense, the code of duelling and the like." A certain type of structure, plus early training—*slanting*—accounts for adult performance. (p. 2)

Emotions. Watson believed that, along with structure and the basic reflexes, humans inherited the emotions of fear, rage, and love. In infants fear was elicited by loud noises and loss of support (for example, falling), rage by restricting the infant's freedom of movement, and love by stroking or patting the infant. Through learning, these emotions came to be elicited by stimuli other than those that originally elicited them. Furthermore, all adult emotions such as hate, pride, jealousy, and shame were derived from rage, fear, and love.

Watson believed that each basic emotion had a characteristic pattern of visceral and glandular responses that was triggered by an appropriate stimulus. Also, each basic emotion had a pattern of overt responses associated with it. With fear there was a catching of the breath, clutching with the hands, closing of the eyes, and crying. With rage there was a stiffening of the body, and slashing and striking movements. With love there was smiling, gurgling, cooing, and an extension of the arms. For Watson, the three important aspects of emotions were the stimuli that elicited the emotions, the internal reactions, and the external reactions. Feelings and sensations were not important, and removing them from emotional behavior converted James's account of emotions to Watson's account.

In order to demonstrate how emotions could be displaced to stimuli other than those that had originally elicited the emotions, Watson and Rosalie Rayner performed an experiment in 1920 on an 11-month-old infant named Albert. They showed Albert a white rat, and he expressed no fear of it. In fact, he reached out and tried to touch it. As Albert reached for the rat, a steel bar behind him was struck with a hammer. The loud, unexpected noise caused Albert to jump and fall forward. Again Albert was offered the rat, and just as he touched it, the steel bar behind him was again struck. Again Albert jumped, and this time he began to cry. So as not to disturb Albert too much, further testing was postponed for a week. A week later, when the rat was again presented to Albert, Albert was less enthusiastic and attempted to keep his distance from it. Five more times Watson and Rayner placed the rat near Albert and struck the steel bar; and Albert, who had at first been attracted to the rat, was now frightened of it. According to Watson and Rayner (1920):

> The instant the rat was shown the baby began to cry. Almost instantly he turned sharply to the left, fell over on his left side, raised himself on all fours and began to crawl away so rapidly that he was caught with difficulty before reaching the edge of the table. (p. 5)

Five days later, Watson and Rayner found that the fear of the rat was just as strong as it had been at the end of testing, and that the fear had generalized to other furry objects such as a rabbit, a dog, a fur coat, and a Santa Claus mask. Watson had clearly demonstrated how experience rearranged the stimuli that caused

emotional responses. He felt that all adult emotional reactions developed by the same mechanism that had operated in the experiment with Albert—that is, contiguity.

Watson and Rayner found that Albert's fear of the rat was still present a month after Albert's training. They intended to eliminate Albert's fear, but before they could do so he was removed from the hospital in which he was living. It was left to Mary Cover Jones, under Watson's supervision, to show how a child's fear could be systematically eliminated. Watson believed that his earlier research on Albert had showed how fear was produced in a child, and he felt strongly that no further research of that kind was necessary. Instead, he would find children who had already developed a fear and would try to eliminate it. The researchers found such a child—a three-year-old boy named Peter who was intensely frightened of white rats, rabbits, fur coats, frogs, fish, and mechanical toys.

Watson and Jones first tried showing Peter other children playing fearlessly with objects that he was frightened of, and there was some improvement. (This is a technique called modeling, which Bandura and his colleagues employ today.) At this point, Peter came down with scarlet fever and had to go to the hospital. Following recovery, he and his nurse were attacked by a dog on their way home from the hospital, and all of Peter's fears returned in magnified form. Watson and Jones decided to try to uncondition Peter. Peter ate lunch in a room 40 feet long. One day as Peter was eating lunch, a rabbit in a wire cage was displayed far enough away from him so that Peter was not disturbed. The researchers made a mark on the floor at that point. Each day they moved the rabbit a bit closer to Peter, until one day it was sitting beside Peter as Peter ate. Finally, Peter was able to eat with one hand and play with the rabbit with the other. The results generalized, and most of Peter's other fears were also eliminated or reduced. This is one of the first examples of what we now call **behavior therapy**. In 1924 Jones published the results of the research with Peter, and in 1974 she published more of the details surrounding the research.

Child rearing. Watson was an extremely popular writer and speaker, and he dealt with many topics; but his favorite topic, and the one that he considered to be most important, was children. Unable to continue his laboratory studies after being forced out of the profession of psychology, he decided to share his thoughts about children with the public by writing *Psychological Care of the Infant and Child* (1928). The book was extremely popular (it sold 100,000 copies in a few months), and in many ways Watson was the Dr. Spock of the 1920s and 1930s. Watson's advice (1928) was to treat children as small adults:

> Never hug and kiss them, never let them sit on your lap. If you must, kiss them once on the forehead when they say good night. Shake hands with them in the morning. Give them a pat on the head if they have made an extraordinary good job of a difficult task. Try it out. In a week's time you will find how easy it is to be perfectly objective with your child and at the same time kindly. You will be utterly ashamed at the mawkish, sentimental way you have been handling it. (pp. 81–82)

Watson goes on (1928):

> When I hear a mother say, "Bless its little heart" when it falls down, or stubs its toe, or suffers some other ill, I usually have to walk a block or two to let off steam. (p. 82)

Watson also had a great deal to say about sex education, urging that children be given frank, objective information about sex; and he often expressed his gratitude to Freud for breaking down the myth and secrecy surrounding sex. None other than Bertrand Russell reviewed Watson's book on child rearing. Though Russell felt that Watson's emphasis on the environment was extreme and that Watson had gone a bit too far in banning hugging and kissing, he heaped praise on the book. But this did not impress most psychologists. Cohen (1979) says:

> The honesty in sex education which Watson demanded seemed wholly admirable to Russell. Watson had also revived Plato's argument that perhaps it would be best for parents and children not to know each other. While this was bound to shock the American public, Russell believed this was an issue that was worth discussing. He ended by saying that no one since Aristotle had actually made as substantial a contribution to our knowledge of ourselves as Watson had—high praise indeed, from a man who was then regarded as one of the greatest minds in the world! None of this impressed most psychologists who complained that Watson had demeaned himself, which was only to be expected, and demeaned their science, which was only to be deplored. (p. 218)

Along with the functionalists and most other subsequent behaviorists, Watson firmly believed that psychology should be useful in everyday life, and he often applied his behaviorism to himself and his children. Though behaviorism might have shortcomings, Watson felt that it could make for a better life than traditional beliefs could. In his book *Behaviorism* (1925) he says:

> I think behaviorism does lay a foundation for saner living. It ought to be a science that prepares men and women for understanding the first principles of their own behavior. It ought to make men and women eager to rearrange their own lives, and especially eager to prepare themselves to bring up their own children in a healthy way. I wish I had time more fully to describe this, to picture to you the kind of rich and wonderful individual we should make of every healthy child; if only we could let it shape itself properly and then provide for it a universe unshackled by legendary folk lore of happenings thousands of years ago; unhampered by disgraceful political history; free of foolish customs and conventions which have no significance in themselves, yet which hem the individual in like taut steel bands. (p. 248)

Learning. Although Watson was very impressed by Thorndike's early animal research, he felt that Thorndike's Law of Effect was too mentalistic. After all, what was a "satisfying state of affairs" but a feeling or a state of consciousness? Also, although Watson sought to make Pavlov's work the cornerstone of his behaviorism, he never shared Pavlov's (and Bechterev's) belief in the importance of reinforcement. For Watson, the important thing about conditioning was that it caused events to be associated in time; that is, it caused contiguity. To employ the concept of reinforcement was unnecessary. Instead of relying on Thorndike's Law of Effect or Pavlov and Bechterev's principle of reinforcement, Watson explained learning in terms of the ancient principles of contiguity, frequency, and recency.

Watson pointed out that in a learning situation, a trial always ended with the animal making the correct response. This meant that the correct response tended to occur more frequently than incorrect responses, and that the more often a response was made, the higher the probability that it would be made again (the law of frequency). Thus, the final response an organism made in a learning situation would be the response it would tend to make when it was next in that situation (the law of recency). In the classical conditioning situation, the conditioned stimulus and the unconditioned stimulus became associated (elicited the same kind of response) simply because they occurred at about the same time (the law of contiguity). We shall see in the next chapter that Guthrie, a neobehaviorist, took much the same position on learning as Watson did.

The mind-body problem. By the time Watson had begun to formulate his theory, there were four views on the mind-body relationship. One was an *interactionist* view of the kind Descartes and sometimes William James had accepted. According to this position, the mind could influence the body, and what happened to the body influenced the mind. That is, the mind and the body interacted. A second position was *psychophysical parallelism*, according to which mental and bodily events were parallel, with no interaction between them. In a third view, *epiphenomenalism*, mental events were the by-product of bodily events but did not cause be-

havior. That is, bodily events caused mental events, but mental events could not cause bodily events. During Watson's time, epiphenomenalism was probably the most commonly held view concerning the mind-body relationship. A fourth position involved rejecting the existence of mental events (consciousness) altogether. This position was called *physical monism*. In his early writings, Watson accepted consciousness as an epiphenomenon, as is evident in the following passage from "Psychology as the Behaviorist Views It" (1913):

> Will there be left over in psychology a world of pure psychics, to use Yerkes' term? I confess I do not know. The plans that I most favor for psychology lead practically to the ignoring of consciousness in the sense that the term is used by psychologists today. I have virtually denied that this realm of psychics is open to experimental investigation. I don't wish to go further into the problem at present because it leads inevitably over into metaphysics. If you will grant the behaviorist the right to use consciousness in the same way as other natural scientists employ it—that is, without making consciousness a special object of observation—you have granted all that my thesis requires. (p. 174)

Later, in his debate with McDougall (which will be discussed below), Watson switched to a physical monist position. Consciousness, he said, "has never been seen, touched, smelled, tasted, or moved. It is a plain assumption just as unprovable as the old concept of the soul" (Watson and McDougall, 1929, p. 26).

Most of today's behaviorists accept Watson's earlier position on consciousness—that since consciousness is an epiphenomenon, it cannot cause behavior. Therefore, while attempting to explain behavior, one can ignore consciousness. Skinner and his followers, however, maintain a belief in physical monism.

Watson's Influence

Watson's version of behaviorism no longer exists as such, but in spirit it lives on in the work of such psychologists as B. F. Skinner. Watson

William McDougall

accepted it for him. Watson died on September 25, 1958, at the age of 80.

Even though Watson's position became extremely popular, there were always prominent psychologists who opposed him. One of his most persistent adversaries was William McDougall.

WILLIAM McDOUGALL: ANOTHER KIND OF BEHAVIORISM

William McDougall was born in 1871 in Lancashire, England, where his father owned a chemical factory. Educated in private schools in England and Germany, McDougall entered the University of Manchester when he was only 15 years old. Four years later he started his medical training at Cambridge, and finally obtained his medical degree from St. Thomas's Hospital in London in 1897, at the age of 26. After a trip to the Far East, McDougall went to the University of Göttingen in Germany to study experimental physiology in the laboratory where Johannes Müller had worked for forty years. However, it was the reading of William James's work that got McDougall interested in psychology, and he always considered himself a disciple of James. Upon his return from Germany, he accepted a position at University College in London to teach experimental psychology. He moved to Oxford University in 1904, and remained there until World War I. During the war he served as a major in the medical corps and was in charge of treating soldiers with mental problems. After the war, he was psychoanalyzed by the famous psychoanalyst Carl Jung.

In 1920, McDougall accepted an invitation from Harvard to fill the position once held by William James and then by Hugo Münsterberg. McDougall stayed at Harvard until 1928; then he moved to Duke University in North Carolina, where he remained until his death in 1938. In his lifetime

influenced modern psychology mainly by making it more objective, more willing to rely on things that were observable. Watson's attempt to rid psychology of the notion of consciousness, although temporarily successful, failed in the long run. Even though there are still psychologists who choose to ignore consciousness and to relate environmental experience and behavior, as Watson attempted to do, there are even more psychologists who are busy exploring the very cognitive processes that Watson ignored, deplored, or denied.

In 1957 the American Psychological Association awarded Watson one of its prestigious gold medals in recognition of his significant contributions to psychology. Watson was very pleased with the award, but because of poor health he was unable to receive it in person; his son Billy

McDougall wrote 24 books and more than 160 articles.

Definition of Psychology

Although McDougall spent a great deal of time arguing with Watson, he was among the first to redefine psychology as the *science of behavior*. By no means, however, did McDougall attempt to eliminate the study of consciousness. As early as 1905, in his book *Physiological Psychology*, McDougall said:

> Psychology may be best and most comprehensively defined as the positive science of the conduct of living creatures. . . . Psychology is more commonly defined as the science of mind, or as the science of mental or psychical processes, or of consciousness, or of individual experience. Such definitions are ambiguous, and without further elaboration are not sufficiently comprehensive. They express the aims of a psychologist who relies solely upon introspection, the observation and analysis of his own experience, and who unduly neglects the manifestations of the mental life afforded by the conduct of his fellow-creatures. . . . To define psychology as the science of experience or of consciousness is therefore to exclude the study of these unconscious factors, whereas the definition stated above brings all these within the scope of psychology without excluding the study of any part of experience or element of consciousness, for all experience affects conduct. (pp. 1–2)

In 1908, in his book *Introduction to Social Psychology*, McDougall elaborated on his conception of psychology:

> Psychologists must cease to be content with the sterile and narrow conception of their science as the science of consciousness, and must boldly assert its claim to be the positive science of the mind in all its aspects and modes of functioning, or, as I would prefer to say, the positive science of conduct or behavior. Psychology must not regard the introspective description of the stream of consciousness as its whole task, but only as a preliminary part of its work. Such introspective description, such "pure psychology," can never constitute a science, or at least can never rise to the level of an explanatory science; and it can never in itself be of any great

value to the social sciences. The basis required by all of them is a comparative and physiological psychology relying largely on objective methods, the observation of the behavior of men and of animals of all varieties under all possible conditions of health and disease. . . . Happily this more generous conception of psychology is beginning to prevail. (p. 15)

Thus, at about the same time that Watson was making his first public statement of his behaviorism, McDougall was also questioning the value of introspection and calling for the objective study of the behavior of both humans and lower animals. Unlike Watson, however, McDougall did not deny the importance of mental events. McDougall felt that one could study such events objectively by observing their influence on behavior.

Purposive Behavior

The kind of behavior that McDougall studied was quite different from the reflexive behavior that the Russians and, in a more general way, Watson studied. McDougall studied purposive behavior, which differs from reflexive behavior in the following ways (McDougall 1923, pp. 44–46):

1. Purposive behavior is spontaneous. That is, unlike reflexive behavior, it need not be elicited by a known stimulus.
2. In the absence of environmental stimulation, it persists for a relatively long time.
3. It varies. Although the goal of purposive behavior remains constant, the behavior used to attain that goal may vary. If an obstacle is encountered, an alternative route is taken to reach the goal.
4. Purposive behavior terminates when the goal is attained.
5. Purposive behavior becomes more effective with practice. That is, the useless aspects of behavior are gradually eliminated. Trial-and-error behavior is purposive, not reflexive.

McDougall, then, saw behavior as goal-directed and stimulated by some instinctual motive. He believed that any behaviorist who ignored the purposive nature of behavior was missing its most important aspect.

The Importance of Instincts

As we have just seen, McDougall did not believe that purposive behavior was stimulated by the environment. Rather, it was stimulated by instinctual energy. A belief in instincts formed the core of McDougall's theory, and McDougall (1908) defined an instinct as

> an inherited or innate psycho-physical disposition which determines its possessor to perceive and to pay attention to, objects of a certain class, to experience an emotional excitement of a particular quality upon perceiving such an object, and to act in regard to it in a particular manner, or, at least, to experience an impulse to such action. (p. 29)

According to McDougall, every organism, including humans, is born with a number of instincts that provide the motivation to act in certain ways. Each instinct has three components:

1. *Perception.* When an instinct is active, the person will attend to stimuli related to its satisfaction. For example, a hungry person will attend to food-related events in the environment.

2. *Behavior.* When an instinct is active, the person will tend to do those things that will lead to its satisfaction. That is, the person will engage in goal-directed or purposive behavior until satisfaction is attained.

3. *Emotion.* When an instinct is active, the person will respond with an appropriate emotion to those environmental events that are related to the satisfaction or the failure to satisfy the instinct. For example, while hungry, a person will respond to

food or food-related events (for example, the odor of food) with positive emotions (for example, the feeling of happiness), and to those events that prevent satisfaction (for example, not having any money) with negative emotions (for example, sadness).

According to McDougall, most behavior can be explained as the result of human instincts and the emotions associated with them. His theory was hedonistic, since it claimed that both human behavior and animal behavior reflect a constant attempt to satisfy inborn needs. In this sense, McDougall's theory was much like Freud's, to which McDougall had responded favorably. The importance McDougall assigned to the instincts and their associated emotions is exemplified in the following passage (1908):

> By the conative or impulsive force of some instinct (or of some habit derived from an instinct), every train of thought . . . is borne along towards its end, and every bodily activity is initiated and sustained. The instinctive impulses determine the ends of all activities and supply the driving power by which all mental activities are sustained, and the most highly developed mind is but a means towards these ends, is the instrument by which these impulses seek their satisfactions, while pleasure and pain do but serve to guide them in their choice of means.
>
> Take away these instinctive dispositions with their powerful impulses, and the organism would become incapable of activity of any kind. (p. 44)

Although McDougall's list of instincts varied through the years, Table 12.1 presents the list he proposed in *Outline of Psychology* (1923, p. 324).

Sentiments

When more than one instinct is focused on the same object, a **sentiment** is formed. For example, one's mate can become associated with several instincts, such as sex, gregariousness, and

TABLE 12.1 McDougall's list of instincts.

Instinct	Emotion accompanying the instinct
Escape	Fear
Combat	Anger
Repulsion	Disgust
Parental (protective)	Love and tenderness
Appeal (for help)	Distress, feeling of helplessness
Mating	Lust
Curiosity	Feeling of mystery, of strangeness, of the unknown
Submission	Feeling of subjection, inferiority, devotion, humility; negative self-feeling
Assertion	Feeling of elation, superiority, masterfulness, pride; positive self-feeling
Gregariousness	Feeling of loneliness, isolation, nostalgia
Food-seeking	Appetite or craving
Construction	Feeling of creativeness, of making, of productivity
Laughter	Amusement, carelessness, relaxation

paternalism. The same is true of one's country or one's self. McDougall considered *self-regard* to be the most important sentiment because it was related to so many other things, and he felt that a healthy personality resulted when self-assertion and submission were in balance. McDougall claimed that sentiments, rather than isolated instincts, motivated most adult behavior. That is, combinations of instincts caused most behavior.

The Battle of Behaviorism

At this point we find two of the world's most famous psychologists saying opposite things. On the one hand, we have McDougall saying that the instincts are the motivators of all animal behavior, including that of humans. On the other hand, we have Watson saying that instincts do not exist on the human level, and that psychology should rid itself of the term *instinct*. Another major difference between Watson and McDougall concerned their views of the learning process. As we have seen, Watson rejected the importance of reinforcement in learning, saying that learning could be explained in terms of the associative principles of contiguity, frequency, and recency. For McDougall, habits of thought and behavior served the instincts; that is, they were formed because they satisfied some instinct. McDougall believed that reinforcement in the form of need-reduction was an important aspect of the learning process, and he expressed his view as follows:

In the developed human mind there are springs to action of another class, namely, acquired habits of thought and action. An acquired mode of activity becomes by repetition habitual, and the more frequently it is repeated the more powerful becomes the habit as a source of impulse or motive power. Few habits can equal in this respect the principle instincts; and habits are in a sense derived from, and secondary to, instincts; for in the absence of instincts, no thought and no action could ever be achieved or repeated, and no habits of thought or action could be formed. Habits are formed only in the service of the instincts. (1908, p. 43)

The time was right for a debate between McDougall and Watson, and debate they did. On February 5, 1924, the two men confronted each other before the Psychological Club in Washington, D.C., and more than 300 people attended. In 1929 Watson and McDougall published the proceedings under the title *The Battle of Behaviorism.* Cohen (1979, p. 234) notes that though McDougall was narrowly voted the loser, he was not too upset; he reasoned that because Watson was better looking than he was, most of the women in the audience had voted for Watson. Unfortunately we can offer only a sample from their lengthy debate. Watson said:

> He then who would introduce consciousness, either as an epiphenomenon or as an active force interjecting itself into the physical and chemical happenings of the body, does so because of spiritualistic and vitalistic leanings. The Behaviorist cannot find consciousness in the test tube of his science. He finds no evidence anywhere for a stream of consciousness, not even for one so convincing as that described by William James. He does, however, find convincing proof of an ever-widening stream of behavior. (Watson and McDougall, 1929, p. 26)

McDougall responded to Watson's inability to account for the most satisfying human experiences, for example, the enjoyment of music:

> I come into this hall and see a man on this platform scraping the guts of a cat with hairs from the tail of a horse; and, sitting silently in

attitudes of rapt attention, are a thousand persons who presently break out into wild applause. How will the Behaviorist explain these strange incidents: How explain the fact that the vibrations emitted by the cat-gut stimulate all the thousand into absolute silence and quiescence; and the further fact that the cessation of the stimulus seems to be a stimulus to the most frantic activity? Common sense and psychology agree in accepting the explanation that the audience heard the music with keen pleasure, and vented their gratitude and admiration for the artist in shouts and hand clappings. But the Behaviorist knows nothing of pleasure and pain, of admiration and gratitude. He has relegated all such "metaphysical entities" to the dust heap, and must seek some other explanation. Let us leave him seeking it. The search will keep him harmlessly occupied for some centuries to come. (Watson and McDougall, 1929, p. 63)

Neither Watson's position nor McDougall's has survived intact. For the moment, however, the student of psychology is more likely to know about Watson than about McDougall. Whether this remains the case, only time will tell.

SUMMARY

Several years before Watson's formal founding of the school of behaviorism, there were many psychologists with strong leanings toward behaviorism who insisted that psychology be defined as the science of behavior. Thorndike, for example, could as easily be labeled a behaviorist as a functionalist. Also, several Russians whom Sechenov had influenced were calling for a completely objective psychology devoid of any mentalistic concepts. Pavlov, for example, sought to explain *all* human behavior in terms of stimuli, sensory and brain mechanisms, and behavior. He saw all behavior, whether learned or innate, as reflexive. According to Pavlov, the innate associations between unconditioned stimuli and unconditioned responses were soon supplemented by learned associations between conditioned stimuli and conditioned responses.

For Pavlov, even responses to symbols (words) were reflexive. Reflexive responses to physical stimuli constituted the first-signal system, whereas reflexive responses to symbols constituted the second-signal system. Bechterev was also a reflexologist who sought a completely objective psychology. But unlike Pavlov, who studied internal reflexes such as salivation, Bechterev studied overt behavior. Bechterev felt that his technique was superior to Pavlov's because it required no operation, it could be used easily on humans, it minimized unwanted reactions from the subject, overt behavior could be easily measured, and satiation was not a problem. The kind of reflexology American psychologists adopted was more like Bechterev's than like Pavlov's.

Several factors molded Watson's behavioristic outlook. First, many of the functionalists at Chicago and elsewhere were studying behavior directly, without the use of introspection. Second, Loeb had shown that some of the behavior of simple organisms and plants was tropistic (that is, it was an automatic reaction to environmental conditions.) Third, animal research that related behavior to various experimental manipulations was becoming very popular. In fact, before his founding of the school of behaviorism, Watson was a nationally recognized expert on the white rat. Watson began to formulate his behavioristic ideas as early as 1902, and in 1904 he shared them with Angell, whose reaction was negative. Watson first publicly stated his behavioristic views at a colloquium at Yale in 1908. The response was again negative. In 1913 Watson gave a lecture entitled "Psychology as the Behaviorist Views It" at Columbia University. The publication of this lecture in the *Psychological Review* in 1913 marks the formal beginning of the school of behaviorism. In 1920, scandal essentially ended Watson's career as a professional psychologist, although afterwards he published articles in popular magazines, gave radio talks, and revised some of his earlier works.

Watson found support for his position in Russian objective psychology, but he rejected the Russian emphasis on physiology and reinforcement. Like the Russians, however, Watson rejected all reference to mental events. For Watson, the goal of psychology was to predict and control behavior by determining how behavior was related to environmental events. Watson even saw thinking as a form of behavior—behavior consisting of minute movements of the tongue and larynx. Early in Watson's theorizing, instincts played a prominent role in explaining human behavior. Later, Watson said that humans possessed instincts but that learned behavior soon replaced instinctive behavior. Watson's final position on instincts was that they had no influence on human behavior. He did say, however, that a person's physical structure was inherited, and that the interaction between structure and environmental experience determined many personality characteristics. Also, the emotions of fear, rage, and love were inherited, and experience greatly expanded the stimuli that elicited these emotions. The experiment with Albert showed the process by which previously neutral stimuli could come to elicit fear. Later, along with Mary Cover Jones, Watson showed how fear could become disassociated from a stimulus.

Watson advised parents not to pamper children but to treat them as small adults, and he urged that open, honest, and objective sex education be given to children. Watson accepted only two principles of learning: contiguity and frequency. That is, the more often two or more events were experienced together, the stronger the association between those events became. On the mind-body question, Watson's final position was that of a physical monist. Watson had a profound influence on psychology, an influence that continues in modern psychology in the form of neobehaviorism.

Even in Watson's time, his was not the only kind of behaviorism. One of Watson's most formidable adversaries was McDougall, who agreed with Watson that psychology should be the science of behavior but felt that purposive and instinctive behavior should be emphasized. Although McDougall defined psychology as the science of behavior, he did not deny the importance of mental events, and he felt that they could be studied through their influence on behavior. Whereas Watson had concluded that instincts played no role in human behavior, McDougall made instincts the cornerstone of his theory. For McDougall, an instinct was an innate disposition that, when active, caused a person to attend to a certain class of events, to feel emotional excitement when perceiving those events, and to act relative to those events in such a way as to satisfy the instinctual need. When the instinctual need was satisfied, the whole chain of events terminated. Thus, for McDougall, instincts and purposive behavior went hand in hand. McDougall believed that the reason humans learned habits was that habits satisfied an instinctual need. In the famous debate between Watson and McDougall, Watson was narrowly declared the winner.

DISCUSSION QUESTIONS

1. Make the case that prior to Watson's formulations, behaviorism was very much "in the air" in America.

2. Discuss the relationship between American behaviorism and the work of Sechenov, Pavlov, and Bechterev.

3. What was the major difference between Pavlov's work and Bechterev's?

4. List the factors that steered Watson toward behaviorism.

5. For Watson, what was the goal of psychology?

6. Summarize Watson's explanation of thinking.

7. For Watson, what was the role of instinct in human behavior?

8. Summarize Watson's views on emotion. What emotions did Watson think were innate? How did emotions become attached to various stimuli or events? What research did Watson perform to validate his views?

9. Describe the procedure Mary Cover Jones used to extinguish a fear.

10. What advice did Watson give on child rearing?

11. How did Watson explain learning?

12. Employing the notion of structure, explain why Watson felt that genetics could influence personality.

13. Summarize McDougall's theory. What kind of behavior did McDougall study, and what did he assume to be the cause of that behavior?

14. Discuss McDougall's concept of sentiment. According to McDougall, what role did sentiments play in human behavior?

15. What were the major points of disagreement between McDougall and Watson?

GLOSSARY

Association reflex Bechterev's term for what Pavlov called a conditioned reflex.

Bechterev, Vladimir M. (1857–1927) Like Pavlov, looked upon all human behavior as reflexive. However, Bechterev studied skeletal reflexes rather than the glandular reflexes that Pavlov studied.

Behaviorism The school of psychology founded by J. B. Watson that insists on the objective study of behavior.

Behavior therapy The use of learning principles in treating emotional problems.

Conditioned reflex A learned reflex.

Conditioned response A response elicited by a conditioned stimulus.

Conditioned stimulus A previously biologically neutral stimulus that, through experience, comes to elicit a certain response.

Discrimination The process by which, after either prolonged training or differential reinforcement, an organism makes a conditioned response only to the stimulus used during training or to stimuli very similar to it.

Extinction The elimination or reduction of a conditioned response that results when a conditioned stimulus is presented but is not followed by the unconditioned stimulus.

First-signal system The physical stimuli that elicit conditioned and unconditioned responses.

Generalization The process in which stimuli similar to the one used during conditioning also become capable of eliciting conditioned responses.

Higher-order conditioning The procedure whereby a conditioned stimulus is used as a reinforcer in order to establish additional conditioning.

McDougall, William (1871–1938) Pursued a kind of behaviorism very different from Watson's. McDougall's behaviorism emphasized purposive and instinctive behavior.

Pavlov, Ivan P. (1849–1936) Shared Sechenov's goal of creating a totally objective psychology. Pavlov focused his study on the conditioned and unconditioned stimuli that controlled behavior and on the physiological processes that they gave rise to. For Pavlov, all human behavior was reflexive.

Primary reinforcer An unconditioned stimulus.

Radical environmentalism The belief that most if not all human attributes are a product of experience.

Sechenov, Ivan M. (1829–1905) The father of Russian objective psychology. Sechenov sought to explain all human behavior in terms of stimuli and physiological mechanisms, without recourse to mentalism of any kind.

Second-signal system The symbols that elicit conditioned responses.

Sentiment The feeling that arises when one object satisfies more than one instinct.

Spontaneous recovery The reappearance of a conditioned response after a delay following extinction.

Tropism The automatic orienting response that Loeb studied in plants and simple animals.

Unconditioned reflex An unlearned reflex.

Unconditioned response An innate response elicited by the unconditioned stimulus that is naturally associated with it.

Unconditioned stimulus A stimulus that elicits an unconditioned response.

Watson, John B. (1878–1958) The founder of behaviorism. Watson saw as psychology's goal the prediction and control of behavior. In his final position, he denied the existence of mental events and concluded that instincts played no role in human behavior; experience molded the basic emotions and the physical structure we were born with into our personality. Watson's theory of learning consisted of the laws of contiguity and frequency. On the mind-body question, Watson ended up as a physical monist, believing that thought was nothing but implicit muscle movement.

CHAPTER 13

Neobehaviorism

BEHAVIORISM AND THE PHILOSOPHY OF SCIENCE

By the 1930s, most psychologists were convinced that in order to be scientific, psychology needed something that could be objectively and reliably measured, and they generally agreed that that something was overt behavior. The kind of behavior psychologists studied, however, varied widely. Those following the Russian tradition focused on reflexive behavior, which could be correlated with physical stimulation. Others studied the purposive behavior of the kind McDougall described. Still others studied behavior just as it occurred, without worrying about its causes. Even during Watson's time, however, it became apparent that in order to account for behavior adequately, psychology had to use theory. After all, physics, the science that psychology had tried for so long to model itself after, was highly theoretical. But even when using theory, psychology would follow the other sciences by insisting that abstract concepts be linked to observable phenomena. That is, an unobservable concept, such as habit, intelligence, or even learning, could be used only if it could be systematically linked to some form of overt behavior.

Operational Definitions

In 1927 the physicist Percy W. Bridgman wrote *The Logic of Modern Physics*, in which he proposed that every abstract concept in physics be defined in terms of the procedures used to measure the concept. He called such a definition an **operational definition**. Thus, concepts such as energy and force would be defined in terms of the operations or procedures followed in determining the quantity of energy or force. In this way there could be no ambiguity as to what the term meant. The insistence that all abstract scientific terms be operationally defined was called **operationism**.

Operationism soon took hold in psychology, and many insisted that the concepts psychologists used be either operationally defined or abandoned. Soon, concepts like anxiety, intelligence, drive, learning, personality, and motivation were being operationally defined by those who used them. Because operational definitions described the kind of behavior that could be used to quantify an abstract concept, operationism was clearly in accordance with psychology's new emphasis on behavior. For example, learning could be operationally defined as making X number of successive correct turns in a T-maze, and anxiety and intelligence could be operationally defined as scores on performance tests. Later in this chapter we shall see other examples of operational definitions, when we consider the neobehaviorists.

Logical Positivism

As we saw in Chapter 5, Auguste Comte (1798–1857) insisted that one could obtain valid information about the world only by studying nature directly. He was one of the earliest opponents of introspection. In *A Positive Philosophy* reprinted long after his death, he offers the following objection to introspection (1896):

In order to observe, your intellect must pause from activity, and yet it is this very activity you want to observe. If you cannot effect the pause you cannot observe; if you do effect it, there is nothing to observe. The results of such a method are in proportion to its absurdity. (p. 11)

For Comte, therefore, introspection was useless, since he believed that psychology should study only what it could see and measure. This position was called *positivism*. Watson, and to a large extent the Russian psychologists, attempted to follow it.

A more recent development was **logical positivism**, which was not as extreme as Comte's positivism. For the logical positivist, it was permissible to use abstract concepts as long as they were tied systematically to something that was directly observable. That is, theoretical terms could be used if they were operationally defined. This development in the philosophy of science paved the way for much more complex forms of behaviorism. Leahey (1980) describes the impact of logical positivism on psychology:

> The immediate impact of logical positivism and operationism on psychology was tremendous. They seemed to promise psychologists that theory could be just as objective and nonmentalistic as the experimental methods of classical conditioning and trial-and-error learning. Before logical positivism, any psychological theory seemed to demand reference to mind, and so smacked of the old psychology. [Logical] positivism seemed to show that theoretical terms could be completely defined by observable behavior, while operationism made it possible to expunge surplus mentalistic meanings. The way seemed open for slow and steady progress on the problems of psychology. (p. 306)

Not all psychologists—and indeed not all behaviorists—followed the new approach, but many did. We shall consider some behaviorists who did follow logical positivism and some who did not.

Soon after its founding, behaviorism began dividing into different camps. The camps differed in regard to the kind of behavior they studied, the role of reinforcement, and the rules by which behavior became associated with stimuli; but they all insisted that in order to be scientific, they must study behavior. To exemplify the behavioristic camps, we will consider the positions of Tolman, Hull, Guthrie, and Skinner—positions that exemplify **neobehaviorism**. According to Segal and Lachman (1972), the neobehavioristic theorists differed from Watson mainly in their attempt to offer a comprehensive explanation for the behavior they observed. Although Watson had embraced Russian reflexology and associationistic principles, his system lacked the explanatory and predictive features that he himself felt were so important. His research often generated facts that appeared to have no relationship to each other. Also, the neobehaviorists shared the belief that most human behavior was learned, and therefore that psychology should concentrate its efforts on the learning process.

EDWARD CHASE TOLMAN

Edward Chase Tolman (1886–1959) was born in Newton, Massachusetts, in a Quaker home, and pacifism was a constant theme running through his life. He earned his B.A. from the Massachusetts Institute of Technology in 1911, and his M.A. (1912) and Ph.D. (1915) from Harvard. While still a graduate student, he traveled to Germany and studied for a short time with Koffka, one of the founders of Gestalt psychology. (As we shall see in the next chapter, Gestalt psychology was highly mentalistic and nativistic.) Although Gestalt psychology influenced him, Tolman became a behaviorist.

Kind of Behavior Studied

Tolman (perhaps incorrectly) referred to Watson's psychology as "twitchism" because he felt it concentrated on isolated responses to specific stimuli. Watson contended that even the most complex human behavior could be explained in terms of S-R reflexes. Tolman referred to such reflexes as **molecular behavior**. Instead of studying these "twitches," Tolman decided to follow McDougall and study **purposive behavior**, calling such behavior **molar behavior** to contrast it with molecular behavior. In his major work, *Purposive Behavior in Animals and Men* (1932), Tolman describes *molar behavior*:

> A rat running a maze; a cat getting out of a puzzle box; a man driving home to dinner; a child hiding from a stranger; a woman doing her washing or gossiping over the telephone; a pupil marking a mental-test sheet; a psychologist reciting a list of nonsense syllables; my friend and I telling one another our thoughts and feelings—*these are behaviors (Qua Molar).* And it must be noted that in mentioning no one of them have we referred to, or, we blush to confess it, for the most part even known, what were the exact muscles and glands, sensory nerves, and motor nerves involved. For these responses somehow had other sufficiently identifying properties of their own. (p. 8)

Because Tolman chose to study molar behavior, his position is often referred to as **purposive behaviorism**. Although Tolman's approach differed from Watson's in several major ways, Tolman was still very much a behaviorist and was completely opposed to the use of introspection. To guard against even the possibility of indirect introspection, Tolman used only rats as experimental subjects. And even though Tolman's theory was mentalistic, Tolman painstakingly tied all his concepts to observable behavior. In other words, he operationally defined all of his theoretical terms.

The Use of Intervening Variables

By introducing the use of intervening variables, Tolman brought abstract scientific theory into psychology. It was clear that environmental events influenced behavior; the problem was to understand *why* they did. One could remain entirely descriptive and simply note what organisms did in certain situations, but for

Edward Chase Tolman

Tolman this was unsatisfactory. The following is a simplified diagram of Tolman's approach:

Independent Variables
(Environmental Events)
↓
Intervening Variables
(Theoretical Concepts)
↓
Dependent Variables
(Behavior)

Thus, for Tolman, environmental experience gave rise to internal, unobservable events, which in turn caused behavior. In order to account fully for the behavior, then, one had to know both the environmental events *and* the internal (or intervening) events that they gave rise to. The most important intervening variables that Tolman postulated were cognitive or mental in nature. It is often said that metaphysically Tolman was a mentalist, but methodologically he was a behaviorist. What made Tolman a different kind of mentalist was his insistence that his intervening variables, even those that were presumed to be mental, be operationally defined, or tied to observable events.

Though Tolman used several intervening variables, we will discuss only his most important, the **cognitive map**. Everyone knows that a rat learns to solve a maze; the question is, how does it do so? Tolman's explanation was mentalistic. As an example, when an animal is first placed in the start box of a T-maze, the experience is entirely new, and therefore the animal can use nothing from its prior experience. As the animal runs the maze, it sometimes turns right at the choice point and sometimes left. Let us say that the experimenter has arranged the situation so that turning left is reinforced with food. At some point, the animal formulates a weak **hypothesis** that turning one way leads to food and turning another way does not. In the early stages of hypothesis formation, the animal may pause at the choice point as if to "ponder" the alternatives. Tolman referred to this apparent pondering as *vicarious trial and error* because instead of behaving overtly in a trial-and-error fashion, the animal appeared to be engaged in mental trial and error. If the early hypothesis "If I turn left I will find food" is valid, the animal will develop the **expectancy** "When I turn left I will find food." If the expectancy is consistently confirmed, the animal will develop the **belief** "Every time I turn left in this situation, I will find food." Consistent confirmation of an expectancy results in a belief. Through this process a cognitive map of the situation develops. A cognitive map is an awareness of all the possibilities in a situation. For example, if I leave the start box, I will find the choice point; if I turn left at the choice point, I will find food; if I turn right, I will not, and so on.

So for Tolman, hypotheses, expectations, beliefs, and finally a cognitive map, intervened between experience and behavior. Rather than just describing an organism's behavior, they *explained* it. Tolman was careful, however, to test his theoretical assumptions through experimentation. Tolman's research program was one of the most creative a psychologist ever devised (for details, see Hergenhahn, 1982).

Position on Reinforcement

Tolman was *not* a reinforcement theorist. He believed that learning occurred constantly, with or without reinforcement and with or without motivation. About as close as Tolman came to a concept of reinforcement was **confirmation**. Through the confirmation of an hypothesis, expectancy, or belief, the cognitive map developed or was maintained. The animal learned what led to what in the environment: it learned that if it did such and such, such and such would follow; or that if it saw one stimulus (S_1), a second stimulus (S_2) would follow. For this reason, Tolman's position is called an S-S theory rather than an S-R theory.

Learning versus Performance

According to Tolman's theory, an organism learned constantly as it observed its environment. But whether the organism used what it learned, and if so how, was determined by the organism's motivational state. For example, a food-satiated rat might not leave the start box of a maze or might wander casually through the maze, even though it had previously learned what had to be done to obtain food. Thus, for Tolman, motivation influenced performance but not learning. Tolman defined **performance** as the translation of learning into behavior.

In one of his famous **latent learning** experiments, Tolman dramatically demonstrated the distinction between learning and performance. Tolman and Honzik (1930) ran an experiment using three groups of rats as subjects. Subjects in Group One were reinforced with food each time they correctly traversed a maze. Subjects in Group Two wandered through the maze but were not reinforced if they reached the goal box. Subjects in Group Three were treated like subjects in Group Two until the eleventh trial,

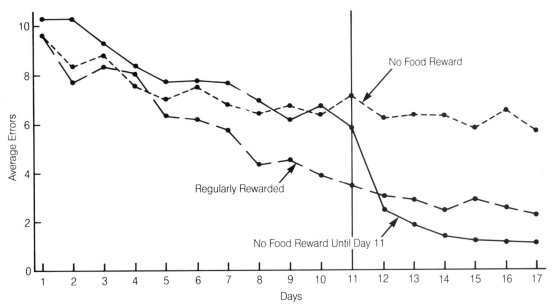

FIGURE 13.1 The results of the Tolman and Honzik experiment on latent learning. (Tolman and Honzik, 1930. Used by permission.)

when they began receiving reinforcement in the goal box. Subjects in all three groups were deprived of food before being placed in the maze. Tolman's hypothesis was that subjects in all groups were learning the maze as they wandered through it. If his hypothesis was correct, subjects in Group Three should perform as well as subjects in Group One from the twelfth trial on. This was because before the eleventh trial, subjects in Group Three had already learned how to arrive at the goal box, and finding food there on the eleventh trial had given them an incentive for acting upon this information. As Figure 13.1 shows, the experiment supported Tolman's hypothesis. Learning appeared to remain latent until the organism had a reason to use it.

ALBERT BANDURA

Tolman's theory is still very influential. In many ways, in fact, Tolman is responsible for the current widespread interest in cognitive psychology. Tolman's influence on contemporary

learning theory can be clearly seen in the work of **Albert Bandura** (1925–   ). Like Tolman, Bandura believes that organisms (including humans) learn by observing what leads to what in the environment. According to Bandura, we can learn either by observing the consequences of our own behavior or by observing the consequences of other people's behavior. Thus, in Bandura's account of **observational learning, vicarious experience** (observing the outcome of the behavior of others) is as important as observing the outcome of **direct** (personal) **experience**. Like Tolman, Bandura also believes that reinforcement is a performance, not a learning variable, and that what we learn are expectancies. For Bandura, the most important expectancy that we learn is the **self-efficacy expectancy**, which is what we *think* we are capable of doing in a given situation. If we think we are capable of doing what needs to be done, we are much more likely to try to do it. For example, if one feels capable of interacting with members of the opposite sex, one will try to do so; if one feels incapable, one will avoid such

ALBERT BANDURA

Albert Bandura

in the same room as the client, thus showing the client that there is nothing to fear by the snake's presence. Modeling has been very effective in changing self-efficacy expectancies and thus allowing individuals to engage in activities that they previously avoided. Bandura's book *Social Learning Theory* (1977) provides an excellent overview of his views on observational learning.

CLARK L. HULL

Born in New York, **Clark L. Hull** (1884–1952) grew up in Michigan. He received his Ph.D. from the University of Wisconsin in 1918 and remained there until 1929, when he moved to Yale. He remained at Yale until his death in 1952.

Borrowing the technique of using intervening variables from Tolman, Hull used them even more extensively than Tolman did. Hull was the first (and last) psychologist to attempt to apply a comprehensive scientific theory to the study of learning, creating a highly complex **hypothetico-deductive theory** that he hoped would be self-correcting. Hull first reviewed the research that had been done on learning; then he summarized that research in the form of general statements or postulates. From these postulates, he inferred theorems that yielded testable propositions. In his most famous book, *Principles of Behavior* (1943), Hull explains why his system should be self-correcting:

> Empirical observation, supplemented by shrewd conjecture, is the main source of the primary principles or postulates of a science. Such formulations, when taken in various combinations together with relevant antecedent conditions, yield inferences or theorems, of which some may agree with the empirical outcome of the conditions in question, and some may not. Primary propositions yielding logical deductions which consistently agree with the observed empirical outcome are retained, whereas those which disagree are rejected or modified. As the sifting of this trial-and-error process continues, there gradually emerges a

interactions. In Bandura's view, the major goal of psychotherapy is to change self-efficacy expectancies.

The major tool Bandura and his colleagues use in changing such expectancies is **modeling**, a procedure in which the client is shown a person similar to himself or herself performing some action that the client feels incapable of performing, and is encouraged to try it. With extreme aversions, like phobias, the modeling proceeds in small steps, and the desired behavior is slowly approximated. For example, if one has a snake phobia, a first step toward eliminating the phobia might be simply to have a snake limited series of primary principles whose joint implications are progressively more likely to agree with relevant observations. Deductions made from these surviving postulates, while never absolutely certain, do at length become highly trustworthy. This is in fact the present status of the primary principles of the major physical sciences. (p. 382)

In Hull's final statement of his theory (1952), he listed 17 postulates and 133 theorems, but we can review only a few of his more important concepts here.

Reinforcement

Unlike Watson and Tolman, Hull was very much a reinforcement theorist. For Hull, a biological need created a *drive* in the organism, and the diminution of this drive constituted **reinforcement**. Thus Hull had a **drive-reduction** theory of reinforcement.

Habit Strength

If a response made in a certain situation led to drive reduction, **habit strength** ($_sH_R$) was said to increase. Hull operationally defined habit strength, an intervening variable, as the number of reinforced pairings between an S (a physical situation) and a response. For Hull, an increase in habit strength constituted learning.

Reaction Potential

Drive was not only a necessary condition for reinforcement, but also an important energizer of behavior. Hull called the probability of a learned response **reaction potential** ($_sE_R$), which was a function of both the amount of drive (D) present and the number of times the response had been previously reinforced in the situation. Hull expressed this relationship as follows:

$$_sE_R = {_sH_R} \times D$$

Clark L. Hull

If either $_sH_R$ or D were zero, the probability of a learned response being made would also be zero.

Hull postulated several other intervening variables, some of which contributed to $_sE_R$ and some of which diminished it. The probability of a learned response was the net effect of all these positive and negative influences, each intervening variable being carefully operationally defined.

Hull's Theory in General

Hull's theory can be seen as an elaboration of Woodworth's S-O-R concept. Using operational definitions, Hull attempted to show how a number of internal events interacted to cause the overt behavior that we observe. By associating reinforcement with those events that were conducive to an organism's survival, Hull's theory was also very much in the Darwinian tradition. It showed not only the influence of Darwin, however, but of Woodworth, Watson, and logical positivism.

Whereas Watson popularized a strictly objective *descriptive* behaviorism, Hull popularized a

PETER GUTHRIE

Edwin Ray Guthrie

strictly objective **scientific behaviorism**. Marx and Hillix (1963) describe Hull's influence:

> Hull's most important contribution to psychology was his demonstration of the possibility of setting one's sights upon the ultimate goal of a thoroughly scientific and systematic behavior theory. He lived his own life in pursuit of that goal and thereby influenced even those who disagreed most vehemently with the substantive and methodological details of his work. No other psychologist has had so extensive an effect on the professional motivation of so many researchers. He popularized the strictly objective behavioristic approach as it had never been popularized previously. (p. 252)

Although Hull's theory was extremely popular in the 1940s and 1950s, it is now generally thought of as having mainly historical value. Hull attempted to create a general behavior theory that all of the social sciences could use to explain human behavior, and his program fit all

the requirements of logical positivism (for example, all of his theoretical concepts were operationally defined). But even though Hull's theory was scientifically respectable, it was relatively sterile. More and more the testable deductions from his theory were criticized for being of little value in explaining behavior beyond the laboratory. Psychologists began to feel hampered by the need to define their concepts operationally and to relate the outcomes of their experiments to a theory such as Hull's. They realized that objective inquiry could take many forms, and that the form suggested by logical positivism had led to a dead end. In many ways, Hull's approach was as unproductive as Titchener's had been. Once again psychology had learned that human behavior was just too complex to be explained by one paradigm and the methodologies that the paradigm dictated.

EDWIN RAY GUTHRIE

Obtaining his Ph.D. from the University of Pennsylvania in 1912, **Edwin Ray Guthrie** (1866–1959) then went to the University of Washington, where he remained until his retirement in 1956. His most important book was *The Psychology of Learning*, published in 1935 and revised in 1952.

One Law of Learning

While Watson explained learning in terms of the laws of contiguity and frequency, Guthrie's theory was even more extreme. Guthrie (1952) felt that all learning could be explained in terms of only one law, the **law of contiguity**:

> A combination of stimuli which has accompanied a movement will on its recurrence tend to be followed by that movement. Note that nothing is here said about "confirmatory waves" or reinforcement or pleasant effects. (p. 23)

This meant that if certain stimuli were present as a response was made, the next time those stimuli appeared the same response would tend to be made. In 1959, Guthrie stated his one principle of learning in a slightly different way: "What is being noticed becomes a signal for what is being done" (p. 186). Guthrie's principle necessitates acceptance of the **recency principle**, which Watson also accepted. According to the recency principle, the final act performed in a certain situation will be performed again if the situation recurs.

One-Trial Learning

Guthrie rejected the ancient law of frequency, which states that the more often a stimulus and a response are paired the stronger the association between them becomes. He believed in **one-trial learning**. For Guthrie, an association between a stimulus and a response gained its full strength upon the first pairing. That is, whether a stimulus and a response were paired one time or a thousand times did not matter; in either case the strength of the relationship between the two was the same. For Guthrie, then, practice did not improve learning.

Practice and Performance

To answer the question of whether practice improved performance, Guthrie distinguished between *movements* and *acts*. Movements were simple muscle contractions, whereas acts were defined in terms of what they accomplished. Examples of acts included writing a letter, throwing a ball, and reading a book. Furthermore, just as acts were composed of many movements, *skills*—such as typing, playing golf, or teaching—were composed of many acts.

Guthrie believed that because acts and skills were composed of many movements, practice improved performance. Though one trial was sufficient for learning any single association between a stimulus and a response (movement), an organism had to make thousands of such associations in order to perform an act—and even more to learn a skill. As Guthrie (1942) says:

> Learning occurs normally in one associative episode. The reason that long practice and many repetitions are required to establish certain skills is that these really require many specific movements to be attached to many different stimulus situations. A skill is not a simple habit, but a large collection of habits that achieve a certain result in many and varied circumstances. (p. 59)

Position on Reinforcement

Like Watson and Tolman, Guthrie was not a reinforcement theorist. He believed that reinforcement prevented *unlearning*. In a learning situation, two general conditions existed: one was the stimulating conditions prior to the presence of reinforcement; the other was the stimulating conditions following reinforcement. In other words, the presence of reinforcement changed the stimulating conditions from S_1 to S_2. Typically, the final thing an organism did in S_1 was to perform the response that the experimenter called "correct." When that response was made, the conditions immediately switched to S_2. The laws of contiguity and recency guaranteed that the final thing the organism did under S_1 was to perform the correct response. The administration of reinforcement switched the stimulating conditions from S_1 to S_2, thus preserving the relationship between S_1 and the correct response. According to Guthrie (1940):

> What encountering the food does is not to intensify a previous item of behavior but to protect that item from being unlearned. The whole situation and action of the animal is so changed by the food that the pre-food situation is shielded from new associations. (p. 145)

In many ways, Guthrie's brand of behaviorism was even more extreme than Watson's.

as an attempt to quantify Guthrie's theory of learning (see, for example, Estes, 1950).

B. F. Skinner

BURRHUS FREDERICK SKINNER

B. F. Skinner (1904–) is undoubtedly the most famous behaviorist in the world today. Born in Susquehanna, Pennsylvania, he obtained his B.A. in English from Hamilton College. He obtained his M.A. (1930) and his Ph.D. (1931) from Harvard University.

Kind of Behavior Studied

Whereas Watson modeled his psychology after Pavlov, Skinner modeled his after Thorndike. Watson and Pavlov attempted to correlate behavior with environmental stimuli. That is, they were interested in reflexive behavior. Skinner called such behavior **respondent behavior** because it was elicited by a known stimulus or stimulus condition. Since both Pavlov and Watson studied the relationship between environmental stimuli (S) and responses (R), their endeavors represent **S-R psychology**. Thorndike, however, studied behavior that was controlled by its consequences. (For example, behavior that had been instrumental in allowing an animal to escape from a puzzle box tended to be repeated when the animal was next placed in the puzzle box.) While Thorndike neither knew nor cared about the origins of such behavior, Skinner called such behavior **operant behavior** because of its functional relationship to the environment. Unlike respondent behavior, which was elicited by known stimulation, operant behavior was simply *emitted* by the organism. It was not that operant behavior was not caused, but that its causes were not known—nor was it important to know them. The most important thing about operant behavior was that it was controlled by its consequences, not elicited by stimulation. Skinner's concentration upon oper-

For Guthrie, all behavior was completely reflexive in that it was elicited by specific stimuli or stimulus combinations. Most radical, however, was Guthrie's rejection of the law of frequency, which Watson and almost everyone else since Aristotle had accepted. Because Guthrie's theory is mechanistic and positivistic, it is a modern example of early French materialism.

Many aspects of Guthrie's theory were compatible with mathematical formulations; and when mathematical models of learning started to become popular in the 1950s, Guthrie's theory formed their basis. For example, William K. Estes' early work, which became the most popular mathematical model of learning, can be seen

ant behavior is one major reason that his brand of behaviorism is *much* different from Watson's.

The Nature of Reinforcement

If an operant response leads to reinforcement, the rate or probability of that response increases. Thus, those responses an organism makes that result in reinforcement are most likely to occur when the organism is next in that situation. This is what is meant by the statement that operant behavior is controlled by its consequences. Reinforcement can be identified only through its effects on behavior. Just because something acts as a reinforcer for one organism under one set of circumstances does not mean that it will be a reinforcer for another organism, or for the same organism under different circumstances. Skinner (1953) says:

> In dealing with our fellow men in everyday life and in the clinic and laboratory, we may need to know just how reinforcing a specific event is. We often begin by noting the extent to which our own behavior is reinforced by the same event. This practice frequently miscarries; yet it is still commonly believed that reinforcers can be identified apart from their effects upon a particular organism. As the term is used here, however, the only defining characteristic of a reinforcing stimulus is that it reinforces. (p. 71)

Thus, for Skinner there is no talk of drive reduction, satisfying states of affairs, or any other mechanisms of reinforcement. A reinforcer is *anything* that, when made contingent on a response, changes the rate or probability with which that response is made. For Skinner, nothing additional needs to be said. He accepts Thorndike's Law of Effect, but not the mentalism that the phrase *satisfying state of affairs* implies.

The Importance of the Environment

While the environment was important for Watson and the Russian reflexologists because it elicited behavior, it is important for Skinner because it *selects* behavior. The reinforcement contingencies that the environment provides determine which behaviors are strengthened and which are not. Change reinforcement contingencies and you change behavior. In his bestselling book *Beyond Freedom and Dignity* (1971), Skinner makes this point as follows:

> The environment is obviously important, but its role has remained obscure. It does not push or pull, it *selects*, and this function is difficult to discover and analyze. The role of natural selection in evolution was formulated only a little more than a hundred years ago, and the selective role of the environment in shaping and maintaining the behavior of the individual is only beginning to be recognized and studied. As the interaction between organism and environment has come to be understood, however, effects once assigned to states of mind, feeling, and traits are beginning to be traced to accessible conditions, and a technology of behavior may therefore become available. It will not solve our problems, however, until it replaces traditional prescientific views, and these views are strongly entrenched. (p. 25)

Thus, Skinner applies Darwinian notions to his analysis of behavior. In any given situation, an organism initially makes a wide variety of responses. Of those responses, only a few will be functional (that is, reinforcing). These effective responses survive and become part of the organism's response repertoire, to be used when that situation next occurs.

The Mind-Body Relationship

Like Watson, Skinner denies the existence of a separate realm of conscious events. He feels that what we call mental events are simply verbal labels given to certain bodily processes. But, says Skinner, even if there were mental events, nothing would be gained by studying them. He reasons that if environmental events give rise to conscious events, which in turn cause behavior, nothing is lost, and a great deal is gained, by simply doing a **functional analysis** of the environment and the behavior. Such an analysis avoids the many problems associated with the study of mental events. These so-called mental events, says Skinner, will someday be explained when we learn what internal physical events people are responding to when they use such terms as *choice*, *will*, and *self* to describe their own behavior. Skinner, then, is a physical monist because he believes that consciousness as a nonphysical entity does not exist. Since we do not at present know what internal events people are responding to when they use mentalistic terminology, we must be content simply to ignore such terms. Skinner (1974) says:

> There is nothing in a science of behavior or its philosophy which need alter feelings or introspective observations. The bodily states which are felt or observed are acknowledged, but there is an emphasis on the environmental conditions with which they are associated and an insistence that it is the conditions rather than the feelings which enable us to explain behavior. (p. 245)

Elsewhere Skinner says, "A completely independent science of subjective experience would have no more bearing on a science of behavior than a science of what people feel about fire would have on the science of combustion" (1974, pp. 220–221), and "There is no place in the scientific position for a self as a true originator or initiator of action" (1974, p. 225). Like Watson, then, Skinner is a radical behaviorist in that he refuses to acknowledge any role of mental events in human conduct. Like the Russian reflexologists, he believes that so-called mental events are nothing but neurophysiological events to which we have assigned mentalistic labels.

Skinner's Attitude toward Theory

Because Skinner's position is nontheoretical, it contrasts with the behavioristic positions of Tolman and Hull. Skinner accepts operationism but rejects logical positivism. He is content to manipulate environmental events (for

example, reinforcement contingencies) and note the effects of these manipulations on behavior, believing that this functional analysis is all that is necessary. For this reason, Skinner's approach is referred to as a **descriptive behaviorism**. There is, Skinner feels, no reason for looking under the skin for explanations of relationships between the environment and behavior. To look for physiological explanations of behavior is a waste of time, since overt behavior occurs whether or not we know its neurophysiological underpinnings. We have already reviewed Skinner's attitude toward mentalistic explanations of behavior. Since Skinner does not care what is going on under the skin either physiologically or mentally, his approach is often referred to as "the empty organism approach." Skinner knows, of course, that the organism is not empty, but he feels that nothing is lost by ignoring events that intervene between the environment and the behavior it selects.

In addition to opposing physiological and mentalistic explanations of behavior, Skinner opposes abstract theorizing like that of Tolman and Hull. In his 1950 article "Are Theories of Learning Necessary?" he says:

> Research designed with respect to theory is also likely to be wasteful. That a theory generates research does not prove its value unless the research is valuable. Much useless experimentation results from theories, and much energy and skill are absorbed by them. Most theories are eventually over-thrown, and the greater part of the associated research is discarded. This could be justified if it were true that productive research requires a theory—as is, of course, often claimed. It is argued that research would be aimless and disorganized without a theory to guide it. The view is supported by psychological texts which take their cue from the logicians rather than empirical science, and describe thinking as necessarily involving stages of hypothesis, deduction, experimental test, and confirmation. But this is not the way most scientists actually work. It is possible to design significant experiments for other reasons, and the possibility to be examined is that such research will lead more directly to the kind of

information which a science usually accumulates. (pp. 194–195)

In his article "A Case Study in Scientific Method" (1956), Skinner describes his nontheoretical approach. He says that he tries something, and if it seems to be leading to something useful he persists. If what he is doing seems to be leading to a dead end, he abandons it and tries something else.

Skinner and Francis Bacon

In Chapter 4 we discussed the great Renaissance thinker Francis Bacon (1561–1626). Bacon was intensely interested in overcoming the mistakes of the past and thus arriving at knowledge that was free of superstition and prejudice. His solution to the problem was to stay very close to what was empirically observable and to avoid theorizing about it. Bacon proposed that science be descriptive and inductive rather than theoretical and deductive. Following Bacon's suggestion, scientists would first gather empirical facts and then infer knowledge from those facts (in contrast to the scientist who first develops an abstract theory and then deduces from it what should be true). Bacon's main point was that in the formulation of theories, a scientist's biases, misconceptions, traditions, and beliefs (perhaps false beliefs) could manifest themselves, and that these very things inhibited a search for objective knowledge. Skinner can be seen as a modern Baconian. Like Bacon, he is a positivist but not a logical positivist.

Applications of Skinnerian Principles

Like Watson, Skinner and his followers have sought to apply their principles to the solution of practical problems. In all of the applications of Skinnerian principles, the general rule is always the same: *Change reinforcement contingencies and you change behavior.* This principle has been used to teach pigeons to play games like table tennis and basketball, and many animals trained through the use of Skinnerian principles have performed at tourist attractions throughout the country. In a defense effort, pigeons were even trained to guide missiles as the missiles sped toward enemy targets (Skinner, 1960). In 1948 Skinner wrote a utopian novel entitled *Walden Two*, in which he demonstrated how his principles could be used in designing a model society. In his *Beyond Freedom and Dignity* (1971), Skinner reviews the reasons that cultural engineering, although possible, has been largely rejected.

In the realm of education, Skinner has developed a teaching technique called *programmed learning*. With programmed learning, material is presented to students in small steps, students are tested over the material that has just been presented, they are given immediate feedback on the accuracy of their answers, and they are allowed to proceed through the material at their own pace. Skinner has been criticizing American education ever since 1953, when he visited his daughter's classroom and concluded that the teacher was violating everything that was known about learning. In his 1984 article "The Shame of American Education," Skinner maintains that many of the problems in our educational system could be solved through the use of operant principles. Skinner's main criticism of American educational practices is that the threat of punishment is used to force students to learn and to behave, instead of the careful manipulation of reinforcement contingencies. This aversive control, Skinner says, creates a negative attitude toward education. Though Skinner and others offer evidence that programmed learning is effective, this evidence remains largely ignored.

Skinner and his followers have applied behavior modification principles to helping individuals with problems ranging from psychosis to smoking, drinking, speech disorders, shyness, phobias, obesity, and sexual disorders. The Skinnerian version of **behavior therapy** assumes that people learn abnormal behavior in the same way that they learn normal behavior. Therefore, "treatment" is a matter of removing the reinforcers that are maintaining the undesirable behavior and arranging the reinforcement contingencies so that they strengthen desirable behavior. In general, the use of Skinnerian principles in treating behavior problems has been very effective (see, for example, Ayllon and Azrin, 1968; Ulrich, Stachnik, and Mabry, 1966; Kazdin and Wilson, 1978; Leitenberg, 1976; Rimm and Masters, 1974; Kazdin, 1980; Craighead, Kazdin, and Mahoney, 1976).

BEHAVIORISM TODAY

The work of all of the neobehaviorists covered in this chapter remains influential in contemporary psychology. Tolman's brand of behaviorism, with its emphasis on purposive behavior and mental constructs, can be viewed as a major reason for the current popularity of cognitive psychology, and Bandura's theory of observational learning can be understood as a direct derivative of Tolman's theory. Guthrie's theory is still at the heart of many mathematically oriented theories of learning (see, for example, Estes, 1950, 1960, 1964). Although Hull did much to promote an objective behavioristic approach, his current influence is due mainly to some of the more esoteric features of his theory that we did not cover in this chapter. His goal of developing a comprehensive behavior theory, however, has given way to the goal of developing theories designed to explain specific phenomena.

Skinner's influence remains strong. As recently as 1974, Skinner wrote *About Behaviorism*, which attempts to correct 20 current misconceptions about behaviorism. In this book, Skinner traces a number of these misconceptions to Watson's early writings—for example, Watson's dependence on reflexive behavior and his de-

nial of the importance of genetic endowment. Skinner's position rectifies both of these "mistakes." Skinner also points out that he does not deny so-called mental processes, but believes that ultimately they will be explained as verbal labels that we attach to certain bodily processes. As evidence of the recent popularity of Skinnerian behaviorism, followers of Skinner have formed their own division of the American Psychological Association (Division 25, the division of the Experimental Analysis of Behavior) and have two of their own journals in which to publish their research, *The Journal of Applied Behavior Analysis* and *Journal for the Experimental Analysis of Behavior*.

In spite of the current manifestations of neobehaviorism mentioned above, contemporary psychology is challenging several themes that behaviorism has typically embraced:

1. Most behavior is learned; therefore, the importance of genetically determined behavior is minimal.

2. Language does not present a special problem, but is just another form of behavior governed by learning principles.

3. The principles governing human and nonhuman learning are the same; therefore, studying animals can teach us about human learning.

4. As causes of behavior, mental events can be either ignored or minimized. (Tolman's theory was an exception to this theme.)

5. All responses that an animal is capable of making are equally modifiable through the application of learning principles.

6. The same principles govern childhood and adult learning.

Those calling themselves sociobiologists have been providing evidence that much animal behavior, including human behavior, is genetically determined (see, for example, Barash, 1979; Wilson, 1978). Several researchers have challenged the contention that language can be understood entirely as learned behavior, saying rather that there is a strong genetic influence in its development (see, for example, Chomsky, 1957, 1959, 1972; Miller, 1965). Accumulating evidence indicates that human and nonhuman learning is so different that little if anything can be learned about human learning by studying nonhuman animals (see, for example, Rogers, 1969; Melton, 1964). The overwhelming interest in cognitive psychology today runs counter to all brands of behaviorism, except Tolman's. Current research indicates that *some* responses an animal makes are more easily modifiable than others, and that an animal's genetic makeup determines the modifiability of a response (see, for example, Seligman, 1970). Also, researchers have found that the same principles of learning do not apply to all animals (see, for example, Bitterman, 1965), and that different principles govern childhood and adult learning (see, for example, Piaget, 1966, 1970; Hebb, 1959). All of these findings are causing abandonment or revision of the tenets of behaviorism.

SUMMARY

Russian psychology did not cause behaviorism, but the two were compatible in outlook, and the same was true for the kind of philosophy of science that prevailed in the 1930s and 1940s. A key component of the philosophy of science at that time was operationism, the belief that all abstract scientific concepts should be operationally defined. An operational definition tied a concept to the procedures followed when measuring the concept. By following operationism, behaviorism could be theoretical and still remain objective. Positivism, which required that scientists deal only with observable data, gave way to logical positivism, which al-

lowed abstract theorizing if all abstract concepts were tied to the empirical world through operational definitions.

Following the lead of the logical positivists, Tolman introduced intervening variables into psychology; and following McDougall, he chose to study purposive behavior. According to Tolman, the learning process progressed from the formation of an hypothesis concerning what led to what in an environment, to an expectancy, and finally to a belief. A set of beliefs constituted a cognitive map, which was Tolman's most important intervening variable. In Tolman's theory, confirmation replaced the notion of reinforcement, and an important distinction was made between learning and performance.

Using intervening variables even more extensively than Tolman did, Hull developed an open-ended, self-correcting, hypothetico-deductive theory of learning. If experimentation supported the deductions from this theory, the theory gained strength; if experimentation did not support the deductions, the part of the theory upon which the deductions were based was revised or rejected. Equating reinforcement with drive reduction, Hull defined habit strength as the number of reinforced pairings between a stimulus and a response. He saw reaction potential as a function of the amount of habit strength and drive present.

For Guthrie there was only one law of learning: the law of contiguity, which states that if two or more things are experienced together they become associated. Furthermore, according to Guthrie, an association occurred at full strength after just one pairing of events. Because an act was composed of a multitude of S-R associations, and a skill was composed of many acts, practice improved performance. For Guthrie, reinforcement changed stimulating conditions, thereby preventing unlearning.

The most influential behaviorist in the world today, Skinner distinguishes between respondent behavior, which is elicited by a known stimulus, and operant behavior, which an organism emits. Skinner is concerned almost exclusively with operant behavior, and his brand of behaviorism is the more positivistic, nontheoretical kind of Watson. For Skinner, reinforcement is anything that changes the rate or probability of a response. Nothing more needs to be known about reinforcement, nor is an understanding of physiology necessary for an understanding of behavior. Skinner urges a study of the functional relationship between behavior and the environment, and like Watson, he is a descriptive behaviorist. The kind of science he accepts is much like the kind Francis Bacon proposed.

Tolman's influence appears in Bandura's work on observational learning and in the current popularity of cognitive psychology. Some aspects of Hull's theory have been useful, but not his comprehensive approach to theory building, since psychologists now seek theories of limited domain. Guthrie's theory has survived mainly as the cornerstone of several mathematical models of learning. Many contemporary psychologists label themselves Skinnerians and are active in both the research and applied aspects of psychology. Contrary to the belief of most behaviorists, however, there is growing evidence for the following: inherited tendencies are powerful determinants of behavior, language is too complex to be explained simply as learned behavior, human learning is qualitatively different from animal learning, some responses an organism can make are more easily modified than others, mental events influence behavior and therefore cannot be ignored, different principles of learning apply to different species of animals, and principles governing childhood learning are different from those governing adult learning. Support for such contentions is causing either revisions in behaviorism or a shift to other perspectives.

DISCUSSION QUESTIONS

1. Describe logical positivism and operationism, and indicate their influence on behaviorism.

2. In what ways was Tolman's brand of behaviorism different from Watson's? In what way(s) did his theory differ from those of the other neobehaviorists?

3. What was Hull attempting to do with his theory? Did he succeed or fail?

4. For Hull, what constituted reinforcement?

5. What was Guthrie's one law of learning? How did Guthrie explain the improvement of performance with practice?

6. How does Skinner distinguish between respondent and operant behavior? On which kind does he concentrate his research?

7. What is meant by the statement that operant behavior is controlled by its consequences?

8. For Skinner, what constitutes a reinforcer?

9. Summarize Skinner's attitude toward the use of theory.

10. Is Skinner a positivist or a logical positivist? Defend your answer.

11. Give examples of how Skinnerian principles have been applied to the solution of practical problems.

12. State the general rule that Skinnerians follow in modifying behavior.

13. Give evidence that the neobehaviorists are still influential in contemporary psychology.

14. What current research findings are causing a weakening or a revision of the behaviorist position?

GLOSSARY

Bandura, Albert (1925–) A contemporary learning theorist who emphasizes the development of expectancies through observational learning, thus following in the tradition of Tolman's theory.

Behaviorism The school of psychology founded by J. B. Watson that insists on the objective study of behavior.

Behavior therapy The use of learning principles in treating emotional problems.

Belief According to Tolman, an expectation that experience has consistently confirmed.

Cognitive map According to Tolman, the mental representation of an environment.

Confirmation The verification of an hypothesis, expectancy, or belief. For Tolman, the notion of confirmation replaced the notion of reinforcement.

Descriptive behaviorism Behaviorism that is positivistic in that it studies only directly observable events and does not employ abstract theory.

Direct experience According to Bandura, the observation of the consequencees of our own behavior.

Drive reduction Hull's proposed mechanism of reinforcement. For Hull, anything that reduced a drive was reinforcing.

Expectancy According to Tolman, an "if-then" proposition that has been tentatively confirmed.

Functional analysis Skinner's approach to research, which involves studying the systematic relationship between behavior and environmental events. Such study focuses on the relationship between reinforcement contingencies and response rate or response probability.

Guthrie, Edwin R. (1866–1959) Developed a brand of behaviorism that was positivistic and parsimonious. Guthrie sought to explain all learning in terms of the law of contiguity.

Habit strength ($_sH_R$) For Hull, the strength of an association between a stimulus and a response. This strength depends upon the number of reinforced pairings between the two.

Hull, Clark L. (1884–1952) Formulated a complex hypothetico-deductive theory in an attempt to explain all learning phenomena.

Hypothesis According to Tolman, an early "if-then" hunch that occurs during the early stages of learning.

Hypothetico-deductive theory A set of postulates from which empirical relationships are deduced (predicted). If the empirical relationships are as predicted, the theory gains strength; if not, the theory loses strength and must be revised.

Latent learning According to Tolman, learning that has occurred but is not translated into behavior.

Law of contiguity If two or more things are experienced together, they become associated.

Logical positivism The philosophy of science according to which theoretical concepts are admissible if they are tied to the observable world through operational definitions.

Modeling The procedure Bandura uses to change self-efficacy expectancies. In modeling, a client is shown a person harmlessly engaging in an activity in which the client is afraid to engage.

Molar behavior Purposive behavior.

Molecular behavior A small segment of behavior, such as a reflex or a habit, that is isolated for study.

Neobehaviorism Behaviorism that, unlike Watson's descriptive behaviorism, seeks a comprehensive explanation of its data and concentrates on a study of the learning process.

Observational learning The kind of learning Bandura studies, which results from attending to environmental events. According to Bandura, we learn what we observe.

One-trial learning In Guthrie's theory, the formation of associations at full strength after just one associative pairing.

Operant behavior Behavior that is emitted by an organism rather than elicited by a known stimulus.

Operational definition A definition that relates an abstract concept to the procedures used to measure it.

Operationism The belief that all abstract scientific concepts should be operationally defined.

Performance The translation of learning into behavior.

Purposive behavior Behavior that is directed toward some goal and that terminates when the goal is attained.

Purposive behaviorism The kind of behaviorism Tolman pursued, which emphasized molar rather than molecular behavior.

Reaction potential ($_sE_R$) For Hull, the probability of a learned response being elicited in a given situation. This probability is a function of the amount of drive and habit strength present.

Recency principle The tendency for that which was done last in a situation to be done again when the situation recurs.

Reinforcement For Hull, drive reduction; for Skinner, anything that increases the rate or the probability of a response; for Guthrie, anything that changes stimulating conditions; for Tolman, the confirmation of an hypothesis, expectation, or belief.

Respondent behavior Behavior that is elicited by a known stimulus.

Scientific behaviorism Behaviorism that uses abstract theory in an effort to explain observable behavior.

Self-efficacy expectancy According to Bandura, the expectations we have concerning our own ability to perform effectively in a given situation.

Skinner, B. F. (1904–) A contemporary behaviorist who believes that psychology should study the functional relationship between environmental events, such as reinforcement contingencies, and behavior. Skinner's work exemplifies the kind of science Francis Bacon suggested.

S-R psychology The kind of psychology insisting that environmental stimuli elicit most if not all behavior. The Russian reflexologists and Watson were S-R psychologists.

Tolman, Edward C. (1886–1959) Created a brand of behaviorism that used mental constructs and emphasized purposive behavior. Although Tolman employed many intervening variables, his most important was the cognitive map.

Vicarious experience The experience of observing the consequences of another person's behavior. According to Bandura, we learn as much by observing which of another person's actions lead to reward and punishment as we do from observing our own direct experience.

CHAPTER 14

Gestalt Psychology

About the same time that the behaviorists were rebelling against structuralism and functionalism in the United States, a group of young psychologists was rebelling against structuralism in Germany. Whereas the focus of the behaviorist's attack was the study of consciousness and the associated method of introspection, the German protesters focused their attack on the structuralist's **elementism**. Consciousness, said the German rebels, could not be reduced to elements without distorting the true meaning of the conscious experience. For them, the investigation of conscious experience through the introspective method was an essential part of psychology, but the kind of conscious experience the structuralists investigated was artificial. These young psychologists believed that we did not experience things in little pieces, but in meaningful, intact configurations. We did not see patches of green, blue, and red; we saw people, cars, trees, and clouds. These meaningful, intact, conscious experiences were what the introspective method should concentrate on. Since the German word for "configuration" or "whole" was **Gestalt**, this new kind of psychology was called **Gestalt psychology**.

According to the Gestalt psychologists, the study of wholes, not parts, should be the major task of psychology. Heidbreder (1933) summarizes what the Gestalt psychologists thought was the proper unit of study for psychology:

> The perception itself shows a character of totality, a form, a Gestalt, which in the very attempt at analysis is destroyed; and this experience, as directly given, sets the problem for psychology.

It is this experience that presents the raw data which psychology must explain, and which it must never be content to explain away. To begin with elements is to begin at the wrong end; for elements are products of reflection and abstraction, remotely derived from the immediate experience they are invoked to explain. *Gestalt* psychology attempts to get back to naive perception, to immediate experience "undebauched by learning"; and it insists that it finds there not assemblages of elements, but unified wholes; not masses of sensations, but trees, clouds, and sky. And this assertion it invites anyone to verify simply by opening his eyes and looking at the world about him in his ordinary everyday way. (p. 331)

The Gestalt psychologists were opposed to any kind of elementism in psychology, whether it be the kind the structuralists practiced in their search for the mental elements, or the kind the behaviorists practiced in their search for S-R associations. The attempt to reduce either consciousness or behavior to the basic elements is called the **molecular approach** to psychology, and psychologists such as Wundt, Titchener, Pavlov, and Watson used such an approach. The Gestalt psychologists argued that a **molar approach** should be taken. Taking the molar approach in studying consciousness would mean concentrating on *phenomenological* experience (that is, mental experience as it occurred to the naive observer without further analysis). Taking the molar approach while studying behavior would mean concentrating on large segments of goal-directed (purposive) behavior. We saw in the last chapter that, under the influence of Gestalt psychology, Tolman and most of the functionalists chose to study this kind of behavior. As we shall see, the Gestalt psychologists attempted to show that in every aspect of psychology it was more beneficial to concentrate on wholes (*Gestalten*) than on parts (atoms, elements). Those taking a molar approach to the study of psychological phenomena are called **holists**, to contrast them with the elementists or atomists, who study complex phenomena by seeking the simpler processes that comprise those phenomena. The Gestalt psychologists were clearly holists.

This switch in emphasis from parts to wholes required a major change from the elementist approach that was popular at the time. Wertheimer (1979) says:

> This formulation involved a radical reorientation: the nature of the parts is determined by the whole rather than vice versa; therefore analysis should go "from above down" rather than "from below up." One should not begin with elements and try to synthesize the whole from them, but study the whole to see what its natural parts are. The parts of a whole are not neutral and inert, but structurally intimately related to one another. That parts of a whole are not indifferent to one another was illustrated, for example, by a soap bubble: change of one part results in a dramatic change in the entire configuration. This approach was applied to the concrete understanding of a wide variety of phenomena in thinking, learning, problem solving, perception, and philosophy, and the movement developed and spread rapidly, with violent criticisms against it from outside, as well as equally vehement attacks on the outsiders from inside. (p. 137)

ANTECEDENTS OF GESTALT PSYCHOLOGY

Whereas behaviorism follows in the tradition of Aristotle, empiricism, materialism, and positivism, Gestalt psychology followed in the tradition of Plato, Descartes, Kant, rationalism, and nativism.

Immanuel Kant

Immanuel Kant (1724–1804) believed that conscious experience was the result of the interaction between sensory stimulation and the faculties of the mind. In other words, the mind added something to our conscious experience that the sensory stimulation did not contain. If the term *faculties of the mind* is replaced by *characteristics of the brain*, there is considerable correspondence between Kant and the Gestalt psychologists. Both believed that conscious experience could not be reduced to sensory stimulation, and for both, conscious experience was different from the elements that made it up. Therefore, to look for a one-to-one correspondence between a sensory event and a mental event was doomed to failure. For Kant and for the Gestalt psychologists, there was an important difference between perception and sensation, a difference that was due to the fact that our minds (Kant) or our brains (the Gestalt psychologists) changed sensory experience, making it more meaningful than it otherwise would be. Thus the world we perceived was never the same as the world we sensed. Because this embellishment of sensory information resulted from innate mechanisms, it was independent of experience.

Ernst Mach

Ernst Mach (1838–1916), a physicist, wrote *Contributions to the Analysis of Sensations* (1886), in which he postulated two perceptions that appeared to be independent of the particular elements that made them up: *space form* and *time form*. For example, one experiences the form of circle whether the actual circle presented is large, small, red, blue, bright, or dull. The experience of "circleness" is therefore an example of space form. The same would be true of any other geometric form. Likewise, a melody is recognizable as the same no matter what key or tempo it is played in. Thus a melody is an example of time form. Mach was making the important point that a wide variety of sensory elements can give rise to the same perception; therefore, perception is independent of any particular cluster of sensory elements.

Christian von Ehrenfels

Elaborating on Mach's notions of space and time forms, **Christian von Ehrenfels** (1859–1932) said that our perceptions contained *Gestalt Qualitäten* (form qualities) that were not contained in isolated sensations. No matter what pattern dots are arranged in, one recognizes the pattern, not the individual dots. Likewise, one cannot experience a melody by attending to individual notes: only when one experiences several notes together does one experience the melody. For both Mach and von Ehrenfels, form was something that emerged from the elements of sensation. Their position was similar to the one John Stuart Mill (1806–1873) had taken many years earlier. With his idea of "mental chemistry," Mill had suggested that when sensations fused, a new sensation totally unlike those of which it was composed could emerge.

Mach and von Ehrenfels also believed that elements of sensation combined and *gave rise* to the experience of form. With his notion of "creative synthesis," Wundt, too, accepted a form of mental chemistry. For Mach, von Ehrenfels, John Stuart Mill, and Wundt, the elements were still necessary in determining the whole or the form; they were still of fundamental importance. As we shall see, the Gestalt psychologists turned this relationship completely around and emphasized the whole. For them, it was the whole that dominated the parts, not the other way around.

William James

Because of his distaste for elementism in psychology, **William James** (1842–1910) can also be seen as a precursor to Gestalt psychology. He said that the approach of the structuralists depended on an artificial and distorted view of mental life. Instead of viewing the mind as consisting of isolated mental elements that were bound together by association, James proposed a stream of consciousness. He felt that this stream should be the object of psychological inquiry, and any attempt to break it up for more detailed analysis must be avoided. The Gestalt psychologists agreed with James's anti-elementist stand, but felt that he had gone too far. The mind, they felt, could indeed be divided for study; it was just that in choosing the mental element for their object of study, the structuralists had made a bad choice. For the Gestalt psychologists, the correct choice was the study of *Gestalten* (plural of *Gestalt*).

Act Psychology

We saw in Chapter 9 that members of the Würzburg school, such as Franz Brentano and Carl Stumpf, favored the kind of introspection that focused on the *acts* of perceiving, sensing, or problem solving. They were against using introspection to search for mental elements, as the structuralists had done, and they directed their more liberal brand of introspection toward intact mental phenomena. The study of meaningful mental phenomena as the naive (untrained) observer experiences them is called **phenomenology**. For the Gestalt psychologists, it was mental phenomena that were studied through introspection. It should come as no surprise that **act psychology** influenced Gestalt psychology, since all three founders of Gestalt psychology (Wertheimer, Koffka, and Köhler) had at one time or another had Carl Stumpf as their teacher. Köhler even dedicated one of his books to Stumpf (1920).

Developments in Physics

Properties of magnetic fields were difficult to understand in terms of the mechanistic-elementist view of Galilean-Newtonian physics, so some physicists turned to a study of force fields, in which all events were interrelated. (Anything that happens in a force field in some way influences everything else in the field.) Köhler was well versed in physics and had even studied for a while with Max Planck, the creator of quantum mechanics, and Max Wertheimer was a personal friend of Albert Einstein. The concepts of relativity and force fields played an important role in the development of Gestalt theory. It has even been said that Gestalt psychology represents an effort to model psychology after Einsteinian physics instead of Newtonian physics. In Einsteinian physics, **field theory** plays a prominent role, and we will have more to say about it later in this chapter.

THE FOUNDING OF GESTALT PSYCHOLOGY

Max Wertheimer (1880–1943) was on a train on his way from Vienna to the Rhine when he had an idea that was to launch Gestalt psychology. The idea was that our perceptions are structured in ways that sensory stimulation is not. That is, our perceptions are more than, or different from, the sensations that make them up. To further explore this notion, Wertheimer got off the train, bought a stroboscope (a device that allows still pictures to be flashed in such a way that the images on them appear to move), and began to experiment. Clearly, Wertheimer was perceiving motion where none actually existed. To examine this phenomenon in more detail, he went to the University of Frankfurt, where a tachistoscope was made available to him. (A tachistoscope is a device that can flash lights on and off for measured fractions of a second.) Flashing two lights successively, Wertheimer found that if the time between the flashes was long (200 milliseconds or longer), the observer perceived two lights flashing on and off successively—which was, in fact, the case. If the interval between flashes was very

short (30 milliseconds or less), both lights appeared to be on simultaneously. But if the interval between the flashes was about 60 milliseconds, it appeared that *one light* was moving from one position to the other. Wertheimer called this apparent movement the **phi phenomenon**, and his 1912 article describing this phenomenon is usually taken as the formal beginning of the school of Gestalt psychology.

Wertheimer's assistants in his research at the University of Frankfurt were Kurt Koffka (1884–1941) and Wolfgang Köhler (1887–1967), both of whom also acted as Wertheimer's subjects in his perception experiments. So closely are Koffka and Köhler linked with the development of Gestalt psychology that they are usually considered cofounders of the school.

Max Wertheimer

Max Wertheimer was born in Prague in 1880. He attended a gymnasium (roughly equivalent to an American high school) until he was 18, at which time he went to the University of Prague to study law. While Wertheimer was attending the University of Prague, his interest shifted from law to philosophy, and during this time he attended lectures by von Ehrenfels. After spending some time at the University of Berlin (1901–1903), where he attended Stumpf's classes, Wertheimer moved to the University of Würzburg, where in 1904 he received his Ph.D. under Külpe's supervision. Being at Würzburg at the time when Külpe and others were locked in debate with Wundt over the existence of "imageless thought" and over what introspection should focus on no doubt affected Wertheimer's thinking. Between 1904 and 1910 Wertheimer held academic positions at the Universities of Prague, Vienna, and Berlin. He was at the University of Frankfurt from 1910 to 1917, the University of Berlin from 1916 to 1929, and again at the University of Frankfurt from 1929 to 1933. In 1933 he emigrated to the United States and taught at the New School for

Social Research in New York until his death in 1943.

Kurt Koffka

Born in Berlin, **Kurt Koffka** (1886–1941) received his Ph.D. from the University of Berlin in 1908, under the supervision of Carl Stumpf. Koffka served as an assistant at Würzburg and at Frankfurt before accepting a position at the University of Giessen in central Germany, where he remained until 1924. During his stay at the University of Frankfurt, Koffka began his long association with Wertheimer and Köhler. In 1924 he came to the Unived States, and after holding visiting professorships at Cornell and the University of Wisconsin, he accepted a position at Smith College in Northampton, Massachusetts, where he remained until his death on November 22, 1941.

In 1922 Koffka wrote an article, in English, on Gestalt psychology. Published in the *Psychological Bulletin*, the article was entitled "Perception: An Introduction to Gestalt Theory." This article is believed to be responsible for most American psychologists erroneously assuming that the Gestalt psychologists were interested only in perception. The truth was that in addition to perception, the Gestalt psychologists were interested in many philosophical issues, in learning, and in thinking. The reason for their early concentration on perception was that Wundt had been concentrating on perception, and he was the primary focus of their attack.

Wolfgang Köhler

Wolfgang Köhler (1887–1967) was born in Reval, Estonia, and received his Ph.D. in 1909 from the University of Berlin. Like Koffka, Köhler worked under the supervision of Carl Stumpf. In 1909 Köhler went to the University of Frankfurt, where a year later he would participate with Wertheimer and Koffka in the research that was to launch the Gestalt movement.

Max Wertheimer

In 1913 the Prussian Academy of Science invited Köhler to go to its anthropoid station on Tenerife, one of the Canary Islands, to study chimpanzees. Shortly after his arrival, the first World War began, and Köhler was marooned for seven years. While at the anthropoid station, Köhler concentrated his study on the nature of learning in chimpanzees. He summarized his observations in the *Mentality of Apes* (1917), which was translated into English in 1927.

Upon his return to Germany, Köhler accepted a professorship at the University of Göttingen (1921–1922), and in 1922 he succeeded Carl Stumpf as chairman of the Department of Psychology at the University of Berlin. This was a prestigious appointment, and it gave Gestalt psychology international recognition. Köhler

ARCHIVES OF THE HISTORY OF AMERICAN PSYCHOLOGY

Kurt Koffka (*l*) and Wolfgang Köhler (*r*)

stayed at the University of Berlin until 1934, when he came to the United States after writing a letter denouncing Nazism to a German newspaper. After lecturing at Harvard for a year, he accepted an appointment at Swarthmore College, where he remained until his retirement. After retiring, he continued his writing and research at Dartmouth College, and he spent considerable time lecturing at European universities. As testimony to the success of early Gestalt theorists, Köhler received a distinguished contribution award from the American Psychological Association in 1956, and he served as president of the association in 1958.

Like behaviorism, Gestalt psychology started as a protest against structuralism; and like the behaviorists, the Gestalt theorists demanded revolutionary changes in psychology. Heid-

breder (1933) describes the early Gestalt position:

> The protest was neither mild in character nor limited in scope. The new school demanded nothing short of a complete revision of psychology. The leaders of the movement were quick to see that the problem involved in the phi phenomenon was present in other common cases of perception. For example, we are continually seeing certain objects as rectangular— table-tops, picture-frames, doors and windows, sheets of paper; but only in a really exceptional case is the image projected on the retina actually rectangular. We see a black object in the sunlight as black, and a white object in the shadow as white, even when conditions have been carefully arranged so that physically the same amount of light is reflected from both objects. We see a man as having the same height whether he is five or ten yards away, though in the one case the retinal image is four times as large as in the other. In all these cases, as in the phi phenomenon, and in literally thousands like them, the obvious and almost pictorial difference between the character of the actual perception and that of the local sensory stimulation throws into sharp relief the problem that, in the opinion of the Gestaltists, the old school had utterly failed to meet. And the same instances show with the utmost clearness the dependence of the perception on the totality of the stimulating conditions. (pp. 330–331)

ISOMORPHISM AND THE LAW OF PRÄGNANZ

A basic question that Wertheimer had to answer was how only two stimuli could cause the perception of motion. Wertheimer did not discover apparent motion; it had been known about for years. In fact, the motion picture had been invented 25 years before Wertheimer's discovery of the phi phenomenon. What was different was Wertheimer's *explanation* of the phenomenon. As we have seen, Mach, von Ehrenfels, and Wundt all recognized that the whole was more than the sum of its parts, but they all assumed that somehow the whole (*Gestalt*) emerged from the characteristics of the parts. That is, after the parts (elements) were attended to, they somehow fused and gave rise to the "whole" experience. This point of view still depended on a form of elementism and its related assumption of association. For example, Wundt's explanation of apparent movement was that the fixation of the eyes changed with each successive presentation of the visual stimulus, and this caused the muscles controlling the eyes to give off sensations identical to those given off when real movement was experienced. Thus, because of past experience with such sensations (association), one experienced what appeared to be movement. Wundt called this creative synthesis, while Helmholtz called it unconscious inference. Both researchers emphasized the role of learning in experiences like the phi phenomenon.

Through an ingenious demonstration, however, Wertheimer showed that explanations based on learning were not plausible. Again using a tachistoscope, he showed that the phi phenomenon could occur in two directions at the same time. Three lights were arranged as shown in the diagram below. The center light was flashed on, and shortly thereafter the two other lights were flashed on, both at the same time. Wertheimer repeated this sequence several times. The center slit of light appeared to fall to the left and right simultaneously, and since the eyes could not move in two directions at the same time, an explanation based on sensations from the eye muscles was untenable.

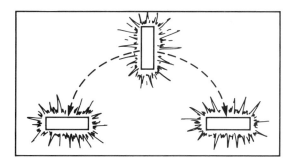

If the experience of psychological phenomena could not be explained by sensory processes, inferences, or fusions, how could it be explained? The Gestalt psychologists' answer was that the brain contained structured fields of forces that existed prior to sensory stimulation. Upon entering such a field, sensory data both modified the structure of the field and was modified by it. What we experienced consciously resulted from the interaction of the sensory data and the force fields in the brain. The situation is similar to one in which metal particles are placed into a magnetic field. The nature of the field will have a strong influence on how the particles are distributed, but the characteristics of the particles will also influence the distribution. For example, larger, more numerous particles will be distributed differently within the field than smaller, less numerous particles. In the case of the mind, the important point is that fields of brain activity *transform* sensory data and give that data characteristics it otherwise would not possess.

Psychophysical Isomorphism

To describe more fully the relationship between the field activity of the brain and conscious experience, the Gestalt psychologists introduced the notion of **psychophysical isomorphism**, which Köhler (1947) describes as follows:

> Experienced order in space is always structurally identical with a functional order in the distribution of underlying brain processes. (p. 61)

Elsewhere Köhler (1969) says,

> Psychological facts and the underlying events in the brain resemble each other in all their structural characteristics. (p. 66)

The Gestalt notion of isomorphism stresses the fact that the brain transforms incoming sensory data, and that we experience the transformed data consciously. The patterns of brain activity and the patterns of conscious experience are structurally equivalent.

The Constancy Hypothesis

With their notion of isomorphism, the Gestalt psychologist were opposing the **constancy hypothesis**, according to which there was a one-to-one correspondence between environmental stimuli and certain sensations. This hypothesis, of course, was the cornerstone of structuralism. The structuralists viewed mental events as the passive reflections of specific environmental events. The Gestalt psychologists totally disagreed with this conception of the brain, instead viewing the brain as itself a Gestalt. They believed that the incoming sensory data interacted with fields of forces within the brain to cause fields of mental activity. Like physical fields, these mental fields were organized configurations. The nature of the mental configurations depended on the totality of the incoming stimulation and the nature of the fields of forces within the brain, and any configurations that occurred in the fields of brain activity would be experienced as perceptions. The organized brain activity dominated our perceptions, *not* the stimuli that entered into that activity. This is the reason it is said that for the Gestalt psychologist the whole is more important than the parts, thus reversing one of psychology's oldest traditions. As we have seen, the Gestalt psychologists said that their analysis proceeded from the top to the bottom instead of from the bottom to the top, as had been the tradition. In other words, they proceeded from the wholes to the parts instead of from the parts to the wholes.

The Law of Prägnanz

What determines the nature of the configurations that occur in the brain and thus in perception? The answer the Gestalt psychologists gave was that the same forces that existed in the physical world, creating configurations such as soap bubbles and magnetic fields, also operated in the brain. The configurations in both the physical world and in the brain always resulted from the total field of interacting forces. Here we have a clear example of how the Gestalt psychologists used field theory from physics as a model for explaining perceptual processes. Fancher (1979) describes this model as follows:

> Toward the end of the nineteenth century it became clear to physicists that many phenomena, particularly of an electrical or magnetic nature, could not be explained as the result of isolated bodies acting upon one another. Instead, whole distributions of forces, or "fields," had to be taken into consideration. To take a very simple example, the fate of a single charged particle could not be predicted in isolation; what happened to it depended on the entire electrical environment, or field, in which it happened to be. . . .
>   Köhler was struck by yet another similarity. The field theorists had noted that physical fields tend over time to organize themselves into increasingly simple configurations. An electric charge, upon a condenser, for example, quickly distributes itself evenly on the entire surface, so that differences of electrical potential exist nowhere on the surface. In general, forces in a field tend to even themselves out as much as possible, so that the final organization is simpler than the original one. This tendency of physical fields to simplify themselves seemed to Köhler to be directly analogous to events in the perceptual field that he and his colleagues had observed.
>   . . . After noting these similarities, Köhler reflected that the organ of perception, the brain, was itself a physical system that distributed and processed electrical charges. He thought that perhaps the similarities between physical and perceptual fields were more than coincidental, and that the phenomena of perception were the direct result of field effects occurring within the brain. (pp. 122–123)

The above notions from field theory are summarized in the **law of Prägnanz**, which was central to all of Gestalt theory. The German word *Prägnanz* means "precision" in English (Sahakian, 1975, p. 205). The law of Prägnanz states that psychological organization will always be as good as conditions allow, because fields of

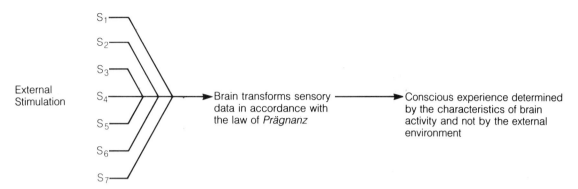

FIGURE 14.1 The Gestalt notion of psychophysical isomorphism. (Hergenhahn, 1982, p. 255. Used by permission of Prentice-Hall, Inc.)

brain activity will always distribute themselves in the simplest way possible under the prevailing conditions, just as other physical field forces do. The law of Prägnanz asserts that all cognitive experiences will tend to be as organized, symmetrical, meaningful, simple, and regular as they can be, given the pattern of brain activity at any given moment. This is what as *"good" as conditions allow* means.

What we experience cognitively, then, is not a function of direct sensory stimulation. Rather, we experience information that results when the brain acts upon sensory information according to the law of Prägnanz. The process of psychophysical isomorphism, as the Gestalt psychologists saw it, is illustrated in Figure 14.1. Clearly this is a nativistic position, but it is not the same kind of nativism that such philosophers as Plato or Descartes represented. For the Gestalt theorists, it was not ideas that were innate, but the organizational ability of the brain. Thus, the Gestalt position was very close to that of Immanuel Kant.

THE PERCEPTUAL CONSTANCIES

The way we respond to objects as if they were the same even though the actual stimulation our senses receive may vary greatly is called **perceptual constancy** (not to be confused with the previously discussed constancy hypothesis). Köhler (1929) says:

> The man approaching us on the street does not grow larger, as for simple optical reasons he should. The circle observed on the oblique plane does not become an ellipse; it seems to remain a circle after its retinal image has become a very flat ellipse. The white object in the shadow remains white, the black paper remains black in full light, though the first may reflect much less light than the second. These three examples have one common property: the physical object *as such* remained constant, while actual stimulation varies according to more or less accidental conditions (of distance, of position, of illumination), our experience agrees with the constancy of the physical object much better than with the varying stimulation produced by it. (p. 80)

The empiricists explained perceptual constancies as the result of learning. The sensations provided by objects seen at different angles, positions, and levels of illumination were different, but through experience we learned to correct for these differences and to respond to the objects as the same. Woodworth (1931) describes what our perceptions would be like, according to the empiricists, if the influence of learning could be removed:

> If we could for a moment lay aside all that we had learned and see the field of view just as the eyes present it, we should see a mere mosaic of variegated spots, free of meaning, of objects, of

FIGURE 14.2 In each illustration, which is the figure and which is the ground? (Illustration at left from Leeper, 1935. Used by permission.)

shapes or patterns. Such is the traditional associationist view of the matter. (pp. 105–106)

The Gestalt theorists disagreed. Köhler, for example, asserted that the constancies were a direct reflection of ongoing brain activity and *not* a result of sensation plus learning. The reason we experienced an object as the same under varied conditions was that the *relationship* between that object and other objects remained the same. Because this relationship was the same, the field of brain activity was also the same, and therefore the mental experience (perception) was the same. The Gestalt theorists' explanation, then, is simply an extension of the notion of psychophysical isomorphism. Using brightness constancy as an example, Bruno (1972) nicely summarizes this point:

[Köhler] said that brightness constancy is due to the existence of a real constancy that is an existing *Gestalt* in the environment. This *Gestalt* is physical—really there as a pattern. It is the *ratio* of brightness of the figure to the brightness of the ground. This ratio remains constant for sunlight and shade. Let us say that a light meter gives a reading of 10 (arbitrary units) for a bikini in the sun. A reading from the grass in the sun is 5. The ratio of figure to ground is 10/5 or 2. Assume now that the girl in the bikini is in the shade, and the light meter gives a

reading of 4 for the bikini. The grass in the shade gives a reading of 2. The ratio of figure to ground is 4/2 or 2—the same ratio as before. The ratio is a constant. The human nervous system responds directly to this constant ratio. The constant ratio in the environment gives rise to a pattern of excitation in the nervous system. As long as the ratio does not change, the characteristics of the pattern of excitation do not change. Thus Köhler explained brightness constancy as a directly perceived *Gestalt* not derived from learning or the association of sensations.

Köhler explained other perceptual constancies involving color, shape, and size in a similar manner. (p. 151)

PERCEPTUAL GESTALTEN

Through the years, the Gestalt psychologists have isolated over 100 configurations (*Gestalten*) into which visual information is arranged. We will sample only a few of them here.

The Figure-Ground Relationship

According to the Gestalt theorists, the most basic kind of perception is the division of the perceptual field into two parts: the *figure*, which is clear and unified and is the object of attention, and the *ground*, which is diffuse and con-

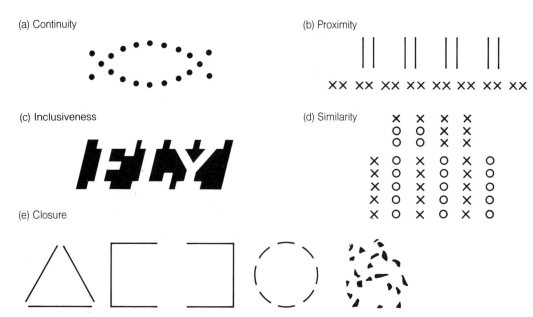

FIGURE 14.3 Examples of (a) principle of continuity; (b) principle of proximity; (c) principle of inclusiveness (Brown and Gilhousen, 1950, renewed © 1978, p. 330; used by permission); (d) principle of similarity; and (e) principle of closure (Sartain et al., 1973; used by permission of Prentice-Hall, Inc.).

sists of everything that is not being attended to. Such a division creates what is called a **figure-ground relationship**. Thus, what is the figure and what is the ground can be changed by shifting one's attention. This can be demonstrated with the illustrations in Figure 14.2. When one attends to the profile of the young woman, the face of the older woman becomes a diffuse background, and vice versa. Likewise, when one focuses attention on the two profiles, one cannot see the vase, and vice versa. The principles discussed below can be considered examples of the figure-ground relationship. They specify the conditions under which visual stimuli are organized into unified figures that stand out from their backgrounds.

Examples of the Figure-Ground Relationship

Stimuli that have continuity with one another will be experienced as a perceptual unit. To describe this principle, Wertheimer also used the terms *intrinsic togetherness, imminent necessity,* and *good continuation.* Figure 14.3a provides an example of this **principle of continuity**. Note that the pattern that emerges cannot be found in any particular dot (element). Rather, because some of the dots seem to be tending in the same direction, one responds to them as a configuration (*Gestalt*). Most people would describe this figure as consisting of two curved lines.

When stimuli are close together they tend to be grouped together as a perceptual unit. This is known as the **principle of proximity**. In Figure 14.3b the Xs tend to be seen in groups of two, instead of as individual Xs. The same is true of the lines.

According to the **principle of inclusiveness**, when there is more than one figure, we are most likely to see the figure that contains the greatest number of stimuli. If, for example, a small figure is embedded in a larger one, we are most likely to see the larger figure and not the smaller. The use of camouflage is an application of this principle. Ships painted the color of water and tanks painted the color of the terrain they operate in blend into the background, thus becoming less susceptible to detection. In Figure 14.3c the word *fly* is difficult to see because so many of its components are part of a larger stimulus complex.

Objects that are similar in some way tend to form perceptual units. This is known as the **principle of similarity**. Twins, for example, stand out in a crowd, and teams wearing different uniforms stand out as two groups on the field. In Figure 14.3d the stimuli that have something in common stand out as perceptual units.

The Gestalt theorists believed in psychophysical isomorphism, according to which our conscious experience is directly related to patterns of brain activity, and the brain activity organizes itself into patterns according to the law of Prägnanz. Thus, the patterns of brain activity are often better organized than the stimuli that enter them. This is clearly demonstrated in the **principle of closure**, according to which incomplete figures in the physical world are perceived as complete ones. As Figure 14.3e shows, even if figures have gaps in them—and thus are not truly circles, triangles, or rectangles—they are nonetheless experienced as circles, triangles, or rectangles. This is because the brain transforms the stimuli into organized configurations that are then experienced cognitively. For the same reason, in Figure 14.3e we see a person on horseback.

SUBJECTIVE AND OBJECTIVE REALITY

As we have seen, the brain acts upon sensory information and arranges it into configurations. What we are conscious of, and therefore act in accordance with, is more a product of the brain than of the physical world. Koffka used this fact to distinguish between the *geographical* and the *behavioral* environments. For him, the **geo-**graphical environment** was the physical environment, while the **behavioral environment** was our subjective interpretation of the geographical environment. Koffka (1935/1963) uses an old German legend to illustrate the important difference between the two environments:

On a winter evening amidst a driving snowstorm a man on horseback arrived at an inn, happy to have reached a shelter after hours of riding over the wind-swept plain on which the blanket of snow had covered all paths and landmarks. The landlord who came to the door viewed the stranger with surprise and asked him whence he came. The man pointed in the direction straight away from the inn, whereupon the landlord, in a tone of awe and wonder, said: "Do you know that you have ridden across the Lake of Constance?" at which the rider dropped stone dead at his feet.

In what environment, then, did the behavior of the stranger take place? The Lake of Constance? Certainly, because it is a true proposition that he rode across it. And yet, this is not the whole truth, for the fact that there was a frozen lake and not ordinary solid ground did not affect his behavior in the slightest. It is interesting for the geographer that this behavior took place in this particular locality, but not for the psychologist as the student of behavior; because the behavior would have been just the same had the man ridden across a barren plain. But the psychologist knows something more: since the man died from sheer fright after having learned what he had "really" done, the psychologist must conclude that had the stranger known before, his riding behavior would have been very different from what it actually was. Therefore the psychologist will have to say: there is a second sense to the word environment according to which our horseman did not ride across the lake at all, but across an ordinary snow-swept plain. His behavior was a riding-over-a-plain, but not a riding-over-a-lake.

What is true of the man who rode across the Lake of Constance is true of every behavior. Does the rat run in the maze *the experimenter* has set up? According to the meaning of the word "in," yes and no. Let us therefore distinguish between a *geographical* and a *behavioral* environment. Do we all live in the same town? Yes, when we mean the geographical, no, when we mean the behavioral. (pp. 27–28)

In other words, our own subjective reality governs our actions more than the physical environment does. This emphasis upon subjective reality is the very heart of existential-humanistic theories in psychology, and we shall therefore return to it in Chapter 17.

THE GESTALT EXPLANATION OF LEARNING

Cognitive Trial and Error

As we have seen, the Gestalt theorists believed that brain activity tended toward a balance or equilibrium in accordance with the law of Prägnanz. If something disrupted this balance, a state of disequilibrium existed until the problem was solved. This cognitive disequilibrium had motivational properties that kept the organism active until it reached a solution. Typically, an organism solved its problems perceptually by scanning the environment and cognitively trying one possible solution and then another, until it reached a solution. Thus, the Gestalt psychologists emphasized *cognitive* trial and error as opposed to *behavioral* trial and error. They believed that organisms came to *see* solutions to problems.

Insightful Learning

The Gestalt psychologist Köhler did much of his work on learning between 1913 and 1917, when he was stranded on one of the Canary Islands during the First World War. In a typical experiment, using apes as subjects, Köhler would place a desired object—for example, a banana—just out of the animal's reach. Then he would place objects such as boxes and sticks, which the animal could use to obtain the banana, in the animal's environment. Thus, by stacking one or more boxes under the banana, or by using a stick, the animal could obtain the banana. In one case, the animal needed to join two sticks together in order to reach a banana.

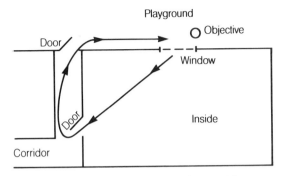

FIGURE 14.4 A typical detour problem. (Köhler, 1925, p. 21. Used by permission.)

In studying learning, Köhler also employed so-called *detour problems*, problems in which the animal could see its goal but could not reach it directly. To solve the problem, the animal had to learn to take an indirect route to the goal. Figure 14.4 shows a typical detour problem. Köhler found that though chickens had great difficulty with such problems, apes solved them with ease.

Köhler noted that during the presolution period, the animals appeared to weigh the situation—that is, to test various hypotheses. (This is what we referred to earlier as cognitive or vicarious trial and error.) Then, at some point, the animal achieved *insight* into the solution and behaved according to that insight. For the Gestalt theorists, a problem could exist in only two stages: it was either unsolved or it was solved—there was no in-between. According to the Gestalt theorists, the reason that Thorndike and others had found what appeared to be incremental learning (learning that occurs a little bit at a time) was that all of the ingredients necessary for the attainment of insight had not been available to the animal. But if a problem was presented to an organism along with those things necessary for the problem's solution, **insightful learning** was possible, And according to the Gestalt theorists, learning characterized by insight was much more desirable than learning achieved through either rote memorization or behavioral trial and error. Hergenhahn

(1982) summarizes the conclusions that the Gestalt theorists reached about insightful learning:

> Insightful learning is usually regarded as having four characteristics: (1) the transition from presolution to solution is sudden and complete; (2) performance based upon a solution gained by insight is usually smooth and free of errors; (3) a solution to a problem gained by insight is retained for a considerable length of time; and (4) a principle gained by insight is easily applied to other problems. (p. 262)

Transposition

Köhler's experiment. To explore further the nature of learning, Köhler used chickens as subjects. He placed a white sheet and a grey sheet of paper on the ground. Both of them were covered with grain. If a chicken pecked at the grain on the white sheet, it was shooed away, but if it pecked at the grain on the grey sheet, it was allowed to eat. After many trials, the chickens learned to peck at only the grain on the grey sheet. The question is, what did the animals learn? Thorndike, Hull, and Skinner would say that reinforcement strengthened the response of eating off the grey paper. To answer the question, Köhler proceeded with phase two of the experiment: he replaced the white paper with a sheet of black paper. Now the choice was between a grey sheet of paper, the one for which the chickens had received reinforcement, and a black sheet. Given the chance, any reinforcement theorist would have probably predicted that the chickens would continue to approach the grey paper. The vast majority of the chickens, however, approached the black paper. Köhler's explanation was that the chickens had not learned a stimulus-response association or a specific operant response, but a *relationship*. In this case, according to Köhler, the animals had learned to approach *the darker of the two sheets* of paper. If, in the second phase of the experiment, Köhler had presented a sheet of paper of a lighter grey than the one the

chickens had been reinforced on, the chickens would have continued to approach the sheet they had previously been fed on, since it would have been the darker of the two. In a sense, the animals were responding to a constancy. Earlier we saw that the Gestalt theorists' explanation of perceptual constancies was that similar ratios between stimuli caused similar cognitive experiences. Köhler showed that a relation between two events remained constant and controlled behavior.

Thus, for the Gestalt psychologist, an organism learned principles or relationships, not specific responses to specific situations. Once it learned a principle, the organism applied it to similar situations. This was called **transposition**, Gestalt psychology's version of transfer of training. The notion of transposition is contrary to Thorndike's identical-elements theory of transfer, according to which the similarity (common elements) between two situations will determine the amount of transfer between them.

The behaviorists' explanation of transposition. The Gestalt-theory explanation of transposition did not go unchallenged. Kenneth Spence, the major spokesman for Hullian psychology, came up with an ingenious alternative explanation. Hergenhahn (1982) summarizes Spence's explanation:

> Suppose, said Spence, that an animal is rewarded for approaching a box whose lid measures 160 sq. cm. and not rewarded for approaching a box whose lid measures 100 sq. cm. Soon the animal will learn to approach the larger box exclusively.
> In phase two of this experiment, the animal chooses between the 160 sq. cm. box and the box whose lid is 256 sq. cm. The animal will usually choose the larger box (256 sq. cm.) even though it had been rewarded specifically for choosing the other (160 sq. cm.) during phase one. . . . This finding seems to support the relational learning point of view.
> Spence's behavioristic explanation of transposition is based on generalization. . . . Spence assumed that the tendency to approach the

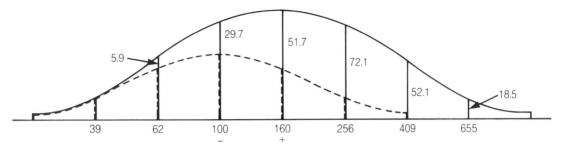

FIGURE 14.5 According to Spence, the algebraic sum of the positive and negative influences determines which of the two stimuli will be approached. (Spence, 1942, p. 249)

positive stimulus (160 sq. cm.) generalizes to other related stimuli. Second, he assumed that the tendency to approach the positive stimulus (and the generalization of this tendency) is stronger than the tendency to avoid the negative stimulus (and the generalization of this tendency). What behavior occurs will be determined by the algebraic summation of the positive and negative tendencies.

[To follow the remainder of Spence's explanation, you will need to refer to Figure 14.5.] Whenever there is a choice between two stimuli, the one eliciting the greatest net approach tendency will be chosen. In the first phase of Spence's experiment, the animal chose the 160 sq. cm. box over the 100 sq. cm. box because the net positive tendency was 51.7 for the former and 29.7 for the latter. In phase two, the 256 sq. cm. box was chosen over the 160 sq. cm. box because the net positive tendency was 72.1 for the former and still 51.7 for the latter. (p. 265)

Spence's explanation had the advantage of predicting the circumstances under which transposition would not occur. As the matter stands today, neither the Gestalt nor the behaviorist explanations can account for all transpositional phenomena; therefore, a comprehensive explanation is still being sought.

PRODUCTIVE THINKING

Wertheimer was concerned with the application of Gestalt theory to education. His book *Productive Thinking* was published in 1945, two years after his death. Under the editorship of Wertheimer's son Michael, this book was later revised and expanded, and it was republished in 1959. The conclusions Wertheimer reached about **productive thinking** were based on personal experience, experimentation, and interviews with individuals considered excellent problem solvers, such as Einstein:

> Those were wonderful days, beginning in 1916, when for hours and hours I was fortunate enough to sit with Einstein, alone in his study, and hear from him the story of the dramatic developments which culminated in the theory of relativity. During those long discussions I questioned Einstein in great detail about the concrete events in his thought. (Wertheimer, 1945/1959, p. 213)

Wertheimer contrasted learning according to Gestalt principles with rote memorization governed by external reinforcement and the laws of association. The former is based on an understanding of the nature of the problem. As we have seen, the existence of a problem creates a cognitive disequilibrium that lasts until the problem is solved. The solution restores a cognitive harmony, and this restoration is all the reinforcement the learner needs. Since learning and problem solving are personally satisfying, they are therefore governed by **intrinsic** (internal) **reinforcement** rather than **extrinsic** (external) **reinforcement**. Wertheimer thought that we were motivated to learn and to solve problems because it was personally satisfying to do so, not because someone or something else rein-forced us for doing so. Since learning governed by Gestalt principles was based on an under-standing of the structure of the problem, it was easily remembered and generalized to other rel-evant situations.

Wertheimer believed that some learning did occur when mental associations, memorization, drill, and external reinforcement were em-ployed, but that such learning was usually triv-ial. He gives as examples of such learning associating a friend's name with his or her tele-phone number, learning to anticipate correctly a list of nonsense syllables, and a dog learning to salivate to a certain sound. Unfortunately, ac-cording to Wertheimer, this is the kind of learn-ing that most schools emphasize.

In Wertheimer's analysis, teaching that em-phasizes logic does not fare any better than rote memorization. Supposedly, logic guarantees that one will reach correct conclusions. Teach-ing based on such a notion, says Wertheimer, assumes that there is a correct way to think, and that everyone should think that way. But like rote memorization, learning and applying the rules of logic stifle productive thinking, since neither activity is based on the realization that problem solving involves the total person and is unique to that person. Hergenhahn (1982) summarizes this point:

> According to Wertheimer, reaching an under-standing involves many aspects of learners, such as their emotions, attitudes, and percep-tions, as well as their intellects. In gaining in-sight into the solution to a problem, a student need not—in fact, should not—be logical. Rather, the student should cognitively arrange and rearrange the components of the problem until a solution based on understanding is reached. Exactly how this is done will vary from student to student. (p. 267)

To demonstrate the difference between rote learning and learning based on understanding, Michael Wertheimer (1980) describes an ex-periment that Katona originally performed in 1940. Katona showed subjects the following 15 digits and told them to study the digits for 15 seconds: 1 4 9 1 6 2 5 3 6 4 9 6 4 8 1. With only these instructions, most people attempt to mem-orize as many digits as possible in the allotted time. Indeed, Katona found that most subjects could reproduce only a few of the correct num-bers; and when tested a week later, most sub-jects remembered none.

Katona asked another group of subjects to look for a pattern or theme running through the numbers. Some individuals in this group realized that the 15 digits represented the squares of the digits from 1 to 9. These subjects saw a principle that they could apply to the problem and were able to reproduce all of the numbers correctly, not only during the experi-ment but for weeks after. In fact, those individ-uals could probably reproduce the series correctly for the rest of their lives. Katona's experiment thus supported Wertheimer's belief that learning and problem solving based on Ge-stalt principles had many advantages over rote memorizaton or problem solving based on for-mal logic.

MEMORY

Although the Gestalt theorists were nativistic in their accounts of learning and perception, they did not deny altogether the influence of experi-ence. They maintained that the tendency to-ward perceptual organization and cognitive equilibrium was derived from the brain's being constructed in such a way as to distribute its activity in the simplest, most concise configura-tion possible under any circumstances. *What* the brain organized, however, was provided by ex-perience. This experiential component of Ge-stalt theory is apparent in the Gestalt theorists' treatment of memory. Of the three founders of Gestalt theory, Koffka wrote the most about memory.

Koffka assumed that each physical event we experienced gave rise to specific activity in the brain. He called the brain activity caused by a specific environmental event a **memory process**. When the environmental event terminated, so did the brain activity it caused. However, a remnant of the memory process—a **memory trace**—remained in the brain. Once the memory trace was formed, all subsequent related experience would involve an interaction between the memory process and the memory trace. For example, when we experience a cat for the first time, the experience will create a characteristic pattern of brain activity; this is the memory process. After the experience is terminated, the brain will register its effects; this is the memory trace. The next time we experience a cat, the memory process elicited will interact with the already existing trace from the first experience. The conscious experience will be the result of both the present memory process *and* the trace of previous related experiences.

According to this analysis, we are aware of and remember things in terms of general rather than specific characteristics. Instead of seeing and remembering such things as cats, clowns, or elephants, we see and remember "catness," "clownness," and "elephantness." This is because the trace of classes of experience records what those experiences have in common—for example, those things that make a cat a cat. With more experience, the trace becomes more firmly established and becomes more and more influential in our perceptions and memories. The individual trace gives way to a **trace system,** which is the consolidation of a number of interrelated experiences. In other words, a trace system will record all of our experiences with, say, cats. The interaction of traces, and trace systems, with ongoing brain activity (memory processes) results in our perceptions and memories being smoother and better organized than they otherwise would be. For example, we remember irregular experiences as regular, incomplete experiences as complete, and unfamiliar experiences as something familiar.

Like everything else Gestalt theory covers,

Kurt Lewin

memory is governed by the law of Prägnanz. The brain operates in such a way as to make memories as meaningful as possible under the circumstances.

KURT LEWIN'S FIELD THEORY

Born in Mogilno, Germany, **Kurt Lewin** (1890–1947) received his Ph.D. in 1914 from the University of Berlin, under the supervision of Carl Stumpf. After several years of military service, for which he earned the Iron Cross, Lewin returned to the University of Berlin and held various positions there until 1932. While he was at the University of Berlin, Lewin worked with Wertheimer, Koffka, and Köhler. Although Lewin is usually not considered a founder of Gestalt psychology, he was an early disciple, and most of his work can be seen as an extension or application of Gestalt principles.

Lewin was a visiting lecturer at Stanford University in 1932, and from 1933 to 1935 he was a visiting lecturer at Cornell. In 1935 he became affiliated with the Child Welfare Station at the University of Iowa as a professor of child psychology, and in 1944 he created and directed the Research Center for Group Dynamics at the Massachusetts Institute of Technology. Although Lewin died only three years after starting his work on group dynamics, the influence of this work was profound and is still evident in psychology today.

Aristotelian versus Galilean Conception of Science

Lewin (1935) distinguished between Aristotle's view of nature, which emphasized inner essences and categories, and Galileo's view, which emphasized outer causation and the dynamics of forces. For Aristotle, various natural objects fell into categories according to their essence, and everything that members of a certain category had in common defined the essence of members of that category. Unless external forces interfered, there was an innate tendency for all members of a category to manifest their essence. In this world of distinct classes, internal forces drove the members of the classes to become what their essence dictated they must become. Aristotle saw uniqueness as a distortion caused by external forces interfering with an object's or organism's natural growth tendencies. He emphasized the common attributes that members of a certain class possessed.

According to Lewin, Galileo revolutionized science when he changed its focus from inner causation to a more comprehensive notion of causation. For Galileo, the behavior of an object or organism was determined by the total forces acting upon the object or organism. For example, whether a body fell or not, and if it fell, how fast it fell, was determined by its total circumstances and not by the innate tendency for

heavy bodies to fall and light ones to rise. For Galileo, causation sprang not from inner essences but from physical forces; thus he eliminated the idea of distinct categories that were characterized by their own essence and its associated inward drive. For Galileo, the interaction of natural forces caused everything that happened; there were no accidents. Even so-called unique events were totally comprehensible if the dynamic forces acting upon them were known.

For Lewin (1935), too much of psychology was still Aristotelian. Psychologists were still seeking inner determinants of behavior, such as instincts, and still attempting to place people in distinct categories, such as normal and abnormal. Lewin also saw stage theories as extensions of Aristotelian thinking; for example, a theory that says two-year-olds act in certain ways and three-year-olds in other ways. Any theory attempting to classify people into types was also seen as exemplifying Aristotelian thinking; for example, a theory that characterizes people as introverts or extroverts. According to Lewin, when Galileo's conception of causation was employed, all of these distinct categories vanished and were replaced with a conception of universal causation (that is, the view that everything that occurs is a function of the total influences occurring at the moment).

In psychology, switching from an Aristotelian to a Galilean perspective could mean deemphasizing such notions as instincts, types, classifications, and even averages (which imply the existence of distinct categories), and emphasizing the complex of dynamic forces acting upon an individual at any given moment. For Lewin, these dynamic forces—and not any kind of inner essences—explained human behavior.

Life Space

Probably the most important concept in all of Lewin's writing was that of **life space**. A person's life space consisted of all of the influences acting on him or her at a given time. These

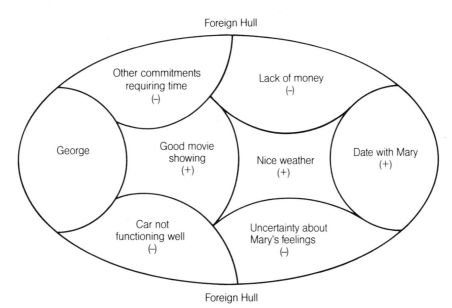

Foreign Hull

FIGURE 14.6 An example of how George's life space might be articulated if he desired a date with Mary.

influences, called **psychological facts**, consisted of an awareness of internal events (for example, hunger, pain, and fatigue), external events (for example, restaurants, restrooms, other people, stop signs, and angry dogs), and recollections of prior experiences (for example, knowing that a particular person was pleasant or unpleasant, or knowing that one's mother tended to say "yes" to certain requests and "no" to others). The only requirement for something to be a psychological fact was that it exist in a person's awareness at the moment. A previous experience was a psychological fact only if one recalled it in the present. Again, Lewin called the totality of psychological facts that existed at any particular time a person's life space.

Topology and Hodological Space

To convey his notions, Lewin borrowed from a branch of geometry called topology. **Topology** represents the relationships among objects and events in a spatial, nonmathematical way. For example, Lewin would represent a person's life space as an ellipse. He designated the person's position in his or her life space with a *P*, and he represented each psychological fact as a region in the life space. Furthermore, he gave each region a *valence*, or sign, depending on the nature of the region's influence on the person. Those regions (psychological facts) that benefited the person were labeled (+), those that inhibited the person were labeled (−), and irrelevant facts received no sign. As a need arose, the life space would be articulated around that need. For example, if George wanted to ask Mary for a date, George's life space might be articulated as shown in Figure 14.6.

The movement (locomotion) of the person through the life space could result from real or imaginary causes. For example, physical movement that brought George closer to Mary would change George's position in his life space, as would coming into a substantial amount of money, receiving an encouraging sign from Mary, or learning that Mary had just become engaged. The field of forces resulting from the various positive and negative influences in the life space created what Lewin called **hodological space**. The nature of this space at any given moment determined the direction and rate of locomotion.

Lewin referred to all events lying outside of the life space as the **foreign hull**. As should be clear, the needs operating at the moment determined which events were part of the life space and which lay in the foreign hull. What was in the foreign hull at one moment might be in the life space at another moment, and vice versa.

Motivation

Like all the Gestalt psychologists, Lewin felt that people sought a cognitive balance. We saw how Köhler used this assumption in his explanation of learning. Lewin used the same assumption in his explanation of motivation. According to Lewin, both biological and psychological needs caused tension in the life space, and the only way to reduce the tension was through satisfaction of the need. Psychological needs, which Lewin called **quasi-needs**, included such intentions as wanting a car, wanting to go to a concert, or wanting to go to medical school. The goal of locomotion was to alleviate the tension caused by a need or a quasi-need.

The Zeigarnik Effect

Doing her Ph.D. work under Lewin's supervision, *Bluma Zeigarnik* (1927) tested Lewin's tension-system hypothesis concerning motivation. According to this hypothesis, needs cause tensions that persist until the needs are satisfied. It was Lewin's custom to have long discussions with his students in a cafe, while drinking coffee and snacking. Apparently the tension-system hypothesis occurred to him as a result of an experience he had during one of these informal discussions. Marrow (1969) reports this experience:

> On one such occasion, somebody called for the bill and the waiter knew just what everyone had ordered. Although he hadn't kept a written reckoning, he presented an exact tally to every-

one when the bill was called for. About a half hour later Lewin called the waiter over and asked him to write the check again. The waiter was indignant. "I don't know any longer what you people ordered," he said. "You paid your bill." In psychological terms, this indicated that a tension system had been building up in the waiter as we were ordering and that upon payment of the bill the tension system was discharged. (p. 27)

In her formal testing of Lewin's hypothesis, Zeigarnik assumed that giving a subject a task to perform would create a tension system, and that completion of the task would relieve the tension. In all, Zeigarnik gave 22 tasks to 138 subjects. The subjects were allowed to finish some of the tasks but not others. Zeigarnik later tested the subjects on their recall of the tasks, and she found that the subjects remembered many more of the *uncompleted* tasks than the completed ones. Her explanation was that for the uncompleted tasks, the associated tension was never reduced; therefore, these tasks remained as intentions, and as such they remained part of the person's life space. The tendency to remember uncompleted tasks better than completed ones has come to be called the **Zeigarnik Effect**.

A year after Zeigarnik did her research, Maria Ovsiankina (1928), who was also working with Lewin, found that individuals would rather resume interrupted tasks than completed ones. Her explanation for this was the same as the one for the Zeigarnik Effect.

Woodworth (1931) gives another example of Lewin's proposed relationship between intention and cognitive tension:

> Suppose I have stuck a letter in my pocket, impressing on myself the necessity of placing it in a letter box when I pass one in the street. I have thus established a bond between the sight of the letter box, as stimulus, and the response of taking the letter out and mailing it. I see a letter box and mail the letter. The associationist or stimulus-response psychologist would cite the case, so far, as a good instance of his doctrine. But now it is also according to the associa-

tion psychology that exercise of this stimulus-response connection should strengthen it. Therefore, when I reach the second letter box my response of reaching in my pocket for the letter will be even stronger. On the contrary, that tendency is probably all wiped out. When I placed the letter in the first box, I said to myself, "That's done," and apparently erased the stimulus-response bond. Lewin urges that the driving force which activated the behavior was not the bond, nor even the letter box as stimulus, but a tension set up when I placed the letter in my pocket with the intention of mailing it. This tension was relieved when the letter was mailed, and the bond had no further influence on my behavior. Had I happened to spy a postman and hand him the letter, that different act would also have relieved the tension.

The behavior in such cases may be brought under the formula of "closing the gap," and so lined up alongside of the tendency to see closed figures; and probably the brain dynamics of the two processes is much the same. When I put the letter in my pocket I had to leave a gap in my behavior, a gap which was filled when the letter was mailed. Filling the gap brought this particular dynamic system into a state of equilibrium with no more force to influence my behavior. (pp. 112–113)

Group Dynamics

In his later years, Lewin extended Gestalt principles to the behavior of groups. He said that each group had a characteristic Gestalt influencing each of its members. Change any element (individual) in the group, and the entire configuration rearranged itself. Among the members of each group, there was what Lewin called a "dynamic interdependence." Lewin's studies of **group dynamics** led to what are now called "encounter groups" and "sensitivity training."

Lundin (1985) describes one of Lewin's studies of group dynamics:

The concept of group dynamics has led to several avenues of research. During World War II, Lewin conducted a number of experiments that attempted to alter group decision-making. At the time, certain food products, such as meat, were rationed. Consequently, housewives were encouraged to buy more accessible products, such as brains, liver, kidneys, and heart and other animal organs not generally considered to be food items. He used two methods—the first was lecturing on the merits of the food, their nutritional values, how they could be tastily prepared, and so on. The second method involved group discussion. The same materials were presented in both cases. In the group discussion, there was participation by the members on the pros and cons of trying and eating and preparing such substances. In a follow-up study only 3 percent of the lecture group took up the suggestions, while 32 percent of the discussion group changed their food habits by trying the formerly unpopular products. Lewin concluded that in the discussion group more forces were made available for a change in behavior. (p. 265–266)

In another study, Lewin, Lippitt, and White (1939) investigated the influence of various kinds of leadership on group performance. Boys were matched and then placed in a *Democratic Group*, in which the leader encouraged group discussion and participated with the boys in making decisions; or an *Authoritarian Group*, in which the leader made all the decisions and told the boys what to do; or a *Laissez-Faire Group*, in which no group decisions were made and the boys could do whatever they wanted. The researchers found that the Democratic Group was highly productive and friendly, the Authoritarian Group was highly aggressive, and the Laissez-Faire Group was unproductive. They concluded that group leadership influenced the Gestalt characterizing the group and, in turn, the attitude and productivity of the group's members.

THE IMPACT OF GESTALT PSYCHOLOGY

Like any school in psychology, Gestalt psychology has had its share of criticism. Critics have said that many of its central terms and concepts

Karl Lashley

to elementism went beyond its critique of structuralism, however, and were applied to S-R behaviorism as well. Gestalt psychology called attention to the usefulness of field concepts and to various problems which might otherwise have been ignored, such as insight in animals and humans, the organized nature of perception and of experience, the richness of genuine thought processes, and in general, to the utility of dealing in larger, molar, organized units, taking full account of their nature and structure. One should not analyze arbitrarily into predetermined elements, since such analysis, the Gestaltists argued, and most psychologists now recognize, may do violence to the intrinsic meaning of the whole.

Although the Gestalt school no longer existed as a major self-conscious movement after the middle of the twentieth century, the issues it raised, and raised successfully, in opposition to the prevalent oversimplified S-R mechanistic, hookup psychology typical especially of American associationistic behaviorism, continued to be central in psychological thought. The Gestalt school had done its job well, leaving a lasting mark on the discipline, in the psychology of cognition, information processing, perception, thinking, and learning, and in motivation, personality, and social psychology—indeed in almost all fields. (pp. 140–141)

THE WORK OF KARL LASHLEY

A colleague and friend of John B. Watson at Johns Hopkins University, **Karl Spencer Lashley** (1890–1958) accompanied Watson on his trip to one of the Florida Keys to study the homing behavior of terns. Receiving his Ph.D. from Johns Hopkins in 1914, Lashley was an early supporter of behaviorism, and he sought to support the associationism upon which behaviorism was based with neurophysiological evidence. But time after time Lashley was frustrated in his efforts to show that the brain worked like a complex switchboard linking sensory impulses to motor reactions. Contrary to his original intention, Lashley gradually showed that brain activity was more like what the Gestalt theorists described than like what the behaviorists described. He found no evidence that

are vague and therefore hard to pin down experimentally. Even the term *Gestalt*, the critics say, has never been defined precisely. The same is true for the law of Prägnanz, for insight, and for cognitive equilibrium. As might be expected, the behaviorists attacked the Gestalt theorists' concern with consciousness, claiming that such a concern was a regression to the old metaphysical position that had caused psychology so many problems.

In spite of these and other criticisms, however, Gestalt theory has clearly influenced almost every aspect of modern psychology. Michael Wertheimer (1979) nicely summarizes this influence:

The Gestalt movement played a significant role in the revolt against structuralism. Its objections stimulation of specific areas of the brain was associated with the elicitation of specific responses. Robinson (1976) summarizes some of Lashley's work:

> Perhaps Lashley's most significant findings were in the areas of learning and memory. He demonstrated in a variety of different experimental settings that the animal's ability to acquire a complex behavioral repertoire and to reproduce it after a long retention interval was not systematically related to specific loci within the cerebral cortex. He remarked whimsically that, after searching for the "engram" of memory for many years, he was forced to conclude that learning was simply not possible! Behind the wry comment was the *caveat* that the brain is not one of La Mettrie's clocks, nor is man Condillac's sentient statue. (p. 377)

Lashley made two major observations that were contrary to the switchboard conception of the brain. One was that loss of ability following destruction of parts of the cortex was related more to the *amount* of destruction than to the *location* of destruction. This finding, called **mass action**, indicated that the cortex worked as a unified whole, as the Gestalt theorists had maintained. The second observation Lashley made was that if surgical destruction of a portion of the cortex caused the loss of an ability, other parts of the cortex would soon take over and the lost function would be regained. This finding, called **equipotentiality**, again indicated that the brain acted as an integrated whole and not as a mechanistic switchboard.

Concerning Lashley's place in the history of psychology, Robinson (1976) says:

> If we were to summarize [Lashley's] role in twentieth-century developments in physiological psychology, we might say that he bore the same relationship to the Pavlovians that Flourens bore to the phrenologists. (p. 376)

As the reader may remember, Flourens's research demonstrated that the cortex was not characterized by localization of function, as the phrenologists had assumed, but functioned as a unit. The Pavlovians (and the behaviorists) assumed a different kind of localization—an asso-

ciation between certain sensory centers and certain motor areas—and Lashley's work showed that this kind of localization did not exist either.

THE WORK OF JEAN PIAGET

Jean Piaget (1896–1980) is generally considered one of the great psychologists. For example, Kagan (1980, p. 246) says, "With Freud, Piaget has been a seminal figure in the sciences of human development." Piaget's work is often offered as a reason for contemporary psychology's widespread interest in cognitive psychology. In several respects, Piaget's work represents an extension of Gestalt principles into the realm of intellectual development.

As we have seen, the Gestalt psychologists believed that preexisting wholes or configurations determined the identity of individual parts. That is, parts did not have an independent identity before they were organized by a field that they entered. This is what is meant by the statement that Gestalt analysis proceeds from the top (preexisting fields of forces in the brain) down (individual sensory elements). The main similarity between the Gestalt theorists and Piaget is the attitude of both toward this part-whole controversy. As Brainerd (1978) says:

> Piaget took the part-whole problem very seriously and concluded that it was absolutely fundamental to all areas of scientific investigation. This fact distinguishes Piaget from most psychologists, who consider neither philosophy nor the part-whole problem very relevant to their work. Apart from Piaget's work, Gestalt psychology is the only other influential school of psychology to have viewed the part-whole problem as fundamental. . . . [Piaget] concluded that all the phenomena that science studies (physical systems, biological systems, social systems, even mathematical systems) are made up of qualitatively *different* "wholes" that impose order and regularity on their "parts." In these systems, there are no parts as such. The parts exist only to the extent that they enter into

the structure of the wholes to which they belong. (p. 3)

Thus, there was a great deal of similarity between Piaget and the Gestalt theorists. A major difference, however, was that the Gestalt theorists tended to lump intelligence with perception, and Piaget sought to show that the two were quite different.

Biographical Sketch

Jean Piaget was born on August 9, 1896, in Neuchâtel, Switzerland. His father was an historian whose specialty was medieval literature. Piaget showed an early interest in nature, and at the age of ten published his first article, a description of an albino sparrow that he had observed in a park. Between the ages of 15 and 18, he published a series of articles on shellfish. A vacation with his godfather, Samuel Cornut, who was a Swiss scholar, broadened Piaget's interests to include such philosophical topics as religion, logic, and epistemology (the study of the nature of knowledge). The combined interests in biology and epistemology were to characterize most of Piaget's subsequent work.

Publishing scientific papers during his adolescence created some unusual problems for the young Piaget. Brainerd (1978) summarizes these difficulties:

> Between 1911 and 1915 Piaget published a series of papers on mollusks based on his studies at the Neuchâtel Museum. These articles made Piaget's name well known in European malacology circles and, eventually, produced conflicts regarding his age. Of these, perhaps the most amusing incident occurred when the director of Geneva's prestigious Museum of Natural History, who knew Piaget only through his published work, wrote to offer him the curatorship of the museum's mollusk collection. Piaget gracefully declined in favor of finishing high school. Piaget's youth also led to less amusing problems. Editors of certain natural history journals in which he had previously published, who were now aware of his age, refused to publish further articles. (p. 2)

Piaget obtained his B.A. degree from the University of Neuchâtel at the age of 18, with a major in biology. Three years later he obtained his Ph.D. from the same institution. Piaget never had a psychology course during his formal education. After completing his Ph.D., however, he worked in a psychiatric clinic in Zurich, where he was exposed to the ideas of Freud, Jung, and other psychologists. Piaget then spent two years studying psychology and philosophy at the Sorbonne in Paris. While in Paris, Piaget accepted a position as research assistant at the Binet Testing Laboratory. His job was to help standardize intelligence tests. As we saw in Chapter 10, this was done by giving the same test items to children of various ages and noting how many items, on the average, children of various ages answered incorrectly. After such norms were devised, it was possible to determine whether a particular child's performance was above, below, or at the average for children of his or her age. Piaget soon became wary of this technique, noting that children of one age tended to make mistakes that were *qualitatively different* from those of children of a different age. He began to investigate how children of various ages embraced the world intellectualy, and concluded that intellectual development proceeded through a succession of qualitatively distinct stages.

Piaget began to publish articles on his own version of the nature of intelligence, and in 1921 he was offered the directorship of the Rousseau Institute in Geneva. At the time, the Rousseau Institute was one of the leading educational research centers in the world; so it was a distinct honor for Piaget, who was then 24 years old, to be its director. In 1924 Piaget accepted a professorship at his alma mater, the University of Neuchâtel, and in 1929 he returned to Geneva, where he was given a professorship of scientific history at the University of Geneva and an assistant directorship of the Rousseau Institute. In 1940 he moved to the University of Geneva full-time as professor of experimental psychology, a position he held until his retirement at the age of 75. Piaget continued his productive research on the nature of intellectual development until his death in 1980.

Piaget's Theory

Genetic epistemology. Piaget's theory is often referred to as **genetic epistemology**, since it purports that intellectual abilities develop as a function of biological maturity and experience. It should be emphasized, however, that the term *genetic* here refers to developmental growth rather than biological inheritance. Thus, *genetic epistemology* has about the same meaning as *developmental knowledge*.

Schemata. According to Piaget, each child was born with a few reflexes with which to interact with the world. He called these reflexes **schemata,** and each schema allowed the child to deal with a class of events. Every child had schemata that allowed it to do such things as suck, reach, look, and grasp. Piaget considered each schema an element in the child's **cognitive structure.** In the early years of life, the child embraced the world in a reflexive manner, using the available schemata. As the child matured, the initial schemata were elaborated and new ones developed. As the schemata developed, the cognitive structure became more complex, and the child's interactions with the world became less reflexive and more cognitive. In other words, in dealing with the world, the child became increasingly dependent on thinking. At all stages of development, however, the child's interactions with the world depended on the available schemata.

Assimilation and accommodation. According to Piaget, if an experience fit a person's existing cognitive structure, assimilation occurred. **Assimilation** was roughly the same thing as recognizing, perceiving, or knowing. If an experience did not fit a person's cognitive structure, an imbalance resulted, and there was a tendency to

modify the cognitive structure so that it could assimilate the new experience. This process, called **accommodation**, was roughly the same thing as learning. Piaget believed that almost every experience a person had must include both assimilation and accommodation, since every experience we had would be at least partially recognizable and partially unlike any experience we had had before.

Equilibration. Piaget thought that **equilibration** was the driving force responsible for intellectual growth. The term refers to our tendency to seek a harmony between our cognitive structures and events in the world. Here we have another point of agreement between Piaget and the Gestalt theorists. Hergenhahn (1982) says:

> Piaget assumed that all organisms have an innate tendency to create a harmonious relationship between themselves and their environment. In other words, all aspects of the organism are geared toward optimal adaptation. Equilibration is this innate tendency to organize one's experiences so as to assure maximal adaptation. Roughly, equilibration can be defined as the continuous drive toward equilibrium or balance. . . . It is his [Piaget's] major motivational concept, which, along with assimilation and accommodation, is used to explain the steady intellectual growth observed in children. (p. 285)

For both Piaget and the Gestalt theorists, a cognitive balance was of supreme importance; and for both, the cognitive/brain structures were biologically based. The Gestalt theorists believed that these structures were innate or that they matured very rapidly, while Piaget believed that structures emerged gradually as a function of biological maturation. Most importantly, however, both the Gestalt theorists and Piaget believed that the brain actively transformed sensory data, and that this transformed data was what we experienced consciously.

Piaget's proposed stages of intellectual development. The following are the stages of intellectual growth as Piaget saw them.

1. *Sensorimotor stage (birth to 2 years).* Adjustments are sensorimotor in nature and deal with the here and now. Symbolic manipulation is absent or at a minimum. Children are egocentric in that they see themselves as the frame of reference for everything.

2. *Preoperational stage (2 to 7 years).* There is some rudimentary symbolization and concept formation. Children begin to classify things in terms of their similarity, and in solving problems they use intuition rather than logic. The child has not yet developed **conservation**, the ability to know that the amount or area of something remains the same even though that thing may be represented in a number of ways. For example, when children at this stage are shown a flat container and a tall, narrow container that are both holding the same amount of water, they tend to say that there is more water in the taller container.

3. *Stage of concrete operations (7 to 11 years).* During this stage, children learn conservation and also develop a number of rather sophisticated concepts. However, they can apply these concepts only to concrete problems that they can deal with directly.

4. *Stage of formal operations (11 years and older).* Thinking is now as sophisticated as it ever will be. Children at this stage can apply complex concepts to both concrete problems and those that are totally abstract.

Like all other stage theories in psychology, Piaget's theory has not gone unchallenged. For the most part, however, research seems to support rather than refute Piaget's theory, which has many supporters today in both psychology and education.

SUMMARY

Attacking both the structuralists and the behaviorists for their elementism, the Gestalt psychologists emphasized configurations that could not be divided without destroying the meaning of the configuration. *Gestalt* is the German word for "whole," "totality" or "configuration." Antecedents to Gestalt psychology included Kant's contention that sensory experience was organized by the faculties of the mind; Mach's contention that the perception of space form and time form were independent of any specific sensory experience; von Ehrenfels's observation that though form qualities emerged from sensory experience, they were different from that experience; J. S. Mill's notion of mental chemistry; James's contention that consciousness was like an ever-moving stream that could not be divided into elements without losing its meaning; act psychology, which emphasized the conscious acts of perceiving, sensing, and problem solving instead of the elements of thought; and the emergence of field theory in physics.

The 1912 publication of Wertheimer's article on the phi phenomenon usually marks the founding of the Gestalt school of psychology. The phi phenomenon indicated that conscious experience was different from sensory experience. Koffka and Köhler worked with Wertheimer on his early perception experiments and are usually considered cofounders of Gestalt psychology. Wertheimer assumed that forces in the brain distributed themselves like any other natural force (that is, symmetrically and evenly), and that these forces determined conscious experience. The contention that the fields of forces in the brain determined consciousness was called psychophysical isomorphism, and the contention that brain activity was always distributed in the most simple, symmetrical, and organized way came to be called the law of Prägnanz. The term *perceptual constancy* referred to the way we responded to objects or events as the same even when we experienced them under a wide variety of circumstances.

According to the Gestalt psychologists, the most basic perception was perception of a figure-ground relationship. Other principles governing perception included those of continuity, by which stimuli following some pattern were seen as a perceptual unit; proximity, by which stimuli that were close together formed a perceptual unit; similarity, by which similar stimuli formed a perceptual unit; inclusiveness, by which a larger perceptual configuration masked smaller ones; and closure, by which incomplete physical objects were experienced psychologically as complete. The Gestalt psychologists distinguished the geographical (physical) environment from the behavioral (subjective) environment. They believed that the behavioral environment, or what we would now call subjective reality, governed behavior.

The Gestalt theorists saw learning as a perceptual phenomenon. For them, the existence of a problem created a psychological tension that persisted until the problem was solved. As long as there was tension, the person engaged in cognitive trial and error in an effort to find the solution to the problem. For the person to find a solution to the problem, insightful learning had to occur. Insightful learning was sudden and complete; it allowed performance that was smooth and free of errors. Also, the person retained it for a long time, and could easily transfer it to similar problems. The utilization of a principle learned in one situation in other similar situations was called transposition.

Productive thinking involved the understanding of principles, rather than the memorization of facts or the utilization of formal logic. The Gestalt psychologists believed that reinforcement for productive thinking came from personal satisfaction, not from events outside of oneself. They thought that memory, like other psychological phenomena, was governed by the law of Prägnanz. Experience activated a brain activity called a memory process, which lasted as long as an experience lasted. After the memory process had terminated, a trace of it remained, and that memory trace would influence subsequent memories of similar objects or events. Eventually, a trace system developed for recording the features that memories of a cer-

tain type had in common. After a memory trace—and to a larger extent, a trace system—had been established, the memory of a specific event would be determined by the memory trace and by the trace system of similar experiences, as well as by one's immediate experience.

Lewin was an early Gestalt psychologist who believed that psychology should not categorize people into types or emphasize inner essences. Rather, Lewin felt psychology should attempt to understand the dynamic field of external forces that motivated human behavior. He felt that such a shift in emphasis would switch psychology from an Aristotelian to a Galilean model of science. According to Lewin, anything influencing a person at a given moment was a psychological fact, and the totality of psychological facts that existed at the moment constituted a person's life space. Lewin believed that both biological and psychological needs created a tension that persisted until the needs were satisfied. The Zeigarnik Effect, or the tendency to remember uncompleted tasks longer than completed ones, supported Lewin's theory of motivation. With his work on group dynamics, Lewin showed that different kinds of group structures created different Gestalts that influenced the performance of group members.

Lashley's research on the brain supported the Gestalt view of cortical functioning instead of the switchboard view of the brain that many behaviorists held. His finding of mass action indicated that, as far as loss of ability was concerned, the amount of cortical destruction was more important than the location of destruction. And his finding of equipotentiality indicated that when a certain cortical area was destroyed, other cortical areas could take over the function lost. Both of these findings were incompatible with a switchboard conception of the brain.

Piaget studied genetic epistemology, or how the nature of a person's intelligence varied as a function of maturational level. Piaget proposed that at birth a person's cognitive structure consisted of only a few genetically determined reflexes. With experience, these reflexes were expanded into complex cognitive schemata that allowed complex interactions with the environment. According to Piaget, if an experience matched one's cognitive structure, assimilation occurred. If an experience could not be assimilated into one's cognitive structure, the cognitive structure changed so that assimilation could occur. This process of change was called accommodation. For Piaget, equilibration, or the need for psychological harmony, was the driving force behind intellectual growth. Piaget believed that intellectual growth proceeded in four stages: the sensorimotor stage, when children interacted with the environment by using their genetically determined reflexes; the preoperational stage, when children used rudimentary concepts in interacting with the environ-

ment; the stage of concrete operations, when children developed conservation and more complex concepts with which to solve problems; and the stage of formal operations, when children could solve both concrete and abstract problems symbolically.

Gestalt psychology played a major role in directing the attention of psychologists away from insignificant bits of behavior and consciousness, and toward the whole person. Much of the existential-humanistic psychology that is so popular today is rooted in Gestalt psychology. As with functionalism, most of the basic features of Gestalt psychology have been assimilated into modern psychology, and therefore Gestalt psychology has lost its distinctiveness as a school.

DISCUSSION QUESTIONS

1. Summarize the disagreements that the Gestalt psychologists had with the structuralists and the behaviorists.

2. Differentiate the molecular approach to psychology from the molar approach.

3. What similarities and differences exist between the positions of Kant, Mach, von Ehrenfels, James, and the act psychologists on the one hand, and the Gestalt theorists on the other?

4. Explain what is meant by the contention that Gestalt theory used Einsteinian physics as its model and empirical-associationistic psychology used Newtonian physics as its model.

5. What is the phi phenomenon? What was its importance in the formation of the Gestalt school of psychology?

6. What is meant by the contention that Gestalt analysis proceeds from the top down?

7. Contrast the Gestalt notion of psychophysical isomorphism with the constancy hypothesis.

8. What is the law of Prägnanz? Describe the importance of this law in Gestalt psychology.

9. What is perceptual constancy? Give an example. How did the Gestalt psychologists explain the perceptual constancies?

10. Briefly define each of the following: figure-ground relationship, principle of continuity, principle of proximity, principle of similarity, principle of inclusiveness, and principle of closure.

11. Distinguish between subjective and objective reality. According to the Gestalt theorists, which is more important in determining our behavior? Give an example.

12. How did the Gestalt psychologists explain learning? In your answer, summarize the characteristics of insightful learning.

13. What is transposition? Summarize the Gestalt and the behavioristic explanations of this phenomenon.

14. For Wertheimer, what represented the best kind of problem solving? Contrast this kind of problem solving with rote memorization and logical problem solving.

15. Summarize the Gestalt explanation of mem-

ory. Include in your answer definitions of *memory process*, *memory trace*, and *trace system*. What does it mean to say that memory is governed by the law of Prägnanz?

16. For Lewin, how did psychology based on Aristotle's view of nature differ from psychology based on Galileo's view of nature?

17. What did Lewin mean by life space? Include in your answer the definition of *psychological fact*.

18. Describe Lewin's use of topology and hodology.

19. Summarize Lewin's theory of motivation. In your answer, distinguish between needs and quasi-needs.

20. What is the Zeigarnik Effect? Describe the research used to demonstrate the effect.

21. Summarize Lewin's work on group dynamics.

22. What was the significance of Lashley's work for Gestalt theory? Include in your answer definitions of the terms *mass action* and *equipotentiality*.

23. What does Piaget's theory have in common with Gestalt theory?

24. Define the terms *schemata, assimilation, accommodation*, and *equilibration*.

25. Summarize Piaget's four proposed stages of intellectual development.

26. Describe the impact Gestalt theory has had on psychology.

GLOSSARY

Accommodation The process whereby one's cognitive structure is modified so as to be able to assimilate an experience. Accommodation is roughly equivalent to learning.

Act psychology Kind of psychology that emphasized the study of mental acts such as perceiving and problem solving, instead of the division of consciousness into elements.

Assimilation The process whereby an experience fits or matches one's cognitive structure. Assimilation is roughly equivalent to perceiving or knowing.

Behavioral environment According to Koffka, subjective reality.

Cognitive structure According to Piaget, the total number of schemata available to a person at a given time.

Conservation According to Piaget, the ability to recognize something as the same even when it is presented in a variety of ways.

Constancy hypothesis The contention that there is a one-to-one correspondence between environmental stimuli and sensations.

Ehrenfels, Christian von (1859–1932) Said that mental forms emerged from various sensory experiences and that these forms were different from the sensory elements that made them up.

Elementism The belief that complex mental or behavioral processes are made up of or derive from simple elements, and that the way to understand these processes is first to find the elements of which they are composed.

Equilibration According to Piaget, the tendency to seek a harmonious relationship between one's cognitive structure and the environment.

Equipotentiality Lashley's finding that when part of the cortex was destroyed, other parts of the cortex could take over the lost function.

Extrinsic reinforcement Reinforcement that comes from a source other than one's self.

Field theory The branch of physics that sees phenomena as part of a set of reciprocally acting influences. In such a set of influences, when something happens to one element in the set, all other elements are influenced. Furthermore, in field theory, the field gives elements within the field their identity.

Figure-ground relationship The most basic kind of perception, consisting of the division of the perceptual field into a figure (that which is attended to) and a ground, which provides the background for the figure.

Foreign hull According to Lewin, all events lying outside of a person's life space.

Genetic epistemology The study of intelligence as a function of maturational level and experience.

Geographical environment According to Koffka, physical reality.

Gestalt The German word meaning "configuration" or "whole."

Gestalt psychology The kind of psychology that studies whole, intact phenomenological experience.

Group dynamics Lewin's extension of Gestalt principles to the study of group behavior.

Hodological space The distribution of the positive and negative influences that characterize a person's life space at any given moment.

Holist One who believes that complex mental or behavioral processes should be studied as such, and not first divided into their elemental components.

Insightful learning Learning that involves perceiving the solution to a problem after a period of cognitive trial and error.

Intrinsic reinforcement The self-satisfaction that comes from solving a problem or learning something.

James, William (1842–1910) Like the other precursors of Gestalt psychology, opposed dividing consciousness into elements. For him, consciousness was to be viewed as a totality with a purpose.

Kant, Immanuel (1724–1804) Said that what we experienced consciously was determined by the interaction of sensory information with the faculties of the mind.

Koffka, Kurt (1886–1941) Worked with Wertheimer on his early perception experiments. Koffka is considered a cofounder of the school of Gestalt psychology.

Köhler, Wolfgang (1887–1967) Worked with Wertheimer on his early perception experiments. Köhler is also considered a cofounder of the school of Gestalt psychology.

Lashley, Karl Spencer (1890–1958) Found evidence, through his neurophysiological research, that the cortex functioned more in accordance with Gestalt principles than associationistic principles.

Law of Prägnanz Because of the tendencies of the fields of forces that occur in the brain, mental events will always tend to be organized, simple, and regular.

Lewin, Kurt (1890–1947) An early Gestalt psychologist, Lewin sought to explain human behavior in terms of the totality of influences acting on people rather than in terms of the manifestation of inner essences.

Life space According to Lewin, the totality of influences acting on a person at any given moment.

Mach, Ernst (1838–1916) Said that some mental experiences were the same even though they were stimulated by a wide range of sensory events. The experiencing of geometric forms (space forms) and melodies (time forms) are examples.

Mass action Lashley's finding that following ablation of various parts of the cortex, loss of ability was determined more by the amount of destruction than by the location of destruction.

Memory process The brain activity caused by the experiencing of an environmental event.

Memory trace The remnant of an experience that remains in the brain after an experience has ended.

Molar approach The attempt to focus on intact mental and behavioral phenomena without dividing those phenomena up in any way.

Molecular approach The attempt to reduce complex phenomena into small units for detailed study. Such an approach is elemenistic.

Perceptual constancy The way we tend to respond to objects as being the same, even when we experience those objects under a wide variety of circumstances.

Phenomenology The study of intact, meaningful mental phenomena.

Phi phenomenon The illusion that light is moving from one location to another. The phi phenomenon is caused by flashing two lights on and off at a certain rate.

Piaget, Jean (1896–1980) Showed how intelligence manifested itself differently in children of different ages.

Preoperational stage (two to seven years) According to Piaget, the second stage of intellectual development, during which rudimentary symbolization and concept formation occurred.

Principle of closure We tend to perceive incomplete physical objects as complete.

Principle of continuity We tend to experience stimuli that follow some predictable pattern as a perceptual unit.

Principle of inclusiveness When a smaller figure is embedded in a larger figure, we are likely to perceive only the larger figure.

Principle of proximity In perception, stimuli that are close together tend to be grouped together.

Principle of similarity Stimuli that are physically similar to one another tend to become perceptual units.

Productive thinking According to Wertheimer, the kind of thinking that pondered principles rather than isolated facts, and that aimed at understanding the solutions to problems rather than memorizing a certain problem-solving strategy or logical rules.

Psychological fact According to Lewin, anything that a person is aware of influencing at any given moment.

Psychophysical isomorphism The Gestalt psychologists' notion that the patterns of activity produced by the brain—rather than sensory experience as such—caused mental experience.

Quasi-needs According to Lewin, psychological rather than biological needs.

Schemata According to Piaget, the elements in one's cognitive structure.

Sensorimotor stage (birth to two years) According to Piaget, the first stage of intellectual development, during which the here and now was emphasized.

Stage of concrete operations (7 to 11 years) According to Piaget, the third stage of intellectual development, during which conservation occurred and the child could solve complex problems as long as he or she could experience them directly.

Stage of formal operations (11 years and older) According to Piaget, the fourth and final stage of intellectual development, during which the child could solve both concrete and abstract problems.

Topology A branch of mathematics, which Lewin used to show pictorially the relationships among psychological facts in a person's life space.

Trace system The consolidation of the enduring features of certain memories of experiences. These experiences concern objects belonging to certain classes, such as boats or trees.

Transposition The application of a principle learned in one situation to other similar situations.

Wertheimer, Max (1880–1943) Founded the school of Gestalt psychology with his 1912 paper on the phi phenomenon.

Zeigarnik Effect The tendency for a person to remember uncompleted tasks longer than completed ones.

CHAPTER 15

Early Treatment of the Mentally Ill and the Events Leading to the Development of Psychoanalysis

When psychology became a science, it became first a science of conscious experience and later a science of behavior. Representatives of psychology's early schools—for example, Wundt, Titchener, and James—were aware of unconscious processes but dismissed them as unimportant. The early behaviorists refused even to admit consciousness into their psychology, so to suggest the study of the unconscious would have been unthinkable. And though Gestalt psychology was mentalistic, it concentrated entirely on conscious processes.

How then could a psychology that emphasized the unconscious mind emerge? The answer is that it did not come from academic or experimental psychology. Indeed, it did not come from the tradition of empiricism and associationism at all, as so much of psychology had. Rather, it came from clinical practice. Those who developed the psychology of the unconscious were not concerned with experimental design or the philosophy of science; nor were they concerned with substantiating the claims of the associationists. Rather, they were concerned with understanding the causes of mental illness and using that understanding to help mentally ill patients.

By emphasizing the importance of unconscious processes as causes of mental illness (and later of most human behavior), this band of individuals set themselves apart not only from the psychologists of the time, but from the medical profession as well. The medical profession had been strongly influenced by the mechanistic-positivistic philosophy, according to which physical events caused all illness. For example, physicians explained abnormal behavior in terms of brain damage or biochemical imbalance. If they used the term *mental illness* at all, it was as a descriptive term, since they believed that all illnesses had physical origins.

The stressing of *psychological* causes of mental illness separated this small group of medical doctors both from their own profession and from academic psychology. Theirs was not an easy struggle, but they persisted, and in the end they had convinced the medical profession, academic psychology, and the public that unconscious processes must be taken into consideration in understanding why people act as they do. Sigmund Freud was the leader of this group of rebels, but before we consider his work in the next chapter, we will consider the way mentally ill patients have been treated through history.

A BRIEF HISTORY OF THE TREATMENT OF THE MENTALLY ILL

In their *History of Psychiatry* (1966), Alexander and Selesnick list three basic trends in psychiatry—the magical, the organic, and the psychological—and we shall use these categories as a framework for our discussion.

The Magical Approach

In primitive times, people attributed most ailments not caused by obvious things like falling down, being attacked by an animal or an enemy, or overeating or overdrinking, to mysterious forces entering the body. Humans did not distinguish between mental and physical disorders, but believed both to be inflicted on a person by some mortal or immortal being. If evil forces entering the body caused illness, then a cure would involve removing those forces. In attempting to coax the invading forces from an inflicted person's body, the primitive medicine man would use appeal, bribery, reverence, and intimidation—and sometimes exorcism, magical rituals, and incantations were employed.

In his famous book *The Golden Bough* (1963), **Sir James Frazer** (1854–1941) discussed **sympathetic magic**, which was extremely important in the cause and treatment of ailments. Frazer distinguished between two kinds of sympathetic magic: *homeopathic* and *contagious*. **Homeopathic magic** was based on the principle of similarity. An example of homeopathic magic is the belief that what one did to a model or image of an enemy would affect the enemy. **Contagious magic**, which was based on the principle of contiguity, involved the belief that what was once close to or part of someone would continue to exert an influence on that person. For example, having an article of clothing that belonged to a person whose actions one was trying to control would increase the likelihood of success. Thus, if two things were similar or were at one time connected, they were thought to influence each other through sympathy. Using these principles, a medicine man would sometimes mimic a patient's symptoms and then model a recovery from them. Frazer (1963) indicates that, to the individuals using them, these magical techniques must have appeared to be very effective:

A ceremony intended to make the wind blow or the rain fall, or to work the death of an enemy, will always be followed, sooner or later, by the occurrence it is meant to bring to pass; and primitive man may be excused for regarding the occurrence as a direct result of the ceremony, and the best possible proof of its efficacy. Similarly, rites observed in the morning to help

the sun to rise, and in the spring to wake the dreaming earth from her winter sleep, will invariably appear to be crowned with success, at least in the temperate zones; for in these regions the sun lights his golden lamp in the east every morning, and year by year the vernal earth decks herself afresh with a rich mantle of green. (p. 68)

Primitive humans, then, saw most illness as caused by evil forces or spirits entering the body. This view of illness was simply an extension of how primitive people viewed everything. According to Alexander and Selesnick (1966):

Wind was destructive; hence he [the primitive human] assumed an angry being who blew it to attack him. Rain was sent by spirits to reward or punish him. Disease was an affliction sent by invisible superhuman beings or was the result of magic manipulations by his enemies. He animated the world around him by attributing to natural events the human motivations that he knew so well from his own subjective experiences. Thus it was logical to him to try to influence natural events by the same methods he used to influence human beings: incantation, prayer, threats, submission, bribery, punishment and atonement. (p. 9)

Bleeding a patient or removing a section of his or her skull were also widely used techniques for allowing evil spirits to escape from the body. Researchers have found that Stone Age people (about a half million years ago) would cut an opening in the skull by chipping away at it with a sharp stone, a procedure known as **trephination**. A picture of two skulls prepared in this way is shown in Figure 15.1. Although trephination was presumably used to allow evil spirits to escape, it may have brought some improvement by relieving pressure caused by bleeding or by a tumor.

The Organic Approach

As early as 3000 B.C. (Sigerist, 1951, p. 201), the Egyptians showed great proficiency in treating superficial wounds and setting fractures. Even with ailments in which the cause was not known,

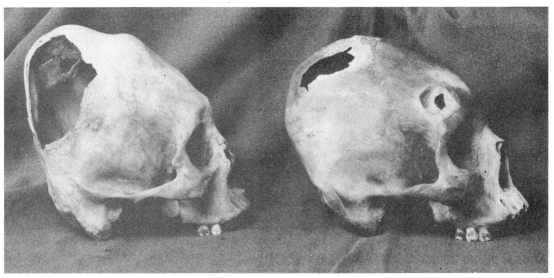

FIGURE 15.1 Prehistoric skulls showing trephination, or the chipping of holes in the skull, presumably to allow evil spirits to escape. (Courtesy of the University Museum, University of Pennsylvania.)

the Egyptians used "natural" treatments such as vapor baths, massage, and herbal remedies. They believed, however, that even the influence of these natural treatments, if there was one, was due to the treatments' effect on evil spirits. The emphasis was clearly on mysterious forces and magic. Even the early Greeks, prior to Hippocrates, believed that God inflicted mental illness upon a person for impiety. The Bible perpetuated this belief, which had much to do with how mentally ill patients were treated until modern times.

Hippocrates (460–380 B.C.) was the first to liberate medicine and psychiatry from their magico-religious background. As we saw in Chapter 2, there was a tendency among the Greeks, starting with Thales, to replace mystical explanations for things wtih naturalistic explanations. Hippocrates applied the naturalistic outlook to the workings of the human body. According to Robinson (1943, p. 51), the work of Hippocrates "marks the greatest revolution in the history of medicine." Esper (1964) agrees:

This was in fact the great contribution of Hippocratic medicine to biological and hence to behavioral science: the introduction of the empirical, naturalistic, objectivistic attitude in the study of human beings. The attempt to hold to or to recapture this attitude seems to me to run through the entire varied history of naturalism, mechanism, materialism, determinism, positivism, anti-metaphysics, pragmatism, behaviorism, physicalism, the "unity of science" movement, etc. The contrasts have been mysticism, metaphysics, vitalism, animism, idealism, dualism, mentalism, supernaturalism, spiritualism, etc. (p. 119)

Hippocrates is known as the Father of Medicine because he was the first to assume that all diseases had natural causes. More specifically, he assumed that the body contained four humors (blood, black bile, yellow bile, and phlegm), and that if they were properly balanced a person would be healthy; if there was an excess or a deficiency of one or more of the humors, an ailment or disease of some sort would occur. The nature of the malady would be a function of the nature of the disbalance.

Since a balance among the humors was normal, there was a natural tendency in each person for a balance to be maintained; and if the balance was disrupted, there was a natural tendency for it to be regained. According to Hippocrates, the best thing a physician could do was to support this natural tendency within each patient. Esper (1964) summarizes Hippocrates' beliefs:

> The healing power of nature strives to restore a disturbed balance; the physician's task is mainly to provide a supportive therapy. Therapeutics followed a policy of watchful waiting upon nature; diet, waters, fresh air, purgation, massage, and supervised exercise were favored over more radical interventions; the influence of climate on health and personality was emphasized. If the physician could not help nature, he was at least to avoid doing injury; this cautious and conservative approach was very wise in view of the scanty knowledge of the time. There was emphasis on the observation and treatment of the total and individual patient. (p. 116)

Hippocrates was hard on those who perpetuated ignorance in medicine. His comments on epilepsy, then called the "sacred disease," are typical:

> I am about to discuss the disease called "sacred." It is not, in my opinion, any more divine or more sacred than other diseases, but has a natural cause, and its supposed divine origin is due to men's inexperience, and to their wonder at its peculiar character. . . . My own view is that those who first attributed a sacred character to this malady were like the magicians, purifiers, charlatans, and quacks of our own day, men who claim great piety and superior knowledge. Being at a loss, and having no treatment which would help, they concealed and sheltered themselves behind superstition, and called this illness sacred, in order that their utter ignorance might not be manifest. (Jones, 1923, Vol. 2, pp. 139, 141)

In addition to arguing that all ailments had natural causes, claiming that nature healed and not physicians, and prescribing treatments such as baths, fresh air, and proper diet, Hippocrates identified several mental illnesses—for example, hysteria, the mental illness that was to become so important in Freud's work. *Hysteria* is a term used to describe a wide variety of disturbances, such as paralysis, loss of sensation, and disturbances of sight and hearing. Hippocrates accepted the earlier Greek and Egyptian contention that hysteria was a uniquely female affliction. *Hystera* is the Greek word for uterus, and it was believed that the symptoms of hysteria were caused by the uterus wandering to various parts of the body. Although later proven false, this view of hysteria represents the organic approach to explaining mental illness.

We will mention only one more of Hippocrates' contributions: his belief that the brain was the seat of the intellect and the emotions. For Hippocrates, the condition of the brain determined whether a person was healthy or not. He says:

> Men ought to know that from the brain, and from the brain only, arise our pleasures, joys, laughs and jests, as well as our sorrows, pains, griefs and tears. Through it, in particular, we think, see, hear, and distinguish the ugly from the beautiful, the bad from the good, the pleasant from the unpleasant. . . . It is the same thing which makes us mad or delirious, inspires us with dread and fear, whether by night or by day, brings sleeplessness, inopportune mistakes, aimless anxieties, absentmindedness, and acts that are contrary to habit. These things that we suffer all come from the brain, when it is not healthy, but becomes abnormally hot, cold, moist, or dry, or suffers any other unnatural affection to which it is not accustomed. (Jones, 1923, Vol. 2, p. 175)

The naturalistic and humane treatment of patients lasted through the time of Galen (A.D. 131–201), who extended Hippocrates' theory of humors into the first personality theory (see Chapter 2). When the Roman Empire fell, however, the humane and rational treatment of physical and mental disorders fell with it.

A Regression to Primitive Beliefs

When the Romans came to power, they adopted much of the Greek emphasis on knowledge and reason, even though they were more concerned with law, technology, and the military than the Greeks were. With the collapse of the Roman Empire, there was an almost complete regression to the nonrational thinking that had characterized the time before the Greek naturalists. Alexander and Selesnick (1966) say:

> The collapse of the Roman security system produced a general regression to belief in the magic, mysticism, and demonology from which, seven centuries before, men had been liberated through Greek genius. (p. 50)
> The psychiatry of the Middle Ages can be scarcely distinguished from prescientific demonology, and mental treatment was synonymous with exorcism. . . . In medieval exorcism Christian mythology and prehistoric demonology found a quaint union. (p. 52)

In 1487 Johann Sprenger and Heinrich Kraemer published a book entitled *Malleus Maleficarum* ("The Witches' Hammer"), which became the textbook of the Inquisition. Before publishing their book, Sprenger and Kraemer sought and received permission from Pope Maximilian, the king of Rome, and members of the theology faculty of the University of Cologne. The book begins by attempting to prove the existence of devils and witches, and indicates that if the authors' arguments do not convince the reader, he or she must be the victim of witchcraft. The second part of the book describes the characteristics and behavior of witches. Many of the attributes the authors assign to witches are clearly those now labeled abnormal behavior. For example, at that time hallucinations, delusions, paranoia, hysteria, catatonia, and mania were all accepted as evidence that a person had been bewitched. The book goes on to suggest how witches are to be tried and punished. The favorite punishment of the time was burning. Since any disease of unknown origin was attributed to witchcraft, a large number of people were suspect. According to the authors, all witchcraft came from sexual lust, which women had much more of than men. Because women were created from the inferior rib of Adam, they were considered

inferior to men in both body and soul, and therefore more likely to be possessed by the devil. The final section of the book describes how witches are made to confess. First mild tortures are to be tried, and if these prove unsuccessful, more extreme measures may be employed.

Alexander and Selesnick (1966) describe the bizarre nature of *Malleus Maleficarum*:

> The *Malleus* includes many descriptions of the incubi, the male demons who seduce women, and of the succubi, the female demons who sexually violate their male captives. In fact, throughout, the book is replete with pornographic sexual orgies occurring between these demons and their human hosts. Not content with these vivid passages, Kraemer and Sprenger go on to satisfy the voyeuristic impulses of the judging inquisitors by recommending that the witch be stripped and her pubic hair shaved before she was presented to the judges. The rationale for shaving the genitals was that the devil would not be able to hide in the pubic hairs. This huntsman's bible, directed against heretics, the mentally ill and women of all stations of life, was responsible for hundreds of thousands of women and children being burned at the stake. (p. 68)

The *Malleus Maleficarum* went through 29 editions and was last published in 1669. It has been estimated that as many as 500,000 people were executed as witches between the fifteenth and the seventeenth centuries (Harris 1974, p. 178). As recently as 1692, 20 people were condemned as witches and sentenced to death in Salem, Massachusetts. During the Renaissance, when advances were being made on so many other fronts, witch-hunting was widespread, and astrology, palmistry, and magic were extremely popular. Conditions were bad for the mentally ill.

When not being tried as witches, many of the mentally ill were locked up in "lunatic asylums." One such asylum was St. Mary of Bethlehem Hospital in London, established in 1547. Known as Bedlam because of the cockney pronunciation of *Bethlehem*, this institution was typical of such institutions at the time. Inmates were chained, beaten, fed only enough to keep them alive, subjected to bloodletting, and put on public display for visitors.

GRADUAL IMPROVEMENT IN THE TREATMENT OF THE MENTALLY ILL

Even during the sixteenth century, when witch hunts and trials were very popular, a few courageous people argued that "witches" were not possessed by demons, spirits, or the devil. They argued that the kind of behavior "witches" displayed was caused by emotional or physical disorders. For example, **Philippus Paracelsus** (1493–1541), a Swiss physician, speculated that hysteria had a sexual origin and that mania was caused by bodily substances influencing the brain. Paracelsus believed that proper medicine could cure all illness, mental or physical. According to Alexander and Selesnick (1966, p. 86), Paracelsus was the second physician to argue against labeling individuals as witches. Agrippa had been the first. Not only did **Cornelius Agrippa** (1486–1535) argue against witchhunts, but he saved many women from the ordeal of a witch trial. In 1563, Agrippa's student **Johann Weyer** (1515–1588) published *The Deception of Demons*, in which he claimed that those labeled as witches were actually mentally disturbed people. Weyer became known to his contemporaries as a crusader against witchhunting, and this was enough for him to be considered weird or even insane.

The view that "witches" were actually mentally ill people also found support from **Reginald Scot** (1538–1599), who wrote *Discovery of Witchcraft* (1584), and from the Swiss psychiatrist **Felix Plater** (1536–1614). In his book *Practice of Medicine*, Plater outlined several different kinds of mental disorders, including consternation, foolishness, mania, delirium, hallucinations, convulsions, drunkenness, hypochondria,

disturbance of sleep, and unusual dreams. The arguments of such people were eventually effective. In 1682, for example, Louis XIV of France abolished the death penalty for witches. But even though mental illness came increasingly to be seen as having natural rather than supernatural causes, it was still poorly understood, and the mentally ill were treated very poorly—if they were treated at all. Bloodletting was still the most popular way of treating all ailments, including mental disorders, and methods were devised for inducing shock in mental patients. One such method was to spin mental patients very rapidly in a chair. These dismal conditions for the mentally ill lasted until the end of the eighteenth century.

Philippe Pinel

Philippe Pinel (1745–1826) came from a family of medical doctors and received his own medical degree in 1773 from the University of Toulouse. Upon beginning his practice, Pinel was upset by the greed and insensitivity of his fellow doctors; so he moved to Paris, where he concentrated on treating that city's poor people. Pinel became interested in the mentally ill when a close friend of his became afflicted with a mental disorder and Pinel was unable to treat him. He read the existing literature on mental illness and consulted with the so-called experts, finding the information on mental illness essentially worthless, except for the work of **Joseph Daquin** (1733–1815). Daquin believed that mental illness was a natural phenomenon that should be studied and treated by means of the methods of natural science. Pinel and Daquin became close friends, and Daquin dedicated the second edition of his book *Philosophy of Madness* (1793) to Pinel.

Pinel began writing influential articles in which he argued for the humane treatment of the mentally disturbed. In 1793 he was appointed director of the Bicêtre Asylum, which had been an institution for the insane since

FIGURE 15.2 Pinel releasing the insane from their chains. (Used by permission of The Bettmann Archive, Inc.)

1660. Upon touring the facility, Pinel found that most of the inmates were chained, and guards patrolled the walls to prevent escape. Pinel asked for permission to release the prisoners from their chains, and although the authorities thought Pinel himself was insane for having such a wish, they reluctantly gave him permission (see Figure 15.2). The first inmate to be unchained was an English soldier who had been at the Bicêtre for 40 years. The soldier had once crushed a guard's skull with his chains and was considered to be a violent person. Upon his release from his chains, the man proved to be nonviolent, and he helped Pinel care for the other inmates. Two years later the soldier was released from Bicêtre. Pinel removed more inmates from their constraints, improved rations, stopped bloodletting, and forbade all harsh treatment such as whirling an inmate in a chair. In his book *Treatise on Insanity* (1801), Pinel says of bloodletting, "The blood of maniacs is sometimes so lavishly spilled, and with so little discernment, as to render it doubtful whether the patient or his physician has the best claim to the appellation of madman" (p. 251).

In addition to unchaining inmates and terminating bloodletting and harsh treatment, Pinel was responsible for many innovations in the treatment of the mentally ill. He segregated different types of patients, encouraged occupational therapy, favored bathing and mild purgatives as physical treatments, and argued effectively against the use of any form of punishment or exorcism. In addition, Pinel was the first to maintain precise case histories and statistics on his patients, including a careful record of cure rates.

Under Pinel's leadership, the number of inmate deaths went way down, and the number of inmates cured and released went way up. His success at Bicêtre led to his 1795 appointment as director of La Salpêtrière, the largest asylum in Europe, housing 8,000 insane women. Following the same procedures he had followed at the Bicêtre, Pinel had equally dramatic success. When he died of pneumonia in 1826, he was given a hero's funeral attended not only by the most influential people in Europe, but also by hundreds of ordinary citizens, including many former patients at the Bicêtre and La Salpêtrière.

Partially because of Pinel's success and partially because of the Zeitgeist, people throughout Europe and the United States began to argue for the humane treatment of the mentally disturbed. In Britain, **William Tuke** (1732–1822), a Quaker, founded the York Retreat for the mentally ill, where inmates were given good food, freedom, respect, medical treatment, recreation, and religious instruction. Tuke designed the York Retreat so that it was more like a farm than a prison. In Florence, Italy, **Vincenzo Chiarugi** (1759–1820) had concluded before Pinel that mental illness had natural causes and that the mentally ill should be spared physical restraint and harsh treatment. Chiarugi's advice for dealing with the mentally ill has a particularly modern ring to it:

> It is a supreme moral duty and medical obligation to respect the insane individual as a person. It is especially necessary for the person who treats the mental patient to gain his confidence and trust. It is best, therefore, to be tactful and understanding and try to lead the patient to the truth and to instill reason into him little by little in a kindly way. . . . The attitude of doctors and nurses must be authoritative and impressive, but at the same time pleasant and adapted to the impaired mind of the patient. . . .Generally it is better to follow the patient's inclinations and give him as many comforts as is advisable

from a medical and practical standpoint. (Mora, 1959, p. 431)

Benjamin Rush

In the United States **Benjamin Rush** (1745–1813), who is often referred to as the first American psychiatrist, wrote *Diseases of the Mind* (1812), in which he lamented that the mentally ill were often treated like criminals or "beasts of prey." Instead, he urged that the mentally ill be unchained and no longer punished. They should experience fresh air and sunlight and be allowed to go for pleasant walks within their institution. Furthermore, Rush contended, the mentally ill should never be on display to the public for the purposes of inhumane curiosity and amusement. Despite his many enlightened views, Rush still advocated bloodletting and the use of rotating and tranquilizing chairs. He believed that bloodletting relieved vascular congestion; that rotating relieved the patient's congested brain; and that strapping a patient's arms and legs in a so-called tranquilizing chair calmed the patient.

Dorothea Lynde Dix

Also in the United States, in 1841 **Dorothea Lynde Dix** (1802–1887) began a campaign to improve the conditions of the mentally ill. Because of unhappy home circumstances, Dix had been forced to leave her home when she was only 10, and when she was 14 she began her career as as schoolteacher. Later, illness forced her to give up her full-time teaching position and take a position teaching women inmates in a Boston prison. It became clear to Dix that many of the women labeled and confined as criminals were really mentally ill, and so Dix began her 40-year campaign to improve the plight of the mentally ill. She traveled from state to state, pointing out the inhumane treatment of the mentally disturbed. Within a 3-year period, Dix visited 18 states and brought about institutional reform in most of them. In 1841, when Dix had begun her campaign, mental hospitals housed only about 15 percent of those needing care; by 1890 that figure had risen to about 70 percent. To a large extent the improvement was due to Dix's efforts.

Although the mentally ill now certainly received better treatment than they had during the Middle Ages and the Renaissance, the reforms involved the patients' physical surroundings and maintenance. Effective treatment for mental illness itself was still lacking. Alexander and Selesnick (1966, p. 115) speculate that there were three reasons for the poor treatment of the mentally ill even *after* it was no longer believed that they were possessed by demons: ignorance of the nature of mental illness, fear of the mentally ill, and the widespread belief that mental illness was incurable.

Back to Organic Explanations

As natural science succeeded, people applied its principles to everything, including humans. When applied to humans, mechanism, determinism, and positivism involved the search for a natural cause for all human behavior, including abnormal behavior. After 2,000 years, conditions had returned to almost the point where they had been about the time of Hippocrates; once again people were emphasizing the brain as the seat of the intellect and the emotions.

This return to naturalism was both good and bad for psychology. It was good because it discouraged mysticism and superstition. No longer did people use evil demons, spirits, or forces to explain mental illness. On the negative side, it discouraged a search for the *psychological factors* underlying mental illness, for it was suggested that a search for such factors was a return to demonology. By the middle of the nineteenth century, the dominant belief was that the cause of all illness, including mental illness, was disordered physiology or brain chemistry. This belief retarded psychology's search for psychological causes of mental illness such as conflict, frustration, emotional disturbance, or other cognitive

Dorothea Dix

THE BETTMANN ARCHIVE, INC.

factors. Under the organic or **medical model of mental illness**, psychological explanations of mental illness were suspect. Since it was generally believed that all disorders had an organic origin, it made sense to classify "mental" diseases just as organic diseases had been classified.

Emil Kraepelin (1856–1926), who had studied with Wundt, attempted to do for mental disorders what Wundt and his colleagues attempted to do for sensations—classify them. In 1883 Kraepelin published a list of mental disorders that was so thorough it has lasted until recent times. Some of the categories of mental disorders that Kraepelin listed, such as mania and depression, had been first mentioned by Hippocrates 2,300 years earlier. Some of the other categories of mental illness Kraepelin listed were primary dementia, which usually appeared during adolescence and was characterized by withdrawal from reality, excessive daydreaming, and inappropriate emotional responses; paranoia, which was characterized by delusions of grandeur or of persecution; and manic depression, which was characterized by cycles of intense emotional outbursts and passive states of depression.

The list of categories of mental illness that many clinicians, psychoanalysts, and psychiatrists currently use as a guide is found in *The Diagnostic and Statistical Manual of Mental Disorders* (1952, 1968, 1980), published by the American Psychiatric Association. Unlike Kraepelin's book, which not only listed various kinds of mental disorders but also attempted to explain the origins of those disorders, the manual published by the American Psychiatric Association is purely descriptive. That is, it simply lists the symptoms that define the various forms of mental illness. Although Kraepelin's classifications brought order to an otherwise chaotic mass of clinical observations, his work is now seen by many as standing in the way of therapeutic progress. People do not fall nicely into the categories that he created, nor are the causes for their disorders always physical in nature, as Kraepelin assumed they were. As Alexander and Selesnick (1966) say of Kraepelin:

> He, whose authority ruled supreme at the turn of the century and the following two decades . . . today is looked upon by the younger generation of psychiatrists as a rigid and sterile codifier of disease categories; even if these were valid, they contribute to neither understanding the causes of diseases nor their prognosis. (p. 184)

Today the tendency in both psychiatry and psychology is to treat the *individual* instead of a label that was placed on the individual by some method of classification such as Kraepelin's or those that the current manual published by the American Psychiatric Association suggests.

The Psychological Model of Mental Illness

The **psychological model of mental illness** places the causes of mental illness in the motives, conflicts, and frustrations of the individual and not in his or her brain chemistry

or physiology. According to Alexander and Selesnick (1966), primitive humans were correct in assuming that the causes of abnormal behavior were psychological rather than physiological, but they were wrong in assuming that the causes were magical and that they lay outside rather than inside the person. Indeed, say Alexander and Selesnick (1966), there has always been, and is now, a tendency to explain abnormal behavior in terms of things beyond our control.

> It appears, indeed, that man has a deep disinclination to understand the disturbances of his behavior in terms of psychology. He undoubtedly shuns the responsibility which results from such understanding and is ready to blame the spirits, the devil, or even mystical fluids in his body for his abnormal behavior instead of recognizing that it is the result of his own feelings, strivings, and inner conflicts. (p. 13)

The battle still rages between those who seek to explain all human behavior in terms of physiology or chemistry (that is, those following a medical model) and those who stress the importance of mental variables such as conflict, frustration, anxiety, fear, and unconscious motivation (those following a psychological model). As we shall see in the next chapter, Freud, who was trained as a mechanistic medical doctor in the tradition of Helmholtz, first attempted to explain personality by using a medical model but was soon forced to switch to a psychological model. Before we turn to Freud, however, we must review a topic that did much to stimulate psychological explanations of mental illness— hypnotism.

THE USE OF HYPNOTISM

Franz Anton Mesmer

It is ironic that the road away from demonology and toward better understanding of mental illness included the work of **Franz Anton Mesmer**

(1734–1815). As we shall see, Mesmer's work was eventually judged unscientific, but at one time his theory of animal magnetism was an improvement over the prevailing superstitions. Mesmer obtained his medical degree in 1766 from the University of Vienna. In his dissertation, which was entiteld "On the Influence of the Planets," he maintained that the planets influenced humans through a force called *animal gravitation*. Considering Newton's theory of universal gravitation, this contention did not seem farfetched.

In the early 1770s, Mesmer met a Jesuit priest named **Maximillian Hell** (quite a name for a priest!) who told Mesmer of cures he had accomplished using a magnet. Mesmer himself then used a magnet to "cure" one of his patients when all of the then conventional forms of treatment had failed. Then Mesmer tried the magnetic treatment on other patients, with equal success. It should be pointed out, however, that the magnetic treatment always involved telling the patient exactly what was expected to occur.

At first, Mesmer assumed that each person's body contained a magnetic force field. In the healthy individual, this force field was distributed evenly throughout the body, but in the unhealthy individual it was unevenly distributed. This uneven distribution of the force field caused symptoms. By using magnets, one could redistribute the force field and restore the patient's health.

Soon Mesmer concluded that it was not necessary to use iron magnets, since anything he touched became magnetized. Goldsmith (1934) quotes Mesmer:

> Steel is not the only object which can absorb and emanate the magnetic force. On the contrary, paper, bread, wool, silk, leather, stone, glass, water, various metals, wood, dogs, human beings, everything that I touched became so magnetic that these objects exerted as great an influence on the sick as does a magnet itself. I filled bottles with magnetic materials just as one does with electricity. (p. 64)

THE BETTMANN ARCHIVE, INC.

Franz Anton Mesmer

Next, Mesmer found that he did not need to use any object at all; simply holding his hand next to a patient's body was enough for the patient to be influenced by Mesmer's magnetic force. Mesmer concluded that although all humans contained a magnetic force field, in some people the field was much stronger than in others. These people were natural healers, and he, of course, was one of them.

When magnetic therapy became popular, Father Hell claimed to be the first to have used it. A great dispute followed, which was covered by the newspapers. During this controversy, which Mesmer (probably unjustly) won, the term **animal magnetism** was first used.

In 1777 Mesmer agreed to treat Fräulein Paradies, a 17-year-old pianist who had been blind since the age of 3. Mesmer claimed that his treatment returned her sight but that she could see only while alone in his presence. The medical community accused Mesmer of being a charlatan, and he was forced to leave Vienna. He fled to Paris where, almost immediately, he attracted an enthusiastic following. He was so popular that he decided to treat patients in groups rather than individually, and still he was effective. By now Mesmer's treatment was filled with ritual. Alexander and Selesnick (1966) describe Mesmer's procedure:

> Mesmer had an astonishing success in Paris—not in academic circles, but with hysterical ladies. For five years Mesmer treated all comers at his clinic. If they were poor there was no charge; if they were wealthy they paid an enormous fee. . . . Mesmer's treatment, which often was conducted on groups of patients at once, was an impressive ceremonial. The patients entered a thickly carpeted, dimly lit room that was mirrored so as to reflect every shadow; soft melodies were heard, and there was a fragrance of orange blossoms. The patients held hands in a circle around the baquent, a tub filled with "magnetized" water. Into this prepared scene would step the healer, clothed in a lilac cloak and waving a yellow wand. In the past, physicians had carried gold cases and worn red cloaks to impress their patients. Why not a purple robe and a yellow wand? Mesmer did not believe there was anything supernatural about what he was doing and explained his rituals in naturalistic terms. What he wanted to accomplish was a "crisis"—the moment when one patient would suddenly scream, break into a cold sweat, and then convulse. Mesmer knew that some of his patients, having witnessed this dramatic scene, would respond with similar symptoms. He did not realize, of course, that this was but mass suggestion. But he knew what revivalists and faith healers throughout the ages had known, namely, that soon after the violent episode tension immediately subsided. (p. 128)

Treating groups increased not only Mesmer's profits but his effectiveness. Because of what was later called the **contagion effect**, many people who would not respond to suggestion when alone with a physician would do so readily after seeing others respond.

As Mesmer's fame grew and thousands came to his clinic, his critics became more severe. The French clergy accused Mesmer of being in consort with the Devil, and the medical profession accused him of being a charlatan. In response to the medical profession's criticisms, Mesmer proposed that 20 patients be chosen at random and ten sent to him for treatment and ten sent to members of the French Academy of Medicine; the results would then be compared. Mesmer's interesting proposal was rejected. In 1781, Queen Marie Antoinette, one of Mesmer's many influential friends, offered Mesmer a château and a lifetime pension if he would disclose the secrets of his success. Mesmer turned down the offer.

Popularity did not satisfy Mesmer personally. What he desparately wanted was the acceptance of the medical profession, which saw Mesmer as a quack. In 1784 the Society of Harmony (a group dedicated to the promotion of animal magnetism) persuaded the king of France to establish a commission to study objectively the effects of animal magnetism. This truly high-level commission consisted of Benjamin Franklin (the commission's presiding officer); Lavoisier, the famous chemist; and Guillotin, the creator of a way to put condemned people to death in a "humane" manner. Much to Mesmer's dismay, the commission concluded that there was no such thing as animal magnetism, and that any positive results from treatment supposedly employing it were due to the imagination. The commission branded Mesmer a mystic and a fanatic. Although many people, some of them prominent, urged Mesmer to continue his work and his writing, the commission's findings had essentially destroyed him, and he sank into oblivion.

Marquis de Puységur

Although the commission's report silenced Mesmer himself, other members of the Society of Harmony continued to use and modify Mesmer's techniques. One such member, **Marquis de Puységur** (1751–1825), discovered that magnetizing did not need to involve the violent crisis that Mesmer's approach necessitated. Simply by placing a person in a peaceful, sleeplike trance, Puységur could demonstrate a number of phenomena. Although the person appeared to be asleep, he or she would still respond to Puységur's voice and follow his commands. When Puységur instructed the magnetized patient to talk about a certain topic, perform various motor activities, or even dance to imagined music, he or she would do so and have no recollection of the events upon waking. Because a sleeplike trance replaced the crisis, Puységur renamed the condition **artificial somnambulism**. He found that the therapeutic results of using this artificial sleep were as good as they had been with Mesmer's crisis approach.

With his new approach, Puységur made many discoveries. As Fancher (1979) says:

> In investigating the properties of artificial somnambulism, Puységur and his colleagues discovered almost all of the properties of the hypnotic state that are known today. They conclusively demonstrated that the state is characterized by drastically increased *suggestibility*. All they had to do was state that certain things were happening, and somnambulistic subjects would begin to behave as if they really were. Paralyses and pains could be artificially produced in various parts of the body, and made to move about at the will of the magnetizer. Parts of the subject's body could be rendered insensitive, so pin pricks, burns, or other painful stimulation could be tolerated without the slightest sign of discomfort.
>
> Puységur also demonstrated the phenomenon now called **post-hypnotic suggestion**, whereby a somnambulistic subject is told to perform a certain act after the trance has ended. When the subject performs it he has often forgotten that the suggestion was ever made, just as he may have forgotten the other events from the trance. These memory deficiencies, now called **post-hypnotic amnesia**, are among the most intriguing and mysterious of all hypnotic effects. Obviously, the forgotten memories have not been completely "lost" because in the post-hypnotic suggestion they retain enough efficacy to produce the suggested response. Furthermore, the post-hypnotic amnesia can be easily overcome if the subject is re-hypnotized, or simply told by the hypnotist that his memory will return. (p. 179, boldface added)

Elliotson, Esdaile, and Braid

Since magnetizing a patient could, by suggestion, make him or her oblivious to pain, a few medical doctors began to look upon magnetism as a possible surgical anaesthetic. **John Elliotson** (1791–1868) suggested that mesmerism be used during surgery, but the medical establishment forbade it, even though other anaesthetics were not available. In 1842, *W. S. Ward* performed a leg amputation in which the patient was magnetized, but some medical doctors accused the patient of being an imposter. Others said that patients should suffer pain during an operation because it helped them recover better (Fancher, 1979, p. 183). In India, **James Esdaile** (1808–1859), a surgeon with the British Army in Calcutta, India, performed more than 250 painless operations on Hindu convicts, but his results were dismissed because his operations had been performed on natives and therefore had no relevance to England. About this time, anaesthetic gases were discovered, and interest in magnetism as an anaesthetic faded almost completely. The use of gases was much more compatible with the training of the physicians of the day than were the mysterious forces involved in magnetism.

James Braid (1795–1860), a prominent Scottish surgeon, was skeptical of magnetism, but after carefully examining a magnetized subject he was convinced that many of the effects were real. Braid proceeded to examine the phenomenon systematically, and in 1843 he wrote *The Rationale of Nervous Sleep*. Braid explained magnetism in terms of prolonged concentration and the physical exhaustion that followed, stressing that the results were explained by the subject's suggestibility rather than by any power that the magnetizer possessed. He renamed the study of the phenomenon neuro-hypnology, which was then shortened to *hypnosis* (*hypnos* being the Greek word for "sleep"). Braid did as much as anyone to make the phenomenon previously known as magnetism or mesmerism respectable within the medical community.

The Nancy School

Convinced of the value of hypnosis, **Auguste Ambroise Liébeault** (1823–1904) wanted to use it in his practice but could find no patient willing to be subjected to it. Eventually he agreed to provide free treatment to any patient willing to undergo hypnotism. A few patients agreed, and Liébeault was so successful with them that his practice was soon threatened by an excess of nonpaying patients. Soon Liébeault was treating all of his patients with hypnotism and accepting whatever fee they could afford. A "school" soon grew up around his work, and since he practiced in a French village just outside of the city of Nancy, it was called the **Nancy School**.

The school attracted a number of physicians; among them **Hippolyte Bernheim** (1840–1919), who became the major spokesperson of the Nancy School. Bernheim contended that *all* humans were suggestible but that some were more suggestible than others, and that highly suggestible people were easier to hypnotize than those less suggestible. Furthermore, Bernheim found that anything a highly suggestible patient believed would improve his or her symptoms usually did so.

Charcot and the Treatment of Hysteria

Contrary to the belief of the members of the Nancy School, **Jean Charcot** (1825–1893) did not believe that suggestibility was a general human trait. Charcot believed that only those people suffering the neurosis called hysteria could

be hypnotized. This belief brought Charcot and his colleagues into sharp conflict with the Nancy School—the former believing that hypnotizability was a sign of mental pathology, the latter believing that it was perfectly normal. The debate was heated and lasted for years.

When Charcot became the director of La Salpêtrière (the institution where Pinel had released the patients from their chains), he immediately converted it into a research center. Though he was flamboyant, Charcot was considered one of the most brilliant physicians in all of Europe. His regular lectures were well attended by both professionals and nonprofessionals. Among those attending were Alfred Binet, William James, and Sigmund Freud. Charcot even became one of Freud's idols.

More and more, Charcot's interests turned to hysteria, an ailment most physicians dismissed as malingering because no one could find an organic cause for its symptoms. In fact, some of the symptoms were anatomically anomalous. Fancher (1979) says:

> Some of these patients experienced paralyses whose characteristics did not conform to the anatomy of the nervous system. In genuine organic paralyses, the boundary between paralyzed and nonparalyzed body areas is never distinct. Some of these patients, however, reported paralyses that were limited to sharply circumscribed parts of their bodies, such as the part of a hand and arm normally covered by a glove. . . . [Such] symptoms without a clear-cut physiological or anatomical base were simply not comprehensible to most nineteenth century physicians. (p. 191)

Charcot dismissed the popular malingering theory and concluded that hysteric patients were suffering real discomfort. Staying within the medical model, however, he concluded that hysteria was caused by an hereditary neurological degeneration that was progressive and irreversible. Since both hysteria and hypnosis produced the same symptoms (for example, paralyses and anaesthesia), Charcot concluded

FIGURE 15.3 Freud observing Charcot demonstrating various hypnotic phenomena. (Used by permission of Culver Pictures, Inc.)

that hypnotizability indicated the presence of hysteria.

Among Charcot's most popular demonstrations were those in which he hypnotized hysteric patients and had them display a wide range of imaginary sensations and physical states. Freud is seen observing such a demonstration in Figure 15.3. Toward the end of his life, Charcot admitted that his theory of suggestibility was wrong and that of the Nancy School was correct. Even so, the prestige of Charcot gave further respectability to hypnosis; and even more importantly, Charcot helped people see hysteria as a real ailment worthy of the concern of physicians.

Pierre Janet

Pierre Janet (1859–1947), Charcot's student and successor, explained hypnosis and hysteria as psychological rather than physiological phenomena. According to Janet, hysterics were born with a neurological weakness that resulted in a lack of psychic cohesiveness. This lack of cohesiveness allowed parts of consciousness to be disassociated from one another, and under extreme conditions this disassociation could result in a "split personality." According to Janet, this disassociation allowed physical symptoms to exist without a person being aware of their origin, and created various hypnotic phenomena such as amnesia and posthypnotic suggestion. Furthermore, the lack of psychic cohesiveness made a person suggestible and therefore hypnotizable. Thus, although Janet's theory is at its roots a physiological one (neurological weakness), it ends up explaining various disorders in psychological terms (psychic cohesiveness and dissociation). This idea of the dissociated mind is compatible with Freud's later distinction between the conscious and the unconscious mind.

OTHER ANTECEDENTS TO THE DEVELOPMENT OF PSYCHOANALYSIS

As we shall see, both hypnotic phenomena and Charcot's concern with hysteria had a strong influence on the development of Freud's theory, but there were several other influences as well.

Gottfried Wilhelm von Leibniz

Gottfried Wilhelm von Leibniz (1646–1716) theorized that the universe was made up of *monads*, or individual entities that could not be divided without losing their identities. As we saw in Chapter 6, sometimes individual monads were so small that one or a few of them could not be perceived although aggregates of them could be. In such a case, consciousness was on a continuum based on the number of monads. When the energy from only a few small monads was available, an unconscious experience, or a **petites perception** occurred. But if enough small monads were present, **apperception**, or conscious experience, occurred. Leibniz was among the first philosophers to suggest that there were levels of awareness ranging all the way from clear perception (apperception) to the unconscious (petites perception). Since Leibniz was an extremely influential philosopher, the notion of levels of consciousness became very popular in Europe.

Johann Friedrich Herbart

Suggesting that there was a *threshold* above which an idea was conscious and below which an idea was unconscious, **Johann Friedrich Herbart** (1776–1841) postulated a conflict model of the mind. Only ideas that were compatible with each other could occur in consciousness. If two incompatible ideas occurred in consciousness,

one of them was forced below the threshold into the unconscious. Unconscious ideas were not passive, and Herbart suggested that they may join forces and force their way above the threshold into consciousness.

Instead of monads, Herbart talked about ideas. For him, ideas were discrete (distinct from one another), active, and strove for expression in consciousness. In other words, ideas struggled against being inhibited into the unconscious. Furthermore, inhibited (unconscious) ideas did not cease to exist. They did lose their clarity, but they continued to exist as a force in the mind. As consciousness changed, different ideas in the unconscious became compatible with it and were no longer resisted (inhibited); therefore, they could enter consciousness. The relationship between the conscious and unconscious was therefore dynamic, in that ideas in the conscious mind and ideas in the unconscious mind changed with the circumstances.

Like Leibniz, Herbart used the term *apperception*, but he used it differently than Leibniz. For both men, *apperception* meant that which we were conscious of. For Leibniz, consciousness resulted when the aggregate of small monads was large enough to cause awareness. For Herbart, however, an idea could become conscious (that is, apperceived) only if it was compatible with the ideas already in one's consciousness. Herbart called the totality of conscious ideas at any given moment the **apperceptive mass**. If an idea was compatible with the apperceptive mass, it was assimilated into consciousness; if not, it was inhibited and forced into the unconscious, where it remained until an apperceptive mass compatible with it occurred. Herbart used the term *repression* to denote the inhibiting force that kept an incompatible idea in the unconscious. Much of Herbart's philosophy appeared later in Freud's theory. As far as the notion of the unconscious is concerned, Boring (1957) says, "Leibniz foreshadowed the entire doctrine of the unconscious, but Herbart actually began it" (p. 257).

Arthur Schopenhauer

Arthur Schopenhauer (1788–1860) believed that humans were governed more by irrational desires than by reason. Since the instincts determined behavior, most humans vaccillated between being in a state of need and being satisfied. The needs of the human species, however, took precedence over the needs of individual humans. According to Schopenhauer, this was why even a person living with a painful terminal disease could not take his or her life; the motive for preservation of the species was more powerful than the circumstances in the life of the individual. Insofar as we sought knowledge and rationality, we entered into conflict with our true irrational nature.

Schopenhauer anticipated Freud's concept of sublimation when he said that we could attain some relief or escape from the irrational forces within us by immersing ourselves in music, poetry, or art. One could also attempt to counteract these irrational forces, especially the sex drive, by living a life of asceticism. Schopenhauer also spoke of repressing undesirable thoughts into the unconscious, and of the resistance one encountered when attempting to recognize repressed ideas. Freud (1938, p. 939) credited Schopenhauer as being the first to discover these processes, but Freud claimed that he had discovered the same processes independently of Schopenhauer.

Much of Freud's theory appears in Schopenhauer's philosophy. In addition to the ideas of sublimation, repression, and resistance, Freud shared Schopenhauer's belief that irrational forces were the prime motivators of human behavior, and that the best we could do was minimize their influence. Both men, therefore, were very pessimistic.

Friedrich Nietzsche

Like Schopenhauer, **Friedrich Nietzsche** (1844–1900) believed that humans were basically irrational. Unlike Schopenhauer, however, Nietzsche felt that the instincts should not be repressed but should be given full expression—even aggressive tendencies. For Nietzsche, the main motive for human behavior was the will to power. A person can fully satisfy this motive by acting as he or she feels—that is, by acting in such a way as to satisfy fully all of the instincts. In *The Antichrist* (1895) Nietzsche says,

> Life itself appears to me as an instinct for growth, for survival, for the accumulation of forces, for power: whenever the will to power fails there is disaster. (No. 6)

Thus, both Schopenhauer and Neitzsche believed that irrational instincts strongly influenced human behavior. Schopenhauer believed that such instincts should be repressed, Nietzsche felt that they should be expressed. Freud was influenced more by Schopenhauer, whereas Alfred Adler, one of Freud's early followers, was influenced more by Nietzsche.

Gustav Theodor Fechner

Like Herbart, **Gustav Theodor Fechner** (1801–1887) employed the concept of threshold in his work. More important to Freud, however, was that Fechner likened the mind to an iceberg, consciousness being the smallest part, or the tip, and the unconscious mind making up the rest. Fechner is the only psychologist whom Freud quoted frequently, and in addition to borrowing the iceberg analogy of the mind from him, Freud also borrowed the notions of mental energy and the death instinct.

Charles Darwin

By showing the continuity between humans and other animals, **Charles Darwin** (1809–1882), strengthened Freud's contention that humans, like "lower" animals, were motivated by instincts rather than by reason. Darwin's conception of humans was compatible with those of Schopenhauer and Nietzsche. Darwin, Freud, Schopenhauer, and Nietzsche all saw humans as animals whose nature conflicted with the demands of civilization.

Hermann von Helmholtz

Representing the thoroughly objective approach to medicine and psychology, **Hermann von Helmholtz** (1821–1894) tolerated no subjectivity or vitalism in the study of humans. His approach, which permeated most of medicine and physiology at the time, had a profound effect on Freud; for although Freud soon abandoned the medical model of mental illness, he never lost his objectivity.

To explain certain perceptual phenomena, Helmholtz used the concept of unconscious inference. His use of the term *unconscious* represented an attempt to show the influence of learning on perception, and bore no resemblance to Freud's use of the term. More important for Freud was Helmholtz's concept of the conservation of energy. Helmholtz demonstrated that an organism was an energy system that could be explained entirely on the basis of physical principles. For example, the amount of energy an organism expended was accounted for by the food that it metabolized. In other words, the energy that came out of an organism depended upon the energy that went into the organism—no life force was left over.

Taking Helmholtz's idea of the conservation of energy and applying it to the mind, Freud assumed that only so much psychic energy was available at any given time, and that it could be distributed in various ways. How this finite amount of energy was distributed in the mind accounted for all human behavior and thought. So whereas Helmholtz applied his principle to physical and biological systems, Freud applied it to a psychological system.

Franz Brentano

Franz Brentano (1838–1917) was one of Freud's teachers at the University of Vienna when Freud was in his early twenties. Brentano taught that motivational factors were extremely important in determining the flow of thought, and that there were major differences between objective reality and subjective reality. This distinction was to play a vital role in Freud's theory. Brentano is known mainly for his "act" psychology, which opposed Wundt's "content" psychology. For Brentano, the *acts* of perceiving, sensing, loving, hating, judging, intending, or wishing were more important than *what* was perceived, sensed, loved, judged, and so on. In other words, Brentano felt that psychology should study the mental processes by which humans interacted with the world, rather than the static *elements* of thought that Wundt and his colleagues sought. Brentano's conception of the mind clearly had much in common with Freud's. Under the influence of Brentano, Freud almost decided to give up medicine and pursue philosophy (which was Brentano's main interest); but *Ernst Brücke* (1819–1892), the mechanistically inclined physiologist, influenced Freud even more than Brentano had, and Freud stayed in medicine.

Karl Eduard von Hartmann

Karl Eduard von Hartmann (1842–1906) wrote a book entitled *Philosophy of the Unconscious* (1869), which remained very popular until the early 1880s. During the time that Freud was studying medicine, and later when he was developing his theory, the idea of the unconscious was quite common in Europe, and no doubt every reasonably educated person knew about it.

Hartmann was strongly influenced by Schopenhauer, but he changed Schopenhauer's concept of the will (irrational instincts) into the concept of the unconscious mind. For Hartmann, there were three kinds of unconsciousness: processes that governed all natural phenomena in the universe; the physiological unconscious, which directed the bodily processes; and the psychological unconscious, which was the source of all behavior. Although Hartmann's position is philosophical and even mystical, it has some elements in common with Freud's theory, especially the notion of the psychological unconscious.

Is the Unconscious a Place?

Even after one concludes that certain material is outside of awareness and therefore unconscious, one must still determine the nature of the unconscious material. Leahey (1980) makes this point as follows:

> We must distinguish . . . the hypothesis of unconscious ideas from the hypothesis of the unconscious. It is obvious that one is unconscious of one's phone number until the occasion to use it arises. But does the idea continue to exist unseen in a mental place called the *unconscious*, or is it no longer a mental entity at all, having disappeared into the neural network? Freud followed von Hartmann and Herbart in positing a mental place called the unconscious where ideas reside when they are not conscious and from which they can affect behavior without our awareness. Leibniz's and Fechner's conceptions were more purely descriptive, saying that some ideas are conscious while others are not-in-consciousness, or are unconscious. For them, there is no place called "the unconscious"; when an idea is unconscious it exists only physiologically, as a brain trace, not psychologically. Wundt and William James differed on much else, but they both accepted the Liebniz-Fechner description of "unconsciousness" and rejected Herbart's concept of a mental place called "unconsciousness." (p. 218)

Thus, most of the ingredients of Freud's theory had evolved over many years. Determinism, the dynamic mind, the importance of the unconscious and irrationality, the similarity between humans and other animals, and the importance of sexual motivation had all been anticipated by others. Freud's unique contribution was his ability to synthesize all of these elements into a comprehensive picture of human nature, a picture that was to have a dramatic impact on Western culture. We turn to Freud and his work in the next chapter.

SUMMARY

The treatment of the mentally ill has gone through three major stages. During the first stage, people saw mental and physical illness as resulting from possession by evil spirits or demons. The healer's job was to rid the body of the negative forces through such methods as appeal, bribery, and magical rituals. Two kinds of sympathetic magic were widely practiced: homeopathic magic, which was based on the belief that what happened to a model or image of a person would also happen to the person himself or herself; and contagious magic, which was based on the belief that what happened to something once close to a person would have an influence on the person. The second stage in the treatment of the mentally ill came about when people saw all mental and physical disorders as having natural causes—and therefore natural cures. Hippocrates, who was among the first to accept this organic approach, saw health as the result of a balance among the four body humors, and illness as an imbalance among them. In order to help patients regain health (a balance), Hippocrates prescribed such things as mineral baths, fresh air, and proper diet.

Naturalistic medicine and psychiatry characterized treatment of physical and mental problems until the collapse of the Roman Empire, when there was a regression to demonology and magic. During the Middle Ages and the Renaissance, the mentally ill were believed to be possessed by evil spirits and were exorcized, punished, or killed. But even during this dark time in history for the mentally ill, there were people who refused to believe that abnormal behavior resulted from possession of the person by demons, spirits, or the Devil. For example, Paracelsus, Agrippa, Weyer, Scot, and Plater argued effectively that abnormal behavior had natural causes and that the mentally ill should be treated humanely. Even when the supernatural explanation of mental illness subsided, however, the mentally ill were still treated harshly in "lunatic asylums" such as Bedlam. Not until the end of the eighteenth century did Tuke, Chiarugi, Rush, Dix, and others help bring about dramatically better living conditions for the mentally ill. Through the efforts of these people, many mentally ill patients were unchained, given better food, provided recreation, fresh air, sunlight, and medical treatment, and treated with respect.

After about 2,000 years, there had been a gradual return to Hippocrates' organic approach to explaining and treating mental illness. According to this approach, all disorders, whether mental or physical, have physical causes—for example, a biochemical imbalance in the brain. This medical model discouraged the search for psychological causes of disorders, since such a search would have exemplified a return to demonology. In 1883 Kraepelin summarized all the categories of mental illness known at that time; he attempted to show the origins of the various disorders and how the disorders should be treated. The current handbook that many clinicians use also describes the various kinds of mental disorders.

The third stage in the history of treating the mentally ill, the psychological approach, came about when people began to see mental illness as the result of such psychological phenomena as frustration, anxiety, and conflict. There is still strong disagreement between those who insist that mental illness be viewed as having organic origins (the medical model) and those who see such illness as psychological in nature (the psychological model).

The work of Mesmer played a crucial role in the transition toward objective psychological explanations of mental illness. Mesmer believed that physical and mental disorders were caused by the uneven distribution of animal magnetism in the patient's body. He also believed that some people had stronger magnetic force fields than others, and that they, like himself, were natural healers. Mesmer contended that his extraordinary powers could redistribute the magnetic fields in clients and thereby cure them. Because of something later to be called the contagion effect, some of Mesmer's clients were more easily "cured" in a group than individually.

Puységur discovered that placing clients in a sleeplike trance, which he called artificial somnambulism, was as effective as Mesmer's crisis-oriented approach for treating disorders. Puységur explained this sleeplike state as the result of suggestibility. He also discovered the phenomena of posthypnotic suggestion and posthypnotic amnesia. Since "magnetizing" patients made them insensitive to pain, several physicians used it as an anaesthetic. This technique was controversial, however, and physicians dropped it when anaesthetic gases such as ether were discovered. By systematically studying hypnosis and attempting to explain it as a biological phenomenon, Braid gave it greater respectability in the medical community. Members of the Nancy School believed that all humans were more or less suggestible, and therefore hypnotizable; Charcot, in contrast, believed that only hysterics were hypnotizable. Unlike other physicians of his day, Charcot treated hysteria as a real rather than an imagined illness. But whereas Charcot viewed hysteria and hypnosis as having physical origins, his successor, Janet, explained both as psychological phenomena.

Other antecedents to the development of

psychoanalysis included Liebniz's contention that some perceptions were conscious and others unconscious; Herbart's contention that ideas incompatible with those already in consciousness (the apperceptive mass) were held in the unconscious until an apperceptive mass with which they were compatible arose; Schopenhauer's contention that we shared instincts with "lower" animals but that we should sublimate, repress, or deny these instincts; Nietzsche's contention that in order to be fully human, we must give full expression to our irrational impulses; Fechner's description of the mind as an iceberg, with the tip corresponding to consciousness; Darwin's observation that humans were continuous with other animals; Helmholtz's principle of the conservation of energy, which Freud later applied to psychic energy; Brentano's view of the mind as consisting of acts rather than static elements; and Hartmann's book on the unconscious, which helped popularize the notion of the unconscious mind throughout Europe. Some use the term *unconscious* to denote a place where ideas that are not in consciousness reside; others use the term simply to denote the status of ideas that we are not aware of.

DISCUSSION QUESTIONS

1. Describe the magical approach to treating mental illness. What belief about the origin of mental illness was this approach based upon?

2. Define and give an example of homeopathic and contagious magic.

3. How did Hippocrates define health and illness? What kinds of things did he prescribe for helping his patients regain health?

4. How were the mentally ill viewed and treated following the collapse of the Roman Empire?

5. Describe some of the kinds of behavior people engaged in that caused them to be labeled as witches.

6. Who were some of the first people to insist that the behavior of so-called witches was really the result of mental illness and should therefore be understood and treated as a natural phenomenon?

7. What is the significance of Philippe Pinel in the history of the treatment of the mentally ill?

8. Describe the reformers of mental institutions, other than Pinel, whom we covered in this chapter.

9. Why did the return to the organic approach to understanding and treating mental illness discourage a search for the psychological causes of mental illness?

10. Why was Kraepelin's listing of the various mental disorders seen as something both positive and negative?

11. Differentiate between the medical model for understanding and treating the mentally ill and the psychological model.

12. According to Mesmer, what caused mental and physical illness? What procedures did Mesmer use to cure such illnesses? What finally happened to Mesmer?

13. What discoveries did Puységur make concerning hypnotism?

14. What was the difference between members of the Nancy School and Charcot concerning the notion of suggestibility?

15. Summarize both Charcot's and Janet's explanations of hysteria and hypnosis.

16. Discuss the contributions of the following people to the development of psychoanalysis: Leibniz, Herbart, Schopenhauer, Nietzsche, Fechner, Helmholtz, Darwin, Brentano, and Hartmann.

17. Distinguish between the unconscious as a place and as a state. Of the people listed in the previous question, which described the unconscious as a place and which described it as a state?

GLOSSARY

Agrippa, Cornelius (1486–1535) The first physician openly to oppose the labeling of individuals as witches. Agrippa felt that so-called witches were people suffering abnormalities that had natural origins.

Animal magnetism A force that Mesmer and others believed was evenly distributed throughout the bodies of healthy people and unevenly distributed in the bodies of unhealthy people.

Apperception According to Leibniz, conscious perception.

Apperceptive mass According to Herbart, the totality of ideas that one is conscious of at any given time.

Artificial somnambulism The sleeplike trance that Puységur created in his patients. It was later called an hypnotic trance.

Bernheim, Hippolyte (1840–1919) A member of the Nancy School of hypnotism who believed that anything a highly suggestible patient believed would improve his or her condition would do so.

Braid, James (1795–1860) Renamed magnetism hypnotism and explained the phenomenon in terms of the suggestibility of the subject rather than in terms of any powers that the hypnotist possessed. Braid did much to make hypnosis respectable to the medical community.

Brentano, Franz (1838–1917) Viewed the mind as consisting of dynamic mental acts rather than static elements. Brentano was one of Freud's teachers.

Charcot, Martin (1825–1893) Disagreed with the contention that all humans could be hypnotized, believing rather that only hysterics could.

Chiarugi, Vincenzo (1759–1820) Even before Pinel, argued for the humane treatment of the mentally ill.

Contagion effect The tendency for people to be more susceptible to suggestion when in a group than when alone.

Contagious magic A kind of sympathetic magic. It involves the belief that what one does to

something that a person once owned or that was close to a person will influence that person.

Daquin, Joseph (1733–1815) Believed that mental illness should be studied through the methods of natural science. Daquin strongly influenced Pinel's thinking.

Darwin, Charles (1809–1882) Showed humans to be continuous with other animals and to possess the same instincts.

Dix, Dorothea Lynde (1802–1887) Caused several states to reform their facilities for the mentally ill by making them more available to those needing them and more humane in their treatment.

Elliotson, John (1791–1868) Suggested that magnetism be used as a surgical anaesthetic.

Esdaile, James (1808–1859) Used hypnotism as an anaesthetic while performing 250 operations on Hindu convicts.

Fechner, Gustav Theodor (1801–1887) Likened the mind to an iceberg, with the tip corresponding to consciousness and the larger part underneath corresponding to the unconscious.

Frazer, Sir James (1854–1941) In his book *The Golden Bough* (1963), described the importance of sympathetic magic to primitive humans.

Hartmann, Karl Eduard von (1842–1906) Wrote a book entitled *Philosophy of the Unconscious* (1869), which remained popular into the 1880s.

Hell, Maximillian The Jesuit priest who called the idea of animal magnetism to Mesmer's attention.

Helmholtz, Hermann von (1821–1894) Attempted to be totally objective in his work by explaining everything in physical terms. Helmholtz saw living organisms as energy systems that were governed by the principle of conservation of energy. Freud applied this principle to mental energy.

Herbart, Johann Friedrich (1776–1841) Had a dynamic conception of the mind. For Herbart, ideas that were incompatible with ideas currently in consciousness were held in the unconscious mind until conscious ideas compatible with them arose. The same idea could at one time exist in consciousness and at another time in the unconscious.

Hippocrates (460–380 B.C.) Argued that all mental and physical disorders had natural causes and that treatment of such disorders should consist of such things as rest, proper diet, and humane counseling,

Homeopathic magic The kind of sympathetic magic involving the belief that doing something to a likeness of a person will influence that person.

Janet, Pierre (1859–1947) Viewed hypnotism as a psychological phenomenon rather than a physical or anatomical one.

Kraepelin, Emil (1856–1926) Published a list of categories of mental illness in 1896. Until recent times, many clinicians used this list in diagnosis.

Leibniz, Gottfried Wilhelm von (1646–1716) Was among the first philosophers to suggest that perception occurred on a continuum ranging from unconscious perceptions (petites perceptions) to conscious perceptions (apperception).

Liébeault, Auguste Ambroise (1823–1904) Founder of the Nancy School of Hypnotism.

Medical model of mental illness The assumption that mental illness results from such biological causes as brain damage, impaired neural transmission, or biochemical abnormalities.

Mesmer, Franz Anton (1734–1815) Used what he thought were his strong magnetic powers to redistribute the magnetic fields of his patients, thus curing them of their ailments.

Nancy School A group of physicians who believed that since all humans were suggestible, all humans could be hypnotized.

Nietzsche, Friedrich (1844–1900) Believed that it was best to give full expression to the irrational aspects of human nature.

Paracelsus, Philippus (1493–1541) Argued that hysteria had a sexual origin and that mania was caused by certain substances entering the brain. Paracelsus was the first physician after Agrippa to argue against labeling people as witches.

Petites perception According to Leibniz, perception that occurs below the level of awareness.

Pinel, Philippe (1745–1826) The first, in modern times, to view the mentally ill as sick people rather than criminals, beasts, or possessed individuals. In the asylums of which he was in charge, Pinel ordered that patients be unchained and treated with kindness in a peaceful atmosphere. Pinel was also responsible for many innovations in the treatment and understanding of the mentally ill.

Plater, Felix (1536–1614) Viewed abnormal behavior as a natural phenomenon. Plater was among the first to delineate several different kinds of mental disorders.

Post-hypnotic amnesia The tendency for a person to forget what happened to him or her while under hypnosis.

Post-hypnotic suggestion A suggestion that a person receives while under hypnosis and acts upon when he or she is again in the waking state.

Psychological model of mental illness The assumption that mental illness results from such psychological causes as conflict, anxiety, faulty beliefs, frustration, or traumatic experience.

Puységur, Marquis de (1751–1825) Found that placing patients in a sleeplike trance was as effective in alleviating ailments as was Mesmer's approach, which necessitated a crisis.

Rush, Benjamin (1745–1813) Often called the first American psychiatrist. Rush advocated the humane treatment of the mentally ill but still clung to some earlier treatments such as bloodletting, tranquilizing, and the use of rotating chairs.

Schopenhauer, Arthur (1788–1860) Believed that humans were controlled mainly by irrational, instinctive forces that they shared with lower animals. According to Schopenhauer, it was best to sublimate, repress, or deny these forces.

Scot, Reginald (1538–1599) Argued that witches were actually mentally disturbed individuals.

Sympathetic magic The belief that by influencing things that are similar to a person or that were once close to that person, one can influence the person. (See also **homeopathic magic** and **contagious magic**.)

Trephination The primitive technique of chipping or drilling holes in a person's skull, presumably to allow evil spirits to escape.

Tuke, William (1732–1822) Founded the York Retreat in Britain. The retreat resembled a farm, and patients there were treated with respect and received good food, medical treatment, recreation, and religious instruction.

Weyer, Johann (1515–1588) Claimed that people labeled as witches were actually mentally disturbed.

CHAPTER 16

Psychoanalysis

SIGMUND FREUD

Sigmund Freud was born May 6, 1856, in Friburg, Moravia (now Pribor, Czechoslovakia). His father, Jakob, was a wool merchant who had ten children. Jakob had already been married twice when he married Amalie Nathansohn, who was 20 years his junior. Since Sigmund was Amalie's first child, he always received special treatment from her. Amalie eventually had five daughters and another son. She lived until 1931, when at the age of 95 she died, only eight years before her son Sigmund.

When Jakob's business failed, the Freuds moved first to Leipzig and then, when Sigmund was 4, to Vienna. From early on Sigmund showed great intellectual ability, and in order to aid his studies, he was the only one in the large household to have an oil lamp and a room of his own. His mother would often serve him his meals in his room, and a piano was taken away from one of his sisters because the music bothered him. Sigmund began reading Shakespeare when he was eight, and while still a young child he taught himself Spanish. Later he added Latin, Greek, Hebrew, Italian, French, and English to his repertoire. Freud always felt that being the indisputable favorite child of his young mother had much to do with his success. Because his mother felt that he was special, he believed that he was special; and therefore much of what he accomplished was due, he felt, to a kind of self-fulfilling prophecy. As Bruno (1972) says:

[Freud] was born with a shock of thick black hair which is supposed to be the sign of the birth of a prophet or sage among the Jewish people. At least Freud's mother was convinced of this, and she sewed him a long "hero's gown" to wear as an infant. Freud's ultimate fame may be an example of what has been called the "self-fulfilling prophecy." A prophecy is made, and then actions are taken to make the prophecy come true. The very making of the prophecy sets the wheels in motion for its ultimate verification. Freud's mother was always convinced that he would be a great man and arranged his childhood, adolescence, and young manhood in such a way that he was encouraged in this direction. He wrote in his own autobiography that his mother's faith in him had much to do with his ultimate success. (pp. 159–160)

Until his final year of high school, Freud was attracted to a career in law or politics, but reading an essay by Goethe aroused his interest in science, and he decided to enroll in the medical school at the University of Vienna. He also made this decision partly because, in anti-Semitic Vienna, medicine and law were the only professions open to Jews. Although Freud enrolled in medical school in 1873, it took him eight years to complete the program; because he had such wide interests, he was often diverted from his medical studies. For example, Franz Brentano caused him to become interested in philosophy, and Freud even helped Brentano translate one of John Stuart Mill's books into German.

According to Freud's own account, the person who influenced him more than anyone else was *Ernst Brücke* (1819–1892). Along with some

Sigmund Freud

Brücke caused Freud to change his career plans and seek a career in medical practice. To help prepare himself, Freud went to study with *Theodor Meynert* (1833–1893), one of the best-known brain anatomists at the time, and Freud soon became a recognized expert at diagnosing various kinds of brain damage.

Many important things happened in Freud's life about this time. In addition to making the decision to practice medicine, Freud was making a name for himself as a neuroanatomist, he had just befriended Joseph Breuer (who, as we shall see, introduced Freud to many of the phenomena that would occupy Freud's attention for the next 50 years), and he had been given the opportunity to visit Charcot in Paris. Freud also just missed becoming internationally famous for reporting the anesthetizing effects of cocaine. In 1884 he began experimenting with cocaine. He took it himself and gave it to his fiancée, his sisters, and various other friends. Feeling that he had discovered an antidepressant that could be widely used in medicine, Freud also noticed that the drug had an anesthetizing action that might be useful during operations. As Freud was making these observations, *Karl Koller* (1857–1944) demonstrated the usefulness of cocaine during eye surgery, and was justifiably given credit for the discovery. Freud was criticized for recommending cocaine as an antidepressant, and he gave up doing so.

of his friends, such as Helmholtz, Brücke founded the mechanist movement in physiology. In Brücke's laboratory Freud studied the reproductive system of male eels and also wrote a number of influential articles on anatomy and neurology. Freud obtained his medical degree in 1881 and continued to work in Brücke's laboratory. Even though doing physiological research was Freud's main interest, he realized that jobs in that area were scarce, low-paying, and generally not available to Jews. Freud's financial concerns became even more acute in 1882, when he became engaged to Martha Bernays. Circumstances and advice from

Joseph Breuer and the case of Anna O. Shortly before Freud obtained his medical degree, he developed a friendship with **Joseph Breuer** (1842–1925), who was another one of Brücke's former students. What Freud learned from Breuer concerning the treatment of a woman referred to as Fräulein Anna O essentially launched psychoanalysis. Because Breuer started treating Anna O in 1880, while Freud was still a medical student, Freud gives Breuer the credit for creating psychoanalysis (1910):

> Granted that it is a merit to have created psychoanalysis, it is not my merit. I was a student,

busy with the passing of my last examinations, when another physician of Vienna, Dr. Joseph Breuer, made the first application of . . . [hypnosis] . . . to the case of an hysterical girl. (pp. 1880–1882)

Fraulein Anna O was a 21-year-old woman who had a variety of symptoms associated with hysteria. At one time or another she had experienced paralysis of the arms or legs, disturbances of sight or speech, nausea, memory loss, and general mental disorientation. Breuer would hypnotize the young woman and then ask her to recall the circumstances under which she had first experienced a particular symptom. For example, one of her symptoms was the perpetual squinting of her eyes. Through hypnosis, Breuer discovered that she had been required to keep a vigil by the bedside of her ill father. The woman's deep concern for her father had brought tears to her eyes, so that when the weak man asked her what time it was, she had to squint in order to see the hands of the clock.

Breuer discovered that each time he traced a symptom to its origin, which was usually some traumatic experience, the symptom disappeared. One by one Anna O's symptoms were relieved in this way. It was as if certain emotionally laden ideas could not be expressed directly but manifested themselves in physical symptoms instead. When such **pathogenic ideas** (ideas that produce physical symptoms) were allowed conscious expression, their energy dissipated, and the symptoms they gave rise to disappeared. Since relief followed the emotional release, which in turn followed the expression of a pathogenic idea, the treatment was called the **cathartic method** (a catharsis is an emotional release). Anna O called the method the "talking cure" or "chimney sweeping." In Breuer's approach, the catharsis occurred during an hypnotic trance.

For more than a year, Breuer saw Anna O for several hours a day. Soon Anna began responding to Breuer as if he were her father, a process later called **transference**. All of the emotions Anna had once expressed toward her father, both positive and negative, she now expressed toward Breuer. Breuer also began developing emotional feelings toward Anna, a process later called **countertransference**. Because his wife became jealous, Breuer decided to give up Anna's treatment. A few hours after Breuer told Anna that he had terminated treatment, Anna developed an hysterical pregnancy, which Breuer agreed to treat with hypnosis. That was the last time Breuer treated her. Afterwards, he and his wife went to Venice on a second honeymoon, and Breuer never treated another hysterical patient.

The story of Anna O usually ends with the revelation that Anna's real name was Bertha Pappenheim and that Breuer's treatment must have been effective, since the woman went on to become a prominent social worker in Germany. Ellenberger (1972), however, has discovered that Anna O had to be institutionalized after Breuer terminated her treatment. In any case, Bertha Pappenheim eventually went on to become a leader in the European feminist movement, a playwright, an author of children's stories, a founder of several schools and clubs for the poor, illegitimate, or wayward young women, and an effective spokesperson against white slavery and abortion. When she died in 1936, tributes came in from throughout Europe, including one from Martin Buber, the famous philosopher and educator. In 1954 the German government issued a stamp in her honor, part of a series paying tribute to "helpers of humanity." How much of Pappenheim's ultimate success can be attributed to Breuer's treatment is still being debated. For 14 interpretations of the case of Anna O, see Rosenbaum and Muroff (1984). In 1895 Freud and Breuer published *Studies on Hysteria*, which contained the case of Anna O. Thus 1895 is taken as the date of the official founding of the school of psychoanalysis.

Freud's visit with Charcot. Because Freud had done so well while studying with Theodor Meynert and because of the reputation he was gaining as a neurophysiologist, in 1885 he was given a small grant to study with Charcot in Paris. Until this visit, although Freud was aware of Breuer's work with Anna O, he remained a mechanistic physiologist; he sought to explain all disorders, including hysteria, in terms of physiology. Like most physicians at the time, Freud saw psychological explanations as nonscientific. As we saw in the last chapter, Charcot also attempted to explain hysteria in terms of neurophysiology and inheritance, but at least Charcot took hysteria seriously—something that set him apart from most of his colleagues. Furthermore, Charcot insisted that hysteria occurred in males as well as females. This contention caused a stir, since from the time of the Greeks it had been assumed that hysteria was caused by a disturbance of the uterus (*hystera* being the Greek word for "uterus").

Freud learned several things from the illustrious Charcot. First, he learned that hysteria was to be taken seriously, something he had already suspected because of Breuer's treatment of Anna O. Second, he learned that both males and females could suffer from hysteria. Third, he overheard Charcot say about hysteria, "But in this kind of case it is always something genital—always, always, always" (reported in Boring, 1957, p. 709). Though Charcot denied making the statement, Freud nonetheless claimed that Charcot had suggested to him the relationship between sexual factors and hysteria. Fourth, all of his life Freud relished Charcot's attitude toward theory. Charcot trusted empirical observation and what actually worked much more than he trusted theory. (Charcot's statement "Theory is fine, but it does not prevent things from existing" is reported in *The Standard Edition of the Complete Psychological Works of Sigmund Freud*, Vol. 3, p. 12.) Freud shared this view to the extent that he revised his theory whenever it conflicted with observation or when important new observations were made. The fifth important thing that Freud learned from Charcot was that one could go

against the established medical community if one had enough prestige. Freud, as we shall see, went contrary to the medical community, but because he did not have the prestige that Charcot had, he paid the price.

Freud returned to Vienna and to his association with Breuer. He used hypnosis in his practice, but he found that very often when a symptom was removed during an hypnotic trance, it would recur later; also, Freud was unable to hypnotize some of his patients. In 1889 he visited Liébeault and Bernheim at the Nancy School in hopes of improving his hypnotic skills. From Liébeault and Bernheim Freud learned about posthypnotic suggestion, observing that an idea planted during hypnosis could influence a person's behavior even when the person was unaware of it. This observation—that intact ideas of which a person was unaware could play an important role in that person's behavior—was to become an extremely important part of psychoanalysis.

The birth of free association. Early in his practice, Freud used all of the traditional methods in treating his patients—including electrotherapy, which involved applying an electric shock to the affected part of the body. Next he tried hypnosis, but found its benefits temporary; and, as we have seen, he could not hypnotize some of his patients. Freud was seeking an alternative to hypnosis when he remembered that, while at the Nancy School, he had observed that the hypnotist would bring back the memory of what had happened during hypnosis by putting his hand on the patient's forehead and saying, "Now you can remember." With this in mind, Freud tried having his patients lie on a couch with their eyes closed but not hypnotized. He would ask the patients to recall the first time they had experienced a particular symptom, and the patients would begin to recollect various experiences but would usually stop short of the goal. In other words, as they approached the recollection of a traumatic experience, they would display **resistance**. At this point, Freud would place his hand on the patient's forehead and declare that additional information was forthcoming, and in many cases it was. Freud found that this **pressure technique** was as effective as hypnosis, and soon he learned that he did not even need to touch his patients; simply encouraging them to speak freely about whatever came to their minds worked just as well. Thus was the method of **free association** born.

With free association, there were still the problems of resistance, transference, and countertransference, but there was the major advantage that the patient was conscious of what was going on. With hypnotism, the patient was unconscious, and therefore whatever information was brought to light during therapy was lost when the patient was aroused from his or her hypnotic trance. With free association, it was often more difficult to arrive at the original traumatic experience, but once it was arrived at, it was available for the patient to deal with in a rational manner. For Freud, the overcoming of resistance and the rational pondering of early traumatic experience were the goals of psychotherapy. This is why he said that true psychoanalysis started only when hypnosis had been discarded (Heidbreder, 1933, p. 379).

Studies on Hysteria. In ***Studies on Hysteria*** (1885), which Freud coauthored with Breuer, the authors put forth a number of the basic tenets of psychoanalysis. They noted that hysteria was caused by traumatic experience that was not allowed adequate expression and therefore manifested itself in physical symptoms. Therefore, symptoms could be taken as *symbolic representations* of underlying traumatic experience that was no longer consciously available to the patient. Because such experience was traumatic, it was *repressed*—that is, actively held in the unconscious, since to ponder it would provoke anxiety. Resistance, then, was a sign that the therapist was on the right track. Also **repression** often resulted from **conflict**, the ten-

dency both to approach and to avoid something considered wrong.

The fundamental point was that repressed experiences or conflicts *did not go away*. Rather, they went on exerting a powerful influence on a person's personality. The only way to deal with repressed material properly was to make it conscious and thereby deal with it rationally. For Freud, the most effective way of making repressed material conscious was through free association. By carefully analyzing the content of the free associations, gestures, and transference, the analyst could determine the nature of the repressed experience and help the patient become aware of it and deal with it. Thus, in *Studies on Hysteria*, Freud clearly outlined his belief in the importance of **unconscious motivation**. Freud and Breuer wrote separate conclusions to the book, and Freud's emphasized the role of sex in unconscious motivation. At the time, Freud contended that a person with a normal sex life could not become neurotic. Breuer disagreed, and the two men parted company. *Studies on Hysteria* was poorly received, and it took 13 years to sell 626 copies, for which each author received about $170 (Watson, p. 499).

Shortly after writing *Studies on Hysteria*, Freud wrote *Project for a Scientific Psychology*, which was published posthumously. In it, Freud attempted to account for both hysterical symptoms and normal behavior in completely physiological terms. He sought to explain psychological phenomena within the materialistic, elementistic framework in which he had been trained. Since Freud was not satisfied with the results of these efforts, he decided to abandon his neurophysiological explanations in favor of psychological explanations.

The seduction theory. In 1886, Freud delivered a paper to the Psychiatric and Neurological Society in Vienna. The paper related the fact that almost without exception, Freud's hysteric patients eventually related a childhood incident in which they had been sexually attacked, usually by a close relative. Freud concluded that such an attack was the basis of all hysteria. As a result of the paper, the medical community laughed at, ridiculed, and in general ostracized Freud.

Soon after presenting the paper, Freud realized that he had made a mistake. In most cases, he concluded, the seduction had not really taken place. Rather, the patients had *imagined* the encounter. But the question remained: Why did the fantasies take a sexual form, and why were they repressed? Freud decided that the imagined incidents were very real to his patients, and therefore just as traumatic as if they had actually occurred. His original belief remained intact: the basis of neuroses was the repression of sexual thoughts, whether the thoughts were based on real or imagined experience.

Some now feel that Freud's original **seduction theory** was correct, and that Freud knew it was correct. One reason for this belief is the current evidence indicating that incest is much more prevalent than was previously believed. Another reason is that recently uncovered documents indicate that Freud may have been attempting to protect his own father. Freud had discovered signs of hysteria in his own brother and sisters, and this would have cast suspicion on his father as a possible seducer. (For an excellent analysis of Freud's seduction theory, and why he may have revised it, see "Finding the Hidden Freud," in *Newsweek*, November 30, 1981).

Freud's Self-Analysis

Freud soon realized that in order to be an effective analyst, he would have to be psychoanalyzed himself. (Later in *The Problem of Lay-Analysis* (1927), Freud insisted that in order to be a qualified psychoanalyst, one need not be a medical doctor, but one needed to be psychoanalyzed. And in addition to being psycho-analyzed, one needed at least two years of supervised practice as a psychoanalyst.) Since no one was available to psychoanalyze Freud, he took on the job himself. In addition to a variety of insecurities, a major motivation for Freud's self-analysis was his reaction to the death of his father in the fall of 1896. Although his father had been very ill and his death was no surprise, Freud found that his father's death affected him especially deeply. For months following the death, Freud experienced severe depression and was unable to work. His reaction was so acute that he decided he had to regard himself as a patient.

Analysis of dreams. Clearly, Freud could not use free association on himself, so he needed another vehicle for his self-analysis. Then Freud made the astonishing discovery that the content of dreams could be viewed in much the same way as hysterical symptoms. That is, both dreams and hysterical symptoms could be seen as symbolic manifestations of repressed traumatic thoughts. If one properly analyzed the symbols of either dreams or hysterical symptoms, one could get at the roots of the problem. **Dream analysis**, then, became a second way of tapping the unconscious mind, and one that was suitable for Freud's self-analysis. Freud even referred to dreams as "the royal road to the unconscious." Freud's self-analysis culminated in what he, and others, considered to be his most important work, *The Interpretation of Dreams* (1900).

Like the physical symptoms of hysteria, dreams required knowledgeable interpretation. During sleep, a person's defenses were down but not eliminated, so a repressed experience reached consciousness only in *disguised* form. Therefore, there was a major difference between what a dream appeared to be about and what it really was about. What a dream appeared to be about was its **manifest content**, and what it really was about was its **latent content**. Freud concluded that every dream was a

wish fulfillment. That is, it was a symbolic expression of a wish that the dreamer could not express or satisfy directly without experiencing anxiety. Wishes expressed in symbolic form during sleep were disguised enough to allow the dreamer to continue sleeping, since a direct expression of the wish involved would produce too much anxiety and disrupt sleep.

According to Freud, dream interpretation was complex business, and only someone well versed in psychoanalytic theory could accomplish the task. One had to understand the **dream work** that disguised the wish actually being expressed in the dream. Dream work included **condensation**, in which one element of a dream symbolized several things in waking life, such as when a family dog symbolized an entire family; and **displacement**, in which instead of dreaming about an anxiety-producing object or event, the dreamer dreamt of something symbolically close to it, such as when one dreamt of a cave instead of a vagina.

Freud felt that the most important dream symbols came from a person's own experience, but that universal dream symbols meant more or less the same thing in everyone's dreams. For example, travel symbolized death; falling symbolized giving in to sexual temptation; boxes, gardens, doors, or balconies symbolized the vagina; and cannons, snakes, trees, swords, church spires, and candles symbolized the penis.

After Freud used dream interpretation to analyze himself, the procedure became an integral part of psychoanalysis. Freud asked his patients to report, and free associate to, any dreams that they had.

The Oedipus complex. One of the major outcomes of Freud's self-analysis was his discovery of the Oedipus (or Oedipal) complex. Remember, one of Freud's major motives for engaging in his self-analysis was his severe reaction to his father's death. Freud's discovery came when he analyzed one of his own recurring dreams that he had first had during childhood. In the dream, Freud's mother was in a sleeping, peaceful posture, and two or more people with birds' beaks on their faces were carrying her into a room. After carrying his mother into the room, the birdlike people placed her on a bed.

Freud free associated to this dream and discovered that the birdlike people symbolized death, because they were like the Egyptian funeral gods he had seen in the family Bible. The expression on his mother's face in the dream was uncharacteristic of her, but very much like the expression Freud had observed on his grandfather's face just before he had died. The figure being carried into the room, then, was a condensed figure symbolizing both Freud's mother and his grandfather. Further free association forced Freud to conclude that the dying grandfather symbolized a dying father, and that secretly he wished his father to be dead. Freud then realized that although he consciously experienced love toward his father, unconsciously he had been hostile toward him since early childhood. Still further free association revealed that the dream was also sexual in nature. One of the things that led Freud to this conclusion was that in German the word for sexual intercourse and the word for bird were very similar. The birdlike people, then, were also a condensed symbol, representing both death and sex. What was the object of this sexual wish that the dream symbolized? Freud concluded that because his mother had been his greatest source of sensual pleasure when he had first had the dream, she was the object of his sexual desire. He called this hostility toward his father and desire for the mother the **Oedipus complex** because in the Greek play, *Oedipus Rex*, Oedipus unknowingly killed his father and married his mother.

Since all male children had a close physical relationship with their mothers (the mother bathed, stroked, nursed, and hugged them), Freud felt that it was natural for male children to have a sexual desire for their mothers. It is important to note, however, that Freud used the term *sexual* in a very general way. A better translation might be "pleasurable" rather than "sexual." For Freud, anything pleasurable was roughly what he meant by "sexual." Heidbreder (1933) nicely summarizes the Freudian use of the word *sex*:

> Freud used the word "sex" in a very general sense. He includes in it not only the specifically sexual interests and activities, but the whole love life—it might almost be said, the whole pleasure life—of human beings. The list of activities that he and his followers have seen as having a sexual significance is almost inexhaustible; but its range and variety may be indicated by the fact that it includes such simple practices as walking, smoking, and bathing, and such complex activities as artistic creation, religious ceremonial, social and political institutions, and even the development of civilization itself. (p. 389)

Since the male child had this intense desire for the mother, he was automatically in competition with the father, who also desired the mother. The reality of the situation (for example, the father being much more powerful than the child) caused the child to repress his amorous desires for the mother and his hostility toward the father. According to Freud, however, repressed ideas did not go away; they continued to manifest themselves in dreams, symptoms, or unusual behavior. For example, it was now clear to Freud that his overreaction to his father's death had been at least partially motivated by the guilt he felt from wishing his father would die.

Freud felt that the Oedipus conflict was universal among male children, and that its remnants in adult life explained much normal and abnormal behavior. One bit of "normal" behavior it explained was that males often married women who were very similar to their mothers. We will discuss what happens to female children at this time of life later in this chapter, when we discuss the psychosexual stages of development.

Now Freud had the vehicle he needed for explaining the seduction fantasies he had observed in so many of his patients. He now saw such fantasies as representing repressed desires to possess the parent of the opposite sex and to eliminate the same-sex parent. Such desires, Freud concluded, were as natural and universal as the need to repress them, and so *infantile sexuality* became an important ingredient in his general theory of unconscious motivation. Attributing sexual desires to children, and claiming that such desires were natural, ran contrary to the Victorian morality of Freud's time, and therefore he was further alienated from the medical establishment.

The Id, the Ego, and the Superego

Early in his theorizing, Freud differentiated among the conscious, the preconscious, and the unconscious. Consciousness consisted of those things we were aware of at any given moment. The **preconscious** consisted of the things we were not aware of but could easily become aware of. For example, memorized phone numbers, friend's names and addresses, and other nontraumatic memories, although typically not in consciousness at any given moment, can easily be conjured up if needed. The unconscious consisted of those memories that were being actively repressed from consciousness, and were therefore made conscious only with great effort. Later Freud summarized and expanded these views with his concepts of the id, the ego, and the superego.

The id. The **id** is the driving force of the personality. It contains all of the **instincts** (although better translations of the word Freud used would be "drives" or "forces"), such as hunger, thirst, and sex. The id is entirely unconscious and is governed by the **pleasure principle**. When a need arises, the id wants immediate gratification of that need. The collective energy associated with the instincts is called **libido**, and libidinal energy accounts for most human behavior.

Associated with every instinct are a *source*, which is a bodily need of some kind; an *aim* of satisfying the need; an *object*, which is anything capable of satisfying the need; and an *impetus*, a driving force whose strength is determined by the magnitude of the need.

The id has only two means of satisfying a need. One is **reflex action**, which is automatically triggered when certain discomforts arise. Sneezing and recoiling from a painful stimulus are examples of reflex actions. The second means of satisfaction available to the id is **wish fulfillment**, in which the id conjures up an image of an object that will satisfy an existing need. But since the id never comes directly into contact with the environment, where do these images come from? Hall (1954) describes Freud's answer:

> Freud speaks of the id as being the true psychic reality. By this he means the id is the primary subjective reality, the inner world that exists before the individual has had experience of the external world. Not only are the instincts and reflexes inborn, but the images that are produced by tension states may also be innate. This means that a hungry baby can have an image of food without having to learn to associate food with hunger. Freud believed that experiences that are repeated with great frequency and intensity in many individuals of successive generations become permanent deposits in the id. (pp. 26–27)

Freud, then, accepted Lamarck's theory of acquired characteristics when explaining how the id was capable of conjuring up images of things in the external world that were capable of satisfying needs.

Because the activities in the id occur independently of personal experience, and because they provide the foundation of the entire personality, Freud referred to them as **primary processes**. The primary processes are irrational, since they are directly determined by a person's need state, they tolerate *no* time lapse

between the onset of a need and its satisfaction, and they exist entirely on the unconscious level. Furthermore, the primary processes can, at best, furnish only temporary satisfaction of a need. For example, thinking about a hamburger is clearly not the same thing as actually eating one; therefore, another aspect of the personality is necessary if the person is to survive.

The ego. The **ego** is aware of *both* the needs of the id and the physical world, and its major job is to coordinate the two. In other words, the ego's job is to match the wishes (images) of the id with their counterparts in the physical environment. For this reason it is said that the ego operates in the service of the id. The ego is also said to be governed by the **reality principle**, since the objects it provides must result in *real* rather than imaginary satisfaction of a need.

When the ego finds an environmental object that will satisfy a need, it invests libidinal energy into the object, thus creating a **cathexis** between the need and the object. A cathexis is an association between a need and something that will satisfy that need. The realistic activities of the ego are called **secondary processes**, and they contrast with the unrealistic primary processes of the id.

If the id and the ego were the only two components of the personality, humans could hardly be distinguished from other animals. Needs would arise, and the ego would seek things in the environment that would satisfy those needs. When there were no needs, humans would be completely inactive. There is, however, a third component of the personality that vastly complicates matters.

The superego. Although the newborn child is completely dominated by its id, it must soon learn that gratification of its needs usually cannot be immediate. More importantly, it must learn that some things are "right" and some things are "wrong." For example, if a child is a member of a family that practices a particular religion, it must learn that certain foods can be eaten and others cannot. It must learn that its parents will tolerate only a certain level of aggression. It often learns that certain words are "bad." It must learn that certain sexual activities are "bad," and therefore must be avoided. For example, the male child must inhibit his sexual desires for his mother and his aggressive tendencies toward his father. Teaching these do's and don'ts is usually what is meant by socializing the child.

As the child internalizes these do's and don'ts it develops a **superego**, which is the moral arm of the personality. When the superego is fully developed, it has two divisions. The **conscience** consists of the internalized experiences for which the child has been consistently punished. Engaging in, or even thinking about engaging in, activities for which he or she has been consistently punished now makes the child feel guilty. The **ego-ideal** consists of the internalized experiences for which the child has been rewarded. Engaging in, or even thinking about engaging in, activities for which he or she has been consistently rewarded makes the child feel good about himself or herself. During the formation of the superego, the seeds of neuroses are planted. Moreover, Freud felt that the widespread practice of punishing children for sexual activity was what made sexual repression such a prominent cause of neuroses. According to Marx and Hillix (1963):

> The early experiences that are most likely to be punished, and hence repressed, involve sex. Therefore, the significant material that will be recovered will concern sex. Even more specifically, we can say that the Oedipal conflict and its resolution will be central to the analysis, and insight into it by the patient central to his recovery. (p. 213)

Freud attributed acquired characteristics to the superego, just as he did to the id, again revealing a Lamarckian tendency. As we have seen, Freud believed that objects associated with need satisfaction through the eons became available to the id as images. Freud also believed that morality was at least in part inherited from cumulative human experience. For example, he believed that modern humans still harbored the guilt a primitive group of brothers had felt when they killed their father. Freud felt that this guilt and the human reaction to it could be found throughout human history. But though Freud believed that the superego had archaic rudiments, he stressed the role of personal experience with reward and punishment in its development.

Once the superego is developed, the child's behavior and thoughts are governed by internalized values, usually those of the parents, and the child is said to be socialized. Feelings of guilt or pride keep the child acting in accordance with the values of society even when authority figures (for example, the parents) are not present.

At this point the job of the ego becomes much more complex. The ego must not only find objects or events that satisfy the needs of the id, but these objects or events must be sanctioned by the superego. In some cases, a cathexis that would be acceptable to the id and ego would cause guilt, and therefore, libidinal energy would be diverted to inhibit the cathexis. The diversion of libidinal energy in an effort to inhibit an association between a need and an object or event is called an **anticathexis**. In such cases, the superego inhibits the association to avoid the feelings of guilt, and the ego inhibits it to postpone need satisfaction until an acceptable object or event can be found. Anticathexis causes a **displacement** from a guilt- or anxiety-producing object or event to one that does not cause anxiety or guilt. In general, displacement involves the substitution of one object or event for another. Figure 16.1 shows an example of displacement where a sexual need is involved. The assumption is that in the adult human the natural cathexis for such a need is sexual intercourse.

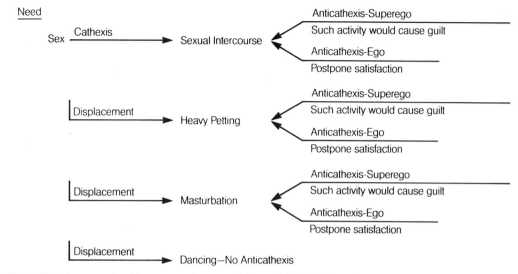

FIGURE 16.1 An example of how an anxiety-provoking activity is displaced by an activity that does not cause anxiety. (Hergenhahn, 1984, p. 22. Used by permission.)

The life and death instincts. In his book *Beyond the Pleasure Principle* (1920), Freud said that the goal of all instincts was to return to the state of minimal tension that existed when they were satisfied. One of life's major goals, then, was to seek a state of no or low tension. Freud called this longing the **life instinct**. He carried his argument a step further by saying that the ultimate condition of nontension was death. Life, he said, started from inorganic matter, and part of us longs to return to that state; therefore, "The goal of all life is death." Freud referred to this longing as the **death instinct**.

So to all the other conflicts that occurred among the id, ego, and superego, Freud added a life-and-death struggle. He called the energy associated with the instincts that preserved life **eros**, and the energy associated with the death instincts **thanatos**. When directed toward one's self, the death instincts manifested themselves as suicide or masochism; when directed outwardly, they manifested themselves in hatred, murder, and general aggression. Freud concluded that aggression was a natural component of human nature and that repressed aggressive

urges became part of the id, just as repressed sexual urges did.

No wonder the ego was referred to as the executive of the personality. One of its jobs was to satisfy the needs of the id in ways that would not alienate the superego. Another job was to minimize the anxiety that arose when one acted contrary to one's internalized values. To combat such anxiety, the ego could employ the ego defense mechanisms.

Anxiety and the Ego Defense Mechanisms

Anxiety. Anxiety is a warning of impending danger, and Freud distinguished three kinds. *Objective anxiety* arises when there is an objective threat to the person's well-being. For example, being physically attacked by another person or an animal would cause objective anxiety. Since the source of this kind of anxiety can be clearly identified, this anxiety is similar to what we call fear. With both feelings, one can usually identify the object causing the feeling. *Neurotic anxiety* arises when the ego feels that it is going to be overwhelmed by the id—in other words, when the needs of the id become so powerful that the ego feels that it will be unable to control them, and that the irrationality of the id will manifest itself in the person's thought and behavior. *Moral anxiety* arises when an internalized value is, or is about to be, violated. Moral anxiety is about the same as shame or guilt. It is the self-punishment that we experience when we act contrary to the values internalized in the super-ego.

Any form of anxiety is extremely uncomfortable, and the individual experiencing it seeks its reduction or elimination, just as one would seek to reduce hunger, thirst, or pain. It is the ego's job to deal with anxiety. To reduce objective anxiety, the ego must deal effectively with the physical environment. To deal with neurotic and moral anxiety, it must use processes that Freud called the **ego defense mechanisms**. Freud believed that all the ego defense mechanisms had two things in common: (1) they all distorted reality, and (2) they operated on the unconscious level—that is, a person was unaware of the fact that he or she was using one. Next we will review a few of the commonly used ego defense mechanisms.

Repression. **Repression** is the fundamental defense mechanism because it is involved in all of the others. Repression occurs when an anxiety-provoking thought is actively held in the unconscious mind. Repressed ideas are constantly seeking conscious expression, and the ego must actively hold them back. Such ideas enter consciousness only when they are disguised enough so as not to cause anxiety. Modified repressed ideas show up in dreams, in symptoms, during free association, and—as we shall see later in this chapter—in many ways in everyday life. So important is repression that Freud said, "The theory of repression is the main pillar upon which rests the edifice of psychoanalysis" (1917, p. 9).

Displacement. Because it is found everywhere in psychoanalytic theory, **displacement** is another very important defense mechanism. In general, displacement involves replacing a goal that provokes anxiety with one that does not. Examples include dancing instead of more direct sexual behavior, aggressing toward a playmate instead of toward one's father, dreaming of grapefruit instead of breasts, and buying an adult, sexually oriented magazine instead of asking a woman out for a date. The ego can accomplish the free substitution of one object for another because the id is entirely unconscious, and can therefore be "fooled" by anything that is symbolically close to the truly desired goal or object.

Sublimation. When a displacement involves substituting a nonsexual goal for a sexual one, the process is called **sublimation**. Freud considered sublimation to be the basis of civilization. Since we cannot express our sexual urges directly, we are forced to express them indirectly in the form of poetry, art, religion, football, baseball, politics, education, and everything else that characterizes civilization. Thus, Freud viewed civilization as a compromise. For civilization to exist, humans must inhibit direct satisfaction of their basic urges. Freud believed that humans were animals that were frustrated by the very civilization that they had created to protect themselves from themselves. One of Freud's later books, *Civilization and Its Discontents* (1930), elaborates on this theme.

Projection. One way to deal with an anxiety-provoking thought is to attribute it to someone or something other than one's self. For example, one sees a strong sexual urge in others rather than in one's self, or attributes failing a test to an ambiguous book, test, or teacher rather than to one's own lack of intelligence or preparation. Such a process is called **projection**. One sees the causes of failure, undesirable urges, and secret desires as "out there" instead of in the self, because seeing them as part of one's self would cause anxiety.

Identification. When one feels frustrated and anxious because one has not lived up to some internalized value, one can symbolically borrow someone else's success. Thus, if one dresses like, behaves like, or talks like a person considered successful, some of that person's success becomes one's own. **Identification** can take many forms. For example, it can manifest itself in one's choice of friends, in a record collection, in wearing a shirt or jacket with a school, company, or team name on it, in a hair style, or in one's personal library.

Rationalization. **Rationalization** involves giving a rational, logical, but false reason for a failure or shortcoming rather than the true reason for it. Alarms not going off, sickness, cars not starting, accidents, and faulty memory can all serve as excuses for missing a test—and they all make sense—but the true reason may have been the dread of failure. Freud would have said that the person may have caused these events unconsciously in order to escape taking a test and thereby possibly experiencing failure. Anytime someone gives a sensible but false reason for his or her behavior instead of the real reason, rationalization is exemplified; and according to Freud, most people's lives do not lack examples of it.

Reaction formation. Sometimes when people have a desire to do something, but doing it would cause anxiety, they do the opposite of what they really want to do. This is what is known as a **reaction formation**. Thus, the male with strong homosexual tendencies becomes a Don Juan type, the mother who hates her child becomes overindulgent, the person with strong communist leanings becomes a super patriot, or the person with strong sexual urges becomes a

preacher concerned with pornography, promiscuity, and the sinfulness of today's youth.

Everyone uses ego defense mechanisms. The difference between the normal and the abnormal person is not the use of the defense mechanisms, but the frequency or intensity of their use. One of Freud's many great contributions to psychology was his insistence that the line between the "normal" person and the "neurotic" was a very thin one. In fact, Freud would say that we are all neurotic but that some of us are more so than others.

The Psychosexual Stages of Development

While Freud considered the entire body to be a source of sexual pleasure, he believed that this pleasure was concentrated on different parts of the body at different stages of development. At any stage, the area of the body on which sexual pleasure was concentrated was called the **erogenous zone**. The erogenous zones gave the stages of development their respective names. According to Freud, the experiences that a child had during each stage would determine, to a large extent, his or her adult personality. For this reason, Freud felt that the foundations for one's adult personality were formed by the time a child was about five years old.

The oral stage. The **oral stage** lasts through about the first year of life, and the erogenous zone is the mouth. Pleasure comes mainly through the lips, tongue, and such activities as sucking and swallowing. If either *overgratification* or *undergratification* (frustration) of the oral needs causes a **fixation** to occur at this level of development, as an adult the child will be an **oral character**. Fixation during the early part of the oral stage results in an *oral-incorporative character*. Such a person tends to be a good listener and an excessive eater, drinker, kisser, or smoker; he or she also tends to be dependent and gullible. A fixation during the latter part of the oral stage, when teeth begin to appear, results in an *oral-sadistic character*. Such a person is sarcastic, cynical, and generally aggressive. He or she also tends to be ambivalent about things and swings from one extreme to another—for example, from being friendly to being hostile, and from being aggressive to being submissive.

The anal stage. The **anal stage** lasts through about the second year of life, and the erogenous zone is the anus-buttocks region of the body. Fixation during this stage results in an **anal character**. During the first part of the anal stage, pleasure comes mainly from activities such as feces expulsion, and a fixation here results in the adult being an *anal-expulsive character*. Such a person tends to be generous, messy, or wasteful. In the latter part of the anal stage, after toilet training has occurred, pleasure comes from being able to withhold feces. A fixation here results in the person becoming an *anal-retentive character*. Such an adult tends to be a collector and to be stingy, orderly, and perhaps perfectionistic.

The phallic stage. The **phallic stage** lasts from about the beginning of the third year to the end of the fifth year, and the erogenous zone is the genital region of the body. During this stage the Oedipus complex occurs: the male child now has an intense desire for his mother and great hostility toward his father, who is his rival for his mother's love. Because the source of the child's pleasurable feelings toward his mother is his penis, and because he sees his father as much more powerful than himself, the male child begins to experience **castration anxiety**, which causes him to repress his sexual and aggressive tendencies. The male child solves this problem by identifying strongly with the father. This does two things: symbolically becoming his father (through identification) allows the child at least to share the mother, and it removes his

father as a threat and reduces the child's castration anxiety. But repressed desires do not disappear; they persist as powerful forces in the unconscious, and thereby remain a major influence in one's life.

The female child's situation is much different from the male's. She experiences what is called the **Electra complex**. Like the male child, the female starts out with a strong attraction and attachment to the mother. She soon learns, however, that she lacks a penis, and she blames the mother for its absence. She now has both positive and negative feelings toward her mother. At about the same time, she learns that her father possesses the valued organ, which she wants to share with him. This causes a sexual attraction toward the father, but the fact that her father possesses something valuable that she does not possess causes her to experience **penis envy**. Thus, the female child also has ambivalent feelings toward her father. To resolve the Electra complex in a healthy way, the female child must repress her hostility toward her mother and her sexual attraction to her father. Thereafter she "becomes" the mother and shares the father.

The repression and strong identification necessary during this stage result in the full development of the superego. When a child identifies with his or her parent of the same sex, the child introjects that parent's morals, standards, and values. Once these things have been introjected, they control the child for the rest of his or her life. For this reason, the final and complete formation of the superego is said to go hand in hand with the resolution of the Oedipal or Electra complex.

The latency stage. The **latency stage** lasts from about the beginning of the sixth year until puberty. Because of the intense repression required during the phallic stage, during the latency stage sexual activity is all but eliminated from consciousness. This stage is characterized by numerous substitute activities, such as schoolwork and peer activities, and by extensive curiosity about the world.

The genital stage. The **genital stage** lasts from puberty through the remainder of one's life. With the onset of puberty, sexual desires become too intense to repress completely, and they begin to manifest themselves. The focus of attention is now on members of the opposite sex. Early manifestations of sexual desires include "crushes," "puppy love," and some experimentation between the sexes. If everything had gone correctly during the preceding stage, this stage will culminate in dating and eventually marriage.

The under- or overgratifications and fixations that a person experiences (or does not experience) during the psychosexual stages will determine the person's adult personality. If the person has adjustment problems later in life, the psychoanalyst looks into these early experiences for solution to the problems. For the psychoanalyst, childhood experience is the stuff of which neuroses or normality are made. Indeed, psychoanalysts believe that "the child is father to the man" (Freud, 1940, p. 64).

The Psychopathology of Everyday Life

According to Freud, all behavior was motivated; so for him it was legitimate to seek the causes of all behavior, whether it be "normal" or "abnormal." Furthermore, he believed that because the causes of behavior were usually unconscious, people seldom knew why they acted as they did. In the *Psychopathology of Everyday Life* (1901), Freud points out that things like slips of the tongue (now known as Freudian slips), forgetting, losing things, and accidents are often unconsciously motivated. Heidbreder (1933) gives several examples:

Freud is never at a loss to find evidence for his theories in the commonplace incidents we dismiss as insignificant or attribute to chance. Slips of the tongue and slips of the pen, forgotten names and forgotten appointments, lost gifts and mislaid possessions, all point to the role of wish and motive. Such happenings, Freud insists, are by no means accidental. The woman who loses her wedding ring wishes that she had never had it. The physician who forgets the name of his rival wishes that name blotted out of existence. The newspaper that prints "Clown Prince" for "Crown Prince" and corrects its error by announcing that of course it meant "Clown Prince," really means what it says. Even untutored common sense has a shrewd suspicion that forgetting is significant; one rarely admits without embarrassment that he failed to keep an appointment because he forgot it. Events of this sort are always determined. They are even overdetermined. Several lines of causation may converge on the same mishap, and physical as well as psychical determinants may be involved. Errors in speech, for example, may be due in part to difficulties of muscular coordination, to transposition of letters, to similarities in words, and the like. But such conditions do not constitute the whole explanation. They do not explain why one particular slip and not another was made—why just that combination of sounds and no other was uttered. A young business man, for example, striving to be generous to a rival, and intending to say "Yes, he is very efficient," actually said, "Yes, he is very officious." Obviously he was slipping into an easy confusion of words, but he was also expressing his real opinion. Desire and indirect fulfillment are at the basis of normal as well as abnormal conduct, and motive determines even those happenings we attribute to chance. (pp. 391–392)

In his book *Jokes and Their Relation to the Unconscious* (1905), Freud indicates that people often use jokes to express sexual and aggressive tendencies. Like dreams, jokes exemplify wish fulfillments. According to Freud, jokes offer a socially approved vehicle for being obscene, aggressive or hostile, cynical, critical, skeptical, or blasphemous. Viewed in this way, jokes offer a way of venting repressed, anxiety-provoking thoughts; so it is no wonder that people find most humorous those things that bother them the most. Freud would say that we laugh most at those things that cause us the most anxiety.

Thus, in his search for the contents of the unconscious mind, Freud made use of free association, dream analysis, slips of the tongue, memory lapses, "accidents," gestures and mannerisms, what the person found humorous, and literally everything else the person did or said. This belief that everything a person does has meaning is exemplified in the following: an acquaintance passing a psychoanalyst says, "Hello," and the psychoanalyst says to himself, "I wonder what he meant by that?" For the psychoanalyst *everything* has meaning.

Freud's View of Human Nature

It should be clear by now that Freud was largely pessimistic about human nature. In *Civilization and Its Discontents* (1930), Freud reacts to the biblical commandment "Thou shalt love thy neighbor as thyself" as follows:

> What is the point of a precept enunciated with so much solemnity if its fulfillment cannot be recommended as reasonable? . . . Not merely is this stranger in general unworthy of my love; I must honestly confess that he has more claim to my hostility and even my hatred. He seems not to have the least trace of love for me and shows me not the slightest consideration. If it will do him any good he has no hesitation in injuring me, nor does he ask himself whether the amount of advantage he gains bears any proportion to the extent of the harm he does to me. Indeed, he need not even obtain an advantage; if he can satisfy any sort of desire by it, he thinks nothing of jeering at me, insulting me, slandering me and showing his superior power; and the more secure he feels and the more helpless I am, the more certainly I can expect him to behave like this to me. . . . Indeed, if this grandiose commandment had run "Love thy neighbour as thy neighbour loves thee," I should not take exception to it. . . .
> The element of truth behind all this, which people are so ready to disavow, is that men are not gentle creatures who want to be loved, and

who at the most can defend themselves if they are attacked; they are, on the contrary, creatures among whose instinctual endowments is to be reckoned a powerful share of aggressiveness. As a result, their neighbour is for them not only a potential helper or sexual object, but also someone who tempts them to satisfy their aggressiveness on him, to exploit his capacity for work without compensation, to use him sexually without his consent, to seize his possessions, to humiliate him, to cause him pain, to torture and to kill him. *Homo homini lupus* (man is a wolf to man). (pp. 110–111)

Another place where Freud shows his pessimism is in *The Future of an Illusion* (1927), which is his major statement on religion. In this book, Freud contends that the basis of religion is the human feeling of helplessness and insecurity. To overcome these feelings, we create a powerful father figure who will supposedly protect us, a father figure symbolized in the concept of God. The problem with this practice, according to Freud, is that it keeps humans operating at a childlike, irrational level. The dogmatic teachings of religion inhibit a more rational, realistic approach to life.

For Freud, our only hope was to come to grips with the repressed forces that motivated us; only then could we live rational lives. Freud said, "Those who do not suffer from the neurosis will need no intoxicant to deaden it" (1927, p. 81). For him, religion was the intoxicant.

Evaluation of Freud's Theory

Criticisms. It should come as no surprise that a theory as broad as Freud's, and one that touched so many aspects of human existence, would receive severe criticism. The common criticisms of Freud and his theory include the following.

1. *Method of data collection.* Freud used his own observations of his own patients as his source of data. There was no controlled experimentation. Not only did his patients not represent the general population, but his

own needs and expectations probably influenced his observations.

2. *Definition of terms.* Freud's theory became popular at a time when psychology was preoccupied with operational definitions. And many, if not most, of Freud's concepts were too nebulous to be measured. For example, how does one quantify psychic energy, castration anxiety, penis envy, or the Oedipal complex in general? How does one determine whether the interpretation of the latent symbols of a dream is valid? Science demands measurement, and many of Freud's concepts were not measurable.

3. *Dogmatism.* As we shall see in the next section, Freud saw himself as the founder and leader of the psychoanalytic movement, and he would tolerate no ideas that conflicted with his own. If a member of his group insisted on disagreeing with him, Freud expelled him from the group.

4. *Overemphasis on sex.* The main reason that many of Freud's early colleagues eventually went their own way was that they felt Freud overemphasized sex as a motive for human behavior. Some felt that to see sexual motivation everywhere, as Freud did, was extreme. The personality theories that other psychoanalytically oriented theorists developed show that human behavior can be explained just as well, if not better, through other than sexual motives.

5. *The self-fulfilling prophecy.* Any theorist, not just Freud, can be criticized for being susceptible to self-fulfilling prophecy. The point is that Freud found what he was looking for simply because he was looking for it. For example, free association is not really free. Rather, it is guided, at least in part, by the analyst's comments and gestures. Furthermore, once a patient is "trained," he or she will begin to tell the analyst exactly what the analyst wants to hear. This criticism also applies to dream interpretation.

6. *Length and cost of psychoanalysis.* Since psychoanalysis usually takes years to complete, it is not available to most troubled people. Only the most affluent can participate. Furthermore, only reasonably intelligent and mildly neurotic people can benefit from psychoanalysis, since patients must be able to articulate their inner experiences and understand the analyst's interpretation of those experiences. Psychoanalysis would not be effective with psychotic patients.

7. *Impossibility of proving psychoanalysis wrong.* One reason that psychoanalytic theory is hard to validate or invalidate is the large number of imprecise and nebulous terms it employs. Another reason is that anyone who criticizes it may be accused of exhibiting personal defensiveness. As Heidbreder (1933) says:

> If the critic rejects the theory, he may be acting in self-defense. If he is friendly toward the theory as a whole, reserving his objections for one or two points, he may simply be employing a more subtle defense, attempting to protect his most sensitive wounds by conceding points that do not greatly concern him. Even if he gives good reasons for the stand he takes, he can never be sure he is not rationalizing. And the critic cannot be sure that he is not adopting such devices, because his motives may be deep in his unconscious. (pp. 400–401)

In Chapter 1 we saw that Karl Popper said Freud's theory was unscientific because it violated the principle of refutability. According to Popper, in order for a theory to be scientific, it must specify observations that, if made, would refute the theory. Unless such observations can be specified, the theory is unscientific. Popper claimed that since Freudian theory could account for *anything* a person did, nothing that a person could do was contrary to what the theory predicted. Let us say, for example, that according to Freudian theory a certain cluster of childhood experiences will make an adult leery of heterosexual relationships. Instead, we find an adult who has had those experiences seeking and apparently enjoying such relationships. The Freudian can simply say that the person is demonstrating a reaction formation. Thus, no matter what happens, the theory is supported.

Contributions. In spite of the above criticisms, most believe that Freud made truly exceptional contributions to psychology. The following are usually listed among them.

1. *Expansion of psychology's domain.* Like no one before him, Freud pointed to the importance of studying unconscious motivation, infantile sexuality, dreams, and anxiety. Freud's was the first comprehensive theory of personality, and every personality theory since his can be seen as a reaction to his theory or to some aspect of it.

2. *Psychoanalysis.* Freud created a new way of dealing with age-old mental disorders. Many still believe that psychoanalysis is the best way to understand and treat neuroses.

3. *Understanding of normal behavior.* Freud not only provided a means of better understanding much abnormal behavior, but also made much normal behavior comprehensible. Dreams, forgetfulness, mistakes, choice of mates, humor, and use of the ego defense mechanisms characterize everyone's life, and Freud's analysis of them makes them less mysterious for everyone.

4. *Generalization of psychology to other fields.* By showing psychology's usefulness in explaining phenomena in everyday life, religion, sports, politics, art, literature, and philosophy, Freud expanded psychology's relevance to almost every sector of human existence. Fancher (1979) says:

> Freud's influence has not been limited to psychology and its related disciplines. His demonstrations of the importance and pervasiveness of unconscious mental factors was so effective that this once revolutionary idea is almost taken for granted today. The best art and literature of our time portrays

human beings as creatures in conflict with themselves, subject to forces beyond their personal conscious control, and unaware of their own identities. While many specific aspects of Freudian theory remain untested or questionable, there can be no doubt that this view of humanity has struck a responsive chord. Sigmund Freud was among the small handful of individuals whose work vitally affected not just a single field of specialization, but also an entire intellectual climate. (p. 248)

Leahey (1980) is even more forceful in his praise of Freud:

> If greatness may be measured by the scope of influence, then Sigmund Freud is without doubt the greatest of psychologists. Scarcely any inquiry into human nature has not felt his touch. His work affected—and affects—literature, philosophy, theology, ethics, aesthetics, political science, sociology, and popular psychology. He revolutionized our thinking about sex. "Freudian slip" is a household world. The modish belief that we all have secret selves with which we must get in touch through the aid of some therapy or belief-system comes from Freud—although he would scorn most such enterprises, for they stress a person's feelings, and Freud valued reason above all else.
>
> Freud, along with Darwin and Marx, is one of the great fathers of the twentieth century Western thought. Freud saw himself as a revolutionary, fighting alone against a condemning world. He explicitly placed himself in the line of Copernicus and Darwin, as one of those who challenged humanity's childish egocentrism and pushed it toward self-sufficient maturity. He was pessimistic about human nature and the dangers of the future, yet his pessimism was hopeful. He wanted us to understand our unconscious, darker nature so that we might subject it to the rule of reason. (p. 216)

As influential as Freud's theory has been, much of it has not withstood the rigors of scientific examination; in fact, much of it is untestable. Why, then, is Freud's theory so often referred to as a milestone in human history? The answer seems to be that scientific methodology is not the only criterion by which to judge a theory. Structuralism, for example, was highly scientific, requiring controlled, systematic experiments to test its hypotheses. Yet structuralism has faded, while psychoanalysis has remained. According to Heidbreder (1933):

> Whenever the Freudian theories have been accepted outside the psychoanalytic fold, they have been received not because they carry the credentials of exact, verifiable evidence, but because they have aroused conviction as convictions are aroused in everyday life—by the feeling that they represent keen observation and shrewd speculation which, in the main, square with the facts. . . .
>
> It is enlightening to compare psychoanalytic psychology with structuralism, in this respect its antithesis. Structuralism, equipped with a highly developed scientific method, and refusing to deal with materials not amendable to that method, admirably illustrates the demand for exactness and correctness by which science disciplines untutored curiosity. Psychoanalysis, with its seemingly inexhaustible curiosity, at present lacks the means, and apparently at times the inclination, to check its exuberant speculation by severely critical tests. But what it lacks in correctness, it gains in vitality, in the comprehensiveness of its view, and in the closeness of its problems to the concerns of everyday life. (pp. 410–411)

To the means by which we evaluate theories, we must add intuition. A theory that, among other things, makes sense personally may survive longer than one that develops and is tested within the realm of science. The extinction of structuralism and the survival of psychoanalysis exemplify this point.

Almost from its beginning, Freud's version of psychoanalysis had its critics, and several people who were originally affiliated with Freud went on to develop their own theories of personality. We shall consider only two such individuals: Carl Jung and Alfred Adler.

CARL JUNG

Born in 1875 in the Swiss village of Kesswyl, **Carl Jung** first became acquainted with Freud's theory when he read *The Interpretation of Dreams*. When Jung tried Freud's ideas in his own prac-

Carl Jung

RINGIER DOKUMENTATIONSZENTRUM

tice, he found them effective. He and Freud began to correspond, and eventually they met in Freud's home in Vienna. Their initial meeting lasted 13 hours, and the two became close friends.

When G. Stanley Hall invited Freud to give a series of lectures at Clark University in 1909, Jung traveled to America with Freud and gave a few lectures of his own. About this time Jung began to express doubts about Freud's emphasis on sexual motivation. These doubts became so intense that in 1912 the two stopped corresponding, and in 1914 they completely terminated their relationship—in spite of the fact that Freud had earlier nominated Jung to be the first president of the International Psychoanalytic Association. The break in the relationship was especially disturbing to Jung, who entered what he called his "dark years," a period of three years during which he was so depressed he could not even read a scientific book. During this time he analyzed his own innermost thoughts, and he emerged from this period with his own distinct theory of personality, which differed markedly from Freud's.

Jung continued to develop his theory until his death in 1961, at the age of 86.

Libido

The major source of difficulty between Freud and Jung was the nature of the libido. Freud defined libido as sexual energy, which he saw as the main driving force of personality. Thus, for Freud, most human behavior was sexually motivated. Jung disagreed, saying that libidinal energy was a creative life force that could be applied to the continuous psychological growth of the individual. According to Jung, libidinal energy was used in a wide range of human endeavors beyond those of a sexual nature, and it could be applied to the satisfaction of both biological *and* philosophical needs. In fact, as one became more proficient at satisfying the former needs, one could use more libidinal energy in dealing with the latter needs. In short, sexual motivation was *much* less important to Jung than it was to Freud.

The Ego

Jung's conception of the ego was very much like Freud's. The ego was the mechanism by which we interacted with the physical environment. It was everything of which we were conscious and was concerned with thinking, remembering and perceiving.

The Personal Unconscious

Combining the Freudian notions of the preconscious and the unconscious, Jung's **personal unconscious** consisted of experiences that had either been repressed or simply forgotten—material from one's lifetime that for one reason or another was not in consciousness. Some of this material was easily retrievable, and some of it was not.

The Collective Unconscious

The **collective unconscious** was Jung's most mystical and controversial concept. Jung believed the collective unconscious to be the deepest and most powerful component of the personality, reflecting the cumulative experiences of humans throughout their entire evolutionary past. According to Jung, it was the "deposit of ancestral experience from untold millions of years, the echo of prehistoric world events to which each century adds an infinitesimally small amount of variation and differentiation" (Jung, 1928, p. 162).

Archetypes. The collective unconscious registered *common* experiences that humans had had through the eons. These common experiences were recorded and were inherited as predispositions to respond emotionally to certain categories of experience. According to Jung, each inherited predisposition contained in the collective unconscious was an **archetype**. Concerning archetypes, Hergenhahn (1984) says:

> These ancestral experiences that are registered in the brain have been called at various times "racial memories," primordial images or more commonly, *archetypes*. An archetype can be defined as an inherited predisposition to respond to certain aspects of the world. Just as the eye and the ear have evolved to be maximally responsive to certain aspects of the environment, so has the brain evolved to cause the person to be maximally responsive to certain categories of experience that humans have encountered over and over again through countless generations. There is an archetype for whatever experiences are universal, those that each member of each generation must experience.
>
> You can generate a list of archetypes yourself by simply answering the question, "What must every human experience in his or her lifetime?" One's answer must include such things as birth, death, the sun, darkness, power, women, men, sex, water, magic, mother, heroes, and pain. There is an inherited predisposition to react to instances of these and other categories of experience. Specific responses are not inherited nor are specific ideas;

all that is inherited is a tendency to deal with universal experiences in *some way*. How the archetypes are responded to depends upon one's life circumstances. (p. 47)

According to Jung, the mind was not a "blank tablet" at birth but contained a structure that had developed in a Lamarckian fashion. That is, experiences of preceding generations were passed on to new generations. The archetypes could be thought of as generic images with which events in one's lifetime interacted. They recorded not only perceptual experiences, but the emotions typically associated with those perceptual experiences. In fact, Jung felt that the emotional component of archetypes was their most important feature. When an experience "communicated with" or was "identified with" an archetype, the emotion elicited was typical of the emotional response people had had to that kind of experience through the eons. For example, each child is born with a generic conception of mother that is the result of the cumulative experiences of preceding generations, and the child will tend to project onto its real mother the attributes of the generic mother-image. This archetype will influence not only how the child views its mother, but how the child responds to her emotionally. For Jung, then, archetypes provided each person with a framework for perceptual and emotional experience. They predisposed people to see things in certain ways, to have certain emotional experiences, and to engage in certain categories of behavior.

Although Jung recognized a large number of archetypes, he elaborated the following ones most fully. The **persona** is the archetype that causes people to present only part of their personality to the public. It is a mask in the sense that the most important aspects of personality are hidden behind it. The **anima** provides the female component of the male personality and a framework within which males can interact with females. The **animus** provides the masculine component of the female personality and

a framework within which females can interact with males. The **shadow**, the archetype that we inherit from our prehuman ancestors, provides us with a tendency to be immoral and aggressive. We project this aspect of our personalities onto the world symbolically as devils, demons, monsters, and evil spirits. The **self** causes people to try to synthesize all of the components of their personalities. It represents the human need for unity and wholeness of the total personality. The goal of life is first to discover and understand the various parts of the personality and then to synthesize them into a harmonious unity. Jung called this unity **self-actualization**.

The Attitudes

Jung described two major orientations or attitudes that people took in relating to the world. One attitude he labeled **introversion**, the other **extroversion**. Jung believed that although every individual possessed both attitudes, he or she usually assumed one of the two attitudes more than the other. The introverted person tended to be quiet, imaginative, and more interested in ideas than in interacting with people. The extroverted person was outgoing and sociable. Jung (1917/1953) describes the two attitudes in more detail:

> The first attitude (introversion) is normally characterized by a hesitant, reflective, retiring nature that keeps itself to itself, shrinks from objects, is slightly on the defensive and prefers to hide behind mistrustful scrutiny. The second (extroversion) is normally characterized by an outgoing, candid, and accommodating nature that adapts easily to a given situation, quickly forms attachments, and, setting aside any possible misgivings, will often venture forth with careless confidence into unknown situations. (p. 44)

Although most people tend toward either introversion or extroversion, Jung believed that the mature, healthy adult personality reflected both attitudes about equally.

Causality and Teleology

Like Freud, Jung was a determinist, but he did not confine his brand of determinism to past experience. Jung felt that in order to truly understand a person, one must understand the person's prior experiences, including those registered in the collective unconscious, *and* the person's goals for the future. Thus, unlike Freud's theory, Jung's involved **teleology** (purpose). For Jung, people were both pushed by the past and pulled by the future.

Dreams

Dreams were very important to Jung, but he interpreted them very differently than Freud. Freud believed that repressed, traumatic experiences revealed themselves in dreams because during sleep one's defenses were reduced. During the waking state, these experiences were actively held in the unconscious mind, since to entertain them consciously would provoke extreme anxiety. Jung believed that everyone had the same collective unconscious, but that individuals differed in their ability to recognize and give expression to the various archetypes. As we have seen, Jung also believed that everyone had an innate tendency to recognize, express, and synthesize the various components of his or her personality, and in so doing to become self-actualized. Even with this tendency, however, most people were never self-actualized. For most individuals, certain components of the personality remained unrecognized and underdeveloped. For Jung, dreams were a means of giving expression to aspects of the psyche that were underdeveloped. If a person did not give adequate expression to the shadow, for example, he or she would tend to have nightmares involving various monsters. Dreams, then, could be used to determine which aspects of the psyche were being given adequate expression and which were not. Another difference between Freud and Jung was that Jung felt series

of dreams should be analyzed, whereas Freud tended to concentrate his analysis on individual dreams.

The Importance of Middle Age

According to Jung, the goal of life is to reach self-actualization, which involves the harmonious blending of all aspects of the personality. Before this blending can occur, however, **individuation** must take place. Individuation is the process by which the various components of the personality are recognized and given expression. The job of recognizing and expressing all of the forces within us is monumental, since these forces usually conflict with each other. The rational conflicts with the irrational, feeling with thinking, masculine tendencies with feminine tendencies, and conscious processes with unconscious processes. The process of individuation occupies most of one's childhood, adolescence, and early adulthood. It is usually not until one reaches his or her late thirties or early forties that a major transformation occurs. Once one has recognized the many conflicting forces in one's personality, one is in a position to synthesize and harmonize them. Self-actualization occurs when all of the discordant elements of personality are given equal expression. In a healthy, integrated individual, each system of the personality is differentiated, developed, and expressed. Although Jung believed that everyone had an innate tendency toward self-actualization, he also believed that people rarely attained that state.

Criticisms and Contributions

Jung's theory has been criticized for embracing occultism, spiritualism, mysticism, and religion. Many saw Jung as unscientific, or even antiscientific, because he used such things as the symbols found in art, religion, and human fantasy to develop and verify his theory. The concept of the archetype, which is central to Jung's theory, has been criticized for being metaphysical and unverifiable. Some have referred to Jung's theory in general as unclear, incomprehensible, inconsistent, and in places contradictory. Finally, Jung has been criticized for employing the Lamarckian notion of the inheritance of acquired characteristics.

In spite of these criticisms, Jungian theory remains popular in psychology. Jung has influential followers throughout the world, and several major cities have Jungian institutes that disseminate his ideas. Jung's notions of introversion and extroversion have stimulated much research and are part of several popular personality tests—for example, the Minnesota Multiphasic Personality Inventory. Most influential in modern psychology, however, is Jung's notion of self-actualization. A number of current humanistically and existentially oriented theories (for example, the theories of Rogers and Maslow) emphasize the self-actualization process. Also compatible with current existential-humanistic theories is Jung's emphasis upon the role of goals in living an effective life. Hall and Lindzey (1978) liken Jung's contributions to those of Freud:

> When all is said and done, Jung's theory of personality as developed in his prolific writings, and as applied to a wide range of human phenomena stands as one of the most remarkable achievements in modern thought. The originality and audacity of Jung's thinking have few parallels in recent scientific history, and no person aside from Freud has opened more conceptual windows into what Jung would choose to call "the soul of man." (p. 149)

ALFRED ADLER

Born on February 17, 1870, in a suburb of Vienna, **Alfred Adler** remembered his childhood as being miserable. He was a sickly child who thought of himself as small and ugly. He also had a severe rivalry with his older brother. All of these recollections may have influenced the kind of personality theory Adler developed. It is always interesting to note how much a theorist's own personality affects the kind of theory he or she creates.

Like Jung, Adler became acquainted with Freudian psychology by reading *The Interpretation of Dreams*. Adler wrote a paper defending Freud's theory and was invited to join the Vienna Psychoanalytic Society, of which he became president in 1910. Differences between Adler and Freud began to emerge, however, and by 1911 they became so pronounced that Adler resigned as president of the Vienna Psychoanalytic Society. After a nine-year association with Freud, the friendship crumbled and the two men never saw each other again. History shows that Freud and Adler never had much in common, and that it was probably a mistake for Adler to join the Freudians to begin with. Freud's biographer, Ernest Jones (1955), summarizes Adler's major disagreements with Freud:

> Sexual factors, particularly those of childhood, were reduced to a minimum: a boy's incestuous desire for intimacy with his mother was interpreted as the male wish to conquer a female masquerading as sexual desire. The concepts of repression, infantile sexuality, and even that of the unconscious itself were discarded. (p. 131)

In 1926 Adler visited the United States and was warmly received. In 1935, partially because of the Nazi menace in Europe, Adler made the United States his permanent home. He died on May 28, 1937, while on a lecture tour in Aberdeen, Scotland.

Organ Inferiority and Compensation

Like Freud, Adler was trained in a mechanistic medical tradition; that is, every disorder, whether physical or mental, was assumed to have a physiological origin. In 1907 Adler published "Organ Inferiority and Its Physical Compensation," in which he presented the view that people were particularly sensitive to disease in organs that were "inferior" to other organs. For example, some people were born with weak eyes, other with weak hearts, still others with weak limbs, and so on. Because of the strain the environment put on these weak parts of the body, the person would develop weaknesses that inhibited normal functioning.

One way to adjust to a weakness was through **compensation**. That is, a person could adjust to a weakness in one part of his or her body by developing strengths in other parts. For example, a blind person could develop especially sensitive auditory skills. Another way to adjust to a weakness was through **overcompensation**, which was the conversion of a weakness into a strength. The usual examples include Teddy Roosevelt, who was a frail child but became a rugged outdoorsman, and Demosthenes, who had a speech impediment but became a great orator. At the time when Adler presented this view, he was a medical doctor, and his observations were clearly in accord with the mechanistic medicine of the time.

Feelings of Inferiority

In 1910 Adler entered the realm of psychology when he noted that compensation and overcompensation could be directed toward *imagined* inferiorities as well as toward real ones. Adler noted that *all* humans began life completely dependent on others for their survival, and therefore with **feelings of inferiority** or weakness. Such feelings motivated people as children, and then as adults, to gain power in order to overcome these feelings. In his early theorizing, Adler emphasized the attainment of power as a means of overcoming feelings of inferiority; later, he suggested that people strove for perfection or superiority in order to overcome these feelings.

Although feelings of inferiority motivate all personal growth and are therefore good, they can also disable rather than motivate some people. These people are so overwhelmed by such feelings that they accomplish nothing, and they are said to have an **inferiority complex**. Thus, feelings of inferiority can act as a stimulus for positive growth or as a disabling force, depending on one's attitude toward them.

Style of Life

The means that one chooses to gain superiority is called a **style of life**. Roughly, a style of life is the same as an identity. It is what a person is known in terms of, the theme that permeates one's entire life. A person chooses a style of life from what is available in the environment. Depending on what is available, one's style of life can be characterized as social, athletic, scholarly, or artistic, to mention only a few possibilities.

To be truly effective, a life-style must contain considerable **social interest**. That is, part of its goal must involve working toward a society that would provide a better life for everyone. Adler called any life-style without adequate social interest a **mistaken style of life**. Since the neurotic typically has a mistaken style of life, the job of the psychotherapist is to replace it with one that contains a healthy amount of social interest.

The Creative Self

Adler departed radically from the theories of Freud and Jung by saying that humans were not victims of their environment or of biological inheritance. Although environment and heredity provide the raw materials of personality, the person is free to arrange those materials in any number of ways. For example, whether feelings of inferiority facilitate growth or disable a person is a matter of personal attitude. If one sees life as meaningless, one is free to invent meaning and then act "as if" it were true. With this concept of the **creative self**, Adler aligned himself with the existential belief that humans were free to choose their own destiny.

Thus, although Adler was an early member of Freud's inner circle, the theory he developed had little, if anything, in common with Freud's. Unlike Freud's theory, Adler's emphasized the conscious mind, social rather than sexual motives, and free will. Much of Adler's thinking was to emerge later in such theories as those of Gordon Allport, George Kelly, Carl Rogers, and Abraham Maslow. All of these theories have in common the existential theme, which is the subject of the next chapter.

SUMMARY

Although Freud was trained in the tradition of mechanistic physiology and originally tried to explain hysteria as a physiological problem, events led him to attempt a psychological explanation of hysteria instead. Freud learned from Breuer that when Breuer's patient Anna O was hypnotized and then asked to remember the circumstances under which a symptom had first occurred, the symptom would at least temporarily disappear. This kind of treatment was called the cathartic method. Thus, Freud learned that some ideas were pathogenic, or capable of causing physical disorders. Freud also learned from Breuer's work with Anna O that the therapist was sometimes responded to as if he were a relevant person in the patient's life, a process called transference. Sometimes the therapist also became emotionally involved with a patient, a process called countertransference. *Studies on Hysteria* (1895), the book that Freud coauthored with Breuer, is usually taken as the formal beginning of the school of psychoanalysis. From his visit with Charcot, Freud learned that hysteria was a serious disorder that occured in both males and females, and that it was probably caused by sexual factors.

When Freud began treating hysterical patients he used hypnosis, but he found that he could not hypnotize some patients, and the ones he could hypnotize received only temporary relief from symptoms. After experimenting with various other therapeutic techniques, Freud fi-

nally settled on free association, whereby he encouraged his patients to say whatever came to their minds without inhibiting any thoughts. By analyzing a patient's symptoms and by carefully scrutinizing a patient's free associations, Freud hoped to discover the repressed memories responsible for a patient's disorder. Since these pathogenic thoughts provoked anxiety, patients resisted allowing them to enter consciousness. Freud originally believed that hysteria resulted from a childhood sexual seduction, but later concluded that the seductions he had discovered were usually patient fantasies.

During his self-analysis, Freud found that dreams contained the same clues concerning the origins of a psychological problem as did physical symptoms or free associations. He distinguished between the manifest content of a dream, or what the dream appeared to be about, and the latent content, or what the dream was actually about. Freud believed that the latent content represented wish fulfillments that a person could not entertain consciously without experiencing anxiety. Dream work disguised the true meaning of a dream. Examples of dream work include condensation, in which several things from a person's life are condensed into one symbol; and displacement, in which a person dreams about something symbolically related to an anxiety-provoking object, person, or event instead of dreaming about whatever it is that actually provokes the anxiety. During his self-analysis Freud discovered the Oedipus complex, which is characterized by a male child's sexual attraction to his mother and hostility toward his father. Freud felt that the Oedipus complex was universal among male children.

According to Freud, the adult mind consisted of an id, an ego, and a superego. The id is entirely unconscious and demands immediate gratification; it is therefore said to be governed by the pleasure principle. The id also contains all of the instincts and the libidinal energy associated with the instincts. Every instinct has a source, which is a bodily deficiency of some kind; an aim of removing the deficiency; an object, which is anything that can be used to remove the deficiency; and an impetus, a driving force whose strength is determined by the magnitude of the deficiency. To satisfy needs, the id has at its disposal only the primary processes of reflex action and wish fulfillment. The ego's job is to find real objects in the environment that can satisfy needs; it is therefore said to be governed by the reality principle. The realistic processes of the ego are referred to as secondary in order to distinguish them from the irrational primary processes of the id. The third component of the mind is the superego, which consists of the conscience, or the internalization of the experiences for which a child has been punished, and the ego-ideal, or the internalization of the experiences for which a child has been rewarded.

The ego's job is to find ways of effectively satisfying needs without violating the values of the superego. When such a way is found, the ego invests energy in it; this is known as a cathexis. If an available way to satisfy a need violates a person's values, energy is expended to inhibit its utilization, in which case an anticathexis occurs. When an anticathexis occurs, the person displaces the anxiety-provoking object or event with one that does not cause anxiety. Freud distinguished between life instincts, the collective energy of which he called eros, and death instincts, the collective energy of which he called thanatos. Freud used the concept of the death instincts to explain such things as suicide, masochism, murder, and general aggression.

Freud distinguished among objective anxiety, the fear of environmental events; neurotic anxiety, the feeling that one is about to be overwhelmed by one's id; and moral anxiety, the feeling caused by violating one or more internalized values. One of the major jobs of the ego is to reduce or eliminate anxiety; to accomplish this, the ego employs the ego defense mecha-nisms, which operate on the unconscious level and distort reality. All of the defense mechanisms depend upon repression, which is the holding of disturbing thoughts in the unconscious. Other ego defense mechanisms are displacement, in which one substitutes something that does not cause anxiety for something that does; sublimation, in which one substitutes something nonsexual for something sexual; projection, in which one attributes anxiety-provoking thoughts to others; identification, in which one gains stature by taking on the traits of illustrious people or institutions; rationalization, in which one gives an apparently logical reason as an excuse for a shortcoming instead of the real reason; and reaction formation, in which a person acts contrary to his or her real desires in order to escape the anxiety that would arise if he or she acted in accordance with the true desires.

During the psychosexual stages of development, the erogenous zone, or the area of the body associated with the greatest amount of pleasure, changes. Freud named the stages of development in terms of their erogenous zones. During the oral stage, either overgratification or undergratification of the oral needs results in a fixation, which in turn causes the individual to become either an oral-incorporative or an oral-sadistic character. Fixation during the anal stage results in the adult being either an anal-expulsive or an anal-retentive character. During the phallic stage, the Oedipus and Electra complexes occur. The Oedipus complex causes the male child to experience castration anxiety, and the Electra complex causes the female child to experience penis envy. The latency stage is characterized by repression of sexual desires and much sublimation. During the genital stage the person comes to possess the personality traits that experiences during the preceding stages have molded.

Freud found considerable evidence for his theory in everyday life. He felt that forgetting, losing things, accidents, and slips of the tongue were all unconsciously motivated. He also thought jokes provided information about repressed experience, since people tended to find only anxiety-provoking material humorous. Freud felt that although we shared the instinctual makeup of other animals, humans had the capacity to understand and harness instinctual impulses by exercising rational thought. To come to grips with the unconscious mind through rationality, however, was an extremely difficult process, and for that reason Freud was not optimistic that rationalism would prevail over our animal nature.

Freud has been criticized for using data from his patients to develop and validate his theory, using nebulous terms that make measurement difficult or impossible, being intolerant of criticism, overemphasizing sexual motivation, creating a method of psychotherapy that is too long and costly to be useful to most troubled people, and creating a theory that is very difficult to test objectively. Also, Freud's theory violates Popper's principle of refutability. Among Freud's contributions are the vast expansion of psychology's domain, a new method of psychotherapy, and a theory that explains much normal as well as abnormal behavior and is relevant to almost every aspect of human existence—for example, religion, philosophy, art, literature, and the theater.

Jung was an early follower of Freud who eventually broke with him because of Freud's emphasis on sexual motivation. Jung saw the libido as a pool of energy that could be used for positive growth throughout one's lifetime, rather than as only sexual energy, as Freud had seen it. Jung distinguished between the personal unconscious, which consisted of experiences from one's lifetime that a person was not conscious of, and the collective unconscious, which represented the recording of universal human experience through the eons of human history. According to Jung, the collective unconscious contained archetypes, or predispositions to respond emotionally to certain experiences in one's life. Among the more fully developed archetypes are the persona, the archetype that causes a person to offer only a small part of his or her personality to other people; the anima, which provides the female component of the male personality; the animus, which provides the male component of the female personality; the shadow, which represents the instinctual makeup that we share with nonhuman animals; and the self, which causes people to seek self-actualization.

Jung distinguished between the attitudes of introversion and extroversion. In dealing with the world, the introvert tends to be quiet, reflective, and socially isolated. The extrovert tends to be socially outgoing, frank, and willing to take a risk. Although most people incline toward either introversion or extroversion, Jung felt it was best if an individual expressed both attitudes equally. Jung stressed the importance of middle age in personality development, because before self-actualization could occur, the individuation process had to take place. Individuation involves discovering the various components of personality and then giving them expression. It is a long, complicated process that usually takes place during childhood, adolescence, and early adulthood. Jung felt that human behavior was both pushed by the past and the present (causality) and pulled by the future (teleology), and he assumed that dreams gave expression to the parts of the personality that were not given adequate expression in one's life. Dream analysis, then, could be used to determine which aspects of the personality were adequately developed and which were not. Also, Jung believed that it was more informative to analyze series of dreams than individual dreams, and he was much more optimistic about human nature than Freud was.

Like Jung, Adler was an early follower of Freud, but for several reasons he went his own way. The theory Adler developed was distinctly different from the theories of both Freud and Jung. Early in his career, Adler noted that a person suffering from some physical disability could either compensate for the disability by strengthening other abilities or, by overcompensating, turn the disability into a strength. Later he discovered that all humans began life feeling inferior because of infant helplessness. Adler believed that most people developed a style of life that allowed them to gain power or approach perfection, and thereby overcome their feelings of inferiority. Some people, however, were overwhelmed by their feelings of inferiority and developed an inferiority complex. According to Adler, healthy styles of life involved a significant amount of social interest, while mistaken styles of life did not. The creative self gave people at least some control over their personal destinies.

DISCUSSION QUESTIONS

1. Define the terms *catharsis, transference,* and *countertransference.*

2. What was the significance of Freud's visit with Charcot for the development of psychoanalysis?

3. What important things did Freud learn when he visited Charcot in Paris?

4. Discuss the importance of resistance in psychoanalysis.

5. What did Freud mean when he said that *true* psychoanalysis began only after hypnosis had been discarded?

6. What was Freud's seduction theory? How did he revise this theory?

7. Explain the significance of dream analysis for Freud. Why did he originally use it? What is the difference between the manifest and the latent content of a dream? List some dream symbols that Freud felt were universal.

8. What is the Oedipus complex and what is its significance in Freud's theory?

9. Describe the nature of the id. What does the id consist of? What principle governs it? What means does it have for satisfying its needs?

10. Differentiate between primary and secondary processes.

11. Give an example showing the interactions among the id, the ego, and the superego.

12. Explain how the superego develops and controls behavior. Include in your answer definitions of *conscience* and *ego-ideal.*

13. Why did Freud feel the need to postulate the existence of death instincts? What kinds of behavior did these instincts account for?

14. Define and give examples of objective, neurotic, and moral anxiety.

15. Define and give an example of each of the following ego defense mechanisms: repression, displacement, sublimation, projection, identification, rationalization, and reaction formation.

16. Explain what Freud meant when he said that civilization was built upon sublimation.

17. List, in order, the psychosexual stages of development. Describe what would cause a fixation on a particular stage. Give an example of an adult personality type that can result from an earlier fixation.

18. Discuss the kind of evidence Freud found for his theory in everyday life.

19. According to Freud, what is the function of religion?

20. Summarize Freud's view of human nature.

21. List the major criticisms of Freud's theory.

22. List the major contributions of Freud's theory.

23. Define each of the following terms from Jung's theory: the collective unconscious, archetype, persona, anima, animus, shadow and the self.

24. Describe the ways that Jung felt archetypes influence an individual's life.

25. What did Jung mean by self-actualization?

26. For Jung, why was middle age so important for personality development? Include in your answer a discussion of the process of individuation.

27. Compare Jung's approach to dream analysis with Freud's.

28. Summarize the criticisms and contributions of Jung's theory.

29. Summarize the main differences between Freud's and Adler's theories of personality.

30. Define each of the following terms from Adler's theory: *feelings of inferiority, inferiority complex, style of life, social interest, mistaken style of life,* and *creative self.*

GLOSSARY

Adler, Alfred (1870–1937) An early follower of Freud who left the Freudian camp and created his own theory of personality, which emphasized the development of a style of life as a means of overcoming feelings of inferiority.

Anal character The personality type that results from fixation on the anal stage of development. If fixation occurs early in the anal stage, the person becomes an anal-expulsive character; such a person gives freely of himself or herself. If fixation occurs late in the anal stage, the person develops an anal-retentive character; such a person tends to be orderly and stingy.

Anal stage of development The second stage of development, which lasts through the second year of life. During the anal stage, the anus-buttocks region of the body constitutes the erogenous zone.

Anima The archetype that provides the female part of the male personality.

Animus The archetype that provides the male part of the female personality.

Anticathexis The investment of psychic energy to prevent the association between needs and anxiety-provoking objects or events.

Anxiety The feeling of impending danger. Freud distinguished three types of anxiety: objective anxiety, which is caused by a physical danger; neurotic anxiety, which is caused by the feeling that one is going to be overwhelmed by his or her id; and moral anxiety,

which is caused by violating one or more values internalized in the superego.

Archetype An inherited predisposition to respond emotionally to certain categories of experience.

Breuer, Joseph (1842–1925) The person Freud credited with the founding of psychoanalysis. Breuer discovered that when the memory of a traumatic event was recalled under hypnosis, there was a release of emotional energy (catharsis), and the symptoms caused by the repressed memory were relieved.

Castration anxiety The fear that a male child has during the phallic stage of development that his father is going to castrate him.

Cathartic method The alleviation of hysterical symptoms by allowing the pathogenic ideas causing these symptoms to be expressed consciously.

Cathexis The investment of psychic energy in those things that satisfy a person's needs. Such an investment of energy creates a relationship between needs and the things that will satisfy the needs.

Collective unconscious Jung's term for the part of the unconscious mind that reflects universal human experience through the ages. For Jung, the collective unconscious was the most powerful component of the personality.

Compensation According to Adler, the making up for a weakness by developing strengths in other areas.

Condensation The kind of dream work that causes several things to be condensed into one dream symbol.

Conflict The simultaneous tendency both to approach and avoid the same object, event, or person.

Conscience The part of the superego consisting of those internalized experiences for which a child has been consistently punished.

Countertransference The process by which a therapist becomes emotionally involved with a patient.

Creative self According to Adler, the component of the personality that allows humans to be at least partially free to choose their own destinies.

Death instincts The instincts that have death as their goal.

Displacement The ego defense mechanism by which a goal that does not provoke anxiety is substituted for one that does. Also, the kind of dream work that causes the dreamer to dream of something symbolically close to anxiety-provoking events rather than dreaming about the anxiety-provoking events themselves.

Dream analysis A major tool that Freud used in studying the contents of the unconscious mind. Freud felt that the symbols dreams contained could yield information about repressed memories, just as hysterical symptoms could. For Jung, dreams provided a mechanism by which inhibited parts of the psyche might be given expression. Therefore, for Jung, dream analysis indicated which aspects of the psyche were underdeveloped.

Dream work The mechanisms that distort the meaning of a dream, thereby making it more tolerable to the dreamer (see also **condensation** and **displacement**).

Ego The component of the personality that is responsible for locating events in the environment that will satisfy the needs of the id.

Ego defense mechanisms Learned, unconscious strategies available to the ego for distorting the anxiety-provoking aspects of reality, thus making those aspects of reality more tolerable.

Ego-ideal The part of the superego consisting of the internalized experiences for which a child has been consistently rewarded.

Electra complex The female counterpart of the male's Oedipus complex.

Erogenous zone The area of the body that is the source of greatest pleasure during a particular stage of development.

Eros The energy associated with the life instincts.

Extroversion The attitude toward life that is characterized by gregariousness and a willingness to take risks.

Feelings of inferiority According to Adler, those feelings that all humans try to escape by becoming powerful or superior.

Fixation Arrested development that results from the undergratification or overgratification of a need during one of the psychosexual stages of development.

Free association Freud's major tool for studying the contents of the unconscious mind. With free association a patient is encourged to express freely everything that comes to his or her mind.

Freud, Sigmund (1856–1939) The developer of a theory of personality that stressed the conflict between the animalistic impulses possessed by humans and the human desire to live in a civilized society.

Genital stage of develoment The final stage of development, which lasts from puberty to the end of one's life.

Id According to Freud, the instinctual energy that is the driving force for the entire personality.

Identification The ego defense mechanism whereby people enhance the feelings they have about themselves by affiliating themselves with people or organizations they perceive to be illustrious.

Individuation The process of discovering and giving expression to the various components of the personality.

Inferiority complex According to Adler, the condition one experiences when feelings of inferiority overwhelm one instead of motivating one toward success.

Instinct According to Freud, the motivational force behind personality. Each instinct has a source, which is a bodily deficiency of some kind; an aim of removing the deficiency; an object, which is anything that is capable of removing the deficiency; and an impetus, a driving force whose strength is determined by the magnitude of the deficiency.

Introversion The attitude toward life that is characterized by social isolation and an introspective nature.

Jung, Carl (1875–1961) An early follower of Freud who finally broke with him because of Freud's emphasis on sexual motivation. Jung eventually developed his own theory, which emphasized the collective unconscious and self-actualization.

Latency stage of development The stage of development that occurs from about the sixth year of life until puberty.

Latent content of a dream What a dream is *actually* about.

Libido For Freud, the collective energy associated with the life instincts. For Jung, the creative life force that provides the energy for personal growth.

Life instincts The instincts that have as their goal the sustaining of life.

Manifest content of a dream What a dream *appears* to be about.

Mistaken style of life According to Adler, any style of life lacking social interest.

Oedipus complex The tendency for a male child, between about the ages of three and five, to be attracted to his mother and hostile toward his father.

Oral character The personality type that results from a fixation on the oral stage of development. If fixation occurs early in the oral stage, the person develops an oral-incorporative character; such a person stresses taking things into his or her body, as in eating, drinking, or smoking. If fixation occurs late in the oral stage, the person develops an oral-sadistic character; such a person is generally aggressive.

Oral stage of development The stage of development that occurs during the first year of life. During this time the mouth, lips, and tongue constitute the erogenous zone.

Overcompensation According to Adler, the conversion of a weakness into a strength.

Pathogenic ideas Ideas that cause physical disorders.

Penis envy According to Freud, the jealousy that results from a female's realization that her father has a penis and she does not.

Persona The archetype that causes people to offer only part of their personality to the public, and thus to keep the larger part hidden.

Personal unconscious Jung's term for the place where material from one's lifetime of which one is currently not conscious resides.

Phallic stage of development The third stage of development, which occurs from about the third year of life through about the fifth year. During this time, the genital region of the body is the erogenous zone.

Pleasure principle The demand for immediate gratification of the needs that arise in the id.

Preconscious The term Freud used in his early theorizing to describe material of which we were not conscious but could become conscious of with relative ease.

Pressure technique A technique that Freud used early in his career. It involved placing his hand on a patient's forehead as a means of overcoming the patient's resistance.

Primary processes Activities that are independent of experience and that the id engages in to satisfy needs. Reflex action and wish fulfillment are primary processes.

Projection The ego defense mechanism by which one attributes an anxiety-provoking thought to someone or something other than one's self.

Rationalization The ego defense mechanism by which one gives a logical, rational, but false reason for a shortcoming rather than the real reason.

Reaction formation The ego defense mechanism by which one does the opposite of what one really wants to do, because doing what one really wanted to do would cause anxiety.

Reality principle The principle governing the ego. The reality principle brings a person into contact with the real environmental objects that will satisfy his or her needs.

Reflex action The genetically determined response mechanisms that the id can employ to remove various discomforts.

Repression The active holding of traumatic memories in the unconscious mind, since pondering them consciously would cause anxiety.

Resistance The tendency for patients to inhibit the recollection of a traumatic experience.

Secondary processes Those processes the ego employs in dealing effectively with the physical environment.

Seduction theory Freud's contention that hysteria was caused by a sexual attack: someone close to or related to the hysteric patient had attacked him or her when the patient was a young child. Freud later concluded that as a child the patient had imagined the attack.

Self The archetype that causes people to seek unity or harmony among the various elements of their personalities.

Self-actualization The harmonious blending of all aspects of the personality.

Shadow The archetype that gives humans the characteristics of nonhuman animals—for example, aggression.

Social interest The concern for other humans and for society that Adler felt characterizes a healthy style of life.

Studies on Hysteria The book Freud and Breuer published in 1895 that is usually viewed as marking the formal beginning of psychoanalysis.

Style of life According to Adler, the way of life that a person chooses in order to overcome feelings of inferiority.

Sublimation The ego defense mechanism that displaces a sexual goal with a nonsexual one. According to Freud, civilization depends upon sublimation.

Superego The internalized values that act as a guide for a person's conduct. If a person acts in accordance with these values, he or she feels good; but if a person violates one or more of these values, he or she feels anxious or guilty.

Teleology The doctrine that states that at least some human behavior is purposive, that is, directed to the attainment of future goals.

Thanatos The energy associated with the death instincts.

Transference The process by which a patient responds to the therapist as if the therapist were a relevant person in the patient's life.

Unconscious motivation The causes of our behavior of which we are unaware.

Wish fulfillment The id's conjuring up of images of those things that will satisfy needs.

CHAPTER 17

Third Force Psychology

In the early 1960s a group of psychologists headed by Abraham Maslow started a movement referred to as **third force psychology**. These psychologists claimed that the other two forces in psychology, behaviorism and psychoanalysis, neglected a number of important human attributes. They said that in applying the techniques used by the natural sciences to the study of humans, behaviorism likened humans to robots, animals, or computers. For the behaviorist there was really nothing unique about humans. The major argument against psychoanalysis was that it concentrated mainly on emotionally disturbed people and on developing techniques for making abnormal people normal. What was lost, according to the third force psychologists, was the healthy individual who wanted to become healthier, as well as an understanding of the conditions that would allow humans to reach their full potential. What was needed was a model of humans that emphasized their positive rather than their negative aspects, and this is what the third force psychologists attempted to provide.

Third force psychology is very popular in psychology today, and its popularity seems to be growing. This kind of psychology contrasts vividly with most other kinds, since it does not assume determinism in explaining human behavior. Rather, it assumes that humans are free to choose their own kind of existence. Instead of attributing the causes of behavior to stimuli, drive states, genetics, or early experience, the third force psychologist claims that the most important cause of behavior is **subjective reality**, or a person's own conscious experience. Since these psychologists do not assume determinism, they are not scientists in the traditional sense, and they make no apology for that. Science in its present form, they say, is not equipped to study, explain, or understand the essence of human nature. When applied to humans, traditional science seeks the *causes* of behavior, whereas third force psychology seeks the *reasons* for behavior. Humans, say the third force psychologists, do what they do because it is reasonable for them to do so under the circumstances. They act rather than react.

Like almost everything else in modern psychology, third force psychology is not new. It can be traced to the romantic movement, which in turn can be traced back to the early Greeks. Two themes from romanticism have combined to form third force psychology: humanism and existentialism. In recent times humanism can be traced to the writings of Rousseau, and existentialism to the writings of Kierkegaard, Nietzsche, and Schopenhauer. But even though elements of both humanism and existential philosophy are found in third force psychology, the two philosophies are by no means the same. After discussing phenomenology, a technique that both existential and humanistic psychology employ, we will review existential psychology and then humanistic psychology, and we will conclude the chapter with a comparison of the two.

PHENOMENOLOGY

Franz Brentano

Phenomenology began with **Franz Brentano** (1838–1917) as an alternative to Wilhelm Wundt's brand of introspection. As we saw in Chapter 9, Wundt's goal was to reduce all mental experience to its basic elements, and thereby discover the building blocks of the mind. Brentano felt that Wundt's elementistic approach distorted the essence of mental experience, and that mental experience consisted of functional acts such as perceiving, judging, and valuing. These acts were mental phenomena that could not be reduced to anything more basic without distorting their meaning. For Brentano, the proper focus for introspective reports was these intact, meaningful acts or mental phenomena—thus the term **phenomenology** for the study of mental phenomena.

In Brentano's brand of phenomenology the concept of **intentionality** was extremely important. Brentano believed that every mental act, whether it be judging, perceiving, valuing, or something else, referred to (intended) something outside of the mind—for example, "I see a tree," "I like my mother," or "That was a good piece of pie." The contents of a mental act could be real or imagined, but the act, according to Brentano, always referred to (intended) something.

In his book *Psychology from an Empirical Standpoint* (1874/1973), Brentano gives the following examples of mental phenomena:

> Every judgment, every recollection, every expectation, every inference, every conviction or opinion, every doubt, is a mental phenomenon. Also to be included under this term is every emotion: joy, sorrow, fear, hope, courage, despair, anger, love, hate, desire, act of will, intention, astonishment, admiration, contempt, etc. (p. 79)

For Brentano, then, mental phenomena consisted of some act or function and of an image of the referent toward which the act was directed.

In Chapter 14, we saw how Brentano's thoughts influenced the development of Gestalt psychology. Next we shall see how Brentano's thoughts were instrumental in the development of modern existentialism mainly through his influence on Edmund Husserl.

Edmund Husserl

Edmund Husserl (1859–1938) studied first at Leipzig, where he attended Wundt's lectures, then transferred to Vienna to study mathematics. At Vienna he came under the influence of Brentano. In 1886, following Brentano's advice, Husserl went to Halle to study with Stumpf, another act psychologist.

Husserl's goal was to take the kind of phenomenology Brentano described and use it to create an objective, rigorous basis for philosophical and scientific inquiry. As Severin (1973) says:

> Husserl's all-absorbing interest was the clarification and validation of knowledge. He envisioned a gigantic phenomenological research project which would eventually integrate all science with philosophy. (p. 275)

Husserl felt that phenomenology could be used to create an objective bridge between the outer, physical world and the inner, subjective world. To form this bridge, Husserl used Brentano's notion of intentionality; and to represent mental acts, Husserl borrowed the technique of bracketing from mathematics. Here is an example of such a representation:

```
(being)   (act)
 | [I]    [see] |        | [the flower] |
    ↑                          ↑
(experience)          (object of experience)
```

Royce and Mos (1981) summarize Husserl's view of the mind:

Husserl's phenomenology identifies consciousness almost completely with intentionalities. Consciousness, with a few exceptional nonintentional experiences . . . consists of mental acts by which certain relations are established between the subject and the object. These acts are called "intentionalities." Consequently, consciousness is not a container filled with sensations and ideas from which the homunculus-ego infers the existence of the external world of objects (resembling a radar operator inferring the presence of planes and ships from the blips on a radar screen). Consciousness is open to the world of real objects; it is in the very relations of the subject to the objects. Consciousness is a dynamic activity (acts) rather than "stuff" . . . it is "doing" rather than "being." (p. 55)

Of prime importance to Husserl was that phenomenology be free of any preconceptions. That is, Husserl believed in reporting exactly what appeared in consciousness, not what *should* be there according to some theory or model. Severin (1973) expands on this point:

> Husserl felt that our minds are so filled with ideas and theories about how things should be that we seldom experience them exactly as they are. If we wish to make certain that our knowledge is valid, we must begin in a special way. Suppose that a traveler in New Guinea discovers a new flower. If he is a phenomenologist, he will banish from mind for the time all names, memories, preconceptions, and theories and not even reflect on whether or not the plant exists. His whole attention will be focused on the thing as he experiences it and only this. As he encounters the flower again and again from different frames of reference, including the use of a microscope, and under a wide variety of circumstances, he will come closer and closer to an understanding of its true nature. One of Husserl's cardinal principles is that things are what they appear to be. (p. 275)

As we saw in Chapter 9, however, Husserl believed that phenomenology could go beyond an analysis of intentionality. A study of intentionality determined how the mind and the physical world interacted, and such a study was essential for the physical sciences. But in addition to an analysis of intentionality, Husserl proposed a kind of introspection that concentrated on the workings of the mind that were independent of the physical world. This second kind of introspection would focus on whatever personal experiences a person had. Whereas intentionality involved the person turned outward, the second kind of introspection would study the person turned inward. The goal of the latter kind of introspection was to describe accurately *all* of a person's subjective experience.

Husserl's phenomenology soon expanded into modern existentialism. Whereas Husserl was mainly interested in epistemology and the nature of consciousness, however, the existentialists were interested in the nature of human existence. The existentialists used phenomenology to study the kinds of experiences humans had as they lived their lives, and their study included *all* experiences, not simply intellectual ones. Van Kaam (1966), an existential psychologist, says, for example:

> Experiences such as responsibility, dread, anxiety, despair, freedom, love, wonder or decision cannot be measured or experimented with . . . they are simply there and can only be explicated in their givenness. (p. 187)

Husserl's phenomenology was converted into existential psychology mainly by his student Martin Heidegger, whose views we will review next.

EXISTENTIAL PSYCHOLOGY

As we saw in Chapter 7, existential philosophy is generally thought of as starting with the writings of Kierkegaard (1813–1855), Nietzsche (1844–1900), and Schopenhauer (1788–1860), because these authors probed the meaning of human existence. All of these philosophers rebelled against the rationalism of Kant and Hegel and tried to restore the importance of feelings and individuality in philosophy. The person most often named as the originator of modern existentialism, however, is Martin Heidegger.

Martin Heidegger

Martin Heidegger (1889–1976) was Husserl's student and then his assistant, and he dedicated his famous book *Being and Time* (1927) to Husserl. Heidegger's work is generally considered the bridge between existential philosophy and **existential psychology**. Many if not most of the terms and concepts that appear in the writings of current existential psychologists can be traced to the writings of Heidegger. Like Husserl, Heidegger was a phenomenologist; but unlike Husserl, Heidegger used phenomenology to examine the totality of human existence.

Heidegger used the term *Dasein* to indicate that a person and the world were inseparable. Literally, **Dasein** means "to be" (*sein*) "there" (*da*), and Heidegger usually described the relationship between a person and the world as "being-in-the-world," using the hyphens to emphasize the interrelatedness of the person and the world. A more dramatic way of stating this relationship is to say that without the world humans would not exist, and without humans the world would not exist. The human mind illuminates the physical world and thereby brings it into existence. As Boss, another contemporary existential psychologist, says:

> Man discloses the world. People are the luminated realm into which all that is to be may actually shine forth, emerge, and appear as phenomena, i.e., as that which shows itself. (1963, p. 70)

What we allow to "shine forth" is reality, and since different people allow different experiences to shine forth, everyone lives in a different world.

It was of major importance to Heidegger that humans could ponder the fact that their existence was finite. For Heidegger, a prerequisite for living an **authentic life** was coming to grips with the fact that "I must someday die." With that realization dealt with, the person could get busy and exercise his or her freedom to create a meaningful existence, an existence that allowed for almost constant personal growth or **becoming**.

Since realizing that one was mortal caused anxiety, however, people often refused to recognize that fact and thereby inhibited a full understanding of themselves and their possibilities. According to Heidegger, this resulted in an **inauthentic life**. Other inauthentic modes of existence included living a traditional, conventional life according to the dictates of society, and emphasizing present activities without concern for the future. The inauthentic person gave up his or her freedom and let others make the choices involved in his or her life.

Heidegger believed that if we did not exercise our personal freedom we experienced **guilt**. Since most people did not fully exercise their freedom to choose, they experienced at least some guilt. All humans could do to minimize guilt was try to live an authentic life—that is, to recognize and live in accordance with their ability to choose their own existence.

Since acceptance of the fact that at some time in the future we would be nothing caused **anxiety**, such acceptance took courage. Heidegger believed that choosing one's existence rather than conforming to the dictates of society, culture, or someone else also took courage. And in general, living an authentic life by accepting all the conditions of existence and making personal choices meant that one must experience anxiety. For Heidegger, anxiety was a necessary part of living an authentic life.

One reason that exercising one's freedom in life caused anxiety was that it made one responsible for the consequences of those choices. The free individual could not blame God, parents, circumstances, genes, or anything else for what happened to him or her. One was responsible for one's own life. Freedom and **responsibility** went hand in hand.

Heidegger did, however, place limits on personal freedom. He said that we were thrown into our particular life by circumstances beyond our control. This **thrownness** determined, for example, whether we were male or female, short or tall, attractive or unattractive, rich or poor, American or Russian, and so on. Thrownness determined the conditions under which we exercised our freedom. According to Heidegger, all humans were free, but the conditions under which that freedom was manifested varied. Thrownness was what placed limits on personal freedom.

Ludwig Binswanger

Ludwig Binswanger (1881–1966) obtained his medical degree from the University of Zurich in 1907, then studied psychiatry under Eugen Bleuler and psychoanalysis under Carl Jung. Binswanger was one of the first Freudian psychoanalysts in Switzerland, and he and Freud remained friends throughout their lives. Under the influence of Heidegger, Binswanger applied phenomenology to psychiatry, and later he became an existential analyst. Binswanger's goal became to integrate the writings of Husserl and Heidegger with psychoanalytic theory. Adopting Heidegger's notion of **Dasein**, Binswanger called his approach to psychotherapy **Daseinanalysis**.

Like most of the existential psychologists, Binswanger emphasized the here-and-now, considering the past or future important only insofar as they manifested themselves in the *present*. In order to understand and help a person, according to Binswanger, one must learn how that person viewed his or her life at the moment. Furthermore, the therapist must try to understand the *particular person's* anxieties, fears, values, thought processes, social relations, and personal meanings, instead of these notions in general. Each person lived in his or her own private, subjective world, which was not generalizable.

Ludwig Binswanger

Binswanger discussed three different modes of existence to which individuals gave meaning through their consciousness. They are the **Umwelt** (the "around world"), the world of things and events; the **Mitwelt** (the "with world"), which consists of our interactions with other humans; and the **Eigenwelt** (the "own world"), which consists of a person's private, inner, subjective experience. To understand a person fully, one must understand all three of his or her modes of existence.

One of Binswanger's most important concepts is that of **world-design**. In general, world-design is how an individual views and embraces the world. World-designs can be open or closed, expansive or constructive, positive or negative, simple or complex, or have any number of other characteristics. In any case, it is through the world-design that one lives one's life, and therefore the world-design touches everything that one does. Hall and Lindzey (1978) present Binswanger's examples of world-designs:

> Binswanger gives examples of some narrowly conceived world-designs that he found in his patients. One patient's design was constructed around the need for continuity. Any disruption of continuity—a gap, tearing, or separating—produced great anxiety. One time she fainted when the heel of her shoe fell off. Separation from the mother also evoked anxiety because it broke the continuity of the relationship. Holding onto mother meant holding onto the world; losing her meant falling into the dreadful abyss of nothingness. . . .
>
> Another patient who had been an active business executive became inactive, dull, and listless. His world-design as a business executive was based on push, pressure, threat, and general world-disharmony. His mode of being-in-the-world was that of bumping up against things and being bumped into. He viewed his fellow humans as being disrespectful, contemptuous, and threatening. When he tried to control his anxiety by keeping his distance from the world, his efforts resulted in exhaustion.
>
> The design for a third patient consisted of the categories of familiarity and strangeness. His existence was constantly being endangered by impersonal hostile powers. He defended himself against these nameless fears by personalizing them as feelings of persecution. (p. 325)

If a world-design is ineffective, in the sense that it results in too much anxiety, fear, or guilt, it is the therapist's job to help the client see that there are other ways of embracing the world, other people, and oneself.

Binswanger agreed with Heidegger that thrownness placed limits upon personal freedom. For Binswanger, the circumstances into which one was thrown determined one's **ground of existence**, which defined the conditions in which one exercised one's personal freedom. No matter what a human's circumstances were, however, he or she aspired to transcend them—that is, not to be victimized by them. Everyone sought **being-beyond-the-world**. By *being-beyond-the-world*, Binswanger was not referring to a life after death, but to the way in which people tried to transform their circumstances by exercising their free will.

By choosing, we change the meanings and values of what we experience. Though physical circumstances may be the same for different people , how they embrace, interpret, value, symbolize, and respond to those circumstances is a matter of individual choice. By exercising our freedom we grow as human beings; and since exercising freedom is an unending process, the developmental process is never completed. Authentic people are always becoming something different from what they were. Thus, becoming characterizes the authentic life, which in turn is characterized by anxiety. Not becoming, or remaining stagnant, characterizes the inauthentic life—as does guilt—since the person does not approach his or her true potential as a human being.

Rollo May

Rollo May (1909–   ) introduced Heideggerian existentialism to American psychology through his edited books *Existence: A New Dimension in Psychiatry and Psychology* (1958) and *Existential Psychology* (1961). Since Binswanger's work has only recently been translated into English, May has been as responsible as anyone for incorporating European existential philosophy (mainly Heidegger's) into American psychology.

May was born in Ada, Ohio. He received a B.A. from Oberlin College in 1930, a Bachelor of Divinity Degree from Union Theological Seminary in 1938, and a Ph.D. in clinical psychology from Columbia University in 1949. Prior to obtaining his Ph.D., May contracted tuberculosis and was very close to death. During this depressing time, he studied Kierkegaard's and Freud's views on anxiety; and upon returning to Columbia, he submitted "The Meaning of Anxiety" as his Ph.D. dissertation. In modified form, this dissertation became May's book *The Meaning of Anxiety* (1950). May's other books include *The Art of Counseling* (1939), *The Springs of Creative Living* (1940), *Man's Search for Himself* (1953), *Psychology and the Human Dilemma* (1967), *Love and Will* (1969), *Power and Innocence* (1972), *Paulus: Reminiscences of a Friendship* (1973), and *The Courage to Create* (1975).

Like most other existential thinkers, May was strongly influenced by Kierkegaard, who had rejected Hegel's belief that the only true identity was found in abstract thought and logic. Kierkegaard proposed **ontology**, which is the study of an individual's existence in the world, or what Heidegger later called *Dasein* (being-in-the-world). May believes, along with the other existentialists, that the most important fact about humans is that they are free. As we have seen, however, freedom does not produce a tranquil life. Freedom carries with it responsibility and uncertainty, and therefore anxiety. The healthy person exercises the freedom to embrace life fully and to approach his or her full potential. Exercising one's freedom means going beyond what one previously was, ignoring the expectations (roles) for one's behavior that others impose, and therefore sometimes acting contrary to traditions, mores, or conventions. All of this causes anxiety, but it is normal, healthy anxiety because it is conducive to personal growth (becoming). **Neurotic anxiety** is not conducive to personal growth, since it results from the fear of freedom. The person experiencing neurotic anxiety lives his or her life in such a way as to reduce or eliminate personal freedom. Such a person conforms to tradition, religious dogma, the expectations of others, or anything else that reduces his or her need to make personal choices. Kierkegaard called the neurotic's situation **shut-upness**. The

ROLLO REESE MAY

Rollo May

neurotic is shut off from himself or herself as well as from other people, and lives an inauthentic life.

If people do not exercise their freedom, they experience **guilt**. According to Kierkegaard, May, and most other existentialists, we can either exercise our free will and experience normal anxiety or not exercise it and feel guilty. Obviously, it is not easy being human, for this conflict between anxiety and guilt is a constant theme in human existence. As May (1953) says,

> The conflict is between every human being's need to struggle toward enlarged self-awareness, maturity, freedom and responsibility, and his tendency to remain a child and cling

Abraham Maslow

to the protection of parents or parental substitutes. (p. 193)

Many of the concepts found in existential psychology will reappear as we consider humanistic psychology. We shall also see, however, that there are important reasons for not equating the two kinds of psychology.

HUMANISTIC PSYCHOLOGY

Abraham Maslow

Although several psychologists through the years can be referred to as humanistic (for example, Adler and Allport), **Abraham Maslow** (1908–1970) was most responsible for making **humanistic psychology** a formal branch of psychology. As we have seen, Maslow contended that the two major branches of psychology, psychoanalysis and behaviorism, had created a narrow and distorted picture of humans. What was needed was a third viewpoint, and that viewpoint was humanistic psychology, which has come to be known as third force psychology.

(We have included existential psychology as part of this third force.) In 1962 Maslow, along with several other psychologists (including Carl Rogers) founded the American Association of Humanistic Psychology.

The humanistic paradigm. The beliefs that those psychologists working within the humanistic paradigm shared include the following: little of value can be learned about humans by studying nonhuman animals; subjective reality is the primary guide for human behavior; studying individuals is more informative than studying what groups of individuals have in common; a major effort should be made to discover those things that expand and enrich human experience; research should seek information that will help to solve human problems; and the goal of psychology should be to formulate a complete description of what it means to be a human being. Such a description would include the importance of language, the valuing process, the full range of human emotions, and the ways humans seek and attain meaning in their lives.

Humanistic psychology, which rejects the notion that psychology should be entirely scientific, sees humans as indivisible wholes. Any attempt to reduce them to habits, cognitive structures, or S-R connections results in a distortion of human nature. According to Maslow (1966), psychologists often use scientific method to cut themselves off from the poetic, romantic, and spiritual aspects of human nature:

> Briefly put, it appears to me that science and everything scientific can be and often is used as a tool in the service of a distorted, narrowed, humorless, de-eroticized, de-emotionalized, desacralized, and de-sanctified *Weltanschauung* (world view). This desacralization can be used as a defense against being flooded by emotion, especially the emotions of humility, reverence, mystery, wonder and awe. (p. 139)

The humanistically oriented psychologists flatly

reject the goal of predicting and controlling human behavior, which so many scientifically inclined psychologists accept. As Maslow (1966) says:

> If humanistic science may be said to have any goals beyond sheer fascination with the human mystery and enjoyment of it, these would be to release the person from external controls and to make him *less* predictable to the observer (to make him freer, more creative, more inner determined) even though perhaps more predictable to himself. (p. 40)

By concentrating on the study of psychologically disturbed individuals, we have created a "crippled" psychology. Maslow (1970) says, "It becomes more and more clear that the study of crippled, stunted, immature, and unhealthy specimens can yield only a cripple psychology and a cripple philosophy" (p. 180). For Maslow, there are exceptional people whose lives cannot be understood simply as the absence of mental disorders. In order to be understood, exceptional people must be studied directly—a point Maslow (1970) makes as follows:

> Health is not simply the absence of disease or even the opposite of it. Any theory of motivation that is worthy of attention must deal with the highest capacities of the healthy and strong man as well as with the defensive maneuvers of crippled spirits. (p. 33)

Maslow's point is not that psychology should stop attempting to be scientific or stop studying and attempting to help those with psychological problems, but that such endeavors tell only part of the story. Beyond this, psychology needs to attempt to understand humans who are in the process of reaching their full potential. We need to know how such people think and what motivates them. Thus, Maslow invested most of his energies in trying to understand exceptional humans.

Maslow's theory of motivation. According to Maslow, human needs are arranged in a hierarchy. The lower the needs in the hierarchy, the

more basic they are, and the more similar they are to the needs of other animals. The higher the needs in the hierarchy, the more distinctly human they are. The following is Maslow's proposed hierarchy of needs:

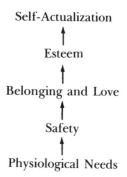

Self-Actualization

↑

Esteem

↑

Belonging and Love

↑

Safety

↑

Physiological Needs

The needs are arranged so that as one satisfies a lower need, one can deal with the next higher need. When one's physiological needs (for example, hunger, thirst, sex) are predictably satisfied, one can deal with the safety needs (for example, protection from the elements, from pain, and from unexpected dangers); when the safety needs are reasonably satisfied, one is free to deal with the belonging and love needs (for example, the need to love and be loved, to share one's life with a relevant other); when the belonging and love needs are adequately satisfied, one is released to ponder the esteem needs (for example, to make a recognizable contribution to the well-being of one's fellow humans); if the esteem needs are met satisfactorily, one is in a position to become self-actualized. By **self-actualization** Maslow means reaching one's full human potential. Since it is impossible for any person to completely reach his or her full potential, Maslow refers to those who have satisfied their esteem needs as *self-actualizing*. (A list of characteristics of self-actualizing people will be given shortly.)

As one climbs the hierarchy, the needs become more fragile. That is, the physiological and safety needs have a long evolutionary history and are therefore very powerful; but the higher needs for love, esteem, and self-actu-alization are "newer" and distinctly human, and therefore do not have as firm a biological foundation. This means that their satisfaction is easily interfered with. The higher up the hierarchy one goes, the truer this is; and therefore the satisfaction of the need for self-actualization—although the need is innate—is easily interfered with. Of self-actualization Maslow (1968) says:

> This inner nature is not strong and overpowering and unmistakable like the instincts of animals. It is weak and delicate and subtle and easily overcome by habit, cultural pressure, and wrong attitudes toward it. (p. 4)

Thus, although all humans have an innate drive to be self-actualized (to reach their full potential as humans), self-actualized people are rare. Another major reason that self-actualization occurs so infrequently is that it requires a great deal of honest knowledge of oneself, and most humans are fearful of such knowledge. Maslow calls the fear of self-knowledge the **Jonah complex**, and he says:

> More than any other kind of knowledge we fear knowledge of ourselves, knowledge that might transform our self-esteem and our self-image. . . . While human beings love knowledge and seek it—they are curious—they also fear it. The closer to the personal it is, the more they fear it. (1966, p. 16)

As we saw earlier, Maslow felt that for too long psychology had emphasized the study of lower animals and psychologically disturbed individuals. To begin to remedy the situation, he studied a number of people he felt were self-actualizing. Among them were Albert Einstein, Albert Schweitzer, Sigmund Freud, Jane Addams, William James, and Abraham Lincoln. Maslow concluded that self-actualizing people had the following characteristics:

1. They perceived reality accurately and fully.

2. They demonstrated a great acceptance of themselves and of others.

3. They exhibited spontaneity and naturalness.

4. They had a need for privacy.

5. They tended to be independent of their environment and culture.

6. They demonstrated a continuous freshness of appreciation.

7. They tended to have periodic mystic or peak experiences. Maslow (1970) describes a peak experience as follows:

> Feelings of limitless horizons opening up to the vision, the feeling of being simultaneously more powerful and also more helpless than one ever was before, the feeling of great ecstasy and wonder and awe, the loss of placing in time and space with, finally, the conviction that something extremely important and valuable had happened, so that the subject is to some extent transformed and strengthened even in his daily life by such experiences. (p. 164)

8. Self-actualizing people were concerned with all humans instead of with only their friends, relatives, and acquaintances.

9. They tended to have only a few friends.

10. They had a strong ethical sense but did not necessarily accept conventional ethics.

11. They had a well-developed but not hostile sense of humor.

12. They were creative.

Although Maslow concluded that his group of self-actualizing people were outstanding humans, he also indicated that they were not without faults. As Maslow (1970) says:

> Our subjects show many of the lesser human failings. They too are equipped with silly, wasteful or thoughtless habits. They can be boring, stubborn, irritating. They are by no means free from a rather superficial vanity, pride, partiality to their own productions, family, friends, and children. Temper outbursts are not rare.
>
> Our subjects are occasionally capable of an extraordinary and unexpected ruthlessness. It must be remembered that they are very strong people. This makes it possible for them to display a surgical coldness when this is called for,

beyond the power of the average man. The man who found that a long-trusted acquaintance was dishonest cut himself off from this friendship sharply and abruptly and without any observable pangs whatsoever. Another woman who was married to someone she did not love, when she decided on divorce, did it with a decisiveness that looked almost like ruthlessness. Some of them recover so quickly from the death of people close to them as to seem heartless. (p. 175)

If a person is functioning at any level other than self-actualization, he or she is said to be deficiency-motivated. That is, the person is seeking specific things to satisfy specific needs, and his or her perceptions are need-directed. Jourard (1974) describes **need-directed perception** as follows:

> Need-directed perception is a highly focused searchlight darting here and there, seeking the objects which will satisfy needs, ignoring everything irrelevant to the need. (p. 68)

Deficiency motivation (D-motivation) leads to need-directed perception (D-perception or D-cognition). Unlike most psychologists, Maslow was mainly interested in what happened to people *after* their basic needs were satisfied. His answer was that people who satisfied their basic needs and became self-actualizing entered into a different mode of existence. Instead of being deficiency-motivated, they were being-motivated (B-motivated). **Being motivation** involves embracing the higher values of life, such as beauty, truth, and justice. Being-motivated people are also capable of B-love, which unlike D-love is nonpossessive and insatiable. Unlike D-perception, **being perception** (B-perception) does not involve seeking specific things in the environment. Therefore, the person interacting with the world through B-perception is open to a wider range of experience than the person who interacts through D-perception.

Maslow's theory is considered humanistic because it assumes that humans have an innate drive to approximate their full potential and to embrace the higher meaning of human exis-

Carl Rogers

LANDMARK PHOTO

tence. Given an optimal environment, all humans would tend toward self-actualization and would seek a harmonious existence with other humans.

Carl Rogers

Carl Rogers (1902–   ) was born in a suburb of Chicago. After graduating from the University of Wisconsin in 1924, Rogers enrolled in the Union Theological Seminary in New York. After two years at the seminary, Rogers's doubts as to whether the religious approach was the most effective way of helping people caused him to transfer to Columbia University, where he earned his M.A. in clinical psychology in 1928 and his Ph.D. in 1931.

After obtaining his Ph.D., Rogers went to work for the Child Study Department of the Society for the Prevention of Cruelty to Children in Rochester, New York. Here Rogers had several experiences that caused him to develop his own brand of psychotherapy. For example, the society was dominated by therapists trained in the psychoanalytic tradition, people who saw their job as gaining an "insight" into the cause of a problem and then sharing that insight with the client. At first Rogers, too, followed this procedure. In one case he concluded that a mother's rejection of her son was the cause of the son's delinquent behavior, but his attempts to share this insight with the mother failed completely. Rogers (1961) describes what happened next:

> Finally I gave up. I told her that it seemed we had both tried, but we had failed. . . . She agreed. So we concluded the interview, shook hands, and she walked to the door of the office. Then she turned and asked, "Do you take adults for counseling here?" When I replied in the affirmative, she said, "Well then, I would like some help." She came to the chair she had left, and began to pour out her despair about her marriage, her troubled relationship with her husband, her sense of failure and confusion, all very different from the sterile "Case History" she had given before. Real therapy began then. . . .
>
> This incident was one of a number which helped me to experience that fact—only fully realized later—that it is the client who knows what hurts, what directions to go, what problems are crucial, what experiences have been deeply buried. It began to occur to me that unless I had a need to demonstrate my own cleverness and learning, I would do better to rely upon the client for the direction of movement in the process. (pp. 11–12)

Eventually Rogers developed a therapeutic technique that has been at various times referred to as client-centered, nondirective, and person-centered. Rogers's approach is based on the belief that a person's subjective experience is the major determinant of behavior, and that only the individual himself or herself is aware of

this experience. Patients use the therapeutic process to better understand, and perhaps change, their own subjective views of themselves, the world, and other people. Because of its emphasis on subjective reality, Rogers's theory, like all the existential-humanistic theories, is referred to as *phenomenological*. As we have seen, a phenomenological theory is one that accepts subjective experience as it occurs to the individual, without attempting to dissect it or analyze it further.

Like Maslow, Rogers postulated an innate human drive toward self-actualization; for this reason, Rogers's theory is also considered humanistic. If people use this *actualizing tendency* as a frame of reference in living their lives, there is a strong likelihood that they will live fulfilling lives and ultimately reach their full potential. Such people are said to be using the **organismic valuing process**. Using this process, a person approaches and maintains experiences that are in accord with the actualizing tendency but terminates and avoids those that are not. Such a person is motivated by his or her own feelings and is living what the existentialists call an authentic life—that is, a life motivated by a person's true inner feelings rather than mores, beliefs, traditions, or conventions imposed by others.

Unfortunately, according to Rogers, not many people live their lives according to the organismic valuing process. A problem arises because of our **need for positive regard**. Positive regard involves receiving such things as love, warmth, sympathy, and acceptance from the people most important to us. If these things were given freely to a child, no problem would arise, but they usually are not. Usually parents (or other relevent people) will give children positive regard only if the children act or think in certain ways. This sets up **conditions of worth**. The children soon learn that in order to feel loved, they must act and think in accordance with the values of the relevant people in their lives. Gradually, as the children internalize these values, the values replace the organismic valuing process as a frame of reference for living life. As long as people live their lives according to someone else's values instead of their own true feelings, experience will be filtered and distorted, and certain experiences that would have been in accord with the organismic valuing process will be denied. Rogers (1966) says:

> In order to hold the love of a parent, the child introjects as his own values and perceptions which he does not actually experience. He then denies to awareness the organismic experiencings that contradict these introjections. Thus, his self-concept contains false elements that are not based on what he is, in his experiencing. (p. 192)

According to Rogers, there is only one way to avoid imposing conditions of worth on people, and that is to give them unconditional positive regard. With **unconditional positive regard**, people are loved and respected for what they truly are; therefore, there is no need for certain experiences to be denied or distorted. Only someone who experiences unconditional positive regard can become a **fully functioning person**. Rogers (1959) says:

> If an individual should *experience* only *unconditional positive regard*, then no *conditions of worth* would develop, self-regard would be unconditional, the needs for *positive regard* and *self-regard* would never be at variance with *organismic evaluation*, and the individual would continue to be *psychologically adjusted*, and would be fully functioning. (p. 224)

When conditions of worth replace the organismic valuing process as a guide for living, the person becomes incongruent. What Rogers calls an **incongruent person** is essentially the same as what the existentialists call an inauthentic person. In both cases, the person is no longer true to his or her own feelings. Rogers sees incongruency as the cause of mental disorders, and he believes, therefore, that the goal of psychotherapy is to help people overcome conditions of worth and again live in accordance with

their oganismic valuing processes. Rogers (1959) describes this goal as follows:

> This, as we see it, is the basic estrangement in man. He has not been true to himself, to his own natural organismic valuing of experience, but for the sake of preserving the positive regard of others has now come to falsify some of the values he experiences and to perceive them only in terms based upon their value to others. Yet this has not been a conscious choice, but a natural—and tragic—development in infancy. The path of development toward psychological maturity . . . is the undoing of this estrangement in man's functioning . . . the achievement of a self which is congruent with experience, and the restoration of a unified organismic valuing process as the regulator of behavior. (pp. 226–227)

When people are living in accordance with their organismic valuing process, they are fully functioning. The fully functioning person embraces life in much the same way as Maslow's self-actualizing person does. Again, such a person is said to be living an authentic life.

George Kelly

George Kelly (1905–1967) is included in the section on humanistic psychology because of his insistence that humans were capable of construing themselves and their world in any number of ways. He urged people who did not like how things look to look at things differently. For Kelly, most personal problems were perceptual problems.

Kelly was born on a farm near Perth, Kansas. During the early pioneering efforts of his family, Kelly developed a pragmatic spirit that remained with him throughout his life. That is, the major criterion he used to judge an idea or a device was whether it worked or not. Kelly earned his B.A. in physics and mathematics from Park College in 1926. He earned his M.A. from the University of Kansas in 1928, with a major in educational sociology and a minor in labor relations. After holding a variety of jobs,

George Kelly

Kelly enrolled in the psychology program at Iowa State University, where he earned a Ph.D. in 1931.

During the Great Depression, Kelly accepted an appointment at Fort Hays Kansas State College. Many people were having emotional problems, and Kelly wanted to help them, but he was not trained as a clinical psychologist. This lack of training in clinical psychology, along with his pragmatic attitude, gave Kelly great latitude in dealing with emotional problems, and this resulted in his unique theory of personality.

Soon after arriving at Fort Hays, Kelly developed traveling clinics that serviced the public school system. The clinics brought Kelly into contact with a wide range of emotional problems that both students and teachers experienced. Soon Kelly made a remarkable observation. Since he was not trained in any particular therapeutic approach, he began to experiment

with a variety of approaches, and he discovered that *anything that caused his clients to view themselves or their problems differently improved the situation*. Whether a proposed explanation was "logical" or "correct" seemed to have little to do with its effectiveness. Kelly (1969) says:

> I began fabricating "insights." I deliberately offered "preposterous interpretations" to my clients. Some of them were about as un-Freudian as I could make them—first proposed somewhat cautiously, of course, and then, as I began to see what was happening, more boldly. My only criteria were that the explanation account for the crucial facts as the client saw them, and that it carry implications for approaching the future in a different way. (p. 52)

In this statement lies the cornerstone of Kelly's position. That is, whether or not a person has a psychological problem is mainly a matter of how that person views things.

Constructive alternativism. Kelly observed that the major goal of scientists was to reduce uncertainty; and since he believed that this was also the goal of all humans, he said all humans were like scientists. But whereas scientists created theories with which they attempted to predict future events, nonscientists created **construct systems** to predict future events. If either a scientific theory or a personal construct system was effective, it adequately predicted the future and thereby reduced uncertainty. And both scientific theories and construct systems were tested empirically. That is, they were checked against reality and were revised until their ability to predict future events or experiences was satisfactory. For Kelly, a construct was a verbal label. Hergenhahn (1984) gives the following example:

> Upon meeting a person for the first time, one might construe that person with the construct "friendly." If the person's subsequent behavior is in accordance with the construct of friendly, then the construct will be useful in anticipating that person's behavior. If the new acquaintance acts in an unfriendly manner, he or she will

need to be construed either with different constructs or by using the other pole . . . of the friendly-unfriendly construct. The major point is that constructs are used to anticipate the future so they must fit reality. Arriving at a construct system that corresponds fairly closely to reality is largely a matter of trial and error. (p. 268)

With his concept of **constructive alternativism**, Kelly aligned himself squarely with the existentialists. Kelly maintained that people were free to choose the constructs they used in interacting with the world. This meant that people could view and interpret events in an almost infinite number of ways, since construing them was an individual matter. No one was a victim of circumstances, nor was anyone a victim of the past; we were free to view things as we wished. Kelly (1955) says:

We take the stand that there are always some alternative constructions available to choose among in dealing with the world. No one needs to paint himself into a corner; no one needs to be completely hemmed in by circumstances; no one needs to be the victim of his biography. (p. 15)

According to Kelly, it was not common experience that made people similar. Rather, it was how they construed reality. If two people employed more or less the same personal constructs in dealing with the world, then they were similar no matter how similar or dissimilar their physical experiences had been. Kelly also said that in order to truly understand another person, we had to know how that person construed things. In other words, we had to know what that person's expectations were, and then we could choose to act in accordance with those expectations. The deepest kind of social interaction occurred when this process was mutual.

Fixed-role therapy. Kelly's approach to therapy reflected his belief that psychological problems were *perceptual problems*, and that the job of the therapist was therefore to help the client *view*

things differently. Usually Kelly began the therapeutic process by having a client write a **self-characterization**. This provided Kelly with information about how the client viewed himself or herself, the world, and other people. Next, Kelly created a role for the client to play for about two weeks. The character in the role was markedly different from the client's self-characterization. The client became an actor, and the therapist became a supporting actor. Kelly called this approach to treating clients **fixed-role therapy**. He hoped that this procedure would help the client discover other possible ways of viewing his or her life. According to Kelly (1964):

What I am saying is that it is not so much what man is that counts as it is what he ventures out to make himself. To make the leap he must do more than disclose himself; he must risk a certain amount of confusion. Then, as soon as he does catch a glimpse of a different kind of life, he needs to find some way of overcoming the paralyzing moment of threat, for this is the instant when he wonders what he really is— whether he is what he just was or is what he is about to be. (p. 147)

In the role of supporting actor, the therapist had to help the client deal with this threatening moment and then provide experiences that validated the client's new construct system. According to Kelly, people with psychological problems had lost their ability to make-believe, an ability that the therapist must help the client regain.

We could just as easily have classified Kelly's theory as existential as humanistic. Clearly, his theory emphasizes the role of free choice in creating the constructs with which we interact with the world. We place Kelly's work in the section on humanistic psychology only because of Kelly's constant hope that healthy humans would open themselves to an ever-increasing variety of experiences, and that neurotic humans would come to embrace the world in less restrictive ways. This hope is clearly humanistic.

COMPARISON OF EXISTENTIAL AND HUMANISTIC PSYCHOLOGY

Existential and humanistic psychology have enough in common to cause them often to be lumped together as existential-humanistic psychology. The following is a list of beliefs that they share.

1. Humans have a free will and are therefore responsible for their own actions. Again, freedom and responsibility go hand in hand.

2. The most appropriate method by which to study humans is phenomenology, the study of intact subjective experience.

3. In order to be understood, the human must be studied as a whole. Elementism of any kind gives a distorted view of human nature.

4. Humans are unique, and therefore anything learned about other animals is irrelevant to the understanding of humans.

5. Each human is unique, since no two have the same subjective reality.

6. Hedonism is not a major motive in human behavior. Instead of seeking pleasure and avoiding pain, humans seek meaningful lives characterized by personal growth.

7. The "self" experiences things and determines how the person will interpret, value, and respond to those things.

8. Living an authentic life is better than living an inauthentic one.

The major difference between existential and humanistic psychology lies in their assumptions about human nature. The humanists assume that humans are basically good, and therefore that if they were placed in a healthy environment, they would naturally live a life in harmony with other humans. For the humanist, the major motivation in life is the actualizing tendency, which is innate and which continually drives a person toward those activities and events conducive to self-actualization. The existentialists, on the other hand, view human nature as essentially neutral. For them, the only thing we are born with is the freedom to choose the nature of our existence. This is what Sartre meant by his famous statement "Existence precedes essence." For Sartre, and most of the existential philosophers, there is no human essence at birth. We are not created in God's or anything else's image, nor do we possess animal instincts. We are free of all these "essences," and therefore free to become what we choose. We become our choices. We can exercise this freedom to create any kind of a life, either good or bad. The major motive in life, according to the existentialist, is to create meaning by effectively making one's choices. A number of existential thinkers have reached the conclusion that without meaning, life is not worth living, but that with meaning, humans can tolerate almost any conditions. Viktor Frankl, in his book *Man's Search for Meaning* (1963), quotes Nietzsche as saying, "He who has a *why* to live can bear with almost any *how*" (p. xiii). Frankl maintains that there is only one motivational force for humans, and that is what he calls the "will to meaning" (p. 154).

Generally, the view of human nature that the humanists hold causes them to be optimistic about humans and their future. If societies could be made compatible with our nature, they say, humans could live together in peace and harmony. The existentialists are more pessimistic. For them, humans have no built-in guidance system but only the freedom to choose. Since we are free, we cannot blame God, our parents, genetics, or circumstances for our misfortune—only ourselves. This responsibility often makes freedom more of a curse than a blessing, and people often choose not to exercise their freedom by conforming to values that others have formulated. In his famous book *Escape from Freedom* (1941), Erich Fromm

(1900–1980) says that often the first thing people do when they acquire freedom is attempt to escape from it by affiliating themselves with someone or something that will reduce or eliminate their choices. The negative aspect of freedom is captured in the following hypothetical situation in which a student in a progressive school asked the teacher: "Do we have to do whatever we want to again today?" It is very difficult to be free.

Another important difference between existential and humanistic psychologists is that for the existentialist, the realization that one's death is inevitable is extremely important. Before a rich full life is possible, one must come to grips with the fact that one's life is finite. The humanistic psychologist does not dwell as much on the meaning of death in human existence. Hall and Lindzey (1978) summarize the pessimism of existential psychology:

> It would be wrong to conclude . . . that existential psychology is primarily optimistic or hopeful about humans. One does not need to read far in Kierkegaard, Nietzsche, Heidegger, Sartre, Binswanger, or Boss to realize that this is far from being the case. Existential psychology is as concerned with death as it is with life. Nothingness yawns always at one's feet. Dread looms as large as love does in the existentialists' writings. There can be no light without shadows. A psychology that makes guilt inborn and an inescapable feature of existence does not offer much solace. "I am free" means at the same time, "I am completely responsible for my existence" . . . becoming a human being is a tough project and few achieve it. (p. 320)

In contrast, Maddi and Costa (1972) summarize the basic optimism of humanistic psychology:

> Humanism, as espoused by third-force adherents, leads to a psychology that is not only centered on the human being but sets a positive value on those of his capabilities and aspirations that seem to distinguish him from lower animals and make him master of his own fate. Choice, will-power, conceptual thought, imagination, introspection, self-criticism, aspirations

for the future, and creativity are important topics in humanism, for they refer to capabilities and interests that seem unique to man as a species. . . .
> Humanism is not only concerned with the characteristics setting man apart from other living things. Also important are the characteristics that set each man apart from other men. Individuality—the thoughts, fantasies, strivings, worries, triumphs, and the tragedies that sum up to one particular person's existence and no one else's—is always a central topic in humanistic positions. . . .
> It should be apparent in all this that humanism takes a very optimistic, laudatory view of man. In the history of philosophical thought, humanism has always made a hero of man, and the contemporary third force in psychology is certainly no exception. (pp. 3–5)

EVALUATION

Modern existential-humanistic psychology began as a protest movement against behaviorism, because behaviorism saw too much similarity between humans and other animals. The protesters contended that behaviorism concentrated on trivial kinds of behavior and ignored or minimized the mental and emotional processes that made humans unique. The existential-humanistic psychologists viewed psychoanalysis as restrictive at best because it focused on abnormal individuals and emphasized unconscious or sexual motivation, while ignoring healthy individuals whose primary motives included personal growth and the improvement of society. They criticized scientific psychology in general because it modeled itself after the physical sciences by assuming determinism and seeking lawfulness among classes of events. It also viewed individual uniqueness, something that was very important to existential-humanistic psychology, as a nuisance. Also, since science and reliable measurement went hand in hand, scientific psychology excluded many important human attributes from study simply because of the difficulty of measuring them.

Processes such as willing, valuing, and seeking meaning are examples of such attributes, as are such emotions as love, guilt, despair, happiness, and hope.

Criticisms

It should come as no surprise that existential-humanistic psychology itself has been criticized. Each of the following has been offered as one of its weaknesses.

1. Existential-humanistic psychology equates behaviorism with the work of Watson and Skinner. Both of these men stressed environmental events as the causes of human behavior and denied or minimized the importance of mental events. Other behaviorists, however, stress mental events in their analysis of behavior—for example, Tolman and Hull.

2. It overlooks the cumulative nature of science by insisting that scientific psychology does not care about the loftier human attributes. The problem is that we are not yet prepared to study such attributes. One must first learn a language before one can compose poetry. The kind of scientific psychology that existential-humanistic psychologists criticize provides the basis for the future study of more complex human characteristics.

3. The description of humans that the existential-humanistic psychologists offer is like the more favorable ones found through the centuries in some poetry, literature, or even religion. It represents a kind of wishful thinking that is not supported by the facts that more objective psychology has accumulated. We should not ignore facts just because they are not to our liking.

4. It criticizes behaviorism, psychoanalysis, and scientific psychology in general, but all three have made significant contributions to the betterment of the human condition. In other words, all three have done the very thing that existential-humanistic psychology sets as one of its major goals. The behaviorists justifiably claim to have brought about improvements in such areas as psychotherapy, education, child rearing, and the management of personal behavior. To brand the entire behavioristic movement as wrong or ineffective because it is based on an "incorrect" assumption about human nature is overly simplistic. Likewise, the psychoanalysts justifiably claim that the information they have provided has vastly improved our understanding of not only mentally ill people but normal people as well. Most behaviorists and psychoanalysts would agree with the weaker criticism that they have had limited success in explaining human behavior.

5. If existential-humanistic psychology rejects scientific method as a means of evaluating propositions about humans, what is to be used in its place? If intuition or reasoning alone are to be used, this enterprise should not be referred to as psychology, but would be more accurately labeled philosophy or even religion. The existential-humanistic approach to studying humans is often characterized as a throwback to psychology's prescientific past.

6. By rejecting animal research, the existential-humanistic psychologists are turning their backs on an extremely valuable source of knowledge about humans. Not to use the insights of evolutionary theory in studying human behavior is at best regressive.

7. Many of the terms and concepts that existential-humanistic psychologists use are so nebulous that they defy clear definition and verification.

Contributions

To be fair to the existential-humanistic psychologists, it must be pointed out that they usually do not complain that behaviorism, psychoanalysis, and scientific psychology have made *no* contributions to the understanding of humans. Rather, their claim has been that behaviorism and psychoanalysis tell only part of the story, and that perhaps some important human attributes cannot be studied using the traditional methods and assumptions of science. As William James said, if existing methods are ineffective for studying certain aspects of human nature, it is not those aspects of human nature that are to be discarded but the methods. The existential-humanistic psychologists do not want to discard scientific inquiry but to expand our conception of science so that scientific inquiry can be used to study the higher human attributes. This desire for a broader conception of science appears in the comments of Rollo May (1967):

> The outlines of a science of man we suggest will deal with man as a symbol-maker, the reasoner, the historical mammal who can participate in his community and who possesses the potentiality of freedom and ethical action. The pursuit of this science will take no less rigorous thought and wholehearted discipline than the pursuit of experimental and natural science at their best, but it will place the scientific enterprise in a broader context. Perhaps it will again be possible to study man scientifically and still see him whole. (p. 199)

We see in contemporary psychology several examples of psychologists who accept the existential-humanistic view of human nature without giving up their faith in scientific method. Walter Mischel, for example, has been instrumental in the formulation of experimentally rigorous social-learning theory. Here he describes his image of human nature and the methods that could be used to study human nature:

> This image is one of the human being as an active, aware problem-solver, capable of profiting from an enormous range of experiences and cognitive capacities, possessed of great potential for good or ill, actively constructing his or her psychological world, interpreting and processing information in potentially creative ways, influencing the world but also being influenced by it lawfully—even if the laws are difficult to discover and hard to generalize. It views the person as so complex and multi-faceted as to defy classifications and comparisons on any single or simple common dimensions, as multiply influenced by a host of determinants, as uniquely organized on the basis of prior experiences and future expectations, and yet as studyable by the methods of science, and continuously responsive to stimulus conditions in meaningful ways. It is an image that has moved a long way from the instinctual drive-reduction models, the static global traits, and the automatic stimulus–response bonds of earlier times. . . . It is an image that highlights the shortcomings of all simplistic theories that view behavior as the exclusive result of any narrow set of determinants, whether these are habits, traits, drives, constructs, instincts, genes, or reinforcers. And yet it is an image that is sure to shift in still unpredictable directions as our understanding and knowledge increase. (1981, pp. 532–533)

This expansion of psychology's domain is existential-humanistic psychology's major contribution to the discipline. In psychology there is now an increased tendency to study the whole person. We are concerned not only with how people learn, think, and mature biologically and intellectually, but with how people formulate plans to attain future goals and why people laugh, cry, and create meaning in their lives. In the opinion of many, the existential-humanistic paradigm has breathed new life into psychology. In the following passage, Hall and Lindzey (1978) mention only existential psychology, but their remarks pertain to humanistic psychology as well.

> Whatever the future of existential psychology may be—and at the present time it appears to have sufficient vigor and vitality to last a long time—it has already served at least one very important function. That function is to rescue psychology from being drowned in a sea of theories that have lost contact with the everyday world and with the "givens" of experience. . . . Existentialism is helping to revitalize a science that many feel has become theoretically

moribund. It has done this by insisting on using a strictly phenomenological methodology. It has tried to see what is actually there and to describe human existence in concrete terms. . . . Whatever the future of existential psychology may be . . . it is clear that now it offers a profoundly new way of studying and comprehending human beings. For this reason, it merits the closest attention by serious students of psychology. (pp. 343–344)

SUMMARY

In the early 1960s a group of psychologists emerged who felt that behaviorism and psychoanalysis, the two major forces in psychology, were neglecting important aspects of human existence. What was needed was a third force that emphasized the positive, creative side of humans. This third force psychology is a combination of existential and humanistic psychology, both of which employ phenomenology. In modern times Brentano and Husserl developed phenomenology, which is the study of intact, meaningful conscious experiences as they occur and without any preconceived notions about the nature of those experiences. Both Brentano and Husserl believed that phenomenal experience could be trusted to represent accurately the physical world. With their concept of intentionality, they indicated that the person and the world came together in consciousness. All conscious acts, they said, intended (referred to) something outside of themselves. An example is the statement "I see that girl." Husserl felt that a careful, objective study of mental phenomena could provide a bridge between philosophy and science. In addition to the kind of phenomenology that focused on intentionality, Husserl proposed a second kind that studied all aspects of subjective experience. Thus, for Husserl, phenomenology could study the mind turned outward or the mind turned inward.

When taken over by the existentialists, phenomenology became a study of the totality of human existence. Such a study focused on the full range of human cognitive experience, including anxiety, dread, fear, joy, guilt, and anguish. Husserl's student Heidegger expanded phenomenology into existential inquiry. Heidegger studied *Dasein*, or being-in-the-world. He believed that humans had a free will but that they were thrown by events beyond their control into their life circumstances. Thrownness determined such things as whether a person was male or female, rich or poor, attractive or unattractive, and so on. It was up to each person to make the most of his or her life no matter what the circumstances. By choosing from among the various alternatives available, we grew as human beings. Choosing, however, required entering the unknown, and this caused anxiety. For Heidegger, then, exercising one's freedom required courage, but only by exercising one's freedom could one live an authentic life—a life that the person had chosen, and therefore a life for which the person was completely responsible. If a person lived his or her life in accordance with other people's values, he or she was living an inauthentic life. For Heidegger, the first step toward living an authentic life was to come to grips with the inevitability of death. Once a person comprehended and dealt with finitude, he or she could proceed to live a rich, full, authentic life.

Binswanger applied Heidegger's philosophical ideas to psychiatry and psychology. Binswanger called his approach to psychotherapy *Daseinanalysis*, or the study of a person's approach to being-in-the-world. Binswanger divided *Dasein* into the *Umwelt* (the physical world), the *Mitwelt* (the social world), and the *Eigenwelt* (the person's perceptions of himself or herself). According to Binswanger, each person embraced life's experiences through a world-design, which was a general orientation toward life. One world-design could portray the world and everything in it as hostile, another could portray it as friendly, and still another could portray some things as hostile and others as friendly. Binswanger attempted to understand his patients' world-designs; and if a patient's world-design was proving to be ineffective, he would suggest alternative, potentially more effective ones. Like Heidegger, Binswanger believed that the circumstances into which one was thrown placed limits on personal freedom. Thrownness created what Binswanger called the ground for existence, from which one had to begin the process of becoming by exercising one's freedom. According to Binswanger, each person attempted to rise above his or her ground for existence and to attain being-beyond-the-world—that is, to rise above current circumstances by transforming them through free choice.

Rollo May was primarily responsible for bringing existential psychology to America. Like the other existential psychologists, May believes that normal, healthy living involves the experience of anxiety, since living an authentic life necessitates venturing into the unknown. If a person cannot cope with normal anxiety, he or she will develop neurotic anxiety and will be driven from an authentic life to a life of conformity, or to a life that is overly restrictive. Furthermore, since the person with neurotic anxiety is not exercising his or her human capacity to choose, he or she experiences guilt. Thus, an authentic life is characterized by normal anxiety, and an inauthentic life by neurotic anxiety and guilt.

Unlike the existential psychologists, the humanistic psychologists believe that humans are basically good, a belief that can be traced back to Rousseau. According to Maslow, the founder of the third force psychology, human needs are arranged in a hierarchy. If one satisfactorily meets the physiological, safety, belonging and love, and esteem needs, then one is in position to become self-actualized. Leading a life characterized by fullness, spontaneity, and creativity, the self-actualizing person is being-motivated rather than deficiency-motivated. That is, since this person has met the basic needs, he or she does not need to seek specific things in the environment. Rather, he or she can embrace the world fully and openly and ponder the higher values of life.

Rogers concluded that the only way to understand a person was to determine how that person viewed things—that is, to determine that person's subjective reality. This view resulted in Rogers's famous client-centered or person-centered therapy. Like Maslow, Rogers postulated an innate actualizing tendency. For this actualizing tendency to be realized, one had to use the organismic valuing process as a frame of reference in living one's life. That is, one had to use one's own inner feelings in determining the value of various experiences. If one lived according to one's organismic valuing process, one was a congruent person and was living an authentic life. Unfortunately, because humans had a need for positive regard, they often allowed the relevant people in their lives to place conditions of worth on them. When conditions of worth replaced the organismic valuing process as a frame of reference for living one's life, the person became incongruent and lived an inauthentic life. According to Rogers, the only way to prevent incongruency was for the person to receive unconditional positive regard from the relevant people in his or her life.

Kelly, who was not trained as a clinical psychologist, tried a number of approaches to dealing with emotional problems. He found that anything that caused his clients to view themselves and their problems differently resulted in improvement. Because of this observation, Kelly concluded that mental problems were really perceptual problems, and he maintained that humans were free to construe the world in any way they chose to. They did this by creating a construct system that was, or should be, tested empirically. A number of constructs could be used to construe any situation. That is, one could always view the world in a variety of ways, so how one viewed it was a matter of personal choice. In fixed-role therapy, Kelly had his clients write a self-characterization; then he would create a role for his client to play that was distinctly different from the client's personality. By offering the client support and help in playing his or her role, Kelly became a supporting actor and helped the client to view himself or herself differently. Once the client saw that there were alternative ways of viewing one's self, one's life, and one's problems, improvement often resulted. According to Kelly, neurotics had lost their ability to make believe.

Existential and humanistic psychology share the following beliefs: humans possess a free will; humans are responsible for their actions; phenomenology is the most appropriate method for studying humans; humans must be studied as whole beings and not divided up in any way; since humans are unique as a species, animal research is irrelevant to an understanding of humans; no two humans are alike; the search for meaning is the most important human motive; there is a "self" to which things happen and which values various experiences; and all humans should aspire to live authentic lives. The major difference between existential and humanistic psychology is that the former views human nature as neutral, whereas the latter views it as basically good. According to the existential psychologist, because we do not have an innate nature or guidance system, we must constantly choose our existence. The existential

psychologist sees freedom as a curse as well as a blessing, and something from which most humans attempt to escape.

Existential-humanistic psychology has been criticized for equating behaviorism with the formulations of Watson and Skinner, and thereby ignoring the work of other behaviorists who stressed the importance of mental events; for failing to understand that psychology's scientific efforts must first concentrate on the simpler aspects of humans before it can study the more complex aspects; for offering a description of humans that may be contrary to the facts; for minimizing or ignoring the positive contributions of behaviorism and psychoanalysis; for suggesting methods of inquiry that go back to psychology's prescientific history; for having more in common with philosophy and religion than with psychology; for overlooking a valuable source of information by rejecting the validity of animal research; and for using terms and concepts so nebulous as to defy clear definition or verification. Existential-humanistic psychology's major contribution has been to expand psychology's domain by urging that all aspects of humans be investigated and that psychology's conception of science be changed to allow objective study of uniquely human attributes.

DISCUSSION QUESTIONS

1. What is third force psychology? What are the other two forces?

2. Describe the phenomenology of Brentano and Husserl.

3. What did Brentano and Husserl mean by *intentionality*?

4. What were the two kinds of phenomenology that Husserl suggested?

5. How did Heidegger expand phenomenology?

6. Discuss the following terms and concepts from Heidegger's theory: *Dasein, authenticity, becoming, responsibility*, and *thrownness*.

7. Describe Binswanger's method of *daseinanalysis*.

8. Discuss the following terms and concepts from Binswanger's theory: *Umwelt, Mitwelt, Eigenwelt, world-design, ground of existence*, and *being-beyond-the-world*.

9. In May's theory, what is the relationship between anxiety and guilt? What is the

difference between normal anxiety and neurotic anxiety?

10. What are the main tenets of humanistic psychology?

11. Summarize Maslow's theory of motivation.

12. List what Maslow found to be the characteristics of self-actualizing people.

13. What is the difference between deficiency motivation and being motivation? Give an example of each.

14. For Rogers, what constituted an incongruent person? In your answer, include a discussion of the organismic valuing process, the need for positive regard, and conditions of worth.

15. According to Rogers what was the only way to avoid incongruency?

16. Why did Kelly maintain that all humans are like scientists?

17. Describe Kelly's concept of constructive alternativism.

18. Describe Kelly's approach to psychotherapy. What did Kelly mean when he said that psychological problems were perceptual problems?

19. What are the similarities and differences between humanistic and existential psychology?

20. Summarize the criticisms of existential-humanistic psychology.

21. In what way(s) has existential-humanistic psychology contributed to modern psychology?

GLOSSARY

Anxiety The feeling that results when one confronts the unknown, as when one contemplates death or when one's choices carry one into new life circumstances. According to the existentialists, one cannot live an authentic life without experiencing anxiety.

Authentic life According to the existentialists, the kind of life that is freely chosen and not dictated by the values of others. In such a life, one's internal feelings, values, and interpretations act as a guide for conduct.

Becoming A characteristic of the authentic life, since the authentic person is always becoming something other than what he or she was. Becoming is the normal, healthy psychological growth of a human being.

Being-beyond-the-world Binswanger's term for becoming. The healthy individual always attempts to transcend what he or she was.

Being motivation For Maslow, the kind of motivation that characterizes the self-actualizing person. Because being motivation is not need-directed, it embraces the full meaning of human existence.

Being perception Perception that embraces fully "what is there," since it is not an attempt to locate specific items that will satisfy needs.

Binswanger, Ludwig (1881–1966) Applied Heidegger's existential philosophy to psychiatry and psychology. For Binswanger, a prerequisite for helping an emotionally disturbed person was determining how that person viewed himself or herself and the world. (See also **daseinanalysis** and **world-design**.)

Brentano, Franz (1838–1917) The modern founder of phenomenology. Brentano's act psychology required the careful analysis of meaningful, intact mental phenomena.

Conditions of worth According to Rogers, the conditions that the relevant people in our lives place on us and that we must meet before these people will give us positive regard.

Constructive alternativism Kelly's notion that it was always possible to view circumstances in a variety of ways.

Construct systems The collection of personal constructs with which people make predictions about future events.

Dasein Heidegger's term for being-in-the-world. The world does not exist without humans, and humans do not exist without the world. Since humans exist in the world, it is there that they must exercise their free will.

Daseinanalysis Binswanger's method of psycho-therapy, which required that the therapist understand the client's world-view. Daseinanalysis examines a person's mode of being-in-the-world.

Deficiency motivation According to Maslow, motivation that is directed toward the satisfaction of some specific need.

Eigenwelt Binswanger's term for a person's private, inner experiences.

Existential psychology The brand of contemporary psychology that was influenced by existential philosophy. The key concepts in existential psychology include freedom, responsibility, anxiety, guilt, and authenticity.

Fixed-role therapy Kelly's brand of therapy, whereby he would assign a role for his clients to play that was distinctly different from the client's self-characterization. With this kind of therapy, the therapist acts much like a supporting actor.

Fully functioning person Rogers's term for a person who is living a congruent or authentic life.

Ground of existence Binswanger's term for the circumstances into which a person is thrown, and according to which he or she must make choices.

Guilt The feeling that results from living an inauthentic life.

Heidegger, Martin (1889–1976) Expanded Husserl's phenomenology to include an examination of the totality of human existence.

Humanistic psychology The branch of psychology that is closely aligned with existential psychology. Unlike existential psychology, however, humanistic psychology assumes that humans are basically good. That is, if negative environmental factors did not stifle human development, humans would live humane lives.

Husserl, Edmund (1859–1938) Proposed two kinds of phenomenology. One kind stressed intentionality and sought to determine the relationship between mental acts and events in the physical world. The second kind involved an analysis of the contents and processes of the mind that were independent of physical events.

Inauthentic life A life lived in accordance with values other than those freely and personally chosen. Such a life is characterized by guilt.

Incongruent person Rogers's term for the person whose organismic valuing process is replaced by conditions of worth as a guide for living.

Intentionality Brentano's notion that every mental act referred to something external to the act.

Jonah complex The fear of self-knowledge.

Kelly, George (1905–1967) Can be labeled as either an existential or a humanistic psychologist. Kelly emphasized that it was always possible to construe one's self and the world in a variety of ways. For Kelly, neurosis was essentially a perceptual problem.

Maslow, Abraham (1908–1970) A humanistic psychologist who emphasized the innate human tendency toward self-actualization. Maslow contended that behaviorism and psychoanalysis provided only a partial understanding of human existence, and that humanistic psychology needed to be added to complete our understanding.

May, Rollo (1909–   ) Psychologist who has been instrumental in bringing European existential philosophy and psychology to America.

Mitwelt Binswanger's term for the realm of social interactions.

Need-directed perception Perception whose purpose is to locate things in the environment that will satisfy a need.

Need for positive regard According to Rogers, the need for positive responses from the relevant people in one's life.

Neurotic anxiety The abnormal fear of freedom that results in a person living a life that minimizes personal choice.

Ontology The study of the nature of existence.

Organismic valuing process According to Rogers, the internal guidance system that a person can use to stay on the track toward self-actualization.

Phenomenology The introspective study of intact, meaningful mental experiences.

Responsibility A necessary by-product of freedom. If we are free to choose our own existence, then we are completely responsible for that existence.

Rogers, Carl (1902–   ) A contemporary humanistic psychologist. (See also **conditions of worth, congruency**, and **organismic valuing process**.)

Self-actualization According to Rogers and Maslow, the innate, human tendency toward wholeness. The self-actualizing person is open to experience and embraces the higher values of human existence.

Self-characterization The self-description that Kelly required of his clients before beginning their therapeutic program.

Shut-upness Kierkegaard's term for the situation of a person living a defensive or inauthentic life.

Subjective reality A person's consciousness.

Third force psychology The psychology consisting of both existential and humanistic psychology. It is concerned with examining the aspects of human existence that behaviorism and psychoanalysis have overlooked.

Thrownness According to Heidegger and Binswanger, the circumstances that characterize a person's existence and that are beyond the person's control.

Umwelt Binswanger's term for the physical world.

Unconditional positive regard According to Rogers, the giving of positive regard without any preconditions.

World-design Binswanger's term for a person's basic orientation toward life.

CHAPTER 18

Psychology Today

PSYCHOLOGY'S ECLECTICISM

Psychology today reflects many of the historical influences that we have considered in this text, but we must avoid the mistake of presentism referred to in Chapter 1. Presentism is the assumption that the present state of a discipline is the discipline's highest, best, and most fully developed state, and that this state evolved out of earlier, less-developed states. While presentism may be valid for some areas of the natural sciences, it does not characterize psychology. Although the many paradigms, theories, philosophical themes, and methodologies covered in this text can be found in one form or another in contemporary psychology, it would be incorrect to conclude that modern psychology evolved from earlier psychology. The term *evolution* implies that psychology began in a diffuse, nebulous state and became increasingly sophisticated over time. The evolutionary model would liken modern psychology to modern humans, and ancient psychology to our apelike ancestors. This model is inaccurate. A more accurate model would be the way languages change as the result of such factors as wars, immigration, commerce, and travel. Such events bring a language into contact with influences that often modify it in various ways. For example, the mixing of two cultures through warfare often leaves the language of each culture with words and phrases—and thus with ideas and concepts—of the other culture. This kind of cross-fertilization seems to characterize the origins of contemporary psychology.

It seems best, then, to view modern psychology as a hybrid discipline that resulted from a variety of influences, including those from philosophy, religion, natural science, and technology. As we shall see, there is no such thing as *a* psychology today—rather, there are *many* psychologies. Somewhere in the many versions of psychology that exist today one can clearly see the influence of nativism, associationism, rationalism, romanticism, empiricism, Newtonian physics, Einsteinian physics, evolutionary theory, and—as we shall see—computer technology.

Psychology today is diverse, but psychology has almost always been diverse. In psychology's long history there has never been a time when all psychologists accepted a single paradigm. Perhaps the closest psychology ever came to being a single-paradigm discipline was during the Dark and Middle Ages, when departures from the view of humans contained in church dogma were simply not tolerated. Some might suggest that behaviorism tended to dominate psychology during the period from about 1920 through the 1950s, but this was not quite the case. Although behaviorism was extremely popular, there were always influential critics of behaviorism and an abundance of alternative views to choose from.

Perhaps what distinguishes modern psychology from earlier psychology is the relatively peaceful coexistence of psychologists holding dissimilar views. During earlier times, when several psychological schools existed simultaneously, there was often open hostility between members of the different schools. The schools were almost like religions, in that the members of one school believed that they were correct and therefore that members of other schools were wrong. Today the schools are gone, and a spirit of *eclecticism* prevails that is reminiscent of the functional approach to psychology that William James suggested. That is, if something is part of the human experience, study it, and use the most effective methods available.

The present concerns of psychology range from the biochemistry of synaptic transmission to meaning in life; methodology ranges from rigorous experimentation to introspection. Some psychologists see this diversity as necessary because of the complexity of humans. Others see it as a sign that psychology has failed to carefully employ scientific method. Still others say that psychology is diverse because it is still in the preparadigmatic stage that characterizes the early development of a science. Thus, psychology is characterized by diversity even regarding opinions as to what its ultimate status can be. Some psychologists believe that psychology can ultimately be a unified science that employs one methodology and one set of principles to study all aspects of humans. Others say that humans can never be adequately studied by using only the methodology that a single paradigm generates.

To describe modern psychology as a diverse discipline does not specify the nature of that diversity. Perhaps two of the best ways to determine what activities psychologists are currenlty engaged in are (1) to scan the tables of contents of several current introductory psychology texts and (2) to note the present divisions of the American Psychological Association.

Contents of Introductory Texts

What follows is a condensation of the tables of contents of 15 introductory psychology texts with copyrights from 1982 on. Here is a summary of the chapters that our sample texts had in common.

- What Is Psychology?
- Psychology as a Science
- Psychology as a Profession
- Biological Correlates of Behavior
- Sensation and Perception
- Altered States of Consciousness
- Learning
- Memory
- Cognition
- Developmental Psychology
- Motivation
- Personality
- Abnormal Psychology
- Psychotherapy
- Social Psychology
- Statistical Methods (usually found in an appendix)

In this list of chapters from introductory texts we see little that is new, at least in terms of psychology's history. Most if not all of the chapters cover topics as old as psychology itself. This is not to say that the work in these areas has not progressed; it is simply to say that psychologists have tended to work on the same topics for a long time.

In viewing current introductory texts one also notices that only a few years ago most introductory texts defined *psychology* as "the science of behavior." Today, however, most texts either define psychology as "the science of behavior and cognition" or are careful to note that their use of the term *behavior* includes both overt and covert (internal) behavior. In other words, the consensus seems to be that psychology is the study of what humans do both internally and externally.

Almost without exception, the definitions of psychology contained in our sample of introductory texts referred to psychology as a sci-

TABLE 18.1 Divisions of the APA and their memberships.

Division	Number of members	Division	Number of members
General Psychology	4553	Philosophical and Theoretical Psychology	524
Teaching Psychology	2193	Experimental Analysis of Behavior	1543
Experimental Psychology	1475	History of Psychology	473
Evaluation and Measurement	1108	Community Psychology	1662
Physiological and Comparative Psychology	751	Psychopharmacology	1037
Developmental Psychology	1225	Psychotherapy	4386
Personality and Social Psychology	3698	Psychological Hypnosis	635
Psychological Study of Social Issues	2632	State Psychological Association Affairs	728
Psychology and the Arts	448	Humanistic Psychology	955
Clinical Psychology	4579	Mental Retardation	934
Consulting Psychology	727	Population and Environmental Psychology	501
Industrial and Organizational Psychology	2009	Psychology of Women	2019
Educational Psychology	3156	Psychologists Interested in Religious Issues	931
School Psychology	2330	Child and Youth Services	865
Counseling Psychology	2595	Health Psychology	1407
Psychologists in Public Service	1221	Psychoanalysis	1175
Military Psychology	565	Clinical Neuropsychology	636
Adult Development and Aging	881	Psychology and Law	581
Engineering Psychology	506	Psychologists in Private Practice	8400
Rehabilitation Psychology	865		
Consumer Psychology	316		

ence. But to refer to psychology as a science is valid only if it is understood that much of psychology is empirical but not experimental, and that some psychologists feel their work is not scientific at all. The latter group would be found in the existential-humanistic camp and would represent only a very small fraction of the total number of psychologists.

To refer to psychology as *empirical* means that most psychologists rely on some kind of observation to test their ideas, but these observations are not necessarily *experimental*. Usually the experimental psychologist makes his or her observations under controlled laboratory conditions, in which some variables are systematically varied, others are carefully measured, and still others are held constant. This kind of experimental activity is usually associated with science. In psychology today, however, many psychologists are empirical but not experimental. For example, the clinician may use changes in mannerisms or speech content to determine the effectiveness of his or her therapy; the social psychologist may observe such phenomena as

NOAM CHOMSKY

Noam Chomsky

Divisions of the APA

The 40 divisions of the American Psychological Association (1981), which are listed in Table 18.1, are another clear indication of the diversity of psychology today. The number of members in each division is also listed, so that the reader may note which areas of psychology are currently the most popular. It is quite common, however, for a psychologist to belong to more than one division.

From the handful of individuals who founded the American Psychological Association in 1892 in Worcester, Massachusetts, under the leadership of G. Stanley Hall, the membership has now grown to over 50,000. There are now more divisions of the American Psychological Association than there were psychologists attending its first meeting.

THE DECLINE OF BEHAVIORISM AND THE RETURN TO COGNITIVE PSYCHOLOGY

As we have seen, except for the periods when the church and later behaviorism dominated psychology, psychology has always entertained a variety of viewpoints that have influenced each other. Moreover, except for the radical behaviorism of such researchers as Pavlov, Watson, and Skinner, psychology has always studied some aspect of cognition. Thus, to say that psychology is *becoming* more cognitively oriented is inaccurate, since except for radical behaviorism, psychology has always been cognitively oriented. Nonetheless, there was a period from about 1920 to about 1950 when it was widely believed that cognitive processes either did not exist or that such processes were the by-product of brain activity and could be ignored. As long as these beliefs were dominant, the study of cognitive processes was inhibited.

patterns of crime, dating practices, or the content of popular music to determine the psychological effects of widespread unemployment; and the developmental psychologist may observe changes in speech as a function of age, or the relationship between child rearing practices and an adolescent's ability to withstand the stresses of puberty. Often uncontrolled empirical observations and experimentation are related—as, for example, when observation of how children seem to be learning in school suggests controlled experimentation on the learning process. The outcome of this experimentation may suggest how to improve the teaching of children in school.

Noam Chomsky's Influence

It is popular these days to search for the event or events that diminished the popularity of radical behaviorism and led to a return to cognitive psychology. Leahey (1980) claims that Noam Chomsky's review of Skinner's book *Verbal Behavior* (1957) was the crucial event. In his review (1959), Chomsky forcefully argues that language is too complex to be explained by operant principles, maintaining that the human brain is genetically programmed to generate language. Each child, says Chomsky, is born with brain structures that make it relatively easy for the child to learn the rules of language. Chomsky argues that children cannot learn these rules if they have to rely solely on principles of association (frequency, contiguity, reinforcement, and so on) as a means of learning. This successful nativistic attack on empirically based behaviorism did much to weaken the latter's influence. Although Chomsky is a linguist and not a psychologist, his views on language acquisition soon displaced the view based on operant principles. Leahey (1980, p. 347) describes Chomsky's impact on contemporary psychology: "Chomsky's review [of Skinner's *Verbal Behavior*] is perhaps the single most influential psychological paper published since Watson's Behaviorist Manifesto of 1913."

Marian Breland

The Work of Marian and Keller Breland

Another severe blow to behaviorists came from the work of Marian and Keller Breland, two of Skinner's former associates. The Brelands started a business called Animal Behavior Enterprises, which involved using operant principles to teach a variety of animals to do a variety of tricks. The trained animals were then put on display at fairs, conventions, amusement parks, and on television. At first the Brelands found their animals to be highly conditionable, but as time passed, instinctive behavior began to interfere with or replace learned behavior. For example, pigs that had learned to place large wooden coins into a "piggy bank" began to perform more slowly, and eventually they would root the coin instead of placing it in the bank, even when doing so delayed or prevented reinforcement. The interference or displacement of learned behavior by instinctive behavior was called *instinctual drift*. The Brelands summarized their findings in an article entitled "The Misbehavior of Organisms" (1961), in which they concluded:

It seems obvious that these animals are trapped by strong instinctive behaviors, and clearly we

FIGURE 18.1 The Dancing Chicken demonstrates instinctual drift. The chicken is not required to "dance" in order to obtain reinforcement. The chicken is simply required to remain near the center of the rotating platform. However, the chicken's instinctive behavior is so strong that it scratches anyway. (Courtesy of Animal Behavior Enteprises, Inc.)

have here a demonstration of the prepotency of such behavior patterns over those which have been conditioned. (p. 85)

The Brelands felt that their observations contradicted three assumptions that the behaviorists usually made: (1) an animal comes to the learning situation as a *tabula rasa*—that is, without any genetic predispositions, (2) differences among various species of animals are unimportant, and (3) any response an animal can make can be conditioned to any stimulus the animal can detect. All of these behavioristic assumptions either deny or minimize the importance of instinctive behavior. Although beginning their careers as behaviorists, the Brelands reached the following conclusion (1961):

After 14 years of continuous conditioning and

observation of thousands of animals, it is our reluctant conclusion that the behavior of any species cannot be adequately understood, predicted, or controlled without knowledge of its instinctive patterns, evolutionary history, and ecological niche. (p. 126)

Since the Brelands' article on the misbehavior of organisms, many other researchers have found support for their conclusions. For example, Seligman (1970) has found that within any given species of animal, some associations are easier to establish than others, and that one species may be able to form an association with ease, while for another species this may be extremely difficult or impossible. According to Seligman, the reason for this is that within a species, animals are biologically prepared to form certain associations and contraprepared to form others, and the same thing is true among the various species. Where an association falls on the prepared-contraprepared continuum determines how easily an animal will learn it. Many examples of how an organism's biological makeup influences what and how easily it can learn may be found in Seligman and Hager (eds.), *Biological Boundaries of Learning* (1972).

The Methodological Behaviorists

Besides the increased number of observations that were contrary to behavioristic assumptions, one should note that not all behaviorists were radical. Some so-called methodological behaviorists emphasized cognitive concepts in their explanation of behavior. As we saw in Chapter 13, Edward Tolman was such a behaviorist. For him, the most important thing organisms (including humans) learned was a *cognitive map* of the environment, which they used in getting from place to place.

Donald Hebb, another influential behaviorist, made the following statement in 1959:

> How are we to learn more about . . . ideational or mediating processes, and the limits of their role in behavior, except by forming hypotheses (as explicit as we can reasonably make them) and then seeing what implications they have for behavior, and whether these implications are borne out in experiment? By all means, if you will, call these central events mediating processes instead of ideas or cell assemblies, but let us get busy and investigate them. (p. 630)

It can be argued that the methodological behaviorists (those willing to use cognitive concepts in their theory) eventually won out over the radical behaviorists (those who refused to entertain cognitive concepts in their theory).

For whatever reason or reasons, radical behaviorism and its opposition to the study of cognitive processes diminished, and cognitive processes have once again become a focus of research in psychology. We have already seen that existential humanistic psychologists use the

Martin Seligman

phenomenological approach, which is clearly cognitive. Those following the existential humanistic paradigm, however, tend either to be antiscientific or to want psychology to create a new human science that does not model itself after the natural sciences. Other kinds of contemporary cognitive psychologists include Piaget's followers and the neo-Freudians, such as Erikson. The newest brand of cognitive psychology, and one of the most scientifically rigorous, is information-processing cognitive psychology. The information-processing approach to studying cognitive processes has been so successful that some are referring to it as psychology's newest paradigm, one that will soon displace all earlier paradigms (for example, Lachman, Lachman, and Butterfield, 1979.) Such an approach warrants closer examination.

INFORMATION-PROCESSING COGNITIVE PSYCHOLOGY

There is no better example of how developments outside of psychology can influence psychology than the recent emergence of the information-processing approach. Most information-processing psychologists note the similarities between humans and computers: both receive input, process that input, have a memory, and produce output. For the information-processing psychologists, the term *input* replaces the term *stimulus*, the term *output* replaces the terms *response* and *behavior*, and terms such as *storage*, *encoding*, *processing*, *capacity*, *retrieval*, *conditional decisions*, and *programs* are used to describe the information-processing events that occur between the input and the output. Most of these terms have been borrowed from computer technology. The information-processing psychologist usually concentrates his or her research on normal, rational thinking and behavior, and views the human as an active seeker and user of information. Within information processing, research is focused on the higher mental processes such as language, thinking, perception, problem solving, concept formation, memory, learning, intelligence, and attention. In answer to the question "How do information-processing psychologists go about studying these things?" Sternberg (1985) says:

> In general, they analyze how people go about solving difficult mental tasks. They often construct explicit models of just how these tasks are solved. These models may take the form of computer programs, flow charts, or other schematizations of the flow of processing during task performance, but their goal is always to understand the processes, strategies, and mental representations that people use in task performance. (p. 3)

As we have seen throughout this book, the assumptions one makes about human nature or some aspect of it will strongly influence how one goes about studying humans. The assumption that the mind or brain either is or acts like a computer demonstrates this point. As Lachman, Lachman, and Butterfield (1979) say:

> Computers take symbolic input, recode it, make decisions about the recorded input, make new expressions from it, store some or all of the input, and give back symbolic output. By analogy, that is most of what cognitive psychology is about. It is about how people take in information, how they recode and remember it, how they make decisions, how they transform their internal knowledge states, and how they transform these states into behavioral outputs. The analogy is important. It makes a difference whether a scientist thinks of humans as if they were laboratory animals or as if they were computers. Analogies influence an experimenter's choice of research questions, and they guide his or her theory construction. They color the scientist's language, and a scientist's choice of terminology is significant. The terms are pointers to a conceptual infrastructure that defines an approach to a subject matter. Calling a behavior a *response* implies something very different from calling it an *output*. It implies different beliefs about the behavior's origin, its history, and its explanation. Similarly, the terms *stimulus* and *input* carry very different implications about how people process them. (p. 99)

Information-processing psychology follows in the rationalistic tradition of Plato, Descartes, Kant, the Gestalt psychologists, and Piaget. Like most rationalist theories, information-processing theory has a strong nativistic component. Lachman, Lachman, and Butterfield (1979) say:

> We do not believe in postulating mysterious instinct to account for otherwise unexplainable behavior, but we do feel that everything the human does is the result of inborn capacities, as well as learning. We give innate capacities more significance than behaviorists did. We think part of the job of explaining human cognition is to identify how innate capacities and the results of experience combine to produce cognitive performance. This leads us, especially in the area of language, to suppose that some aspects of cognition have evolved primarily or exclusively in humans. (p. 118)

Note the similarity between the Gestalt position and the following statement of Lachman, Lachman, and Butterfield: "The human mind has parts, and they interrelate as a *natural system*" (1979, p. 128). Note also the similarity between the positions of Kant and Piaget and another statement of Lachman, Lachman, and Butterfield: "Man's cognitive system is constantly active; it adds to its environmental input and literally *constructs* its reality" (1979, p. 128). The kinship between information-processing psychology and Piaget's theory is especially evident in the following quotation from Piaget (1970), where he is arguing against the empiricists' conception of intelligence as the passive copying and storing of information about the environment:

> This passive interpretation of the act of knowledge is in fact contradicted at all levels of development and, particularly, at the sensorimotor and prelinguistic levels of cognitive adaptation and intelligence. Actually to know objects, the subject must act upon them, and therefore transform them: he must displace, connect, combine, take apart, and reassemble them.
>
> From the most elementary sensorimotor actions (such as pushing and pulling) to the most sophisticated intellectual operations, which are interiorized actions, carried out mentally (e.g., joining together, putting in order, putting in one-to-one correspondence), knowledge is constantly linked with actions or operations, that is, with *transformations*. (pp. 703–704)

According to Lachman, Lachman, and Butterfield (1979, p. 113), information-processing psychology has finished its revolution; it is now a paradigm, and as such has entered a period of normal science. If it is true that psychology has another paradigm, it is a paradigm that, for the moment at least, has limited application. At present, information-processing psychologists tend to concentrate on intelligent human behavior and to ignore emotional behavior, abnormal behavior, and individual differences. This is changing, however, and the paradigm is being employed to study an ever-increasing number of topics—for example, social psychology

(Hendrick, 1977), developmental psychology (Klahr & Wallace, 1976), and clinical psychology (Mahoney, 1974). In the preface to their book *Human Information Processing: An Introduction to Psychology* (2nd ed., 1977), Lindsay and Norman express their belief that the information-processing paradigm has widespread usefulness:

> We believe our extensions of the area of information processing research show how the scientific analysis of this book can help to illuminate many if not all human phenomena. (p. v)

Whether or not the information-processing approach represents a full-fledged paradigm, it has clearly been extremely useful and productive, and all indications are that it is becoming increasingly popular.

IS THERE ANYTHING NEW IN PSYCHOLOGY?

There is no doubt that there are aspects of psychology that are newer and better than they have ever been. As we have just seen, computer technology has provided psychology with a new and useful tool. Improvements in measuring and recording devices, the invention of the electron microscope, and new drugs have provided physiological psychologists with powerful research tools. In addition to providing a model for human cognitive processes, computers allow for complex data analysis that only a few years ago would have been impossible. So the answer to the question "Is there anything new in psychology?" must be yes. But note that our examples were all technological rather than conceptual. When we look at the larger issues, the answer to our question seems to be negative. After listing some advances in our knowledge of how the brain and body function—our greater understanding of simple learning and of memory phenomena and of children's thinking—Leahey (1980) goes on to say:

However, in a broader, conceptual sense progress is harder to demonstrate. The most modern psychology, information processing cognitive psychology, is remarkably similar to Aristotle's account of mind. Both view the acquisition of knowledge as the internalization and processing of information about the environment which is then stored in some form of memory. (p. 385)

In his *History and Systems of Psychology* (1982) James Brennan also concludes:

Despite the elapse of almost 2,500 years since the flowering of Greek thought, very little of original quality has been added. Changes, modifications, and reinterpretations have been offered, but essentially science as we know it today is a study based upon an Aristotelian framework of knowledge. (p. 349)

Emphases change, and the research tools we have to work with sometimes improve, but it seems that psychology is still addressing the same questions it addressed from its very inception. Since we elaborated upon psychology's persistent questions in Chapter 1, we will simply list them here:

- How are the mind and the body related?

- What is the nature of human nature?

- To what extent is human behavior determined, and to what extent is it free?

- What proportion of human ability is genetically determined, and what proportion comes from experience?

- Does the mind merely record and store information or does it actively transform information? In other words, is the mind active or passive?

- What attributes do humans share with other animals? Are humans in any way unique among animals?

- How are humans related to other animals?

- Can psychology be a science?

These are the questions that have guided the efforts of psychologists for well over 2,000 years, and no doubt they will continue to guide their efforts in the future. The last question on the list is one that has plagued psychology at least since the time of Galileo. We will now review a few current answers to that question.

PSYCHOLOGY'S STATUS AS A SCIENCE

We begin with William James's description of psychology as it appeared to him in 1892:

A string of raw facts; a little gossip and a wrangle about opinions; a little classification and generalization on the mere descriptive level; a strong prejudice that we *have* states of mind, and that our brain conditions them: but not a single law in the same sense in which physics shows us laws, not a single proposition from which any consequence can causally be deduced. . . . This is no science, it is only the hope for a science. (p. 335)

More than 40 years later, in her influential book *Seven Psychologies* (1933), Edna Heidbreder offers her description of psychology:

Psychology is, in fact, interesting, if for no other reason, because it affords a spectacle of a science still in the making. Scientific curiosity, which has penetrated so many of the ways of nature, is here discovered in the very act of feeling its way through a region it has only begun to explore, battering at barriers, groping through confusions, and working sometimes fumblingly, sometimes craftily, sometimes excitedly, sometimes wearily, at a problem that is still largely unsolved. For psychology is a science that has not yet made its great discovery. It has found nothing that does for it what atomic theory has done for chemistry, the principle of organic evolution for biology, the laws of motion for physics. Nothing that gives it a unifying principle has yet been discovered or recognized. As a rule, a science is presented, from the standpoint of both subject-matter and development, in the light of its great successes. Its verified hypotheses form the established lines about which it sets its facts in order, and about which it organizes its research. But psychology has not yet won its great unifying victory. It has had flashes of perception, it holds a handful of clues, but it has not yet achieved a synthesis or an insight that is compelling as well as plausible. (pp. 425–426)

Although the views of James and Heidbreder are separated by more than four decades, they are remarkably similar. Have things improved in the 50 years since Heidbreder recorded her thoughts? Rychlak (in Arnold, 1976) concludes that psychology has not been very successful in explaining human behavior because it has been dominated by the empirical, mechanistic, and deterministic model that started with Aristotle and was brought into modern times by the French materialists and British empiricists. Rychlak believes that the Kantian model, with its emphasis on reasoning powers, would have been much more productive. With the current popularity of information-processing cognitive psychology and existential-humanistic pyschology, we see a shift toward the rationalist tradition of Plato, Descartes, Kant, and Leibniz. Only time will tell if a science of psychology based on the rational model of humans will be more productive than the empirical-associationistic model has been.

As we saw in Chapter 1, after addressing the question of whether psychology is a science or not, Sigmund Koch (1981) concludes that psychology is not a single discipline. Rather, it is several disciplines, some of which qualify as science, but most of which do not. Koch believes that it would be more realistic to refer to our discipline as *psychological studies* rather than as *the science of psychology*. The designation *psychological studies* recognizes the diversity of psychology and shows a willingness to use a wide variety of methods while studying humans. Koch (1981) summarizes his views of what psychology should be like:

Because of the immense range of the psychological studies, different areas of study will not only require different . . . methods but will bear affinities to different members of the broad groupings of inquiry as historically conceived. Fields like sensory and biological psychology may certainly be regarded as solidly within the family of the biological and, in some reaches, natural sciences. But psychologists must finally accept the circumstances that extensive and important sectors of psychological study require modes of inquiry rather more like those of the humanities than the sciences, and among these I would include areas traditionally considered "fundamental"—like perception, cognition, motivation, and learning, as well as such more obviously rarefied fields as social psychology, psychopathology, personality, aesthetics, and the analysis of "creativity". . . . I have been inviting a psychology that might show the imprint of a capacity to accept the inevitable ambiguity and mystery of our situation. (p. 269)

We see that in the five decades since Heidbreder's assessment of psychology, the situation has not significantly changed. Psychology is still a collection of different facts, assumptions, methodologies, and goals. It is still not clear how much of psychology is scientific or even can be scientific, and even those who believe psychology can be a science debate over what kind of a science it should be. No matter what else psychology is, it is not now a unified discipline.

Where does all this leave the student of psychology? It seems that psychology is not a place for people with a low tolerance for ambiguity. The diverse and sometimes conflicting points of view that characterize psychology will undoubtedly continue to characterize it in the future. There is growing recognition that psychology must be as diverse as the humans whose behavior it attempts to explain. For those looking for one truth, this state of affairs is distressing. For those willing to ponder several truths, psychology is and will be an exciting field. Because many questions remain unanswered, students of psychology are in a position to contribute to the solution of the remaining mysteries of human existence.

SUMMARY

Contemporary psychology is a hybrid discipline that reflects many influences from philosophy, natural science, and technology. In psychology there is now a spirit of eclecticism, a willingness to employ whatever methods are effective in studying various aspects of humans. Examination of the contents of introductory psychology texts shows that most of the topics covered are as old as psychology itself. Although psychology is still defined as a science in most introductory texts, it is now typically defined as the science of behavior and cognition. It is accurate to define psychology as a science only if one realizes that much psychological research is empirical but not experimental. That is, more often than not propositions are tested by naturalistic observation rather than by controlled laboratory research. Psychology's great diversity is shown in the 40 divisions of the American Psychological Association.

The decline in the popularity of behaviorism and the increased popularity of cognitive psychology go hand in hand. Reasons for behaviorism's decreased popularity include Chomsky's successful attack on Skinner's account of language, the increased evidence for the importance of genetic influences on behavior (which the behaviorists minimized or ignored), and the fact that a number of influential behaviorists themselves found it necessary to employ cognitive concepts. One of the most popular kinds of cognitive psychology today is information-processing cognitive psychology, which uses the computer as an analogy for how humans process information. Like the computer, humans receive input, process that input by using various programs, strategies, memories and plans, and then produce output. The major goal of the information-processing psychologist is to determine the mechanisms that humans employ in processing information. Information-processing psychologists follow in the rationalistic tradition, and their work and assumptions show

similarities to those of Plato, Kant, the Gestalt psychologists, and Piaget. At present, information-processing psychology concentrates on rational, intelligent actions and has little to say about human emotion, abnormal behavior, and individual differences, but it is gradually expanding into these and other areas.

Psychology has provided considerable information about such things as learning, memory, brain functioning, bodily functioning, and childhood thinking, and has refined many of its research tools because of methodological advances. But in a broader sense, psychology continues to respond to questions that the early Greeks posed. Although the emphases have changed from time to time, as well as the research tools and the terminology, psychology continues to seek answers to the same questions. How are the mind and the body related? What is the nature of human nature? Are human behavior and thought processes completely determined, or are we at least partially free to determine our own behavior and thoughts? How much of what we do is determined by genetics and how much by experience? Is the human mind active or passive? How much do humans have in common with other animals? Are humans in any way unique among animals? Do humans act for reasons or is their behavior mechanistically caused? Can psychology be a science?

In 1892 William James concluded that psychology was still hoping to become a science. In 1933 Heidbreder reached more or less the same conclusion. In 1976 Rychlak concluded that psychology had failed as a science because it used an empirical, mechanistic, and deterministic model. Rychlak believes we would fare better if we would use a model emphasizing human rational powers. In 1981 Koch argued that although some aspects of humans are amenable to scientific scrutiny, most are not. Koch suggests that we should label our discipline *psychological studies* rather than *the science of psychology* in recognition of the fact that many aspects of humans can only be investigated through the research techniques of the humanities. Now as throughout history, psychology's status as a science is difficult to determine.

DISCUSSION QUESTIONS

1. Why is it misleading to conclude that psychology evolved into what is today?

2. What is meant by describing contemporary psychology as eclectic?

3. What does one learn about modern psychology by scanning tables of contents of introductory psychology texts and by noting the various divisions of the American Psychological Association?

4. How has the definition of *psychology* changed in recent times?

5. Distinguish between the empirical and experimental methods of verifying psychological propositions.

6. Describe three factors that led to the recent decline in the popularity of behaviorism.

7. What did the Brelands mean by *instinctual drift*?

8. What three behavioristic assumptions did the Breland's feel that their observations contradicted?

9. For Seligman, what was a preparedness-contrapreparedness continuum?

10. Summarize the ways in which computer technology has influenced the development of information-processing psychology.

11. What topics in psychology does the information-processing psychologist concentrate on? Which topics does he or she tend to ignore?

12. What philosophical tradition does information-processing psychology represent? Explain.

13. Give examples of how information-processing psychology is similar to the theories of Kant, Piaget, and the Gestalt psychologists.

14. How would you answer the question "Is there anything new in psychology?"

15. List the persistent questions that psychology has attempted to answer through the centuries.

16. Is psychology a science or not? Defend your answer.

REFERENCES

Alexander, F. G., & Selesnick, S. T. (1966). *The history of psychiatry.* New York: Harper & Row.

Arnold, W. J. (Ed.). (1976). *Nebraska symposium on motivation.* Lincoln, NE: University of Nebraska Press.

Ayllon, T., & Azrin, N. (1968). *The token economy: A motivational system for therapy and rehabilitation.* New York: Appleton-Century-Crofts.

Bacon, F. (1878). *Of the proficience and advancement of learning divine and human.* Vol. 1 of *The works of Francis Bacon.* Cambridge, MA: Hurd and Houghton. (Originally published 1605.)

Bain, A. (1859). *The emotions and the will.* London: Parker.

Bain, A. (1868). *The senses and the intellect* (3rd ed.). London: Longmans, Green. (Originally published 1855.)

Bain, A. (1872). *Mind and body.* London: King.

Bandura, A. (1977). *Social learning theory.* Englewood Cliffs, NJ: Prentice-Hall.

Barash, D. P. (1979). *The whispering within.* New York: Harper & Row.

Bechterev, V. M. (1973). *General principles of human reflexology.* New York: Arno Press. (Originally published 1928.)

Bentham, J. (1961). *An introduction to the principles of morals and legislation.* In *The utilitarians.* New York: Dolphin Books. (Originally published 1879.)

Berkeley, G. (1954). An essay towards a new theory of vision. In *Berkeley: A new theory of vision and other writings.* London: J. M. Dent & Sons Ltd. (Originally published 1709.)

Bernfeld, S. (1949). Freud's scientific beginnings. *American Imago, 6,* 163–196.

Binet, A. (1898). Historique des recherches sur les rapports de l'inteligence avec la grandeur et la forme de la tête. *L'Année Psychologique, 5,* 245–298.

Binet, A. (1900). Recherches sur la technique de la mensuration de la vivante, plus four other memoirs on cephalometry. *L'Année Psychologique, 7,* 314–429.

Binet, A. (1909). *Les idées modernes sur les enfants.* Paris: Flammarion.

Bitterman, M. E. (1965). Phyletic differences in learning. *American Psychologist, 20,* 396–410.

Blucher, J. (Ed.). (1946). Martin Luther, twenty-seven articles respecting the reformation of the Christian state. In Vol. 1 of *Introduction to contemporary civilization in the West.* New York: Columbia University Press.

Blumenthal, A. (1970). *Language and psychology: Historical aspects of psycholinguistics.* New York: Wiley.

Blumenthal, A. (1975). A re-appraisal of Wilhelm Wundt. *American Psychologist, 30,* 1081–1088.

Blumenthal, A. (1979). The founding father we never knew. *Contemporary Psychology, 24,* 547–550.

Boring, E. G. (1950). *A history of experimental psychology.* New York: Appleton-Century-Crofts.

Boring, E. G. (1957). *A history of experimental psychology* (2nd ed.). New York: Appleton-Century-Crofts.

Boring, E. G. (1965). On the subjectivity of important historical dates: Leipzig, 1879. *Journal of the History of the Behavioral Sciences, 1,* 5–9.

Boss, M. (1963). *Psychoanalysis and Daseinanalysis.* New York: Basic Books.

Braid, J. (1843). *The rationale of nervous sleep considered in relation to animal magnetism.* London: Churchill.

Brainerd, C. J. (1978). *Piaget's theory of intelligence.* Englewood Cliffs, NJ: Prentice-Hall.

Breland, K., & Breland, M. (1961). The misbehavior of organisms. *American Psychologist, 16,* 681–684.

Brennan, J. F. (1982). *History and systems of psychology.* Englewood Cliffs, NJ: Prentice-Hall.

Brentano, F. (1973). *Psychology from an empirical standpoint.* O. Kraus (Ed.). English ed., L. L. McAlister (Ed.). New York: Humanities Press. (Originally published 1874.)

Brett, G. S. (1965). *A history of psychology.* (Edited and abridged by R. S. Peters.) (2nd rev. ed.). Cambridge, MA: M.I.T. Press. (Originally published 1953.)

Breuer, J., & Freud, S. (1955). *Studies on hysteria.* Vol. 2 of *The standard edition.* London: Hogarth Press. (Originally published 1895.)

Bridgman, P. W. (1927). *The logic of modern physics.* New York: Macmillan.

Brown, R. (Ed.). (1970). Thomas Reid, An inquiry into the human mind on the principles of common sense. In *Between Hume and Mill: An anthology of British philosophy 1749–1843*. New York: Random House.

Brown, W., & Gilhousen, H. C. (1950). *College psychology*. Englewood Cliffs, NJ: Prentice-Hall.

Brožek, J. (Ed.). (1984). *Explorations in the history of psychology in the United States*. Cranbury, NJ: Associated University Presses.

Bruno, F. J. (1972). *The story of psychology*. New York: Holt, Rinehart & Winston.

Burtt, E. A. (1932). *The metaphysical foundations of modern physical science*. Garden City, NY: Doubleday.

Carr, H. (1925). *Psychology: A study of mental activity*. New York: Longmans, Green.

Cattell, J. McKeen. (1890). Mental tests and measurements. *Mind, 15*, 373–381.

Cattell, J. McKeen. (1904). The conceptions and methods of psychology. *Popular Science Monthly, 66*, 176–186.

Cattell, J. McKeen. (1929). Psychology in America. In *Proceedings and papers: Ninth International Congress of Psychology*. Princeton, NJ: Psychological Review Company.

Chaplin, J. P., & Krawiec, T. S. (1979). *Systems and theories of psychology* (4th ed.). New York: Holt, Rinehart & Winston.

Chomsky, N. (1957). *Syntactic structures*. The Hague: Mouton.

Chomsky, N. (1959). Review of Skinner's *Verbal learning. Language, 35*, 26–58.

Chomsky, N. (1972). *Language and mind* (enlarged ed.). New York: Harcourt Brace Jovanovich.

Coan, R. (1977). *Hero, artist, sage, or saint? A survey of views on what is variously called mental health, normality, maturity, self-actualization, and human fulfillment*. New York: Columbia University Press.

Cohen, D. (1979). *J. B. Watson: The founder of behaviourism*. London: Routledge & Kegan Paul.

Comte, A. (1896). *A positive philosophy*. H. Martineau (Trans.). London: G. Bell.

Cornford, F. M. (1957). *From religion to philosophy: A study of the origins of Western speculation*. New York: Harper & Row.

Cornford, F. M. (Trans.). (1968). *The republic of Plato*. New York: Oxford University Press.

Craighead, W. E., Kazdin, A. E., & Mahoney, M. J. (1976). *Behavior modification: Principles, issues, and applications*. Boston: Houghton Mifflin.

Daquin, J. *Philosophie de la folie*. (1793). Paris: Alican.

Darwin, C. (1859). *On the origin of species by means of natural selection*. London: J. Murray.

Darwin, C. (1871). *The descent of man*. New York: Appleton.

Darwin, C. (1872). *The expression of emotions in man and animals*. London: John Murray.

Darwin, F. (Ed.). (1959). *The autobiography of Charles Darwin and selected letters*. New York: Dover.

Dewey, J. *Psychology*. (1886). New York: American Book.

Dewey, J. (1896). The reflex arc concept in psychology. *Psychological Review, 3*, 357–370.

Ebbinghaus, H. (1902). *Outline of psychology*. Leipzig: Veit & Co.

Ebbinghaus, H. (1913). *On memory: A contribution to experimental psychology*. H. A. Ruger & C. E. Bussenius (Trans.). New York: Teachers College, Columbia University Press. (Originally published 1885.)

Ellenberger, H. F. (1970). *The discovery of the unconscious: The history and evolution of dynamic psychiatry*. New York: Basic Books.

Ellenberger, H. F. (1972). The story of "Anna O": A critical review with new data. *Journal of the History of the Behavioral Sciences, 8*, 267–279.

Engel, L. (1962). Darwin and the Beagle. Editor's introduction to *Charles Darwin, The voyage of the Beagle*. New York: Natural History Library (Doubleday).

Esper, E. A. (1964). *A history of psychology*. Philadelphia; W. B. Saunders Co.

Estes, W. K. (1950). Toward a statistical theory of learning. *Psychological Review, 57*, 94–107.

Estes, W. K. (1960). Learning theory and the new "mental chemistry." *Psychological Review, 67*, 207–223.

Estes, W. K. (1964). All-or-none processes in learning and retention. *American Psychologist, 19*, 16–25.

Evans, R. B. (1984). Brožek, J. (Ed.). *Explorations in the history of psychology in the United States*. Cranbury, NJ: Associated University Presses, Inc.

Fancher, R. E. (1979). *Pioneers of psychology*. New York: Norton.

Fay, J. W. (1939). *American psychology before William James.* New Brunswick, NJ: Rutgers University Press.

Fechner, G. T. (1966). *Elements of psychophysics.* New York: Holt, Rinehart & Winston. (Originally published 1860.)

Fell, H. B. (1960). Fashion in cell biology. *Science, 132,* 1625–1627.

Fisher, S., & Greenberg, R. P. (1977). *The scientific credibility of Freud's theories and therapy.* New York: Basic Books.

Frankl, V. E. (1963). *Man's search for meaning: An introduction to logotherapy.* New York: Washington Square Press, Inc.

Fraser, A. C. (Ed.). (1959). John Locke, *An essay concerning human understanding.* New York: Dover Press. (Originally published 1690.)

Frazer, J. G. (1963). *The golden bough.* New York: Macmillan.

Freud, S. (1910). The origins and development of psychoanalysis. *American Journal of Psychology, 21.*

Freud, S. (1927). *The problem of lay-analyses.* New York: Brentano's.

Freud, S. (1953). *The interpretation of dreams.* Volumes 4 and 5 of *The standard edition.* London: Hogarth. (Originally published 1900.)

Freud S. (1955). *Beyond the pleasure principle.* Vol. 18 of *The standard edition.* London: Hogarth. (Originally published 1920.)

Freud, S. (1960a). *Jokes and their relation to the unconscious.* Vol. 8 of *The standard edition.* London: Hogarth. (Originally published 1905.)

Freud, S. (1960b). *Psychopathology of everyday life.* Vol. 6 of *The standard edition.* London: Hogarth. (Originally published 1901.)

Freud, S. (1961a). *Civilization and its discontents.* Vol. 21 of *The standard edition.* London: Hogarth. (Originally published 1930.)

Freud, S. (1961b). *The future of illusion.* Vol. 22 of *The standard edition.* London: Hogarth. (Originally published 1927.)

Fromm, E. (1941). *Escape from freedom.* New York: Avon Books.

Galton, F. (1853). *Narrative of an explorer in tropical South Africa.* London: Murray.

Galton, F. (1855). *Art of travel.* London: Murray.

Galton, F. (1869). *Hereditary genius: An inquiry into its laws and consequences.* London: Macmillan.

Galton, F. (1874). *English men of science: Their nature and nurture.* London: Macmillan.

Galton, F. (1883). *Inquiries into human faculty and its development.* London: Macmillan.

Galton, F. (1888). Co-relations and their measurement, chiefly from anthropological data. *Proceedings of the Royal Society, 45,* 135–145.

Galton, F. (1884). *Natural inheritance.* London: Macmillan.

Goddard, H. H. (1912). *The Kallikak family, A study in the heredity of feeble-mindedness.* New York: Macmillan.

Goddard, H. H. (1914). *Feeble-mindedness: Its causes and consequences.* New York: Macmillan.

Goethe, J. W. (1898). *Faust: A tragedy.* Bayard Taylor (Trans.). New York: Houghton Mifflin Co. (Originally published 1808.)

Goethe, J. W. (1952). *Sorrows of young Werther.* Chapel Hill, NC: University of North Carolina Press. (Originally published 1774.)

Goldsmith, M. (1934). *Franz Anton Mesmer.* New York: Doubleday.

Gould, S. J. (1976). Darwin and the captain. *Natural History, 85*(1), 32–34.

Gould, S. J. (1981). *The mismeasure of man.* Toronto; George J. McLeod Limited.

Guilford, J. P. (1967). *The nature of human intelligence.* New York: McGraw-Hill.

Guthrie, E. R. (1940). Association and the law of effect. *Psychological Review, 47,* 127–148.

Guthrie, E. R. (1942). Conditioning: A theory of learning in terms of stimulus, response, and association. In N. B. Henry (Ed.), *The forty-first yearbook of the National Society for the Study of Education.* Part 2: *The psychology of learning.* Chicago: University of Chicago Press.

Guthrie, E. R. (1952). *The psychology of learning* (rev. ed.). New York: Harper & Row. (Originally published 1935.)

Guthrie, E. R. (1959). Association by contiguity. In Vol. 2 of S. Koch (Ed.), *Psychology: A study of a science.* New York: McGraw-Hill.

Hadden, A. W. (Trans.). (1912). St. Augustine's "On the trinity." In Benjamin Rand (Ed.), *The classical psychologists.* Boston: Houghton Mifflin.

Hall, C. S. (1954). *A primer of Freudian psychology.* Cleveland: World Publishing.

Hall, C. S., & Lindzey, G. (1978). *Theories of personality* (3rd ed.). New York: Wiley.

Hall, G. S. (1904). *Adolescence: Its psychology and its relation to physiology, anthropology, sociology, sex, crime, religion and education.* 2 vols. New York: Appleton.

Harris, M. (1974). *Cows, pigs, wars and witches: The riddles of culture.* New York: Vintage.

Hartley, D. (1934). *Observations on man, his frame, his duty and his expectations.* London: Thomas Tegg & Sons. (Originally published 1749.)

Hebb, D. (1959). A neuropsychological theory. In Vol. 1 of S. Koch (Ed.), *Psychology: A study of a science.* New York: McGraw-Hill.

Hebb, D. O. (1972). *Textbook of psychology* (3rd ed.). Philadelphia: Saunders.

Heidbreder, E. (1933). *Seven psychologies.* New York: D. Appleton-Century.

Heidegger, M. (1927). *Being and time.* Halle, East Germany: M. Niemeyer.

Hendrick, C. (Ed.). (1977). *Perspectives on social psychology.* Hillsdale, NJ: Lawrence Erlbaum Associates.

Hergenhahn, B. R. (1982). *An introduction to theories of learning.* Englewood Cliffs, NJ: Prentice-Hall.

Hergenhahn, B. R. (1984). *An introduction to theories of personality.* Englewood Cliffs, NJ: Prentice-Hall.

Hulin, W. S. (1934). *A short history of psychology.* New York: Hewey Holt & Co.

Hull, C. L. (1943). *Principles of behavior.* New York: Appleton-Century.

Husserl, E. (1900–1901). *Logical investigations.* Halle, East Germany: M. Niemeyer.

Husserl, E. (1962). *Ideas: General introduction to pure phenomenology.* New York: Collier. (Originally published 1913.)

James, W. (1890). *The principles of psychology.* 2 vols. New York: Henry Holt and Company.

James, W. (1902). *The varieties of religious experience.* New York: Longmans, Green.

James, W. (1907). *Pragmatism: A new name for some old ways of thinking.* New York: Longmans, Green.

James, W. (1920). Letters of William James. In H. James (Ed.), *Letters of William James.* 2 vols. Boston: Atlantic Monthly Press.

James, W. (1961). *Psychology: The briefer course.* New York: Harper & Brothers, 1961. (Originally published by Henry Holt in 1892.)

Jones, E. (1953, 1955, 1957). *The life and work of Sigmund Freud.* 3 vols. New York: Basic Books.

Jones, M. C. (1924). A laboratory study of fear: The case of Peter. *Pedagogical Seminary, 31,* 308–315.

Jones, M. C. **(1974).** Albert, Peter and John B. Watson. *American Psychologist, 29,* 581–583.

Jones, W. H. S. (1923). *Hippocrates.* (Vols. 1 and 2.). New York: Putnam.

Jourard, S. M. (1974). *Healthy personality: An approach from the veiwpoint of humanistic psychology.* New York: Macmillan.

Jowett, B. (1908). *The republic of Plato* (3rd ed.). 2 vols. Oxford: Clarendon Press.

Jowett, B. (Trans.). (1942). *Plato.* Rosyln, NY: Walter J. Black, Inc.

Joynson, R. B. (1970). Breakdown of modern psychology. In M. Marx & F. Goodson (Eds.), *Theories in contemporary psychology.* New York: Macmillan.

Jung, C. G. (1953). Two essays on analytic psychology. In Vol. 7 of *The collected works of C. G. Jung.* Princeton: Princeton University Press. (Originally published 1917.)

Jung, C. G. (1963). *Memories, dreams, reflections.* New York: Pantheon Books; and London: William Collins Sons, Ltd.

Kagen, J. (1980, November). Jean Piaget's contributions. *Phi Delta Kappan.*

Kahl, R. K. (Ed.). (1971). *Selected writings of Hermann von Helmholtz.* Middletown, CT: Wesleyan University Press.

Kant, I. (1965). *Critique of pure reason.* N. K. Smith (Trans.). New York: St. Martin's. (Originally published 1781.)

Kant, I. (1908). Critique of practical reason. In B. Rand (Ed.), *Modern classical philosophers.* Boston: Houghton Mifflin Co. (Originally published 1788.)

Kazdin, A. E. (1980). *Behavior modification in applied settings* (rev. ed.). Homewood, IL: Dorsey Press.

Kazdin, A. E., & Wilson, G. T. (1978). *Evaluation of behavior therapy.* Cambridge, MA: Bollinger.

Keller, F. S. (1973). *The definition of psychology* (2nd ed.). Englewood Cliffs, NJ: Prentice-Hall.

Kelly, G. A. (1955). *The psychology of personal constructs: A theory of personality.* 2 vols. New York: W. W. Norton.

Kelly, G. A. (1964). The language of hypotheses: Man's psychological instrument. *Journal of Individual Psychology, 20,* 137–152.

Kelly, G. A. (1969). The autobiography of a theory. In Brenden Maher (Ed.), *Clinical psychology and personality: Selected papers of George Kelly.* New York: Wiley.

Klahr, D., & Wallace, J. C. (1976). *Cognitive development: An information-processing view.* Hillsdale, NJ: Lawrence Erlbaum Associates.

Koch, S. (1981). The nature and limits of psychological knowledge: lessons of a century qua "science." *American Psychologist, 36* (3), 257–269.

Koffka, K. (1963). *Principles of Gestalt psychology.* New York: Harcourt, Brace & World, Inc. (Originally published 1935.)

Köhler, W. (1925). *The mentality of apes.* London: Routledge and Kegan Paul, Ltd. (Originally published 1917.)

Köhler, W. (1929). *Gestalt psychology.* New York: Liveright.

Köhler, W. (1947). *Gestalt psychology: An introduction to new concepts in modern psychology.* New York: Liveright.

Köhler, W. (1969). *The task of Gestalt psychology.* Princeton, NJ: Princeton University Press.

Kuhn, T. S. (1973). *The structure of scientific revolutions* (2nd ed.). Chicago: The University of Chicago Press, 1973.

Külpe, O. (1909). *Outlines of psychology: Based upon the results of experimental investigation* (3rd ed.). New York: Macmillan. (Originally published 1893.)

Lachman, R., Lachman, J. L., & Butterfield, E. C. (1979). *Cognitive psychology and information processing.* Hillsdale, NJ: Lawrence Erlbaum Associates.

Lafleur, L. J. (Ed. and Trans.). (1960). Rene Descartes, Discourse on method. *Discourse on method and meditations.* New York: Library of Liberal Arts.

Lamarck, J. B. (1914). *Philosophie zoologique.* Hugh Elliot (Trans.). London: Macmillan. (Originally published 1809.)

LaMettrie, J. O. de. (1912). *L'homme machine* (Man, a machine). M. W. Calkins (Trans.). New York: Open Court. (Originally published 1748.)

Leahey, T. H. (1980). *A history of psychology.* Englewood Cliffs, NJ: Prentice-Hall.

Leeper, R. W. (1935). A study of a neglected portion of the field of learning: The development of sensory organization. *Pedagological Seminary and Journal of Genetic Psychology, 46,* 41–75.

Lehrer, K., & Beanblossom, R. (Eds.). (1975). *Thomas Reid's inquiry and essays.* Indianapolis: Bobbs-Merrill.

Leitenberg, H. (Ed.). (1976). *Handbook of behavior modification and behavior therapy.* Englewood Cliffs, NJ: Prentice-Hall.

Lewin, K. (1935). *A dynamic theory of personality: Selected papers.* New York: McGraw-Hill.

Lewin, K., Lippitt, R., & White, R. K. (1939). Patterns of aggressive behavior in experimentally created "social climates." *Journal of Social Psychology, 10,* 271–299.

Lindsay, P. H., & Norman, D. A. (1977). *Human information processing: An introduction to psychology.* New York: Academic Press.

Locke, J. (1975). *An essay concerning human understanding.* P. Nidditch (Ed.). Oxford: Clarendon Press. (Originally published 1690.)

Lundin, R. W. (1979). *Theories and systems of psychology* (2nd ed.). Lexington, MA: D.C. Heath.

Lundin, R. W. (1985). *Theories and systems of psychology* (3rd ed.). Lexington, MA: D. C. Heath.

McDougall, W. (1905). *Physiological psychology.* London: Dent.

McDougall, W. (1908). *Introduction to social psychology.* London: Methuen and Co.

McDougall, W. (1923). *Outline of psychology.* New York: Scribner.

Mach, E. (1914). *Contributions to the analysis of sensations.* La Salle, IL: Open Court. (Originally published 1886.)

McKeon, R. (Ed.). (1941). *The basic works of Aristotle.* New York: Random House.

MacLeod, R. B. (1975). *The persistent problems of psychology.* Pittsburgh, PA: Duquesne University Press.

Maddi, S. R., & Costa, P. T. (1972). *Humanism in personology: Allport, Maslow and Murray.* Chicago: Aldine-Atherton, Inc.

Mahoney, M. J. (1974). *Cognition and behavior modification.* Cambridge, MA: Ballinger.

Malthus, T. (1914). *Essay on the principle of population.* New York: Dutton. (Originally published 1798.)

Marrow, A. J. (1969). *The practical theorist: The life and work of Kurt Lewin.* New York: Basic Books.

Marx, M. H., & Hillix, W. A. (1963). *Systems and theories in psychology.* New York: McGraw-Hill.

Maslow, A. H. (1966). *The psychology of science: A reconnaissance.* New York: Harper & Row.

Maslow, A. H. (1968). *Toward a psychology of being* (2nd ed.). New York: D. Van Nostrand Co.

Maslow, A. H. (1970). *Motivation and personality* (2nd ed.). New York: Harper & Row.

May, R. (1939). *The art of counseling: How to give and gain mental health.* Nashville: Abingdon-Cokesbury.

May, R. (1940). *The springs of creative living: A study of human nature and God.* New York: Abingdon-Cokesbury.

May, R. (1950). *The meaning of anxiety.* New York: Ronald Press.

May, R. (1953). *Man's search for himself.* New York: Norton.

May, R. (Ed.). (1961). *Existential psychology.* New York: Random House.

May, R. (1967). *Psychology and the human dilemma.* New York: D. Van Nostrand Co.

May, R. (1969). *Love and will.* New York: Norton.

May, R. (1972). *Power and innocence: A search for the sources of violence.* New York: Norton.

May, R. (1973). *Paulus: Reminiscences of a friendship.* New York: Harper & Row.

May, R. (1975). *The courage to create.* New York: Norton.

Melton, A. W. (Ed.). (1964). *Categories of human learning.* New York: Academic Press.

Mill, J. (1829). *Analysis of the phenomena of the human mind.* London: Longmans and Dyer.

Mill, J. S. (1956). *A system of logic.* London: Longmans. (Originally published 1843.)

Miller, G. A. (1965). Some preliminaries to psycholinguistics. *American Psychologist, 20,* 15–20.

Mischel, W. (1981). *Introduction to personality* (3rd ed.). New York: Holt, Rinehart & Winston.

Monte, C. F. (1975). *Psychology's scientific endeavor.* New York: Praeger.

Mora, G. (1959). Vincenzo Chiarugi (1759–1820) and his psychiatric reform in Florence in the late eighteenth century. *Journal of the History of Medicine, 14.*

Morgan, C. L. (1891). *An introduction to comparative psychology.* London: W. Scott.

Morgan, C. L. (1900). *Animal life and intelligence.* (Revised as Animal behavior.) London: Edward Arnold. (Originally published 1891.)

Müller, J. (1842). *Handbuch der physiologie des menschen.* (Translated as *Elements of physiology.*) 2 vols. London: Taylor and Walton. (Originally published 1833–1840.)

Münsterberg, H. (1888). *Activity of the will.* Freiburg, West Germany: J. C. B. Mohr.

Münsterberg, H. (1904). *The Americans.* Edwin B. Holt (Trans.). New York: McClure, Phillips & Co.

Münsterberg, H. (1908). *On the witness stand.* New York: Clark Boardman.

Münsterberg, H. (1909). *Psychotherapy.* New York: Moffat, Yard.

Münsterberg, H. (1912). *Vocation and learning.* University City, St. Louis, MO: The People's University.

Münsterberg, H. (1913). *Psychology and industrial efficiency.* New York: Houghton Mifflin.

Murphy, G. (1968). *Psychological thought from Pythagoras to Freud.* New York: Harcourt, Brace & World, Inc.

Murray, G. (1955). *Five stages of Greek religion.* New York: Doubleday.

Mussen, P., & Rosenzweig, R. (1973). *Psychology: An introduction.* Lexington, MA: D. C. Heath & Co.

Nietzsche, F. (1905). *Thus spake Zarathustra.* Thomas Common (Trans.). New York: Modern Library. (Originally published 1893.)

Nietzsche, F. (1931) *The Antichrist* (rev. ed.). New York: Knopf. (Originally published 1895).

Nietzsche, F. (1955). *Beyond good and evil.* Chicago: Henry Regnery. (Originally published 1886.)

Ovsiankina, M. (1928). Die wiederaufnahme von interbrochenen handlungen. *Psychologische Forschung, 2,* 302–389.

Pavlov, I. P. (1928). *Lectures on conditioned reflexes.* New York: Liveright.

Pavlov, I. P. (1955). *Selected works.* Moscow: Foreign Languages Publishing House.

Penfield, W. (1958). *The excitable cortex in conscious man.* Springfield, IL: Charles C. Thomas.

Piaget, J. (1966). *Psychology of intelligence.* Totowa, NJ: Littlefield, Adams.

Piaget, J. (1970). Piaget's theory. In Vol. 1 of P. H. Mussen (Ed.), *Carmichael's manual of child psychology*. New York: Wiley.

Pillsbury, W. B. (1911). *Essentials of psychology*. New York: Macmillan.

Pinel, P. (1962). *A treatise on insanity*. Academy of Medicine—The History of Medicine Series. New York: Hafner. (Originally published 1801.)

Popper, K. (1963). *Conjectures and refutations*. New York: Basic Books.

Porter, N. (1868). *The human intellect: With an introduction upon psychology and the soul*. New York: Scribner.

Rand, B. (1912). *The classical psychologists*. Boston: Houghton Mifflin.

Rimm, D. C., & Masters, J. C. (1974). *Behavior therapy: Techniques and empirical findings*. New York: Academic Press.

Roback, A. A. (1952). *History of American psychology*. New York: Library Publishers.

Robinson, D. N. (1976). *An intellectual history of psychology*. New York: Macmillan.

Robinson, D. N. (1981). *An intellectual history of psychology* (rev. ed.). New York: Macmillan.

Robinson, V. (1943). *The story of medicine*. New York: New Home Library.

Rogers, C. R. (1959). A theory of therapy, personality, and interpersonal relationships, as developed in the client-centered framework. In Vol. 3 of S. Koch (Ed.), *Psychology: A study of a science*. New York: McGraw-Hill.

Rogers, C. R. (1961). *On becoming a person: A therapist's view of psychotherapy*. Boston: Houghton Mifflin.

Rogers, C. R. (1966). Client-centered therapy. In S. Arieti (Ed.), *American handbook of psychiatry*. New York: Basic Books.

Rogers, C. R. (1969). *Freedom to learn*. Columbus, OH: Charles E. Merrill.

Romanes, G. J. (1882). *Animal intelligence*. London: Kegan Paul, Trench.

Romanes, G. J. (1884). *Mental evolution in animals*. New York: Appleton.

Romanes, G. J. (1885). *Mental evolution in man*. London: Kegan Paul.

Rosenbaum, M., & Muroff, M. (Eds.). (1984). *Anna O. Fourteen Contemporary Reinterpretations*. New York: The Free Press.

Rousseau, J. J. (1947). *The social contract*. New York: Macmillan. (Originally published 1762.)

Rousseau, J. J. (1974). *Emile*. New York: Dutton. (Originally published 1762.)

Royce, J. R., & Mos, L. P. (Eds.). (1981). *Humanistic psychology: Concepts and criticisms*. New York: Plenum Press.

Rush, B. (1812). *Diseases of the mind*. Philadelphia: Kimber and Richardson.

Russell, B. (1945). *A history of Western philosophy* (14th ed.). New York: Simon & Schuster.

Russell, B. (1959). *Wisdom of the West*. Garden City, NJ: Doubleday.

Sahakian, W. S. (1975). *History and systems of psychology*. New York: Wiley.

Samelson, F. (1977). World War I intelligence testing and the development of psychology. *Journal of the History of the Behavioral Sciences, 13,* 274–282.

Sargent, S. S., & Stafford, K. R. (1965). *Basic teachings of the great psychologists*. Garden City, NY: Doubleday.

Sartain, J., North, J., Strange, R., & Chapman, M. (1973). *Psychology: Understanding human behavior*. New York: McGraw-Hill.

Schur, M. (1972). *Freud: Living and dying*. New York: International Universities Press.

Schwartz, B., & Lacey, H. (1982). *Behaviorism, science and human nature*. New York: W. W. Norton.

Scot, R. *Discoverie of witchcraft*. (1964). Carbondale, IL: Southern Illinois University Press. (Originally published 1584.)

Sechenov, I. M. (1965). *Reflexes of the brain*. Cambridge, MA: M.I.T. Press. (Originally published 1863.)

Sechenov, I. M. (1973). *I. M. Sechenov: Biographical sketch and essays*. New York: Arno. (Reprinted from I. Sechenov, *Selected works*, 1935.)

Segal, E. M., & Lachman, R. (1972). Complex behavior or higher mental process: Is there a paradigm shift? *American Psychologist, 27,* 46–55.

Seligman, M. E. P. (1970). On the generality of the laws of learning. *Psychological Review, 77,* 406–418.

Seligman, M. E. P., & Hager, J. L. (1972). *Biological boundaries of learning*. New York: Appleton-Century-Crofts.

Severin, F. T. (1973). *Discovering man in psychology: A humanistic approach*. New York: McGraw-Hill.

Sigerist, H. E. (1951). *A history of medicine.* Vol. 1, *Primitive and archaic medicine.* New York: Oxford.

Skinner, B. F. (1948). *Walden two.* New York: Macmillan.

Skinner, B. F. (1950). Are theories of learning necessary? *Psychological Review, 57,* 193–216.

Skinner, B. F. (1953). *Science and human behavior.* New York: Macmillan.

Skinner, B. F. (1956). A case study in scientific method. *American Psychologist, 11,* 221–233.

Skinner, B. F. (1957). *Verbal behavior.* Englewood Cliffs, NJ: Prentice-Hall.

Skinner, B. F. (1960). Pigeons in a pelican. *American Psychologist, 15,* 28–37.

Skinner, B. F. (1971). *Beyond freedom and dignity.* New York: Knopf.

Skinner, B. F. (1974). *About behaviorism.* New York: Knopf.

Skinner, B. F. (1984). The shame of American education. *American Psychologist, 39,* 947–954.

Small, W. S. (1901). Experimental study of the mental processes of the rat. *American Journal of Psychology, 12,* 218–220.

Spence, W. K. (1942). The basis of solution by chimpanzees of the intermediate size problem. *Journal of Experimental Psychology, 131,* 257–271.

Spencer, H. (1855). *The principles of psychology.* New York: Appleton.

Staats, A. W. (1981). Paradigmatic behaviorism, unified theory, unified theory construction methods, and the Zeitgeist of separatism. *American Psychologist, 36,* 239–256.

Sternberg, R. J. (Ed.). (1985). *Human abilities: An information-processing approach.* New York: W. H. Freeman.

Stevens, S. S. (1951). Psychology and the science of science. In M. H. Marx (Ed.), *Psychological theory: Contemporary readings.* New York: Macmillan.

Stumpf, C. (1883–1890). *Psychology of tone.* 2 vols. Leipzig: S. Hirzel.

Taylor, R. (1963). *Metaphysics.* Englewood Cliffs, NJ: Prentice-Hall.

Terman, L. M. (1916). *The measurement of intelligence.* Boston: Houghton Mifflin.

Terman, L. (1926). *Genetic studies of genius.* Vol. 1, *Mental and physical traits of a thousand gifted children.* Stanford, CA: Stanford University Press.

Thorndike, E. L. (1898). Animal intelligence: An experimental study of the associative processes in animals *Psychological Review,* Monograph Suppl., *2,* No. 8.

Thorndike, E. L. (1911). *Animal intelligence.* New York: Macmillan.

Thorndike, E. L. (1924). Mental discipline in high school studies. *Journal of Educational Psychology, 15,* 1–22, 83–98.

Titchener, E. B. (1896). *An outline of psychology.* New York: Macmillan.

Titchener, E. B. (1898). The postulates of a structural psychology. *Philosophical Review, 7,* 449–465.

Titchener, E. B. (1910). *A textbook of psychology.* New York: Macmillan.

Titchener, E. B. (1921). In memory of Wilhelm Wundt, by his American students. *The Psychological Review, 28,* 153–188.

Tolman, E. C. (1932). *Purposive behavior in animals and men.* New York: Naiburg.

Tolman, E. C., & Honzik, C. H. (1930). Introduction and removal of reward, and maze performance in rats. *University of California Publications in Psychology, 4,* 257–273.

Ulrich, R., Stachnik, T., & Mabry, J. (Eds.). (1966). *Control of human behavior.* (Vols 1 and 2). Glenview, IL: Scott, Foresman.

Van Kaam, A. (1966). *Existential foundations of psychology.* Pittsburgh, PA: Duquesne University Press.

Veith, I. (1965). *Hysteria: The history of a disease.* Chicago: University of Chicago Press.

Watson, J. B. (1913). Psychology as the behaviorist views it. *Psychological Review, 20,* 158–177.

Watson, J. B. (1914). *Behavior: An introduction to comparative psychology.* New York: Holt, Rinehart & Winston.

Watson, J. B. (1919). *Psychology from the standpoint of a behaviorist.* Philadelphia: J.B. Lippincott.

Watson, J. B. (1930). *Behaviorism* (rev. ed.). New York: W.W. Norton. (Originally published 1925.)

Watson, J. B. (1926). What the nursery has to say about instincts. In C. Murchison (Ed.), *Psychologies of 1925.* Worchester, MA: Clark University Press.

Watson, J. B. (1928). *Psychological care of infant and child.* New York: W. W. Norton.

Watson, J. B., & Lashley, K. S. (1915). Homing and related activities of birds. Vol. 7. Carnegie Institution, Department of Marine Biology.

Watson, J. B., & McDougall, W. (1929). *The battle of behaviorism*. New York: W. W. Norton.

Watson, J. B., & Rayner, R. (1920). Conditioned emotional reactions. *Journal of Experimental Psychology, 3*, 1–14.

Watson, R. I. (1971). Prescriptions as operative in the history of psychology. *Journal of the History of Psychology, 7*, 311–322.

Watson, R. I. (1978). *The great psychologists* (2nd ed.). New York: J. B. Lippincott.

Weimer, W. B. (1973). Psycholinguistics and Plato's paradoxes of the Meno. *American Psychologist, 28*, 15–33.

Wertheimer, Max. (1912). Experimentelle studien über das sehen von bewegung. *Zeitschrift für Psychologie, 61*, 161–265.

Wertheimer, Max. (1959). *Productive thinking* (enlarged ed.). Michael Wertheimer (Ed.). New York: Harper and Brothers Publishers. (Originally published 1945.)

Wertheimer, Michael. (1970). *A brief history of psychology*. New York: Holt, Rinehart & Winston.

Wertheimer, Michael. (1979). *A brief history of psychology* (rev. ed.). New York: Holt, Rinehart & Winston.

Wertheimer, Michael. (1980). Gestalt theory of learning. In G. M. Gazda & R. J. Corsini (Eds.), *Theories of learning: A comparative approach.* Ithaca, IL: F. E. Peacock Publishers, Inc.

Weyer, J. (1563). *De praestigiis daemonum*. Basel, Switzerland: Per Joannem Oporinum.

Wilson, E. O. (1978). *On human nature*. Cambridge, MA: Harvard University Press.

Wolf, T. H. (1973). *Alfred Binet*. Chicago: University of Chicago Press.

Woodworth, R. S. (1931). *Contemporary schools of psychology*. New York: Ronald Press.

Wundt, W. (1862). *Contributions toward a theory of sense perception*. Leipzig: Winter.

Wundt, W. (1904). *Principles of physiological psychology*. London: Swan Sonnenschein. (Originally published 1874.)

Wundt, W. (1897). *Outlines of psychology*. Leipzig: Englemann.

Wundt, W. (1900–1909). *Völkerpsychologie*. 10 vols. Leipzig: Engelmann.

Yerkes, R. M. (1923). Testing the human mind. *Atlantic Monthly, 121*, 358–370.

Zeigarnik, B. (1927). Über behalten von erledigten und unerledigten handlungen. *Psychologische Forschung, 9*, 1–85.

NAME INDEX

SUBJECT INDEX